# From Malin Head to Mizen Head

## The Definitive Guide to Local Government in Ireland

KEVIN RAFTER
and
NOEL WHELAN

**BLACKWATER PRESS**

## BE BETTER

TSB Bank aims to be better than the rest. Better service. Better rates and charges. A better attitude to customer requirements.

## BE OPEN

The fact that TSB Bank opens lunchtimes and opens longer will come as no surprise to anyone who knows us. It's something we've been happily doing for years. But being open is more than about hours. It's also about attitude. If you've got a need, you'll find we've got the answer.

## BE CLOSER

TSB Bank likes to maintain a close relationship with all its customers.

IT'S WHAT YOUR BANK SHOULD

To help with plans or problems, big or small. To treat each one as an individual who deserves the very best we have to offer.

## BE MORE

TSB Bank can now offer its very special welcome at a broader network of branches. 70 in all – all over the country.

## BELONGING

TSB Bank is very much a part of your community, very much a part of the people who are and will become our customers.

## BE WITH US

Today, you're not far away from a TSB Bank branch. Better get to know us. Before long.

# Contents

Printed in Ireland at the press of the publishers.

©Blackwater Press 1992
8 Airton Road
Tallaght
Dublin 24.

Editors: Anna O'Donovan,
John O'Connor

Typeset by: Typelink Ltd

ISBN 0 86121 4218

Photographs have been provided by many sources including:
Lensmen, Irish Times, Cork Examiner, Newspics, Limerick Leader, Connaught Tribune and Donegal Democrat.

# Acknowledgements

This book has been written to update the information available on both the political and administrative aspects of Irish local government. It follows on from the Brennan Guide of 1986 and will hopefully prove an invaluable reference book on the local elections of June 1992. It will be of use to anyone interested in Irish political life, particularly politics at local level.

Compiling and writing "From Malin Head to Mizen Head" has been an enormous undertaking over the last number of months. It would never have reached publication stage without the generous support and practical help from so many individuals, all of whom we are exrtemely thankful to.

We are indebted to several individuals for the key professional advice they gave, especially Paddy Troy (Solicitor) and Gerry Feehily (Accountant). Both Paddy and Gerry deserve special mention, without their enthusiastic support and "never say die" attitude producing this book would have proven impossible.

John O'Connor in Blackwater Press deserves special thanks for the committment he showed in taking on board the project when it was only an idea. Without his support, it would never have appeared.

Thanks are due to Gerry Proctor and Barbara in Typelink who designed the book and made the impossible possible. We are also thankful to Sean Hendrickx and Noel McCarthy in Link Services who made the project financially viable.

We are grateful to Professor Brian Farrell, Dr. Michael Gallagher, Yvonne Galligan and Dick Roche, all of whom readily agreed to write articles for the book. Thanks are also due not only for the quality of these pieces but also for the fact that they all were returned within deadline.

Thanks are due to the staff of the Press Offices of the main political parties - Niamh O'Connor of Fianna Fail, Mary Cummins of Fine Gael, Fergus Finlay and Sinead Bruton of Labour, Stephan O'Byrne of The Progressive Demorcrats and Tony Heffernan of Democratic Left.

The General Secretaries of Fianna Fail, Fine Gael and Labour were generous with the time and provided invaluable assistance. To Pat Farrell, Ivan Doherty and Ray Kavanagh, respectively, special thanks are due.

The staff of the National Library of Ireland and Trinity College Library are to be thanked for their patience in photocopying endless back issues of the national and provincial newspapers from June 1991.

Special thanks goes to Seamus Purcel, Dermot Rafter, Sean Sherwin, John Whelan, Vincent Fagan, Kevin Macourt, Cora Enright, Denis M O'Brien, Alan and Sandra in Ryehill House. We are most grateful to Barbara O'Dywer who read the illegible and Oorla Gallagher who did more than we could ever have asked. All of these individuals were involved in this project somewhere along the way and helped to make our task easier.

We would also like to thank the Whelan and Rafter families for all their support during this project.

Kevin Rafter   Noel Whelan
November 1992

Kevin Rafter wrote the county analysis pieces for: Clare, Donegal, Kildare, Leitrim, Limerick CC, Limerick BC, Longford, Louth, Meath, Roscommon, Sligo, Tipperary NR, Tipperary SR, Waterford CC, Waterford BC, Westmeath and Wexford.

Noel Whelan wrote the county analysis pieces for Carlow, Cavan, Cork CC, Cork BC, Dublin CC, Dublin BC, Galway CC, Galway BC, Kerry, Kilkenny, Laois, Mayo, Monaghan, Offaly and Wicklow.

# Introduction

Brian Farrell — Professor of Politics at University College Dublin and presenter of the RTE Current Affairs Programme "Farrell".

Elections are among the most popular of Irish sporting activities. Our particularly sophisticated mode of proportional representation, by means of the single transferable vote, offers an almost infinite range of possibilities for elaborate calculations of where the last seat may fall; it stimulates some exquisitely calibrated bets. But the excitement generated by national contests rarely spills over into local elections.

A substantial part of the reason, perhaps, lies in the lack of any proper "form book". In 1986, for the first time, that gap was filled by Seamus Brennan's pioneering study. "From Malin Head to Mizen Head" is a worthy successor to, and considerable expansion on, Brennan's Key. It is, indeed, as the sub-title claims, the Definitive Guide to Local Government in Ireland.

Noel Whelan and Kevin Rafter have put us all in their debt with this comprehensive and essential reference book on the 1991 Local Elections. There are detailed statistics on the contests in all 177 local electoral areas. These go beyond the carefully organised tables for each count. They include an analysis of the campaigns in each area, the issues involved, the

comprehensive overview of the contests and a valuable "Who's Who" of the nation's local representatives. In particular, the fortunes of women candidates are examined and the obstacles to their successful selection honestly and objectively considered.

It is impossible to ruffle through the pages of this major contribution to Irish Politics and not recognise the extraordinary wealth of talent, commitment, energy and ambition that motivates so many men, and an increasing number of women, to offer their services to fellow citizens. It is a measure of a self-induced "democratic deficit" that their efforts are not matched by a corresponding willingness to participate by voters. There are some striking and disturbing variations in participation rates.

The turn out of barely 40% in the capital (including the comprehensively mythical "Dublin 4", embracing Dublin South and Dun Laoire) suggests a casual detachment - perhaps, semi-detachment - from public affairs in one of the most affluent areas of the whole country. The comparison between the 37% turn-out in Rathmines and the capacity of frequently politically denigrated "redneck" Leitrim and Roscommon, to produce over 70% turn-outs, is eloquent testimony to the

need to be sceptical about cliched comparisons between "advanced" and "backward" areas of Ireland.

At the same time, these regional variations also illustrate not only real differences between communities which, however disadvantaged (not least by the ravages of emigration), empowerment, and the anonymous conglomerations and impersonally disconnected suburban sprawls in which so many Irish people now live. They also underline the need to reform local government structures so as to encourage a revival of local democracy, stimulate citizen involvement and free communities from the strait-jacket of an excessively centralised system.

Here is a treasure house of information on which to build such an endeavour; a reference work that will be indispensable for all involved in public administration, voluntary and community effort and politics, both locally and nationally. Also, I hope, a "form-book" that will entice more people to participate, not merely as spectators, but as active players in the noble and necessary sport of politics.

Brian Farrell.

# The local elections of June 1991

BY MICHAEL GALLAGHER

Lecturer in the Department of Political Science at Trinity College Dublin.

In a country as centralised as the Republic of Ireland, local elections have an importance that is as much symbolic as real. Although the battles around the country are keenly fought, few could claim that it really matters very much which party or group of parties controls most county councils, apart perhaps from Dublin city, the only area where the parties' policies at local level might make any impact on voting behaviour.

As far as most candidates and campaigners are concerned, there are two factors involved that are much more important than where power on the county council may lie after the elections. Both relate not to the local elections being contested but to the next general election. The first is that the political parties use the local elections as training grounds for the next Dáil election. Local elections offer a useful opportunity to find out where the organisation needs improving, and they also give activists a chance to work off some of their energy. Since the results of local elections are almost invariably interpreted in terms of the standing of the parties nationally, the parties want to achieve a good showing to be able to claim that they are gaining support from the electorate and to keep up morale among members.

The second factor is that individual candidates have a powerful incentive to poll strongly because, as is well known, the road to the Dáil often runs through the council chamber. Of the 166 TDs elected in June 1989, 118 (71 per cent) had belonged to a local council before entering the Dáil. Becoming a county councillor helps in two ways: not only does it enable the councillor to show what he or she is made of in terms of ability to deal with the needs of constituents, but, in addition, a strong

> The political parties use the local elections as training grounds for the next Dáil election.

performance at a local election increases one's chance of winning a nomination to stand as a candidate when the next general election comes around.

Because of this, local elections in Ireland are taken much more seriously than the very limited powers of local authorities might lead one to expect. In the weeks leading up to 27 June 1991, the parties bombarded the provincial press with advertisements and the 1,974 candidates pressed the flesh as relentlessly as if their political futures depended on the outcome—as in some cases they did.

## THE CAMPAIGN

The parties approached the local elections with varying expectations. Fianna Fáil was in generally confident mood, its standing in the national opinion polls still above the level of support that it had won in the previous general election two years earlier. The events that were ultimately to undermine the position of Charles Haughey as party leader had yet to emerge, and, for the first time since 1974, the incumbent government did not have to go into the local elections at a low point in its fortunes. On the other hand, no-one doubted that Fianna Fáil would lose seats at the elections, because it had done so well at the previous local elections. These had taken place in June 1985, when the Fine Gael-Labour coalition had been deeply unpopular, and Fianna Fáil had advanced dramatically from 347 seats out of 806 in 1979 to 437 seats out of 883. Gratifying as this had been at the time, it meant that the party was bound to lose ground in 1991, and that it would be placed on the defensive when trying to explain its performance to the media.

For the same reasons, it might have been expected that Fine Gael would be approaching the 1991 local elections in optimistic mood. The party's disastrous showing in 1985 should have meant that the only way was up. However, things were not quite so simple. The 29.8 per cent of the votes it had won in 1985 might have been seen as calamitous at the time, but it compared rather well with its performances at the subsequent general elections (27.1 per cent in 1987, 29.3 per cent in 1989), not to mention Austin Currie's 17 per cent at the 1990 presidential election. The last of these had brought about the ousting of Alan Dukes as party leader and his replacement by John Bruton, but this had had no discernible impact on the party's support, which remained stubbornly in the low 20s in the opinion polls. Consequently, the very real possibility existed that Fine Gael would now slip back further from what had been seen in 1985 as rock bottom.

Both left-wing parties anticipated gains from the elections. Labour, like its senior coalition partner, had felt the full force of the electorate's hostility in 1985, when it had been reduced to a mere 59 seats. Unlike Fine Gael, it now seemed to be on the road to recovery, as the polls showed it a few modest percentage points above its 1985 vote and its morale had been boosted by the success of Mary Robinson in the presidential election 7 months earlier. The Workers' Party also claimed a share of the credit for that result, and is expected to continue its seemingly inexorable advance by electing new councillors who could support its 7 TDs

"The political landscape was changed significantly with the retirement of Charles Haughey . . ." seen here launching Fianna Fail's local election campaign in June 1991.

and, in some cases, eventually join their ranks.

Finally, both the PDs and the Greens went into the elections hoping to elect their first county councillors. The PDs had been founded six months after the 1985 local elections, and although a number of sitting councillors had joined the new party, these representatives were open to the charge that they had never received a mandate as PD councillors. In addition, the party had suffered in the 1989 general election from the fact that some of its TDs had lacked a support base of party councillors who could give it added presence on the ground, and it may also have been fixed with an image of high-minded aloofness from the mundane reality of constituency work. It was therefore important for the PDs to show that they were a serious political force that was there for the long haul, and not merely a "head without a body" party that was not very active outside Leinster House. On a humbler scale, the Greens had no county or county borough councillors, but, following the election

> One aspect that caused little surprise was the low turnout: only 55.1 per cent of the electorate came out and cast valid votes.

to the Dáil of Roger Garland in 1989 and Trevor Sargent's strong showing in the European Parliament election in Dublin, they hoped that a solid performance at local level could lay the foundations for several more Dáil seats at the next general election.

Inevitably, the parties were hard pressed to come up with specifically local policies, and the opposition in particular tended to concentrate on national issues such as unemployment. Nevertheless, opinion polls found that voters claimed to see local issues as more important: in an MRBI / Irish

Times survey at the start of the campaign 47 per cent of respondents declared that local issues were most important compared with 30 per cent opting for national issues, a feeling that was particularly marked in rural areas. However, an IMS / Irish Independent poll suggested that what people meant by "local issues" was really the impact locally of matters that in fact are decided mainly at national level, since issues such as the state of the health services and of the roads were picked out as most important from a list offered to respondents.

**THE RESULTS**

When the votes were counted, the overall picture conformed broadly to what had been generally expected, but there were a few surprises. One aspect that caused little surprise was the low turnout: only 55.1 per cent of the electorate came out and cast valid votes. Turnout at the 1967 local elections had been 69 per cent, but interest in local contests has been declining steadily since then. In Dublin city and in the South Dublin and Dun Laoghaire areas, turnout was little more than 40 per cent. This might be partly attributable to the relatively high ratio of electors to councillors in the Dublin region— Dublin has about a third as many TDs as councillors, whereas in some rural areas there are far fewer TDs in relation to councillors. For example, the counties of Sligo and Leitrim returned 4 TDs at the 1989 general election, but they had 47 councillors between them. Far fewer votes are needed to elect a rural councillor than to elect one in Dublin, and the greater remoteness of local government is no doubt one reason why voters in the capital tend to be less likely to vote at local elections.

For Fianna Fáil, the results were worse than anticipated. The party had known that it would lose seats, but it had not expected to lose so many. It lost control of most of the county councils on which it had previously had a majority, and suffered particularly heavy losses in areas where the PDs were strongly established, such as Cork and Limerick, and in Dublin, where a number of its councillors had attracted unfavourable publicity over the rezoning of land. Its share of the votes was below the 39.2 per cent it had won in 1979, a performance that had been

| RESULT OF THE 1991 LOCAL ELECTIONS | | | | | | |
|---|---|---|---|---|---|---|
| | Candidates | Seats | Change from 1985 | % vote | Change from 1985 local elections | Change from 1989 election |
| Fianna Fáil | 643 | 357 | -80 | 37.9 | -7.6 | -6.2 |
| Fine Gael | 471 | 270 | -13 | 26.4 | -3.4 | -2.9 |
| Labour | 202 | 90 | +31 | 10.6 | +2.9 | +1.1 |
| Progressive Democrats | 125 | 37 | +37 | 5.0 | +5.0 | -0.5 |
| Workers' Party | 82 | 24 | +4 | 3.7 | +0.5 | -1.3 |
| Green Party | 60 | 13 | +13 | 2.0 | +1.9 | +0.5 |
| Sinn Féin | 60 | 7 | -3 | 1.7 | -1.6 | +0.5 |
| Others | 331 | 85 | +11 | 12.7 | +2.1 | +8.8 |
| **Total** | **1974** | **883** | **0** | **100.0** | **0** | **0** |

For John Bruton "this performance raised doubts about his continued leadership" of Fine Gael.

seen at the time as a reflection of widespread discontent with the Fianna Fáil government of Jack Lynch. Lynch lasted only a further six months as Fianna Fáil leader, an achievement that Charles Haughey was to better by only two months. While Haughey might have survived had it not been for the sequence of strange incidents that took place over the ensuing months, Fianna Fáil's poor showing in the local elections left him in a weaker position to fight off the renewed challenge to his leadership when it came.

Fine Gael also sustained a demoralising setback. It managed to lose both votes and seats relative to 1985, and its 26.4 per cent of the votes compared starkly with the 34.9 per cent it had won in 1979, the last time local elections had been held while Fianna Fáil was in government. The results provided tangible evidence that the

> Far fewer votes are needed to elect a rural councillor than to elect one in Dublin

party had not found a way out of the morass in which it seemed to have been floundering for the previous six or seven years. Particularly striking was its weak performance in the major urban areas of the country: it won just 15.9 per cent of the votes in the county

boroughs, with only 13 per cent in Waterford and 14 per cent in Dublin. Only in the rural areas did it poll respectably, and even there its strength was uneven, with only two counties (Longford and Roscommon) giving it more than 40 per cent of the votes. As John Bruton's first test, this performance raised doubts about his continued leadership of the party if Fine Gael should fare badly at the next general election.

On the left, fortunes were mixed. Labour gained votes, relative to both the 1985 local elections and to the 1989 general election, and party morale was encouraged accordingly. It won more votes than any other party on Limerick Corporation, thanks to the acquisition of Jim Kemmy in 1990, and became the largest party there and the second largest on Dublin Corporation. However, it should be remembered that the two baselines—the 1985 local elections and the 1989 general election—marked very low points in Labour's fortunes, and that Labour's 1991 performance was not especially good in a longer-term context. For example, its 10.6 per cent of the votes in 1991 compared unfavourably with the 11.8 per cent won in the 1979 local elections, the 12.8 per cent won in 1974 and the 14.8 per cent won in 1967. While the party was pleased to win 10 seats out of 52 on Dublin Corporation in 1991, this was still below the 11 out of 42 it had won in 1979. However, such historical comparisons are not the stuff of contemporary political debate, and the prevailing impression was that the 1991 local elections had been good for

Labour.

The Workers' Party, in contrast, was not encouraged by the outcome. It did make small gains in both votes and seats relative to 1985, but at that time it had had only 2 TDs and was still struggling to establish itself as a serious political force. By 1991 it had advanced to 7 TDs and was thinking in altogether bigger terms. In 1989 it had outpolled Labour in Dublin at both the general and European Parliament elections, and had won 6 Dáil seats in the capital to Labour's 2. In the light of all this, its result in 1991 was a major disappointment. It won fewer votes than in 1989, and was outpolled by Labour in all the major urban areas except Waterford. It is impossible to say to what extent this result contributed to the split that led to the establishment of Democratic Left nine months later,

> The PDs, like Labour, regarded the elections as a success story, but, again like Labour, jubilation should have been rather less than unbounded.

but, had the party performed more successfully in the local elections, the internal strains and stresses would almost certainly have been fewer.

The PDs, like Labour, regarded the elections as a success story, but, again like Labour, jubilation should have been rather less than unbounded. The party defied those who believed that it would be swept aside, but its achievement was more in the nature of clinging on bravely than asserting itself as a major national political force. Its performance was very uneven. It polled strongly in some areas where it already had TDs, especially in Galway, Limerick and Dublin South-West. However, it won no seats at all on 17 of the 29 county councils, and its vote in both Cork and in Dublin city (just 3.4 per cent of the votes) was below expectations. The party was entitled to celebrate the

**John O'Gorman of the Christian Principles Party pounds the flesh in the Artane area. He was unsuccessful in his attempt receiving 248 votes.**

election of its first councillors, but the jury is still out on the long-term future of the PDs.

Smaller parties invariably fare better at local than at general elections, since, with no significant issues at stake, voters can protest against the government or the major parties, so it would be imprudent to read too much into the fortunes of the rest of the field. Nevertheless, the Greens were understandably pleased with their performance, and by outpolling both the PDs and the Workers' Party in Dublin county they gave themselves hope of an extra Dáil seat or two at the next general election. Sinn Féin, in contrast, continued its seemingly inexorable decline into irrelevance in southern politics. Much of the post-election publicity focussed on the election of a large number of independent candidates,

and especially the success of the four "pothole" candidates in Cavan. While such candidates rarely try, let alone

> Smaller parties
> invariably fare
> better at local
> than at general
> elections

manage, to mobilise the same support at Dáil elections, the election of Tom Foxe in Roscommon in 1989 might persuade

some of them to try their luck at the next general election.

Finally, it is worth mentioning one other aspect of the new councils that attracted some attention, namely the increase in the number of women councillors. Whereas in 1985 women had made up only 8.1 per cent of the new councillors, this figure advanced to 11.4 per cent in 1991. As at previous elections, women fared less well than men (the average male candidate won 719 first preferences compared with 631 for the average female candidate) and did much better in Dublin (where they took 25.2 per cent of the first preferences) than in the rest of the country (they won 14.2 per cent of the votes nationwide). Given the role of local councils in the process of recruitment to the Dáil, this very modest increase in the number of women councillors does not suggest that a dramatic growth in the number of women TDs is likely in the near future.

Looking more broadly ahead to the next general election, it would be unwise to attach too much importance to the results of the 1991 local elections. The political landscape was changed significantly with the retirement of Charles Haughey in February 1992, and Fianna Fáil in particular will argue that the 37.9 per cent of the votes it won in 1991 has no bearing on its likely general election performance. The political careers of some individuals may have been launched or effectively ended by what happened on 27 June 1991, but the political parties know that the next general election will be a battle of a different order.

### REFERENCES:

Rona Fitzgerald, **"The 1991 local elections in the Republic of Ireland"**, Irish Political Studies 7 (1992), pp. 99-104.

Michael Gallagher, **"Local elections and electoral behaviour in the Republic of Ireland"**, Irish Political Studies 4 (1989), pp. 21-42.

Yvonne Galligan, **"Women in Irish politics"**, pp. 182-99 in John Coakley and Michael Gallagher (eds), Politics in the Republic of Ireland (Galway: PSAI Press, 1992).

Michael Marsh and Rick Wilford, **"Irish Political Data 1991"**, Irish Political Studies 7 (1992), pp. 139-163.

**"Well, holy God!" — Independent candidate, Tommy Byrne checks the figures with friends at the count in Drogheda. Tommy missed a seat by 18 votes.**

# County by county

| | Turnout | Fianna Fail | Fine Gael | Labour | PDs | Workers Party | Green Party | Sinn Fein | Others |
|---|---|---|---|---|---|---|---|---|---|
| 1991 Local Election | | 37.8 | 26.6 | 10.6 | 4.9 | 3.7 | 2.4 | 2.1 | 11.9 |
| 1989 General Election | | 44.0 | 29.2 | 9.6 | 5.6 | 4.9 | 1.5 | 1.2 | 5.5 |
| 1985 Local Election | | 45.5 | 29.8 | 7.6 | — | 3.0 | — | 3.3 | 10.8 |
| Connaught /Ulster | | 41.6 | 32.4 | 2.3 | 3.6 | 0.8 | 0.1 | 3.0 | 16.2 |
| Dublin | | 31.4 | 17.8 | 14.5 | 5.7 | 8.7 | 7.4 | 3.2 | 11.4 |
| Leinster (ex Dublin) | | 39.5 | 26.7 | 13.9 | 3.6 | 1.9 | 0.9 | 1.9 | 11.5 |
| Munster | | 38.4 | 28.7 | 11.1 | 6.4 | 3.4 | 1.5 | 1.0 | 9.7 |
| Carlow | 58.3 | 39.4 | 20.9 | 23.3 | 2.5 | — | — | — | 3.9 |
| Cavan | 66.5 | 42.8 | 35.5 | 1.2 | — | — | — | 2.6 | 17.9 |
| Clare | 65.3 | 48.5 | 21.6 | 7.3 | 6.1 | — | — | 1.1 | 15.4 |
| Cork County | 59.1 | 36.7 | 35.4 | 6.1 | 5.5 | 4.3 | 2.2 | 0.4 | 9.5 |
| Cork Co. Borough | 51.9 | 29.0 | 20.3 | 12.6 | 8.3 | 9.9 | 5.1 | 2.4 | 12.1 |
| Donegal | 60.8 | 36.2 | 24.7 | 2.3 | — | 2.5 | 0.7 | 5.2 | 28.4 |
| Dublin Co. Borough | 42.7 | 32.5 | 14.5 | 12.8 | 3.4 | 9.4 | 5.9 | 4.7 | 16.8 |
| Dublin Fingal | 48.8 | 31.6 | 20.2 | 17.5 | 5.9 | 4.1 | 9.7 | 0.5 | 10.4 |
| South Dublin | 41.4 | 29.6 | 18.5 | 18.2 | 9.1 | 8.7 | 5.0 | 3.7 | 7.7 |
| Dun Laoghaire/Rathdown | 42.1 | 30.3 | 23.8 | 12.6 | 8.2 | 10.9 | 11.4 | 1.2 | 1.6 |
| Galway County | 63.2 | 45.0 | 28.0 | 0.5 | 10.8 | 0.6 | — | 0.4 | 14.8 |
| Galway Co. Borough | 49.0 | 27.4 | 20.3 | 13.2 | 22.1 | 2.9 | — | — | 14.2 |
| Kerry | 65.8 | 44.1 | 26.2 | 16.6 | .7 | — | 1.7 | 1.2 | 9.5 |
| Kildare | 48.4 | 33.4 | 20.8 | 17.7 | 6.9 | 3.8 | 3.7 | 2.1 | 11.7 |
| Kilkenny | 63.6 | 43.2 | 33.3 | 16 | 3.0 | 2.1 | — | — | 2.5 |
| Laois | 64.6 | 49.3 | 34.1 | 7.2 | 4.1 | — | — | — | 5.3 |
| Leitrim | 75.3 | 43.4 | 35.4 | — | — | — | — | 9.0 | 12.2 |
| Limerick County | 64.2 | 43.3 | 32.1 | 4.1 | 15.5 | — | 1.10 | 0.6 | 3.3 |
| Limerick Co. Borough | 57.5 | 20.3 | 22.0 | 22.9 | 13.2 | 3.6 | 0.3 | 1.0 | 16.7 |
| Longford | 61.9 | 37.5 | 40.7 | — | 1.3 | — | — | — | 20.5 |
| Louth | 55.9 | 34.7 | 21.2 | 12.0 | 4.6 | 0.7 | — | 9.4 | 17.5 |
| Mayo | 68.3 | 47.1 | 41.5 | 3.6 | 1.5 | — | — | — | 6.4 |
| Meath | 51.0 | 44.8 | 26.5 | 11.8 | 3.2 | 2.8 | 0.6 | 2.3 | 8 |
| Monaghan | 65.0 | 40.1 | 32.8 | — | — | 1.0 | — | 13.9 | 12.2 |
| Offaly | 61.3 | 41.4 | 31.1 | 6.8 | 4.1 | — | 1.2 | 2.3 | 13.0 |
| Roscommon | 73.1 | 40.1 | 40.3 | — | — | — | — | — | 19.5 |
| Sligo | 68.0 | 44.5 | 34.3 | 3.3 | 1.0 | — | — | 1.6 | 15.4 |
| Tipperary North | 68.1 | 45.5 | 35.9 | 10.1 | 3.7 | — | — | 1.3 | 3.5 |
| Tipperary South | 66.3 | 37.8 | 28.7 | 17.5 | 4.4 | 0.2 | — | 0.5 | 10.8 |
| Waterford County | 62.6 | 43.3 | 32.3 | 14.0 | 2.0 | 2.7 | — | — | 5.7 |
| Waterford Co. Borough | 61.1 | 19.0 | 13.3 | 20.5 | 8.2 | 22.0 | — | 2.8 | 14.2 |
| Westmeath | 60.4 | 43.8 | 27.3 | 18.3 | 1.8 | 0.1 | — | — | 8.7 |
| Wexford | 57.7 | 40.2 | 30.2 | 12.6 | 2.6 | 2.1 | — | — | 12.4 |
| Wicklow | 56.7 | 32.2 | 14.6 | 19.2 | 3.4 | 5.3 | 2.5 | 1.7 | 21.1 |
| FINAL TOTALS | 51.1 | 37.8 | 26.6 | 10.6 | 4.9 | 3.7 | 2.4 | 2.1 | 11.9 |

# first preference vote

## NATIONAL PERCENTAGE VOTING

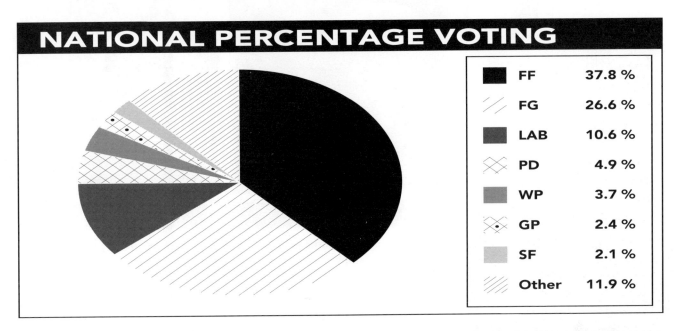

| | | |
|---|---|---|
| ■ | FF | 37.8 % |
| ▨ | FG | 26.6 % |
| ▨ | LAB | 10.6 % |
| ▧ | PD | 4.9 % |
| ▨ | WP | 3.7 % |
| ▨ | GP | 2.4 % |
| ▨ | SF | 2.1 % |
| ▨ | Other | 11.9 % |

## DUBLIN PERCENTAGE VOTING

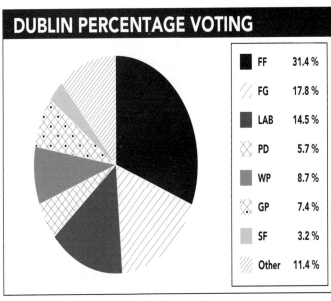

| | | |
|---|---|---|
| ■ | FF | 31.4 % |
| ▨ | FG | 17.8 % |
| ▨ | LAB | 14.5 % |
| ▧ | PD | 5.7 % |
| ▨ | WP | 8.7 % |
| ▨ | GP | 7.4 % |
| ▨ | SF | 3.2 % |
| ▨ | Other | 11.4 % |

## LEINSTER (EXCL DUBLIN) PERCENTAGE VOTING

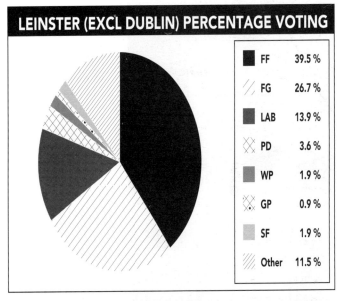

| | | |
|---|---|---|
| ■ | FF | 39.5 % |
| ▨ | FG | 26.7 % |
| ▨ | LAB | 13.9 % |
| ▧ | PD | 3.6 % |
| ▨ | WP | 1.9 % |
| ▨ | GP | 0.9 % |
| ▨ | SF | 1.9 % |
| ▨ | Other | 11.5 % |

## MUNSTER PERCENTAGE VOTING

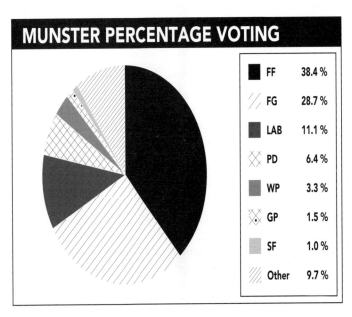

| | | |
|---|---|---|
| ■ | FF | 38.4 % |
| ▨ | FG | 28.7 % |
| ▨ | LAB | 11.1 % |
| ▧ | PD | 6.4 % |
| ▨ | WP | 3.3 % |
| ▨ | GP | 1.5 % |
| ▨ | SF | 1.0 % |
| ▨ | Other | 9.7 % |

## CONNACHT/ULSTER PERCENTAGE VOTING

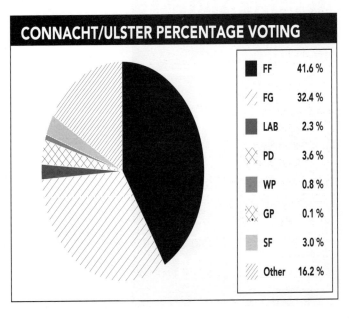

| | | |
|---|---|---|
| ■ | FF | 41.6 % |
| ▨ | FG | 32.4 % |
| ▨ | LAB | 2.3 % |
| ▧ | PD | 3.6 % |
| ▨ | WP | 0.8 % |
| ▨ | GP | 0.1 % |
| ▨ | SF | 3.0 % |
| ▨ | Other | 16.2 % |

# The Parties . . . The

FIANNA FAIL

FINE GAEL

## EMPLOYMENT

"Reorientation of industrial policy towards greater emphasis on the creation of employment. Jobs to follow from a sustained high level of economic performance over a long period."

Creation of all party "National Jobs Forum". Change in industrial policy towards jobs creation, and not the creation of profits.

## CRIME

Increased numbers of Gardai with greater resources. Programme of law reform building on changes since 1987.

Each county and county borough council to set up a crime and police committee which would meet monthly with local gardai.

## HOUSING

Series of new schemes involving shared ownership, rent subsidies and improvement grants. Mortgage allowances for tenant purchasers of private dwellings.

Five-year-plan to refurbish all flat complexes. Schemes to aid elderly people including senior citizen's protected dwellings.

## ENVIRONMENT

"Tough measures and positive incentives". An action programme geared to the year 2000 with £1bn in funds available.

National environmental plan concentrating on litter and pollutant reduction.

## HEALTH

New and extended hospitals in Dublin, Cavan and Mullingar as well as other centres. An increase of 2,000 in health care staff.

Seek end to "two-tier" health system. Use National Lottery money to reduce waiting lists. Maximum waiting time guarantee for all public patients.

## LOCAL GOVT. REFORM

Increased powers for county and county borough councils. Eight new regional authorities to be "put in place as soon as possible."

Propose a single greater Dublin Authority to govern all of Dublin city and county. Would establish a Dublin transport authority and streets commission. Keep remainder of existing structures.

# Promises . . . The Pledges . . .

| LABOUR | PROGRESSIVE DEMOCRATS | WORKERS PARTY |
|---|---|---|
| Change industrial policy to retain value added in Ireland and reduce profit expatriation. A "creative and dynamic role" for the public sector in job creation. | Want to reduce "excessive burden" of income tax and PRSI. Seek overhaul of industrial policy to get greater employment return. | State support for indigenous industry. Grants to be given only where there are definite plans for job creation. |
| Greater resources for the Gardai. Better support for victims of crime. Rehabilitation of young offenders. | More Gardai on the beat. More neighbourhood watch schemes. Update of criminal code. | Establish police liaison committees made up of public representatives, gardai and local community members. |
| Seek "the doubling of social housing provisions each year for the next 3 years" — a target of 6,000 dwellings being built by 1994. Increased funds to refurbish existing local authority housing. | Abolishment of ground rents, within 5 years, for all domestic housing. | "Black list of land developers as part of a campaign to ensure proper completion of estates." Greater advice on energy efficiency and conservation. |
| Outlaw planning abuse. Transport review for Dublin. Ban the use of CFCs within 3 years. | End of planning compensation. New waste control strategy. Independent environmental protection agency to be set up. | Make more hospital beds available. Greater democratic input in service. |
| Abolition of income ceiling for health contributions and use this money to end the problems such as waiting lists. | Greater value for money. "Statutory or institutional link up" with elected representatives by bodies controlling health services. | Citizen's Rights Charter. Increased transparency. Workers participation schemes to address problem of "low staff morale and inefficient service." |
| Ministers' powers to be reduced with immediate devolution of functions to local authorities. | Regional authorities to be directly elected. 150 new district councils, each catering for 30,000 people in Dublin City and Cork City and 20,000 people in the rest of the country. | Propose a single greater Dublin Authority to govern all of Dublin city and county. Would establish a Dublin transport authority and streets commission. Keep remainder of existing structures. |

# Oireachtas Members and the Local Elections

Of the 166 TDs elected in the 1989 General Election 118 (71%) had been members of a local council before entering Dail Eireann. 108 of the Deputies were candidates in the Local Elections of June 1991.

Several of Fianna Fail's successful councillors in 1985 were unable to contest the elections of 1991 due to being appointed to Ministerial posts in the period inbetween. Legislation introduced in 1991 prohibited Ministers and Ministers of State from holding local authority seats. Those excluded from being candidates included Ministers Michael Smith, Terry Leydon and Michael J. Noonan, all of whom were elected in 1985 but held ministerial positions in June 1991.

In total, almost half of Fianna Fail's TDs were candidates while over three quarters of Fine Gael's Dail Deputies contested the local elections in June 1991. Many Fine Gael TDs, who did not run in the 1985 elections were in the field on this occasion. Included in this list was Michael Noonan from Limerick.

### SUCCESSFUL TDs

| Party | Dail Seats | TDs contesting 1991 Local Elections | TDs elected |
|---|---|---|---|
| FF | 77 | 38 | 37 |
| FG | 55 | 43 | 41 |
| Lab | 16 | 16 | 15 |
| PD | 6 | 3 | 3 |
| WP | 7 | 6 | 6 |
| Others | 5 | 2 | 2 |
| **TOTAL** | **166** | **108** | **104** |

### SUCCESSFUL SENATORS

| Party | Senate Seats | Senators contesting 1991 Local Elections | Senators elected |
|---|---|---|---|
| FF | 32 | 25 | 25 |
| FG | 16 | 13 | 7 |
| Lab | 4 | 3 | 3 |
| PD | 3 | 3 | 3 |
| Others | 5 | 1 | 1 |
| **TOTAL** | **60** | **45** | **39** |

All of the Labour Party's Deputies were candidates in the local elections including party leader Dick Spring,

Fianna Fail's Brian Cowen who resigned his seat on Offaly County Council when appointed Minister for Labour in February 1992.

Willie O'Dea, a poll topper in Limerick Borough Council who resigned his seat when appointed Junior Minister in February 1992.

successful in the Tralee electoral area. Deputy Michael Moynihan was the only Labour TD who failed to be elected although there was some consolation with the successful return of his daughter Breeda in the Killarney area. All of the Worker's Party TDs, with the exception of their party leader, contested the local elections and all were elected.

The leading vote-getter among the 108 TDs, and in the country, was Tony Gregory while Noel Dempsey received the highest number of quotas. The Meath Deputy was the only candidate in the country to receive over 2 quotas.

Two Dail Deputies, Labour's Brian O'Shea and Padraic McCormack of Fine Gael were returned to two areas.

Of the 60 senators in the Oireachtas 45 were candidates in the 1991 Local Elections. Six of these Senators failed to get elected, all from Fine Gael.

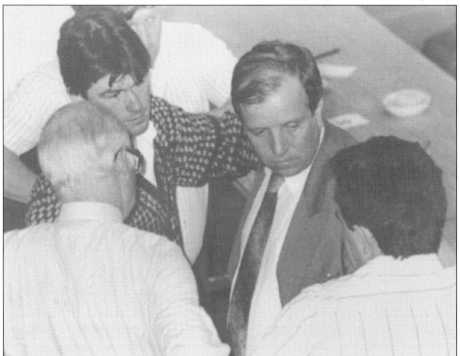

"Disappointed Senator". Fine Gael Senator Joe O'Reilly who lost his Councillor seat in Cavan ponders what might have been.

# The Poll Toppers . . .

## BASED ON NUMBER OF FIRST PREFERENCE VOTES

| | Candidate | Party | Area | Votes |
|---|---|---|---|---|
| 1. | T. Gregory | NP | North Inner City | 4094 |
| 2. | N. O'Keeffe | FF | Mallow | 3419 |
| 3. | S. Loftus | NP | Clontarf | 3411 |
| 4. | M. Creed | FG | Bandon | 3267 |
| 5. | C. Hederman | NP | Pembroke | 3126 |
| 6. | B. O'Keeffe | FF | Cork South | 3081 |
| 7. | J. O'Donoghue | FF | Killorglin | 2979 |
| 8. | S. Haughey | FF | Artane | 2976 |
| 9. | D. Spring | LB | Tralee | 2960 |
| 10. | L. Fitzgerald | FF | Donaghmede | 2894 |

Tony Gregory TD who was the only candidate in the country to exceed 4000 first preference votes.

Carmencita Hederman the leading votegetter among the Senators who contested the 1991 local elections

Michael Creed TD Fine Gael's leading votegetter with 3,267 first preference votes.

Ned O'Keeffe TD Fianna Fail's leading votegetter with 3,419 first preference votes.

## BASED ON NUMBER OF QUOTAS RECEIVED

| | Candidate | Party | Area | Votes |
|---|---|---|---|---|
| 1. | N. Dempsey | FF | Trim | 2.01 |
| 2. | M. Dollard | LB | Mullingar Urban | 1.98 |
| 3. | T. Gregory | NP | North Inner City | 1.93 |
| 4. | L. Aylward | FF | Piltown | 1.89 |
| 5. | M. Lowry | FG | Thurles | 1.85 |
| 6. | J. Dunne | FF | Portlaoise | 1.83 |
| 7. | J. O'Donoghue | FF | Killorglin | 1.74 |
| 8. | S. Ryan | LB | Swords | 1.74 |
| 9. | D. Spring | LB | Tralee | 1.63 |
| 10. | J. Moloney | FF | Tinnahinch | 1.59 |

Noel Dempsey TD who was the only candidate in the country to exceed two quotas.

Mick Dollard, of the Labour Party, who was only a handful of votes off two quotas.

Michael Lowry TD who was Fine Gael's leading votegetter per quota throughout the country with 1.85 quotas in Thurles.

John O'Donoghue TD who was the seventh best votegetter in the county in terms of both first preference votes and also quotas.

# Women and the 1991 Local Elections

## BY YVONNE GALLIGAN

**Lecturer in Politics at the Institute of Public Administration, Dublin.**

It was anticipated that the 1991 local election would see women make a significant breakthrough into local government in the Republic of Ireland. This expectation, held mainly by women political activists and media commentators, stemmed from the encouragement given to women's participation in political life by the victory of Mary Robinson just seven months previously. This hope rested on the assumption that a significant women's vote had been instrumental in voting Mary Robinson into the office of President and was available for translation into votes for women candidates in the local election. It was relatively unjustified as there was no evidence of a strong feminist vote in either the Presidential election or in the 1991 local election.

In any event, the election of 103 women to local councils around the country represented a modest increase of 29 women councillors over the results of the previous local elections held in 1985. The hoped for breakthrough, which, in order to be significant, was estimated as requiring the election of between 220 and 290 women (one quarter to one third of the council seats), did not occur. Nonetheless, the campaign and its result gives a snapshot of the representation of women in local politics at an interesting point in time. In looking at this event, some of the reasons for the rather modest performance of women become apparent.

### THE INVOLVEMENT OF WOMEN IN THE 1991 LOCAL ELECTION

There were 285 women candidates among the total of 1,973 individuals running for local government seats in 1991. This was both the highest number and proportion of women to contest the five local elections held in the last 25 years. The progressive increase in the numbers of women standing for local councils over this period can be seen in Table 1 below. Yet, it is significant to note that despite this consistent increase in women's candidatures in 1991, there were almost six men candidates to each woman seeking election.

This leads on to the related question of which party provided the most opportunities for women to be selected

> **There were almost six men candidates to each woman seeking election**

as candidates in the 1991 local elections. The pattern of women's selection by party is illustrated in Table 2. This shows that Fianna Fail and Fine Gael between them chose 141, or almost half of the women candidates in this election. In terms of the balance between men and women party candidates, the Green Party and the Workers' Party selected the most women in proportion to the size of their overall party ticket, at around one third and one quarter respectively. The Progressive Democrats followed, with 20 per cent women candidates. Only 13

> **The newer parties are considerably more open to selecting women than the older parties**

per cent of the total candidates fielded by the three long-established parties - Fianna Fail, Fine Gael and Labour - were women. In contrast, the more recently established Progressive Democrats, Greens and Workers' Party achieved a selection rate of 25 per cent women from

## TABLE 1: WOMEN'S REPRESENTATION IN LOCAL GOVERNMENT, 1967-91

| Year of Elect. | Total Cand. | Women Cand. | % Women Cand. | Seats | Women Elected | Women as % of Total Councillors |
|---|---|---|---|---|---|---|
| 1967 | n.a. | 63 | n.a. | 795 | 26 | 3.2 |
| 1974 | 1811 | 86 | 4.7 | 795 | 42 | 5.2 |
| 1979 | 1812 | n.a. | n.a. | 806 | 55 | 6.8 |
| 1985 | 1958 | 229 | 11.7 | 883 | 71 | 8.1 |
| 1991 | 1973 | 285 | 14.4 | 883 | 103 | 11.7 |

The figures relate to County Councils and County Borough Councils. Urban District Councils and Town Commissions are not included.

n.a. = not available.
Source: Manning, 1987: 160; Randall and Smyth, 1987: 206; Department of the Environment official returns, 1974, 1979, 1991.

### TABLE 2: WOMEN CANDIDATES BY PARTY AFFILIATION, 1991

| Party | Total Candidates | Women Candidates | Women as % of Total Candidates | Total Councillors | Women Councillors | Women as % of Total Councillors |
|---|---|---|---|---|---|---|
| Fianna Fail | 644 | 71 | 11.0 | 357 | 34 | 6.7 |
| Fine Gael | 471 | 70 | 14.9 | 270 | 32 | 11.9 |
| Labour | 201 | 29 | 14.4 | 90 | 14 | 15.6 |
| Progressive Democrats | 125 | 25 | 20.0 | 37 | 12 | 32.4 |
| Green Party | 60 | 21 | 35.0 | 13 | 5 | 38.5 |
| Workers' Party | 82 | 20 | 24.4 | 24 | 4 | 16.7 |
| Sinn Fein | 61 | 3 | 5.0 | 7 | — | — |
| Others | 329 | 46 | 14.0 | 85 | 12 | 14.1 |
| Total | 1973 | 285 | 14.4 | 883 | 103 | 11.7 |

**Source: Department of the Environment, Local Elections 1991, Dublin: Stationery Office.**

among their total candidates . This suggests that the newer parties are considerably more open to selecting women than the older parties. In the case of the Greens and Workers' Party, this can be seen as a reflection of their respective internal policies of attempting to achieve gender equality. In the case of the PDs, the party offered women opportunities for becoming politically involved without their first having to overcome ingrained organisational and attitudinal barriers to the selection of women candidates. As a result, these parties can present more opportunities for the selection of women and

newcomers to politics than the older parties. Indeed, it has long been recognised by both politicians and political analysts that the selection process is one of the most difficult obstacles for women to negotiate. Anything which removes some of the barriers for women in securing selection considerably increases their success rate at selection conventions. The patterns of women's candidatures at the 1991 local election bears out this observation.

However, in countering the charge that there were not sufficient women selected to contest the 1991 local

election, the political parties invariably point to the fact that few women make themselves available for selection due to their family commitments. While this indeed is a major consideration, recent research on women's representation in local politics from both Northern Ireland and the Republic suggests that a positive and supportive attitude of party leaders towards women's candidature is of considerable significance in determining the extent of women's success at the selection stage.

In terms of geographical distribution, over one quarter (26.6 per cent) of the candidates in Dublin city and county were women, while in the rest of the country women accounted for slightly over one in eight (12.8 per cent) of the candidates. Given that the majority of women standing for election held party affiliations, this suggests that parties are considerably more open to selecting women candidates in the Dublin region than in other parts of the country. This certainly held true for the Green Party and the Workers' Party, who ran respectively 13 (61.9 per cent ) and 12 (60.0 per cent) of their women candidates in this part of the country. This was followed by Labour and the Progressive Democrats, who fielded 12 (41.3 per cent) and 10 (40.0 per cent) of their women candidates in Dublin city and county. Fianna Fail and Fine Gael selected 22 (31.0 per cent) and 21 (30.0 per cent) of their women candidates in Dublin. Two of the three women candidates for Sinn Fein contested in Dublin.

Fellow PD members Liz O'Donnell, who was successful in Rathmines, and Jeananne Crowley who was defeated in Pembroke.

## THE PERFORMANCE OF WOMEN IN 1991 - SOME PATTERNS:

The analysis so far suggests that the most favourable formula for the selection and electoral success of women in the 1991 local election rested on a combination of being a candidate from one of the newer parties and standing in a Dublin electoral area. Taking a closer look at the party element of this equation, it is evident that, as with men candidates, the electoral fortunes of women were inextricably linked with the overall level of voter support for each party. Table 3 summarises the relevant trends. Thus, Fianna Fail women fared badly in the 1991 local elections, reflecting the drop in electoral support for that party. The Green Party and the Progressive Democrats, at 38.5 and 32.4 per cent respectively, had the highest proportion of women councillors elected. Both parties were the beneficiaries of substantial voter support. The PDs were, of course, contesting local government seats for the first time in 1991. The proportion of women councillors elected for the Workers' Party (16.7 per cent), Labour (15.6 per cent) and Fine Gael (11.6 per cent) was considerably less than that of the PD and Green women. One reason for this lies in the fact that Labour and Fine Gael did not select proportionally as many women candidates as the two newer parties. Consequently, they did not have sufficient women in strategic positions to benefit from either an increase in their vote or the operation of PR. The success rate of women who ran as independents

> ## There may be some credence in the view that voters gave a slight preference to men candidates over women in 1991

or for one of the minor parties was, at 14 per cent, in this range.

Overall, though, women candidates did not fare as well as their male counterparts. Just over one third (35 per cent) of the women who ran were

elected, while men had an almost even chance (46 per cent) of succeeding in their bid to win a local government seat. This suggests that there may be some credence in the view that voters gave a slight preference to men candidates over women in 1991. If one looks at the rate of success of incumbents, it is possible to see whether there is any basis for making this statement.

The incumbency factor is one of considerable importance in predicting the likelihood of candidate success. Generally, it is considered very difficult to unseat a candidate already holding political office. This is true for the 1991

local election. Over one third of all candidates (684 or 34.7 per cent) were running for re-election. Of these, one tenth were women. Of the 68 women councillors who went forward for re-election, 56 were returned, giving an incumbency success rate for women of 82 per cent. This is lower than the overall success rate for incumbents, which was 90.3 per cent. Thus, there is an indication that it is slightly more difficult for women councillors to hold on to their seats. This trend must, however, be treated with caution for two reasons. First, as there were far fewer women councillors seeking re-election

## TABLE 3: WOMEN ELECTED PER PARTY PER COUNCIL

| Council | Seats | FF | FG | LB | PD | WP | GP | SF | NP | Total |
|---|---|---|---|---|---|---|---|---|---|---|
| Carlow | 21 | 1 | 1 | | | | | | | 2 |
| Cavan | 25 | | 1 | | | | | | 2 | 3 |
| Clare | 32 | | 2 | | 1 | | | | 2 | 5 |
| Cork Corp. | 31 | 1 | | | 1 | 1 | | | | 3 |
| Cork | 48 | 1 | 1 | 2 | | | | | | 4 |
| Donegal | 29 | 1 | 1 | | | | | | | 2 |
| Dublin Corp. | 52 | 3 | 1 | 2 | 1 | 1 | 2 | | 1 | 11 |
| Dublin Fingal | 24 | 1 | 3 | 2 | 1 | | | | | 7 |
| Dublin South | 26 | 2 | 2 | | 3 | | | 1 | | 8 |
| Dun Laoghaire | 28 | 1 | 2 | 3 | 1 | | | 1 | | 8 |
| Galway Corp. | 15 | | 1 | | 1 | | | | | 2 |
| Galway | 30 | 2 | | | 1 | | | | | 3 |
| Kerry | 27 | | | 2 | | | | | | 2 |
| Kildare | 25 | | 1 | | | 1 | | | 1 | 3 |
| Kilkenny | 26 | 1 | 2 | | | | | | | 3 |
| Laois | 25 | 2 | | | 1 | | | | | 3 |
| Leitrim | 22 | 1 | 1 | | | | | | | 2 |
| Limerick Corp. | 17 | | | 1 | | | | | | 1 |
| Limerick | 28 | 1 | 1 | 1 | | | | | | 3 |
| Longford | 21 | | 2 | | | | | | 1 | 3 |
| Louth | 26 | | | | 1 | | | | | 1 |
| Mayo | 31 | 1 | | | | | | | | 1 |
| Meath | 29 | 1 | 1 | | | | | | 1 | 3 |
| Monaghan | 20 | 2 | | | | | | | | 2 |
| Offaly | 21 | 1 | 1 | 1 | | | | | | 3 |
| Roscommon | 26 | | 1 | | | | | | 1 | 2 |
| Sligo | 25 | | 2 | | | | | | 1 | 3 |
| Tipperary North | 21 | 1 | 1 | | | | | | | 2 |
| Tipperary South | 26 | | 1 | | | | | | | 1 |
| Waterford Corp. | 15 | | | | | | | | | 0 |
| Waterford | 23 | | 1 | | | | | | | 1 |
| Westmeath | 23 | | | | | | | | | 0 |
| Wexford | 21 | | 2 | | | | | | | 13 |
| Wicklow | 24 | | | | | 1 | 1 | | 1 | 3 |
| Total 34 | 883 | 24 | 32 | 14 | 12 | 4 | 5 | 0 | 12 | 103 |
| Total Elected | | 357 | 270 | 90 | 37 | 24 | 13 | 7 | 85 | 883 |
| % Women | | 6.7 | 11.9 | 15.6 | 32.4 | 16.7 | 38.5 | 0 | 14.1 | 11.7 |

than men, there is a risk of distortion in the proportionate figures. Second, the lower incumbency return rate for women could be accounted for by the poor electoral performance of Fianna Fail being reflected in the loss of seats held by women councillors. Until there are more equal proportions of men and women incumbents contesting an election, it is difficult to determine whether a gender bias on the part of voters or party electoral performance is the more significant factor in assessing apparent differences between the overall re-election rates and the success with which women councillors retain their seats.

Finally, four of the five (80.0 per cent) Green Party women councillors were elected in Dublin. Six (50.0 per cent) Progressive Democrat women councillors won their seats in Dublin as did six (42.8) successful Labour women. Women candidates from Fianna Fail, the Workers' Party and Fine Gael did not achieve significant electoral success in the capital. Seven (33.3 per cent) of Fianna Fail's women councillors were returned in Dublin, one (25.0 per cent) Workers' Party woman candidate gained a seat and seven (22.5 per cent) women councillors were elected in Dublin for Fine Gael.

### THE RESULTS - SOME TRENDS:

There is a discernible pattern in the distribution of women councillors following the 1991 elections. There is at least one woman on 32 of the 34 councils for which elections were held on this occasion. Only two councils,

## TABLE 4: WOMEN ELECTED: 1991 V 1985

| Council | Seats | 1991 | % | 1985 | % | Seats | % |
|---|---|---|---|---|---|---|---|
| Carlow | 21 | 2 | 9.5 | 3 | 14.3 | -1 | -4.8 |
| Cavan | 25 | 3 | 12.0 | 0 | 0.0 | +3 | +12.0 |
| Clare | 32 | 5 | 15.6 | 2 | 6.3 | +3 | +9.3 |
| Cork Corp. | 31 | 3 | 9.7 | 3 | 9.7 | 0 | 0.0 |
| Cork | 48 | 4 | 8.3 | 2 | 4.2 | +2 | +4.1 |
| Donegal | 29 | 2 | 6.9 | 1 | 3.4 | +1 | +3.5 |
| Dublin Corp. | 52 | 11 | 21.2 | 7 | 13.5 | +4 | +7.7 |
| Dublin Fingal | 24 | 7 | 29.2 | 7 | 29.2 | 0 | 0.0 |
| Dublin South | 26 | 8 | 30.8 | 5 | 19.2 | +3 | +11.6 |
| Dun Laoghaire | 28 | 8 | 28.6 | 9 | 32.1 | -1 | -3.5 |
| Galway Corp. | 15 | 2 | 13.3 | 4 | 26.7 | -2 | -13.4 |
| Galway | 30 | 3 | 10.0 | 0 | 0.0 | +3 | +10.0 |
| Kerry | 27 | 2 | 7.4 | 1 | 3.7 | +1 | +3.7 |
| Kildare | 25 | 3 | 12.0 | 1 | 4.0 | +2 | +8.0 |
| Kilkenny | 26 | 3 | 11.5 | 3 | 11.5 | 0 | 0.0 |
| Laois | 25 | 3 | 12.0 | 1 | 4.0 | +2 | +8.0 |
| Leitrim | 22 | 2 | 9.1 | 1 | 4.5 | +1 | +4.6 |
| Limerick Corp. | 17 | 1 | 5.9 | 1 | 5.9 | 0 | 0.0 |
| Limerick | 28 | 3 | 10.7 | 2 | 7.1 | +1 | +3.6 |
| Longford | 21 | 3 | 14.3 | 1 | 4.8 | +2 | +9.5 |
| Louth | 26 | 1 | 3.8 | 0 | 0.0 | +1 | +3.8 |
| Mayo | 31 | 1 | 3.2 | 1 | 3.2 | 0 | 0.0 |
| Meath | 29 | 3 | 10.3 | 2 | 6.9 | +1 | +3.4 |
| Monaghan | 20 | 2 | 10.0 | 1 | 5.0 | +1 | +5.0 |
| Offaly | 21 | 3 | 14.3 | 2 | 9.5 | +1 | +4.8 |
| Roscommon | 26 | 2 | 7.7 | 1 | 3.8 | +1 | +3.9 |
| Sligo | 25 | 3 | 12.0 | 2 | 8.0 | +1 | +4.0 |
| Tipperary North | 21 | 2 | 9.5 | 2 | 9.5 | 0 | 0.0 |
| Tipperary South | 26 | 1 | 3.8 | 2 | 7.7 | -1 | -6.7 |
| Waterford Corp. | 15 | 0 | 0.0 | 1 | 6.7 | -1 | -6.7 |
| Waterford | 23 | 1 | 4.3 | 0 | 0.0 | +1 | +4.3 |
| Westmeath | 23 | 0 | 0.0 | 2 | 8.7 | -2 | -8.7 |
| Wexford | 21 | 3 | 14.3 | 2 | 9.5 | +1 | +4.8 |
| Wicklow | 24 | 3 | 12.5 | 2 | 8.3 | +1 | +4.2 |
| **Total** | **883** | **103** | **11.7** | **74** | **8.4** | **+29** | **+3.3** |

Waterford Corporation and Westmeath County Council, have no women councillors. This situation is an improvement on the 1985 pattern, where there were six councils without a single elected woman representative.

In contrast, 11 women were elected to Dublin Corporation, making this body the one with the largest number of women councillors. However, if one looks at the proportional balance of men and women on the 32 councils, Dublin South has the highest proportion of women (30.8 per cent), followed by Dublin Fingal (29.2 per cent) and Dun Laoghaire (28.6 per cent). Dublin Corporation then follows at 21.2 per cent.

Significantly fewer women were returned to local councils outside the Dublin region. Clare County Council had, at five, the highest number of women and at 15.6 per cent, the highest proportion of women of all the councils

"Smiling Faces". Alice Glenn who lost her seat on Dublin Corporation.

outside Dublin. However, Cavan County Council, Dublin South and Galway County Council showed the highest increases on the 1985 results at 12.0, 11.6 and 10.0 per cent respectively. Overall, compared with the outcome in 1985, women were returned in greater numbers to 22 councils, maintained their representation on six authorities and decreased on a further six local bodies.

Almost one quarter of the women councillors elected in 1991 stated their primary occupation as housewife (24 or 23.3 per cent). This was followed by teacher (17 or 16.5 per cent), public representative (13 or 12.6 per cent), TD (7 or 6.7 per cent) and Senator (5 or 4.8 per cent). This occupational profile is different to the overall picture for councillors, where farmer (18 per cent), TD (12 per cent) and teacher (10.5 per cent) are the three occupations occurring with the greatest frequency.

Following the local elections, there were 16 co-options to fill vacancies arising from either death or resignations of elected councillors. Two of these co-options were women, bringing the total number of women councillors to 105.

In conclusion, the 1991 local election did not result in an influx of women into

## WOMEN ELECTED: TOP VOTEGETTERS BY VOTES

| Names | Party | L.E.A. | Votes |
|---|---|---|---|
| 1. C. Hederman | NP | Pembroke | 3126 |
| 2. E. Fitzgerald | LB | Stillorgan | 1800 |
| 3. O. Bennett | FF | Ballyfermot | 1774 |
| 4. M. Coughlan | FF | Donegal | 1747 |
| 5. L. O'Donnell | PD | Rathmines | 1635 |
| 6. A. Ormonde | FF | Rathfarnham | 1582 |
| 7. R. Shortall | LB | Drumcondra | 1579 |
| 8. A. Reape | FF | Ballina | 1578 |
| 9. B. Coffey | FF | Dun Laoghaire | 1547 |
| 10. M. Wallace | FF | Dunshaughlin | 1469 |

local government. This was due in part to an over-estimation of the effects of the 'Robinson factor', which fuelled an expectation that women would be elected in greater numbers than before to local councils. In reality, though, the relatively disappointing performance of women at this election was in large measure due to the overall low rate of selection of women candidates by the major parties. It was given a further set-back by the poor overall performance of both Fianna Fail and Fine Gael in the election. Finally, with the exception of a small number of electoral areas in the

Dublin region, there was no substantial evidence of a 'women's vote' in the 1991 local election. On the positive side, the gradual increase in women's representation in local politics continued. 1991 may yet be seen as a consolidating rather than a mould-breaking election for women. However, in order to increase the numbers of women in local politics, a substantial commitment from the longer-established parties, Fianna Fail and Fine Gael in particular, to ensuring the selection of a considerably higher proportion of women is required.

**Fianna Fail Minister Mary O'Rourke, with party colleagues contesting the 1991 local elections.**

# Irish Local Government: Controlled to a virtual standstill

BY DICK ROCHE

Lecturer in Public Administration at University College Dublin and
Fianna Fail TD for Wicklow.

Basil Chubb in his seminal work on local government in Ireland comments that most Irish people almost certainly approve of the idea of idea of local democracy, though they do not feel very strongly about it.

> There can be no doubt that local government is the Cinderella of Ireland's public administration. It is legally subordinate

The same thought comes across more pithily in a comment by T. J. Barrington who compares Irish local government to an ancient monument. The people, while not prepared to see the monument destroyed are content to let it crumble away.

There can be no doubt that local government is the cinderella of Ireland's pubic administration. It is legally subordinate to central government, the creature of statute, lacking a basis in either the 1992 Constitution or in Bunreacht na hEireann, its 1937 successor. Local government has never received the benign treatment afforded to the State sponsored sector.

Since the foundation of the State, a number of distinct trends have marked and marred both the relationship between central and local government and the evolution of local government itself. These are:

- a continuous move from small to larger local authorities;

- a continuous trends towards centralisation and bureaucratisation;

- a growth in controls and controllers.

- the continuing dilution of the autonomy of local authorities.

## THE ABOLITION OF SMALLER AUTHORITIES & CENTRALISATION OF FUNCTIONS

The first two trends can be taken together. The trends towards centralisation which has been a feature of all aspects of Irish Public Administration is particularly evident in the local government sector. Since the very foundation of the authorities to bigger authorities, to sub-regional authorities and regional authorities.

One of the first acts of native government was to abolish 185 rural district councils and to absorb them into the existing county council structure. At the same time 127 Boards of Guardians were absorbed into 32 Boards of Health and Public Assistance.

In time with the exception of the Unified Health Boards in the four metropolitan cities, these too were abolished and their functions were taken over by the County Councils. At the beginning of the 1970s, the function health was transferred from county to Regional Health Board level.

In the first three decades of self-government other, more subtle, changes which had the same effect were the downgrading of the Town Commissioners and Joint Drainage Boards and Committees, both of which lost their rating authority status with the Drainage Committees eventually disappearing.

At the foundation of the State, Ireland had 158 rating authorities and 401 other or minor local authorities. Twenty five years later we had 85 rating authorities and less than 160 other authorities. With the final disappearance of Drainage Committees, this was to fall to just over 120.

Throughout this period, it was fashionable to argue that we had too many local authorities in terms of population when, in fact, we were moving to a position where we had far less local government than our neighbours, particularly than our European neighbours, on a population basis.

While the abolition of the smaller authorities became the most visible sign of the taming and emasculation of local government, a more insidious force was in operation in the background-the reduction of the autonomy of local authorities in general and the displacement of democratic local government by bureaucratic local government.

## CENTRALISATION & BUREAUCRATISATION

As early as 1923 in the Local Government Temporary Provisions Act, the Minister for Local Government was given the power to dissolve troublesome local authorities. In the early years of the State, local authorities lost control of their staffing. With the establishment of the Local Appointments' Commission, the recruitment of senior positions was centralised. At the same time the recruitment of junior personnel became the subject of more specific regulation.

In the same year as the Commission came into effect, 1926, another idea of an immeasurable impact on local government also emerged - the concept of the City and County Manager. The managerial system which applies in local government can rightly be said to be only uniquely Irish experiment in public administration. The concept made its appearance in the report of the Greater Dublin Commission. The Commission which was set up in 1924 when Dublin and Cork Corporations found themselves abolished, recommend a division between the political and administrative sides of local government with the appointment of managers to take charge of the latter.

The managerial system was established in 1928 in the City of Cork. Between that date and 1941,it spread throughout the county. While there can be no doubt that the arrival of the managerial system represented progress and modernisation in administrative terms, it, in equal measure, marked the beginning of decline in the role of the

> Local government law is complex and the controls which apply are myriad

democratically elected representative.

The managerial Acts sought to incorporate into Irish local government law a dichotomy between policy and administration which cannot exist in fact. The innovation met with spirited opposition in its early years. A series of amending Bills were introduced. All failed until in 1955 the City and County Management (Amendment) Act found its way onto the statute books. That Act was intended to restore the balance between bureaucracy and democracy. It did little more than genuflect in the direction of a system whose days were over. As recently as last year in the interests of preventing what some termed abuse, the central element of that Act - the Council's right to direct a manager - was itself wound further back.

Since the enactment of the Managerial Acts, the democratic portion of local government has steadily declined and the bureaucratic has grown. Now our local authorities look more and more like some hybrid offshoot of an agency of central government.

### CONTROLS & CONTROLLERS

It is more difficult to portray the growth of controls and controllers. However, more important than the evolution of both is the fact of their existence and their impact.

Dick Roche, second from left, chats with party colleagues, former Taoiseach Charles Haughey, Dermot Ahern and Sean Calleary. All but Haughey have been local government representatives.

Local government law is complex and the controls which apply are myriad. In 1943, the late Justice Gavan Duffy characterised the Irish system as jungle - a tangled mass of statutes rules and orders.

From the foundation of the State central, control by ministerial departments grew steadily to the point where in the late 1950s it had become in Chubb's words 'ubiquitous, unsystematic and uneven'. There has been some codification and tidying up since, however, the general description is still apt.

Herman Finer in his work 'English Local Government', a book which has long since fallen from fashion, provides a useful taxonomy. His list can be applied to the Irish case with some minor modifications. Taking Finer's list we have the following departmental and ministerial controls. Taking first the administrative controls.

### —TUTELARY POWERS

From the same latin base as Tutor, mentor or guide. In many ways this is the most subtle form of control exercised through the notes, comments and explanations of legislation and regulation which flow continuously from central government to local government. (Interestingly, in the French systems, the perfect - a position with similarities to the county managerial system to the County Manager exercises a 'tutelle administrative' or supervisory role over local government units.)

### —RULES, ORDERS & REGULATIONS

Most laws on local government leave it to the central department to detail the precise intention of the law in Rules Orders and Regulations. These are so tightly drawn that, with their explanatory memorandum, they severely limit any chance of local inventiveness arising at the implementation stage.

> A Minister can call on the local authority to make a report to him or her on any matter

### —SANCTIONS & APPROVALS

While many laws or schemes may grant a general power to the local authority, the Minister retains the right to grant the final sanction or approval. Thus, for example, bylaws are made by the local authorities subject to confirmation from the Central Department. Decisions to amend boundaries require ministerial approval, although the individual authorities concerned are the only ones truly affected. Sanctions are required in a whole series of areas.

## —INSPECTION

There exists a great duplicating layer of technical inspectors, engineers, fire fighting inspectors, etc. whose effectiveness or purpose of detailed inspection must be questioned.

## APPEALS

While less important than in the pre-Bord Pleanala days, there still exist areas, where ministerial appeals remain. In certain staff matters, for example, there is a right of appeal to the Minister.

## REPORTS & ENQUIRIES

A Minister can call on the local authority to make a report to him or her on any matter. In the same area of control, Ministers can appoint an enquiry or even a sworn enquiry. Another variation in the same theme is the British practice of appointing advisory bodies, a devise described by Finer as 'one of the more fruitful contributions of the 20th Century'.

In addition to administrative controls, a series of Financial control mechanisms also exists including,

## APPROVALS

In major works a whole series of approvals are required before preparing tenders, going to tender and accepting tenders. Where local authorities are raising loans approval from the 'parent' department and the Department of Finance is required. The approval system for VEC school building undoubtedly rank as one of the more tediously bureaucratic in operation in any developed administration.

## AUDIT

The local government audit, conducted by auditors appointed by the Minister, is particularly comprehensive and has novel features such as the surcharge and the right of the public to draw to the Auditors attention a matter in the local authority accounts. The audit is another novel feature in that is advertised inviting members of the public to make an input, something which does not happen in the audit of central departments or state sponsored bodies.

## CASH LIMITS

The financial provisions legislation introduced in 1978 brought two new forms of financial control. Under Section 10 of the legislation, the Minister for the Environment was empowered to limit the level of year on year increase in the rate in the pound struck by local authorities. While the rating system had been in terminal disarray for two decades before this change, the Section 10 provisions marked a final step away from one of the most fundamental principles of local government-the principle which linked the charge for local services to the beneficiaries of local service by giving local elected representatives, ultimately answerable to the people, responsibility, for the levels of local taxation.

An equally important departure from the principle was to be found in Section 11 of the same legislation which gave the Minister the right to determine the amount that could be spent on any particular expenditure programme-a

> Since 1978, the most fundamental control which has been imposed on local government has been the tightening of budgets

function which can be regarded as central to one of the new few remaining real powers residing in the elected council-the power to adopt the estimates of expenditure. The point can, of course, be made here that Ministers had long possessed the power to strike down a Council which adopted an estimate or struck a rate which was regarded as inadequate.

A further important departure from principle was signalled in the initial proposals for service charges in 1983. These proposed that the Manager rather than the elected Council set the level of charges. While this proposal was amended, it is significant that a government composed of parties who had decried the shift in balance of authority away from the elected Council, could even contemplate such a fundamental departure.

Since 1978 the most fundamental control which has been imposed on local government has been the tightening of budgets. While changes in the financial relationships between central and local authorities, in particular, the abolition of circular flows of funds means that the effective cutback in real terms is somewhat less than the lurid projected losses highlighted in many managers reports, there is no contesting the fact, in the decade and a half since the 'abolition of the rates' there has been a swinging cutback in the overall budgets of all local Councils in real terms.

Parallel, with the real term loss of funding and in spite of promises to move to more block grant allocations, another financial reality faced in the same period by local government is a dramatic diminution of the element of discretion which the elected councils have within their own budgets. Increasingly committed expenditure on which there can be no variation has grown while the discretionary element (of discretion which the elected councils have within their own budgets) has dwindled. While Councils still adopt estimates increasingly, the estimate procedure is a rubber stamping exercise.

## LEGAL CONTROLS

In addition to administration and financial controls, the local government system must cope with legal controls. The legal basis of local government-its nature as a creature of statute, has historically been one of the major constraints.

The ultra vires doctrine which flowed from the legal basis of local government has been portrayed as a major constraint on local authorities.

Ultra vires meant that each action of a local authority had to be capable of defence by reference to a specific statutory authority

Where statutory authority could not be adduced, application of ultra vires could result ultimately in either a High Court injunction restraining performance or a disallowance and surcharge by the local government auditor.

The 1971 White Paper proposed the 'abolition' of ultra vires and its replacement by a positive statement of the powers of local authorities. As a mark of the glacial pace of progress in local government it was not until 1991 that legislation was actually enacted to curb ultra vires. Section 6 of the 1991 Act is designed to give local authorities more discretion and more flexibility of action in local government matters. It provides authorities with a general

# Why should you let this woman tell you what to do with your money?

You may be wondering what to do with that lump sum you just received. You may want to save for a holiday, a new car or for that special occasion. Whatever the reason, you'll be looking for sound advice so that your money works harder for you.

Working out the most suitable savings or investment plan calls for expert advice. At Bank of Ireland we can ensure that you are guided through the range of options most suited to your needs, from short-term savings to longer-term investments.

By combining the resources of Bank of Ireland, ICS Building Society, Lifetime Assurance, Investment Bank of Ireland and Davy Stockbrokers we know we can plan together to help make it happen for you.

The woman on the left may be the one. Or the man who works next to her. Whichever of our 11,000 employees you do business with, you can be certain that they will advise you in confidence and without obligation.

Now, can we tell you what to do with your money?

**Bank of Ireland**

Helping to make things happen.

competence with regard to type of administration outlined in the section. While this is a welcome change, arguably it falls short of a complete removal of ultra vires and it will take time before its impact can be measured. The Minister has promised further legislation in the next year.

There are, of course, general legal controls too. The local authorities like any other corporate person are subject to the courts. While nobody can argue that this is other than it should be, one has the inescapable feeling that in our many court battles that have taken place, the judges do not always provide a sympathetic ear to the local authorities.

## OTHER AREAS OF CONTROL

There are of course other areas of control. Local authorities are not just administrative organs, they are institutions with a democratic element. The public, through the ballot box, exercise ultimate control on this element. Local government is, therefore, more subject to public pressure and to lobbying than either the commercial or non-commercial state sponsored bodies or the administrators of the departments of State.

There are, in addition to this, unique if somewhat obscure, controls which the public can exercise. The public has, for example, a right to inspect the books of a local authority. They can not only request access to books, but while not often used, do not apply elsewhere in public administration.

## MULTIPLICITY OF CONTROLLERS

Local government in Ireland does not suffer only from a multiplicity of controls, it also has a multiplicity, indeed a bewildering array, of controllers. The Minister for the Environment is the main controller but colleagues also get in on the act. Local authorities must answer to the Ministers for Education (VECs, grants etc.); Agriculture (County Committees of Agriculture); Health (Health Boards and Public Health); Defence (Civil Defence); Marine (Foreshore); Ombudsman, to their own elected representatives and to the public.

Local government is in effect controlled to a virtual standstill.

Irish local government is not unique in being controlled. The French system while subject to major changes in recent years still has the Prefect in operation, linking the local to central government. The English system has more direct elective control and it also has tight spending controls exercised from the centre. In the United States there are in fact a number of different models of local administration some strong and some weak.

What is unique in the Irish system is that it applies, at the same time, all the controls which exists in other systems with some additions. This lead the

> # Historically, there has always been a tension between local and central administration in Ireland

Radcliffe Maude Commission in the U.K. to observe that Ireland's was the most controlled of all the local government systems it examined.

The question is why? The answer to that is a complex one.

Historically, there has always been a tension between local and central administration in Ireland. Immediately prior to the birth of the nation the political nature of local government was exploited by the men and women who went on to scale the political heights in the new state. They, in turn, faced the same problems-the use of local government by political opponents, and so it has continued to this day. The fact is that local government is political. Parties and persons who are excluded from government can command control at local level. It is hardly surprising if political opponents in government do not go to the trouble to enhance their opponents, power bases.

There is also the fact that local government is often the stepping stone to national politics. Self preservation means that people who made the transition, invariably after some hardship, are prone to be less than generous when it comes to endowing future competitors with additional power and authority.

It is not, however, all defensive posturing from the top. The members of local councils become little more than mini Dala where Members focus on things they cannot change while ignoring the things that they can.

While the managerial system was the subject of a spirited opposition in its first decade, it has to be said that local authority members in recent decades have been accommodated all too well to it. The point has long been reached where local representatives have willingly accepted a position of role representatives in command.

There are also a number of philosophical attitudes which pervade public administration in Ireland and which have had an impact.

There is an almost touching belief in the concept of economies of scale in Irish public administration, a belief which contrary to all the evidence, sees big as beautiful. Thus one has the sustained attack on the VEC system-a policy of movement which transcends politics and which is firmly set on replacing the 38 VECs with a lesser number of bigger sub-regional bodies. The same attitude is visible in health administration where administrators have an ongoing agenda of centralisation which is not necessarily by politicians.

There is also a belief in central administrative circles that the only effective way to control expenditure is from the centre, and that in a sense local government agencies cannot be trusted to contain themselves. In part, this is because the managers of central government have failed to keep abreast of management development and thus have failed to evolve mechanisms which regulate but do not stifle.

Finally, there is the conditioning of both the public and indeed the politicians to accepting that local government is secondary. For far too long there has been a corrosive cynicism in this nation about politics, politicians and public service. Commentators who have conspicuously failed to contribute anything to the life of the nation, continuously denigrate those who have at least tried. Local government which is accessible, not overly endowed with efficiency and operating on a shoestring, provides the cynical commentator with an all too easy target.

The Minister has promised further reforms and legislation we need to change more than the law.

# The Question of Local Service Charges

**BY KEVIN RAFTER**

They called it the 'Foxe Factor' in Roscommon but it is a feature not exclusive to that constituency, in the place of 'Foxe' and 'Roscommon' insert 'Gilligan' and 'Limerick', 'Gorman and Meath' . . . The main political parties like to see the election of such Council Members as a product of the 'anti-this, that, and the other thing vote'. While this contains an element of truth, to ignore this feature and dismiss it as a quirk of local elections would be wholly incorrect. The big 'protest' issue in the 1991 local elections was the local service charges, the inequities of the charging system and Fianna Fail's broken promise of 1985.

Local authorities are financed from property rates, state fundings and other miscellaneous sources of income. Domestic rates were abolished in 1977 with any shortfall being made good by Central Government grants. In 1978, the Government sought to place limitations on the amount which it was obliged to give councils to replace the revenue lost due to the abolition of domestic rates. Further measures were later taken to absolve central government of the responsibility of matching quid-pro-quo the forgone domestic rates revenue. With the basis for valuation of agricultural land declared unconstitutional in 1982, many local authorities were placed in a difficult financial position.

To ameliorate this situation and fill the financial gap, the 1983 Local Government (Financial Provisions) Act (No. 2) increased the powers of local authorities to impose charges for

> The big 'protest' issue in the 1991 local election was that of local service charges

certain domestic services such as refuse collection, water and sewage. Up to 1985, the power to make decisions on charges rested with the manager of a particular area. However, in October of that year a Ministerial Order was introduced, under the 1983 Act, making such decisions the responsibility of the councillors of a given area.

With greater competition for scarcer Central Government funds, and increased demands for and cost of, services provided, local authorities throughout the country have had to increase, and extend, the extent of charges for certain local services. Today, Dublin County Council and Dublin Corporation are the only local authorities in the country which do not impose any local charges for domestic services.

Dublin's status as capital city places it at an advantage over other areas. Last year almost half of the £250 million levied in commercial rates in the state were collected in Dublin. This money — approximately £35 million for the County Council and £80 million for the Corporation — allows the Dublin region's officials to provide local services without the need to apply local charges.

The other authorities, including Dun Laoghaire Corporation, are obliged to levy domestic service charges to supplement the income which they receive from central government.

These charges have been imposed in an ad hoc and uneven manner as the accompanying table clearly indicates. Moreover, there does not appear to be any linkage whatsoever between the level of service provided and value for money.

In a report for the Barrington Committee, the London based Institute of Fiscal Studies, observed that the principle of 'horizontal equity' was not being adhered to with the present local changes framework. This is because "people living in different authorities may pay different

**Donegal Councillors Colm Gallagher and James McBrearty with Donegal County Secretary Tom O'Reilly.**

levels of charges for a similar level of service." For example with regard to refuse collection it can cost from 25 pence to 50 pence per tag (one tag per rubbish bag) in different local authority areas. In Galway County Council it costs 50 pence per tag in

> ## Charges have been imposed in an ad hoc and uneven manner . . .

Connemara for a fortnightly collection, while in the remainder of that local authority area, householders are charged £75 to £80 per annum to have their refuse collected on a weekly basis.

The Institute's Report also noted that "there appears to be no clear criteria for the determination and setting of charges, and the level of charges in different authorities does not appear to be related to the cost of the relevant service."

> ## The contentious local service charge issue will remain on the political agenda

The uneven levying of service charges by local authorities is a product of the 1978 abolition of domestic rates. Unfortunately, the issue of financing local government was not within the terms of reference of the Barrington Committee. Therefore the contentious local service charge issue will remain on the political agenda until an independent source of local revenue is decided upon.

| County Council | Water | Refuse | Sewerage |
|---|---|---|---|
| Carlow | £54 | 25p per tag | |
| Cavan | £71.50 | £27.50 | £27 |
| Clare | £95 | £37 | £27.50 |
| Cork North | £63.60 | 50p per tag | N/C |
| Cork South | £51-£76 | £36 | N/C |
| Cork West | £69 | — | N/C |
| Donegal | £40 | £40 | N/C |
| Galway | £85 | 50p per tag Connemara | N/C |
| Kerry | £80 | 50p per tag | N/C |
| Kildare | £55 | £50 | N/C |
| Kilkenny | £62 | 25p per tag | N/C |
| Laoighis | £65 | N/C | N/C |
| Leitrim | £80 | £30 | £10 |
| Limerick | £42-£71 | 33p per tag | N/C |
| Longford | £75 | N/C | N/C |
| Louth | £75 | 50p per tag | £20 |
| Mayo | £78 | £40-£52 | N/C |
| Meath | £80 | £60 (privatised) | N/C |
| Monaghan | £60 | £20 | N/C |
| Offaly | £65 | 25p per tag | £15 |
| Roscommon | £75 | £30 fortnightly, £40 weekly | N/C |
| Sligo | £50 | £50 | £40 |
| Tipperary NR | £96 | N/C | £30 |
| Tipperary SR | £75 | £35 | N/C |
| Waterford | £98 | 25p per tag | N/C |
| Westmeath | £92 | £26 | £26 |
| Wexford | £80 | 33p per tag | N/C |
| Wicklow | £49 | £44 | £49 |
| **DUBLIN** | | | |
| Dublin Co. Council | N/C | N/C | N/C |
| Dublin Corporation | N/C | N/C | N/C |
| Dun Laoghaire Corporation (VB) | £47-£130 | N/C | N/C |
| **OTHER BOROUGH CORPORATIONS** | | | |
| Cork (VB) | £56-£137 | £16 | N/C |
| Galway (VB) | £30 | N/C | £13 |
| Limerick (VB) | £24.75-£73.35 | £24.75-£73.35 | N/C |
| *Waterford (VB) | £18.75-£56.25 | N/C | N/C |

N/C - No Charge.   VB - Valuation Based   * Waterford applies a developmental, as distinct from a water, refuse or sewerage charge. Figures are 1991 based.

# Financial services tailored to suit your requirements.

At Woodchester Crédit Lyonnais Bank, one of Ireland's largest and fastest growing financial services groups, personal and business loans are one of our strong suits.

Our expert staff can tailor just about any loan or leasing package to fit your needs.

From leases for cars, office equipment and agricultural machinery to personal finance loans for home improvements, holidays and educational fees.

We also provide made-to-measure insurance premium loans, commercial property finance and professional practice finance.

Plus currency deposit and foreign exchange services. And the highest rates on fixed income, demand and monthly income deposit accounts.

So whatever your financial needs, Woodchester Crédit Lyonnais Bank has a loan or leasing package to suit you.

Give us a call today and try us on for size.

# CARLOW COUNTY COUNCIL

## CARLOW COUNTY COUNCIL RESULTS

| PARTY | 1991 % of votes | 1991 Seats obtained | 1985 % of votes | 1985 Seats obtained |
|---|---|---|---|---|
| Fianna Fail | 39.3 | 9 | 44.3 | 10 |
| Fine Gael | 31.0 | 7 | 29.7 | 7 |
| Labour | 23.3 | 4 | 18.7 | 3 |
| Progressive Dem. | 2.5 | 1 | — | — |
| Workers Party | — | — | 0.5 | — |
| Other | 3.9 | — | 6.8 | 1 |
| **TOTAL SEATS** | | **21** | | **21** |

## CARLOW

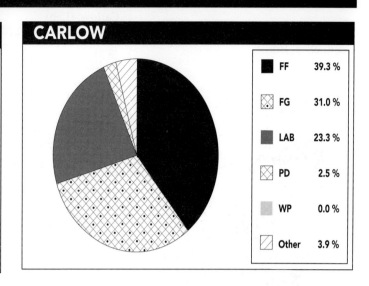

| | |
|---|---|
| FF | 39.3 % |
| FG | 31.0 % |
| LAB | 23.3 % |
| PD | 2.5 % |
| WP | 0.0 % |
| Other | 3.9 % |

**County Offices, Carlow**
**Telephone: (0503) 31126**
**Total population: 40,988**
**Rateable valuation: £297,274.55**
**Rate: £25.43**
**County Council meetings: First Monday in each month**
**(excl. August)**

*County Manager*: Matthew O'Connor
*County Secretary*: J. Kearney
*Finance Officer* Vacant
*County Engineer*: F. O'Feighan
*County Development Officer*: J. Lane
*Administrative Officer*: G. O'Brien
*Senior Staff Officers*:
*Roads and Planning*: D. McDonnell
*Rates and County Checker*: R. Forde
*Housing*: J. Watters
*County Librarian*: T. King
*Library*: Dublin Street, Carlow
*Telephone*: (0503) 31126
*County Solicitor*: F. Lanigan
*County Coroner*: Dr Brendan Doyle,
*Chief Fire Officer*: Seamus Grogan
*Senior Executive Engineers*:
*Roads*: S. O'Connor
*Housing*: P. Connolly
*Planning and Development*: L. Fitzgerald
*Sanitary-Environment*: J. Higginson
*Veterinary Inspector*: Elizabeth McCollum

Matt O'Connor was educated at the Patrician College, Ballyfin and later at University College, Cork.

He began his Local Authority career as a clerical officer with Offaly County Council. He later served as Town Clerk with both Birr and Dungarvan Urban District Councils.

He was Senior Staff Officer with Cork Corporation before joining the Western Health Board as Senior Executive Officer.

He later returned to a career in Local Government and Cork Corporation. He was Assistant City Manager in Cork before his appointment in 1990 as County Manager in Carlow.

He is responsible for a budget in excess of £15 million per annum and a staff of 257.

Matt O'Connor is married with two sons and his hobbies include music, gardening and golf.

## BORRIS

|      | 1991 | 1985 | '85 to '91 Swing |
|------|------|------|------|
| FF   | 48.7 | 43.4 | 5.3  |
| FG   | 22.2 | 25.3 | -3.1 |
| Lab  | 29.2 | 31.3 | -2.1 |

DOYLE, Michael,
Courtnellan, Borris,
County Carlow. (FG)
Farmer. 0503-73510.

KINSELLA, Mary,
Kilbrannish, Bunclody,
County Wexford. (FF)
Teacher. 054-77750

MEANEY, Michael,
Courtnellan, Borris,
County Carlow. (Lab)
Farmer. 0503-73366

WALSH, Brendan,
Tinnahinch, Graiguenamanagh,
County Kilkenny. (FF)
Solicitor. 0503-24155

## CARLOW

|      | 1991 | 1985 | '85 to '91 Swing |
|------|------|------|------|
| FF   | 40.5 | 44.0 | -3.5 |
| FG   | 32.1 | 29.1 | 3.0  |
| Lab  | 15.2 | 4.1  | 11.1 |
| PD   | 8.3  | —    | 8.3  |
| SF   | 0.0  | 5.0  | -5.0 |
| IND  | 3.8  | 17.8 | -14.0 |

ALCOCK, Declan,
96 Pearse Road, Graiguecullen,
Carlow. (FG)
Barman. 0503-32523.

BROWNE, John,
Ballinacarrig,
Carlow. (FG)
Dail Deputy. 0503-31579.

CARPENTER, Paddy,
10 Barrack Street,
Carlow. (FF)
Publican. 0503-43049.

HURLEY, Des,
30 St Fiacc's Terrace, Graiguecullen,
Carlow. (Lab)
Self-employed. 0503-32489

LACEY, Walter,
19 Avondale Drive,
Carlow. (PD)
Depot Supervisor. 0503-43274

MURNANE, Jimmy,
80 Fr Maher Road, Graiguecullen,
Carlow. (FF)
Flooring Contractor. 0503-31470

NOLAN, Matthew J,
Strawhall,
Carlow. (FF)
Dail Deputy. 0503-31777.

## MUINEBHEAG

|      | 1991 | 1985 | '85 to '91 Swing |
|------|------|------|------|
| FF   | 33.7 | 39.0 | -5.3 |
| FG   | 19.1 | 24.7 | -5.6 |
| Lab  | 39.9 | 35.2 | 4.7  |
| Ind  | 7.3  | 1.1  | 6.2  |

McDONALD, Arthur,
Kilcarrig Street, Bagenalstown,
County Carlow. (FF)
Farmer. 0503-21048.

McDONALD, Mary,
St Lazerian's Street, Leighlinbridge,
County Carlow. (FG)
0503-21936.

McNALLY, John,
9 Barrett Street, Muinebheag,
County Carlow. (Lab)
Unemployed. 0503-21857.

NOLAN, Enda,
Park Tinryland,
Carlow. (FF)
Manufacturer. 0503-41184

TOWNSEND, Jim,
Ballybar Upper,
Carlow. (Lab)
Farmer. 0503-416197

## TULLOW

|      | 1991 | 1985 | '85 to '91 Swing |
|------|------|------|------|
| FF   | 36.2 | 51.7 | -15.5 |
| FG   | 50.5 | 40.1 | 10.4 |
| Lab  | 9.8  | 8.2  | 1.6  |
| Ind  | 3.5  | —    | 3.5  |

DEERING, Michael,
Ballybit, Rathvilly,
County Carlow. (FG)
Farmer. 0503-61124

HUNTER, Fred,
Raheen, Tobinstown,
Tullow,
County Carlow. (FG)
Farmer. 0503-61173

KENNEDY, Arthur,
Main Street, Hacketstown,
County Carlow. (FF)
Chemist. 0508-71282

O'TOOLE, Pat,
12 Shillelagh Grove, Tullow,
County Carlow. (FG)
Builder. 0503-51940

PENDER, John,
"Grangeview", Friarstown,
Carlow. (FF)
Farmer. 0503-63760.

**Des Hurley (Lab.)**
**Carlow Rural**

**Joun Browne (FG)**
**Carlow**

**Brendan Walsh (FF)**
**Borris**

**John Pender (FF)**
**Tullow**

# The PD's and Labour Party have cause to celebrate in Carlow

Carlow's four electoral areas and 21 seats were contested by 43 candidates. Fianna Fail were to loose one of their ten seats. The only outgoing Independent seat was not contested. The P.D.'s and Labour Party were to gain a seat each.

Labour indeed has much to cheer about, four of their five candidates were elected and they were to hold the balance of power in the new Council. All three outgoing labour Councillors were returned on the first count.

Michael Meaney topped the poll in Borris with 310 votes to spare over the quota, while in the Muinebeag electoral area, the Party put in an unprecedented performance to take the first two seats. John McNally and Jim Townsend, both outgoing Councillors got 980 and 818 first preference votes respectively. The outgoing Labour trio will be joined on

the new Council by Des Hurley, who took the second seat in the Carlow Town area.

Indeed the Party came close to a grand slam with Michael Hickey just losing out in the Tullow area. He secured 389 first preferences and was in fifth position right to the last count when he lost out to Fianna Fail Arthur Kennedy by just 48 votes.

Fianna Fail now hold nine seats on the County Council, three of them new Councillors. Outgoing Councillor Liam Murphy, who had served on the Council for 36 years, lost his seat to new comer Brendan Walsh in the Borris area.

In Muinebeag, two newcomers Arthur McDonald and Enda Nolan, held onto the Party's two seats, but outgoing Councillor Martin Nevin lost out. Enda Nolan, aged 30, regained the seat vacated by his recently deceased father

and former Minister Tom Nolan. Tom had first secured the seat for Fianna Fail in 1958.

Enda's elder brother, local Fianna Fail deputy M.J. Nolan was to have a close call in the Carlow electoral area, however. Here Paddy Carpenter was Fianna Fail's strongest performer with 560 votes, followed by the colourful Jimmy Murnane. Deputy M.J. Nolan secured 379 first preference and struggled to retain his seat against Party colleague Roddy Kelly. The Carlow town based T.D. was 83 votes ahead on the final count however, and was declared elected without even reaching the quota.

M.J. had the unwelcome distinction of securing the lowest first preference vote of any TD who contested the election.

In Muinebeag Mary McDonald held onto the Party's one seat while in Tullow the Party took three out of the five seats. Michael Deering again topped the poll. Pat O'Toole, the Tullow based builder held his seat, but new comer Fred Hunter from the Tobinstown area replaced outgoing Councillor Brendan Brophy.

For the Progressive Democrats, the Carlow result brought much to celebrate. Independent poll topper Michael Kearns had joined them in 1986, but decided not to contest these Local Elections. In an upset, however Walter Lacey polled 436 and went on to take the fifth seat for the P.D.'s.

Fine Gael held their own in Carlow in these Local Elections. The Party's sitting Deputy John Browne topped the poll in the Carlow area, while newcomer Declan Alcock, a binman from Graiguecullen also took a seat for the Party at the expense of a fellow party man. Outgoing Councillor Walter Lacey held on to his Carlow town seat to the delight of Fine Gael.

**Padraig Flynn, Minister of the Environment in June 1991, on the campaign trail with Fianna Fail Carlow Councillor Jimmy Murnane.**

# BORRIS ELECTORAL AREA

TOTAL ELECTORATE 5,866. VALID POLL 3,498.

NO. OF MEMBERS 4. QUOTA 700

| Names of Candidates | First Count | Second Count | | Third Count | | Fourth Count | |
|---|---|---|---|---|---|---|---|
| | | Transfer of Meaney's surplus | | Transfer of Moore's votes | | Transfer of Redmond's votes | |
| | Votes | | Result | | Result | | Result |
| DOYLE, Michael (F.G.) | 498 | +79 | 577 | +19 | 596 | +212 | 808 |
| KINSELLA, Mary (F.F.) | 575 | +61 | 636 | +105 | 741 | — | 741 |
| MEANEY, Michael (Lab.) | 1,020 | -320 | 700 | — | 700 | — | 700 |
| MOORE, David (F.F.) | 267 | +41 | 308 | -308 | — | — | — |
| MURPHY, Liam (F.F.) | 317 | +44 | 361 | +85 | 446 | +47 | 493 |
| REDMOND, Ciaran (F.G.) | 278 | +35 | 313 | +18 | 331 | -331 | — |
| WALSH, Brendan (F.F.) | 543 | +60 | 603 | +52 | 655 | +12 | 667 |
| Non-transferable papers not effective | — | — | — | +29 | 29 | +60 | 89 |
| TOTAL: | 3,498 | — | 3,498 | — | 3,498 | — | 3,498 |

Elected: Meaney, Michael (Lab.); Kinsella, Mary (F.F.); DOYLE, Michael (F.G.); Walsh, Brendan (F.F.)

# CARLOW ELECTORAL AREA

TOTAL ELECTORATE 10,567. VALID POLL 5,223. NO. OF MEMBERS 7. QUOTA 653.

| Names of Candidates | First Count | Second Count | | Third Count | | Fourth Count | | Fifth Count | | Sixth Count | | Seventh Count | | Eighth Count | | Ninth Count | | Tenth Count | | Eleventh Count | |
|---|---|---|---|---|---|---|---|---|---|---|---|---|---|---|---|---|---|---|---|---|---|
| | | Transfer of Prendergast's surplus | | Transfer of Browne's votes | | Transfer of Brady's votes | | Transfer of C. Whelan's votes | | Transfer of Hurley's votes | | Transfer of Carpenter's votes | | Transfer of McDonald's votes | | Transfer of Governey's votes | | Transfer of S. Whelan's votes | | Transfer of Alcock's votes | |
| | Votes | | Result | | Result | | Result | | Result | | Result | | Result | | Result | | Result | | Result | | Result |
| ALCOCK, Declan (F.G.) | 413 | +1 | 414 | +14 | 428 | +12 | 440 | +10 | 450 | +10 | 460 | +2 | 462 | +24 | 486 | +84 | 570 | +169 | 739 | -86 | 653 |
| BRADY, James | 201 | +1 | 202 | +2 | 204 | -204 | — | — | — | — | — | — | — | — | — | — | — | — | — | — | — |
| BROWNE, John (F.G.) | 756 | — | 756 | -103 | 653 | — | 653 | — | 653 | — | 653 | — | 653 | — | 653 | — | 653 | — | 653 | — | 653 |
| CARPENTER, Paddy (F.F.) | 560 | +15 | 575 | +13 | 588 | +60 | 648 | +25 | 673 | — | 673 | -20 | 653 | — | 653 | — | 653 | — | 653 | — | 653 |
| GOVERNEY, Paddy (F.G.) | 255 | +2 | 257 | +21 | 278 | +11 | 289 | +10 | 299 | +7 | 306 | +2 | 308 | +14 | 322 | -322 | — | — | — | — | — |
| HURLEY, Des (Lab.) | 557 | +1 | 558 | +5 | 563 | +29 | 592 | +115 | 707 | -54 | 653 | — | 653 | — | 653 | — | 653 | — | 653 | — | 653 |
| KELLY, Rody (F.F.) | 314 | +11 | 325 | +7 | 332 | +12 | 344 | +18 | 362 | +1 | 363 | +1 | 364 | +64 | 428 | +16 | 444 | +30 | 474 | +21 | 495 |
| LACEY, Walter (P.D.) | 436 | +3 | 439 | +12 | 451 | +24 | 475 | +24 | 499 | +14 | 513 | +3 | 516 | +26 | 542 | +53 | 595 | +101 | 696 | — | 696 |
| McDONALD, Joe (F.F.) | 243 | +10 | 253 | +3 | 256 | +7 | 263 | +14 | 277 | +5 | 282 | — | 282 | -282 | — | — | — | — | — | — | — |
| MURNANE, Jimmy (F.F.) | 545 | +6 | 551 | +3 | 554 | +12 | 566 | +10 | 576 | +4 | 580 | +2 | 582 | +32 | 614 | +21 | 635 | +14 | 649 | +15 | 664 |
| NOLAN, M. J. (F.F.) | 379 | +10 | 389 | +6 | 395 | +11 | 406 | +7 | 413 | +1 | 414 | +2 | 416 | +73 | 489 | +35 | 524 | +39 | 563 | +15 | 578 |
| PRENDERGAST, Sean (F.F.) | 73 | -73 | — | — | — | — | — | — | — | — | — | — | — | — | — | — | — | — | — | — | — |
| WHELAN, Cecil (Lab.) | 238 | +4 | 242 | +3 | 245 | +12 | 257 | -257 | — | — | — | — | — | — | — | — | — | — | — | — | — |
| WHELAN, Sean (F.G.) | 253 | +8 | 261 | +14 | 275 | — | 275 | +14 | 289 | +12 | 301 | +7 | 308 | +28 | 336 | +71 | 407 | -407 | — | — | — |
| Non-transferable papers not effective | — | +1 | 1 | — | 1 | +14 | 15 | +10 | 25 | — | 25 | +1 | 26 | +21 | 47 | +42 | 89 | +54 | 143 | +35 | 178 |
| TOTAL: | 5,223 | — | 5,223 | — | 5,223 | — | 5,223 | — | 5,223 | — | 5,223 | — | 5,223 | — | 5,223 | — | 5,223 | — | 5,223 | — | 5,223 |

Elected: Browne, John (F.G.); Hurley, Des (Lab); Carpenter Paddy (F.F.); Alcock, Declan (F.G);. Lacey, Walter (P.D.); Murnane, Jimmy (F.F.); Nolan, M.J. (F.F.)

# MUINEBHEAG ELECTORAL AREA

TOTAL ELECTORATE 7,033. VALID POLL 4,509. NO. OF MEMBERS 5. QUOTA 752

| Names of Candidates | First Count Votes | Second Count Transfer of McNally's surplus | Result | Third Count Transfer of Curran's and Dillon's votes | Result | Fourth Count Transfer of Townsend's surplus | Result | Fifth Count Transfer of Maher's votes | Result | Sixth Count Transfer of Brennan's votes | Result | Seventh Count Transfer of Cullen's votes | Result | Eighth Count Transfer of Foley's votes | Result | Ninth Count Transfer of McDonald's surplus | Result |
|---|---|---|---|---|---|---|---|---|---|---|---|---|---|---|---|---|---|
| BRENNAN, Ann (F.G.) | 246 | +4 | 250 | +2 | 252 | +21 | 273 | +38 | 311 | -311 | — | — | — | — | — | — | — |
| CULLEN, Eddie (F.F.) | 292 | +14 | 306 | +6 | 312 | +2 | 314 | +7 | 321 | +9 | 330 | -330 | — | — | — | — | — |
| CURRAN, John (Non-Party) | 56 | +18 | 74 | -74 | — | — | — | — | — | — | — | — | — | — | — | — | — |
| DILLON, William (Non-Party) | 9 | +3 | 12 | -12 | — | — | — | — | — | — | — | — | — | — | — | — | — |
| FOLEY, Denis (Non-Party) | 264 | +34 | 298 | +31 | 329 | +7 | 336 | +40 | 376 | +33 | 409 | +28 | 437 | -437 | — | — | — |
| MAHER, Stephen (F.G.) | 224 | +22 | 246 | +3 | 249 | +1 | 250 | -250 | — | — | — | — | — | — | — | — | — |
| McDONALD, Arthur (F.F.) | 496 | +72 | 568 | +13 | 581 | +8 | 589 | +25 | 614 | +17 | 631 | +82 | 713 | +138 | 851 | -99 | 752 |
| McDONALD, Mary (F.G.) | 392 | +17 | 409 | +4 | 413 | +9 | 422 | +87 | 509 | +142 | 651 | +44 | 695 | +100 | 795 | — | 795 |
| McNALLY, John (Lab.) | 980 | —228 | 752 | — | 752 | — | 752 | — | 752 | — | 752 | — | 752 | — | 752 | — | 752 |
| NEVIN, Martin (F.F.) | 305 | +27 | 332 | +5 | 337 | +7 | 344 | +17 | 361 | +10 | 371 | +104 | 475 | +52 | 527 | +29 | 556 |
| NOLAN, Enda (F.F.) | 427 | +17 | 444 | +7 | 451 | +11 | 462 | +16 | 478 | +48 | 526 | +33 | 559 | +34 | 593 | +41 | 634 |
| TOWNSEND, Jim (Lab.) | 818 | — | 818 | — | 818 | -66 | 752 | — | 752 | — | 752 | — | 752 | — | 752 | — | 752 |
| Non-transferable papers not effective | — | — | — | +15 | 15 | — | 15 | +20 | 35 | +52 | 87 | +39 | 126 | +133 | 239 | +29 | 268 |
| TOTAL: | 4,509 | — | 4,509 | — | 4,509 | — | 4,509 | — | 4,509 | — | 4,509 | — | 4,509 | — | 4,509 | — | 4,509 |

Elected: McNally, John (Lab.); Townsend, Jim (Lab.); McDonald, Arthur (F.F.); McDonald, Mary (F.G.); Nolan, Enda ((F.F.))

# TULLOW ELECTORAL AREA

TOTAL ELECTORATE 6,338. VALID POLL 3,957. NO. OF MEMBERS 5. QUOTA 660.

| Names of Candidates | First Count Votes | Second Count Transfer of Leonard's surplus | Result | Third Count Transfer of Dunne's votes | Result | Fourth Count Transfer of Pender's votes | Result | Fifth Count Transfer of Deering's votes | Result | Sixth Count Transfer of Brophy's votes | Result | Seventh Count Transfer of Condon's votes | Result |
|---|---|---|---|---|---|---|---|---|---|---|---|---|---|
| BROPHY, Brendan (F.G.) | 317 | +6 | 323 | +4 | 327 | +3 | 330 | +5 | 335 | -335 | — | — | — |
| CONDON, Paddy (F.F.) | 252 | +33 | 285 | +55 | 340 | +4 | 344 | +2 | 346 | +22 | 368 | -368 | — |
| DEERING, Michael (F.G.) | 683 | — | 683 | — | 683 | — | 683 | -23 | 660 | — | 660 | — | 660 |
| DUNNE, Mary Ann (F.F.) | 165 | +21 | 186 | -186 | — | — | — | — | — | — | — | — | — |
| HICKEY, Michael (Lab.) | 389 | +18 | 407 | +23 | 430 | +2 | 432 | +3 | 435 | +47 | 482 | +55 | 537 |
| HUNTER, Fred (F.G.) | 449 | +10 | 459 | +13 | 472 | — | 472 | +6 | 478 | +91 | 569 | +48 | 617 |
| KENNEDY, Arthur (F.F.) | 358 | +12 | 370 | +47 | 417 | +13 | 430 | +2 | 432 | +20 | 452 | +133 | 585 |
| LEONARD, Bill (Non-Party) | 140 | -140 | — | — | — | — | — | — | — | — | — | — | — |
| O'TOOLE, Pat (F.G.) | 548 | +3 | 551 | +1 | 552 | +1 | 553 | +5 | 558 | +122 | 680 | — | 680 |
| PENDER, John (F.F.) | 656 | +2 | 658 | +29 | 687 | -27 | 660 | — | 660 | — | 660 | — | 660 |
| Non-transferable papers not effective | — | +35 | 35 | +14 | 49 | +4 | 53 | — | 53 | +33 | 86 | +132 | 218 |
| TOTAL: | 3,957 | — | 3,957 | — | 3,957 | — | 3,957 | — | 3,957 | — | 3,957 | — | 3,957 |

Elected: Deering, Michael (F.G.); Pender, John (F.F.); O'Toole, Pat (F.F.); Hunter, Fred (F.G.); Kennedy, Arthur (F.F.)

# The ENFO Centre provides free public access to information on all environmental topics

## INFORMATION ON THE ENVIRONMENT

17 St Andrew Street
Dublin 2

Tel 01-6793144
Fax 01-6795204

OUR EXTENSIVE INFORMATION
RESOURCES ARE AT YOUR DISPOSAL.

Open Monday to Saturday
from 10 am to 5 pm

- information leaflets
- query-answering service
- reference library
- videos to view or borrow
- exhibitions
- access to international databases
- environmental impact statements
- reports of the U.S. Environmental Protection Agency
- access to INFOTERRA

**A public service - at your service !**

ENFO is a service of the Department of the Environment.

# CAVAN COUNTY COUNCIL

## CAVAN COUNTY COUNCIL RESULTS

| PARTY | 1991 % of votes | 1991 Seats obtained | 1985 % of votes | 1985 Seats obtained |
|---|---|---|---|---|
| Fianna Fail | 42.8 | 11 | 53.5 | 14 |
| Fine Gael | 35.5 | 9 | 36.4 | 10 |
| Labour | 1.2 | — | — | — |
| Progressive Dem. | — | — | — | — |
| Workers Party | — | — | — | — |
| Other | 20.5 | 5 | 10.1 | 1 |
| TOTAL SEATS | | 25 | | 25 |

## CAVAN

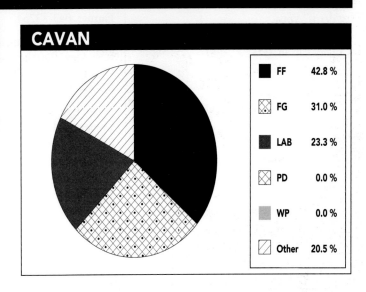

| | | |
|---|---|---|
| FF | 42.8 % |
| FG | 31.0 % |
| LAB | 23.3 % |
| PD | 0.0 % |
| WP | 0.0 % |
| Other | 20.5 % |

Courthouse, Cavan
Telephone: (049) 31799
Fax: (049) 61565
Total population: 52,756
Rateable valuation: £368,744.70
Rate: £24.91
County Council meetings: second Monday each month

*County Manager*: B. Johnston
*County Secretary*: P. Hayden
*Finance Officer*: J. McLoughlin
*County Engineer*: J. Tiernan
*Administrative Officers*
*Planning and Sanitation*: M. Keavney
*Housing, General and Personnel*: M. Donnelly
*Senior Staff Officers*
*Accounts*: D. Maguire
*Computer*: P. Fox
*County Development Officer*: V. Reynolds
*County Librarian*: Josephine M. Brady
*County Coroner*: S. Kelly
*Chief Fire Officer*: V. Maguire
*Law Agent*: G. Maloney
*Senior Executive Engineers*:
*Roads*: J. Neary
*Sanitary Services*: D. Fallon
*Senior Executive (Planning)*: C.T. Davis
*Executive Engineers*: J. Lennon, P. Gallagher, P. Lafferty, F.
Cleary, P. Cork, B. Smith, P.J. Duggan, G. Finn, F. Gibbons, P.
Coleman

Brian Johnston was born in 1942 and educated at St. Patrick's College, Cavan and Queens University in Belfast from where he received a Commerce degree. He has also undertaken courses in Public Administration and Marketing with the I.P.A and the I.M.I respectively. He is married to Mary Dunne and they have three sons and five daughters.

He began his career in local government as Clerical Officer in Cavan County Council. His career has taken him from positions in local authorities in Mayo, Longford, Louth and Wicklow. He worked in Wicklow for eleven years before returning to Cavan County Council as Manager in 1989.

As well as being responsible for a local authority area with a population of some 53,000 people, Brian Johnston is a director of the Cavan County Enterprises Fund and is involved in the County and City Managers Association.

Brian Johnston's principal hobby is golf. He is a member of the Cavan Golf Club and an honorary member of the Wicklow Golf Club.

## BAILIEBOROUGH

|      | 1991 | 1985 | '85 to '91 Swing |
|------|------|------|------------------|
| FF   | 44.9 | 59.8 | -14.9            |
| FG   | 33.1 | 29.8 | 3.3              |
| Ind  | 17.9 | 5.5  | 12.4             |

BOYLE, Aiden,
16 Market Street, Cootehill,
County Cavan. (FG)
Shopkeeper. 049-52357

COLEMAN, May,
Drutamon, Canningstown, Cootehill,
County Cavan. (NP)
Housewife. 042-60269

GILES, Michael,
Barrack Street, Bailieborough,
County Cavan. (FF)
Publican. 042-65467

KELLY, Clifford,
Church Street, Kingscourt,
County Cavan. (FF)
Public Representative. 042-67393

RYAN, Timothy,
Bailieborough,
County Cavan. (FG)
Agricultural Advisor. 042-65210

SMITH, Michael,
Market Street, Cootehill,
County Cavan. (FF)
Auctioneer. 049-52391

TURNER, Winston,
Lear, Bailieborough,
County Cavan. (NP)
Farmer. 042-65175

## BALLYJAMESDUFF

|      | 1991 | 1985 | '85 to '91 Swing |
|------|------|------|------------------|
| FF   | 46.0 | 47.7 | -1.7             |
| FG   | 43.1 | 41.1 | 2.0              |
| Ind  | 10.9 | 11.2 | -0.3             |

BOYLAN, Dessie,
Latnadronagh, Crosserlough,
County Cavan. (FG)
Farmer. 049-36283

BRADY, Daniel,
Drumcor, Loughduff,
County Cavan. (FF)
Farmer. 043-83234

FITZSIMONS, Francie,
Rasudden, Ballyjamesduff,
County Cavan. (FF)
Farmer. 049-44184.

HARTEN, Seamus,
Crenew, Kilnaleck,
County Cavan. (NP)
Farmer. 049-36315

MINEY, Philip,
Kiltrasna, Corlesmore, Ballinagh,
County Cavan. (FG)
Farmer.

O'REILLY, Paddy Jr,
Murmod, Virginia,
County Cavan. (FG)
Farmer. 049-47372.

## BELTURBET

|      | 1991 | 1985 | '85 to '91 Swing |
|------|------|------|------------------|
| FF   | 43.2 | 55.2 | -12.0            |
| FG   | 25.3 | 34.5 | -9.2             |
| SF   | 7.3  | 10.3 | -3.0             |
| Ind  | 24.2 |      | 24.2             |

FEELEY, Eddie,
Stranamort, Blacklion,
County Cavan. (FF)
Farmer. 072-53125

FITZPATRICK, Matthew,
Drummanny Beg, Milltown, Belturbet,
County Cavan. (NP)
Farmer. 049-34130

MAGUIRE, Mary,
Drummany, Killeshandra,
County Cavan. (FG)
Housewife. 049-34599

SMITH, Sean,
Gowlagh South, Bawnboy,
County Cavan. (FF)
Farmer. 049-23322

VESEY, Anthony P.,
Drumbarlum, Belturbet,
County Cavan. (FF)
Office Manager. 049-22525

## CAVAN

|      | 1991 | 1985 | '85 to '91 Swing |
|------|------|------|------------------|
| FF   | 43.2 | 55.2 | -12.0            |
| FG   | 25.3 | 34.5 | -9.2             |
| SF   | 7.3  | 10.3 | -3.0             |
| Ind  | 24.2 | —    | 24.2             |

BOYLAN, Andrew,
Butlersbridge,
Cavan. (FG)
Dáil Deputy. 049-31747

CONATY, Patrick J. (Jnr),
Killynebber,
Cavan. (FF)
Health Board Employee. 049-32821.

MURRAY, Gerry,
Lavey, Stradone,
County Cavan. (FF)
Farmer. 049-30172.

O'BRIEN, Andy,
Crubany,
Cavan. (FG)
Retired Teacher. 049-31324

O'REILLY, Paddy,
79 Church Street,
Cavan. (FG)
Sales Representative. 040-32336

SMITH, Dolores,
Newtown, Carrickaboy,
County Cavan. (NP)
Teacher.

SMITH, T. P.,
Ardamagh, Ballyhaise,
County Cavan. (FF)
Builder. 049-38175

**Eddie Feeley (FF)**
**Belturbet**

**May Coleman (NP)**
**Bailieborough**

**Tim Ryan (FG)**
**Bailieborough**

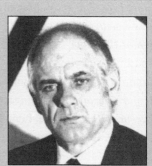
**Michael Giles (FF)**
**Bailieborough**

# Main parties potholed

The long term Fine Gael and Fianna Fail dominance of Cavan politics suffered a shaking of earthquake proportions with the emergence of the Cavan Road Action Group (CRAG) in the 1991 Local Elections.

Cavan had traditionally been a battle ground preserved for the two main Parties. Between them the two Parties held all but one of the seats on the outgoing Council. In 1985 Fianna Fail had regained control for the first time in 27 years winning 14 of the 25 seats. For six years they had rotated the Cavan County Council Chair between their own members with Fine Gael holding the Vice Chair in each case.

This time out, 42 candidates in total contested the four electoral areas of Bailieboro, Ballyjamesduff, Belturbet and Cavan.

As the votes were counted the Drumalee Sports Complex became a focus of national media attention when all four of the C.R.A.G. candidates were elected. The CRAG Group had been campaigning for many months for an improvement in Cavan's considerable network of County Roads. First for the pot hole candidates was Dolores Smith who secured just over 1,000 first preference on her first outing in the Cavan Electoral Area. Fellow pot holer Matthew Fitzpatrick clocked up another 1,071 first preferences. Fitzpatrick, a Drumabeg farmer, had almost 200 votes to spare over Fianna Fail's Sean Smith to top the poll in the Belturbet Area.

In Ballieboro Winston Turner became the third CRAG candidate to top the poll while Seamus Hart another CRAG man came in fourth in Ballyjamesduff and also secured a seat.

Fianna Fail suffered most, losing three seats in all in a campaign where the conditions of the Cavan Roads had been the dominant issue. They lost seats in Bailieboro, Ballyjamesduff and Cavan. Throughout that County their vote was down almost 11%.

In Cavan Gerry Murray and T.P. Smith took seats for the Party while outgoing Councillor Pat Conaty and Diarmuid Wilson nephew of Local T.D. and Tanaiste John Wilson fought neck and neck until the last count for the final seat in the 7 seater with Conaty finally winning out.

In Ballyjamesduff Donal Brady was the only outgoing Fianna Fail Councillor running. He secured re-election with newcomer Francie Fitzsimons also getting one of the six seats. The decision of the two other outgoing Councillors not to run and the strength of the pot hole factor left Fianna Fail with only two seats in this area.

> As the votes were counted, the Drumalee Sports Complex became a focus of national media attention

In Bailieboro Michael Gilles was Fianna Fail's best performer getting 850 votes, just two more than party colleague Clifford Kelly, and both were comfortably elected. The Party's two remaining outgoing Councillors were Cootehill Auctioneer Michael Smith and Turlough Smith. The Cootehill man was to take the final seat by 125 votes on the ninth count.

In Belturbet, Fianna Fail held their three seats and it was Fine Gael who was to lose out to the Cavan Roads Action Group. May Maguire who had been co-opted to replace her husband Joseph, was the Party's best performer and won the Party's only seat in the Belturbet area.

Local Fine Gael T.D. Andrew Boylan was also re-elected along with veteran Councillor and former Senator Andy O'Brien and Paddy O'Leary in the Cavan area. The surprise here was the loss of the seat by Fine Gael's outgoing Councillor Senator Joe O'Reilly who had been strong on the Fine Gael party ticket in the 1989 General Election.

Fine Gael also retained its three seats from Ballyjamesduff with Paddy O'Reilly son of the former T.D. putting in a superb performance with 876 votes to become the only non CRAG candidate to top the poll in Cavan. Second in the poll and taking the second seat was Fine Gael's outgoing Councillor Dessie Boylan but the other outgoing Councillor Robert Fossett lost out to Party colleague Philip Miney.

In Bailieboro, Fine Gael held its two seats also and an impressive showing by Cootehill shopkeeper Aidan Boyle gave rise to a change in personnel. Gerard Lynch a co-opted member of the outgoing Council was re-elected, but Denis Reynolds lost out to Boyle.

The Labour Party has never featured significantly in Cavan and they had a candidate in only one of the four Electoral Areas.

Sinn Fein contested the Cavan area and Belturbet area gaining less then 4% of the vote in each case. Except in cases of high emotion, such as the H.Block controversy, Sinn Fein's core support in Cavan is of little consequence. Neither Sinn Fein nor the Labour Party appear likely to make a breakthrough in Cavan politics even at local level.

Cavan County Council's one non-pot hole Independent seat survived the election campaign although this time it was held by Mary Coleman who was elected in the Bailieboro area to replace her husband David.

Finally, what are the implications of the CRAG success for the next General Election poll? In all, the three candidates secured almost 3,700 first preference votes, yet despite this strong performance, speculation of their chances of coming near a seat in the next General Election are greatly exaggerated. CRAG reflects the protest vote on a subject of great annoyance in an Election where the future of the Government was not at risk.

Their support is solely Cavan based in the Cavan/Monaghan five seater and John Wilson (Fianna Fail), and Bill Cotter (Fine Gael), both Cavan based, are likely to be the strongest Party performers in any such National contest. If the pot hole issue should persist a CRAG candidate may come forward and may gather enough support, although it is unlikely that this will be enough to win a Dail seat.

# BAILIEBOROUGH ELECTORAL AREA

TOTAL ELECTORATE 11,113. VALID POLL 7,461. NO. OF MEMBERS 7. QUOTA 933.

| | First Count Votes | Second Count Transfer of Turner's surplus | Result | Third Count Transfer of Patterson's votes | Result | Fourth Count Transfer of Kelly's surplus | Result | Fifth Count Transfer of Reynold's votes | Result | Sixth Count Transfer of Boyle's surplus | Result | Seventh Count Transfer of Ryan's surplus | Result | Eighth Count Transfer of McDermott's votes | Result | Ninth Count Transfer of Giles' votes | Result |
|---|---|---|---|---|---|---|---|---|---|---|---|---|---|---|---|---|---|
| BOYLE, Aiden (F.G.) | 863 | +3 | 866 | +29 | 895 | +1 | 896 | +225 | 1,121 | -188 | 933 | — | 933 | — | 933 | — | 933 |
| COLEMAN, May | 683 | +5 | 688 | +22 | 710 | — | 710 | +31 | 741 | +90 | 831 | +53 | 884 | +32 | 916 | +9 | 925 |
| GILES, Michael (F.F.) | 850 | +2 | 852 | +9 | 861 | +1 | 862 | +9 | 871 | +6 | 877 | +3 | 880 | +148 | 1,028 | -95 | 933 |
| KELLY, Clifford (F.F.) | 848 | +1 | 849 | +91 | 940 | -7 | 933 | — | 933 | — | 933 | — | 933 | — | 933 | — | 933 |
| McDERMOTT, Francis (F.F.) | 525 | +2 | 527 | +10 | 537 | +1 | 538 | +36 | 574 | +12 | 586 | +14 | 600 | -600 | — | — | — |
| PATTERSON, Jim (F.G.) | 424 | +1 | 425 | -425 | — | — | — | — | — | — | — | — | — | — | — | — | — |
| REYNOLDS, Denis (F.G.) | 434 | +2 | 436 | +99 | 535 | +1 | 536 | -536 | — | — | — | — | — | — | — | — | — |
| RYAN, Timothy (F.G.) | 746 | +5 | 751 | +139 | 890 | +2 | 892 | +162 | 1,054 | — | 1,054 | -121 | 933 | — | 933 | — | 933 |
| SMITH, Michael (F.F.) | 579 | +2 | 581 | +7 | 588 | +1 | 589 | +25 | 614 | +17 | 631 | +3 | 634 | +169 | 803 | +60 | 863 |
| SMITH, Turlough (F.F.) | 551 | +2 | 553 | +5 | 558 | — | 558 | +26 | 584 | +10 | 594 | +10 | 604 | +108 | 712 | +26 | 738 |
| TURNER, Winston (Non-Party) | 958 | -25 | 933 | — | 933 | — | 933 | — | 933 | — | 933 | — | 933 | — | 933 | — | 933 |
| Non-transferable papers not effective | — | — | — | +14 | 14 | — | 14 | +22 | 36 | +53 | 89 | +38 | 127 | +143 | 270 | — | 270 |
| TOTAL: | 7,461 | — | 7,461 | — | 7,461 | — | 7,461 | — | 7,461 | — | 7,461 | — | 7,461 | — | 7,461 | — | 7,461 |

Elected: Turner, Winston (Non-Party); Kelly, Clifford (F.F.); Boyle, Aiden (F.G.); Ryan, Timothy (F.G.); Giles, Michael (F.F.); Coleman, May; Smith, Michael (F.F.)

# BALLYJAMESDUFF ELECTORAL AREA

TOTAL ELECTORATE 9,442. VALID POLL 6,091. NO. OF MEMBERS 6. QUOTA 871.

| Names of Candidates | First Count Votes | Second Count Transfer of Fausset's votes | Result | Third Count Transfer of Boylan's surplus | Result | Fourth Count Transfer of Sheridan's votes | Result | Fifth Count Transfer of Brady's surplus | Result |
|---|---|---|---|---|---|---|---|---|---|
| BOYLAN, Dessie (F.G.) | 711 | +283 | 994 | -123 | 871 | — | 871 | — | 871 |
| BRADY, Daniel (F.F.) | 690 | +12 | 702 | +1 | 703 | +236 | 939 | -68 | 871 |
| FAUSSET, Robert (F.G.) | 547 | -547 | — | — | — | — | — | — | — |
| FITZSIMONS, Francie (F.F.) | 654 | +63 | 717 | +10 | 727 | +103 | 830 | +42 | 872 |
| HARTEN, Seamus (Non-Party) | 664 | +68 | 732 | +20 | 752 | +125 | 877 | — | 877 |
| MINEY, Philip (F.G.) | 669 | +57 | 726 | +86 | 812 | +46 | 858 | +6 | 864 |
| O'DWYER, Aidan (F.F.) | 647 | +29 | 676 | +2 | 678 | +101 | 779 | +20 | 799 |
| O'REILLY, Paddy Jr. (F.G.) | 876 | — | 876 | — | 876 | — | 876 | — | 876 |
| SHERIDAN, Patrick (F.F.) | 633 | +19 | 652 | +4 | 656 | -656 | — | — | — |
| Non-transferable papers not effective | — | +16 | 16 | — | 16 | +45 | 61 | — | 61 |
| TOTAL | 6,091 | — | 6,091 | — | 6,091 | — | 6,091 | — | 6,091 |

Elected: O'Reilly, Paddy (Jr). (F.G.); Boylan, Dessie (F.G.); Brady, Daniel (F.F.); Harten, Seamus (Non-Party); Fitzsimons, Francie (F.F.); Miney, Philip (F.G.)

# BELTURBET ELECTORAL AREA

TOTAL ELECTORATE 7,763. VALID POLL 5,488. NO. OF MEMBERS 5. QUOTA 915

| Names of Candidates | First Count Votes | Second Count Transfer of M. Fitzpatrick's surplus Result | Third Count Transfer of Tiernan's votes Result | Fourth Count Transfer of M. Smith's votes Result | Fifth Count Transfer of S. Smith's surplus Result | Sixth Count Transfer of Neary's votes Result | Seventh Count Transfer of S. Fitzpatrick's votes Result |
|---|---|---|---|---|---|---|---|
| DOLAN, Eamonn (F.G.) | 432 | +16 448 | +2 450 | +13 463 | +1 464 | +61 525 | +127 652 |
| FEELEY, Eddie (F.F.) | 696 | +4 700 | +9 709 | +20 729 | +8 737 | +98 835 | +23 858 |
| FITZPATRICK, Matthew (Non-Party) | 1,071 | -156 915 | — 915 | — 915 | — 915 | — 915 | — 915 |
| FITZPATRICK, Seamus F.G | 392 | +33 425 | +13 438 | +28 466 | +1 467 | +26 493 | -493 — |
| MAGUIRE, Mary (F.G.) | 564 | +27 591 | +55 646 | +67 713 | +9 722 | +35 757 | +123 880 |
| NEARY, Peadar (S.F.) | 400 | +17 417 | +5 422 | +19 441 | +2 443 | -443 — | — — |
| SMITH, Mary | 256 | +11 267 | +11 278 | -278 — | — — | — — | — — |
| SMITH, Sean (F.F.) | 885 | +13 898 | +71 969 | — 969 | -54 915 | — 915 | — 915 |
| TIERNAN, Pat (F.F.) | 204 | +8 212 | -212 — | — — | — — | — — | — — |
| VESEY, Anthony, P. (F.F.) | 588 | +27 615 | +43 658 | +72 730 | +33 763 | +88 851 | +158 1,009 |
| Non-transferable papers not effective | — | — — | +3 3 | +59 62 | — 62 | +135 97 | +62 259 |
| TOTAL: | 5,488 | — 5,488 | — 5,488 | — 5,488 | — 5,488 | — 5,488 | — 5,488 |

Elected: Fitzpatrick, Matthew (Non-Party); Smith, Sean ((F.F.)), Vesey, Anthont P. ((F.F.)); Maguire, Mary ((F.G.)); Feeley, Eddie ((F.F.))

# CAVAN ELECTORAL AREA

TOTAL ELECTORATE 11,865. VALID POLL 7,416. NO. OF MEMBERS 7. QUOTA 928

| Names of Candidates | First Count Votes | Second Count Transfer of D. Smith's surplus Result | Third Count Transfer of M. Smith's votes Result | Fourth Count Transfer of Ennis' votes Result | Fifth Count Transfer of Murray's surplus Result | Sixth Count Transfer of Dolan's votes Result | Seventh Count Transfer of Elliott's votes Result | Eighth Count Transfer of J.O'Reilly's votes Result | Ninth Count Transfer of O'Brien's surplus Result |
|---|---|---|---|---|---|---|---|---|---|
| BOYLAN, Andrew (F.G.) | 895 | +11 906 | +12 918 | +19 937 | — 937 | — 937 | — 937 | — 937 | — 937 |
| CONATY, Patrick J. Jr. (F.F.) | 497 | +4 501 | +9 510 | +18 528 | +4 532 | +46 578 | +199 777 | +38 815 | +16 831 |
| DOLAN, Paul (Lab.) | 320 | +4 324 | +9 333 | +46 379 | +1 380 | -380 — | — — | — — | — — |
| ELLIOTT, Breda (F.F.) | 367 | +1 368 | +4 372 | +9 381 | +10 391 | +31 422 | -422 — | — — | — — |
| ENNIS, Joe (S.F.) | 292 | +4 296 | +6 302 | -302 — | — — | — — | — — | — — | — — |
| MURRAY, Gerry (F.F.) | 891 | +14 905 | +7 912 | +45 957 | -29 928 | — 928 | — 928 | — 928 | — 928 |
| O'BRIEN, Andy (F.G.) | 670 | +6 676 | +12 688 | +24 712 | +1 713 | +55 768 | +38 806 | +228 1,034 | -106 928 |
| O'REILLY, Joe (F.G.) | 529 | +12 541 | +2 543 | +26 569 | +3 572 | +42 614 | +17 631 | -631 — | — — |
| O'REILLY, Paddy (F.G.) | 641 | +4 645 | +6 651 | +18 669 | — 669 | +73 742 | +46 788 | +165 953 | — 953 |
| SMITH, Dolores (Non-Party) | 1,001 | -73 928 | — 928 | — 928 | — 928 | — 928 | — 928 | — 928 | — 928 |
| SMITH, Mary | 106 | +4 110 | -110 — | — — | — — | — — | — — | — — | — — |
| SMITH, T.P. (F.F.) | 654 | +5 659 | +14 673 | +47 720 | +5 725 | +28 753 | +47 800 | +29 829 | +12 841 |
| WILSON, Diarmuid James (F.F.) | 553 | +4 557 | +25 582 | +24 606 | +5 611 | +37 648 | +51 699 | +38 737 | +8 745 |
| Non-transferable papers not effective | — | — — | +4 4 | +26 30 | — 30 | +68 98 | +24 122 | +133 255 | +70 325 |
| TOTAL: | 7,416 | — 7,416 | — 7,416 | — 7,416 | — 7,416 | — 7,416 | — 7,416 | — 7,416 | — 7,416 |

Elected: Smith, Dolores (Non-Party); Murray, Gerry (F.F.); Boylan, Andrew (F.G.); O'Brien, Andy (F.G.); O'Reilly, Paddy (F.G.); Smith, T.P. (F.F.); Conaty, Patrick J. Jr. (F.F.)

# Whatever

Whether you're leading an orchestra, or banging your own drum, the Take Five range of single and multi-user

# your tune

accounting and payroll software will harmonise your business. Selected by IBM as the preferred accounting

# Take Five can

packages for IBM PS/1 and PS/2 computers, Take Five Classic and Professional will improve your efficiency with seven integrated modules as standard each finely tuned to your individual business style and timing.

# orchestrate

Priced from £650 to £2,500, the all new Guaranteed Irish Take Five accounting and payroll software by G.F.K. Technology, is just your number.

# your business.

Don't waste a second. Be informed. Telephone G.F.K. Technology now on 599655 for your personal information pack.

# CLARE COUNTY COUNCIL

## CLARE COUNTY COUNCIL RESULTS

| PARTY | 1991 % of votes | 1991 Seats obtained | 1985 % of votes | 1985 Seats obtained |
|---|---|---|---|---|
| Fianna Fail | 48.5 | 17 | 53.5 | 17 |
| Fine Gael | 21.6 | 8 | 23.4 | 8 |
| Labour | 7.3 | 1 | 5.2 | 2 |
| Progressive Dem. | 6.1 | 1 | — | — |
| Workers Party | — | — | — | — |
| Other | 16.5 | 5 | 10.1 | 5 |
| TOTAL SEATS | | 32 | | 32 |

## CLARE

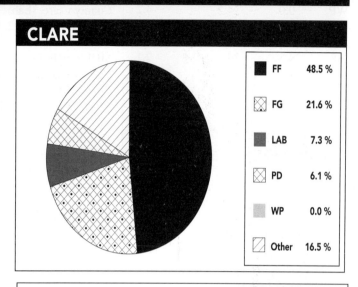

| | | |
|---|---|---|
| ■ FF | 48.5 % | |
| ▨ FG | 21.6 % | |
| ■ LAB | 7.3 % | |
| ▨ PD | 6.1 % | |
| ▨ WP | 0.0 % | |
| ▨ Other | 16.5 % | |

New Road, Ennis
Telephone: (065) 21616
Fax: (065) 28233
Total population: 91,343
Rateable valuation: £727,840
Rate: £29.4690

**County Council meetings: second Monday each month**

*County Manager*: Michael Nunan
*Assistant County Manager*: R. 'O Ceallaigh
*County Secretary*: Vacant
*Finance Officer*: Eamonn Kelly
*County Engineer*: J. J. Coyne
*Administrative Officers*:
Housing, Roads, General Purposes and
*Personnel*: Timothy Caffrey
*Planning, Sanitary Services, Environment and*
*Fire Service*: Michael McNamara
*Senior Staff Officers*:
*Housing*: Pat Shannon
*Roads, Stores and Machinery*: G. Glennon
*Computers*: Martin Nolan
*Internal Audit*: Caroline Curley
*County Librarian*: N. Crowley
*County Solicitor*: M. Houlihan
*County Coroner*: Dr T.A. Daly
*Chief Fire Officer*: M. Raftery
*Civil Defence Officer*: N. Carmody
*Social Worker*: C. McInerney
*Senior Executive Engineers*:
J. J. Coyne
H. McKiernan
*Planner*: C. Lynch.

**Michael Nunan**

Michael Nunan has been Manager of Clare County since 1984. Originally from Limerick where he was born in 1929, he started his career as a Clerical Assistant with his native County Council in 1948 and twelve years later was promoted to Staff Officer.

In 1969 he left Limerick to become County Accountant with Leitrim County Council. He moved again three years later to Dublin County Council in 1972 and was appointed Senior Administrative Officer. A year later he become County Secretary to Carlow County Council where he stayed five years before beginning a five year stint as Assistant County Manager with Cork County Council 1978 to 1983. He then joint the ranks of County Managers, firstly briefly with Roscommon 1983 -84 and then to Clare.

As Clare County Manager, Nunan employs a staff of over 700 and has an annual budget of almost £30 million pounds. His county also includes several of the countries biggest rate payers, outside of Cork and Dublin. These include Shannon Airport, Shannon Industrial Estate and more recently the ESB's coal burning station at Money Point.

Nunan is married to Thelma (nee O'Brien), has three children and was educated at St. Andrews Secondary School Co. Limerick.

## ENNIS

|     | 1991 | 1985 | '85 to '91 Swing |
| --- | --- | --- | --- |
| FF  | 35.1 | 46.9 | -11.8 |
| FG  | 15.4 | 21.4 | -6.0 |
| Lab | 10.5 | 5.1  | 5.4 |
| WP  | 0.0  | 4.2  | -4.2 |
| PD  | 11.0 | —    | 11.0 |
| SF  | 3.5  | —    | 3.5 |
| Ind | 24.5 | 22.4 | 2.1 |

CONSIDINE, Peter,
26 Abbey Street, Ennis,
County Clare. (FF)
Publican. 065-29054

BRENNAN, Thomas,
Prairie House, Clonroadmore, Ennis,
County Clare. (NP)
Electrician. 065-20909

GREENE, Raymond,
Cloughleigh Road, Ennis,
County Clare. (FF)
Nurse. 065-28742

MULQUEEN, Anna,
2 Parnell Street, Ennis,
County Clare. (FG)
Baker. 065-24356

## ENNISTYMON

|     | 1991 | 1985 | '85 to '91 Swing |
| --- | --- | --- | --- |
| FF  | 53.1 | 46.9 | -11.8 |
| FG  | 23.6 | 25.3 | -1.7 |
| Lab | 17.7 | 14.7 | 3.0 |
| Ind | —    | 0.7  | -0.7 |

HENCHY, Frank,
Golf Links Road, Lahinch,
County Clare. (FG)
Teacher. 065-81066.

KILLEEN, Tony,
Kilnaboy, Corofin,
County Clare. (FF)
Teacher. 065-27895

LAFFERTY, Martin,
Lisdoonvarna,
County Clare. (Lab)
Teacher. 065-74052.

MULKERE, Enda,
Carrownacloghy, Crusheen,
County Clare. (FF)
SFADCO. 065-27177.

NAGLE, Jimmy,
Church Street, Ennistymon,
County Clare. (FF)
Publican. 065-71040.

## KILLALOE

|     | 1991 | 1985 | '85 to '91 Swing |
| --- | --- | --- | --- |
| FF  | 52.9 | 57.4 | -4.5 |
| FG  | 26.1 | 25.9 | 0.2 |
| Lab | 7.3  | —    | 7.3 |
| PD  | 11.0 | —    | 11.0 |
| SF  | 2.7  | —    | 2.7 |
| Ind | 0.0  | 16.7 | -16.7 |

BEGLEY, Michael,
Clonlara,
County Clare. (FF)
Publican. 061-354170.

BUGLER, Paddy,
Kilrateera, Mountshannon,
County Clare. (FG)
Farmer. 0619-21418.

GORMAN, Joe,
Cratloe,
County Clare. (FF)
Farmer.

MANNION, Mary,
Knockballynameath, Parteen,
County Clare. (PD)
Teacher. 061-349884.

McMAHON, Tony,
Parkroe, Blackwater,
County Clare. (FG)
Farmer. 061-49807.

WILEY, Colm,
Coolready, Bodyke,
County Clare. (FF)
Company Manager. 0619-21264.

## KILRUSH

|     | 1991 | 1985 | '85 to '91 Swing |
| --- | --- | --- | --- |
| FF  | 60.2 | 53.1 | 7.1 |
| FG  | 27.1 | 31.9 | -4.8 |
| Ind | 12.7 | 15.0 | -2.3 |

CHAMBERS, Bill,
Kilmacduane, Cooraclare,
County Clare. (FF)
Farmer.

KEANE, Jackie,
Gortglass, Cranny,
County Clare. (FG)*

KELLY, P.J.,
Lissycasey,
County Clare. (FF)
Teacher. 065-34197

TAYLOR-QUINN, Madeline,
Francis Street, Kilrush,
County Clare. (FG)
Dáil Deputy. 065-51656

KEANE, Patrick,
Circular Road, Kilkee,
County Clare. (FF)
Farmer.

**Madeline Taylor-Quinn (FG)**
**Kilrush**

**Frank Henchy (FG)**
**Ennistymon**

**Mary Mannion (PD)**
**Killaloe**

**Flan Garvey (FF)**
**Miltown Malbay**

PRENDEVILLE, Tom,
Cappa, Kilrush,
County Clare. (FF)
Teacher. 065-51517

* KEANE, Jackie RIP
Replaced by KEANE, Cissie, Gortglass,
Cranny, County Clare. (FG)

### MILTOWN MALBAY

| | 1991 | 1985 | '85 to '91 Swing |
|---|---|---|---|
| FF | 46.6 | 49.7 | -3.1 |
| FG | 15.0 | 16.0 | -1.0 |
| Lab | 23.3 | — | 23.3 |
| Ind | 15.1 | 34.3 | -19.2 |

BREEN, James,
Ballyknock, Kilnamona,
County Clare. (FF)
De Beers Employee. 065-28180

BURKE, Patrick J.,
Clounlaheen, Doonogan,
County Clare. (NP)
Farmer.

CAREY, Donal,
3 Thomond Villas, Clarecastle,
County Clare. (FG)
Dáil Deputy. 065-29191

CURTIN, Christy,
Clonbony, Miltown Malbay,
County Clare. (NP)
Teacher. 065-84342

GARVEY, Flan,
Inagh,
County Clare. (FF)
Teacher.

HILLERY, Michael,
Spanish Point, Miltown Malbay,
County Clare. (FF)
Agricultural Advisor. 065-84323

### SHANNON

| | 1991 | 1985 | '85 to '91 Swing |
|---|---|---|---|
| FF | 35.4 | 51.6 | -16.2 |
| FG | 18.4 | 16.6 | 1.8 |
| Lab | 7.5 | 16.2 | -8.7 |
| Ind | 28.9 | 15.6 | 13.3 |

HILLERY, Sean,
The Pharmacy,
Shannon Town Centre, Shannon,
County Clare. (FF)
Pharmacist. 061-72130

MAKOWSKI, Bridget,
16 Tradaree Court,
Shannon,
County Clare. (NP)
Public Rep. 061-364300

McCARTHY, Patricia,
13 Caragh Park, Shannon,
County Clare. (NP)
Self-employed. 061-61725

McMAHON, Pat,
Ennis Road, Newmarket-on-Fergus,
County Clare. (FF)
Publican. 061-368182

SCANLAN, Sonny,
Ballyhannon, Quin,
County Clare. (FG)
Farmer.

**The executive members of the General Council of County Councils pictured with the 1991 Council Chairpersons.**

# Fianna Fail dominance in Clare remains

While the Fianna Fáil heyday in Clare may be a thing of the past, with the party having the same number of Dail seats as Fine Gael, at local level, however, their dominance of old still remains. They returned seventeen seats, the same number as in 1985, on this ocassion, thus securing their majority on the County Council. Fine Gael also held their own, regaining their eight Councillors. The Progressive Democrats gained a seat as Labour's representation dropped by one while five Independents, the same number as in 1985, were returned.

The downgrading and threatened closure of Ennis County Hospital surprisingly did not cause Fianna Fail any seat loss in the Ennis Electoral Area. While Fianna Fail's vote slipped alarmingly by almost 12% two councillors were still returned, as in the last local elections. One of these, Peter Considine, had been narrowly beaten for a seat in 1985 and was co-opted onto the council prior to the 1991 election in the place of party colleague, Frank Barrett.

The poll was topped once again by Independent, Thomas Browne who increased his vote since 1985. The real surprise was the near loss of Fine Gael's single seat in the Ennis Area. Outgoing Fine Gael Councillor, Michael Howard was replaced on the Council by party colleague Anna Mulqueen who had to fight off the very strong challenge of Progressive Democrat candidate, Frankie Neylon. Mulqueen ended up scrapping home by a mere 28 vote margin over Neylon. Mulqueen's election meant that all the candidates returned in the Ennis Area are also members of the town's UDC.

In the Ennistimon Electoral Area all five outgoing councillors were returned with four of the five being elected on the first count and the fifth, Fianna Fail's Jimmy Nagle elected on the third count safely ahead of the other two candidates in the field. Tony Killeen of Fianna Fail again topped the poll this time with 1,355

first preference votes. The Progressive Democrats performed poorly and would have been disappointed that their candidate received a mere 307 votes.

Overall the Progressive Democrat performance in Clare was unexceptional. Their big success story, however, was in the Killaloe Electoral Area where PD candidate, Mary Mannion, polled an impressive 1094 votes in being elected. The poll was topped by Fianna Fail's Colm Wiley who was one of four outgoing representatives who were re-elected in Killaloe. The others were his party colleague Joe Gorman and the two Fine Gael Councillors - Tony McMahon and Paddy Budler. Michael Begley was the Fianna Fail newcomer in the area making good any disappointment

> The Stop-Over issue was undoubtedly the main cause of the 16% swing against Fianna Fail in the Shannon Area

remaining from 1985 when he was beaten for the last seat.

Kilrush was one of the best Fianna Fail results in the country. The party vote increased by just over 7% and they gained a seat at the expense of outgoing Independent Councillor William O'Looney. Fianna Fail newcomer, Patrick Keane, joined party colleagues Bill Chambers, Sean Keating and poll-topper P.J. Kelly on the Council. Surprisingly Fine Gael TD Madeline Taylor-Quinn had to wait until the sixth count to be returned and was over 200 votes behind her running mate, outgoing Councillor Jackie Keane, who himself was just 9 votes short of replacing P.J. Kelly at the top of the poll.

The Miltown Malbay Electoral Area returned the 6 Councillors elected in 1985 with 4 of the 6 being re-elected on the first count. Independent Councillor Christy Curtin increased his vote to head the poll on this occasion. He was joined by another Independent Patrick Burke who had topped the poll in 1985. Fianna Fail's share of the vote was down but they still held their own.

Michael Hillery, a nephew of former President Dr. Partick Hillery, was Fianna Fail's chief vote-getter increasing his first preferences by some 515 votes. Fine Gael had to be content with only one seat in Miltown Malbay with Deputy Donal Carey being elected. Like his Dail partner, Taylor-Quinn in Kilrush, Carey's showing was unimpressive taking the fifth seat on the sixth count.

The Stop-Over issue was undoubtedly the main cause of the 16% swing against Fianna Fail in the Shannon Area resulting in the loss of 1 of the 3 seats they gained in 1985. Pat McMahon of Fianna Fail was replaced at the top of the poll by Patricia McCarthy who was returned in 1985 for the Labour Party, but canvassed as an Independent on this occasion. McCarthy was one of two Independents elected in the Shannon Area the other was UDC member Brigid Makowski who increased her vote on 1985 to secure election this time. Given the urban make-up of Shannon and the contentious stop-over issue, the Progressive Democrats would have been hoping for a better performance from their 2 candidates in this area.

While the Fianna Fail dominance in the Banner County is long gone they will be glad to have held their majority on the County Council. This does not, however, give much hope to them of gaining the third seat in Clare in the next general election. The Fianna Fail vote is weak in areas of urban population such as Shannon and Ennis where their vote dropped by 12% and 16% respectively, from the 1985 Local Elections.

The Progressive Democrats can only be deeply disappointed with their showing in Clare returning only 1 councillor in a constituency in which they, not so long ago, targeted for a Dail seat. It would seem unlikely that there will be any changes in party strength after the next general election, given the performance of the two possible gainers - FF and PD. If there is to be a change it will probably be at the expense of Fine Gael's two sitting TDs both of whom had poor outings in the 1991 locals.

# ENNIS ELECTORAL AREA

TOTAL ELECTORATE 10,739. VALID POLL 5,431. NO. OF MEMBERS 4. QUOTA 1,087.

| Names of Candidates | First Count Votes | Second Count Transfer of Brennan's surplus | Result | Third Count Transfer of Kenny's votes | Result | Fourth Count Transfer of McCarthy's votes | Result | Fifth Count Transfer of Nevin's votes | Result | Sixth Count Transfer of Howard's votes | Result | Seventh Count Transfer of Corley's votes | Result | Eighth Count Transfer of Greene's surplus | Result | Ninth Count Transfer of Neylon's votes | Result |
|---|---|---|---|---|---|---|---|---|---|---|---|---|---|---|---|---|---|
| BRENNAN, Tommy (Non-Party) | 1,212 | -125 | 1,087 | — | 1,087 | — | 1,087 | — | 1,087 | — | 1,087 | — | 1,087 | — | 1,087 | — | 1,087 |
| CONSIDINE, Peter (F.F.) | 702 | +20 | 722 | +13 | 735 | +14 | 749 | +121 | 870 | +62 | 932 | +94 | 1,026 | +30 | 1,056 | +210 | 1,266 |
| CORLEY, MICHAEL (Lab.) | 569 | +16 | 585 | +14 | 599 | +31 | 630 | +18 | 648 | +46 | 694 | -694 | — | — | — | — | — |
| GREENE, Raymond (F.F.) | 942 | +24 | 966 | +24 | 990 | +49 | 1,039 | +81 | 1,120 | — | 1,120 | — | 1,120 | -33 | 1,087 | — | 1,087 |
| HOWARD, Michael (F.G.) | 391 | +14 | 405 | +13 | 418 | +18 | 436 | +10 | 446 | -446 | — | — | — | — | — | — | — |
| KENNY, Frank | 118 | +2 | 120 | -120 | — | — | — | — | — | — | — | — | — | — | — | — | — |
| McCARTHY, Tony | 190 | +6 | 196 | +11 | 207 | -207 | — | — | — | — | — | — | — | — | — | — | — |
| MULQUEEN, Anna (F.G.) | 445 | +16 | 461 | +16 | 477 | +14 | 491 | +8 | 499 | +236 | 735 | +234 | 969 | +1 | 970 | +318 | 1,288 |
| NEVIN, Josie (F.F.) | 263 | +7 | 270 | +4 | 274 | +13 | 287 | -287 | — | — | — | — | — | — | — | — | — |
| NEYLON, Frankie (P.D.) | 599 | +20 | 619 | +14 | 633 | +20 | 653 | +35 | 688 | +50 | 738 | +202 | 940 | +2 | 942 | -942 | — |
| Non-transferable papers not effective | — | — | — | +11 | 11 | +48 | 59 | +14 | 73 | +52 | 125 | +164 | 289 | +2 | 289 | +414 | 703 |
| TOTAL: | 5,431 | — | 5,431 | — | 5,431 | — | 5,431 | — | 5,431 | — | 5,431 | — | 5,431 | — | 5,431 | — | 5,431 |

Elected: Brennan, Tommy (Non-Party); Greene, Raymond (F.F.); Mulqueen, Anna (F.G.); Considine, Peter (F.F.)

# ENNISTIMON ELECTORAL AREA

TOTAL ELECTORATE 9,891. VALID POLL 6,435. NO. OF MEMBERS 5. QUOTA 1,073.

| Names of Candidates | First Count Votes | Second Count Transfer of Killeen's surplus | Result | Third Count Transfer of Henchy's surplus | Result |
|---|---|---|---|---|---|
| HENCHY, Frank (F.G.) | 1,258 | — | 1,258 | -185 | 1,073 |
| KILLEEN, Tony (F.F.) | 1,355 | -282 | 1,073 | — | 1,073 |
| LAFFERTY, Martin (Lab.) | 1,142 | — | 1,142 | — | 1,142 |
| MORAN, Noel (P.D.) | 307 | +25 | 332 | +29 | 361 |
| MULKERE, Enda (F.F.) | 1,128 | — | 1,128 | — | 1,128 |
| JIMMY, Nagle (F.F.) | | | | | |
| O'CONNOR, PADDY (F.G.) | 260 | +21 | 281 | +156 | 437 |
| Non-transferable papers not effective | — | — | — | — | — |
| TOTAL: | 6,435 | — | 6,435 | — | 6,435 |

Elected:- Killeen, Tony (F.F.); Henchy, Frank (F.G.); Lafferty, Martin (Lab.); Mulkere, Enda (F.F.); Nagle, Jimmy (F.F.)

# KILLALOE ELECTORAL AREA

TOTAL ELECTORATE 13,913. VALID POLL 9,917. NO. OF MEMBERS 6. QUOTA 1,417

| Names of Candidates | First Count Votes | Second Count Transfer of Foley's votes (Result) | | Third Count Transfer of Ginivan's votes (Result) | | Fourth Count Transfer of Conlon's votes (Result) | | Fifth Count Transfer of Liley's surplus (Result) | | Sixth Count Transfer of P. Hayes' votes (Result) | | Seventh Count Transfer of B. Hayes' votes (Result) | | Eighth Count Transfer of Mannion's surplus (Result) | | Ninth Count Transfer of Begley's surplus (Result) | |
|---|---|---|---|---|---|---|---|---|---|---|---|---|---|---|---|---|---|
| BEGLEY, Michael (F.F.) | 1,071 | +41 | 1,112 | +157 | 1,269 | +17 | 1,286 | +4 | 1,290 | +80 | 1,370 | +107 | 1,477 | — | 1,477 | -60 | 1,417 |
| BUGLER, Paddy (F.G.) | 1,019 | +17 | 1,036 | +19 | 1,055 | +202 | 1,257 | +1 | 1,258 | +129 | 1,387 | +44 | 1,431 | — | 1,431 | — | 1,431 |
| CONLON, Eugene (F.G.) | 566 | +5 | 571 | +7 | 578 | -578 | — | — | — | — | — | — | — | — | — | — | — |
| FOLEY, Tony | 272 | -272 | — | — | — | — | — | — | — | — | — | — | — | — | — | — | — |
| GINIVAN, Eddie (F.F.) | 524 | +18 | 542 | -542 | — | — | — | — | — | — | — | — | — | — | — | — | — |
| GORMAN, Joe (F.F.) | 998 | +9 | 1,007 | +70 | 1,077 | +24 | 1,101 | — | 1,101 | +93 | 1,194 | +24 | 1,218 | +32 | 1,250 | +10 | 1,260 |
| HAYES, Brendan patrick (Lab.) | 723 | +39 | 762 | +40 | 802 | +19 | 821 | +2 | 823 | +8 | 831 | -831 | — | — | — | — | — |
| HAYES, Pat (F.F.) | 657 | +20 | 677 | +51 | 728 | +48 | 776 | +3 | 779 | — | — | — | — | — | — | — | — |
| MANNION, Mary (P.D.) | 1,094 | +18 | 1,112 | +74 | 1,186 | +39 | 1,225 | +1 | 1,226 | +29 | 1,255 | +411 | 1,666 | -249 | 1,417 | — | 1,417 |
| McMAHON, Tony (F.G.) | 999 | +11 | 1,010 | +75 | 1,085 | +91 | 1,176 | — | 1,176 | +13 | 1,189 | +81 | 1,270 | +129 | 1,399 | +20 | 1,419 |
| TORPEY, Michael (F.F.) | 617 | +8 | 625 | +31 | 656 | +129 | 785 | +1 | 786 | +330 | 1,116 | +42 | 1,158 | +22 | 1,180 | +15 | 1,195 |
| WILEY, Colm (F.F.) | 1,377 | +52 | 1,429 | — | 1,429 | — | 1,429 | -12 | 1,417 | — | 1,417 | — | 1,417 | — | 1,417 | — | 1,417 |
| Non-transferable papers not effective | — | +34 | 34 | +18 | 52 | +9 | 61 | — | 61 | +97 | 158 | +122 | 280 | +66 | 346 | +15 | 361 |
| TOTAL: | 9,917 | — | 9,917 | — | 9,917 | — | 9,917 | — | 9,917 | — | 9,917 | — | 9,917 | — | 9,917 | — | 9,917 |

# KILRUSH ELECTORAL AREA

TOTAL ELECTORATE 11,610. VALID POLL 8,023. NO. OF MEMBERS 6. QUOTA 1,147.

| Names of Candidates | First Count Votes | Second Count Transfer of O'Shea's votes (Result) | | Third Count Transfer of O'Brien's votes (Result) | | Fourth Count Transfer of Horgan's votes (Result) | | Fifth Count Transfer of O'Looney's votes (Result) | | Sixth Count Transfer of Prendeville's surplus (Result) | | Seventh Count Transfer of Taylor-Quinn's surplus (Result) | | Eighth Count Transfer of J. Keane's surplus (Result) | | Ninth Count Transfer of Kelly's surplus (Result) | |
|---|---|---|---|---|---|---|---|---|---|---|---|---|---|---|---|---|---|
| CHAMBERS, Bill (F.F.) | 963 | +1 | 964 | +14 | 978 | +63 | 1,041 | +81 | 1,122 | +29 | 1,151 | — | 1,151 | — | 1,151 | — | 1,151 |
| HORGAN, Mossie (Non-Party) | 380 | +11 | 391 | +7 | 398 | -398 | — | — | — | — | — | — | — | — | — | — | — |
| KEANE, Jackie (F.G.) | 1,072 | +1 | 1,073 | +116 | 1,189 | — | 1,189 | — | 1,189 | — | 1,189 | — | 1,189 | -42 | 1,147 | — | 1,147 |
| KEANE, Patrick (F.F.) | 924 | +3 | 927 | +12 | 939 | +37 | 976 | +48 | 1,024 | +11 | 1,035 | +13 | 1,048 | +4 | 1,052 | +9 | 1,061 |
| KEATING, Seán (F.F.) | 877 | — | 877 | +9 | 886 | +37 | 923 | +49 | 972 | +21 | 993 | +26 | 1,019 | +25 | 1,044 | +5 | 1,049 |
| KELLY, P.J. (F.F.) | 1,080 | — | 1,080 | +37 | 1,117 | +18 | 1,135 | +26 | 1,161 | — | 1,161 | — | 1,161 | — | 1,161 | -14 | 1,147 |
| O'BRIEN, Tom (F.G.) | 257 | — | 257 | -257 | — | — | — | — | — | — | — | — | — | — | — | — | — |
| O'LOONEY, William | 603 | +9 | 612 | +5 | 617 | +74 | 691 | -691 | — | — | — | — | — | — | — | — | — |
| O'SHEA, John Joseph (Non-Party) | 35 | -35 | — | — | — | — | — | — | — | — | — | — | — | — | — | — | — |
| PRENDEVILLE, Tom (F.F.) | 987 | +5 | 992 | +3 | 995 | +52 | 1,047 | +251 | 1,298 | -151 | 1,147 | — | 1,147 | — | 1,147 | — | 1,147 |
| TAYLOR-QUINN, Madeleine (F.G.) | 845 | +3 | 848 | +50 | 898 | +76 | 974 | +170 | 1,144 | +90 | 1,234 | -87 | 1,147 | — | 1,147 | — | 1,147 |
| Non-transferable papers not effective | — | +2 | 2 | +4 | 6 | +41 | 47 | +66 | 113 | — | 113 | +48 | 161 | +13 | 174 | — | 174 |
| TOTAL: | 8,023 | — | 8,023 | — | 8,023 | — | 8,023 | — | 8,023 | — | 8,023 | — | 8,023 | — | 8,023 | — | 8,023 |

Elected: Keane, Jackie (F.G.); Prendeville, Tom (F.F.); Kelly, P.J. (F.F.); Taylor-Quinn, Madeleine (F.G.); Chambers, Bill (F.F.); Keane, Patrick (F.F.)

# MILLTOWN MALBAY ELECTORAL AREA

TOTAL ELECTORATE 10,040. VALID POLL 7,179. NO. OF MEMBERS 6. QUOTA 1,026

| Names of Candidates | First Count Votes | Second Count Transfer of Curtin's surplus | (Result) | Third Count Transfer of Hillery's surplus | (Result) | Fourth Count Transfer of Burke's surplus | (Result) | Fifth Count Transfer of Breen's surplus | (Result) | Sixth Count Transfer of McNamara's votes | (Result) | Seventh Count Transfer of Pilkington's votes | (Result) |
|---|---|---|---|---|---|---|---|---|---|---|---|---|---|
| BREEN, James (F.F.) | 1,072 | — | 1,072 | — | 1,072 | — | 1,072 | -46 | 1,026 | — | 1,026 | — | 1,026 |
| BURKE, Patrick J. | 1,085 | — | 1,085 | — | 1,085 | -59 | 1,026 | — | 1,026 | — | 1,026 | — | 1,026 |
| CAREY, Donal (F.G.) | 848 | +88 | 936 | +11 | 947 | +13 | 960 | +11 | 971 | +131 | 1,102 | — | 1,102 |
| CURTIN, Christy | 1,416 | -390 | 1,026 | — | 1,026 | — | 1,026 | — | 1,026 | — | 1,026 | — | 1,026 |
| GARVEY, Flan (F.F.) | 592 | +127 | 719 | +66 | 785 | +22 | 807 | +21 | 828 | +33 | 861 | +98 | 959 |
| HANRAHAN, Bernard (F.F.) | 549 | +31 | 580 | +15 | 595 | +6 | 601 | +10 | 611 | +41 | 652 | +22 | 674 |
| HILLERY, Michael (F.F.) | 1,132 | — | 1,132 | -106 | 1,026 | — | 1,026 | — | 1,026 | — | 1,026 | — | 1,026 |
| McNAMARA, Peadar (Lab.) | 256 | +43 | 299 | +3 | 302 | +8 | 310 | +3 | 313 | -313 | — | — | — |
| PILKINGTON, Dick (F.G.) | 229 | +101 | 330 | +11 | 341 | +10 | 351 | +1 | 352 | +24 | 376 | -376 | — |
| Non-transferable papers not effective | — | — | — | — | — | — | — | — | — | +84 | 84 | +256 | 340 |
| TOTAL: | 7,179 | — | 7,179 | — | 7,179 | — | 7,179 | — | 7,179 | — | 7,179 | — | 7,179 |

Elected: Curtin, Christy; Hillery, Michael (F.F.); Burke, Patrick J.; Breen, James (F.F.); Carey, Donal (F.G.); Garvey, Flan (F.F.).

# SHANNON ELECTORAL AREA

TOTAL ELECTORATE 10,717. VALID POLL 6,408. NO. OF MEMBERS 5. QUOTA 1,069

| Names of Candidates | First Count Votes | Second Count Transfer of Flannigan's votes | (Result) | Third Count Transfer of Hammond's votes | (Result) | Fourth Count Transfer of McGrath's votes | (Result) | Fifth Count Transfer of McCabe's votes | (Result) | Sixth Count Transfer of Lambert's votes | (Result) | Seventh Count Transfer of Cusack's votes | (Result) | Eighth Count Transfer of Casey's votes | (Result) | Ninth Count Transfer of McMahon's surplus | (Result) | Tenth Count Transfer of O'Shaughnessy's votes | (Result) | Eleventh Count Transfer of O'Loughlin's votes | (Result) |
|---|---|---|---|---|---|---|---|---|---|---|---|---|---|---|---|---|---|---|---|---|---|
| CASEY, Tom (P.D.) | 453 | +4 | 457 | +8 | 465 | +69 | 534 | +23 | 557 | +15 | 572 | +28 | 600 | -600 | — | — | — | — | — | — | — |
| CUSACK, Mary (F.G.) | 336 | +2 | 338 | +42 | 380 | — | 380 | +3 | 383 | +5 | 388 | -388 | — | — | — | — | — | — | — | — | — |
| FLANNIGAN, Peter (Non-Party) | 140 | -140 | — | — | — | — | — | — | — | — | — | — | — | — | — | — | — | — | — | — | — |
| HAMMOND, Dermot (F.G.) | 167 | +2 | 169 | -169 | — | — | — | — | — | — | — | — | — | — | — | — | — | — | — | — | — |
| HILLERY, Seán (F.F.) | 496 | +6 | 502 | +5 | 507 | +17 | 524 | +7 | 531 | +94 | 625 | +47 | 672 | +76 | 748 | +40 | 788 | +136 | 924 | +405 | 1,329 |
| LAMBERT, Geraldine (F.F.) | 290 | +7 | 297 | +3 | 300 | +5 | 305 | +5 | 310 | -310 | — | — | — | — | — | — | — | — | — | — | — |
| MAKOWSKI, Brigid (Non-Party) | 545 | +63 | 608 | +13 | 621 | +11 | 632 | +6 | 638 | +50 | 688 | +11 | 699 | +27 | 726 | +8 | 734 | +221 | 955 | +49 | 1,004 |
| McCABE, J.J. (Non-Party) | 204 | — | 204 | +2 | 206 | +2 | 208 | -208 | — | — | — | — | — | — | — | — | — | — | — | — | — |
| McCARTHY, Patricia (Non-Party) | 963 | +22 | 985 | +35 | 1,020 | +53 | 1,073 | — | 1,073 | — | 1,073 | — | 1,073 | — | 1,073 | — | 1,073 | — | 1,073 | — | 1,073 |
| McGRATH, Mary (P.D.) | 174 | +3 | 177 | +10 | 187 | -187 | — | — | — | — | — | — | — | — | — | — | — | — | — | — | — |
| McMAHON, Pat (F.F.) | 941 | +6 | 947 | +1 | 948 | +1 | 949 | +33 | 982 | +47 | 1,029 | +11 | 1,040 | +182 | 1,222 | -153 | 1,069 | — | 1,069 | — | 1,069 |
| O'LOUGHLIN, Pat (F.F.) | 540 | +2 | 542 | +1 | 543 | +3 | 546 | +54 | 600 | +34 | 634 | +18 | 652 | +39 | 691 | +42 | 733 | +36 | 769 | -769 | — |
| O'SHAUGHNESSY, Tom (Lab.) | 481 | +16 | 497 | +14 | 511 | +17 | 528 | +16 | 544 | +40 | 584 | +28 | 612 | +57 | 669 | +17 | 686 | -686 | — | — | — |
| SCANLAN, Sonny (F.G.) | 678 | +2 | 680 | +29 | 709 | +6 | 715 | +49 | 764 | +7 | 771 | +209 | 980 | +129 | 1,109 | — | 1,109 | — | 1,109 | — | 1,109 |
| Non-transferable papers not effective | — | +5 | 5 | +6 | 11 | +3 | 14 | +12 | 26 | +18 | 44 | +36 | 80 | +90 | 170 | +46 | 216 | +293 | 509 | +315 | 824 |
| TOTAL: | 6,408 | — | 6,408 | — | 6,408 | — | 6,408 | — | 6,408 | — | 6,408 | — | 6,408 | — | 6,408 | — | 6,408 | — | 6,408 | — | 6,408 |

Elected: McCarthy, Patricia (Non-Party); McMahon, Pat (F.F.); Scanlan, Sonny (F.G.); Hillery, Seán (F.F.); Makowski, Brigid (Non-Party)

# ROAD MAINTENANCE SERVICES LTD.

## Contractors to Local Authorities for:

**Ralumac**

**Bitupave Slurry Seal**

**Retread Process      Surface Dressing**

**Shellgrip**

**Road Planing**

**Road Marking      Joint Sealing**

**Suction Sweeping**

Bluebell Industrial Estate,
Dublin 12.
Telephone: (01) 783245
Telefax: (01) 522464

Oranmore,
Co. Galway.
Telephone: (091) 94659
Telefax: (091) 94675

Quartertown Mills,
Mallow,
Co. Cork.
Telephone: (022) 21684
Telefax: (022) 42125

# CORK BOROUGH COUNCIL

## CORK CO. BOROUGH COUNCIL RESULTS

| | 1991 | | 1985 | |
|---|---|---|---|---|
| PARTY | % of votes | Seats obtained | % of votes | Seats obtained |
| Fianna Fail | 29.0 | 9 | 41.1 | 13 |
| Fine Gael | 18.8 | 6 | 26.9 | 8 |
| Labour | 14.2 | 6 | 10.6 | 5 |
| Progressive Dem. | 8.4 | 3 | — | — |
| Workers Party | 9.9 | 3 | 5.7 | 2 |
| Other | 19.7 | 4 | 15.7 | 3 |
| TOTAL SEATS | | 31 | | 31 |

## CORK

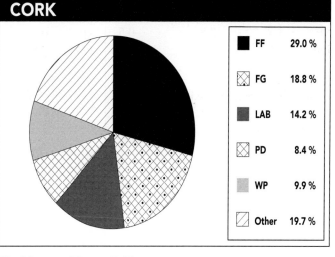

| | | |
|---|---|---|
| ■ | FF | 29.0 % |
| ▨ | FG | 18.8 % |
| ■ | LAB | 14.2 % |
| ▨ | PD | 8.4 % |
| ▨ | WP | 9.9 % |
| ▨ | Other | 19.7 % |

**City Hall, Cork**
**Telephone:(021) 966222**
**Fax:(021) 314238**
**Rateable valuation: £1,014,321**
**Municipal rate: £33.76**
**Borough Council meetings: second and fourth Monday of each month**

*City Manager:* Thomas P. Rice
*Assistant City Managers:* Niall Bradley, Maurice Moloney
*City Engineer:* William A. Fitzgerald
*City Architect:* Cornelius Hegarty
*Town Planning Officer:* John O'Donnell (Acting)
*Law Agent:* David O'Hagen
*Chief Fire Officer:* Denis O'Mahony
*Finance Officer:* Thomas Hunter McGowan
*Personnel Officer:* Vincent Barrett
*Collector of Municipal Rates:* Kathleen Lynch
*City Librarian:* Hanna O'Sullivan
*Chief Veterinary Inspector:* Patrick Maloney
*City Coroner:* Cornelius Riordan
*Personnel Officer:* Vincent Barrett
*City Engineer:* William A. Fitzgerald
*Senior Engineer:* Edward Stoker (Environment)
*Senior Engineer:* John J. O'Sullivan (Sanitary)
*Roads:* Harling Hayes
*Road Safety:* Josephine Daly
*City Architect:* Cornelius Hegarty
*Senior Executive Building Surveyor:* Ernest Burns (Acting)
*Senior Executive Engineer:* John Dromey
*Town Planning Officer:* John O'Donnell (Acting)
*Law Agent:* David O'Hagen
*Senior Executive Solicitor:* Deborah Hegarty
*Chief Fire Officer:* Denis O'Mahony
*Senior Staff Officer:* John O'Brien

The position of Cork County Manager is presently vacant. It was advertised in the national press job sections in late October 1992.

The individual sought would be required "for developing and implementing a medium and long term strategy for the county in the physical, social, economic and cultural areas."

The position needs experience of administration at a sufficiently high level and a knowledge of public administration in Ireland.

The appointment is for a period of seven years and carries a current salary of £45,768.

## NORTH-CENTRAL

|     | 1991 | 1985 | '85 to '91 Swing |
|-----|------|------|------|
| FF  | 25.8 | 33.8 | -8.0 |
| FG  | 21.0 | 27.2 | -6.2 |
| LAB | 13.3 | 13.1 | 0.2 |
| WP  | 8.0  | 5.0  | 3.0 |
| PD  | 4.5  | —    | 4.5 |
| GP  | 2.2  | —    | 2.2 |
| SF  | 3.3  | 3.8  | -0.5 |
| Ind | 22.1 | 20.0 | 2.1 |

ALLEN, Bernard (Ald),
7 Mount Prospect, Shanakiel,
Cork. (FG)
Dáil Deputy. 021-46689

O'CALLAGHAN, Joe,
2 Lapp's Quay,
Cork. (Lab)
Trade Union Official.

O'FLYNN, Noel,
Kilnap,
Mallow Road, Cork. (FF)
Businessman. 021-305677

O'LEARY, Con,
1 St. Rita's Avenue, Gurranabraher,
Cork. (NP)
Shopkeeper.

WALLACE, Damien,
63 Merrion Court, Montenotte,
Cork. (FF)
Insurance Broker. 021-307465

## NORTH-EAST

|     | 1991 | 1985 | '85 to '91 Swing |
|-----|------|------|------|
| FF  | 23.0 | 40.5 | -17.5 |
| FG  | 21.7 | 22.5 | -0.8 |
| LAB | 13.3 | 13.1 | 0.2 |
| WP  | 17.3 | 9.9  | 7.4 |
| PD  | 15.9 | —    | 15.9 |
| GP  | 7.9  | —    | 7.9 |
| SF  | 0.0  | 4.9  | -4.9 |
| Ind | 0.8  | 9.1  | -8.3 |

BROSNAN, Tim,
7 St Christophers Road, Montenotte,
Cork. (FF)
Pensions Consultant

BURKE, Liam,
"The Grove", Douglas Hall,
Cork. (FG)
Auctioneer. 021-892707

KELLEHER, John (Ald),
34 Silverheights Drive, Mayfield,
Cork. (Elected WP, now DL)
Teacher.

NASH, Frank,
1 Goulding's Cottages, Dillons Cross,
Cork. (Lab)
Self-employed. 021-500895

QUILL, Máirín,
1 Wellesley Terrace, Wellington Road,
Cork. (PD)
Dáil Deputy. 021-502099

## NORTH-WEST

|     | 1991 | 1985 | '85 TO '91 Swing |
|-----|------|------|------|
| FF  | 38.0 | 51.3 | -13.3 |
| FG  | 11.4 | 21.2 | -9.8 |
| LAB | 21.9 | 11.3 | 10.6 |
| WP  | 14.6 | 10.1 | 4.5 |
| PD  | 4.1  | —    | 4.1 |
| GP  | 3.9  | —    | 3.9 |
| SF  | 5.3  | 5.1  | 0.2 |
| Ind | 0.9  | 1.0  | -0.1 |

McCARTHY, David,
8 Hillcrest Avenue, Blarney Road,
Cork. (FF)
Public Representative

O'SULLIVAN, Gerry (Ald),
17 Bakers Road, Gurranabraher,
Cork. (Lab)
Dáil Deputy. 021-303235

HOMAN, Jimmy,
38 Kerryhall Road, Fairhill,
Cork. (WP)
Docker.

O'LEARY, Michael,
"Mogeely", Glasheen Road,
Cork. (FG)
Barrister.

WALLACE, Dan,
13, Killeens Place, Farranree,
Cork. (FF)
Dail Deputy. 021-307465*

* Resigned when appointed Minister for
State, Feb. 1992. Replaced by: Falvey,
Tim, 367 Blarney Street, Cork. (FF)

## SOUTH-CENTRAL

|     | 1991 | 1985 | '85 to '91 Swing |
|-----|------|------|------|
| FF  | 35.3 | 42.1 | -6.8 |
| FG  | 12.6 | 23.0 | -10.4 |
| LAB | 20.5 | 12.2 | 8.3 |
| WP  | 15.7 | 6.0  | 9.7 |
| PD  | 2.7  | —    | 2.7 |
| SF  | 0.0  | 6.8  | -6.8 |
| Ind | 13.2 | 9.9  | 3.3 |

CREGAN, Denis,
7 Elm Grove, Ballinlough,
Cork. (FG)
Businessman. 021-291863

**John Kelleher (DL)**
**Cork**

**Frank Nash (Lab)**
**North East Ward**

**Liam Burke (FG)**
**North East Ward**

**Frank Crowley (FG)**
**Cork City**

LYNCH, Kathleen,
3 Brookfield Park, The Lough,
Cork. (Elected WP, now DL)
Housewife. 021-317911

MARTIN, Michael (Ald),
16 Silver Manor, Ballinlough,
Cork. (FF)
Dáil Deputy. 021-964673

MURRAY, John,
17 Gregg Road, Gillabbey Street,
Cork. (Lab)
Self-employed. 021-270774

O'DRISCOLL, Tom,
95 Fr. Dominic Road, Ballyphehane,
Cork. (FF)
Teacher. 021-317190

## SOUTH-EAST

|     | 1991 | 1985 | '85 TO '91 Swing |
|-----|------|------|------------------|
| FF  | 21.8 | 37.4 | -15.6 |
| FG  | 20.0 | 36.5 | -15.6 |
| LAB | 7.1  | 7.3  | -0.2 |
| WP  | 4.4  | 4.1  | 0.3 |
| PD  | 12.1 | —    | 12.1 |
| GP  | 9.8  | —    | 9.8 |
| SF  | 3.3  | —    | 3.3 |
| Ind | 20.7 | 14.7 | 6.0 |

AHERNE, Chrissie,
9 Dunlocha Cottages, Blackrock,
Cork. (FF)
Housewife. 021-292125

BEAUSANG, Sean,
22 Richmond Estate, Blackrock Road,
Cork. (NP)
Teacher. 021-295181

BOYLE, Dan,
45 Capwell Avenue, Turners Cross,
Cork. (GP)
Community Worker.

CORR, Jim (Ald),
"Kakuri", Hettyfield, Douglas Road,
Cork. (FG)
Teacher. 021-291400

O'FLYNN, Joe,
Connolly Hall, Lapps Quay,
Cork. (Lab)
Trade Union Official. 021-357700

WYSE, Pearse,
"Shanoon", Dunmore Lawn,
Boreenmanna Road,
Cork. (PD)
Dáil Deputy. 021-295493

## SOUTH-WEST

|     | 1991 | 1985 | '85 TO '91 Swing |
|-----|------|------|------------------|
| FF  | 31.7 | 42.7 | -11.0 |
| FG  | 23.8 | 28.3 | -4.5 |
| LAB | 12.4 | 10.5 | 1.9 |
| WP  | 4.0  | —    | 4.0 |
| PD  | 10.4 | —    | 10.4 |
| GP  | 5.8  | —    | 5.8 |
| SF  | 2.1  | 2.9  | -0.8 |
| Ind | 9.9  | 15.6 | -5.7 |

BERMINGHAM, Brian,
12 Woodbrook Grove, Bishopstown,
Cork. (PD)
Teacher. 021-543775

DENNEHY, John (Ald),
"Avondale", Westside Estate, Togher,
Cork. (FF)
Dáil Deputy. 021-962908

HOURICAN, P.J.,
20 Fremont Drive, Bishopstown,
Cork. (FG)
Builder.

MURRAY, Pat,
"Saint Francis", Rossa Avenue,
Bishopstown,
Cork. (NP)
Teacher.

O'SULLIVAN, Toddy,
"Farnoge", Lough Villas, The Lough,
Cork. (Lab)
Dáil Deputy. 021-962788

"The Comeback Man" – Michael O'Leary celebrates his election to Cork Corporation.

**John Dennehy (FF)**
**South West Area**

**Bernard Allen (FG)**
**North Central Area**

**Michael Martin (FF)**
**South Central**

**Chrissie Aherne (FF)**
**South East**

# Candidates break ranks over Service Charges

Service Charges was the central issue to the Local Elections Campaign in Cork City. Whether they had any real bearing on the voters' decision in the polling booths, it is impossible to say, but it certainly was the media issue and the issue which shaped the presentation of both the personal and the Party Campaigns.

Added impeteas was given to the emotiveness of the Service Charge issue by the jailing of five Cork citizens a few months before the Campaign for non payment of the controversial levy.

Fianna Fail had promised to abolish the levy in the 1985 Local Elections and now was to get a lot of stick from the other Parties and from the Cork Council Trade Unions for failing to do so. Fianna Fail members of the Corporation had supported the charges since 1985 arguing that the charges raised, £2.2 m which the Corporation could ill afford to do without. Their candidates defended their position with the point that

abolition of the charges could mean the loss of Corporation jobs, a massive increase in commercial rates or even failure to strike any rate and the abolition of the elected body.

One Fianna Fail candidate however, refused to toe the agreed Party line. Colourful North City Motor Factors businessman Noel O'Flynn, a candidate for the Party in the North West Ward had earlier in the year paid the fines of a service charge protester to get him out of jail and vowed to vote against the levy if elected to the Corporation.

If Fianna Fail had problems holding a party line on the charges, Fine Gael too had its problems with the issue. For the Fine Gael Corporation members, including Bernard Allen T.D., the problem was brought to a head by the Party's decision at national level, to back the Workers Party Dail motion calling for the abolition of the charges in the middle of the Local Election Campaign.

Party H.Q. had made it known that it

was up to each local Fine Gael Council Group to determine their own local policy, the Fine Gael Corporation candidates subsequently reversed their previously held position and promised to vote against service charges in the newly elected Corporation.

All other Parties, Labour, Workers Party and the Greens and the majority of Independents nailed their colours to the No Charges mast. Spare a thought however for the Cork South Central Workers Party (now Democratic Left) candidate, Kathleen Lynch, who was unfortunate enough to have the same name as the City Official's signing the demand notices for the charges and so occasionally got an earful at the doorstep of a few confused householders.

Other issues also presented themselves to candidates. Unemployment in Cork in June 1991 was running at just over 19% with 17,000 out of work while the City had a list of 1,700 waiting for Corporation housing.

In the weeks prior to polling, Fianna Fail had attempted to stem an expected mid term protest vote by announcing the go ahead for the £60m down stream crossing, while Finance Minister Reynolds paid a special visit to the City to announce the transfer of the Central Statistics Office Headquarters and staff to the Southern City.

Cork City has six Local Electoral areas, three on each side of the River Lee. In all, eight, candidates put themselves in front of the City's 89,000 plus electors for the 31 seats on Cork Corporation.

Fianna Fail had won 13 out of these seats in the 1985 Local Elections. In 1986, four of these Councillors had switched to join the newly formed Progressive Democrats.

Fianna Fail entered the campaign with nine out-going Councillors. Against the National trend, and to the surprise of even its own organisation, they returned to the new Council with nine seats, losing one in the South West Ward and gaining one in the North Central Ward. There were however personality changes for the Party.

Paud Black lost out to be replaced in the North Central Ward by the afore mentioned O'Flynn who was joined by young Damian Wallace, the 23 year old son of Deputy Dan Wallace. Danny himself topped the poll with just 10 votes under the quota in the North West

"Father and Son" - Damien and Danny Wallace celebrate their success in both being elected to Cork Corporation

Ward and so the father and son team made history to become the first parent-child combination to sit on the benches of Cork City Hall.

Fine Gael had little reason to celebrate at their disappointing performance in the City. They went in to the Election with eight Corporation seats and came out of it with only six.

Bernard Allen T.D. topped the poll comfortably in the North Central Ward but secured the Party's only seat there, Liam Bourke held on to his seat in the North East Ward, as did P.J. Hourihan in the South West Ward, while Jim Corr despite the fact, that during the Campaign, he had persisted in his support of services charges, topped the poll with 1,315 first preferences in the South East Ward.

The big personality story of the Fine Gael camp however, was the election of former Labour Leader and Tanaiste Michael O'Leary. O'Leary who had stepped down from active politics in 1989 had re-emerged in his native Cork, where he has been practising as a Barrister on the Southern circuit and his candidature for the Local Elections had been a national news item. His return to Local Politics was a close call, however and he just managed to beat Fianna Fail's Jim Falvey for the last seat on the North West Ward by only 27 votes. Labour in Cork as elsewhere had cause to celebrate

picking up an extra seat and increasing its share of the vote to 14.2%. Its Deputies Toddy and Gerry O'Sullivan were elected comfortably as were

outgoing Councillor Joe O'Callaghan. Outgoing City Mayor Frank Nash had to wait until the last count on the North East Ward, however, to secure his seat.

The P.D.'s had high hopes for this their first Local Election Campaign in Cork City. This campaign was hampered by the fact that one of their four outgoing Councillors, Eoin Curtin, was not contesting. Another problem for

the Party was the surprise decision of the South Side T.D. Pierce Wyse to transfer to the South East Ward instead of running in his traditional base of South Central.

Cork had been considered a stronghold, for the flagging Party, with two sitting T.D.'s, a third of their Dail Representation but gains like those, they secured in Limerick and Dublin, did not materialise in Cork. Wyse, and Dail colleague Maureen Quill were easily returned and the Party's other outgoing Councillor Brian Bermingham, after looking dead and buried at one stage in the count, also held on.

The Green's had their first Cork County Councillor elected in the person of Dan Boyle. A lot of his support could be contributed to his high profile campaign against the controversial landfill site on the Kinsale Road.

Independents Patrick Murray and Sean Busang were also elected.

On the Southside, Fianna Fail's T.D.'s John Dennehy and Micheal Martin both topped the poll and both returned comfortably while Martin's surplus enabled the Party to pick up an extra seat in the form of Tom O'Driscoll. Former Lord Mayor Chrissie Ahern just passed Pierce Wyse by 5 votes to top the poll in the South East Ward for the Party.

**"A word in your ear"** - **Charles Haughey and Bertie Ahern at a Fianna Fail rally in Cork during the June 1991 local elections.**

# NORTH-CENTRAL ELECTORAL AREA

TOTAL ELECTORATE 13,853. VALID POLL 7,386. NO. OF MEMBERS 5. QUOTA 1,232

| Names of Candidates | First Count Votes | Second Count Transfer of Maloney's votes | Result | Third Count Transfer of Allen's surplus | Result | Fourth Count Transfer of Burke's votes | Result | Fifth Count Transfer of Murphy's votes | Result | Sixth Count Transfer of Kelly's votes | Result | Seventh Count Transfer of D. O'Leary's votes | Result | Eighth Count Transfer of Black's votes | Result | Ninth Count Transfer of Harris' votes | Result | Tenth Count Transfer of Sheehan's votes | Result | Eleventh Count Transfer of Buckley's votes | Result | Twelfth Count Transfer of Leary's votes | Result |
|---|---|---|---|---|---|---|---|---|---|---|---|---|---|---|---|---|---|---|---|---|---|---|---|
| ALLEN, Bernard (F.G.) | 1,291 | − | 1,291 | -59 | 1,232 | − | 1,232 | − | 1,232 | − | 1,232 | − | 1,232 | − | 1,232 | − | 1,232 | − | 1,232 | − | 1,232 | − | 1,232 |
| BLACK, Paud (F.F.) | 285 | − | 285 | +3 | 288 | +3 | 291 | +4 | 295 | +19 | 314 | +5 | 319 | -319 | — | — | — | — | — | — | — | — | — |
| BUCKLEY, Dave (P.D.) | 334 | +2 | 336 | +5 | 341 | +10 | 351 | +8 | 359 | +23 | 382 | +16 | 398 | +26 | 424 | +13 | 437 | +43 | 480 | -480 | — | — | — |
| BURKE, Brendan (G.P.) | 161 | +4 | 165 | +2 | 167 | -167 | — | — | — | — | — | — | — | — | — | — | — | — | — | — | — | — | — |
| HARRIS, Collette (W.P.) | 247 | +10 | 257 | +1 | 258 | +24 | 282 | +5 | 287 | +6 | 293 | +28 | 321 | +5 | 326 | -326 | — | — | — | — | — | — | — |
| KELLY, Declan (Non-Party) | 180 | +2 | 182 | +1 | 183 | +10 | 193 | +10 | 203 | -203 | — | — | — | — | — | — | — | — | — | — | — | — | — |
| LEAHY, Denis (W.P.) | 344 | +14 | 358 | +2 | 360 | +15 | 375 | +12 | 387 | +8 | 395 | +42 | 437 | +7 | 444 | +189 | 633 | +14 | 647 | +47 | 694 | +56 | 750 |
| LEARY, Donie (Non-Party) | 381 | +5 | 386 | +2 | 388 | +10 | 398 | +23 | 421 | +17 | 438 | +28 | 466 | +8 | 474 | +15 | 489 | +22 | 511 | +43 | 554 | -554 | — |
| MALONEY, Pat | 98 | -98 | — | — | — | — | — | — | — | — | — | — | — | — | — | — | — | — | — | — | — | — | — |
| MURPHY, Bernie (Non-Party) | 169 | +8 | 177 | +1 | 178 | +10 | 188 | -188 | — | — | — | — | — | — | — | — | — | — | — | — | — | — | — |
| O'CALLAGHAN, Joe (Lab.) | 971 | +19 | 990 | +7 | 997 | +23 | 1,020 | +27 | 1,047 | +16 | 1,063 | +26 | 1,089 | +21 | 1,110 | +37 | 1,147 | +58 | 1,205 | +64 | 1,269 | − | 1,269 |
| O'FLYNN, Noel (F.F.) | 903 | +2 | 905 | +4 | 909 | +8 | 917 | +15 | 932 | +9 | 941 | +11 | 952 | +106 | 1,058 | +8 | 1,066 | +23 | 1,089 | +56 | 1,145 | +101 | 1,246 |
| O'LEARY, Con (Non-Party) | 802 | +10 | 812 | +5 | 817 | +13 | 830 | +26 | 856 | +30 | 886 | +41 | 927 | +13 | 940 | +21 | 961 | +40 | 1,001 | +60 | 1,061 | +171 | 1,232 |
| O'LEARY, Don (S.F.) | 242 | +11 | 253 | +1 | 254 | +7 | 261 | +14 | 275 | +3 | 278 | -278 | — | — | — | — | — | — | — | — | — | — | — |
| SHEEHAN, Maebh (F.G.) | 263 | +2 | 265 | +21 | 286 | +13 | 299 | +8 | 307 | +15 | 322 | +10 | 332 | +9 | 341 | +7 | 348 | -348 | — | — | — | — | — |
| WALLACE, Damian (F.F.) | 715 | +3 | 718 | +4 | 722 | +10 | 732 | +10 | 742 | +25 | 767 | +14 | 781 | +84 | 865 | +9 | 874 | +33 | 907 | +76 | 983 | +65 | 1,048 |
| Non-transferable papers not effective | — | +6 | 6 | − | 6 | +11 | 17 | +26 | 43 | +32 | 75 | +57 | 132 | +40 | 172 | +27 | 199 | +115 | 314 | +134 | 448 | +161 | 609 |
| TOTAL: | 7,386 | − | 7,386 | − | 7,386 | − | 7,386 | − | 7,386 | − | 7,386 | − | 7,386 | − | 7,386 | − | 7,386 | − | 7,386 | − | 7,386 | − | 7,386 |

Elected: Allen, Bernard (F.G.); O'Callaghan, Joe (Lab.); O'Flynn, Noel (F.F.); O'Leary, Con (Non-Party); Wallace, Damian (F.F.)

# NORTH-WEST ELECTORAL AREA

TOTAL ELECTORATE 14,357. VALID POLL 7,244. NO. OF MEMBERS 5. QUOTA 1,208

| Names of Candidates | First Count Votes | Second Count Transfer of G. O'Sullivan's surplus | Result | Third Count Transfer of Murray's votes | Result | Fourth Count Transfer of Riordan's votes | Result | Fifth Count Transfer of Hickey's votes | Result | Sixth Count Transfer of J. O'Sullivan's votes | Result | Seventh Count Transfer of Coughlan's votes | Result | Eighth Count Transfer of Flynn's votes | Result | Ninth Count Transfer of Magner's votes | Result | Tenth Count Transfer of Homan's surplus | Result |
|---|---|---|---|---|---|---|---|---|---|---|---|---|---|---|---|---|---|---|---|
| COUGHLAN, Jack (P.D.) | 297 | +1 | 298 | +3 | 301 | +11 | 312 | +21 | 333 | +42 | 375 | -375 | — | — | — | — | — | — | — |
| FALVEY, Tim (F.F.) | 735 | +3 | 738 | +6 | 744 | +4 | 748 | +17 | 765 | +13 | 778 | +61 | 839 | +38 | 877 | +48 | 925 | +20 | 945 |
| FLYNN, Thomas (S.F.) | 384 | +1 | 385 | +4 | 389 | +1 | 390 | +1 | 391 | +15 | 406 | +6 | 412 | -412 | — | — | — | — | — |
| HICKEY, Pat (F.G.) | 215 | +1 | 216 | − | 216 | +38 | 254 | -254 | — | — | — | — | — | — | — | — | — | — | — |
| HOMAN, Jimmy (W.P.) | 1,058 | +6 | 1,064 | +12 | 1,076 | +4 | 1,080 | +8 | 1,088 | +57 | 1,145 | +20 | 1,165 | +167 | 1,332 | − | 1,332 | -124 | 1,208 |
| MAGNER, Pat (Lab.) | 334 | +18 | 352 | +10 | 362 | +3 | 365 | +11 | 376 | +55 | 431 | +43 | 474 | +35 | 509 | -509 | — | — | — |
| McCARTHY, Dave (F.F.) | 821 | +5 | 826 | +3 | 829 | +6 | 835 | +3 | 838 | +30 | 868 | +30 | 898 | +80 | 978 | +46 | 1,024 | +23 | 1,047 |
| MURRAY, Philip | 63 | +1 | 64 | -64 | — | — | — | — | — | — | — | — | — | — | — | — | — | — | — |
| O'LEARY, Michael (F.G.) | 437 | +2 | 439 | +4 | 443 | +83 | 526 | +167 | 693 | +39 | 732 | +126 | 858 | +14 | 872 | +88 | 960 | +12 | 972 |
| O'SULLIVAN, Gerry (Lab.) | 1,253 | -45 | 1,208 | − | 1,208 | − | 1,208 | − | 1,208 | − | 1,208 | − | 1,208 | − | 1,208 | − | 1,208 | − | 1,208 |
| O'SULLIVAN, John T. (G.P.) | 279 | +2 | 281 | +6 | 287 | +18 | 305 | +9 | 314 | -314 | — | — | — | — | — | — | — | — | — |
| RIORDAN, David (F.G.) | 170 | +1 | 171 | +2 | 173 | -173 | — | — | — | — | — | — | — | — | — | — | — | — | — |
| WALLACE, Dan (F.F.) | 1,198 | +4 | 1,202 | +7 | 1,209 | − | 1,209 | − | 1,209 | − | 1,209 | − | 1,209 | − | 1,209 | − | 1,209 | − | 1,209 |
| Non-transferable papers not effective | — | — | — | +7 | 7 | +5 | 12 | +17 | 29 | +63 | 92 | +89 | 181 | +78 | 259 | +327 | 586 | +69 | 655 |
| TOTAL: | 7,244 | − | 7,244 | − | 7,244 | − | 7,244 | − | 7,244 | − | 7,244 | − | 7,244 | − | 7,244 | − | 7,244 | − | 7,244 |

Elected: O'Sullivan, Gerry (Lab.); Wallace, Dan (F.F.); Homan, Jimmy (W.P.); McCarthy, Dave (F.F.); O'Leary, Michael (F.G.)

## NORTH-EAST ELECTORAL AREA

TOTAL ELECTORATE 12,462. VALID POLL 6,034. NO. OF MEMBERS 5. QUOTA 1,006

| Names of Candidates | First Count Votes | Second Count Transfer of Howe's votes | Result | Third Count Transfer of Kelleher's surplus | Result | Fourth Count Transfer of McAuliffe's votes | Result | Fifth Count Transfer of Houlihan's votes | Result | Sixth Count Transfer of McGee's votes | Result | Seventh Count Transfer of Quill's surplus | Result | Eighth Count Transfer of McRory's votes | Result |
|---|---|---|---|---|---|---|---|---|---|---|---|---|---|---|---|
| BROSNAN, Tim (F.F.) | 654 | +2 | 656 | +2 | 658 | +14 | 672 | +86 | 758 | +32 | 790 | +11 | 801 | +268 | 1,069 |
| BURKE, Liam (F.G.) | 711 | +1 | 712 | +3 | 715 | +84 | 799 | +21 | 820 | +191 | 1,011 | — | 1,011 | — | 1,011 |
| HOULIHAN, Bird (F.F.) | 306 | +1 | 307 | +3 | 310 | +6 | 316 | -316 | — | — | — | — | — | — | — |
| HOWE, James (Harry) (Non-Party) | 46 | -46 | — | — | — | — | — | — | — | — | — | — | — | — | — |
| KELLEHER, John (W.P.) | 1,045 | — | 1,045 | -39 | 1,006 | — | 1,006 | — | 1,006 | — | 1,006 | — | 1,006 | — | 1,006 |
| MacCARTHY-MORROGH, Donogh (G.P.) | 478 | +22 | 500 | +9 | 509 | +17 | 526 | +12 | 538 | +44 | 582 | +9 | 591 | +32 | 623 |
| McAULIFFE, Tadgh (F.G.) | 297 | — | 297 | +2 | 299 | -299 | — | — | — | — | — | — | — | — | — |
| McGEE, Betty (F.G.) | 304 | +2 | 306 | +1 | 307 | +64 | 371 | +8 | 379 | -379 | — | — | — | — | — |
| McRORY, Pat (F.F.) | 429 | — | 429 | +2 | 431 | +25 | 456 | +73 | 529 | +16 | 545 | +8 | 553 | -553 | — |
| NASH, Frank (Lab.) | 803 | +9 | 812 | +13 | 825 | +45 | 870 | +29 | 899 | +51 | 950 | +9 | 959 | +122 | 1,081 |
| QUILL, Mairin (P.D.) | 961 | +4 | 965 | +4 | 969 | +36 | 1,005 | +54 | 1,059 | — | 1,059 | -53 | 1,006 | — | 1,006 |
| Non-transferable papers not effective | — | +5 | 5 | — | 5 | +8 | 13 | +33 | 46 | +45 | 91 | +16 | 107 | +131 | 238 |
| TOTAL: | 6,034 | — | 6,034 | — | 6,034 | — | 6,034 | — | 6,034 | — | 6,034 | — | 6,034 | — | 6,034 |

Elected: Kelleher, John (W.P.); Quill, Mairín (P.D.); Burke, Liam (F.G.); Nash, Frank (Lab.); Brosnan, Tim (F.F.)

## SOUTH-WEST ELECTORAL AREA

TOTAL ELECTORATE 16,790. VALID POLL 8,271. NO. OF MEMBERS 5. QUOTA 1,379

| Names of Candidates | First Count Votes | Second Count Transfer of Dennehy's surplus | Result | Third Count Transfer of McBarron's votes | Result | Fourth Count Transfer of McCarthy's votes | Result | Fifth Count Transfer of Hennigan's votes | Result | Sixth Count Transfer of Morrissey's votes | Result | Seventh Count Transfer of Delaney's votes | Result | Eighth Count Transfer of Whyte's votes | Result |
|---|---|---|---|---|---|---|---|---|---|---|---|---|---|---|---|
| BERMINGHAM, Brian (P.D.) | 861 | +24 | 885 | +2 | 887 | +21 | 908 | +40 | 948 | +37 | 985 | +126 | 1,111 | +158 | 1,269 |
| DELANEY, Jillian (G.P.) | 478 | +10 | 488 | +34 | 522 | +59 | 581 | +21 | 602 | +22 | 624 | -624 | — | — | — |
| DENNEHY, John (F.F.) | 1,662 | -283 | 1,379 | — | 1,379 | — | 1,379 | — | 1,379 | — | 1,379 | — | 1,379 | — | 1,379 |
| HENNIGAN, Sean (F.F.) | 306 | +91 | 397 | +9 | 406 | +2 | 408 | -408 | — | — | — | — | — | — | — |
| HOURICAN, P.J. (F.G.) | 925 | +11 | 936 | +2 | 938 | +8 | 946 | +32 | 978 | +58 | 1,036 | +44 | 1,080 | +440 | 1,520 |
| LONG, Jerry (F.F.) | 652 | +51 | 703 | +16 | 719 | +13 | 732) | +249 | 981 | +20 | 1,001 | +43 | 1,044 | +23 | 1,067 |
| McBARRON, James (S.F.) | 171 | +6 | 177 | -177 | — | — | — | — | — | — | — | — | — | — | — |
| McCARTHY, Jerry (W.P.) | 328 | +5 | 333 | +34 | 367 | -367 | — | — | — | — | — | — | — | — | — |
| MORRISSEY, Dan (F.G.) | 384 | +22 | 406 | +7 | 413 | +19 | 432 | +3 | 435 | -435 | — | — | — | — | — |
| MURRAY, Patrick (Non-Party) | 817 | +13 | 830 | +30 | 860 | +74 | 934 | +23 | 957 | +35 | 992 | +229 | 1,221 | +107 | 1,328 |
| O'SULLIVAN, Toddy (Lab.) | 1,029 | +46 | 1,075 | +27 | 1,102 | +130 | 1,232 | +16 | 1,248 | +138 | 1,386 | — | 1,386 | — | 1,386 |
| WHYTE, Kenneth (F.G.) | 658 | +4 | 662 | +3 | 665 | +7 | 672 | +13 | 685 | +80 | 765 | +59 | 824 | -824 | — |
| Non-transferable papers not effective | — | — | — | +13 | 13 | +34 | 47 | +11 | 58 | +45 | 103 | +123 | 226 | +96 | 322 |
| TOTAL: | 8,271 | — | 8,271 | — | 8,271 | — | 8,271 | — | 8,271 | — | 8,271 | — | 8,271 | — | 8,271 |

Elected: Dennehy, John (F.F.); O'Sullivan, Toddy (Lab.); Hourican, P.J. (F.G.); Murray, Patrick (Non-Party); Bermingham, Brian (P.D.)

# SOUTH-EAST ELECTORAL AREA

TOTAL ELECTORATE 20,230. VALID POLL 10,140. NO. OF MEMBERS 6. QUOTA 1,449

| Names of Candidates | First Count Votes | Second Count Transfer of O'Sullivan's votes Result | Third Count Transfer of Dennehy's votes Result | Fourth Count Transfer of O'Brien's votes Result | Fifth Count Transfer of M. MacCarthy's votes Result | Sixth Count Transfer of McNicholl Murphy's votes Result | Seventh Count Transfer of Corr's votes Result | Eighth Count Transfer of Burke's surplus Result | Ninth Count Transfer of Heffernan's votes Result | Tenth Count Transfer of White's votes Result | Eleventh Count Transfer of S. McCarthy's votes Result | Twelfth Count Transfer of T.McCarthy's votes Result |
|---|---|---|---|---|---|---|---|---|---|---|---|---|
| AHERNE, Chrissie (F.F.) | 1,027 | +14 1,041 | +9 1,050 | +41 1,091 | +86 1,177 | +13 1,190 | +4 1,194 | +27 1,221 | +25 1,246 | +53 1,299 | +32 1,331 | +78 1,409 |
| BEAUSANG, Sean (Non-Party) | 923 | +6 929 | +36 965 | +5 970 | +18 988 | +22 1,010 | +5 1,015 | +27 1,042 | +55 1,097 | +88 1,185 | +95 1,280 | +206 1,486 |
| BOYLE, Daniel (G.P.) | 989 | +5 994 | +8 1,002 | +21 1,023 | +16 1,039 | +15 1,054 | +3 1,057 | +70 1,127 | +55 1,182 | +73 1,255 | +133 (1388) | +130 1,518 |
| BURKE, Liam (S.F.) | 333 | — 333 | +17 350 | +1 351 | +10 361 | — 361 | — 361 | — — | — — | — — | — — | — — |
| CORR, Jim (F.G.) | 1,315 | +36 1,351 | +2 1,353 | +16 1,369 | +7 1,376 | +152 1,528 | -79 1,449 | — (1,449) | — 1,449 | — 1,449 | — 1,449 | — 1,449 |
| COUNIHAN, Donal J. (F.F.) | 743 | +3 746 | +1 747 | +32 779 | +59 838 | +8 846 | +3 849 | +11 860 | +23 883 | +22 905 | +13 918 | +94 1,012 |
| DENNEHY, Paddy (Non-Party) | 199 | +4 203 | -203 — | — — | — | — | — | — | — | — | — | — |
| HEFFERNAN, Frank (F.G.) | 338 | +16 354 | +1 355 | — 355 | — 355 | +56 411 | +48 459 | +6 465 | -465 — | — | — | — |
| MacCARTHY, Maurice (F.F.) | 240 | +4 244 | +23 267 | +31 298 | -298 — | — | — | — | — | — | — | — |
| McCARTHY, Sean (W.P.) | 442 | +3 445 | +14 459 | +7 466 | +13 479 | +2 481 | — 481 | +58 539 | +11 550 | +26 576 | -576 — | — |
| McCARTHY, Ted (Non-Party) | 628 | +6 634 | +9 643 | +4 647 | +7 654 | +8 662 | +4 666 | +18 684 | +59 743 | +59 802 | +36 838 | -838 — |
| McNICHOLL MURPHY, Jean (F.G.) | 295 | +33 328 | +3 331 | — 331 | +1 332 | -332 — | — | — | — | — | — | — |
| O'BRIEN, Denis (F.F.) | 203 | +2 205 | +1 206 | -206 — | — | — | — | — | — | — | — | — |
| O'FLYNN, Joe (Lab.) | 723 | +11 734 | +21 755 | +10 765 | +18 783 | +13 796 | +2 798 | +23 821 | +32 853 | +42 895 | +154 1,049 | +119 1,168 |
| O'SULLIVAN, Marie (F.G.) | 172 | -172 — | — | — | — | — | — | — | — | — | — | — |
| WHITE, Rose (Non-Party) | 348 | +11 359 | +40 399 | +1 400 | +27 427 | +10 437 | +3 440 | +53 493 | +18 511 | -511 — | — | — |
| WYSE, Pearse (P.D.) | 1,222 | +11 1,233 | +6 1,239 | +27 1,266 | +17 1,283 | +28 1,311 | +7 1,318 | +13 1,331 | +94 1,425 | -481 1,473 | — 1,473 | — 1,473 |
| Non-transferable papers not effective | — | +7 7 | +12 19 | +10 29 | +19 48 | +5 53 | — 53 | +55 108 | +93 201 | +100 301 | +113 414 | +211 625 |
| TOTAL: | 10,140 | — 10,140 | — 10,140 | — 10,140 | — 10,140 | — 10,140 | — 10,140 | — 10,140 | — 10,140 | — 10,140 | — 10,140 | — 10,140 |

Elected: Corr, Jim (F.G.); Wyse, Pearse (P.D.); Boyle, Daniel (G.P.); Beausang, Séan (Non-Party); Aherne, Chrissie (F.F.); O'Flynn, Joe (Lab.)

# SOUTH-CENTRAL ELECTORAL AREA

ELECTORATE 12,765. VALID POLL 7,213. NO. OF MEMBERS 5. QUOTA 1,203

| Names of Candidates | First Count Votes | Second Count Transfer of Martin's surplus Result | Third Count Transfer of Cotter's votes Result | Fourth Count Transfer of Walsh's votes Result | Fifth Count Transfer of Kennedy's votes Result | Sixth Count Transfer of McSweeney's votes Result | Seventh Count Transfer of Carrington's votes Result | Eighth Count Transfer of Collins' votes Result | Ninth Count Transfer of O'Connell's votes Result |
|---|---|---|---|---|---|---|---|---|---|
| CARRINGTON, Hannah (Bawn) (F.F.) | 221 | +95 316 | — 316 | +10 326 | +17 343 | +11 354 | -354 — | — — | — — |
| COLLINS, Fidelma (F.G.) | 328 | +16 344 | +2 346 | +25 371 | +8 379 | +12 391 | +17 408 | -408 — | — — |
| COTTER, A.J. | 26 | +3 29 | -29 — | — — | — | — | — | — | — |
| CREGAN, Denis (Dino) (F.G.) | 581 | +40 621 | +4 625 | +32 657 | +28 685 | +28 713 | +19 732 | +250 982 | +85 1,067 |
| DAWSON, Pat (Lab.) | 523 | +26 549 | +1 550 | +18 568 | +38 606 | +21 627 | +23 650 | +21 671 | +119 790 |
| KENNEDY, Bernie (Non-Partty) | 222 | +8 230 | +9 239 | +9 248 | -248 — | — | — | — | — |
| LYNCH, Kathleen (W.P.) | 1,136 | +61 1,197 | +6 1,203 | — 1,203 | — 1,203 | — 1,203 | — 1,203 | — 1,203 | — 1,203 |
| MARTIN, Micheal Antoin (F.F.) | 1,746 | -543 1,203 | — 1,203 | — 1,203 | — 1,203 | — 1,203 | — 1,203 | — 1,203 | — 1,203 |
| McSWEENEY, Damien (Non-Party) | 268 | +17 285 | +2 287 | +17 304 | +29 333 | -333 — | — | — | — |
| MURRAY, John (Lab.) | 955 | +33 988 | +2 990 | +22 1,012 | +42 1,054 | +65 1,119 | +16 1,135 | +35 1,170 | +120 1,290 |
| O'CONNELL, Con (Non-Party) | 434 | +13 447 | — 447 | +20 467 | +33 500 | +112 612 | +13 625 | +23 648 | -648 — |
| O'DRISCOLL, Tom (F.F.) | 581 | +218 799 | +2 801 | +24 825 | +20 845 | +18 863 | +222 1,085 | +26 1,111 | +54 1,165 |
| WALSH, Noel (P.D.) | 192 | +13 205 | — 205 | -205 — | — | — | — | — | — |
| Non-transferable papers not effective | — | — — | +1 1 | +28 29 | +33 62 | +66 128 | +44 172 | +53 225 | +270 495 |
| TOTAL: | 7,213 | — 7,213 | — 7,213 | — 7,213 | — 7,213 | — 7,213 | — 7,213 | — 7,213 | — 7,213 |

Elected: Martin, Micheal Antóin (F.F.); Lynch, Kathleen (W.P.); Murray, John (Lab.); O'Driscoll, Tom (F.F.); Cregan, Denis (Dino) (F.G.)

# CORK COUNTY COUNCIL

## CORK COUNTY COUNCIL RESULTS

| PARTY | 1991 % of votes | 1991 Seats obtained | 1985 % of votes | 1985 Seats obtained |
|---|---|---|---|---|
| Fianna Fail | 36.6 | 19 | 47.0 | 24 |
| Fine Gael | 35.4 | 20 | 38.4 | 19 |
| Labour | 6.1 | 4 | 2 | 2 |
| Progressive Dem. | 5.5 | 1 | — | — |
| Workers Party | 4.3 | 1 | 3.7 | 1 |
| Other | 12.1 | 3 | 6.2 | 2 |
| TOTAL SEATS | | 48 | | 48 |

## CORK

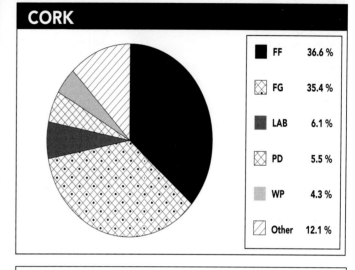

| | |
|---|---|
| ■ FF | 36.6 % |
| ⊠ FG | 35.4 % |
| ■ LAB | 6.1 % |
| ⊠ PD | 5.5 % |
| ▨ WP | 4.3 % |
| ▨ Other | 12.1 % |

County Hall, Carrigrohane Road, Cork
Telephone:(021) 276891
Telex: 75404
Fax: (021) 276321
Total population: 412,623
County (excl. Cork city): 279,427
Cork city: 136,000
Rateable valuation (County): £2,022,197.30
Rates: North:£34.38
Rates: South:£34.38   West: £34.38
County Council meetings: second and fourth Monday of each month at 11.30

*County Manager:*
*County Secretary:* O. O'Donovan (Acting)
*County Engineer:* C. B. Devlin (Acting)
*Financial Controller:* P. Deasy
*Personnel Officer:* T. Manley
*Development Officer:* T. 2O Murchú
*Administrative Officers:*
*General Purposes:* O. O'Donovan
*Rate Collection:* D. O'Callaghan
*Motor Taxation:* J. Kennedy
*Internal Audit:* K. Casey
*Housing and Sanitary: North:* J. R. Holohan *South:* Vacancy*West:* D. Daly
*Planning:* M. O'Donovan, J. McAleer
*Finance:* D. Hearun (Acting)
*Senior Staff Officers:*
*County Housing:* P. J. Corcoran
*Personnel:* Vacant
*Computer:* M. Murphy, M. Rogers
*Rates and Franchise:* P. NicSuibhne
*Engineering:*
 *North:* M. O'Connor  *South:* D. McCarthy  *West:* S. Ryan
*Land Purchase:* W. G. O'Mahony
*Housing and Sanitary:* E. K. Costello, M. Fitzgerald
*Finance:* E. O'Mahony (Acting)
*County Librarian:* R. Flanagan
*County Solicitor:* M. Roche
*County Coroners:*
Finbarr McCarthy, Cornelius O'Connell, Dr C. G. Quigley
*Chief Fire Officer:* Gerard Malone
*County Architect:* G. O'Callaghan
*Senior Executive Architects:* W. A. Houlihan, D. Heffernan
*Senior Executive Engineer:* M. Lavelle

Thomas Rice is a Dubliner, who for over six years has been Cork County Manager. Unusally for a County Manager, Rice began his career not in local administration but in what was then the Department of Local Government He spent nineteen years at the Customs House, 1952 - 1971, firstly as Executive Officer and then Assistant Principal in the Department.

In 1971 he was appointed as Tipperary North Riding County Secretary. He remained there until his first appointment in Cork as Assistant County Manager from 1974 - 1976. He left Cork in 1976, to begin a six year spell as Tipperary South County Manager. He was Limerick City Manager from 1983 until he returned to take up his present Cork City post in 1987.

A very qualified public administrator, Rice is a former Vice Chairman of the County Managers Association. He was educated at St. Patrick's,

**Thomas P. Rice**

Drumcondra and Collaiste Mhuire in Dublin, holds a diploma in Public Administration from U.C.D. and a Certificate in Govern-ment and Accountancy Finance from the College of Commerce in Rathmines.

Born in 1934, he is married to Mary Hamilton and has six children, four daughters and two sons. He enjoys walking, travelling and a game of golf at Cork Golf Club.

## BANDON

| | 1991 | 1985 | '85 to '91 Swing |
|---|---|---|---|
| FF | 37.8 | 43.7 | -5.9 |
| FG | 48.5 | 49.7 | -1.2 |
| PD | 6.7 | — | 6.7 |
| GP | 3.6 | — | 3.6 |
| Ind | 3.3 | 6.6 | -3.3 |

CALLANAN, Peter,
Ballymountain, Innishannon,
County Cork. (FF)
Farmer. 021-75192.

COLEMAN, Alan,
Ballinacourtha, Belgooley,
County Cork. (FF)
Farmer. 021-771319

CREED, Michael,
Codrum, Macroom,
County Cork. (FG)
Dáil Deputy. 026-41177

LUCEY, Eddie,
Kilbrogan, Bandon,
County Cork. (FG)
Retired Teacher. 023-41651

METCALF, Frank,
Knockane, Ovens,
County Cork. (FG)
Carpenter. 021-331183

MOYNIHAN, Donal,
Gortnascarty, Ballymakeera, Macroom,
County Cork. (FF)
Farmer. 026-45019

MURPHY, Kevin,
Killany House, Kinsale,
County Cork. (FG)
Farmer. 021-772590

## CORK NORTH

| | 1991 | 1985 | '85 to '91 Swing |
|---|---|---|---|
| FF | 46.8 | 54.3 | -7.5 |
| FG | 27.2 | 34.9 | -7.7 |
| Lab | 9.8 | 6.6 | 3.2 |
| WP | 3.8 | — | 3.8 |
| PD | 9.5 | — | 9.5 |
| GP | 2.8 | — | 2.8 |
| SF | 0.0 | 4.2 | -4.2 |

FLEMING, Daniel,
Dawstown, Blarney,
County Cork. (FF)
Auctioneer. 021-385524

McNAMARA, Annette,
Stoneview, Blarney,
County Cork. (FF)
Teacher. 021-385663

O'SULLIVAN, Sheila,
Staff Home, St. Stephens Hospital,
Glanmire,
Co. Cork (Lab)
Hospital Worker.

RYAN, Tomas,
"Ardfield", Dripsey,
County Cork. (FG)
Sales Representative. 021-334235

## CORK SOUTH

| | 1991 | 1985 | '85 to '91 Swing |
|---|---|---|---|
| FF | 43.8 | 54.0 | -10.2 |
| FG | 22.5 | 29.8 | -7.3 |
| Lab | 11.9 | 10.9 | 1.0 |
| WP | 4.4 | — | 4.4 |
| PD | 10.6 | 10.6 | |
| Ind | 6.9 | 5.3 | 1.6 |

BRENNAN, Graham,
Raheens, Carrigaline,
County Cork. (FG)
Fire Officer. 021-372942.

CANTY, Derry,
24 Beech Road, Muskerry Est, Ballincollig,
County Cork. (PD)
Decorator. 021-871383.

COGAN, Barry,
Rosebank, Church Hill, Carrigaline,
County Cork. (FF)
TV Dealer. 021-372035.

COTTER, Sylvester P.,
Hill House, Rochestown,
County Cork. (FG)
Farmer. 021-364035.

DESMOND, Paula,
Ballinrea Road, Carrigaline,
County Cork. (Lab)
Public Representative. 021-372239

O'KEEFFE, Batt,
8 Westcliffe, Ballincollig,
County Cork. (FF)
Senator/Lecturer. 021-871393

## KANTURK

| | 1991 | 1985 | '85 to '91 Swing |
|---|---|---|---|
| FF | 42.8 | 52.8 | -10.0 |
| FG | 44.3 | 42.3 | 2.0 |
| Lab | 8.5 | 4.9 | 3.6 |
| PD | 3.8 | — | 3.8 |
| Ind | 0.6 | — | 0.6 |

BIGGANE, Billy,
Charleville,
County Cork. (FG)
Auctioneer.

CROWLEY, Frank,
Strand Street, Kanturk,
County Cork. (FG)
Dáil Deputy. 022-27157

KELLY, Laurence,
Main Street, Kanturk,
County Cork. (FF)
Dáil Deputy. 029-50828

MURPHY, Gerard,
New Street, Newmarket,
County Cork. (FG)
Postmaster.

MURPHY, John B.,
'The Shamrock', Millstreet Town,
County Cork. (FF)
Publican. 029-79058

ROCHE, Jack,
Clough, Rockchapel,
County Cork. (FF)
Project Manager. 068-44169

## MALLOW

| | 1991 | 1985 | '85 to '91 Swing |
|---|---|---|---|
| FF | 34.0 | 46.7 | -12.7 |
| FG | 31.6 | 30.1 | 1.5 |
| LAB | 1.9 | 2.3 | -0.4 |
| WP | 18.7 | 17.4 | 1.3 |
| PD | 4.9 | — | 4.9 |
| GP | 2.1 | — | 2.1 |
| Ind | 6.8 | 3.5 | 3.3 |

**Michael Pat Murphy (NP)**
**Schull**

**Noel Collins (NP)**
**Midleton**

**Batt O'Keeffe (FF)**
**Cork South**

**Sylvester P. Cotter (FG)**
**Cork South**

BRADFORD, Paul,
Mourneabbey, Mallow,
County Cork. (FG)
Dáil Deputy. 022-29375.

JOYCE, Carey Patrick,
Acres, Fermoy,
County Cork. (FF)
Farmer. 025-38182

O'CALLAGHAN, Conor,
'Annard', Brigown Road, Mitchelstown,
County Cork. (FG)
Solicitor.

O'KEEFFE, Ned,
Ballylough, Mitchelstown,
County Cork. (FF)
Dáil Deputy. 021-871393

O'RIORDAN, Ted,
22 Lisheen Row, Mallow,
County Cork. (FF)
Dairygold Employee. 022-22451

PYNE, Aileen D.,
"Kerrymist", Duntahane Road, Fermoy,
County Cork. (FG)
Teacher. 025-32043

SHERLOCK, Joe,
20 Blackwater Drive, Mallow,
County Cork. (Elected WP, now DL)
Dáil Deputy. 022-29375.

## MIDLETON

|     | 1991 | 1985 | '85 to '91 Swing |
| --- | --- | --- | --- |
| FF  | 24.7 | 38.3 | -13.6 |
| FG  | 24.0 | 36.1 | -12.1 |
| Lab | 6.5  | 3.6  | 2.9 |
| WP  | 2.5  | 3.6  | -1.1 |
| PD  | 2.3  | —    | 2.3 |
| GP  | 2.3  | —    | 2.3 |
| Ind | 37.8 | 18.4 | 19.4 |

AHERN, Maurice,
"Avanbloom", Carrigogna, Midleton,
County Cork. (FF)
Financial Consultant. 021-632183

AHERN, Matt,
Monagoul, Ballymacode,
County Cork. (FG)
Farmer. 024-98145.

COLLINS, Noel,
"St Jude's", Midleton,
County Cork. (NP)
Social Worker.

HEGARTY, Michael,
Moanroe, Ladysbridge,
County Cork. (FG)
Farmer.

HEGARTY, Paddy,
Ballinvoher, Cloyne,
County Cork. (NP)
Farmer. 021-652578

MULVIHILL, John,
Tay Road, Ballywilliam, Cobh,
County Cork. (Lab)
Factory Employee. 021-812603.

## SKIBBEREEN

|     | 1991 | 1985 | '85 to '91 Swing |
| --- | --- | --- | --- |
| FF  | 30.6 | 49.4 | -18.8 |
| FG  | 39.4 | 39.3 | 0.1 |
| Lab | 9.1  | 8.9  | 0.2 |
| PD  | 5.9  |      | 5.9 |
| GP  | 5.4  |      | 5.4 |
| SF  | 2.9  | 2.4  | 0.5 |
| Ind | 6.8  |      | 6.8 |

CALNAN, Michael J.,
Kilbarry Road, Dunmanway,
County Cork. (Lab)
Teacher. 023-45329.

McCARTHY, John Cal,
Cool House, Rossmore, Clonakilty,
County Cork. (FG)
Farmer.

O'DONOVAN, Tadg,
Glenafael, Mardyke Road, Skibbereen,
County Cork. (FG)
Publican. 028-21170

O'NEILL, Tom,
Chapel Street, Dunmanway,
County Cork. (FF)
Funeral Director. 023-45121

O'ROURKE, Donal F.,
"Ross Cove", Gallanes, Clonakilty,
County Cork. (FF)
Teacher. 023-33776

O'SULLIVAN, Jim,
Island View, Inchydoney, Clonakilty,
County Cork. (FG)
Farmer.

O'SULLIVAN, D. F.,
Schull Road, Skibbereen,
County Cork. (FF)
Vintner. 023-21329

## SCHULL

|     | 1991 | 1985 | '85 to '91 Swing |
| --- | --- | --- | --- |
| FF  | 38.4 | 40.4 | -2.0 |
| FG  | 41.4 | 41.6 | -0.2 |
| Lab | 6.0  | 4.1  | 1.9 |
| SF  |      | 1.8  | -1.8 |
| Ind | 14.2 | 12.1 | 2.1 |

CALLAGHAN, Vivian,
Bantry Bay Hotel,
Wolfe Tone Square, Bantry,
Co. Cork. (FF)
Hotelier. 027-50062.

HARRINGTON, Michael,
Church Gate, Castletownbere,
County Cork. (FG)
Businessman. 027-70011.

MURPHY, Michael Pat,
Harbour View, Schull,
County Cork. (NP)
Farmer. 028-28200.

O'DONOVAN, Denis,
Montrose House, Slip, Bantry,
County Cork. (FF)
Senator. 027-51541.

SHEEHAN, Patrick Joseph,
Main Street, Goleen,
County Cork. (FG)
Dáil Deputy. 028-35236

"Pull up a chair" — waiting for the voters at a polling booth in Schull.

# Fine Gael are now the biggest party on Cork County Council

After Dublin, Cork was the largest County Council contest in the 1991 poll and now after the restructuring of Local Government in the Capital, Cork with 48 seats will have the largest number of members in its County Hall.

It must be remembered that Cork County Council oversees an area including all the territory of the Cork North West, Cork South West and Cork East Dail constituencies as well as the rural section of Cork North and South Central. In all, there are eight electoral areas.

Over 200,000 Corkonians were registered to vote on June 27th in Cork County, just over 60,000 did so, a turnout of just 29.7% the third lowest in the Country.

When votes were actually counted the collapse of the Fianna Fail vote was most striking. The Party support in the County dropped by almost 11% to a low of 36.3%, and even allowing for the fact that the Party was in Government and that it entered the battle this time in Skibbereen without Joe Walsh T.D. and in Cork North Central without Denis Lyons T.D, its performance still represented a major disappointment. It was even 3% below the Party's previous Local Elections performances in Government in 1979 when they managed at least 39.37%.

The Cork County Council result too had its personalities and news makers. Fianna Fail Mitchelstown Deputy Ned O'Keeffe put the Dail bar controversy behind him in a sweeping poll topping performance with some 3,419 first preferences. Almost 1,000 votes above the quota it was the highest Fianna Fail vote in the country. He ran in the Mallow Electoral area where he battled with two other high profile Deputies, Fine Gael's Paul Bradford (2,761) and the Workers Party Joe Sherlock (2,650). Other poll topping sitting Fine Gael

Deputies included Michael Creed, Fine Gael in Bandon, Frank Crowley from Kanturk and the colourful P.J. Sheehan in Schull.

The major upset for Fine Gael in the campaign however, was the election of former Fine Gael Junior Minister, Paddy Hegarty, as an Independent at the top of the poll in Midleton. Hegarty, the former Fine Gael T.D. for Cork East had lost out at the 1987 General Elections and had announced before the 1991 poll that he would contest as an Independent. The subsequent Paddy Hegarty versus Fine Gael show-down had been one of the talking points of the election coverage with Fine Gael Party Leader John Bruton even finding it necessary to write to every registered Fine Gael member in the Midleton Electoral area warning them of the consequences of supporting the Ballinbaher man. Many had felt that Hegarty's election would have cost Fine Gael a seat as it turned out Fianna Fail were to lose a seat.

The Midleton area also produced another surprise with the election of the first Labour Party Councillor there in decades. Their candidate in the area, Cobh based John Mulvihill, wasn't expected to perform well since the party's candidate in 1985 only secured 596 votes. As the boxes were emptied however, Mulvihill had totted up over 1,000 first preference and with help from Green and Workers Party transfers he held in until the 13th count when he was ahead of Fianna Fail's Tom Brosnan with 300+ votes and so took the sixth and final seat without reaching the quota.

Another talking point of the Campaign was what would be the fate of outgoing Council Chairman Vivian O'Callaghan. The former Fianna Fail Senator and Bantry Bay Hotelier was the second longest serving member of the outgoing Council with 20 years Local Government membership, including seven different years as Chairman of Cork Council. O'Callaghan was one of a

"Taking a break" - Joe Sherlock, then of the Worker's Party, takes time out from the count in Mallow to chat with young supporters.

three man Fianna Fail ticket in the Schull Electoral Area with Senator Denis O'Donovan and former Councillor Dan R. Harrington.

Senator O'Donovan was elected on the first count, just an unlucky 13 votes behind poll topper Fine Gael Deputy P.J. Sheehan. Despite some commentators prediction O'Callaghan's first count total was 200 votes ahead of Harrington and he maintained the lead to take the final seat in the electoral area after just five counts.

In the Cork North area Fianna Fail saw off a strong Labour challenge to hold on to their two seats despite being without Denis Lyons, who, as Minister of State for Tourism could not contest.

Throughout the five week campaign, Labour's Sheila O'Sullivan had been seen as strong and on the day she secured yet another surprise seat gain for Labour but at the expense of Fine Gael. Fine Gael had decided to run a tight vote management strategy with just two candidates in a bid to hold on to their two seats but George Osborne was to lose out.

On the Fianna Fail side the strategy had been four candidates for two seats, a risky strategy especially since two of the candidates Donal O'Connell and Councillor Tom Joyce came from the same area. In the end both Joyce and O'Connell where to lose out with Dan Fleming and new face Ann McNamara being elected for the Party.

Fianna Fail's performance in the Skibbereen Electoral Area was also watched with interest, with the then Minister of State at the Department of Agriculture, Joe Walsh, not contesting. Walsh had secured over two quotas in the 1985 Election and is Fianna Fail's only T.D. for the Cork South West constituency.

The Government Party suffered the most dramatic decline of its vote in Skibbereen with the percentage slipping from 49% to 30% yet the Party still held on to its three seats. The man chosen to fill the Ministers shoes was school

teacher and Fianna Fail National Executive member Donal O'Rourke who was comfortably elected.

Outgoing Fine Gael Councillor John Carroll-McCarthy was also easily returned topping the poll with some 600 votes above the quota. His other outgoing Fine Gael colleague Mary Bourke had failed to get a Fine Gael nomination. She was replaced in the Council by Skibbereen Publican Tadgh O'Donovan.

The two O'Sullivan's, D.F. for Fianna Fail and Jim for Fine Gael where elected on the seventh and ninth count respectively. Councillor Tom O'Neill Fianna Fail, had to sweat it out until the final count but also got elected.

The Progressive Democrats performance in Cork county was also disappointing for them. This was their first Local Elections Campaign and they had hoped to plant a strong local base in Cork County. In all they ran ten candidates but between them they could only secure 5.5% of the first preferences in the County. The Party returned to the new Council with just one seat, won by Derek Carthy in the Cork South Electoral Area.

Disappointing for the P.D.'s also was the loss of businessman John Kevin Colman. Colman had been the power broker of the June 1990 Council A.G.M. and it was his vote that secured the Council Chair for Fianna Fail's Vivian O'Callaghan and in the process he secured a Council Vice Chair for himself. In 1985 he contested the Locals as a Fine Gael Councillor in the Cork South Area, this time he was the P.D. candidate in Bandon. With a first count tally of just 605 votes he was eliminated on the eighth count.

Fine Gael's performance in the Bandon Area was excellent. The Party's Deputy Michael Creed came in with 900 votes above the quote on the first count and the Party won four of the seven seats.

Fianna Fail got the remaining three seats with Peter Calleran, Alan Colman and former T.D. Donal Moynihan. The fourth man on the ticket, outgoing Councillor Jim Long was below his 1985 tally on the first count and so lost out.

In the other half of the Cork North West Dail Constituency, Kanturk, the two large Parties also divided the seats evenly between them securing three seats each. Fine Gael Deputy Frank Crowley topped the toll and indeed was the first member elected to the new County Council early in the afternoon of Friday 28th. Billy Beggane and Gerard Murphy took the other two Fine Gael seats. Fianna Fail Jack Roche was their top performer here with 2,067 first preferences followed 379 votes later by Kanturk Larry Kelly T.D. with John B. Shamrock-Murphy only 100 votes behind him. All three were returned but the Party lost its fourth seat here with Fine Gael the beneficiaries.

The overall result left Fine Gael as the largest Group on Cork County Council. They gained one seat and had 20 members in the new Council. Fianna Fail lost five seats and returned with only 19. Labour doubled their seats to four with the P.D.'s and Paddy Hegarty holding the other two seats.

# BANDON ELECTORAL AREA

TOTAL ELECTORATE 30,218. VALID POLL 19,127. NO. OF MEMBERS 7. QUOTA 2,391

| Names of Candidates | First Count Votes | Second Count Transfer of Creed's surplus Result | Third Count Transfer of Callanan's surplus Result | Fourth Count Transfer of Moynihan's surplus Result | Fifth Count Transfer of Collin's votes Result | Sixth Count Transfer of Ryan's votes Result | Seventh Count Transfer of Lucey's surplus Result | Eighth Count Transfer of J.K. Coleman's votes Result | Ninth Count Transfer of Giles' votes Result | Tenth Count Transfer of Kelleher's votes Result | Eleventh Count Transfer of Murphy's surplus Result | Twelfth Count Transfer of Metcalfe's surplus Result |
|---|---|---|---|---|---|---|---|---|---|---|---|---|
| CALLANAN, Peter (F.F.) | 2,797 | — 2,797 | -406 2,391 | — 2,391 | — 2,391 | — 2,391 | — 2,391 | — 2,391 | — 2,391 | — 2,391 | — 2,391 | — 2,391 |
| COLEMAN, Alan (F.F.) | 916 | +7 923 | +168 1,091 | +15 1,106 | +15 1,121 | +123 1,244 | +4 1,248 | +155 1,403 | +94 1,497 | +88 1,585 | +11 1,596 | +18 1,614 |
| COLEMAN, John Kevin (P.D.) | 605 | +8 613 | +35 648 | +2 650 | +11 661 | +51 712 | +6 718 | -718 — | — — | — — | — — | — — |
| COLLINS, Frank | 170 | +5 175 | +12 187 | +1 188 | -188 — | — — | — — | — — | — — | — — | — — | — — |
| CREED, Michael (F.G.) | 3,267 | -876 2,391 | — 2,391 | — 2,391 | — 2,391 | — 2,391 | — 2,391 | — 2,391 | — 2,391 | — 2,391 | — 2,391 | — 2,391 |
| GILES, Paula (G.P.) | 695 | +29 724 | +35 759 | +4 763 | +24 787 | +71 858 | +6 864 | +100 964 | -964 — | — — | — — | — — |
| KELLEHER, Jerry (P.D.) | 672 | +233 905 | +5 910 | +22 932 | +4 936 | +15 951 | +14 965 | +158 1,123 | +171 1,294 | -1,294 — | — — | — — |
| LONG, James (F.F.) | 1,004 | +57 1,061 | +89 1,150 | +78 1,228 | +10 1,238 | +23 1,261 | +4 1,265 | +44 1,309 | +92 1,401 | +186 1,587 | +1 1,588 | +19 1,607 |
| LUCEY, Eddie (F.G.) | 2,347 | +142 2,489 | — 2,489 | — 2,489 | — 2,489 | — 2,489 | -98 2,391 | — 2,391 | — 2,391 | — 2,391 | — 2,391 | — 2,391 |
| METCALFE, Frank (F.G.) | 1,366 | +364 1,730 | +5 1,735 | +4 1,739 | +9 1,748 | +30 1,778 | +64 1,842 | +75 1,917 | +171 2,088 | +340 2,428 | — 2,428 | -37 2,391 |
| MOYNIHAN, Donal (F.F.) | 2,519 | — 2,519 | — 2,519 | -128 2,391 | — 2,391 | — 2,391 | — 2,391 | — 2,391 | — 2,391 | — 2,391 | — 2,391 | — 2,391 |
| MURPHY, Kevin (F.G.) | 2,301 | +26 2,327 | +49 2,376 | +1 2,377 | +56 2,433 | — 2,433 | — 2,433 | — 2,433 | — 2,433 | — 2,433 | -42 2,391 | — 2,391 |
| RYAN, Dermot | 468 | +5 473 | +8 481 | +1 482 | +17 499 | -499 — | — — | — — | — — | — — | — — | — — |
| Non-transferable papers not effective | — | — — | — — | — — | +42 42 | +186 228 | — 228 | +186 414 | +436 850 | +680 1,530 | +30 1,560 | — 1,560 |
| TOTAL: | 19,127 | — 19,127 | — 19,127 | — 19,127 | — 19,127 | — 19,127 | — 19,127 | — 19,127 | — 19,127 | — 19,127 | — 19,127 | — 19,127 |

Elected: Creed, Michael (F.G.); Callanan, Peter (F.F.); Moynihan, Donal (F.F.); Lucey, Eddie (F.G.); Murphy, Kevin (F.G.); Metcalfe, Frank (F.G.); Coleman, Alan (F.F.)

# CORK SOUTH ELECTORAL AREA

TOTAL ELECTORATE 33,222. VALID POLL 14,021. NO. OF MEMBERS 6. QUOTA 2,004.

| Names of Candidates | First Count Votes | Second Count Transfer of O'Keeffe's surplus Result | Third Count Transfer of Ward's votes Result | Fourth Count Transfer of Lancaster's votes Result | Fifth Count Transfer of C. O'Mahony's votes Result | Sixth Count Transfer of Kelly's votes Result | Seventh Count Transfer of Buwalda-Wagner's votes Result | Eighth Count Transfer of Cogan's surplus Result | Ninth Count Transfer of B. O'Mahony's votes Result | Tenth Count Transfer of Meany's votes Result | Eleventh Count Transfer of Desmond's surplus Result |
|---|---|---|---|---|---|---|---|---|---|---|---|
| BRENNAN, Braham (F.G.) | 953 | +14 967 | +52 1,019 | +8 1,027 | +28 1,055 | +45 1,100 | +61 1,161 | +16 1,177 | +246 1,423 | +216 1,639 | +79 1,718 |
| BUWALDA-WAGNER, Mary (F.F.) | 785 | +130 915 | +5 920 | +8 928 | +15 943 | +24 967 | -967 (—) | — — | — — | — — | — — |
| CANTY, Derry (P.D.) | 758 | +173 931 | +98 1,029 | +155 1,184 | +29 1,213 | +349 1,562 | +54 1,616 | +9 1,625 | +123 1,748 | +119 1,867 | +51 1,918 |
| COGAN, Barry (F.F.) | 1,613 | +293 1,906 | +12 1,918 | +17 1,935 | +30 1,965 | +36 2,001 | +399 2,400 | -396 2,004 | — 2,004 | — 2,004 | — 2,004 |
| CONNOLE, Mary (F.F.) | 656 | +194 850 | +4 854 | +6 860 | +62 922 | +59 981 | +177 1,158 | +220 1,378 | +48 1,426 | +87 1,513 | +25 1,538 |
| COTTER, Sylvester P. (F.G.) | 968 | +14 982 | +51 1,033 | +10 1,043 | +18 1,061 | +142 1,203 | +54 1,257 | +10 1,267 | +341 1,608 | +57 1,665 | +42 1,707 |
| DESMOND, Paula (Lab.) | 1,194 | +36 1,230 | +8 1,238 | +250 1,488 | +212 1,700 | +73 1,773 | +69 1,842 | +31 1,873 | +106 1,979 | +448 2,427 | -423 2,004 |
| KELLY, Peter (P.D.) | 724 | +16 740 | +9 749 | +10 759 | +49 808 | -808 — | — — | — — | — — | — — | — — |
| LANCASTER, Tony (Lab.) | 475 | +49 524 | +54 578 | -578 — | — — | — — | — — | — — | — — | — — | — — |
| MEANEY, Kevin (Non-Party) | 967 | +29 996 | +14 1,010 | +14 1,024 | +150 1,174 | +30 1,204 | +86 1,290 | +30 1,320 | +47 1,367 | -1,367 — | — — |
| O'KEEFFE, Batt (F.F.) | 3,081 | -1,077 2,004 | — 2,004 | — 2,004 | — 2,004 | — 2,004 | — 2,004 | — 2,004 | — 2,004 | — 2,004 | — 2,004 |
| O'MAHONY, Barry (F.G.) | 828 | +49 877 | +126 1,003 | +23 1,026 | +22 1,048 | +17 1,065 | +9 1,074 | +3 1,077 | -1,077 — | — — | — — |
| O'MAHONY, Con (W.P.) | 613 | +20 633 | +14 647 | +44 691 | -691 — | — — | — — | — — | — — | — — | — — |
| WARD, Liam (F.G.) | 406 | +60 466 | -466 — | — — | — — | — — | — — | — — | — — | — — | — — |
| Non-transferable papers not effective | — | — — | +19 (19) | +33 (52) | +76 128 | +33 161 | +58 219 | +77 296 | +166 462 | +440 902 | +226 1,128 |
| TOTAL: | 14,021 | — 14,021 | — 14,021 | — 14,021 | — 14,021 | — 14,021 | — 14,021 | — 14,021 | — 14,021 | — 14,021 | — 14,021 |

Elected: O'Keeffe, Batt (F.F.); Cogan, Barry (F.F.); Desmond, Paula (Lab.); Canty, Derry (P.D.); Brennan, Braham (F.G.); Cotter, Sylvester P. (F.G.)

# CORK NORTH ELECTORAL AREA

TOTAL ELECTORATE 19,771. VALID POLL 9,261. NO. OF MEMBERS 4. QUOTA 1,853.

| Names of Candidates | First Count Votes | Second Count Transfer of Hyland's and Corbett's votes | Result | Third Count Transfer of Burns' votes | Result | Fourth Count Transfer of O'Connell's votes | Result | Fifth Count Transfer of Osborne's votes | Result | Sixth Count Transfer of Ryan's surplus | Result |
|---|---|---|---|---|---|---|---|---|---|---|---|
| BURNS, Michael (P.D.) | 884 | +88 | 972 | -972 | (—) | — | — | — | — | — | — |
| CORBETT, Patrick (W.P.) | 353 | -353 | — | — | — | — | — | — | — | — | — |
| FLEMING, Daniel (F.F.) | 1,253 | +32 | 1,285 | +72 | 1,357 | +319 | 1,676 | +83 | 1,759 | +101 | 1,860 |
| HYLAND, Thomas (G.P.) | 257 | -257 | — | — | — | — | — | — | — | — | — |
| JOYCE, Tom (F.F.) | 975 | +32 | 1,007 | +146 | 1,153 | +329 | 1,482 | +42 | 1,524 | +39 | 1,563 |
| McNAMERA, Annette (F.F.) | 1,137 | +65 | 1,202 | +95 | 1,297 | +172 | 1,469 | +49 | 1,518 | +58 | 1,576 |
| O'CONNELL, Donal (F.F.) | 968 | +16 | 984 | +102 | 1,086 | -1,086 | — | — | — | — | — |
| OSBORNE, George (F.G.) | 953 | +37 | 990 | +153 | 1,143 | +80 | 1,223 | -1,223 | — | — | — |
| O'SULLIVAN, Sheila (Lab.) | 912 | +243 | 1,155 | +223 | 1,378 | +76 | 1,454 | +137 | 1,591 | +265 | 1,856 |
| RYAN, Tomas (F.G.) | 1,569 | +35 | 1,604 | +94 | 1,698 | +43 | 1,741 | +813 | 2,554 | -701 | 1,853 |
| Non-transferable papers not effective | — | +62 | 62 | +87 | 149 | +67 | 216 | +99 | 315 | +238 | 553 |
| TOTAL: | 9,261 | — | 9,261 | — | 9,261 | — | 9,261 | — | 9,261 | — | 9,261 |

Elected: Ryan, Tomas (F.g.); Fleming, Daniel (F.F.); O'Sullivan, Sheila (Lab.); McNamera, Annette (F.F.)

# KANTURK ELECTORAL AREA

TOTAL ELECTORATE 22,012. VALID POLL 15,604. NO OF MEMBERS 6. QUOTA 2,230

| Names of Candidates | First Count Votes | Second Count Transfer of Curtin's votes | Result | Third Count Transfer of Crowley's surplus | Result | Fourth Count Transfer of O'Riordan's votes | Result | Fifth Count Transfer of Barry's votes | Result | Sixth Count Transfer of Donegan's votes | Result | Seventh Count Transfer of Kelly's surplus | Result |
|---|---|---|---|---|---|---|---|---|---|---|---|---|---|
| BARRY, Charles (F.G.) | 1,168 | +5 | 1,173 | +111 | 1,284 | +41 | 1,325 | -1,325 | — | — | — | — | — |
| BIGGANE, Billy (F.G.) | 1,652 | +10 | 1,662 | +53 | 1,715 | +20 | 1,735 | +333 | 2,068 | +303 | 2,371 | — | 2,371 |
| CASHIN, Billy (Lab.) | 1,327 | +31 | 1,358 | +56 | 1,414 | +81 | 1,495 | +128 | 1,623 | +101 | 1,724 | +9 | 1,733 |
| CROWLEY, Frank (F.G.) | 2,610 | — | 2,610 | -380 | 2,230 | — | 2,230 | — | 2,230 | — | 2,230 | — | 2,230 |
| CURTIN, Dan | 89 | -89 | — | — | — | — | — | — | — | — | — | — | — |
| DONEGAN, Michael (F.F.) | 1,377 | +18 | 1,395 | +10 | 1,405 | +13 | 1,418 | +21 | 1,439 | -1,439 | — | — | — |
| KELLY, Laurence (F.F.) | 1,686 | +7 | 1,693 | +36 | 1,729 | +33 | 1,762 | +49 | 1,811 | +606 | 2,417 | -187 | 2,230 |
| MURPHY, Gerard (F.G.) | 1,480 | — | 1,480 | +63 | 1,543 | +130 | 1,673 | +480 | 2,153 | +45 | 2,198 | +14 | 2,212 |
| MURPHY, John B., The Shamrock (F.F.) | 1,555 | +2 | 1,557 | +11 | 1,568 | +181 | 1,749 | +79 | 1,828 | +230 | 2,058 | +164 | 2,222 |
| O'RIORDAN, Sean (P.D.) | 593 | +8 | 601 | +15 | 616 | -616 | — | — | — | — | — | — | — |
| ROCHE, Jack (F.F.) | 2,067 | +4 | 2,071 | +25 | 2,096 | +66 | 2,162 | +145 | 2,307 | — | 2,307 | — | 2,307 |
| Non-transferable papers not effective | — | +4 | 4 | — | 4 | +51 | 55 | +90 | 145 | +154 | 299 | — | 299 |
| TOTAL: | 15,604 | — | 15,604 | — | 15,604 | — | 15,604 | — | 15,604 | — | 15,604 | — | 15,604 |

Elected: Crowley, Frank (F.G.); Roche, Jack (F.F.); Kelly, Laurence (F.F.); Biggane, Billy (F.G.); Murphy, John B. The Shamrock (F.F.); Murphy, Gerard (F.G.)

# MALLOW ELECTORAL AREA

TOTAL ELECTORATE 31,118. VALID POLL 19,540. NO. OF MEMBERS 7. QUOTA 2,443

| Names of Candidates | First Count Votes | Second Count Transfer of O'Keeffe's surplus Result | Third Count Transfer of Bradford's surplus Result | Fourth Count Transfer of Sherlock's surplus Result | Fifth Count Transfer of Guinevan's votes Result | Sixth Count Transfer of Curtis' votes Result | Seventh Count Transfer of Bartley's Result |
|---|---|---|---|---|---|---|---|
| BARTLEY, Jim (G.P.) | 410 | +13  423 | +6  429 | +6  435 | +33  468 | +43  511 | -511  — |
| BRADFORD, Paul (F.G.) | 2,761 | —  2,761 | -318  2,443 | —  2,443 | —  2,443 | —  2,443 | —  2,443 |
| BRODERICK, Michael | 655 | +21  676 | +34  710 | +15  725 | +6  731 | +21  752 | +28  780 |
| CONROY, Tom | 667 | +17  684 | +27  711 | +30  741 | +7  748 | +115  863 | +56  919 |
| CURTIS, Tadhg (Lab.) | 372 | +9  381 | +3  404 | +35  439 | +3  442 | -442  — | —  — |
| FITZGERALD, John (W.P.) | 453 | +55  508 | +2  510 | +25  535 | +5  540 | +23  563 | +27  590 |
| GUINEVAN, John (P.D.) | 361 | +17  378 | +5  383 | +2  385 | -385  — | — | — |
| JOYCE, Carey Patrick (F.F.) | 1,633 | +408  2,041 | +10  2,051 | +7  2,058 | +84  2,142 | +16  2,158 | +60  2,218 |
| KELLEHER, Brendan (F.F.) | 780 | +87  867 | +10  877 | +9  886 | +9  895 | +11  906 | +5  911 |
| LANE, Michael (F.G.) | 794 | +19  813 | +63  876 | +2  878 | +8  886 | +6  892 | +20  912 |
| LEAMY, Naois (P.D.) | 603 | +35  638 | +15  653 | +11  664 | +88  752 | +20  772 | +31  803 |
| O'CALLAGHAN, Conor (F.G.) | 1,313 | +117  1,430 | +43  1,473 | +6  1,479 | +28  1,507 | +15  1,522 | +21  1,543 |
| O'DONOVAN, Tadhg (W.P.) | 557 | +12  569 | +2  571 | +30  601 | +14  615 | +21  636 | +51  687 |
| O'KEEFFE, Ned (F.F.) | 3,419 | -976  2,443 | —  2,443 | —  2,443 | —  2,443 | —  2,443 | —  2,443 |
| O'RIORDAN, Ted (F.F.) | 806 | +137  943 | +25  968 | +21  989 | +5  994 | +44  1,038 | +13  1,051 |
| PYNE, Aileen D. (F.G.) | 1,306 | +29  1,335 | +53  1,388 | +8  1,396 | +65  1,461 | +29  1,490 | +114  1,604 |
| SHERLOCK, Joe (W.P.) | 2,650 | —  2,650 | —  2,650 | -207  2,443 | —  2,443 | —  2,443 | —  2,443 |
| Non-transferable papers not effective | — | —  — | —  — | —  — | +30  30 | +78  108 | +85  193 |
| TOTAL: | 19,540 | —  19,540 | —  19,540 | —  19,540 | —  19,540 | —  19,540 | —  19,540 |

| Eighth Count Transfer of Fitzgerald's votes Result | Ninth Count Transfer of Broderick's votes Result | Tenth Count Transfer of Leamy's votes Result | Eleventh Count Transfer of O'Donovan's votes Result | Twelfth Count Transfer of Lane's votes Result | Thirteenth Count Transfer of Joyce's surplus Result | Fourteenth Count Transfer of Pyne's surplus Result | Fifteenth Count Transfer of Conroy's votes Result |
|---|---|---|---|---|---|---|---|
| —  — | —  — | —  — | —  — | —  — | —  — | —  — | —  — |
| —  2,443 | —  2,443 | —  2,443 | —  2,443 | —  2,443 | —  2,443 | —  2,443 | —  2,443 |
| +5  785 | -785  — | —  — | —  — | —  — | —  — | —  — | —  — |
| +11  930 | +51  981 | +64  1,045 | +65  1,110 | +17  1,127 | +5  1,132 | +3  1,135 | -1,135  — |
| -590  — | —  — | —  — | —  — | —  — | —  — | —  — | —  — |
| +29  2,247 | +19  2,266 | +127  2,393 | +124  2,517 | —  2,517 | -74  2,443 | —  2,443 | —  2,443 |
| +4  915 | +193  1,108 | +57  1,165 | +6  1,171 | +18  1,189 | +8  1,197 | +1  1,198 | +90  1,288 |
| +3  915 | +73  988 | +35  1,023 | +12  1,035 | -1,035  — | —  — | —  — | —  — |
| +18  821 | +65  886 | -886  — | —  — | —  — | —  — | —  — | —  — |
| +142  1,685 | +63  1,748 | +137  1,885 | +23  1,908 | +178  2,086 | +3  2,089 | +70  2,159 | +103  2,262 |
| +213  900 | +10  910 | +18  928 | -928  — | —  — | —  — | —  — | —  — |
| —  2,443 | —  2,443 | —  2,443 | —  2,443 | —  2,443 | —  2,443 | —  2,443 | —  2,443 |
| +7  1,058 | +27  1,085 | +92  1,177 | +14  1,191 | +10  1,201 | +11  1,212 | +2  1,214 | +278  1,492 |
| +8  1,612 | +38  1,650 | +90  1,740 | +216  1,956 | +563  2,519 | —  2,519 | -76  2,443 | —  2,443 |
| —  2,443 | —  2,443 | —  2,443 | —  2,443 | —  2,443 | —  2,443 | —  2,443 | —  2,443 |
| +150  343 | +246  589 | +266  855 | +468  1,323 | +249  1,572 | +47  1,619 | —  1,619 | +664  2,283 |
| —  19,540 | —  19,540 | —  19,540 | —  19,540 | —  19,540 | —  19,540 | —  19,540 | —  19,540 |

Note: In the second table, the rows correspond in order to: BARTLEY, BRADFORD, BRODERICK, CONROY, CURTIS, FITZGERALD, GUINEVAN, JOYCE, KELLEHER, LANE, LEAMY, O'CALLAGHAN, O'DONOVAN, O'KEEFFE, O'RIORDAN, PYNE, SHERLOCK, Non-transferable papers not effective, TOTAL.

Elected: O'Keeffe, Ned (F.F.); Bradford, Paul (F.G.); Sherlock Joe (W.P.); Joyce, Carey Patrick (F.F.); Pyne, Aileen D. (F.G.); O'Callaghan, Conor (F.G.); O'Riordan, Ted (F.F.).

# MIDLETON ELECTORAL AREA

TOTAL ELECTORATE 28,321. VALID POLL 15,536. NO. OF MEMBERS 6. QUOTA 2,220

| Names of Candidates | First Count Votes | Second Count Transfer of P.Hegarty's surplus Result | Third Count Transfer of Twomey's votes Result | Fourth Count Transfer of Cashman's votes Result | Fifth Count Transfer of Owen's votes Result | Sixth Count Transfer of Quinlan's votes Result | Seventh Count Transfer of Joy's votes Result | Eighth Count Transfer of Collins' surplus Result | Ninth Count Transfer of Bickerdike's votes Result | Tenth Count Transfer of Kidney's votes Result | Eleventh Count Transfer of Bell's votes Result | Twelfth Count Transfer of Jeffery's votes Result | Thirteenth Count Transfer of Foster's votes Result |
|---|---|---|---|---|---|---|---|---|---|---|---|---|---|
| AHERN, Matt (F.G.) | 1,559 | +59 1,618 | +6 1,624 | +8 1,632 | +2 1,634 | +4 1,638 | +31 1,669 | +6 1,675 | +58 1,733 | +40 1,773 | +52 1,825 | +301 2,126 | +41 2,167 |
| AHERN, Maurice (F.F.) | 1,639 | +21 1,660 | +5 1,665 | +27 1,692 | +5 1,697 | +4 1,701 | +33 1,734 | +20 1,754 | +11 1,765 | +52 1,817 | +48 1,865 | +57 1,922 | +345 2,267 |
| BELL, Sean (G.P.) | 350 | +11 361 | +9 370 | +5 375 | +19 394 | +17 411 | +49 460 | +8 468 | +92 560 | +43 603 | -603 — | — | — |
| BICKERDIKE, Bob (Non-Party) | 371 | +14 385 | +2 387 | +4 391 | +10 401 | +33 434 | +7 441 | +1 442 | -442 — | — | — | — | — |
| BROSNAN, John (F.F.) | 1,131 | +28 1,159 | +6 1,165 | — 1,165 | +4 1,169 | +1 1,170 | +27 1,197 | +3 1,200 | +98 1,298 | +43 1,341 | +52 1,393 | +15 1,408 | +229 1,637 |
| CASHMAN, Tom (W.P.) | 186 | +3 189 | — 189 | -189 — | — | — | — | — | — | — | — | — | — |
| COLLINS, Noel (Non-Party) | 2,059 | +54 2,113 | +7 2,120 | +51 2,171 | +11 2,182 | +19 2,201 | +87 2,288 | -68 2,220 | — 2,220 | — 2,220 | — 2,220 | — 2,220 | — 2,220 |
| FOSTER, Kevin (F.F.) | 1,062 | +10 1,072 | +33 1,105 | +2 1,107 | +18 1,125 | +50 1,175 | +8 1,183 | +1 1,184 | +4 1,188 | +102 1,290 | +36 1,326 | +12 1,338 | -1,338 — |
| HEGARTY, Michael (F.G.) | 1,402 | +47 1,449 | +5 1,454 | +11 1,465 | +4 1,469 | +8 1,477 | +48 1,525 | +8 1,533 | +9 1,542 | +34 1,576 | +64 1,640 | +310 1,950 | +55 2,005 |
| HEGARTY, Paddy | 2,552 | -332 2,220 | — 2,220 | — 2,220 | — 2,220 | — 2,220 | — 2,220 | — 2,220 | — 2,220 | — 2,220 | — 2,220 | — 2,220 | — 2,220 |
| JEFFERY, George (F.G.) | 768 | +29 797 | +8 805 | +1 806 | +4 810 | +5 815 | +35 850 | +5 855 | +3 858 | +11 869 | +46 915 | -915 — | — |
| JOY, Michael (P.D.) | 362 | +10 372 | +11 383 | +8 391 | +5 396 | +4 400 | -400 — | — | — | — | — | — | — |
| KIDNEY, William David | 441 | +12 453 | +20 473 | +5 478 | +5 483 | +25 508 | +7 515 | +3 518 | +23 541 | -541 — | — | — | — |
| MULVIHILL, John (Lab.) | 1,003 | +22 1,025 | +27 1,052 | +16 1,068 | +79 1,147 | +125 1,272 | +28 1,300 | +4 1,304 | +47 1,351 | +99 1,450 | +104 1,554 | +38 1,592 | +366 1,958 |
| OWENS, Leo (W.P.) | 196 | +3 199 | +3 202 | +37 239 | -239 — | — | — | — | — | — | — | — | — |
| QUINLAN, Maurice Hurbert | 288 | +5 293 | +21 314 | +1 315 | +36 351 | -351 — | — | — | — | — | — | — | — |
| TWOMEY, Jack | 167 | +4 171 | -171 — | — | — | — | — | — | — | — | — | — | — |
| Non-transferable papers not effective | — | — | +8 8 | +13 21 | +37 58 | +56 114 | +40 154 | +9 163 | +97 260 | +117 377 | +201 578 | +182 760 | +302 1,062 |
| TOTAL: | 15,536 | — 15,536 | — 15,536 | — 15,536 | — 15,536 | — 15,536 | — 15,536 | — 15,536 | — 15,536 | — 15,536 | — 15,536 | — 15,536 | — 15,536 |

# SKIBBEREEN ELECTORAL AREA

TOTAL ELECTORATE 22,677. VALID POLL 15,305. NO. OF MEMBERS 7. QUOTA 1,914

| Names of Candidates | First Count Votes | Second Count Transfer of McCarthy's surplus Result | Third Count Transfer of De Búrca's and O'Sé's votes Result | Fourth Count Transfer of Lehane's votes Result | Fifth Count Transfer of J. Collins' votes Result | Sixth Count Transfer of R. O'Neill's votes Result | Seventh Count Transfer of D.F.O'Sullivan's surplus Result | Eighth Count Transfer of O'Rourke's surplus Result | Ninth Count Transfer of J.O'Sullivan's surplus Result | Tenth Count Transfer of M. Collins' votes Result |
|---|---|---|---|---|---|---|---|---|---|---|
| CALNAN, Michael J. (Lab.) | 1,387 | +24 1,411 | +32 1,443 | +106 1,549 | +43 1,592 | +44 1,636 | +2 1,638 | +13 1,651 | +4 1,655 | +327 1,982 |
| COLLINS, John | 544 | +5 549 | +69 618 | +18 636 | -636 — | — | — | — | — | — |
| COLLINS, Michael (F.G.) | 1,058 | +65 1,123 | +8 1,131 | +119 1,250 | +18 1,268 | +40 1,308 | — 1,308 | +4 1,312 | +1 1,313 | -1,313 — |
| DE BÚRCA, Seamus (S.F.) | 144 | +1 145 | -145 — | — | — | — | — | — | — | — |
| LEHANE, Donal | 497 | +11 508 | +14 522 | -522 — | — | — | — | — | — | — |
| McCARTHY, John Cal (F.G.) | 2,346 | -432 1,914 | — 1,914 | — 1,914 | — 1,914 | — 1,914 | — 1,914 | — 1,914 | — 1,914 | — 1,914 |
| O'DONNELL, Mary (G.P.) | 828 | +17 845 | +72 917 | +42 959 | +160 1,119 | +183 1,302 | +9 1,311 | +33 1,344 | +14 1,358 | +66 1,424 |
| O'DONOVAN, Tadgh (F.G.) | 1,179 | +48 1,227 | +13 1,240 | +20 1,260 | +119 1,379 | +106 1,485 | +11 1,496 | +10 1,506 | +6 1,512 | +479 1,991 |
| O'NEILL, Ray (P.D.) | 901 | +51 952 | +25 977 | +36 1,013 | +54 1,067 | -1,067 — | — | — | — | — |
| O'NEILL, Tom (F.F.) | 1,231 | +16 1,247 | +25 1,272 | +88 1,360 | +18 1,378 | +62 1,440 | +6 1,446 | +34 1,480 | +12 1,492 | +190 1,682 |
| O'ROURKE, Donal F. (F.F.) | 1,768 | +35 1,803 | +33 1,836 | +19 1,855 | +10 1,865 | +259 2,124 | — 2,124 | -210 1,914 | — 1,914 | — 1,914 |
| Ó SÉ, Donncadh (S.F.) | 294 | — 294 | -294 — | — | — | — | — | — | — | — |
| O'SULLIVAN, D. F. (F.F.) | 1,688 | +22 1,710 | +70 1,780 | +26 1,806 | +137 1,943 | — 1,943 | -29 1,914 | — 1,914 | — 1,914 | — 1,914 |
| O'SULLIVAN, Jim (F.G.) | 1,440 | +137 1,577 | +33 1,610 | +11 1,621 | +20 1,641 | +248 1,889 | +1 1,890 | +83 1,973 | -59 1,914 | — 1,914 |
| Non-transferable papers not effective | — | — | +45 45 | +37 82 | +57 139 | +125 264 | — 264 | +33 297 | +22 319 | +251 570 |
| TOTAL: | 15,305 | — 15,305 | — 15,305 | — 15,305 | — 15,305 | — 15,305 | — 15,305 | — 15,305 | — 15,305 | — 15,305 |

Elected: McCarthy, John Cal (F.G.); O'Sullivan, D.F. (F.F.); O'Rourke, Donal F. (F.F.); O'Sullivan, Jim (F.G.); O'Donovan, Tadgh (F.G.); Calnan, Michael J. (Lab.); O'Neill, Tom (F.F.)

# SCHULL ELECTORAL AREA

TOTAL ELECTORATE 13,584. VALID POLL 9,545. NO. OF MEMBERS 5. QUOTA 1,591

| Names of Candidates | First Count Votes | Second Count Transfer of Sheehan's surplus | Result | Third Count Transfer of O'Donovan's surplus | Result | Fourth Count Transfer of Kingston's votes | Result | Fifth Count Transfer of D.R. Harrington's votes | Result |
|---|---|---|---|---|---|---|---|---|---|
| CALLAGHAN, Vivian (F.F.) | 1,022 | +14 | 1,036 | +95 | 1,131 | +114 | 1,245 | +273 | 1,518 |
| HARRINGTON, Dan R. (F.F.) | 812 | +5 | 817 | +34 | 851 | +39 | 890 | -890 | — |
| HARRINGTON, Michael (F.G.) | 1,256 | +42 | 1,298 | +7 | 1,305 | +64 | 1,369 | +473 | 1,842 |
| KINGSTON, Matt (Lab.) | 575 | +14 | 589 | +20 | 609 | -609 | — | — | — |
| MURPHY, Michael Pat (Non-Party) | 1,360 | +92 | 1,452 | +50 | 1,502 | +135 | 1,637 | — | 1,637 |
| O'DONOVAN, Denis (F.F.) | 1,827 | — | 1,827 | -236 | 1,591 | — | 1,591 | — | 1,591 |
| O'SHEA, John Patrick (F.G.) | 853 | +82 | 935 | +30 | 965 | +186 | 1,151 | +26 | 1,177 |
| SHEEHAN, Patrick Joseph (F.G.) | 1,840 | -249 | 1,591 | — | 1,591 | — | 1,591 | — | 1,591 |
| Non-transferable papers not effective | — | — | — | — | — | +71 | 71 | +118 | 189 |
| TOTAL: | 9,545 | — | 9,545 | — | 9,545 | — | 9,545 | — | 9,545 |

Elected: Sheehan, Patrick Joseph (F.G.); O'Donovan, Denis (FF.); Murphy, Michael Pat (Non-Party); Harrington, Michael (F.G.); Callaghan, Vivian (F.F.)

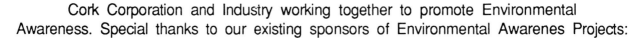

# WITH PHONELINK, YOU CAN CONDUCT EVERYDAY BANKING TRANSACTIONS BY PHONE.

# WITHOUT SPEAKING.

Introducing Phonelink. A unique service from AIB Bank.

Now you can conduct a range of routine banking transactions conveniently and in complete confidence.

By simply dialling on a telephone – you don't have to speak – you can check the balance and transactions on your account, pay bills and even transfer funds.

Seven days and seven nights a week. From any phone, anywhere.

All you do is dial in code numbers and a computer activated voice will respond to your requests. You can ask for details of your last five transactions. Or order statements. You can pay ESB, Telecom and AIB VISA bills. Transfer funds from one account to another or find out if a cheque has been presented yet.

But actions speak louder than words. Call into any AIB Bank branch and we'll give you a demonstration of how simple Phonelink is to use.

# PHONELINK
## *You bring out the best in us*

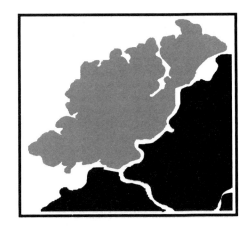

# DONEGAL COUNTY COUNCIL

## DONEGAL COUNTY COUNCIL RESULTS

| PARTY | 1991 % of votes | 1991 Seats obtained | 1985 % of votes | 1985 Seats obtained |
|---|---|---|---|---|
| Fianna Fail | 36.2 | 11 | 35.9 | 11 |
| Fine Gael | 24.7 | 9 | 29.6 | 9 |
| Labour | 2.3 | 1 | 0.7 | — |
| Progressive Dem. | — | — | — | — |
| Workers Party | 2.5 | 1 | 2.2 | 1 |
| Other | 34.3 | 7 | 31.6 | 8 |
| **TOTAL SEATS** | | **29** | | **29** |

## DONEGAL

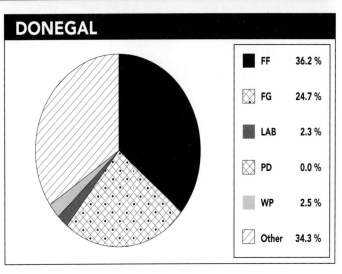

| | |
|---|---|
| FF | 36.2 % |
| FG | 24.7 % |
| LAB | 2.3 % |
| PD | 0.0 % |
| WP | 2.5 % |
| Other | 34.3 % |

**County House, Lifford**
**Telephone: (074) 41066**
**Fax: (074) 41205**
**Total population: 129,428**
**Rateable valuation(County): £555,870.20**
**Rate: £35.05**
**County Council meetings: last Monday in each second month**
*County Manager:* S. Dooley

*Assistant County Manager:* W. Moloney
*County Secretary:* L. Kelly
*Finance Officer:* Vacant
*County Engineer:* J. McShane
*Administrative Officers:*
*Capital Works:* S. O'Donnell
*Personnel, Housing, Rates, Motor Taxation,*
*General Purposes:* E. Sweeney
*Planning:* L. Kelly
*Senior Staff Officers:*
*Housing:* S. Sheridan
*Rates:* F. Coyle
*Finance:* T. McCrossan
*County Librarian:* L. Ronayne, County Library, High Road,
*Letterkenny Telephone:* (074) 21968
*County Solicitor:* E. T. McMullin.
*County Development Officer:* P. Bolger
*County Coroners:* Dr John V. Gallagher, Dr F. C. Friel, L. Coyle,
Dr J. A. Farrelly
*Chief Fire Officer:* F. Kerrane
*Civil Defence Officer:* D. O'Regan
*Senior Executive Engineers:*
*Roads:* J. McInerney, H. Ritchie (Acting), T. Bradley, A.
O'Doherty
*Sanitary Services:* K. Cunnane, P. Doherty
*Planning:* G. Convie, G. Moynihan
*Housing:* J. Canney
*Machinery:* J. Holohan
*Senior Executive Architect:* M. J. Swanton

## BUNCRANA

| | 1991 | 1985 | '85 to '91 Swing |
|---|---|---|---|
| FF | 55.8 | 38.1 | 17.7 |
| FG | 25.7 | 30.8 | -5.1 |
| Lab | — | 1.8 | -1.8 |
| SF | 11.6 | 11.1 | 0.5 |
| Ind | 6.9 | 18.2 | -11.3 |

CONAGHAN, Hugh,
Monfad, Newtowncunningham,
County Donegal. (FF)
Public Representative. 074-56297.

FERRY, Jim,
21 Upper Main Street, Buncrana,
County Donegal. (SF)
Barman.

GILL, Seamus,
55 Lower Main Street, Buncrana,
County Donegal. (FG)
Wholesaler. 077-61064.

KEAVENEY, Paddy,
"Loreto", Moville,
County Donegal. (FF)
Undertaker. 077-82177

McGONAGLE, Denis A.,
Tiernaleague, Carndonagh,
County Donegal. (FF)
Sales Representative. 077-74607

McGUINNESS, Bernard J.,
Culdaff,
County Donegal. (FG)
Farmer. 077-79116

## DONEGAL

| | 1991 | 1985 | '85 to '91 Swing |
|---|---|---|---|
| FF | 52.0 | 52.0 | -0.0 |
| FG | 30.0 | 38.5 | -8.5 |
| SF | — | 7.9 | -7.9 |
| Ind | 18.1 | 1.6 | 16.5 |

COUGHLAN, Mary,
Cranny, Inver,
County Donegal. (FF)
Dail Deputy. 073-36002

GALLAGHER, Colm,
Mountcharles,
County Donegal. (FG)
Businessman. 073-353302

KENNEDY, Peter,
25 St Joseph's Avenue,
Donegal Town,
County Donegal. (FF)
Sales Representative. 073-21294

McBREARTY, James,
Bogagh, Carrick,
County Donegal.(FF)
Teacher. 073-39074.

McENIFF, Sean,
Derlua, Bundoran,
County Donegal. (FF)
Company Director. 072-41257

O'KELLY, Francis J.,
Bundrowes House, Bundoran,
County Donegal. (FG)
Vet. 072-41238.

## GLENTIES

| | 1991 | 1985 | '85 to '91 Swing |
|---|---|---|---|
| FF | 31.2 | 31.5 | -0.3 |
| FG | 28.6 | 27.6 | 1.0 |
| WP | 12.2 | 10.1 | 2.1 |
| SF | — | 2.0 | -2.0 |
| Ind | 6.9 | 18.2 | -11.3 |

BOYLE, Connell,
Dooey House, Lettermacaward,
County Donegal. (FG)
Farmer. 075-44108

BRENNAN, Francis,
Main Street, Glenties,
County Donegal. (FF)
Auctioneer. 075-51235.

COLL, Fred,
Derrybeg,
County Donegal. (NP)
Builder. 075-31218

DOOHAN, Maureen,
Shamrock Lodge, Falcarragh,
County Donegal. (FG)
Teacher. 074-35197

KELLY, Padraig,
Falcarragh,
County Donegal. (NP)
Teacher.

RODGERS, Seamus,
Annagry West,
Annagry,
County Donegal. (Elected WP, now DL)
Trade Union Official. 075-48198

**Seamus Gill (FG)**
**Buncrana**

**Francis Brennan (FF)**
**Glenties**

**Paddy Keaveney (FF)**
**Buncrana**

**Seamus Rodgers (DL)**
**Glenties**

## LETTERKENNY

| | 1991 | 1985 | '85 to '91 Swing |
|---|---|---|---|
| FF | 21.8 | 33.0 | -11.2 |
| FG | 19.2 | 25.6 | -6.4 |
| LAB | 9.6 | 1.4 | 8.2 |
| GP | 2.8 | — | 2.8 |
| SF | 6.9 | 9.1 | -2.2 |
| Ind | 39.8 | 30.9 | 8.9 |

DEVENNY, Jim,
Dooish, Newtowncunningham,
County Donegal. (DPP)
Farmer.

HARKIN, Danny,
Kiltoal, Convoy, Lifford,
County Donegal. (NP)
Businessman. 074-47117

HARTE, Paddy,
The Diamond, Raphoe,
County Donegal. (FG)
Dáil Deputy. 074-45187

MALONEY, Sean,
39 McNeely Villas, Letterkenny,
County Donegal. (Lab)
Trade Union Official. 074-21123

McGLINCHEY, Bernard,
Bluebanks, Kilmacrennan,
County Donegal. (FF)
Businessman. 074-21088

McGOWAN, Patrick,
Edenmore, Lifford,
County Donegal. (FF)
Senator. 074-41553

REID, J.J.,
Railway Road, Letterkenny,
County Donegal. (FG)
Farmer. 074-31065

## MILLFORD

| | 1991 | 1985 | '85 to '91 Swing |
|---|---|---|---|
| FF | 29.0 | 21.4 | 7.6 |
| FG | 19.4 | 24.6 | -5.2 |
| SF | 3.9 | 3.5 | 0.4 |
| Ind | 47.7 | 50.5 | -2.8 |

BLANEY, Harry,
Rossnakill, Letterkenny,
County Donegal. (NP)
Farmer. 074-59014

LOUGHREY, Joachim A.,
82 Upper Main Street, Letterkenny,
County Donegal. (FG)
Auctioneer. 074-50050

McGINLEY, Noel,
Ballyboes, Creeslough,
County Donegal. (FF)
Garage Owner. 074-38032

O'DONNELL, Edward,
Ballykeerin, Kilmacrennan, Letterkenny,
County Donegal. (NP)
Wool Merchant. 074-39043

**Former Taoiseach Charles Haughey with representatives of LAMA and the British Association of Councillors at Government Buildings on the occasion of the first joint LAMA/BAC Local Authority Conference.**

# Labour take first seat in Donegal

Local services charges , the closure of border roads and the MMDS television system were the main issues raised by voters in Donegal. Nevertheless, both Fianna Fail and Fine Gael held their own on the County Council as Labour gained their first seat and Sinn Fein lost 1 of the 2 seats they won in 1985.

Party representation in the Buncrana Electoral Area was, as it was, going into the election with the only change in Councillors being the election for Sinn Fein of Jim Ferry replacing his party colleague Eddie Fullerton who had been murdered by the UVF prior to the elections.

Fianna Fail, in fact, gained a seat on 1985 in the Buncrana Area due to the defection of former TD Paddy Keaveney from Neil Blaney's Independent Fianna Fail. Hugh Conaghan, who lost his Dail seat in 1989, topped the poll for Fianna Fail although talk of him challenging sitting TD Jim McDaid at the next general election may be premature as Conaghan was returned on a lower first preference than in 1985. Fine Gael's two outgoing Councillors, Bernard McGuinness and Seamus Gill, were both re-elected despite the 5% drop in Fine Gael support. Independent Fianna Fail's attempt to regain the seat lost by the defection of Keaveney proved unsuccessful with their

vote declining by over 2%.

No new faces appeared to threaten the six outgoing Councillors in the Donegal Electoral Area. The only change on 1985 was the election of Deputy Mary Coughlan who replaced her late father, Cathal. For the Fianna Fail TD it was her first time taking part in a local election and she was elected on the first count with 54 votes to spare. Interestingly, her poll topping vote was 40% lower than that of her late father's in 1985.

The Glenties Electoral Area was probably the most exciting of the 5 areas in Donegal County Council. Fianna Fail's representation dropped to a single Councillor in Francis Brennan. The absence of Deputy Pat 'the Cope' Gallagher's name from the ballot paper in this area was believed to have had a bearing on the Fianna Fail performance. Although the fact that Fianna Fail's vote was exactly the same as in 1985 and Fine Gael's 2 seats were won with less votes than Fianna Fail's single seat, would appear to indicate that poor strategy, and not the 'Gallagher factor', was responsible for the Fianna Fail loss.

Seamus Rodgers of the Worker's Party was the first candidate elected in The Glenties although the honour of topping the poll went to Connell Boyle of Fine Gael who was returned along with party colleague Maureen Doohan.

One talking point in the Glenties was the return to the Council of Fred Coll after an absence of six years. Coll was a Fine Gael Councillor from 1979 to 1985. In winning back his seat, as an Independent this time, Coll actually received less votes than in 1985 when he was beaten. Independent Fianna Fail held on to their seat with newcomer Padraig Kelly being elected alongside Maureen Doohan and Fred Coll on the last count, all without reaching the quota. Fine Gael's Doohan held off James Breslin of Fianna Fail by 72 votes.

Both Fine Gael's and Fianna Fail's two outgoing Councillors were returned in Letterkenny. The other three seats in this seven seat electoral area were divided evenly between Labour, the Donegal Progressive Party (DPP) and Blaney's Fianna Fail.

The election of hospital employee Sean Maloney for Labour marked a new departure in Donegal politics and may be a reflection for the first time of the political power of Donegal's urban areas. In Letterkenny town Maloney topped the poll in almost all polling booths. Maloney's father had in fact been a Labour candidate in the Letterkenny UDC elections in the late 1950s.

Jim Devenney of the DPP headed the poll and in holding the seat orginally won by retiring DPP Councillor Willie Buchanan he increased the party's vote. The DPP strength is based in East Donegal and is largely a Protestant vote. Paddy Harte TD and outgoing Councillor JJ Reid were returned for Fine Gael although both were re-elected on the final count, along with Fianna Fail's Bernard McGlinchey, without reaching the quota. For Deputy Harte this would have being a cause of some disappointment and concern. The same can be said for Fianna Fail Senator Paddy McGowan who topped the poll in 1985. He had to wait until the sixth count on this occasion. JJ Reid of Fine Gael hung on by 168 votes from Sinn Fein's Liam Mac Elhinney who lost his seat.

Milford had only 8 candidates contesting it's 4 seats and all 4 outgoing Councillors were returned by the end of the fourth count. The poll was headed by Independent candidate and outgoing Councillor Eddie O'Donnell, the first time in nearly 60 years that a Blaney name was not at the top of the poll in this area. Neil Blaney's brother Harry was returned on the third count. Both Noel McGinley of Fianna Fail and Fine Gael's Joachim Loughrey were also elected in Milford.

**Joachim Loughrey, Chairperson Donegal C.C., and County Manager, Seamus Dooly, welcome President Mary Robinson to Donegal.**

# BUNCRANA ELECTORAL AREA

TOTAL ELECTORATE 19,588. VALID POLL 11,598. NO. OF MEMBERS 6. QUOTA 1,657.

| Names of Candidates | First Count Votes | Second Count Transfer of Gillespie's votes Result | | Third Count Transfer of Conaghan's surplus Result | | Fourth Count Transfer of McGroarty's votes Result | | Fifth Count Transfer of Diggin's votes Result | | Sixth Count Transfer of McGuinness' surplus Result | | Seventh Count Transfer of J.N. Doherty's votes Result | | Eighth Count Transfer of McLaughlin's votes Result | |
|---|---|---|---|---|---|---|---|---|---|---|---|---|---|---|---|
| CONAGHAN, Hugh (F.F.) | 1,733 | — | 1,733 | -76 | 1,657 | — | 1,657 | — | 1,657 | — | 1,657 | — | 1,657 | — | 1,657 |
| DIGGIN, Philip | 579 | +32 | 611 | +6 | 617 | +6 | 623 | -623 | — | — | — | — | — | — | — |
| DOHERTY, Albert | 798 | +66 | 864 | +7 | 871 | +9 | 880 | +119 | 999 | +3 | 1,002 | +29 | 1,031 | +209 | 1,240 |
| DOHERTY, Joseph Neil (F.F.) | 740 | +19 | 759 | +33 | 792 | +6 | 798 | +125 | 923 | +3 | 926 | -926 | — | — | — |
| FERRY, Jim (S.F.) | 1,344 | +46 | 1,390 | +8 | 1,398 | +7 | 1,405 | +96 | 1,501 | +2 | 1,503 | +165 | 1,668 | — | 1,668 |
| GILL, Seamus (F.G.) | 958 | +4 | 962 | +4 | 966 | +55 | 1,021 | +117 | 1,138 | +61 | 1,199 | +149 | 1,348 | +36 | 1,384 |
| GILLESPIE, Conal Joseph | 403 | -403 | — | — | — | | | | | | | | | | |
| KEAVENEY, Paddy (F.F.) | 1,082 | +136 | 1,218 | +11 | 1,229 | +191 | 1,420 | +25 | 1,445 | +16 | 1,461 | +163 | 1,624 | +127 | 1,751 |
| McGONAGLE, Denis Anthony (F.F.) | 1,046 | +7 | 1,053 | +3 | 1,056 | +8 | 1,064 | +20 | 1,084 | — | 1,084 | +97 | 1,181 | +338 | 1,519 |
| McGROARTY, Mary (F.G.) | 503 | +33 | 536 | +1 | 537 | -537 | — | | | | | | | | |
| McGUINNESS, Bernard John (F.G.) | 1,524 | +20 | 1,544 | +1 | 1,545 | +201 | 1,746 | — | 1,746 | -89 | 1,657 | — | 1,657 | — | 1,657 |
| McLAUGHLIN, John Henry (F.F.) | 888 | +11 | 899 | +2 | 901 | +18 | 919 | +24 | 943 | +4 | 947 | +43 | 990 | -990 | — |
| Non-transferable papers not effective | — | +29 | 29 | — | 29 | +36 | 65 | +97 | 162 | — | 162 | +280 | 442 | +280 | 722 |
| TOTAL: | 11,598 | — | 11,598 | — | 11,598 | — | 11,598 | — | 11,598 | — | 11,598 | — | 11,598 | — | 11,598 |

Elected: Conaghan, Hugh (F.F.); McGuinness, Bernard John (F.G.); Ferry, Jim (S.F.); Keaveney, Paddy (F.F.); McGonagle, Denis Anthony (F.F.); Gill, Seamus (F.G.)

# DONEGAL ELECTORAL AREA

TOTAL ELECTORATE 18,138. VALID POLL 11,850. NO. OF MEMBERS 6. QUOTA 1,693

| Names of Candidates | First Count Votes | Second Count Transfer of Coughlan's surplus Result | | Third Count Transfer of T. Kennedy's votes Result | | Fourth Count Transfer of Mulhern's votes Result | | Fifth Count Transfer of Byrne's votes Result | | Sixth Count Transfer of O'Neill's votes Result | | Seventh Count Transfer of Murphy's votes Result | | Eighth Count Transfer of Boyle's votes Result | | Ninth Count Transfer of Kelly's votes Result | | Tenth Count Transfer of McEniff's surplus Result | | Eleventh Count Transfer of McShane's votes Result | |
|---|---|---|---|---|---|---|---|---|---|---|---|---|---|---|---|---|---|---|---|---|---|
| BOYLE, John James (F.G.) | 552 | +4 | 556 | +4 | 560 | +3 | 563 | +6 | 569 | +2 | 571 | +106 | 677 | -677 | — | — | — | — | — | — | — |
| BYRNE, Tony | 318 | +1 | 319 | +10 | 329 | +4 | 333 | -333 | — | — | — | | | | | | | | | | |
| COUGHLAN, Mary (F.F.) | 1,747 | -54 | 1,693 | — | 1,693 | — | 1,693 | — | 1,693 | — | 1,693 | — | 1,693 | — | 1,693 | — | 1,693 | — | 1,693 | — | 1,693 |
| GALLAGHER, Colm (F.G.) | 1,196 | +9 | 1,205 | +62 | 1,267 | +6 | 1,273 | +11 | 1,284 | +9 | 1,293 | +36 | 1,329 | +186 | 1,515 | +49 | 1,564 | — | 1,564 | +254 | 1,818 |
| KELLY, Donal | 569 | +2 | 571 | +8 | 579 | +22 | 601 | +67 | 668 | +126 | 794 | +5 | 799 | +18 | 817 | -817 | — | — | — | — | — |
| KENNEDY, Peter (F.F.) | 1,168 | +17 | 1,185 | +25 | 1,210 | — | 1,210 | +3 | 1,213 | +14 | 1,227 | +21 | 1,248 | +26 | 1,274 | +46 | 1,320 | +20 | 1,340 | +16 | 1,356 |
| KENNEDY, Tom | 202 | +2 | 204 | -204 | — | — | — | | | | | | | | | | | | | | |
| McBREARTY, James (F.F.) | 1,026 | +3 | 1,029 | +6 | 1,035 | +2 | 1,037 | +92 | (1,129) | +4 | 1,133 | +41 | 1,174 | +30 | 1,204 | +20 | 1,224 | +9 | 1,233 | +331 | 1,564 |
| McCLOSKEY, Paddy (F.F.) | 732 | +6 | 738 | +3 | 741 | +3 | 744 | +16 | 760 | +1 | 761 | +148 | 909 | +129 | 1,038 | +20 | 1,058 | +5 | 1,063 | +61 | 1,124 |
| McENIFF, Sean (F.F.) | 1,484 | +5 | 1,489 | +7 | 1,496 | +51 | 1,547 | +3 | 1,550 | +123 | 1,673 | +6 | 1,679 | +7 | 1,686 | +207 | 1,893 | -200 | 1,693 | — | 1,693 |
| McSHANE, Patrick (F.G.) | 718 | +1 | 719 | +1 | 720 | — | 720 | +76 | 796 | +7 | 803 | +82 | 885 | +137 | 1,022 | +26 | 1,048 | +1 | 1,049 | -1,049 | — |
| MULHERN, Michael D (Dessie) (Non-Party) | 220 | +1 | 221 | +5 | 226 | -226 | — | — | — | | | | | | | | | | | | |
| MURPHY, Tommy (Non-Party) | 456 | +2 | 458 | +5 | 463 | +14 | 477 | +30 | 507 | +23 | 530 | -530 | — | — | — | | | | | | |
| O'KELLY, Francis Joseph (F.G.) | 1,085 | +1 | 1,086 | +5 | 1,091 | +30 | 1,121 | +3 | 1,124 | +47 | 1,171 | +9 | 1,180 | +25 | 1,205 | +132 | 1,337 | +53 | 1,390 | +125 | 1,515 |
| O'NEILL, Joe | 377 | — | 377 | +26 | 403 | +62 | 465 | +7 | 472 | -472 | — | — | — | | | | | | | | |
| Non-transferable papers not effective | — | — | — | +37 | 37 | +29 | 66 | +19 | 85 | +116 | 201 | +76 | 277 | +119 | 396 | +317 | 713 | +112 | 825 | +262 | 1,087 |
| TOTAL: | 11,850 | — | 11,850 | — | 11,850 | — | 11,850 | — | 11,850 | — | 11,850 | — | 11,850 | — | 11,850 | — | 11,850 | — | 11,850 | — | 11,850 |

Elected: Coughlan, Mary (F.F.); McEniff, Sean (F.F.); Gallagher, Colm (F.G.); McBrearty, James (F.F.); O'Kelly, Francis Joseph (F.G.); Kennedy, Peter (F.F.).

# LETTERKENNY ELECTORAL AREA

TOTAL ELECTORATE 24,915. VALID POLL 13,782. NO. OF MEMBERS 7. QUOTA 1,723.

| Names of Candidates | First Count Votes | Second Count Transfer of O'Donnell's votes Result | Third Count Transfer of Patterson's votes Result | Fourth Count Transfer of Devenney's surplus Result | Fifth Count Transfer of Brophy's votes Result | Sixth Count Transfer of Blake's votes Result | Seventh Count Transfer of Gillespie's votes Result | Eighth Count Transfer of Larkin's votes Result | Ninth Count Transfer of Maloney's surplus Result | Tenth Count Transfer of Meehan's votes Result |
|---|---|---|---|---|---|---|---|---|---|---|
| BLAKE, P.J. | 424 | +14 438 | +6 444 | — 444 | +29 473 | -473 — | — — | — — | — — | — — |
| BROPHY, Rorie (G.P.) | 382 | +15 397 | +7 404 | +1 405 | -405 — | — — | — — | — — | — — | — — |
| DEVENNEY, Jim D.P.P. | 1,775 | — 1,775 | — 1,775 | -52 1,723 | — 1,723 | — 1,723 | — 1,723 | — 1,723 | — 1,723 | — 1,723 |
| GILLESPIE, Ellen (Non-Party) | 439 | +1 440 | +4 444 | +2 446 | +71 517 | +27 544 | -544 — | — — | — — | — — |
| HARKIN, Danny | 1,489 | +2 1,491 | +21 1,512 | +7 1,519 | +15 1,534 | +24 1,558 | +82 1,640 | +130 1,770 | — 1,770 | — 1,770 |
| HARTE, Paddy (F.G.) | 1,309 | +55 1,364 | +38 1,402 | +25 1,427 | +49 1,476 | +51 1,527 | +38 1,565 | +27 1,592 | +9 1,601 | +112 1,713 |
| LARKIN, James | 520 | +17 537 | +4 541 | — 541 | +12 553 | +57 610 | +22 632 | -632 — | — — | — — |
| MacELHINNEY, Liam (S.F.) | 946 | +4 950 | +6 956 | — 956 | +15 971 | +11 982 | +46 1,028 | +39 1,067 | +8 1,075 | +141 1,216 |
| MALONEY, Sean (Lab.) | 1,317 | +27 1,344 | +18 1,362 | +2 1,364 | +106 1,470 | +155 1,625 | +58 1,683 | +126 1,809 | -86 1,723 | — 1,723 |
| McGLINCHEY, Bernard (F.F.) | 1,087 | +16 1,103 | +72 1,175 | +1 1,176 | +28 1,204 | +50 1,254 | +40 1,294 | +124 1,418 | +28 1,446 | +117 1,563 |
| McGOWAN, Paddy (F.F.) | 1,611 | +3 1,614 | +75 1,689 | +2 1,691 | +13 1,704 | +23 1,727 | — 1,727 | — 1,727 | — 1,727 | — 1,727 |
| MEEHAN, Charles | 844 | +3 847 | +11 858 | +3 861 | +5 866 | +7 873 | +7 880 | +85 965 | +15 980 | -980 — |
| O'DONNELL, Joseph P (F.G.) | 203 | -203 — | — — | — — | — — | — — | — — | — — | — — | — — |
| PATTERSON, Billy (F.F.) | 300 | +6 306 | -306 — | — — | — — | — — | — — | — — | — — | — — |
| REID, J. J. (F.G.) | 1,136 | +28 1,164 | +18 1,182 | +9 1,191 | +24 1,215 | +18 1,233 | +85 1,318 | +20 1,338 | +11 1,349 | +35 1,384 |
| Non-transferable papers not effective | — | +12 12 | +26 38 | — 38 | +38 76 | +50 126 | +166 292 | +81 373 | +15 388 | +575 963 |
| TOTAL: | 13,782 | — 13,782 | — 13,782 | — 13,782 | — 13,782 | — 13,782 | — 13,782 | — 13,782 | — 13,782 | — 13,782 |

Elected: Devenney, Jim (D.P.P.); McGowan, Paddy (F.F.); Maloney, Sean (Lab); Harkin, Danny; Harte, Paddy (F.G.); McGlinchey, Bernard (F.F.); Reid, J.J. (F.G.)

# GLENTIES ELECTORAL AREA

TOTAL ELECTORATE 19,969. VALID POLL 11,639. NO. OF MEMBERS 6. QUOTA 1,663.

| Names of Candidates | First Count Votes | Second Count Transfer of McGarvey's votes Result | Third Count Transfer of J. Doherty's votes Result | Fourth Count Transfer of J. Boyle's votes Result | Fifth Count Transfer of Rodgers' surplus Result | Sixth Count Transfer of O'Colla's votes Result | Seventh Count Transfer of P. Doherty's votes Result |
|---|---|---|---|---|---|---|---|
| BOYLE, Connell (F.G.) | 1,528 | +1 1,529 | +18 1,547 | +156 1,703 | — 1,703 | — 1,703 | — 1,703 |
| BOYLE, John | 635 | +3 638 | +35 673 | -673 — | — — | — — | — — |
| BRENNAN, Francis (F.F.) | 1,427 | +14 1,441 | +12 1,453 | +139 1,592 | +37 1,629 | +48 1,677 | — 1,677 |
| BRESLIN, James (F.F.) | 1,010 | +27 1,037 | +40 1,077 | +29 1,106 | +8 1,114 | +185 1,299 | +64 1,363 |
| COLL, Fred (Non-Party) | 899 | +16 915 | +98 1,013 | +9 1,022 | +5 1,027 | +204 1,231 | +282 1,513 |
| DOHERTY, Jimmy | 543 | +4 547 | -547 — | — — | — — | — — | — — |
| DOHERTY, Padraig (F.G.) | 873 | +12 885 | +36 921 | +12 933 | +1 934 | +90 1,024 | -1,024 — |
| DOOHAN, Maureen (F.G.) | 932 | +114 1,046 | +15 1,061 | +9 1,070 | +3 1,073 | +24 1,097 | +338 1,435 |
| KELLY, Pádraig | 1,175 | +110 1,285 | +54 1,339 | +107 1,446 | +6 1,452 | +37 1,489 | +37 1,526 |
| McGARVEY, Hugh (F.F.) | 483 | -483 — | — — | — — | — — | — — | — — |
| Ó COLLA, Feardorcha Seosamh (F.F.) | 709 | +78 787 | +52 839 | +3 842 | +1 843 | -843 — | — — |
| RODGERS, Seamus (W.P.) | 1,425 | +28 1,453 | +146 1,599 | +125 1,724 | -61 1,663 | — 1,663 | — 1,663 |
| Non-transferable papers not effective | — | +76 76 | +41 117 | +84 201 | — 201 | +255 456 | +303 759 |
| TOTAL: | 11,639 | — 11,639 | — 11,639 | — 11,639 | — 11,639 | — 11,639 | — 11,639 |

Elected: Rodgers, Seamus (W.P.); Boyle, Connell (F.G.); Brennan, Francis (F.F.); Kelly, Pádraig; Coll, Fred (Non-Party); Doohan, Maureen (F.G.)

# MILLFORD ELECTORAL AREA

TOTAL ELECTORATE 12,016. VALID POLL 8,144. NO. OF MEMBERS 4. QUOTA 1,629.

| Names of Candidates | First Count Votes | Second Count Transfer of Doherty's votes **Result** | | Third Count Transfer of Diver's votes **Result** | | Fourth Count Transfer of McGee's votes **Result** | |
|---|---|---|---|---|---|---|---|
| BLANEY, Harry | 1,540 | +73 | 1,613 | +28 | 1,641 | — | 1,641 |
| DIVER, Lexie (F.G.) | 653 | +6 | 659 | -659 | — | — | — |
| DOHERTY, Patrick (S.F.) | 315 | -315 | — | — | — | — | — |
| GRIER, Lizzie (F.F.) | 857 | +30 | 887 | +88 | 975 | +63 | 1,038 |
| LOUGHREY, Joachim Anthony (F.G.) | 926 | +9 | 935 | +363 | 1,298 | +72 | 1,370 |
| McGEE, Sean | 732 | +82 | 814 | +23 | 837 | -837 | — |
| McGINLEY, Noel (F.F.) | 1,506 | +25 | 1,531 | +66 | 1,597 | +254 | 1,851 |
| O'DONNELL, Edward | 1,615 | +52 | 1,667 | — | 1,667 | — | 1,667 |
| Non-transferable papers not effective | — | +38 | 38 | +91 | 129 | +448 | 577 |
| TOTAL: | 8,144 | — | 8,144 | — | 8,144 | — | 8,144 |

Elected: O'Donnell, Edward; Blaney, Harry; McGinley, Noel (F.F.); Loughrey, Joachim Anthony (F.G.).

# If you've got The Irish Times, you've got the full story.

# DUBLIN BOROUGH COUNCIL

## DUBLIN BOROUGHH COUNCIL RESULTS

| PARTY | 1991 % of votes | 1991 Seats obtained | 1985 % of votes | 1985 Seat obtained |
|---|---|---|---|---|
| Fianna Fail | 33.0 | 20 | 41.8 | 26 |
| Fine Gael | 14.0 | 6 | 20.0 | 13 |
| Labour | 12.8 | 10 | 9.0 | 2 |
| Progressive Dem. | 3.4 | 1 | — | — |
| Workers Party | 9.4 | 5 | 9.4 | 6 |
| Other | 27.4 | 10 | 19.8 | 5 |
| TOTAL SEATS | | 52 | | 52 |

## DUBLIN

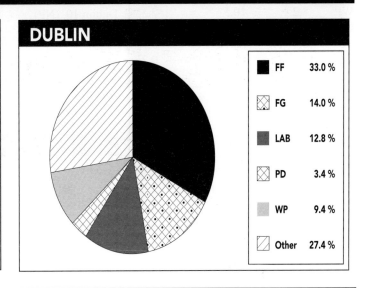

| | | |
|---|---|---|
| ■ | FF | 33.0 % |
| ⊠ | FG | 14.0 % |
| ■ | LAB | 12.8 % |
| ⊠ | PD | 3.4 % |
| ▨ | WP | 9.4 % |
| ▧ | Other | 27.4 % |

Dublin Corporation
City Hall, Dublin 2
Telephone: (01) 6796111
Population: 477,675
Rateable valuation: £5,670,056.35
Municipal rate: £27.95
Council meetings: First Monday of each month at 18.45
City Manager and Town Clerk: F. J. Feely
Personnel Officer: H. Niall
Finance Officer and Treasurer: M. Redmond
City Manager's Department
Administrative Officer: A. McHugh
Public Relations Officer: N. Carroll
Public Libraries Department
City Librarian: D. Ellis-King
Law Department
Law Agent: A. Barry
City Coroner: Dr. B. Farrell
Finance Officer and Treasurer's Department
Finance Officer and Treasurer: M.Redmond
Data Processing Controller: F. Davis
Administrative Officers: E. Brady, J.Doherty,
T.O'Shaughnessy, P.Lawlor, M.Dawson
Engineering Department
Principal Officer: W. Soffe
Administrative Officers: P. O'Shea, V. Moore,
T. O'Donoghue (Acting)
Dublin Chief Engineer(Engineering Services):
J. Fenwick
Senior Engineers:
Design and Construction: M. Murphy
Waterworks: M. Phillips (Acting)
Sewers and Main Drainage: D. Gallagher (Acting)
Mechanical: D. Berkery

At 62 years of age, Frank Feeley is Ireland's most important and undoubtedly best known local government official. Prior to the present local authority reform in Dublin, he was Dublin County and City Manager with administrative responsibility for an area with a population of over 1 million people and an annual budget of almost 500 million pounds as well as a staff of well over ten thousand individuals. Even when the new Dublin local government structures are up and running, Feeley, as Dublin City Manager, will command a staff, budget and range of responsibilities well in excess of many Department Secretaries.

He is a true Dubliner. He was born in 1931 and educated at the Christian Brothers School at Synge Street and later at the School of Accountancy in Glasgow. He also has qualifications from the Chartered Associations of Certified Accountants and is presently President of the Institute of Public Administration.

His career has been exclusively Dublin based beginning as a Principal officer in the finance section of Dublin Corporation in1949. He worked his way up through the Corporation ranks becoming Assistant City and County Manager in 1969 - 1979 until taking up the position of City and County Manager in 1979.

Feely is married to Ita Deegan, has one son and two daughters and enjoys oil painting, golf and reading.

His work for the City and County, which Councillors of all parties agree, often goes beyond the call of duty, has not gone unrecognised. He was the receipent of the Lord Mayor's award in 1989 and has received an honorary doctorate from Dublin University, Trinity College. Frank Feeley will probably be best remembered in the public mind as the brains and driving force behind the Dublin Millennium.

## ARTANE

|  | 1991 | 1985 | '85 to '91 Swing |
|---|---|---|---|
| FF | 37.9 | 44.3 | -6.4 |
| FG | 5.3 | 8.0 | -2.7 |
| Lab | 21.2 | 17.9 | 3.3 |
| WP | 8.2 | 10.5 | -2.3 |
| GP | 4.5 | 0.4 | 4.1 |
| SF | 10.4 | 6.7 | 3.7 |
| Ind | 12.4 | 12.2 | 0.2 |

BOURKE, Paddy,
13 Montrose Grove, Artane,
Dublin 5. (Lab)
Unemployed. 01-474065

BROUGHAN, Tommy,
23 Riverside Road, Coolock,
Dublin 17. (Lab)
Teacher.

GREEN, Ita,
9 St. Assam's Drive, Raheny,
Dublin 5. (FF)
Librarian. 01-314458

HAUGHEY, Sean (Ald),
Abbeyville, Kinsealy,
County Dublin. (FF)
Senator. 01-450111

## BALLYFERMOT

|  | 1991 | 1985 | '85 to '91 Swing |
|---|---|---|---|
| FF | 24.3 | 34.4 | -10.1 |
| FG | 13.2 | 16.2 | -3.0 |
| Lab | 20.5 | 7.9 | 12.6 |
| WP | 13.2 | 17.5 | -4.3 |
| GP | 2.8 | 0.5 | 2.3 |
| SF | 5.5 | 8.3 | -2.8 |
| Ind | 20.4 | 15.2 | 5.2 |

BENNETT, Olga,
104 Inchicore Road,
Dublin 8. (FF)
Senator.

CONAGHAN, Michael (Ald),
33 Lally Road, Ballyfermot,
Dublin 10. (Lab)
Teacher.

JACKSON, Vincent,
38 Drumfinn Avenue, Ballyfermot,
Dublin 10. (NP)
Carpenter. 01-6262541

MacGIOLLA, Tomás,
Dáil Éireann, Leinster House,
Dublin 2. (WP)
Dáil Deputy. 01-6267429

## CABRA

|  | 1991 | 1985 | '85 to '91 Swing |
|---|---|---|---|
| FF | 38.9 | 43.2 | -4.3 |
| FG | 14.2 | 19.1 | -4.9 |
| Lab | 7.2 | 4.3 | 2.9 |
| WP | 4.2 | 3.9 | 0.3 |
| GP | 4.6 | 1.7 | 2.9 |
| SF | 7.9 | 9.3 | -1.4 |
| Ind | 23.1 | 18.5 | 4.6 |

FARRY, Patrick J,
"Brushlee",
141 Howth Road, Sutton,
Dublin 13. (FF)
Solicitor. 01-309766

FITZPATRICK, Dr. Dermot (Ald),
80 Navan Road,
Dublin 7. (FF)
Dail Deputy. 01-387515

MITCHELL, Jim,
Dail Eireann, Leinster House,
Dublin 2. (FG)
Dail Deputy. 01-904574

## CLONTARF

|  | 1991 | 1985 | '85 to '91 Swing |
|---|---|---|---|
| FF | 34.6 | 44.5 | -9.9 |
| FG | 20.8 | 25.4 | -4.6 |
| Lab | 6.8 | 5.3 | 1.5 |
| WP | 4.2 | 4.6 | -0.4 |
| GP | 1.2 | 2.0 | -0.8 |
| Ind | 32.2 | 18.2 | 14.1 |

BRUTON, Richard,
210 Griffith Avenue,
Dublin 9. (FG)
Dail Deputy. 01-368185

CALLELY, Ivor,
"Lansdale House",
7 St Lawrence Road, Clontarf,
Dublin 3.
Dail Deputy. 01-313059

DUBLIN BAY LOFTUS, Sean (Ald),
"Nephin", 5 Seafield Avenue, Clontarf,
Dublin 3. (NP)
Barrister. 01-332134

McDOWELL, Derek,
3 Dunluce Road, Clontarf,
Dublin 3. (Lab)
Solicitor. 01-336138

STAFFORD, John,
60 North Strand Road,
Dublin 3. (FF)
Dáil Deputy. 01-334044

## CRUMLIN

|  | 1991 | 1985 | '85 to '91 Swing |
|---|---|---|---|
| FF | 27.5 | 42.2 | -14.7 |
| FG | 24.6 | 25.5 | -0.9 |
| Lab | 14.9 | 13.8 | 1.1 |
| WP | 19.9 | 11.4 | 8.5 |
| GP | 6.0 | — | 6.0 |
| SF | 3.3 | 5.3 | -2.0 |
| Ind | 3.8 | 1.8 | 2.0 |

Ciaran Cuffe (Greens)
South Inner City

Eamonn Walsh (Lab)
Terenure

Ita Greene (FF)
Artane

Richard Bruton (FG)
Clontarf

BRISCOE, Ben,
Dáil Éireann, Leinster House,
Dublin 2. (FF)
Dáil Deputy. 01-6288426

BYRNE, Eric,
Dáil Éireann, Leinster House,
Dublin 2. (Elected DL, now WP)
Dáil Deputy. 01-682559

CONNOLLY, Joe,
39 Hughes Road South, Walkinstown,
Dublin 12. (Lab)
Sports Administrator. 01-501914

MITCHELL, Gay (Ald),
Lord Mayor, Mansion House,
Dawson Street,
Dublin 2. (FG)
Dáil Deputy. 01-972475

## DONAGHMEDE

|     | 1991 | 1985 | '85 to '91 Swing |
|-----|------|------|------|
| FF  | 42.2 | 54.0 | -11.8 |
| FG  | 9.0  | 15.3 | -6.3 |
| Lab | 18.7 | 13.3 | 5.4 |
| WP  | 13.1 | 6.1  | 7.0 |
| PD  | 4.4  |      | 4.4 |
| GP  | 5.5  | 1.2  | 4.3 |
| Ind | 7.1  | 10.1 | -3.0 |

BRADY, Martin,
37 Grangemore Drive,
Dublin 13. (FF)
Telecom Employee. 01-484509

FITZGERALD, Liam (Ald),
117 Tonlegee Road, Raheny,
Dublin 5. (FF)
Dáil Deputy. 01-470632

KENNY, Sean,
44 Woodbine Road, Raheny,
Dublin 5. (Lab)
Executive Officer. 01-761845.

McCARTAN, Pat,
Dáil Éireann, Leinster House,
Dublin 2. (Elected WP, now DL)
Dáil Deputy. 01-723836

O'NEILL, Sadhbh,
Flat 1, 61 Philipsburgh Avenue,
Fairview,
Dublin 3. (GP)
Student. 01-331621

## DRUMCONDRA

|     | 1991 | 1985 | '85 to '91 Swing |
|-----|------|------|------|
| FF  | 37.1 | 44.7 | -7.6 |
| FG  | 13.5 | 23.4 | -9.9 |
| Lab | 17.8 | 7.1  | 10.7 |
| WP  | 9.6  | 11.3 | -1.7 |
| PD  | 2.9  | —    | 2.9 |
| GP  | 6.4  | 1.6  | 4.8 |
| SF  | 5.0  | 6.7  | -1.7 |
| Ind | 7.7  | 5.2  | 2.5 |

AHERN, Noel (Ald),
25 Church Avenue, Drumcondra,
Dublin 9. (FF)
Clerical Officer. 01-363333

BARRETT, Michael,
102 Glasnevin Avenue,
Dublin 11. (FF)
Dáil Deputy. 01-422480

BRADY, Brendan,
20 Home Farm Road, Drumcondra,
Dublin 9. (FG)
Engineer. 01-777465

O'BRIEN, Eamonn,
58 Knowth Court, Ballymun,
Dublin 11. (WP)
Bus Driver.

SHORTHALL, Roisín,
12 Iveragh Road, Whitehall,
Dublin 9. (Lab)
Teacher.

## FINGLAS

|     | 1991 | 1985 | '85 to '91 Swing |
|-----|------|------|------|
| FF  | 42.5 | 42.3 | 0.2 |
| FG  | 12.4 | 12.4 | -0.0 |
| Lab | 9.1  | 6.7  | 2.4 |
| WP  | 11.2 | 23.1 | -11.9 |
| PD  | 7.8  | —    | 7.8 |
| GP  | 4.6  | 1.7  | 2.9 |
| SF  | 7.7  | 6.6  | 1.1 |
| Ind | 4.7  | 7.2  | -2.5 |

CAREY, Pat (Ald),
69 Bourne View, Ashbourne,
County Meath. (FF)
Teacher. 01-350544

FLAHERTY, Mary,
Dáil Éireann, Leinster House,
Dublin 2. (FG)
Dáil Deputy. 01-976620

O'NEILL, Lucia,
159 Mellows Road, Finglas West,
Dublin 11. (WP)
Library Assistant.

TAAFFE, Tony,
Mayne, Clonee,
County Meath. (FF)
Solicitor.

## NORTH INNER CITY

|     | 1991 | 1985 | '85 to '91 Swing |
|-----|------|------|------|
| FF  | 25.9 | 42   | -16.1 |
| FG  | 6.7  | 13.4 | -6.7 |
| Lab | 8.7  | 5.4  | 3.3 |
| WP  | 5.6  | 5.2  | 0.4 |
| PD  | 3.1  | —    | 3.1 |
| GP  | 3.9  | 0.9  | 3.0 |
| SF  | 11.3 | 7.8  | 3.5 |
| IND | 34.8 | 25.3 | 9.5 |

**Paddy Bourke (Lab)**
**Artane**

**Michael Mulcahy (FF)**
**South Inner City**

**Gay Mitchell (FG)**
**Crumlin**

BURKE, Christy,
11 Cherrymount Crescent, Marino,
Dublin 3. (SF)
Sinn Féin Employee. 01-308783

COSTELLOE, Joe,
75 Lower Sean McDermott Street,
Dublin 1. (Lab)
Senator. 01-365698

GREGORY, Tony (Ald),
5 Sackville Gardens, Ballybough,
Dublin 3.
Dáil Deputy. 01-729910

KETT, Tony,
54 Whitethorn Road, Artane,
Dublin 5. (FF)
Administrator. 01-318821

STAFFORD, Thomas,
99 Amiens Street,
Dublin 1. (FF)
Funeral Director. 01-364933

## PEMBROKE

|     | 1991 | 1985 | '85 to '91 Swing |
|-----|------|------|------|
| FF  | 24.4 | 34.2 | -9.8 |
| FG  | 18.3 | 28.9 | -10.6 |
| Lab | 10.9 | 7.8  | 3.1 |
| WP  | 5.9  | 6.1  | -0.2 |
| PD  | 7.7  | —    | 7.7 |
| GP  | 7.8  | 4.2  | 3.6 |
| SF  | 1.6  | —    | 1.6 |
| Ind | 23.3 | 18.8 | 4.5 |

DOYLE, Joe,
14 Simmonscourt Terrace, Donnybrook,
Dublin 4. (FG)
Dáil Deputy. 01-692391

HEDERMAN, Carmencita (Ald),
92 Upper Leeson Street,
Dublin 4. (NP)
Senator. 01-680889

RYAN, Eoin,
19 Vavasour Square,
Bath Avenue, Sandymount,
Dublin 4. (FF)
Senator. 01-600082

WHEELER, Claire,
27 Oaklands Park, Ballsbridge,
Dublin 4. (GP)
Engineer.

## RATHMINES

|     | 1991 | 1985 | '85 to '91 Swing |
|-----|------|------|------|
| FF  | 30.4 | 38.9 | -8.5 |
| FG  | 18.4 | 38.9 | -20.5 |
| Lab | 10.7 | 7.6  | 3.1 |
| WP  | 10.0 | 5.9  | 4.1 |
| PD  | 14.7 |      | 14.7 |
| GP  | 11.7 | 3.8  | 7.9 |
| Ind | 4.1  | 4.9  | -0.8 |

DONNELLY, Michael (Ald),
33 Glendoher Avenue, Rathfarnham,
Dublin 14. (FF)
Accountant. 01-931074

FREHILL, Mary,
48 Penrose Street,
Dublin 4. (Lab)
Rehab Executive. 01-686802

GORMLEY, John,
71 St. Magdelene Terrace,
Dublin 4. (GP)
Language School Director. 01-607032

O'DONNELL, Liz,
34 Ormond Road,
Dublin 6. (PD)
Lawyer. 01-960610

## SOUTH INNER CITY

|     | 1991 | 1985 | '85 to '91 Swing |
|-----|------|------|------|
| FF  | 25.9 | 32.3 | -6.4 |
| FG  | 11.3 | 15.6 | -4.3 |
| Lab | 11.4 | 10.2 | 1.2 |
| WP  | 12.9 | 10.7 | 2.2 |
| GP  | 10.7 | 1.4  | 9.3 |
| SF  | 8.5  | 8.4  | 0.1 |
| Ind | 19.2 | 22.5 | -3.3 |

CUFFE, Ciarán,
81 Dame Street,
Dublin 2. (GP)
Architect.

LYNCH, Brendan,
25 Donore Road, South Circular Road,
Dublin 8. (NP)
Compositor. 01-540240

MOONEY, Mary,
Rooske Road, Dunboyne,
County Meath. (FF)
Public Representative.

MULCAHY, Michael,
The Law Library,
PO Box 2424, The Four Courts,
Dublin 7. (FF)
Barrister.

QUINN, Ruairí (Ald),
Dáil Éireann, Leinster House,
Dublin 2. (Lab)
Dáil Deputy. 01-839563

**Martin Brady (FF)**
**Donaghmede**

**Ruairi Quinn (Lab)**
**South Inner City**

**Eoin Ryan (FF)**
**Pembroke**

**Carmencita Hederman (NP)**
**Pembroke**

# Labour Party victorious in Dublin city

Labour pulled off an impressive success in Dublin City, increasing their seats by 400%, coming ahead of Fine Gael as the second largest Party on the Corporation and in the process denying Fianna Fail the control of the Council.

The 1985 Local Elections had been a disaster for Labour in the capital. Then in Government, in an unpopular Coalition with Fine Gael, they had returned after the election with just 2 seats, while their rivals on the left, the Workers Party, had won six seats.

This time, Labour were to make no mistakes. In a carefully managed campaign they ran half as many candidates as they had in 1985 and converted 12.8% of the first preferences into over 19% of the seats. They increased their seat numbers from 2 to 10 and indeed were unluckly not to secure a further three seats.

Labour pulled off an impressive two out of four seats in Artane despite running without outgoing Councillor Michael O'Halloran. Paddy Burke and Tommy Broughan became the two Labour Councillors for the area, where they won an extra seat at the expense of the Workers Party.

In the Ballyfermot, Clontarf, Crumlin, North Inner City, Rathmines and South Inner City areas, Labour ran only one candidate, to good effect picking up one seat in each area. Their seat in South Inner City was taken by the man, who as Director of Elections, had masterminded their Dublin Campaign Ruairi Quinn. As a Government Minister in 1985, he could not contest the Local Elections, but this time polled 1,215 first preference to take the first seat.

It was Quinn who directed the Party Campaign in the Robinson Presidential Election and the Dublin City performance in the 1991 Locals can be credited to the boost in Party morale and indeed Party personnel which the

Robinson victory had brought.

In Donaghmede, Sean Kenny was

> Labour's Dublin city performance can be credited to the boost in Party morale and indeed Party personnel which the Robinson victory had brought

elected for Labour with help from running mate Anne Carter. Kenny went on to be elected as Dublin Lord Mayor in 1991-92 by the Rainbow Alliance. His impressive 2,097 first preference tally and this heightened profile will put him in a strong position in the Dublin North

East four seater in the next Dail Elections.

In Drumcondra, teacher Roisin Shorthall took a seat for the Party while her running mate, the curiously named Desmond O'Malley, also polled exceptionally well.

If Dublin City was a success for Labour, it was a disaster for their partners in the 1982-1987 Coalition Fine Gael. The 1985 Elections had been a disappointment for Fine Gael, their 20% vote had been one of their lowest ever in the capital. It was to drop considerably in these elections.

The Fine Gael vote dropped a full 6%, despite the fact that they are now in opposition and they lost seven seats. They returned to the City hall as only the third largest group with just six seats.

Fine Gael's Dublin City performance was their worst in the country and they now have no Councillors in half of the City's twelve electoral areas.

Five of their members of the new Council are T.D.'s, Richard Bruton (Clontarf), Gay Mitchell (Crumlin), Joe Doyle (Pembroke), Mary Flaherty (Crumlin) and Jim Mitchell, who had moved to Dublin Central in order to establish a base for the next General Election, just managed to take the last seat in Cabra. Brenda Brady in Drumcondra is the only Fine Gael member of Dublin Corporation not a Dail Deputy.

If the implications for Fine Gael strength in Dublin Local Government are clear, the prospects for Fine Gael are

**"Nail Biting Stuff"** - Jim Mitchell of Fine Gael ,who took the final seat in the Cabra Area on the13th count

also ominous in those five Dublin Dail Constituencies, all or part of which are in the corporation area.

The chances of Fine Gael retaining Garret Fitzgerald's seat in Dublin South East, for example look very slim. The 4 seat Dail Constituency is made up of Pembroke and Rathmines and part of South Inner City. Fine Gael lost it's seat in South Inner City and both its' seats in the Rathmines electoral area.

Fine Gael leader in the Senate, Maurice Manning had moved his political base to Rathmines and was seen as the Party's new challenger for the Garret Fitzgerald seat in the next General Election. He secured only 777 first preferences, just under a third of the quota and failed to get elected.

Fine Gael won 2 seats in Rathmines in 1985 but with Maurice Manning's disappointing performance and the collapse of outgoing Councillor Michael McShane's vote, it became one of the City's six areas without a Fine Gael representative in City Hall. Even the performance of the Party's other South East T.D. Joe Doyle cannot be said to be impressive. He polled 1,673 first preferences, just under two thirds of a quota and had to wait to take the third seat after Independent Senator Carmacita Hederman and Fianna Fail Senator Eoin Ryan in Pembroke.

For Fianna Fail, the Dublin Corporation result will certainly be a disappointment. They had twenty six seats on the old Council, they have twenty seats on the new. Yet the slippage in Dublin City was nothing like the disaster in Dublin County. Their city vote was down almost 9% on the exceptional high of 1985. However, in light of the Labour onslaught, the Greens factor and the fact that they contested this time without poll toppers Bertie Ahern T.D. Vincent Brady T.D. and Jim Tunney T.D., it can be viewed as a credible exercise in damage limitation.

The Party had six poll toppers, Senator Sean Haughey put in a very impressive performance in Artane with 2,976 first preference, almost 800 above the quota, while outgoing Party colleague Ita Green also polled well and the Party held onto its two seats.

In Donaghmede, Fianna Fail TD Liam Fitzgerald also topped the poll. He secured one of the highest polls in the City with a 2,894 first preference while Fianna Fail newcomer and Telcom Official Martin Brady polled an impressive 2,086 on his first outing and took the second seat.

In Cabra, Fianna Fail Dublin Central Deputy Dermot Fitzgerald topped the poll and was returned along with

## The Fianna Fail slippage in Dublin city was nothing like the disaster in Dublin county

outgoing Councillor Paddy Farry.

In Finglas, Pat Carey outgoing and newcome Tony Taaffe took the first two seats for Fianna Fail.

The fourth area in which the Party took the first and second seats was in Drumcondra where Noel Ahern, brother of the Minister, polled 2,745 votes, an impressive 1.16 quota, while the local Fianna Fail Deputy for Dublin North West Michael Barrett T.D. took the second seat with 1,902 first preferences.

Fianna Fail also managed to retain the two seats in Clontarf due largely to the fact that two of the party's Dublin T.D.'s had moved into this area. Deputy Ivor Callely had moved across from Drumcondra in order to anchor himself more firmly in the Dublin North Central constituency. He secured 2,792 first perference, to come in second behind Independent Sean "Dublin Bay" Loftus. John Stafford meanwhile had moved

across to Clontarf from North Inner City. The redrawing of Dail constituencies will see him contesting in Dublin North Central constituency in the next General Election. He got 1,747 first tallies and took the last seat ahead of sitting Fianna Fail Councillor for the area Joe Burke.

Meanwhile Stafford's brother Thomas contested North Inner City in his place and along with the outgoing Tony Kett, held onto the Party's two seats.

In Ballyfermot Senator Olga Bennett held on, but Michael Delaney lost out. In Crumlin where outgoing Councillor Andy O'Callaghan was not contesting the Party's other outgoing Councillor sitting Deputy for Dublin South Central Ben Briscoe's vote dropped over 1,100 on 1985 but he mananged to take the final seat.

Fianna Fail held its two out of four in South Inner City where former T.D. Mary Mooney and Councillor Michael Mulcahy were returned.

The 1985 Local Elections had seen good gains by the Workers Party in Dublin Corporation and these gains were repeated in the the 1987 and 1989 General Elections. Dublin City was the Workers Party strong hold - four of their six Dail Deputies were from the Corporation area.

The 1991 Local Elections proved to be a set back, however, the Party had seven Councillors on the old Council but despite the fact that they were expected to make further gains, they returned to City Hall with only six seats. They won a seat in Donaghmede, but lost one in both Artane and South Inner City.

Proinsias De Rossa as an M.E.P. was

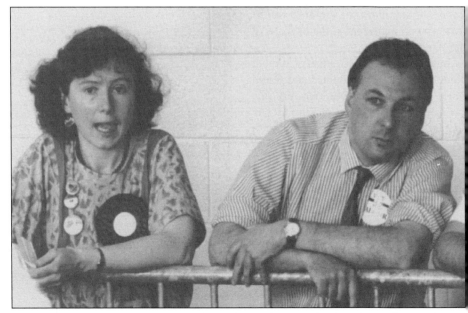

**"Green over Red" - Green Party candidate Claire Wheeler who just pipped Dermot Lacey of the Labour Party by 37 votes to take the final seat in the Pembroke Area.**

> ## In hindsight the Green's breakthrough in Dublin should not have been such a surprise

not contesting these Elections, the party vote in his Finglas base dropped a massive 12% as a result, but the replacement candidate Lucia O'Neill managed to hold on to take the final seat.

Worker's Party North East Deputy Pat McCartan had moved from the Artane to the Donaghmede Electoral area. He did pick up a new seat in Donaghmede but his replacement in Artane failed to hold onto the Party's seat there.

Former Leader Tomas MacGiolla struggled to win the last seat for the Party in the Ballyfermot electoral area.

The Worker's Party other Dublin Deputy, Eric Byrne, put on a very impressive performance in the Crumlin area, taking 2,081 first preferences while outgoing Councillor Eamon O'Brien held onto his seat in Drumcondra.

The other big surprise of the Elections in Dublin City was the phenomenal performance of the Green Party who now have four members on Dublin Corporation. They had contested the 1985, election, and it must not be forgotten, had put in a very good performance in some areas. The 1987 and especially the 1989 General Election had seen their support strengthen and the election of their first T.D. In hindsight the Greens breakthrough in Dublin Corporation should not have been seen as such a surprise.

What was a surprise however, was the number of Green Councillors elected and the manner in which they attained their seats. John Gormley, one of the leading figures in the Party at national level, had come close to a Dail seat in Dublin South East for the party in 1989. He took an impressive 1,302 first preferences and the forth seat in Rathmines.

Gormley's 1989 General Election performance was also reflected by the strength of the Party support in South Inner City, where Ciaran Cuffe had run

for the Party in 1985. Cuffe ran again this time, increased his vote by over 9% and took the second seat ahead of four outgoing Councillors.

A major surprise however, was the Party vote in Pembroke where Clare Wheelan, thanks especially to transfers from the P.D.'s Seamus Crowley, edged out Labour's Dermot Lacey by just 37 votes to take the last seat. Lacey had been unlucky to lose out in 1985 and indeed this time was 418 votes ahead of Wheelan on the first count, but the phenomenal ability of Green candidate to attract transfers from all quarters was to see them take a seat in this Ward.

The other major surprise was the election of Sadhbh O'Neill in Donaghmede. She had been abroad on a working holiday in the States for the duration of the campaign and had not even voted for herself. However she managed to take the last seat by just two votes.

Dublin City has always had a small number of very high profile Independent Councillors. The most remarkable individual performance in the County was put in by Independent Councillor and Dublin Central T.D. Tony Gregory in the North Inner City Ward. He got 4,096 first preferences, the highest in the Country, 1.93 quotas and almost a third of all the votes cast in the electoral area. Although the absence of Fianna Fail's 1985 poll topper in the area of Bertie Ahern, would have strengthened Gregory's vote, the result is still an impressive personal victory and

dismisses any doubt that Gregory will be one of Dublin Central's four T.D.'s after the next national poll.

Carmacita Hederman topped the poll once again in Pembroke. In the process, the former Lord Mayor polled the highest female vote in the country with 3,126. In the constituency of Dublin South East where Garrett Fitzgerald's retirement leaves a vacancy next time out, the Independent Senator's name could feature for a seat, especially if it was to appear on the ticket of any of the parties.

Sean "Dublin Bay" Loftus, the man who describes himself as the "first Green Councillor", topped the poll in Clontarf, ahead of two Fianna Fail T.D.'s, while in South Inner City Brendan Lynch retained his Independent seat.

Newcomer to the Independent benches in City Hall this time is Vincent "Ballyfermot" Jackson who polled almost 0.7 of a quota on the first count to take the third seat in Ballyfermot four seater.

The Progressive Democrat's performance was not as impressive as they might have hoped. They had put their hopes in three celebrities, actor Jean Anne Crowley in Pembroke, Dublin footballer Barney Rock in Finglas and women's rights campaigner Liz O'Donnell in Rathmines. Rock never really featured, Crowley came close to getting a seat but Liz O'Donnell was elected in Rathmines and is the Party's only member on Dublin Corporation.

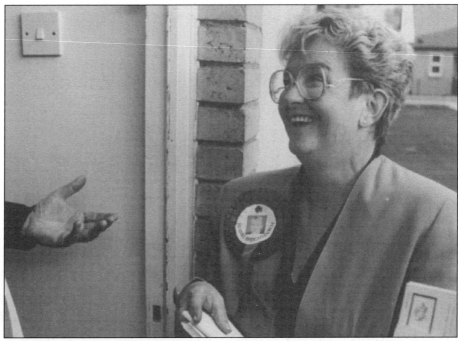

"On the doors steps" - Niamh Breathnach of the Labour Party who topped the poll in the Blackrock Area receiving 1,303 votes.

# ARTANE ELECTORAL AREA

TOTAL ELECTORATE 26,692. VALID POLL 10,916. NO. OF MEMBERS 4. QUOTA 2,184

| Names of Candidates | First Count Votes | Second Count Transfer of Haughey's surplus Result | Third Count Transfer of Quinn's votes Result | Fourth Count Transfer of McCoy's votes Result | Fifth Count Transfer of Marsh's votes Result | Sixth Count Transfer of O'Gorman's votes Result | Seventh Count Transfer of Dowling's votes Result | Eighth Count Transfer of Howard's votes Result | Ninth Count Transfer of Moore's votes Result | Tenth Count Transfer of Maher's votes Result | Eleventh Count Transfer of McGrath's votes Result | Twelfth Count Transfer of Curry's votes Result |
|---|---|---|---|---|---|---|---|---|---|---|---|---|
| BOURKE, Paddy (Lab.) | 1,236 | +32 1,268 | +12 1,280 | +14 1,294 | +12 1,306 | +16 1,322 | +25 1,347 | +9 1,356 | +134 1,490 | +111 1,601 | +128 1,729 | +240 1,969 |
| BROUGHAN, Tommy (Lab.) | 1,083 | +41 1,124 | +16 1,140 | +24 1,164 | +10 1,174 | +21 1,195 | +67 1,262 | +20 1,282 | +91 1,373 | +72 1,445 | +138 1,583 | +490 2,073 |
| CURRY, John (W.P.) | 896 | +23 919 | +13 932 | +17 949 | +3 952 | +9 961 | +51 1,012 | +38 1,050 | +44 1,094 | +91 1,185 | +142 1,327 | -1,327 — |
| DOWLING, Joe | 277 | +11 288 | +11 299 | +28 327 | +4 331 | +15 346 | -346 — | — — | — — | — — | — — | — — |
| GREEN, Ita (F.F.) | 815 | +406 1,221 | +5 1,226 | +26 1,252 | +1 1,253 | +55 1,308 | +23 1,331 | +388 1,719 | +54 1,773 | +110 1,883 | +116 1,999 | +90 2,089 |
| HAUGHEY, Sean (F.F.) | 2,976 | -792 2,184 | — 2,184 | — 2,184 | — 2,184 | — 2,184 | — 2,184 | — 2,184 | — 2,184 | — 2,184 | — 2,184 | — 2,184 |
| HOWARD, Jim (F.F.) | 348 | +191 539 | +2 541 | +13 554 | +4 558 | +9 567 | +14 581 | -581 — | — — | — — | — — | — — |
| McCOY, Austin (Non-Party) | 209 | +8 217 | +5 222 | -222 — | — — | — — | — — | — — | — — | — — | — — | — — |
| McGRATH, Finian | 509 | +18 527 | +10 537 | +30 567 | +2 569 | +36 605 | +54 659 | +19 678 | +62 740 | +141 881 | -881 — | — — |
| MAHER, Bronwen (G.P.) | 493 | +12 505 | +11 516 | +18 534 | +3 537 | +44 581 | +39 620 | +18 638 | +82 720 | -720 — | — — | — — |
| MARSH, Philip (F.G.) | 225 | +6 231 | +2 233 | +16 249 | -249 — | — — | — — | — — | — — | — — | — — | — — |
| MOORE, Kathy (F.G.) | 354 | +12 366 | +2 368 | +11 379 | +197 576 | +26 602 | +19 621 | +5 626 | -626 — | — — | — — | — — |
| O'GORMAN, John | 248 | +5 253 | +10 263 | +6 269 | +2 271 | -271 — | — — | — — | — — | — — | — — | — — |
| O'TOOLE, Larry (S.F.) | 1,137 | +21 1,158 | +10 1,168 | +6 1,174 | +7 1,181 | +12 1,193 | +13 1,206 | +46 1,252 | +22 1,274 | +31 1,305 | +114 1,419 | +187 1,606 |
| QUINN, Vincent | 110 | +6 116 | -116 — | — — | — — | — — | — — | — — | — — | — — | — — | — — |
| Non-transferable papers not effective | — | — — | +7 7 | +13 20 | +4 24 | +28 52 | +41 93 | +38 131 | +137 268 | +164 432 | +243 675 | +320 995 |
| TOTAL: | 10,916 | — 10,916 | — 10,916 | — 10,916 | — 10,916 | — 10,916 | — 10,916 | — 10,916 | — 10,916 | — 10,916 | — 10,916 | — 10,916 |

Elected: Haughey, Seán (F.F.); Green, Ita (F.F.); Broughan, Tommy (Lab.); Bourke, Paddy (Lab.)

# BALLYFERMOT ELECTORAL AREA

TOTAL ELECTORATE 26,145. VALID POLL 11,393. NO. OF MEMBERS 4. QUOTA 2,279

| Names of Candidates | First Count Votes | Second Count Transfer of Ryan's & & Norton's votes Result | Third Count Transfer of Armelin's votes Result | Fourth Count Transfer of L. Kavanagh's votes Result | Fifth Count Transfer of Guidon's votes Result | Sixth Count Transfer of Delaney's votes Result | Seventh Count Transfer of Doyle's votes Result | Eighth Count Transfer of N. Kavanagh's votes Result | Ninth Count Transfer of Conaghan's surplus Result | Tenth Count Transfer of Bennett's surplus Result | Eleventh Count Transfer of McManus' votes Result | Twelfth Count Transfer of Craig's votes Result |
|---|---|---|---|---|---|---|---|---|---|---|---|---|
| ARMELIN, Cecilia (G.P.) | 286 | +1 287 | -287 — | — — | — — | — — | — — | — — | — — | — — | — — | — — |
| BENNETT, Olga (F.F.) | 1,774 | +78 1,852 | +44 1,896 | +10 1,906 | +37 1,943 | +277 2,220 | +43 2,263 | +59 2,322 | — 2,322 | -43 2,279 | — 2,279 | — 2,279 |
| CONAGHAN, Michael (Lab.) | 2,130 | +7 2,137 | +60 2,197 | +43 2,240 | +30 2,270 | +27 2,297 | — 2,297 | — 2,297 | -18 2,279 | — 2,279 | — 2,279 | — 2,279 |
| CORCORAN, Tom (F.G.) | 694 | +6 700 | +11 711 | +9 720 | +16 736 | +10 746 | +21 767 | +14 781 | +6 787 | +3 790 | +526 1,316 | +100 1,416 |
| CRAIG, Gregg (F.F.) | 627 | +30 657 | +10 667 | +5 672 | +18 690 | +142 832 | +16 848 | +37 885 | +3 888 | +22 910 | +30 940 | -940 — |
| DELANEY, Michael (F.F.) | 493 | +43 536 | +5 541 | +3 544 | +25 569 | -569 — | — — | — — | — — | — — | — — | — — |
| DOYLE, Marion | 495 | +9 504 | +25 529 | +13 542 | +40 582 | +9 591 | -591 — | — — | — — | — — | — — | — — |
| GUIDON, Paul (Non-Party) | 419 | +21 440 | +11 451 | +6 457 | -457 — | — — | — — | — — | — — | — — | — — | — — |
| JACKSON, Vincent | 1,575 | +32 1,607 | +17 1,624 | +8 1,632 | +105 1,737 | +37 1,774 | +326 2,100 | +175 2,275 | +1 2,276 | +6 2,282 | — 2,282 | — 2,282 |
| KAVANAGH, Linda (W.P.) | 423 | +2 425 | +21 446 | -446 — | — — | — — | — — | — — | — — | — — | — — | — — |
| KAVANAGH, Noel (S.F.) | 569 | +9 578 | +12 590 | +15 605 | +24 629 | +7 636 | +42 678 | -678 — | — — | — — | — — | — — |
| MacGIOLLA, Tomas (W.P.) | 919 | +24 973 | +35 1,008 | +328 1,336 | +72 1,408 | +23 1,431 | +85 1,516 | +159 1,675 | +3 1,678 | +5 1,683 | +99 1,782 | +166 1,948 |
| McMANUS, Charlie (F.G.) | 680 | +12 692 | +20 712 | +1 713 | +9 722 | +12 734 | +4 738 | +15 753 | +3 756 | +1 757 | -757 — | — — |
| NORTON, Reginald Dennis (Non-Party) | 47 | -47 — | — — | — — | — — | — — | — — | — — | — — | — — | — — | — — |
| RYAN, Robert (F.F.) | 232 | -232 — | — — | — — | — — | — — | — — | — — | — — | — — | — — | — — |
| Non-transferable papers not effective | — | +5 5 | +16 21 | +5 26 | +81 107 | +25 132 | +54 186 | +219 405 | +2 407 | +6 413 | +102 515 | +674 1,189 |
| TOTAL: | 11,393 | — 11,393 | — 11,393 | — 11,393 | — 11,393 | — 11,393 | — 11,393 | — 11,393 | — 11,393 | — 11,393 | — 11,393 | — 11,393 |

Elected: Conaghan, Michael (Lab.); Bennett, Olga (F.F.); Jackson, Vincent; MacGiolla, Tomás (W.P.)

# CABRA ELECTORAL AREA

TOTAL ELECTORATE 24,124. VALID POLL 10,905. NO. OF MEMBERS 3. QUOTA 2,727

| Names of Candidates | First Count Votes | Second Count Transfer of Price's votes Result | Third Count Transfer of Speed's votes Result | Fourth Count Transfer of O'Shea's votes Result | Fifth Count Transfer of McEvoy's votes Result | Sixth Count Transfer of Kearney's votes Result | Seventh Count Transfer of Tiernan's votes Result | Eighth Count Transfer of Baker's votes Result | Ninth Count Transfer of Finnegan's votes Result | Tenth Count Transfer of O'Byrne's votes Result | Eleventh Count Transfer of Coultry's votes Result | Twelfth Count Transfer of Clerkin's votes Result | Thirteenth Count Transfer of Fitzpatrick's surplus Result |
|---|---|---|---|---|---|---|---|---|---|---|---|---|---|
| BAKER, Jo (G.P.) | 498 | +11 509 | +5 514 | +15 529 | +40 569 | +10 579 | +59 638 | -638 — | — — | — — | — — | — — | — — |
| CLERKIN, Seán (Non-Party) | 1,136 | +6 1,142 | +4 1,146 | +15 1,161 | +16 1,177 | +17 1,194 | +23 1,217 | +85 1,302 | +59 1,361 | +27 1,388 | +218 1,606 | -1,606 — | — — |
| COULTRY, Seán (Non-Party) | 770 | +5 775 | +10 785 | +39 824 | +48 872 | +13 885 | +53 938 | +88 1,026 | +153 1,179 | +47 1,226 | -1,226 — | — — | — — |
| FARRY, Patrick J. (F.F.) | 1,516 | +2 1,518 | +6 1,524 | +17 1,541 | +16 1,557 | +14 1,571 | +20 1,591 | +37 1,628 | +65 1,693 | +340 2,033 | +121 2,154 | +279 2,433 | +167 2,600 |
| FINNEGAN, Mick (S.F.) | 603 | — 603 | +162 765 | +17 782 | +37 819 | +24 843 | +20 863 | +14 877 | -877 — | — — | — — | — — | — — |
| FITZPATRICK, Dr. Dermot (F.F.) | 1,802 | +5 1,807 | +8 1,815 | +18 1,833 | +26 1,859 | +32 1,891 | +30 1,921 | +41 1,962 | +63 2,025 | +439 2,464 | +110 2,574 | +415 2,989 | -262 2,727 |
| KEARNEY, John (F.G.) | 386 | +2 388 | +7 395 | +22 417 | +24 441 | -441 — | — — | — — | — — | — — | — — | — — | — — |
| McEVOY, Gaye | 273 | +9 282 | +2 284 | +44 328 | -328 — | — — | — — | — — | — — | — — | — — | — — | — — |
| MITCHELL, Jim (F.G.) | 1,164 | +5 1,169 | +6 1,175 | +13 1,188 | +18 1,206 | +249 1,455 | +42 1,497 | +61 1,558 | +26 1,584 | +34 1,618 | +80 1,698 | +306 2,004 | +67 2,071 |
| O'BYRNE, Willie (F.F.) | 922 | +4 926 | +5 931 | +27 958 | +17 975 | +25 1,000 | +12 1,012 | +13 1,025 | +64 1,089 | -1,089 — | — — | — — | — — |
| O'SHEA, Ambrose | 275 | +3 278 | +1 279 | -279 — | — — | — — | — — | — — | — — | — — | — — | — — | — — |
| PRICE, Brendan (Non-Party) | 65 | -65 — | — — | — — | — — | — — | — — | — — | — — | — — | — — | — — | — — |
| RAFFERTY, Cecilia (Lab.) | 786 | +6 792 | +17 809 | +31 840 | +37 877 | +26 903 | +227 1,130 | +205 1,335 | +75 1,410 | +50 1,460 | +278 1,738 | +215 1,953 | +28 1,981 |
| SPEED, Anne (S.F.) | 256 | +3 259 | -259 — | — — | — — | — — | — — | — — | — — | — — | — — | — — | — — |
| TIERNAN, Carol (W.P.) | 453 | +3 456 | +21 477 | +17 494 | +30 524 | +8 532 | -532 — | — — | — — | — — | — — | — — | — — |
| Non-transferable papers not effective | — | +1 1 | +5 6 | +4 10 | +19 29 | +23 52 | +46 98 | +94 192 | +372 564 | +152 716 | +419 1,135 | +391 1,526 | — 1,526 |
| TOTAL: | 10,905 | — 10,905 | — 10,905 | — 10,905 | — 10,905 | — 10,905 | — 10,905 | — 10,905 | — 10,905 | — 10,905 | — 10,905 | — 10,905 | — 10,905 |

Elected: Fitzpatrick, Dr. Dermot (F.F.); Farry, Patrick J. (F.F.); Mitchell, Jim (F.G.)

# CLONTARF ELECTORAL AREA

TOTAL ELECTORATE 37,155. VALID POLL 18,561. NO. OF MEMBERS 5. QUOTA 3,094

| Names of Candidates | First Count Votes | Second Count Transfer of Loftus' surplus Result | Third Count Transfer of Reeves' votes Result | Fourth Count Transfer of Nugent's votes Result | Fifth Count Transfer of Ó Fiacháin's votes Result | Sixth Count Transfer of Coonagh's votes Result | Seventh Count Transfer of Dooney's votes Result | Eighth Count Transfer of Rawson's votes Result | Ninth Count Transfer of Noonan's votes Result | Tenth Count Transfer of Lee's votes Result | Eleventh Count Transfer of Bruton's surplus Result |
|---|---|---|---|---|---|---|---|---|---|---|---|
| BRUTON, Richard (F.G.) | 2,393 | +45 2,438 | +8 2,446 | +26 2,472 | +53 2,525 | +121 2,646 | +69 2,715 | +157 2,872 | +205 3,077 | +1,121 4,198 | -1,104 3,094 |
| BURKE, Joe (F.F.) | 1,713 | +8 1,721 | +5 1,726 | +12 1,738 | +9 1,747 | +33 1,780 | +32 1,812 | +35 1,847 | +215 2,062 | +85 2,147 | +94 2,241 |
| CALLELY, Ivor (F.F.) | 2,792 | +30 2,822 | +4 2,826 | +42 2,868 | +59 2,927 | +54 2,981 | +51 3,032 | +78 3,110 | — 3,110 | — 3,110 | — 3,110 |
| COONAGH, Patricia | 559 | +17 576 | +10 586 | +39 625 | +45 670 | -670 — | — — | — — | — — | — — | — — |
| DOONEY, TRIONA (W.P.) | 767 | +13 780 | +6 786 | +33 819 | +16 835 | +84 919 | -919 — | — — | — — | — — | — — |
| LEE, Dr. Pat (F.G.) | 1,361 | +26 1,387 | +7 1,394 | +17 1,411 | +35 1,446 | +23 1,469 | +21 1,490 | +68 1,558 | +163 1,721 | -1,721 — | — — |
| LOFTUS, Sean Dublin Bay (Non-Party) | 3,411 | -317 3,094 | — 3,094 | — 3,094 | — 3,094 | — 3,094 | — 3,094 | — 3,094 | — 3,094 | — 3,094 | — 3,094 |
| McDOWELL, Derek (Lab.) | 1,225 | +22 1,247 | +7 1,254 | +33 1,287 | +28 1,315 | +59 1,374 | +418 1,792 | +364 2,156 | +187 2,343 | +118 2,461 | +366 2,827 |
| NOONAN, Dominic | 1,048 | +17 1,065 | +14 1,079 | +22 1,101 | +45 1,146 | +73 1,219 | +38 1,257 | +178 1,435 | -1,435 — | — — | — — |
| NUGENT, Kate (Non-Party) | 348 | +36 384 | +13 397 | -397 — | — — | — — | — — | — — | — — | — — | — — |
| O FIACHÁIN, Éamonn (Non-Party) | 376 | +37 413 | +4 417 | +53 470 | -470 — | — — | — — | — — | — — | — — | — — |
| RAWSON, Steve (G.P.) | 725 | +43 768 | +11 779 | +62 841 | +82 923 | +132 1,055 | +186 1,241 | -1,241 — | — — | — — | — — |
| REEVES, Michael John (Non-Party) | 96 | +4 100 | -100 — | — — | — — | — — | — — | — — | — — | — — | — — |
| STAFFORD, John (F.F.) | 1,747 | +19 1,766 | +7 1,773 | +21 1,794 | +46 1,840 | +27 1,867 | +31 1,898 | +68 1,966 | +258 2,224 | +189 2,413 | +126 2,539 |
| Non-transferable papers not effective | — | — — | +4 4 | +37 41 | +52 93 | +64 157 | +73 230 | +293 523 | +407 930 | +208 1,138 | +518 1,656 |
| TOTAL: | 18,561 | — 18,561 | — 18,561 | — 18,561 | — 18,561 | — 18,561 | — 18,561 | — 18,561 | — 18,561 | — 18,561 | — 18,561 |

Elected: Loftus, Sean Dublin Bay (Non-Party); Callely, Ivor (F.F.); Bruton, Richard (F.G.); McDowell, Derek (Lab.); Stafford, John (F.F.)

# CRUMLIN ELECTORAL AREA

TOTAL ELECTORATE 28,341. VALID POLL 10,469. NO. OF MEMBERS 4. QUOTA 2,094

| Names of Candidates | First Count Votes | Second Count Transfer of Mitchell's surplus Result | Third Count Transfer of Tuffy's votes Result | Fourth Count Transfer of McGovern's votes Result | Fifth Count Transfer of McGinley's votes Result | Sixth Count Transfer of Concannon's votes Result | Seventh Count Transfer of Murray's votes Result | Eighth Count Transfer of Bowers' votes Result |
|---|---|---|---|---|---|---|---|---|
| BOWERS, Mary (G.P.) | 623 | +8 631 | +2 633 | +94 727 | +47 774 | +156 930 | +16 946 | -946 — |
| BRISCOE, Ben (F.F.) | 1,477 | +13 1,490 | +107 1,597 | +25 1,622 | +47 1,669 | +51 1,720 | +186 1,906 | +121 2,027 |
| BYRNE, Eric (W.P.) | 2,081 | +19 2,100 | — 2,100 | — 2,100 | — 2,100 | — 2,100 | — 2,100 | — 2,100 |
| CONCANNON, Seamus | 401 | +4 405 | +7 412 | +40 452 | +53 505 | -505 — | — — | — — |
| CONNOLLY, Joe (Lab.) | 1,557 | +16 1,573 | +12 1,585 | +63 1,648 | +111 1,759 | +120 1,879 | +33 1,912 | +416 2,328 |
| McGINLEY, Ruairi (F.G.) | 299 | +117 416 | +11 427 | +13 440 | -440 — | — — | — — | — — |
| McGOVERN, Martin (S.F.) | 342 | +3 345 | +4 349 | -349 — | — — | — — | — — | — — |
| MITCHELL, Gay (F.G.) | 2,287 | -193 2,094 | — 2,094 | — 2,094 | — 2,094 | — 2,094 | — 2,094 | — 2,094 |
| MURRAY, Damien (F.F.) | 453 | +6 459 | +60 519 | +16 535 | +14 549 | +30 579 | -579 — | — — |
| O'MOORE, Etáin Maire (F.F.) | 617 | +5 622 | +117 739 | +19 758 | +22 780 | +32 812 | +289 1,101 | +117 1,218 |
| TUFFY, Pat (F.F.) | 332 | +2 334 | -334 — | — — | — — | — — | — — | — — |
| Non-transferable papers not effective | — | — — | +14 14 | +79 93 | +146 239 | +116 355 | +55 410 | +292 702 |
| TOTAL: | 10,469 | — 10,469 | — 10,469 | — 10,469 | — 10,469 | — 10,469 | — 10,469 | — 10,469 |

Elected: Mitchell, Gay (F.G.); Byrne, Eric (W.P.); Connolly, Joe (Lab.); Briscoe, Ben (F.F.)

# DONAGHMEDE ELECTORAL AREA

TOTAL ELECTORATE 36,307. VALID POLL 14,798. NO. OF MEMBERS 5. QUOTA 2,467

| Names of Candidates | First Count Votes | Second Count Transfer of Fitzgerald's surplus Result | Third Count Transfer of Connolly's votes Result | Fourth Count Transfer of Daly's votes Result | Fifth Count Transfer of Brady's surplus Result | Sixth Count Transfer of Pitts' votes Result | Seventh Count Transfer of Carter's votes Result | Eighth Count Transfer of Kenny's surplus Result | Ninth Count Transfer of McLoughlin's votes Result | Tenth Count Transfer of Clerkin's votes Result | Eleventh Count Transfer of Loscher's votes Result | Twelfth Count Transfer of Monaghan's votes Result | Thirteenth Count Transfer of McCartan's surplus Result |
|---|---|---|---|---|---|---|---|---|---|---|---|---|---|
| BRADY, Martin (F.F.) | 2,086 | +161 2,247 | +57 2,304 | +263 2,567 | -100 2,467 | — 2,467 | — 2,467 | — 2,467 | — 2,467 | — 2,467 | — 2,467 | — 2,467 | — 2,467 |
| CARTER, Anne (Lab.) | 675 | +14 689 | +11 700 | +18 718 | +2 720 | +31 751 | -751 — | — — | — — | — — | — — | — — | — — |
| CLERKIN, Gerry | 686 | +13 699 | +46 745 | +9 754 | +1 755 | +24 779 | +32 811 | +17 828 | +19 847 | -847 — | — — | — — | — — |
| CONNOLLY, James J. | 372 | +3 375 | -375 — | — — | — — | — — | — — | — — | — — | — — | — — | — — | — — |
| COSGRAVE, Niamh (F.G.) | 691 | +9 700 | +16 716 | +17 733 | +1 734 | +104 838 | +48 886 | +20 906 | +470 1,376 | +111 1,487 | +61 1,548 | +203 1,751 | +34 1,785 |
| DALY, Rose (F.F.) | 487 | +60 547 | +20 567 | -567 — | — — | — — | — — | — — | — — | — — | — — | — — | — — |
| FITZGERALD, Liam Joseph (F.F.) | 2,894 | -427 2,467 | — 2,467 | — 2,467 | — 2,467 | — 2,467 | — 2,467 | — 2,467 | — 2,467 | — 2,467 | — 2,467 | — 2,467 | — 2,467 |
| KENNY, Sean (Lab.) | 2,097 | +50 2,147 | +30 2,177 | +28 2,205 | +6 2,211 | +84 2,295 | +414 2,709 | -242 2,467 | — 2,467 | — 2,467 | — 2,467 | — 2,467 | — 2,467 |
| LOSCHER, Angela (W.P.) | 704 | +3 707 | +13 720 | +16 736 | +1 737 | +16 753 | +65 818 | +53 871 | +15 886 | +60 946 | -946 — | — — | — — |
| McCARTAN, Pat (W.P.) | 1,233 | +23 1,256 | +21 1,277 | +12 1,289 | +3 1,292 | +48 1,340 | +81 1,421 | +82 1,503 | +56 1,559 | +210 1,769 | +638 2,407 | +128 2,535 | -68 2,467 |
| McLOUGHLIN, Barney (F.G.) | 643 | +6 649 | +18 667 | +29 696 | +3 699 | +111 810 | +7 817 | +8 825 | -825 — | — — | — — | — — | — — |
| MONAGHAN, Brian A. (F.F.) | 773 | +67 840 | +34 874 | +120 994 | +77 1,071 | +59 1,130 | +18 1,148 | +8 1,156 | +63 1,219 | +88 1,307 | +50 1,357 | -1,357 — | — — |
| O'NEILL, Sadhbh (G.P.) | 809 | +11 820 | +41 861 | +25 886 | +5 891 | +145 1,036 | +50 1,086 | +54 1,140 | +90 1,230 | +165 1,395 | +108 1,503 | +252 1,755 | +32 1,787 |
| PITTS, Eamonn (P.D.) | 648 | +7 655 | +19 674 | +17 691 | +1 692 | -692 — | — — | — — | — — | — — | — — | — — | — — |
| Non-transferable papers not effective | — | — — | +49 49 | +13 62 | — 62 | +70 132 | +36 168 | — 168 | +112 280 | +213 493 | +89 582 | +774 1,356 | +2 1,358 |
| TOTAL: | 14,798 | — 14,798 | — 14,798 | — 14,798 | — 14,798 | — 14,798 | — 14,798 | — 14,798 | — 14,798 | — 14,798 | — 14,798 | — 14,798 | — 14,798 |

Eelected: Fitzgerald, Liam Joseph (F.F.); Brady, Martin (F.F.); Kenny, Sean (Lab.); McCartan, Pat (W.P.); O'Neill, Sadhbh (G.P.)

# DRUMCONDRA ELECTORAL AREA

TOTAL ELECTORATE 33,237. VALID POLL 14,164. NO. OF MEMBERS 5. QUOTA 2,361

| Names of Candidates | First Count Votes | Second Count Transfer of Ahern's surplus | Result | Third Count Transfer of Gormley's & E. P. Murphy's votes | Result | Fourth Count Transfer of Ó Cionnaith's votes | Result | Fifth Count Transfer of Lydon's votes | Result | Sixth Count Transfer of Fitzpatrick's votes | Result | Seventh Count Transfer of Foley's votes | Result |
|---|---|---|---|---|---|---|---|---|---|---|---|---|---|
| AHERN, Noel (F.F.) | 2,745 | -384 | 2,361 | — | 2,361 | — | 2,361 | — | 2,361 | — | 2,361 | — | 2,361 |
| BARRETT, Michael (F.F.) | 1,902 | +221 | 2,123 | +16 | 2,139 | +4 | 2,143 | +111 | 2,254 | +39 | 2,293 | +283 | 2,576 |
| BRADY, Brendan (F.G.) | 964 | +21 | 985 | +13 | 998 | +2 | 1,000 | +9 | 1,009 | +58 | 1,067 | +16 | 1,083 |
| FARRELL, Tom (F.G.) | 432 | +6 | 438 | +8 | 446 | — | 446 | +6 | 452 | +35 | 487 | +6 | 493 |
| FITZPATRICK, Terry (P.D.) | 407 | +6 | 413 | +4 | 417 | +3 | 420 | +5 | 425 | -425 | — | — | — |
| FOLEY, Mary (F.F.) | 319 | +56 | 375 | +1 | 376 | +1 | 377 | +63 | 440 | +13 | 453 | -453 | — |
| GLENN, Alice (Non-Party) | 909 | +19 | 928 | +33 | 961 | +5 | 966 | +10 | 976 | +72 | 1,048 | +31 | 1,079 |
| GORMLEY, Brian | 105 | +1 | 106 | -106 | — | — | — | — | — | — | — | — | — |
| HAMILTON, Dermot Anthony (G.P.) | 900 | +9 | 909 | +51 | 950 | +6 | 966 | +12 | 978 | +66 | 1,044 | +25 | 1,069 |
| LYDON, Peter (F.F.) | 294 | +15 | 309 | +3 | 312 | +1 | 313 | -313 | — | — | — | — | — |
| MURPHY, Eamonn Patrick | 74 | — | 74 | -74 | — | — | — | — | — | — | — | — | — |
| MURPHY, Eileen (S.F.) | 710 | +3 | 713 | +2 | 715 | +6 | 721 | +22 | 743 | +5 | 748 | +11 | 759 |
| NOLAN, Eddie (F.G.) | 518 | +5 | 523 | +4 | 527 | +3 | 530 | +8 | 538 | +22 | 560 | +11 | 571 |
| O'BRIEN, Eamonn (W.P.) | 1,091 | +5 | 1,096 | +10 | 1,106 | +222 | 1,328 | +24 | 1,352 | +18 | 1,370 | +6 | 1,376 |
| O CIONNAITH, Seán (W.P.) | 273 | +1 | 274 | +6 | 280 | -280 | — | — | — | — | — | — | — |
| O'MALLEY, Desmond (Lab.) | 942 | +2 | 944 | +8 | 952 | +11 | 963 | +25 | 988 | +20 | 1,008 | +3 | 1,011 |
| SHORTALL, Roisín (Lab.) | 1,579 | +14 | 1,593 | +10 | 1,603 | +12 | 1,615 | +8 | 1,623 | +50 | 1,673 | +24 | 1,697 |
| Non-transferable papers not effective | — | — | — | +11 | 11 | +4 | 15 | +10 | 25 | +27 | 52 | +37 | 89 |
| TOTAL: | 14,164 | — | 14,164 | — | 14,164 | — | 14,164 | — | 14,164 | — | 14,164 | — | 14,164 |

| Eighth Count Transfer of Barrett's surplus | Result | Ninth Count Transfer of Farrell's votes | Result | Tenth Count Transfer of Nolan's votes | Result | Eleventh Count Transfer of Eileen Murphy's votes | Result | Twelfth Count Transfer of O'Malley's votes | Result | Thirteenth Count Transfer of Shortall's surplus | Result | Fourteenth Count Transfer of Glenn's votes | Result |
|---|---|---|---|---|---|---|---|---|---|---|---|---|---|
| — | 2,361 | — | 2,361 | — | 2,361 | — | 2,361 | — | 2,361 | — | 2,361 | — | 2,361 |
| -215 | 2,361 | — | 2,361 | — | 2,361 | — | 2,361 | — | 2,361 | — | 2,361 | — | 2,361 |
| +19 | 1,102 | +242 | 1,344 | +419 | 1,763 | +15 | 1,778 | +34 | 1,812 | +11 | 1,823 | +358 | 2,181 |
| +6 | 499 | -499 | — | — | — | — | — | — | — | — | — | — | — |
| — | — | — | — | — | — | — | — | — | — | — | — | — | — |
| — | — | — | — | — | — | — | — | — | — | — | — | — | — |
| +39 | 1,118 | +40 | 1,158 | +60 | 1,218 | +69 | 1,287 | +26 | 1,313 | +7 | 1,320 | -1,320 | — |
| — | — | — | — | — | — | — | — | — | — | — | — | — | — |
| +23 | 1,092 | +30 | 1,122 | +44 | 1,166 | +122 | 1,288 | +55 | 1,343 | +15 | 1,358 | +347 | 1,705 |
| — | — | — | — | — | — | — | — | — | — | — | — | — | — |
| — | — | — | — | — | — | — | — | — | — | — | — | — | — |
| +8 | 767 | +4 | 771 | +2 | 773 | -773 | — | — | — | — | — | — | — |
| +7 | 578 | +92 | 670 | -670 | — | — | — | — | — | — | — | — | — |
| +3 | 1,379 | +18 | 1,397 | +26 | 1,423 | +158 | 1,581 | +280 | 1,861 | +52 | 1,913 | +99 | 2,012 |
| — | — | — | — | — | — | — | — | — | — | — | — | — | — |
| +2 | 1,013 | +6 | 1,019 | +19 | 1,038 | +171 | 1,209 | -1,209 | — | — | — | — | — |
| +14 | 1,711 | +38 | 1,749 | +57 | 1,806 | +46 | 1,852 | +594 | 2,446 | -85 | 2,361 | — | 2,361 |
| +94 | 183 | +29 | 212 | +43 | 255 | +192 | 447 | +220 | 667 | — | 667 | +516 | 1,183 |
| — | 14,164 | — | 14,164 | — | 14,164 | — | 14,164 | — | 14,164 | — | 14,164 | — | 14,164 |

Elected: Ahern, Noel (F.F.); Barrett, Michael (F.F.); Shortall, Roisín (Lab.); Brady, Brendan (F.G.); O'Brien, Eamonn (W.P.).

# FINGLAS ELECTORAL AREA

TOTAL ELECTORATE 25,496. VALID POLL 12,002. NO. OF MEMBERS 4. QUOTA 2,401

| Names of Candidates | First Count Votes | Second Count Transfer of Carey's and Clarke's surplus votes Result | Third Count Transfer of Atkinson's votes Result | Fourth Count Transfer of Keegan's votes Result | Fifth Count Transfer of Wilson's votes Result | Sixth Count Transfer of Doolan's votes Result | Seventh Count Transfer of Fisher's votes Result | Eighth Count Transfer of Cloak's votes Result | Ninth Count Transfer of Jordan's votes Result | Tenth Count Transfer of Meagher's votes Result | Eleventh Count Transfer of Fleming's votes Result | Twelfth Count Transfer of Grant's votes Result | Thirteenth Count Transfer of Rock's votes Result |
|---|---|---|---|---|---|---|---|---|---|---|---|---|---|
| ATKINSON, Brendan | 45 | +1 46 | -46 — | — — | — — | — — | — — | — — | — — | — — | — — | — — | — — |
| CAREY, Pat (F.F.) | 2,774 | -373 2,401 | — 2,401 | — 2,401 | — 2,401 | — 2,401 | — 2,401 | — 2,401 | — 2,401 | — 2,401 | — 2,401 | — 2,401 | — 2,401 |
| CLARKE, Frank (Non-Party) | 32 | +3 35 | -35 — | — — | — — | — — | — — | — — | — — | — — | — — | — — | — — |
| CLOAK, Noel (F.F.) | 251 | +66 317 | +13 330 | +2 332 | +1 333 | +5 338 | +18 356 | -356 — | — — | — — | — — | — — | — — |
| DOOLAN, Gerard (Non-Party) | 147 | +3 150 | +15 165 | +17 182 | +1 183 | -183 — | — — | — — | — — | — — | — — | — — | — — |
| FISHER, Lily | 258 | +5 263 | +7 270 | +6 276 | +3 279 | +17 296 | -296 — | — — | — — | — — | — — | — — | — — |
| FLAHERTY, Mary (F.G.) | 1,359 | +34 1,393 | +6 1,399 | +9 1,408 | +63 1,471 | +21 1,492 | +50 1,542 | +46 1,588 | +16 1,604 | +85 1,689 | +52 1,741 | +146 1,887 | +350 2,237 |
| FLEMING, Harry (S.F.) | 921 | +21 942 | +3 945 | +9 954 | +1 955 | +7 962 | +5 967 | +16 983 | +14 997 | +35 1,032 | -1,032 — | — — | — — |
| GRANT, Pat (F.F.) | 852 | +71 923 | +7 930 | +6 936 | +2 938 | +11 949 | +42 991 | +126 1,117 | +16 1,133 | +36 1,169 | +97 1,266 | -1,266 — | — — |
| JORDAN, Samuel (W.P.) | 465 | +12 477 | +5 482 | +8 490 | +1 491 | +10 501 | +8 509 | +9 518 | -518 — | — — | — — | — — | — — |
| KEEGAN, Billy (Non-Party) | 83 | +4 87 | +3 90 | -90 — | — — | — — | — — | — — | — — | — — | — — | — — | — — |
| MEAGHER, Aidan (G.P.) | 550 | +9 559 | +3 562 | +7 569 | +7 576 | +19 595 | +53 648 | +6 654 | +26 680 | -680 — | — — | — — | — — |
| O'NEILL, Lucia (W.P.) | 880 | +16 896 | +1 897 | +11 908 | +7 915 | +6 921 | +12 933 | +8 941 | +354 1,295 | +164 1,459 | +196 1,655 | +103 1,758 | +131 1,889 |
| ROCK, Barney (P.D.) | 940 | +19 959 | +4 963 | +5 968 | +20 988 | +27 1,015 | +30 1,045 | +30 1,075 | +19 1,094 | +94 1,188 | +113 1,301 | +122 1,423 | -1,423 — |
| TAAFFE, Tony (F.F.) | 1,228 | +84 1,312 | +6 1,318 | +5 1,323 | +9 1,332 | +12 1,344 | +33 1,377 | +69 1,446 | +16 1,462 | +44 1,506 | +110 1,616 | +531 2,147 | +246 2,393 |
| TORMEY, Bill (Lab.) | 1,090 | +23 1,113 | +2 1,115 | +3 1,118 | +11 1,129 | +23 1,152 | +15 1,167 | +14 1,181 | +27 1,208 | +98 1,306 | +138 1,444 | +69 1,513 | +295 1,808 |
| WILSON, Miriam (F.G.) | 127 | +2 129 | +1 130 | +1 131 | -131 — | — — | — — | — — | — — | — — | — — | — — | — — |
| Non-transferable papers not effective:- | — | — | +5 5 | +1 6 | +5 11 | +25 36 | +30 66 | +32 98 | +30 128 | +124 252 | +326 578 | +295 873 | +401 1,274 |
| TOTAL: | 12,002 | — 12,002 | — 12,002 | — 12,002 | — 12,002 | — 12,002 | — 12,002 | — 12,002 | — 12,002 | — 12,002 | — 12,002 | — 12,002 | — 12,002 |

Elected: Carey, Pat (F.F.); Taaffe, Tony (F.F.); Flaherty, Mary (F.G.); O'Neill, Lucia (W.P.)

# NORTH INNER CITY ELECTORAL AREA

TOTAL ELECTORATE 28,917. VALID POLL 12,715. NO. OF MEMBERS 5. QUOTA 2,120

| Names of Candidates | First Count Votes | Second Count Transfer of Gregory's surplus Result | Third Count Transfer of Dillon's votes Result | Fourth Count Transfer of Kearney's votes Result | Fifth Count Transfer of Lowth's votes Result | Sixth Count Transfer of Allen's votes Result | Seventh Count Transfer of Beggs' votes Result | Eighth Count Transfer of McKenna's votes Result | Ninth Count Transfer of Healy's votes Result |
|---|---|---|---|---|---|---|---|---|---|
| ALLEN, Tom (P.D.) | 396 | +101 497 | +5 502 | +7 509 | +52 561 | -561 — | — — | — — | — — |
| BEGGS, Ernie (F.F.) | 593 | +88 681 | +3 684 | +10 694 | +7 701 | +58 759 | -759 — | — — | — — |
| BURKE, Christy (S.F.) | 1,437 | +433 1,870 | +11 1,881 | +28 1,909 | +44 1,953 | +62 2,015 | +101 2,116 | +73 2,189 | — 2,189 |
| COSTELLO, Joe (Lab.) | 1,103 | +348 1,451 | +11 1,462 | +21 1,483 | +43 1,526 | +96 1,622 | +53 1,675 | +224 1,899 | +347 2,246 |
| DILLON, Erick | 71 | +47 118 | -118 — | — — | — — | — — | — — | — — | — — |
| GREGORY, Tony | 4,094 | -1,974 2,120 | — 2,120 | — 2,120 | — 2,120 | — 2,120 | — 2,120 | — 2,120 | — 2,120 |
| HEALY, Deirdre (F.G.) | 603 | +99 702 | +9 711 | +153 864 | +16 880 | +61 941 | +23 964 | +99 1,063 | -1,063 — |
| JENNINGS, Mike (W.P.) | 711 | +238 949 | +8 957 | +15 972 | +29 1,001 | +38 1,039 | +40 (1,079 | +169 1,248 | +105 1,353 |
| KEARNEY, Dave (F.G.) | 253 | +37 290 | +2 292 | -292 — | — — | — — | — — | — — | — — |
| KETT, Tony (F.F.) | 1,545 | +163 1,708 | +1 1,709 | +18 1,727 | +24 1,751 | +55 1,806 | +330 2,136 | — 2,136 | — 2,136 |
| LOWTH, Tony | 257 | +100 357 | +27 384 | +8 392 | -392 — | — — | — — | — — | — — |
| McKENNA, Patricia (G.P.) | 499 | +144 643 | +17 660 | +11 671 | +85 756 | +50 806 | +24 830 | -830 — | — — |
| STAFFORD, Thomas (F.F.) | 1,153 | +176 1,329 | +12 1,341 | +11 1,352 | +40 1,392 | +63 1,455 | +130 1,585 | +72 1,657 | +155 1,812 |
| Non-transferable papers not effective | — | — — | +12 12 | +10 22 | +52 74 | +78 152 | +58 210 | +193 403 | +456 859 |
| TOTAL: | 12,715 | — 12,715 | — 12,715 | — 12,715 | — 12,715 | — 12,715 | — 12,715 | — 12,715 | — 12,715 |

Elected: Gregory, Tony; Kett, Tony (F.F.); Burke, Christy (S.F.); Costello, Joe (Lab.); Stafford, Thomas (F.F.)

## PEMBROKE ELECTORAL AREA

TOTAL ELECTORATE 33,502. VALID POLL 13,585. NO. OF MEMBERS 4. QUOTA 2,718

| Names of Candidates | First Count Votes | Second Count Transfer of Hederman's surplus Result | Third Count Transfer of Merriman's votes Result | Fourth Count Transfer of Ó Snodaigh's votes Result | Fifth Count Transfer of Murphy's votes Result | Sixth Count Transfer of Byrne's votes Result | Seventh Count Transfer of Crilly's votes Result | Eighth Count Transfer of Egan's votes Result | Ninth Count Transfer of O'Loughlin's votes Result | Tenth Count Transfer of Ryan's surplus Result | Eleventh Count Transfer of Crowley's votes Result | Twelfth Count Transfer of Doyle's surplus Result |
|---|---|---|---|---|---|---|---|---|---|---|---|---|
| BYRNE, Kathryn (F.F.) | 687 | +23 710 | +4 714 | +12 726 | +4 730 | -730 — | — — | — — | — — | — — | — — | — — |
| CRILLY, Tom (W.P.) | 486 | +9 495 | +2 497 | +15 512 | +224 736 | +18 754 | -754 — | — — | — — | — — | — — | — — |
| CROWLEY, Jeananne (P.D.) | 1,045 | +85 1,130 | +7 1,137 | +5 1,142 | +10 1,152 | +51 1,203 | +32 1,235 | +96 1,331 | +35 1,366 | +85 1,451 | -1,451 — | — — |
| DOYLE, Joe (F.G.) | 1,673 | +71 1,744 | +8 1,752 | +2 1,754 | +12 1,766 | +42 1,808 | +63 1,871 | +579 2,450 | +86 2,536 | +126 2,662 | +419 3,081 | -363 2,718 |
| EGAN, William (F.G.) | 814 | +39 853 | — 853 | +2 855 | +3 858 | +20 878 | +22 900 | -900 — | — — | — — | — — | — — |
| HEDERMAN, Carmencita (Non-Party) | 3,126 | -408 2,718 | — 2,718 | — 2,718 | — 2,718 | — 2,718 | — 2,718 | — 2,718 | — 2,718 | — 2,718 | — 2,718 | — 2,718 |
| LACEY, Dermot (Lab.) | 1,478 | +35 1,513 | +6 1,519 | +25 1,544 | +20 1,564 | +22 1,586 | +248 1,834 | +52 1,886 | +51 1,937 | +45 1,982 | +177 2,159 | +128 2,287 |
| MERRIMAN, Jim (Non-Party) | 42 | +16 58 | -58 — | — — | — — | — — | — — | — — | — — | — — | — — | — — |
| MURPHY, Angie (W.P.) | 321 | +6 327 | +2 329 | +10 339 | -339 — | — — | — — | — — | — — | — — | — — | — — |
| O'LOUGHLIN, Ciaran (F.F.) | 857 | +13 870 | +4 874 | +20 894 | +9 903 | +286 1,189 | +20 1,209 | +30 1,239 | -1,239 — | — — | — — | — — |
| O SNODAIGH, Aengus (S.F.) | 220 | +2 222 | — 222 | -222 — | — — | — — | — — | — — | — — | — — | — — | — — |
| RYAN, Eoin (F.F.) | 1,776 | +33 1,809 | +3 1,812 | +20 1,832 | +23 1,855 | +233 2,088 | +74 2,162 | +36 2,198 | +916 3,114 | -396 2,718 | — 2,718 | — 2,718 |
| WHEELER, Claire (G.P.) | 1,060 | +76 1,136 | +17 1,153 | +85 1,238 | +26 1,264 | +31 1,295 | +136 1,431 | +60 1,491 | +50 1,541 | +114 1,655 | +524 2,179 | +145 2,324 |
| Non-transferable papers not effective | — | — — | +5 5 | +26 31 | +8 39 | +27 66 | +159 225 | +47 272 | +101 373 | +26 399 | +331 730 | +90 820 |
| TOTAL: | 13,585 | — 13,585 | — 13,585 | — 13,585 | — 13,585 | — 13,585 | — 13,585 | — 13,585 | — 13,585 | — 13,585 | — 13,585 | — 13,585 |

Elected: Hederman, Carmencita (Non-Party); Ryan, Eoin (F.F.); Doyle, Joe (F.G.); Wheeler, Claire (G.P.)

# RATHMINES ELECTORAL AREA

TOTAL ELECTORATE 30,397. VALID POLL 11,111. NO. OF MEMBERS 4. QUOTA 2,223

| Names of Candidates | First Count Votes | Second Count Transfer of Richards' votes | Result | Third Count Transfer of Canney's votes | Result | Fourth Count Transfer of Chambers' votes | Result | Fifth Count Transfer of Mooney's votes | Result | Sixth Count Transfer of McShane's votes | Result | Seventh Count Transfer of Cosgrave's votes | Result | Eighth Count Transfer of Allen's votes | Result | Ninth Count Transfer of Hanafin's votes | Result |
|---|---|---|---|---|---|---|---|---|---|---|---|---|---|---|---|---|---|
| ALLEN, Jim (W.P.) | 1,113 | +3 | 1,116 | +14 | 1,130 | +43 | 1,173 | +9 | 1,182 | +29 | 1,211 | +31 | 1,242 | -1,242 | — | — | — |
| CANNEY, Mick | 118 | +4 | 122 | -122 | — | — | — | — | — | — | — | — | — | — | — | — | — |
| CHAMBERS, Padraig (Non-Party) | 256 | +27 | 283 | +21 | 304 | -304 | — | — | — | — | — | — | — | — | — | — | — |
| COSGRAVE, Terry (F.G.) | 757 | +3 | 760 | +4 | 764 | +20 | 784 | +3 | 787 | +114 | 901 | -901 | — | — | — | — | — |
| DONNELLY, Michael (F.F.) | 1,985 | +9 | 1,994 | +2 | 1,996 | +40 | 2,036 | +122 | 2,158 | +51 | 2,209 | +53 | 2,262 | — | 2,262 | — | 2,262 |
| FREEHILL, Mary (Lab.) | 1,188 | +6 | 1,194 | +19 | 1,213 | +48 | 1,261 | +7 | 1,268 | +33 | 1,301 | +75 | 1,376 | +566 | 1,942 | +140 | 2,082 |
| GORMLEY, John (G.P.) | 1,302 | +10 | 1,312 | +44 | 1,356 | +71 | 1,427 | +8 | 1,435 | +22 | 1,457 | +54 | 1,511 | +290 | 1,801 | +173 | 1,974 |
| HANAFIN, Mary (F.F.) | 1,083 | +3 | 1,086 | +4 | 1,090 | +7 | 1,097 | +128 | 1,225 | +24 | 1,249 | +33 | 1,282 | +99 | 1,381 | -1,381 | — |
| McSHANE, Michael (F.G.) | 507 | +1 | 508 | +1 | 509 | +9 | 518 | +4 | 522 | -522 | — | — | — | — | — | — | — |
| MANNING, Maurice (F.G.) | 777 | — | 777 | +1 | 778 | +10 | 788 | +3 | 791 | +208 | 999 | +560 | 1,559 | +46 | 1,605 | +137 | 1,742 |
| MOONEY, Derek Simon (F.F.) | 309 | +3 | 312 | — | 312 | +5 | 317 | -317 | — | — | — | — | — | — | — | — | — |
| O'DONNELL, Liz (P.D.) | 1,635 | +6 | 1,641 | +9 | 1,650 | +21 | 1,671 | +24 | 1,695 | +28 | 1,723 | +74 | 1,797 | +93 | 1,890 | +264 | 2,154 |
| RICHARDS, Harry | 81 | -81 | — | — | — | — | — | — | — | — | — | — | — | — | — | — | — |
| Non-transferable papers not effective | — | +6 | 6 | +3 | 9 | +30 | 39 | +9 | 48 | +13 | 61 | +21 | 82 | +148 | 230 | +667 | 897 |
| TOTAL: | 11,111 | — | 11,111 | — | 11,111 | — | 11,111 | — | 11,111 | — | 11,111 | — | 11,111 | — | 11,111 | — | 11,111 |

Eelected: Donnelly, Michael (F.F.); O'Donnell, Liz (P.D.); Freehill, Mary (Lab.); Gormley, John (G.P.)

# SOUTH INNER CITY ELECTORAL AREA

TOTAL ELECTORATE 28,161. VALID POLL 10,651. NO. OF MEMBERS 5. QUOTA 1,776

| Names of Candidates | First Count Votes | Second Count Transfer of Merriman's votes | Result | Third Count Transfer of Doyle's votes | Result | Fourth Count Transfer of Gray's votes | Result | Fifth Count Transfer of Dunne's votes | Result | Sixth Count Transfer of Smith's votes | Result | Seventh Count Transfer of Gallagher's votes | Result | Eighth Count Transfer of Ó Muireagáin's votes | Result | Ninth Count Transfer of Burke's votes | Result |
|---|---|---|---|---|---|---|---|---|---|---|---|---|---|---|---|---|---|
| BURKE, Peter (F.G.) | 812 | — | 812 | +5 | 817 | +207 | 1,024 | +6 | 1,030 | +20 | 1,050 | +52 | 1,102 | +34 | 1,136 | -1,136 | — |
| CUFFE, Ciarán (G.P.) | 1,141 | +2 | 1,143 | +7 | 1,150 | +36 | 1,186 | +11 | 1,197 | +30 | 1,227 | +123 | 1,350 | +200 | 1,550 | +239 | 1,789 |
| DOYLE, Christy (Non-Party) | 71 | +2 | 73 | -73 | — | — | — | — | — | — | — | — | — | — | — | — | — |
| DUNNE, Gerry (F.F.) | 429 | +3 | 432 | +2 | 434 | +10 | 444 | -444 | — | — | — | — | — | — | — | — | — |
| GALLAGHER, John | 788 | +1 | 789 | +11 | 800 | +8 | 808 | +12 | 820 | +3 | 823 | -823 | — | — | — | — | — |
| GRAY, Bernadette (F.G.) | 396 | — | 396 | +9 | 405 | -405 | — | — | — | — | — | — | — | — | — | — | — |
| LYNCH, Brendan (Non-Party) | 1,165 | +7 | 1,172 | +9 | 1,181 | +27 | 1,208 | +13 | 1,221 | +9 | 1,230 | +175 | 1,405 | +113 | 1,518 | +145 | 1,663 |
| MERRIMAN, Jim (Non-Party) | 22 | -22 | — | — | — | — | — | — | — | — | — | — | — | — | — | — | — |
| MOONEY, Mary (F.F.) | 1,102 | +2 | 1,104 | +2 | 1,106 | +30 | 1,136 | +219 | 1,355 | +43 | 1,398 | +125 | 1,523 | +93 | 1,616 | +101 | 1,717 |
| MULCAHY, Michael (F.F.) | 1,223 | +1 | 1,224 | +4 | 1,228 | +22 | 1,250 | +137 | 1,387 | +43 | 1,430 | +58 | 1,488 | +114 | 1,602 | +86 | 1,688 |
| O'CONNOR, Brian (W.P.) | 778 | +1 | 779 | +2 | 781 | +8 | 789 | +3 | 792 | +320 | 1,112 | +82 | 1,194 | +165 | 1,359 | +63 | 1,422 |
| Ó MUIREAGÁIN, Micheal (S.F.) | 909 | — | 909 | +6 | 915 | +3 | 918 | +6 | 924 | +42 | 966 | +76 | 1,042 | -1,042 | — | — | — |
| QUINN, Ruairi (Lab.) | 1,215 | +1 | 1,216 | +5 | 1,221 | +40 | 1,261 | +15 | 1,276 | +93 | 1,369 | +87 | 1,456 | +139 | 1,595 | +285 | 1,880 |
| SMITH, Andy (W.P.) | 600 | +1 | 601 | +3 | 604 | +6 | 610 | +1 | 611 | -611 | — | — | — | — | — | — | |
| Non-transferable papers not effective | — | +1 | 1 | +8 | 9 | +8 | 17 | +21 | 38 | +8 | 46 | +45 | 91 | +184 | 275 | +217 | 492 |
| TOTAL: | 10,651 | — | 10,651 | — | 10,651 | — | 10,651 | — | 10,651 | — | 10,651 | — | 10,651 | — | 10,651 | — | 10,651 |

Elected: Quinn, Ruairi (Lab.); Cuffe, Ciaran (G.P.); Mooney, Mary (F.F.); Mulcahy, Michael (F.F.); Lynch, Brendan (Non-Party)

# DUBLIN
# COUNTY COUNCIL

## FINGAL RESULTS

| PARTY | 1991 % of votes | 1991 Seats obtained | 1985 % of votes | 1985 Seat obtained |
|---|---|---|---|---|
| Fianna Fail | 33.0 | 20 | 41.8 | 26 |
| Fine Gael | 14.0 | 6 | 20.0 | 13 |
| Labour | 12.8 | 10 | 9.0 | 2 |
| Progressive Dem. | 3.4 | 1 | — | — |
| Workers Party | 9.4 | 5 | 9.4 | 6 |
| Other | 27.4 | 10 | 19.8 | 5 |
| TOTAL SEATS | | 52 | | 52 |

## DUBLIN FINGAL

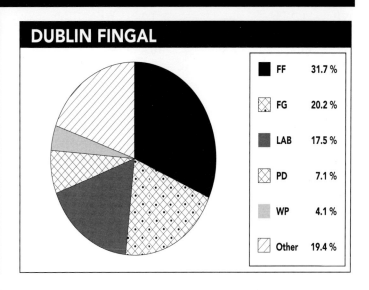

| | |
|---|---|
| ■ FF | 31.7 % |
| ⊠ FG | 20.2 % |
| ■ LAB | 17.5 % |
| ⊠ PD | 7.1 % |
| WP | 4.1 % |
| ⧄ Other | 19.4 % |

## DUN LAOGHAIRE RESULTS

| PARTY | 1991 % of votes | 1991 Seats obtained | 1985 % of votes | 1985 Seat obtained |
|---|---|---|---|---|
| Fianna Fail | 30.3 | 8 | 38.1 | 13 |
| Fine Gael | 23.8 | 7 | 34.1 | 11 |
| Labour | 12.6 | 5 | 12.1 | 3 |
| Progressive Dem. | 8.2 | 2 | — | — |
| Workers Party | 10.9 | 3 | 4.6 | 1 |
| Other | 14.2 | 3 | 11.1 | — |
| TOTAL SEATS | | 28 | | 28 |

## SOUTH DUBLIN RESULTS

| PARTY | 1991 % of votes | 1991 Seats obtained | 1985 % of votes | 1985 Seat obtained |
|---|---|---|---|---|
| Fianna Fail | 29.1 | 7 | 42.1 | 13 |
| Fine Gael | 18.5 | 6 | 25.3 | 8 |
| Labour | 17.4 | 4 | 12.0 | 2 |
| Progressive Dem. | 9.1 | 4 | — | — |
| Workers Party | 8.7 | 3 | 7.1 | 2 |
| Other | 17.2 | 2 | 13.5 | 1 |
| TOTAL SEATS | | 26 | | 26 |

## BALBRIGGAN

| | 1991 | 1985 | '85 to '91 Swing |
|---|---|---|---|
| FF | 35.4 | 43.2 | -7.8 |
| FG | 11.1 | 26.8 | -15.7 |
| Lab | 23.2 | 16.1 | 7.1 |
| WP | 1.2 | — | 1.2 |
| PD | 5.5 | — | 5.5 |
| GP | 13.2 | 2.8 | 10.4 |
| SF | — | 3.9 | -3.9 |
| Ind | 10.4 | 7.2 | 3.2 |

BOLAND, Cathal,
10 Churchfield Lawns, Skerries,
County Dublin. (FG)
Manager. 01-491008

FARRELL, Ken,
Chapel Lane, The Green, Lusk,
County Dublin. (Lab)
Station Foreman.

GILBRIDE, Sean,
18 Greenlawns, Skerries,
County Dublin. (FF)
Teacher. 01-490253

LARKIN, Jack,
39 Dublin Street, Balbriggan,
County Dublin. (FF)
Auctioneer. 01-411006

SARGENT, Trevor,
37 Tara Cove, Balbriggan,
County Dublin. (GP)
Teacher. 01-412371

## CASTLEKNOCK

| | 1991 | 1985 | '85 to '91 Swing |
|---|---|---|---|
| FF | 26.9 | 43.8 | -16.9 |
| FG | 27.9 | 32.8 | -4.9 |
| Lab | 4.1 | 4.3 | -0.2 |
| WP | 2.6 | 3.9 | -1.3 |
| PD | 14.7 | — | 14.7 |
| GP | 5.3 | 2.5 | 2.8 |
| Ind | 18.5 | 12.7 | 5.8 |

LYONS, Sean,
30 Coolmine Woods, Clonsilla,
Blanchardstown,
County Dublin. (NP)
Teacher. 01-213116

MORRISSEY, Tom,
34 Castleknock View, Castleknock,
Dublin 15. (FG)
Company Director.

RYAN, Ned,
95 Castleknock Park, Castleknock,
Dublin 15. (FF)
Company Director. 01-214213

TERRY, Sheila,
65 College Grove, Castleknock,
Dublin 15. (PD)
Housewife. 01-214169

## HOWTH

| | 1991 | 1985 | '85 to '91 Swing |
|---|---|---|---|
| FF | 27.9 | 39.0 | -11.1 |
| FG | 32.7 | 37.7 | -5.0 |
| Lab | 6.5 | 3.3 | 3.2 |
| WP | 9.2 | 3.8 | 5.4 |
| PD | 13.3 | — | 13.3 |
| GP | 10.4 | 2.3 | 8.1 |
| Ind | — | 13.9 | -13.9 |

COSGRAVE, Michael J.,
22 College Street, Baldoyle,
Dublin 13. (FG)
Dáil Deputy. 01-322554

CREAVEN, Liam,
43 St. Fintans Park, Sutton,
Dublin 13. (FF)
Newsagent. 01-325379

HEALY, David,
54 Evora Park, Howth,
County Dublin. (GP)
Weaver.

MAHER, Joan,
19 Bayside Square East, Sutton,
Dublin 13. (FG)
Public Representative. 01-324291

## MALAHIDE

| | 1991 | 1985 | '85 to '91 Swing |
|---|---|---|---|
| FF | 39.8 | 49.0 | -9.2 |
| FG | 24.3 | 22.9 | 1.4 |
| Lab | 14.4 | 15.7 | -1.3 |
| PD | 8.9 | — | 8.9 |
| GP | 9.7 | — | 9.7 |
| Ind | 2.9 | 12.4 | -9.5 |

KENNEDY, Michael,
84 The Dunes, Portmarnock,
County Dublin. (FF)
Insurance Broker.

MALONE, Bernie,
Elmhill, Grove Road, Malahide,
County Dublin. (Lab)
Solicitor. 01-453085

OWEN, Nora,
17 Ard na Mara, Malahide,
County Dublin. (FG)
Dail Deputy. 01-451041

WRIGHT, G.V.,
58 The Moorings, Malahide,
County Dublin. (FF)
Senator. 01-452642

Trevor Sargent (Greens)
Fingal

Marian McGennis (FF)
Fingal

Eamon Gilmore (DL)
Dun Laoghaire/Rathdown

Colm Breatnach (DL)
Dun Laoghaire/Rathdown

## MULHUDDART

|     | 1991 | 1985 | '85 to '91 Swing |
| --- | ---- | ---- | ---------------- |
| FF  | 25.2 | 42.5 | -17.3 |
| FG  | 17.8 | 28.2 | -10.4 |
| Lab | 12.9 | 2.9  | 10.0 |
| WP  | 10.3 | 15.1 | -4.8 |
| GP  | 2.6  | —    | 2.6 |
| SF  | 4.0  | —    | 4.0 |
| Ind | 27.1 | 11.3 | 15.8 |

BURTON, Joan,
81 Old Cabra Road,
Dublin 7. (Lab)
Lecturer. 01-388711

HIGGINS, Joe,
Orchard Avenue, Clonsilla,
County Dublin. (NP)
Office Worker. 01-201753

McGENNIS, Marian,
204 Edgewood Lawn, Blanchardstown,
Dublin 15. (FF)
Public Representative.

## SWORDS

|     | 1991 | 1985 | '85 to '91 Swing |
| --- | ---- | ---- | ---------------- |
| FF  | 31.3 | 54.6 | -23.3 |
| FG  | 10.7 | 18.2 | -7.5 |
| Lab | 40.6 | 20.6 | 20.0 |
| WP  | 4.0  | —    | 4.0 |
| GP  | 6.7  | —    | 6.7 |
| Ind | 6.7  | 6.6  | 0.1 |

DEVITT, Anne,
Lispopple, Swords,
County Dublin. (FG)
Teacher. 01-404280

GALLAGHER, Cyril,
16 Glasmore Park, Swords,
County Dublin. (FF)
Technician. 01-403329

KELLEHER, Tom,
4 Highfield Downs, Swords,
County Dublin. (Lab)
Teacher. 01-402425

RYAN, Sean,
1 Burrow Road, Portrane, Donabate,
County Dublin. (Lab)
Dáil Deputy. 01-436254

## CLONDALKIN

|     | 1991 | 1985 | '85 to '91 Swing |
| --- | ---- | ---- | ---------------- |
| FF  | 33.4 | 53.8 | -20.4 |
| FG  | 18.3 | 17.3 | 1.0 |
| Lab | 8.3  | 9.9  | -1.6 |
| WP  | 8.9  | 6.7  | 2.2 |
| PD  | 17.7 | —    | 17.7 |
| GP  | 4.5  | 1.5  | 3.0 |
| SF  | 2.4  | 7.3  | -4.9 |
| Ind | 9.3  | 12   | -2.7 |

McGRATH, Colm,
2 Moyle Park, Clondalkin,
Dublin 22. (FF)
Businessman.

RIDGE, Therese,
4 St. Patricks Avenue, Clondalkin,
Dublin 22. (FG)
Public Representative. 01-592164

TYNDALL, Colm,
15 St. Brigids Drive, Clondalkin,
Dublin 22. (PD)
Insurance Broker. 01-591376

## GREENHILLS

|     | 1991 | 1985 | '85 to '91 Swing |
| --- | ---- | ---- | ---------------- |
| FF  | 23.8 | 42.5 | -18.7 |
| FG  | 14.3 | 19.2 | -4.9 |
| Lab | 31.8 | 6.4  | 25.4 |
| WP  | 13.8 | 11.1 | 2.7 |
| GP  | 4.5  | 1.5  | 3.0 |
| SF  | 2.4  | 7.3  | -4.9 |
| Ind | 9.3  | 12   | -2.7 |

FARRELL, Margaret,
6 St. Aongus Crescent,
Tymon North, Tallaght,
Dublin 24. (FF)
Housewife.

KEATING, Michael,
26 Tamerisk Park, Kilnamanagh,
Dublin 24. (FG)
Public Representative.

TAYLOR, Mervyn,
4 Springfield Road, Templeogue,
Dublin 6. (Lab)
Dáil Deputy.

TIPPING, Don,
20 St. Anthony's Crescent,
Walkinstown,
Dublin 12. (Elected WP, now DL)
Telecom Employee.

## LUCAN

|     | 1991 | 1985 | '85 to '91 Swing |
| --- | ---- | ---- | ---------------- |
| FF  | 26.3 | 39.9 | -13.6 |
| FG  | 16.6 | 30.5 | -13.9 |
| Lab | 21.2 | 16.6 | 4.6 |
| WP  | 6.7  | 10.4 | -3.7 |
| GP  | 5.0  | 1.7  | 3.3 |
| SF  | 7.9  | —    | 7.9 |
| Ind | 16.2 | 0.9  | 15.3 |

**Betty Coffey (FF)**
**Dun Laoghaire/Rathdown**

**Larry Gordon (Greens)**
**Dun Laoghaire/Rathdown**

**Niamh Bhreathnach (Lab)**
**Dun Laoghaire/Rathdown**

**Joan Burton (Lab)**
**Fingal**

BRADY, Peter,
43 Dodsboro, Lucan,
County Dublin. (FG)
Company Manager.

HANRAHAN, Finbarr,
"Ardagh", Main Road, Lucan,
County Dublin. (FF)
Teacher. 01-6281710

O'CONNELL, Gus,
47 Palmerstown Green, Palmerstown,
Dublin 20. (NP)
Training Manager.

O'HALLORAN, John,
19 St. Marks Grove, Rowlagh,
Dublin 22. (Lab)
Baker. 01-6262299

### RATHFARNHAM

|     | 1991 | 1985 | '85 to '91 Swing |
|-----|------|------|------|
| FF  | 35.4 | 43.1 | -7.7 |
| FG  | 28.3 | 38.2 | -9.9 |
| Lab | 4.6  | 5.9  | -1.3 |
| PD  | 8.6  | —    | 8.6  |
| GP  | 14.0 | 5.9  | 8.1  |
| Ind | 9.1  | 6.9  | 2.2  |

MULDOON, Mary,
'Run na Gaoithe',
34A Dargle Wood, Knocklyon,
Dublin 16. (FG)
Teacher. 01-946601

MULLARNEY, Máire,
Millhouse,
Whitechurch Road, Rathfarnham,
Dublin 14. (GP)
Journalist. 01-931219

ORMONDE, Ann,
28 Home Villas,
Dublin 4. (FF)
Teacher. 01-687896

SHATTER, Alan,
57 Delbrook Manor, Dundrum,
Dublin 16. (FG)
Dail Deputy. 01-610317

### TALLAGHT/OLDBAWN

|     | 1991 | 1985 | '85 to '91 Swing |
|-----|------|------|------|
| FF  | 30.4 | 43.5 | -13.1 |
| FG  | 13.5 | 22.4 | -8.9 |
| Lab | 18.9 | 7.0  | 11.9 |
| WP  | 13.5 | 6.0  | 7.5  |
| PD  | 12.7 | —    | 12.7 |
| GP  | 3.7  | 2.1  | 1.6  |
| SF  | 5.7  | 9.5  | -3.8 |
| Ind | 1.8  | 9.5  | -7.7 |

CASS, Breda,
40 Monalea Wood, Firhouse,
Dublin 24. (PD)
Housewife. 01-516892

HANNON, John,
11 Knocklyon Heights, Firhouse Road,
Dublin 16. (FF)
Company Director. 01-942045

RABBITTE, Pat,
56 Monastery Drive,
Dublin 22. (Elected WP, now DL)
Dáil Deputy. 01-593191

### TALLAGHT/RATHCOOLE

|     | 1991 | 1985 | '85 to '91 Swing |
|-----|------|------|------|
| FF  | 29.6 | 35.2 | -5.6 |
| FG  | 9.3  | 10.7 | -1.4 |
| Lab | 11.6 | 22.5 | -10.9 |
| WP  | 20.3 | 14.5 | 5.8  |
| PD  | 16.8 | —    | 16.8 |
| GP  | —    | 0.9  | -0.9 |
| SF  | 6.4  | 12.6 | -6.2 |
| Ind | 6.0  | 3.6  | 2.4  |

BILLANE, Mick,
17 Bawnlea Green, Jobstown, Tallaght,
Dublin 24. (Elected WP, now DL)
Machine Operator.

O'CONNOR, Charles,
32 Ashgrove, Tallaght,
Dublin 24. (FF)
Community Worker. 01-514087

QUINN, Catherine,
47 Beechwood Lawns, Rathcoole,
County Dublin. (PD)
Housewife. 01-589718

### TERENURE

|     | 1991 | 1985 | '85 to '91 Swing |
|-----|------|------|------|
| FF  | 25.6 | 38.3 | -12.7 |
| FG  | 23.9 | 31.5 | -7.6 |
| Lab | 23.7 | 14.3 | 9.4  |
| WP  | 4.2  | 3.7  | 0.5  |
| PD  | 10.9 | —    | 10.9 |
| GP  | 6.6  | 2.2  | 4.4  |
| Ind | 5.1  | 10.0 | -4.9 |

ARDAGH, Sean,
23 Grosvenor Court, Templeville Road,
Dublin 6W. (FF)
Accountant. 01-551389

KEANE, Cáit,
26 Rushbrook Court, Templeogue,
Dublin 6W. (PD)
Teacher. 01-509878

LAING, Stanley,
86 Templeville Road, Terenure,
Dublin 6W. (FG)
Public Representative. 01-905571

UPTON, Pat,
1 College Drive, Templeogue,
Dublin 6W. (Lab)
Senator. 01-909653

**Ann Ormonde (FF)**
South Dublin

**Pat Rabbitte (DL)**
South Dublin

**John Hannon (FF)**
South Dublin

**Michael J. Cosgrove (FG)**
South Dublin

WALSH, Eamonn,
133 Limekiln Green, Walkinstown,
Dublin 12. (Lab)
Teacher. 01-504772

## BALLYBRACK

|    | 1991 | 1985 | '85 to '91 Swing |
|----|------|------|-------|
| FF | 21.2 | 31.8 | -10.6 |
| FG | 22.5 | 30.5 | -8.0 |
| Lab | 10.0 | 9.9 | 0.1 |
| WP | 24.5 | 9.0 | 15.5 |
| PD | 10.4 | — | 10.4 |
| GP | 11.5 | 2.6 | 8.9 |
| SF | — | 4.8 | -4.8 |
| Ind | — | 11.4 | -11.4 |

CONROY, Dr. Richard,
Silveracre House, Grange Road,
Dublin 16. (FF)
Senator. 01-931196

GILMORE, Eamon,
24 Corbawn Close, Shankill,
County Dublin. (Elected WP, now DL)
Dáil Deputy. 01-821363

LOHAN, Larry,
3 Woodlands Avenue, Dun Laoghaire,
County Dublin. (PD)
Teacher. 01-2853084

MARREN, Donal,
17 Rock Lodge, Killiney,
County Dublin. (FG)
Teacher. 01-2853160

SMYTH, Frank,
Brookville, Commons Road,
Loughlinstown,
County Dublin. (Lab)
Company Manager. 01-2825339

## BLACKROCK

|    | 1991 | 1985 | '85 to '91 Swing |
|----|------|------|-------|
| FF | 31.0 | 36.8 | -5.8 |
| FG | 20.2 | 39.1 | -18.9 |
| Lab | 16.1 | 14.2 | 1.9 |
| WP | 10.3 | 3.9 | 6.4 |
| PD | 12.4 | — | 12.4 |
| GP | 6.1 | 6.0 | 0.1 |
| Ind | 4.0 | — | 4.0 |

BHREATHNACH, Niamh,
12 Anglesea Avenue, Blackrock,
County Dublin. (Lab)
Teacher. 01-2889321

DOCKRELL, John H.,
13 Knocksinna Crescent,
Dublin 18. (FG)
Lawyer. 01-606888

MADIGAN, Paddy,
"Algoa", Westminster Road, Foxrock,
Dublin 18. (FF)
Solicitor. 01-895182

REEVES Betty,
16 Rosehill,
Careysford Avenue, Blackrock,
County Dublin. (GP)
Housewife. 01-2886897

## CLONSKEAGH

|    | 1991 | 1985 | '85 to '91 Swing |
|----|------|------|-------|
| FF | 28.0 | 41.6 | 28.0 |
| FG | 38.2 | 42.3 | 38.2 |
| Lab | 9.3 | 6.3 | -90.7 |
| WP | 4.8 | 3.9 | 4.8 |
| GP | 14.9 | 5.9 | 14.9 |
| SF | — | — | -51.3 |
| Ind | 4.9 | — | -20.3 |

BROCK, Seamus,
167 Mulvey Park, Dundrum,
Dublin 14. (FF)
Company Representative.

GREENE, Richard,
58 The Palms, Roebuck Road,
Dublin 14. (Elected GP, now NP)
Teacher. 01-2831484

HAND, Tom,
The Haven, Farranboley Park, Dundrum,
Dublin 14. (FG)
Public Representative. 01-980246

## DUNDRUM

|    | 1991 | 1985 | '85 to '91 Swing |
|----|------|------|-------|
| FF | 48.7 | 51.3 | -2.6 |
| FG | 22.3 | 25.2 | -2.9 |
| Lab | 13.4 | 9.9 | 3.5 |
| WP | 5.9 | 5.9 | -0.0 |
| GP | 9.7 | 2.7 | 7.0 |
| SF | 0.0 | 4.2 | -4.2 |
| Ind | 0.0 | 0.8 | -0.8 |

BUCKLEY, Frank,
4 Highfield Drive, Marley Grange,
Dublin 16. (Lab)
Teacher. 01-941273

ELLIOTT, Mary,
23 Broadford Lawn, Ballinteer,
Dublin 16. (FG)
Housewife. 01-941128

FOX, Tony,
93 Mountainview Park, Rathfarnham,
Dublin 14. (FF)
Tailor. 01-980816

KITT, Tom,
3 Pine Valley Drive, Rathfarnham,
Dublin 16. (FF)*

*Resigned when appointed Minister for
State, Feb. 1992.
Replaced by MATTHEWS Trevor,
46 Willow Road, Meadow Brook,
Dundrum,
Dublin 16. (FF)
01-2986975

**G. V. Wright (FF)**
Fingal

**Nora Owen (FG)**
Fingal

**Alan Shatter (FG)**
South Dublin

**Pat Upton (Lab)**
South Dublin

## DUN LAOIRE

|     | 1991 | 1985 | '85 to '91 Swing |
|-----|------|------|------|
| FF  | 24.6 | 29.0 | -4.4 |
| FG  | 22.1 | 35.5 | -13.4 |
| Lab | 10.1 | 16.6 | -6.5 |
| WP  | 10.8 | 3.3  | 7.5 |
| PD  | 11.9 | —    | 11.9 |
| GP  | 11.5 | 2.4  | 9.1 |
| SF  | 6.1  | 8.7  | -2.6 |
| Ind | 2.9  | 4.5  | -1.6 |

BREATHNACH, Colm,
41 Montpelier Parade, Monkstown,
County Dublin. (Elected WP, now DL)
Teacher.

COFFEY, Betty,
40 Northumberland Avenue,
Dun Laoghaire,
County Dublin. (FF)
Public Representative. 01-809369

COSGRAVE, Liam T.,
33 Hillside, Dalkey,
County Dublin. (FG)
Senator. 01-844029

DILLION-BYRNE, Jane,
Silchester House, Glenageary,
County Dublin. (Lab)
Public Representative.

KEOGH, Helen,
12 Beech Court, Killiney,
County Dublin. (PD)
Senator. 01-28

## GLENCULLEN

|     | 1991 | 1985 | '85 to '91 Swing |
|-----|------|------|------|
| FF  | 34.4 | 47.0 | -12.6 |
| FG  | 23.6 | 35.5 | -11.9 |
| Lab | 7.8  | 6.9  | 0.9 |
| WP  | 15.2 | 6.2  | 9.0 |
| PD  | 8.3  | —    | 8.3 |
| GP  | 10.7 | 4.4  | 6.3 |

BARRETT, Sean,
"Avondale", Ballinclea Road, Killiney,
County Dublin. (FG)
Dáil Deputy. 01-2852077

BUTLER, Larry,
6 Hainault Park,
Foxrock, Dublin 18. (FF)
Businessman. 01-2896320

O'CALLAGHAN, Denis,
49 Rathsallagh Park, Shankill,
County Dublin. (Elected WP now DL)
Postal Worker. 01-2822436

## STILLORGAN

|     | 1991 | 1985 | '85 to '91 Swing |
|-----|------|------|------|
| FF  | 28.7 | 38.1 | -9.4 |
| FG  | 22.6 | 31.8 | -9.2 |
| Lab | 22.2 | 16.9 | 5.3 |
| PD  | 13.8 | —    | 13.8 |
| GP  | 12.7 | 5.5  | 7.2 |
| Ind | —    | 7.7  | -7.7 |

FITZGERALD, Eithne,
9 Clonard Avenue,
Dublin 16. (Lab)
Economist. 01-988345

GORDON, Larry,
56 South Avenue, Mount Merrion,
County Dublin. (GP)
Teacher.

LYDON, Don,
34 Clonmore Road, Mount Merrion,
County Dublin. (FF)
Senator. 01-888741

MITCHELL, Olivia,
18 Ballawley Court, Sandyford Road,
Dublin 16. (FG)
Public Representative. 01-953033

**Mary Harney with three Progressive Democrate candidates in Dublin. Colm Tyndall (first left) was elected in Clondalkin.**

# Fianna Fail and Fine Gael suffer big losses in Dublin County Council

Dublin County Council going into the 1991 local elections was by far the most populated and most socially economically, and politically diverse of all County Council jurisdictions. From 1985-1991, 78 County Councillors gathered at least twice monthly in the County Council chambers at Upper O'Connell Street to oversee Local Government for the capital.

The reform of Dublin's Local Government structure and the eventual establishment of three separate Councils will alleviate the problem associated with an authority of 78 members. However, the true significance of the 1991 Election will not be seen until these three Councils of Fingal, South Dublin and Dunlaoghaire/Rathdown meet for the first time. Only then will the differences in party strength in the three different Councils clearly be visible.

The most striking feature of the results in Dublin County is that all the parties performed differently in different parts of the county. The only consistency is that Fianna Fail lost seats. They had thirty nine seats and absolute control on the old Dublin County Council but they returned to the new Council with just twenty three. Fianna Fail lost sixteen seats in total - five in the new Dunlaoghaire/Rathdown area, six in Dublin South and five in Fingal.

Fine Gael also lost seats, seven in all, four of the seven in Dun Laoghaire/Rathdown area and two in Dublin South. While their vote dropped 7.5% in Fingal, they only lost one seat there. Relative to their Dublin Corporation performance, Fine Gael's showing was not as poor, although there are four County Areas where Fine Gael has no Councillors - Mulhuddard, Tallaght, Rathcoole and Tallaght/Oldbawn.

The Labour performances although

> The Labour performance although not as impressive as in Dublin Corporation was also successful

not as successful as their Dublin Corporation result was also impressive. They picked up six extra seats - two extra in each of the three Councils.

The Workers Party won one new seat in Dublin South and two new seats in Dunlaoghaire/Rathdown, with good performances by Pat Rabbitte and Eamon Gilmore, the party's two T.D.'s in these respective areas. Strangely, however, the Worker's Party has never featured in the North and North East part of Dublin, which will eventually form the Council area of Fingal. They got just over 4% of the vote in these areas and they will have no members on Fingal County Council.

The P.D. performance was also varied across the three Councils. They took 7% of the vote in Fingal but only one seat. Despite the fact that they once had a Dail seat in both the Dublin South and Dunlaoghaire area, they will have only two of the twenty eight seats on the Dunlaoghaire/Rathdown Council. The only real success for the PDs in Dublin was their performance in the Dublin South Council, where they took four seats, an excellent performance in Mary

**Barney Rock who was unsuccessful for the Progressive Democrats in Finglas.**

**Bertie Ahern on the election trail in Dublin during the 1991 local elections.**

Boland lost his seat to Sheila Terry of the P.D.s. While in Mulhuddard the Blanchardstown Shopping Centre controversy severally effected the support of both Fianna Fail and Fine Gael. Fine Gael lost their only seat in the area while Marian McGennis of Fianna Fail became their only representative in that area. Another Councillor elected here was Joe Higgins who had been expelled from the Labour Party over the militant issue. He ran as an Independent and topped the poll.

Dublin South County Council is in many ways a misnomer. The Council is made up of representatives from the Local Electoral areas of Clondalkin, Greenhills, Lucan, Rathfarnham, Tallaght/Oldbawn, Tallaght/Rathcoole and Terenure.

Four of these areas make up the new Dail five seater constituency of Dublin South West. Terenure is also partly in Dublin South West, Lucan is mainly in Dublin West, while Rathfarnham is the only electoral area that is a component of the Dublin South Dail Constituency.

Mary Harney did what most P.D. T.D.'s had hoped to do in these elections in giving herself a strong local base, as one P.D. Councillor was elected in each of Dublin South West's local electoral areas. 26 year old Colm Tyndall captured a seat for the party in impressive style in Clondalkin while Housewife Catherine Quinn won a seat in Tallaght/Rathcoole. In Terenure, Cait Keane who got 1,128 first preference votes, was in third place on the first

Harney's Dail base.

The Greens proved as successful in the County as they were in the City. They won one seat on Dublin South, two seats in Fingal and three seats on Dunlaoghaire/Rathdown.

Fingal has twenty four members and seventy two candidates, contested the 1991 poll. It has six electoral areas, three of which, Swords, Malahide and Balbriggan, make up the Dail constituencies of Dublin North. This was a three seater in the 1989 General Elections but will be a four seater when the next Dail poll is held. A look at the results in these three areas throws some interesting pointers as to who is best positioned to take the extra seat.

Labour's sitting T.D. for the area, Sean Ryan put in an impressive performance in Swords getting a massive 2,667 first preferences and succeeded in bringing in running mate Tom Kellegher. Although Ryan's strong showing was helped by the inability of the area's other local T.D. Ray Burke to run, nevertheless it was still a personal triumph.

Although Fianna Fail's potential is difficult to quantify from the local election results, they would certainly

seem to be in with the best chance of winning the seat and Senator G.V. Wright who topped the poll with 1,929 first preferences in Malahide is a possible contender.

However, one person who will also put in challenge for a Dail seat in the new four seater is Trevor Sargent of the Greens. He had performed exceptionally in the 1989 General and European Elections and surprised few by taking a Council seat in his native Balbriggan at Fianna Fail's expense. Given the ability of the Greens to attract the large numbers of transfers, the School Principal could be in there with a strong chance.

The remainder of Fingal is made up of parts of Dublin West and one Electoral area from Dublin North East - Howth. In Howth, the decision of Fianna Fail Councillor Eilish Rickard not to stand, severely hampered the party's chances of holding their two seats and the Green Party were to be the beneficiaries.

In the Dublin West area of Castleknock and Mulhuddard, Fianna Fail suffered major set-backs. In Castleknock, outgoing Fianna Fail County Council Chairman Tommy

> # Fianna Fail's performance in South Dublin was disastrous

count and went on to win the last seat in this five seater. In Tallaght/Oldbawn, Breda Cass, who had been an outgoing Fine Gael Councillor, ran for the P.D.'s and took a seat after a close run with former colleague Fine Gael's Senator Larry McMahon.

The other Deputy who could be happy with the South Dublin result was Pat Rabbitte. Rabbitte moved his elected

**Tommy Boland, the outgoing Chairman of Dublin County Council, who was unsuccessful in June 1991.**

make up the Dunlaoghaire Dail Constituency.

Fine Gael's Dublin South TD Nuala Fennell had a disappointing performance in the Clonskeagh Electoral area. They had won 2 seats here in 1985 and when outgoing Gina Menzies decided not to run, Fennell was drafted in, but she failed to win a seat.

In Dunlaoghaire, Fennell's Fine Gael Oireachtas colleagues did much better. Sean Barrett TD, who was not a member of the outgoing Council, ran and topped the poll in Glencullen while Senator Liam Cosgrove, an outgoing Councillor for the Dunlaoghaire area,

> ## The Green's performance in Dun Laoghaire was very impressive

headed the poll in his area.

The Workers Party too, had much to celebrate as they picked up two new seats with a particularly impressive performance by their Deputy Eamon Gilmore who topped the poll in Ballybrack.

The P.D.'s picked up two seats with Larry Lohan taking a seat in Ballybrack, while Senator Helen Keogh won a seat as predicted in Dunlaoghaire.

The Green's performance was by far the most impressive, however, as they won three seats and were unlucky not to win six. They took seats in Stillorgan and Blackrock while, former Fianna Fail Anti Extradition Campaigner, Richard Greene won a seat for the Green Party in Clonskeagh. In addition their candidates in Ballybrack, Dundrum and Glencullen survived until the last count and in each case just missed out on winning these final seats.

Fine Gael took the chair of Dublin County Council in 1991/92, but with the patchwork breakdown of party support in the three new Local Authorities, it still remains to be seen what alliances will be formed to control these new Councils of Fingal, Dublin South and Dunlaoghaire/ Rathdown.

area from Tallaght/Rathcoole to Tallaght/Oldbawn in an attempt by the Workers Party to broaden their base in this constituency. Rabbitte took the second seat in the Tallaght/Oldbawn 3 seater while despite his absence, his party topped the poll in Tallaght/Rathcoole with his replacement Mick Billane, getting an impressive 1,217 first count votes.

For Fianna Fail, however, South Dublin was a near disaster. Fianna Fail lost a seat in six out of the seven electoral areas in South Dublin - the only exception being in Terenure were they held onto one out of five seats. The biggest shock for Fianna Fail was in Lucan where their vote dropped 13.7% and, in one of the biggest upsets in the country, Dublin West T.D. Liam Lawlor lost his Council seat.

Fine Gael lost two seats as their likely candidate in Dublin South West for the

next Dail Election, Michael Keating, polled disappointingly and just managed to take the last seat in the Greenhills area.

Dublin South West is one of only two constituencies in the county without a Fine Gael T.D. After the revision of the Dail Constituency, it will change from being a four seater to a five seater and Fine Gael would wish to be in the best position to take this extra seat. Their chances were not helped by their disappointing performance in the Local Elections as they now have no Councillor in either Tallaght/Rathcoole or Tallaght/Oldbawn.

The new twenty eight Dunlaoghaire/Rathdown Council has seven electoral areas. Three of these areas - Dundrum, Clonskeagh and Stillorgan are in Dublin South while the remaining four Dunlaoghaire, Glencullen, Ballybrack and Blackrock

# BALLYBRACK ELECTORAL AREA

TOTAL ELECTORATE 24,818. VALID POLL 9,950. NO. OF MEMBERS 5. QUOTA 1,659.

| Names of Candidates | First Count Votes | Second Count Transfer of Gilmore's surplus | Result | Third Count Transfer of Long's votes | Result | Fourth Count Transfer of Hammond's votes | Result | Fifth Count Transfer of Treanor's votes | Result | Sixth Count Transfer of Batt's votes | Result | Seventh Count Transfer of Culleton's votes | Result | Eighth Count Transfer of Butler's votes | Result | Ninth Count Transfer of Brophy's votes | Result | Tenth Count Transfer of Marren's surplus | Result |
|---|---|---|---|---|---|---|---|---|---|---|---|---|---|---|---|---|---|---|---|
| BATT, Sylvie (W.P.) | 333 | +223 | 556 | +12 | 568 | +19 | 587 | +22 | 609 | -609 | — | — | — | — | — | — | — | — | — |
| BLAKE, Maggie (G.P.) | 640 | +16 | 656 | +18 | 674 | +19 | 693 | +310 | 1,003 | +166 | 1,169 | +57 | 1,226 | +64 | 1,290 | +100 | 1,390 | +87 | 1,477 |
| BROPHY, Colm (F.G.) | 684 | +14 | 698 | +13 | 711 | +10 | 721 | +19 | 740 | +22 | 762 | +164 | 926 | +21 | 947 | -947 | — | — | — |
| BUTLER, Noírin (F.F.) | 534 | +6 | 540 | +71 | 611 | +106 | 717 | +21 | 738 | +18 | 756 | +20 | 776 | -776 | — | — | — | — | — |
| CONROY, Dr. Richard (F.F.) | 784 | +12 | 796 | +69 | 865 | +191 | 1,056 | +21 | 1,077 | +20 | 1,097 | +22 | 1,119 | +481 | 1,600 | +70 | 1,670 | — | 1,670 |
| CULLETON, Barbara (F.G.) | 579 | +10 | 589 | +8 | 597 | +16 | 613 | +22 | 635 | +12 | 647 | -647 | — | — | — | — | — | — | — |
| GILMORE, Eamon (W.P.) | 2,104 | -445 | 1,659 | — | 1,659 | — | 1,659 | — | 1,659 | — | 1,659 | — | 1,659 | — | 1,659 | — | 1,659 | — | 1,659 |
| HAMMOND, Owen (F.F.) | 428 | +16 | 444 | +82 | 526 | -526 | — | — | — | — | — | — | — | — | — | — | — | — | — |
| LOHAN, Larry (P.D.) | 1,035 | +15 | 1,050 | +15 | 1,065 | +31 | 1,096 | +44 | 1,140 | +33 | 1,173 | +67 | 1,240 | +58 | 1,298 | +130 | 1,428 | +103 | 1,531 |
| LONG, Noel (F.F.) | 362 | +17 | 379 | -379 | — | — | — | — | — | — | — | — | — | — | — | — | — | — | — |
| MARREN, Donal (F.G.) | 972 | +27 | 999 | +21 | 1,020 | +33 | 1,053 | +23 | 1,076 | +42 | 1,118 | +258 | 1,376 | +46 | 1,422 | +509 | 1,931 | -272 | 1,659 |
| SMYTH, Frank (Lab.) | 995 | +73 | 1,068 | +38 | 1,106 | +42 | 1,148 | +49 | 1,197 | +198 | 1,395 | +33 | 1,428 | +36 | 1,464 | +67 | 1,531 | +82 | 1,613 |
| TREANOR, Vincent (G.P.) | 500 | +16 | 516 | +14 | 530 | +21 | 551 | -551 | — | — | — | — | — | — | — | — | — | — | — |
| Non-transferable papers not effective | — | — | — | +18 | 18 | +38 | 56 | +20 | 76 | +98 | 174 | +26 | 200 | +70 | 270 | +71 | 341 | — | 341 |
| TOTAL: | 9,950 | — | 9,950 | — | 9,950 | — | 9,950 | — | 9,950 | — | 9,950 | — | 9,950 | — | 9,950 | — | 9,950 | — | 9,950 |

Elected: Gilmore, Eamon (W.P.); Marren, Donal (F.G.); Conroy, Dr. Richard (F.F.); Smyth, Frank(Lab.); Lohan, Larry (P.D.)

# BLACKROCK ELECTORAL AREA

TOTAL ELECTORATE 19,450. VALID POLL 8,109. NO. OF MEMBERS 4. QUOTA 1,622.

| Names of Candidates | First Count Votes | Second Count Transfer of Dunphy's surplus | Result | Third Count Transfer of Walker's votes | Result | Fourth Count Transfer of Cotter's votes | Result | Fifth Count Transfer of Davis' votes | Result | Sixth Count Transfer of White's votes | Result | Seventh Count Transfer of Breathnach's surplus | Result | Eighth Count Transfer of Elliott's votes | Result | Ninth Count Transfer of Dockrell's surplus | Result |
|---|---|---|---|---|---|---|---|---|---|---|---|---|---|---|---|---|---|
| BHREATHNACH, Niamh (Lab.) | 1,303 | +14 | 1,317 | +37 | 1,354 | +36 | 1,390 | +148 | 1,538 | +401 | 1,939 | -317 | 1,622 | — | 1,622 | — | 1,622 |
| BRADY, Anne (F.F.) | 784 | +7 | 791 | +36 | 827 | +305 | 1,132 | +55 | 1,187 | +34 | 1,221 | +25 | 1,246 | +124 | 1,370 | +29 | 1,399 |
| COTTER, Michael (F.F.) | 641 | +6 | 647 | +14 | 661 | -661 | — | — | — | — | — | — | — | — | — | — | — |
| DAVIS, Evelynne (P.D.) | 697 | +11 | 708 | +28 | 736 | +25 | 761 | -761 | — | — | — | — | — | — | — | — | — |
| DOCKRELL, John H. (F.G.) | 839 | +7 | 846 | +23 | 869 | +19 | 888 | +136 | 1,024 | +41 | 1,065 | +33 | 1,098 | +691 | 1,789 | -167 | 1,622 |
| DUNPHY, Michael (G.P.) | 309 | -309 | — | — | — | — | — | — | — | — | — | — | — | — | — | — | — |
| ELLIOTT, Áine (F.G.) | 798 | +8 | 806 | +29 | 835 | +14 | 849 | +120 | 969 | +83 | 1,052 | +44 | 1,096 | -1,096 | — | — | — |
| MADIGAN, Paddy (F.F.) | 1,089 | +12 | 1,101 | +38 | 1,139 | +197 | 1,336 | +57 | 1,393 | +103 | 1,496 | +28 | 1,524 | +56 | 1,580 | +25 | 1,605 |
| REEVES, Betty (G.P.) | 492 | +219 | 711 | +75 | 786 | +22 | 808 | +174 | 982 | +209 | 1,191 | +179 | 1,370 | +144 | 1,514 | +113 | 1,627 |
| WALKER, Marie | 324 | +3 | 327 | -327 | — | — | — | — | — | — | — | — | — | — | — | — | — |
| WHITE, Marian (W.P.) | 833 | +17 | 850 | +34 | 884 | +25 | 909 | +32 | 941 | -941 | — | — | — | — | — | — | — |
| Non-transferable papers not effective | — | +5 | 5 | +13 | 18 | +18 | 36 | +39 | 75 | +70 | 145 | +8 | 153 | +81 | 234 | — | 234 |
| TOTAL: | 8,109 | — | 8,109 | — | 8,109 | — | 8,109 | — | 8,109 | — | 8,109 | — | 8,109 | — | 8,109 | — | 8,109 |

Names of candidates elected: Bhreathnach, Niamh (Lab.); Dockrell, John H. (F.G.); Reeves, Betty (G.P.); Madigan, Paddy (F.F.)

# CLONSKEAGH ELECTORAL AREA

TOTAL ELECTORATE 14,294. VALID POLL 5,893. NO. OF MEMBERS 3. QUOTA 1,474.

| Names of Candidates | First Count | Second Count Transfer of Wood's votes | Result | Third Count Transfer of Dockrell's votes | Result | Fourth Count Transfer of Nolan's votes | Result | Fifth Count Transfer of Gilbert's votes | Result |
|---|---|---|---|---|---|---|---|---|---|
| | votes | | | | | | | | |
| BROCK, Seamus (F.F.) | 956 | +14 | 970 | +9 | 979 | +79 | 1,058 | +522 | 1,580 |
| DOCKRELL, Maurice | 288 | +10 | 298 | -298 | — | — | — | — | — |
| FENNELL, Nuala (F.G.) | 809 | +14 | 823 | +114 | 937 | +157 | 1,094 | +69 | 1,163 |
| GILBERT, Tim (F.F.) | 694 | +7 | 701 | +20 | 721 | +34 | 755 | -755 | — |
| GREENE, Richard (G.P.) | 876 | +63 | 939 | +106 | 1,045 | +360 | 1,405 | +112 | 1,517 |
| HAND, Tom (F.G.) | 1,443 | +39 | 1,482 | — | 1,482 | — | 1,482 | — | 1,482 |
| NOLAN, Peter (Lab.) | 547 | +128 | 675 | +30 | 705 | -705 | — | — | — |
| WOODS, Chris (W.P.) | 280 | -280 | — | — | — | — | — | — | — |
| Non-transferable papers not effective | — | +5 | 5 | +19 | 24 | +75 | 99 | +52 | 151 |
| TOTAL: | 5,893 | — | 5,893 | — | 5,893 | — | 5,893 | — | 5,893 |

Elected: Hand, Tom (F.G.); Brock, Seamus (F.F.); Greene, Richard (G.P.)

# DUNDRUM ELECTORAL AREA

TOTAL ELECTORATE 17,467. VALID POLL 7,889. NO. OF MEMBERS 4. QUOTA 1,578

| Names of Candidates | First Count | Second Count Transfer of Kitt's surplus | Result | Third Count Transfer of Brady's votes | Result | Fourth Count Transfer of Lawlor's votes | Result | Fifth Count Transfer of Corcoran's votes | Result | Sixth Count Transfer of Fox's surplus | Result |
|---|---|---|---|---|---|---|---|---|---|---|---|
| | Votes | | | | | | | | | | |
| BRADY, Pat (W.P.) | 464 | +11 | 475 | -475 | — | — | — | — | — | — | — |
| BUCKLEY, Frank (Lab.) | 1,055 | +45 | 1,100 | +271 | 1,371 | +31 | 1,402 | +86 | 1,488 | +55 | 1,543 |
| CORCORAN, Austen (F.G.) | 528 | +33 | 561 | +18 | 579 | +21 | 600 | -600 | — | — | — |
| ELLIOTT, Mary (F.G.) | 1,231 | +75 | 1,306 | +34 | 1,340 | +59 | 1,399 | +419 | 1,818 | — | 1,818 |
| FOX, Tony (F.F.) | 1,273 | +264 | 1,537 | +34 | 1,571 | +345 | 1,916 | — | 1,916 | -338 | 1,578 |
| KITT, Tom (F.F.) | 2,203 | -625 | 1,578 | — | 1,578 | — | 1,578 | — | 1,578 | — | 1,578 |
| LAWLOR, Siobhán (F.F.) | 367 | +159 | 526 | +8 | 534 | -534 | — | — | — | — | — |
| RYAN, Jim (G.P.) | 768 | +38 | 806 | +104 | 910 | +59 | 969 | +60 | 1,029 | +79 | 1,108 |
| Non-transferable papers not effective | — | — | — | +6 | (6) | +19 | 25 | +35 | 60 | +204 | 264 |
| TOTAL: | 7,889 | — | 7,889 | — | 7,889 | — | 7,889 | — | 7,889 | — | 7,889 |

Elected: Kitt, Tom (F.F.); Fox, Tony (F.F.); Elliott, Mary (F.G.); Buckley, Frank (Lab.)

# DÚN LAOGHAIRE ELECTORAL AREA

TOTAL ELECTORATE 27,220. VALID POLL 11,356. NO. OF MEMBERS 5. QUOTA 1,893.

| Names of Candidates | First Count Votes | Second Count Transfer of Merriman's and Pierce's votes Result | Third Count Transfer of O'Rafferty's votes Result | Fourth Count Transfer of Ó'Murchú's votes Result | Fifth Count Transfer of Henderson's votes Result | Sixth Count Transfer of Fitzpatrick's votes Result | Seventh Count Transfer of Coffey's surplus Result | Eighth Count Transfer of Sexton's votes Result | Ninth Count Transfer of Harvey's votes Result |
|---|---|---|---|---|---|---|---|---|---|
| BREATHNACH, Colm (W.P.) | 1,227 | +5 1,232 | +12 1,244 | +9 1,253 | +18 1,271 | +224 1,495 | +17 1,512 | +64 1,576 | +93 1,669 |
| COFFEY, Betty (F.F.) | 1,547 | +3 1,550 | +18 1,568 | +194 1,762 | +57 1,819 | +139 1,958 | -65 1,893 | — 1,893 | — 1,893 |
| COSGRAVE, Liam T. (F.G.) | 1,759 | +100 1,859 | +28 1,887 | +16 1,903 | — 1,903 | — 1,903 | — 1,903 | — 1,903 | — 1,903 |
| DILLON-BYRNE, Jane (Lab.) | 1,149 | +21 1,170 | +40 1,210 | +14 1,224 | +78 1,302 | +59 1,361 | +11 1,372 | +81 1,453 | +142 1,595 |
| FITZPATRICK, Kevin (S.F.) | 688 | +7 695 | +5 700 | +12 712 | +4 716 | -716 — | — — | — — | — — |
| HARVEY, William (Bill) (F.F.) | 861 | — 861 | +9 870 | +106 976 | +43 1,019 | +51 1,070 | +27 1,097 | +23 1,120 | -1,120 — |
| HENDERSON, Brendan T. (F.G.) | 474 | +73 547 | +22 569 | +1 570 | -570 — | — — | — — | — — | — — |
| KEOGH, Helen (P.D.) | 1,346 | +34 1,380 | +40 1,420 | +11 1,431 | +149 1,580 | +19 1,599 | +3 1,602 | +88 1,690 | +157 1,847 |
| MacDOWELL, Vincent (G.P.) | 700 | +8 708 | +83 791 | +10 801 | +55 856 | +66 922 | +4 926 | +514 1,440 | +126 1,566 |
| MERRIMAN, Jim (Non-Party) | 15 | -15 — | — — | — — | — — | — — | — — | — — | — — |
| Ó'MURCHÚ, Labhrás (F.F.) | 384 | +1 385 | +8 393 | -393 — | — — | — — | — — | — — | — — |
| O'RAFFERTY, Tomás (Non-Party) | 320 | +10 330 | -330 — | — — | — — | — — | — — | — — | — — |
| PIERCE, Donna (F.G.) | 275 | -275 — | — — | — — | — — | — — | — — | — — | — — |
| SEXTON, Jane (G.P.) | 611 | +26 637 | +53 690 | +13 703 | +75 778 | +60 838 | +3 841 | -841 — | — — |
| Non-transferable papers not effective | — | +2 2 | +12 14 | +7 21 | +91 112 | +98 210 | — 210 | +71 281 | +602 883 |
| TOTAL: | 11,356 | — 11,356 | — 11,356 | — 11,356 | — 11,356 | — 11,356 | — 11,356 | — 11,356 | — 11,356 |

Elected: Cosgrave, Liam T. (F.G.); Coffey, Betty (F.F.); Keogh, Helen (P.D.); Breathnach, Colm (W.P.); Dillon-Byrne, Jane (Lab.)

# GLENCULLEN ELECTORAL AREA

TOTAL ELECTORATE 18,775. VALID POLL 7,557. NO. OF MEMBERS 3. QUOTA 1,890.

| Names of Candidates | First Count Votes | Second Count Transfer of Brennan's votes Result | Third Count Transfer of Carroll's votes Result | Fourth Count Transfer of Cox's votes Result | Fifth Count Transfer of Ó'Síocháin's votes Result | Sixth Count Transfer of Barrett's surplus Result | Seventh Count Transfer of Murphy's votes Result | Eighth Count Transfer of Butler's surplus Result |
|---|---|---|---|---|---|---|---|---|
| BARRETT, Sean (F.G.) | 1,272 | +23 1,295 | +307 1,602 | +116 1,718 | +269 1,987 | -97 1,890 | — 1,890 | — 1,890 |
| BRENNAN, John (F.F.) | 267 | -267 — | — — | — — | — — | — — | — — | — — |
| BUTLER, Larry (F.F.) | 1,239 | +140 1,379 | +58 1,437 | +40 1,477 | +123 1,600 | +26 1,626 | +789 2,415 | -525 1,890 |
| CARROLL, Sam (F.G.) | 509 | +12 521 | -521 — | — — | — — | — — | — — | — — |
| COX, Deirdre (Lab.) | 588 | +3 591 | +24 615 | -615 — | — — | — — | — — | — — |
| McKINSTRY, Alastair (G.P.) | 809 | +9 818 | +35 853 | +151 1,004 | +212 1,216 | +47 1,263 | +149 1,412 | +182 1,594 |
| MURPHY, Jim (F.F.) | 1,094 | +66 1,160 | +18 1,178 | +16 1,194 | +43 1,237 | +7 1,244 | -1,244 — | — — |
| O'CALLAGHAN, Denis (W.P.) | 1,149 | +10 1,159 | +15 1,174 | +215 1,389 | +53 1,442 | +17 1,459 | +101 1,560 | +62 1,622 |
| Ó'SÍOCHÁIN, Seán (P.D.) | 630 | +3 633 | +55 688 | +64 752 | -752 — | — — | — — | — — |
| Non-transferable papers not effective | — | +1 (1) | +9 10 | +13 23 | +52 75 | — 75 | +205 280 | +281 561 |
| TOTAL: | 7,557 | — 7,557 | — 7,557 | — 7,557 | — 7,557 | — 7,557 | — 7,557 | — 7,557 |

Elected: Barrett, Sean (F.G.); Butler, Larry (F.F.); O'Callaghan, Denis (W.P.)

# STILLORGAN ELECTORAL AREA

TOTAL ELECTORATE 19,000. VALID POLL 8,108. NO. OF MEMBERS 4. QUOTA 1,622

| Names of Candidates | First Count Votes | Second Count Transfer of Fitzgerald's surplus | Result | Third Count Transfer of Cranley's votes | Result | Fourth Count Transfer of Mitchell's surplus | Result | Fifth Count Transfer of Ryan's votes | Result | Sixth Count Transfer of Boyhan's votes | Result | Seventh Count Transfer of Murphy's votes | Result | Eighth Count Transfer of Gordon's surplus | Result |
|---|---|---|---|---|---|---|---|---|---|---|---|---|---|---|---|
| BOYHAN, Victor (P.D.) | 533 | +12 | 545 | +29 | 574 | +48 | 622 | +24 | 646 | -646 | — | — | — | — | — |
| CRANLEY, Eugene (F.G.) | 448 | +8 | 456 | -456 | — | — | — | — | — | — | — | — | — | — | — |
| FITZGERALD, Eithne (Lab.) | 1,800 | -178 | 1,622 | — | 1,622 | — | 1,622 | — | 1,622 | — | 1,622 | — | 1,622 | — | 1,622 |
| GORDON, Larry (G.P.) | 1,032 | +61 | 1,093 | +24 | 1,117 | +37 | 1,154 | +27 | 1,181 | +108 | 1,289 | +492 | 1,781 | -159 | 1,622 |
| HICKEY, Paddy (F.F.) | 940 | +11 | 951 | +10 | 961 | +6 | 967 | +163 | 1,130 | +34 | 1,164 | +116 | 1,280 | +83 | 1,363 |
| LYDON, Don (F.F.) | 924 | +10 | 934 | +24 | 958 | +7 | 965 | +205 | 1,170 | +34 | 1,204 | +195 | 1,399 | +76 | 1,475 |
| MITCHELL, Olivia (F.G.) | 1,387 | +54 | 1,441 | +332 | 1,773 | -151 | 1,622 | — | 1,622 | — | 1,622 | — | 1,622 | — | 1,622 |
| MURPHY, Anna (P.D.) | 582 | +14 | 596 | +26 | 622 | +49 | 671 | +38 | 709 | +425 | 1,134 | -1,134 | — | — | — |
| RYAN, Carmel (F.F.) | 462 | +8 | 470 | +3 | 473 | +4 | 477 | -477 | — | — | — | — | — | — | — |
| Non-transferable papers not effective | — | — | — | +8 | 8 | — | 8 | +20 | 28 | +45 | 73 | +331 | 404 | — | 404 |
| TOTAL: | 8,108 | — | 8,108 | — | 8,108 | — | 8,108 | — | 8,108 | — | 8,108 | — | 8,108 | — | 8,108 |

Elected: Fitzgerald, Eithne (Lab.); Mitchell, Olivia (F.G.); Gordon, Larry (G.P.); Lydon, Don (F.F.)

# BALBRIGGAN ELECTORAL AREA

TOTAL ELECTORATE 19,705. VALID POLL 10,653. NO. OF MEMBERS 5. QUOTA 1,776.

| Names of Candidates | First Count Votes | Second Count Transfer of Farrell's surplus | Result | Third Count Transfer of Brady's and McCarthy's votes | Result | Fourth Count Transfer of Gallen's votes | Result | Fifth Count Transfer of McKittrick's votes | Result | Sixth Count Transfer of Dineen's votes | Result | Seventh Count Transfer of Shield's votes | Result | Eighth Count Transfer of Sargent's surplus | Result | Ninth Count Transfer of Maxwell's votes | Result | Tenth Count Transfer of Murray's votes | Result | Eleventh Count Transfer of Davis' votes | Result |
|---|---|---|---|---|---|---|---|---|---|---|---|---|---|---|---|---|---|---|---|---|---|
| BOLAND, Cathal (F.G.) | 871 | +7 | 878 | +4 | 882 | +133 | 1,015 | +22 | 1,037 | +100 | 1,137 | +31 | 1,168 | +23 | 1,191 | +75 | 1,266 | +191 | 1,457 | +222 | 1,679 |
| BRADY, Séan (Non-Party) | 78 | — | 78 | -78 | — | — | — | — | — | — | — | — | — | — | — | — | — | — | — | — | — |
| DAVIS, Joe (Lab.) | 608 | +45 | 653 | +42 | 695 | +27 | 722 | +16 | 738 | +16 | 754 | +101 | 855 | +42 | 897 | +27 | 924 | +184 | 1,108 | -1,108 | — |
| DINEEN, Liam (Non-Party) | 532 | +3 | 535 | +18 | 553 | +4 | 557 | +6 | 563 | -563 | — | — | — | — | — | — | — | — | — | — | — |
| FARRELL, Ken (Lab.) | 1,865 | -89 | 1,776 | — | 1,776 | — | 1,776 | — | 1,776 | — | 1,776 | — | 1,776 | — | 1,776 | — | 1,776 | — | 1,776 | — | 1,776 |
| GALLEN, Patricia (F.G.) | 313 | +1 | 314 | +10 | 324 | -324 | — | — | — | — | — | — | — | — | — | — | — | — | — | — | — |
| GERAGHTY, Jim (F.F.) | 916 | +6 | 922 | +1 | 923 | +2 | 925 | +92 | 1,017 | +55 | 1,072 | +28 | 1,100 | +3 | 1,103 | +87 | 1,190 | +32 | 1,222 | +38 | 1,260 |
| GILBRIDE, Séan (F.F.) | 1,104 | +3 | 1,107 | +7 | 1,114 | +12 | 1,126 | +78 | 1,204 | +63 | 1,267 | +39 | 1,306 | +12 | 1,318 | +145 | 1,463 | +91 | 1,554 | +117 | 1,671 |
| LARKIN, Jack (F.F.) | 711 | +1 | 712 | +15 | 727 | +17 | 744 | +45 | 789 | +7 | 796 | +66 | 862 | +18 | 880 | +287 | 1,167 | +142 | 1,309 | +180 | 1,489 |
| McCARTHY, Anne (W.P.) | 123 | +2 | 125 | -125 | — | — | — | — | — | — | — | — | — | — | — | — | — | — | — | — | — |
| McKITTRICK Wilbur (F.F.) | 374 | +7 | 381 | +5 | 386 | +1 | 387 | -387 | — | — | — | — | — | — | — | — | — | — | — | — | — |
| MAXWELL, John C. (F.F.) | 665 | +1 | 666 | +2 | 668 | +6 | 674 | +57 | 731 | +1 | 732 | +15 | 747 | +5 | 752 | -752 | — | — | — | — | — |
| MURRAY, David (P.D.) | 585 | +2 | 587 | +8 | 595 | +43 | 638 | +10 | 648 | +33 | 681 | +85 | 766 | +64 | 830 | +49 | 879 | -879 | — | — | — |
| SARGENT, Trevor (G.P.) | 1,405 | +8 | 1,413 | +51 | 1,464 | +43 | 1,507 | +25 | 1,532 | +198 | 1,730 | +227 | 1,957 | -181 | 1,776 | — | 1,776 | — | 1,776 | — | 1,776 |
| SHIELDS, Gertie (Non-Party) | 503 | +3 | 506 | +28 | 534 | +31 | 565 | +7 | 572 | +62 | 634 | -634 | — | — | — | — | — | — | — | — | — |
| Non-transferable papers not effective | — | — | — | +12 | 12 | +5 | 17 | +29 | 46 | +28 | 74 | +42 | 116 | +14 | 130 | +82 | 212 | +239 | 451 | +551 | 1,002 |
| TOTAL: | 10,653 | — | 10,653 | — | 10,653 | — | 10,653 | — | 10,653 | — | 10,653 | — | 10,653 | — | 10,653 | — | 10,653 | — | 10,653 | — | 10,653 |

Elected: Farrell, Ken (Lab.); Sargent, Trevor (G.P.); Boland, Cathal (F.G.); Gilbride, Seán (F.F.); Larkin, Jack (F.F.)

# CASTLEKNOCK ELECTORAL AREA

TOTAL ELECTORATE 15,777. VALID POLL 7,434. NO. OF MEMBERS 4. QUOTA 1,487.

| Names of Candidates | First Count Votes | Second Count Transfer of Malone's votes | Result | Third Count Transfer of Byrne's votes | Result | Fourth Count Transfer of Condron's votes | Result | Fifth Count Transfer of Tuffy's votes | Result | Sixth Count Transfer of Caldwell's votes | Result | Seventh Count Transfer of Gogarty's votes | Result | Eighth Count Transfer of Lyons' surplus | Result | Ninth Count Transfer of Loftus' votes | Result | Tenth Count Transfer of Morrissey's surplus | Result | Eleventh Count Transfer of Terry's surplus | Result |
|---|---|---|---|---|---|---|---|---|---|---|---|---|---|---|---|---|---|---|---|---|---|
| BOLAND, Tom (F.F.) | 752 | +1 | 753 | +8 | 761 | +7 | 768 | +2 | 770 | +184 | 954 | +35 | 989 | +4 | 993 | +44 | 1,037 | +75 | 1,112 | +52 | 1,164 |
| BYRNE, Willie (Lab.) | 136 | +1 | 137 | -137 | — | — | — | — | — | — | — | — | — | — | — | — | — | — | — | — | — |
| CALDWELL, Miley (F.F.) | 439 | +3 | 442 | +4 | 446 | +4 | 450 | +5 | 455 | -455 | — | — | — | — | — | — | — | — | — | — | — |
| CONDRON, Patricia (W.P.) | 196 | +1 | 197 | +16 | 213 | -213 | — | — | — | — | — | — | — | — | — | — | — | — | — | — | — |
| GOGARTY, Paul Nicholas (G.P.) | 391 | — | 391 | +3 | 394 | +54 | 448 | +101 | 549 | +27 | 576 | -576 | — | — | — | — | — | — | — | — | — |
| LOFTUS, Eithne (F.G.) | 780 | +45 | 825 | +4 | 829 | +4 | 833 | +20 | 853 | +25 | 878 | +72 | 950 | +8 | 958 | -958 | — | — | — | — | — |
| LYONS, Seán | 1,378 | +18 | 1,396 | +16 | 1,412 | +34 | 1,446 | +77 | 1,523 | — | 1,523 | — | 1,523 | -36 | 1,487 | — | 1,487 | — | 1,487 | | 1,487 |
| MALONE, Patrick (F.G.) | 123 | -123 | — | — | — | — | — | — | — | — | — | — | — | — | — | — | — | — | — | — | — |
| MORRISSEY, Tom (F.G.) | 1,172 | +41 | 1,213 | +4 | 1,217 | +11 | 1,228 | +21 | 1,249 | +10 | 1,259 | +74 | 1,333 | +5 | 1,338 | +476 | 1,814 | -327 | 1,487 | | 1,487 |
| RYAN, Ned (F.F.) | 807 | +5 | 812 | +3 | 815 | +3 | 818 | +5 | 823 | +119 | 942 | +36 | 978 | +3 | 981 | +68 | 1,049 | +75 | 1,124 | +57 | 1,181 |
| TERRY, Sheila (P.D.) | 1,093 | +6 | 1,099 | +7 | 1,106 | +15 | 1,121 | +51 | 1,172 | +42 | 1,214 | +187 | 1,401 | +16 | 1,417 | +266 | 1,683 | — | 1,683 | -196 | 1,487 |
| TUFFY, Joanna (Lab.) | 167 | +2 | 169 | +70 | 239 | +77 | 316 | -316 | — | — | — | — | — | — | — | — | — | — | — | — | — |
| Non-transferable papers not effective | — | — | — | +2 | (2) | +4 | (6) | +34 | 40 | +48 | 88 | +172 | 260 | — | 260 | +104 | 364 | +177 | 541 | +87 | 628 |
| TOTAL: | 7,434 | — | 7,434 | — | 7,434 | — | 7,434 | — | 7,434 | — | 7,434 | — | 7,434 | — | 7,434 | — | 7,434 | — | 7,434 | — | 7,434 |

Elected: Lyons, Seán; Morrissey, Tom (F.G.); Terry, Sheila (P.D.); Ryan, Ned (F.F.).

# HOWTH ELECTORAL AREA

TOTAL ELECTORATE 16,807. VALID POLL 7,592. NO. OF MEMBERS 4. QUOTA 1,519

| Names of Candidates | First Count Votes | Second Count Transfer of Rudden's votes | Result | Third Count Transfer of Barry's votes | Result | Fourth Count Transfer of Kenny's votes | Result | Fifth Count Transfer of Beary's votes | Result | Sixth Count Transfer of Cosgrave's surplus | Result | Seventh Count Transfer of Peers' votes | Result | Eighth Count Transfer of Clune's votes | Result | Ninth Count Transfer of Creaven's surplus | Result |
|---|---|---|---|---|---|---|---|---|---|---|---|---|---|---|---|---|---|
| BARRY, Frank (Lab.) | 497 | +5 | 502 | -502 | — | — | — | — | — | — | — | — | — | — | — | — | — |
| BEARY, Tom (F.F.) | 519 | +50 | 569 | +42 | 611 | +6 | 617 | -617 | — | — | — | — | — | — | — | — | — |
| BEHAN, Niall (W.P.) | 695 | +16 | 711 | +197 | 908 | +15 | 923 | +30 | 953 | +2 | 955 | +136 | 1,091 | +40 | 1,131 | +59 | 1,190 |
| CLUNE, Dymphna (F.F.) | 550 | +39 | 589 | +8 | 597 | +28 | 625 | +268 | 893 | +8 | 901 | +63 | 964 | -964 | — | — | — |
| COSGRAVE, Michael Joe (F.G.) | 1,342 | +59 | 1,401 | +56 | 1,457 | +45 | 1,502 | +43 | 1,545 | -26 | 1,519 | — | 1,519 | — | 1,519 | — | 1,519 |
| CREAVEN, Liam (F.F.) | 703 | +119 | 822 | +19 | 841 | +36 | 877 | +176 | 1,053 | +7 | 1,060 | +106 | 1,166 | +618 | 1,784 | -265 | 1,519 |
| HEALY, David (G.P.) | 789 | +8 | 797 | +72 | 869 | +45 | 914 | +24 | 938 | +5 | 943 | +212 | 1,155 | +120 | 1,275 | +179 | 1,454 |
| KENNY, Michael (P.D.) | 500 | +3 | 503 | +19 | 522 | -522 | — | — | — | — | — | — | — | — | — | — | — |
| MAHER, Joan (F.G.) | 1,141 | +14 | 1,155 | +49 | 1,204 | +51 | 1,255 | +45 | 1,300 | +1 | 1,301 | +240 | 1,541 | — | 1,541 | — | 1,541 |
| PEERS, Noel (P.D.) | 511 | +29 | 540 | +30 | 570 | +294 | 864 | +21 | 885 | +3 | 888 | -888 | — | — | — | — | — |
| RUDDEN, Eugene (F.F.) | 345 | -345 | — | — | — | — | — | — | — | — | — | — | — | — | — | — | — |
| Non-transferable papers not effective | — | +3 | (3) | +10 | 13 | +2 | 15 | +10 | 25 | — | 25 | +131 | 156 | +186 | 342 | +27 | 369 |
| TOTAL: | 7,592 | — | 7,592 | — | 7,592 | — | 7,592 | — | 7,592 | — | 7,592 | — | 7,592 | — | 7,592 | — | 7,592 |

Elected: Cosgrave, Michael Joe (F.G.); Maher, Joan (F.G.); Creaven, Liam (F.F.); Healy, David (G.P.).

# MALAHIDE ELECTORAL AREA

TOTAL ELECTORATE 16,431. VALID POLL 8,346. NO. OF MEMBERS 4. QUOTA 1,670.

| Names of Candidates | First Count Votes | Second Count Transfer of Wright's surplus Result | | Third Count Transfer of Hancox's votes Result | | Fourth Count Transfer of Keaveney's votes Result | | Fifth Count Transfer of Webberley's votes Result | | Sixth Count Transfer of O'Brien's votes Result | | Seventh Count Transfer of Dunne's votes Result | | Eighth Count Transfer of Jones' votes Result | |
|---|---|---|---|---|---|---|---|---|---|---|---|---|---|---|---|
| DUNNE, Pat (F.F.) | 472 | +109 | 581 | +22 | 603 | +19 | 622 | +7 | 629 | +21 | 650 | -650 | — | — | — |
| HANCOX, John (F.G.) | 211 | +2 | 213 | -213 | — | — | — | — | — | — | — | — | — | — | — |
| JONES, Terri (F.G.) | 670 | +2 | 672 | +33 | 705 | +27 | 732 | +94 | 826 | +22 | 848 | +22 | 870 | -870 | — |
| KEAVENEY, Angela | 241 | +3 | 244 | +8 | 252 | -252 | — | — | — | — | — | — | — | — | — |
| KENNEDY, Michael (F.F.) | 923 | +63 | 986 | +19 | 1,005 | +44 | 1,049 | +45 | 1,094 | +12 | 1,106 | +419 | 1,525 | +207 | 1,732 |
| MALONE, Bernie (Lab.) | 1,198 | +19 | 1,217 | +51 | 1,268 | +30 | 1,298 | +65 | 1,363 | +112 | 1,475 | +52 | 1,527 | +175 | 1,702 |
| NAGLE, Alan (G.P.) | 813 | +14 | 827 | +29 | 856 | +59 | 915 | +42 | 957 | +90 | 1,047 | +35 | 1,082 | +140 | 1,222 |
| O'BRIEN, Bill (P.D.) | 394 | +7 | 401 | +4 | 405 | +10 | 415 | +78 | 493 | -493 | — | — | — | — | — |
| OWEN, Nora (F.G.) | 1,148 | +37 | 1,185 | +40 | 1,225 | +18 | 1,243 | +36 | 1,279 | +190 | 1,469 | +64 | 1,533 | +297 | 1,830 |
| WEBBERLEY, Mary (P.D.) | 347 | +3 | 350 | +3 | 353 | +21 | 374 | -374 | — | — | — | — | — | — | — |
| WRIGHT, G.V. (F.F.) | 1,929 | -259 | 1,670 | — | 1,670 | — | 1,670 | — | 1,670 | — | 1,670 | — | 1,670 | — | 1,670 |
| Non-transferable papers not effective | — | — | — | +4 | (4) | +24 | 28 | +7 | 35 | +46 | 81 | +58 | 139 | +51 | 190 |
| TOTAL: | 8,346 | — | 8,346 | — | 8,346 | — | 8,346 | — | 8,346 | — | 8,346 | — | 8,346 | — | 8,346 |

Elected: Wright, G.V. (F.F.); Owen, Nora (F.G.); Kennedy, Michael (F.F.); Malone, Bernie (Lab.)

# MULHUDDART ELECTORAL AREA

TOTAL ELECTORATE 13,768. VALID POLL 6,520. NO. OF MEMBERS 3. QUOTA 1,631.

| Names of Candidates | First Count Votes | Second Count Transfer of Clarke's and Leahy's votes Result | | Third Count Transfer of McGuinness' votes Result | | Fourth Count Transfer of Fleming's votes Result | | Fifth Count Transfer of Heffernan's votes Result | | Sixth Count Transfer of Reynold's votes Result | | Seventh Count Transfer of Fahey's votes Result | | Eighth Count Transfer of Lunney's votes Result | |
|---|---|---|---|---|---|---|---|---|---|---|---|---|---|---|---|
| BURTON, Joan (Lab.) | 844 | +12 | 856 | +31 | 887 | +29 | 916 | +18 | 934 | +84 | 1,018 | +56 | 1,074 | +425 | 1,499 |
| CLARKE, Frank (Non-Party) | 35 | -35 | — | — | — | — | — | — | — | — | — | — | — | — | — |
| FAHEY, Jim (F.F.) | 620 | +31 | 651 | +11 | 662 | +8 | 670 | +15 | 685 | +45 | 730 | -730 | — | — | — |
| FLEMING, Jim (F.G.) | 254 | +1 | 255 | +13 | 268 | -268 | — | — | — | — | — | — | — | — | — |
| HEFFERNAN, Jim (S.F.) | 264 | +3 | 267 | +8 | 275 | +7 | 282 | -282 | — | — | — | — | — | — | — |
| HIGGINS, Joe | 1,281 | +13 | 1,294 | +22 | 1,316 | +31 | 1,347 | +117 | 1,464 | +117 | 1,581 | +71 | 1,652 | — | 1,652 |
| LEAHY, P.J. (F.F.) | 123 | -123 | — | — | — | — | — | — | — | — | — | — | — | — | — |
| LUNNEY, Ollie (W.P.) | 672 | +10 | 682 | +24 | 706 | +12 | 718 | +53 | 771 | +66 | 837 | +31 | 868 | -868 | — |
| McGENNIS, Marian (F.F.) | 903 | +52 | 955 | +14 | 969 | +62 | 1,031 | +23 | 1,054 | +45 | 1,099 | +437 | 1,536 | +106 | 1,642 |
| McGUINNESS, Anthony (G.P.) | 168 | +9 | 177 | -177 | — | — | — | — | — | — | — | — | — | — | — |
| REYNOLDS, Tom | 450 | +9 | 459 | +32 | 491 | +16 | 507 | +20 | 527 | -527 | — | — | — | — | — |
| SHEEHAN, Marian (F.G.) | 906 | +14 | 920 | +13 | 933 | +87 | 1,020 | +5 | 1,025 | +126 | 1,151 | +49 | 1,200 | +89 | 1,289 |
| Non-transferable papers not effective | — | +4 | 4 | +9 | 13 | +16 | 29 | +31 | 60 | +44 | 104 | +86 | 190 | +248 | 438 |
| TOTAL: | 6,520 | — | 6,520 | — | 6,520 | — | 6,520 | — | 6,520 | — | 6,520 | — | 6,520 | — | 6,520 |

Elected: Higgins, Joe; McGennis, Marian (F.F.); Burton, Joan (Lab.)

# SWORDS ELECTORAL AREA

TOTAL ELECTORATE 17,053. VALID POLL 7,684. NO. OF MEMBERS 4. QUOTA 1,537

| Names of Candidates | First Count Votes | Second Count Transfer of Ryan's surplus | Result | Third Count Transfer of Crosbie's and McCormack's votes | Result | Fourth Count Transfer of O'Brien's votes | Result | Fifth Count Transfer of Hobson's votes | Result | Sixth Count Transfer of Mulvihill's votes | Result | Seventh Count Transfer of Nolan's votes | Result | Eighth Count Transfer of Kelleher's surplus | Result | Ninth Count Transfer of Gallagher's votes | Result |
|---|---|---|---|---|---|---|---|---|---|---|---|---|---|---|---|---|---|
| CROSBIE, Noel | 108 | +18 | 126 | -126 | — | — | — | — | — | — | — | — | — | — | — | — | — |
| DEVITT, Anne (F.G.) | 689 | +94 | 783 | +92 | 875 | +18 | 893 | +95 | 988 | +77 | 1,065 | +203 | 1,268 | +48 | 1,316 | +8 | 1,324 |
| GALLAGHER, Cyril (F.F.) | 872 | +91 | 963 | +35 | 998 | +5 | 1,003 | +43 | 1,046 | +450 | 1,496 | +66 | 1,562 | — | 1,562 | -25 | 1,537 |
| HOBSON, Elaine (Non-Party) | 406 | +60 | 466 | +41 | 507 | +55 | 562 | -562 | — | — | — | — | — | — | — | — | — |
| KELLEHER, Tom (Lab.) | 453 | +553 | 1,006 | +28 | 1,034 | +120 | 1,154 | +97 | 1,251 | +36 | 1,287 | +312 | 1,599 | -62 | 1,537 | — | 1,537 |
| McCORMACK, Tommy (F.G.) | 133 | +29 | 162 | -162 | — | — | — | — | — | — | — | — | — | — | — | — | — |
| MULVIHILL, Larry (F.F.) | 727 | +94 | 821 | +19 | 840 | +17 | 857 | +30 | 887 | -887 | — | — | — | — | — | — | — |
| NOLAN, Tony (G.P.) | 514 | +94 | 608 | +32 | 640 | +78 | 718 | +175 | 893 | +44 | 937 | -937 | — | — | — | — | — |
| O'BRIEN, Tim (W.P.) | 306 | +60 | 366 | +14 | 380 | -380 | — | — | — | — | — | — | — | — | — | — | — |
| O'CONNOR, Margaret (F.F.) | 809 | +37 | 846 | +8 | 854 | +63 | 917 | +46 | 963 | +214 | 1,177 | +108 | 1,285 | +14 | 1,299 | +17 | 1,316 |
| RYAN, Sean (Lab.) | 2,667 | -1,130 | 1,537 | — | 1,537 | — | 1,537 | — | 1,537 | — | 1,537 | — | 1,537 | — | 1,537 | — | 1,537 |
| Non-transferable papers not effective | — | — | — | +19 | 19 | +24 | 43 | +76 | 119 | +66 | 185 | +248 | 433 | — | 433 | — | 433 |
| TOTAL: | 7,684 | — | 7,684 | — | 7,684 | — | 7,684 | — | 7,684 | — | 7,684 | — | 7,684 | — | 7,684 | — | 7,684 |

Elected: Ryan, Sean (lab.); Kelleher, Tom (Lab.); Gallagher, Cyril (F.F.); Devitt, Anne (F.G.)

# CLONDALKIN ELECTORAL AREA

TOTAL ELECTORATE 20,425. VALID POLL 7,544. NO. OF MEMBERS 3. QUOTA 1,887.

| Names of Candidates | First Count Votes | Second Count Transfer of Duffy's and O'Connor's votes | Result | Third Count Transfer of Coffey's votes | Result | Fourth Count Transfer of Smyth's votes | Result | Fifth Count Transfer of Delaney's votes | Result | Sixth Count Transfer of Dowds' votes | Result | Seventh Count Transfer of Sherwin's votes | Result |
|---|---|---|---|---|---|---|---|---|---|---|---|---|---|
| COFFEY, Vincent (S.F.) | 315 | +25 | 340 | -340 | — | — | — | — | — | — | — | — | — |
| CONLON, Donna (W.P.) | 671 | +58 | 729 | +80 | 809 | +4 | 813 | +130 | 943 | +349 | 1,292 | +64 | 1,356 |
| DELANEY, Conor (G.P.) | 400 | +36 | 436 | +60 | 496 | +22 | 518 | -518 | — | — | — | — | — |
| DOWDS, Robert (Lab.) | 626 | +53 | 679 | +32 | 711 | +10 | 721 | +73 | 794 | -794 | — | — | — |
| DUFFY, Maurice (Non-Party) | 178 | -178 | — | — | — | — | — | — | — | — | — | — | — |
| McGRATH, Colm (F.F.) | 1,104 | +8 | 1,112 | +24 | 1,136 | +121 | 1,257 | +23 | 1,280 | +36 | 1,316 | +711 | 2,027 |
| O'CONNOR, Marie | 123 | -123 | — | — | — | — | — | — | — | — | — | — | — |
| RIDGE, Therese (F.G.) | 1,378 | +53 | 1,431 | +28 | 1,459 | +38 | 1,497 | +66 | 1,563 | +170 | 1,733 | +150 | 1,883 |
| SHERWIN, Catherine (F.F.) | 986 | +18 | 1,004 | +24 | 1,028 | +154 | 1,182 | +47 | 1,229 | +30 | 1,259 | -1,259 | — |
| SMYTH, Pat (F.F.) | 431 | +5 | 436 | +5 | 441 | -441 | — | — | — | — | — | — | — |
| TYNDALL, Colm (P.D.) | 1,332 | +23 | 1,355 | +20 | 1,375 | +72 | 1,447 | +97 | 1,544 | +103 | 1,647 | +216 | 1,863 |
| Non-transferable papers not effective | — | +22 | 22 | +67 | 89 | +20 | 109 | +82 | 191 | +106 | 297 | +118 | 415 |
| TOTAL: | 7,544 | — | 7,544 | — | 7,544 | — | 7,544 | — | 7,544 | — | 7,544 | — | 7,544 |

Elected: McGrath, Colm (F.F.); Ridge, Therese (F.G.); Tyndall, Colm (P.D.)

# GREENHILLS ELECTORAL AREA

TOTAL ELECTORATE 16,819. VALID POLL 6,590. NO. OF MEMBERS 4. QUOTA 1,319.

| Names of Candidates | First Count Votes | Second Count Transfer of Taylor's surplus | Result | Third Count Transfer of Earley's votes | Result | Fourth Count Transfer of O'Brien's votes | Result | Fifth Count Transfer of Larkin's votes | Result | Sixth Count Transfer of Hanrahan's votes | Result | Seventh Count Transfer of Byrne's votes | Result | Eighth Count Transfer of O'Connor's votes | Result | Ninth Count Transfer of Farrell's surplus | Result |
|---|---|---|---|---|---|---|---|---|---|---|---|---|---|---|---|---|---|
| BYRNE, Bob | 611 | +17 | 628 | +17 | 645 | +6 | 651 | +62 | 713 | +23 | 736 | -736 | — | — | — | — | — |
| EARLEY, Dessie (S.F.) | 157 | +5 | 162 | -162 | — | — | — | — | — | — | — | — | — | — | — | — | — |
| FARRELL, Margaret (F.F.) | 525 | +12 | 537 | +12 | 549 | +6 | 555 | +25 | 580 | +248 | 828 | +115 | 943 | +469 | 1,412 | -93 | 1,319 |
| HANRAHAN, Michael (F.F.) | 468 | +11 | 479 | +26 | 505 | +6 | 511 | +12 | 523 | -523 | — | — | — | — | — | — | — |
| KEATING, Michael (F.G.) | 720 | +25 | 745 | +9 | 754 | +121 | 875 | +44 | 919 | +27 | 946 | +120 | 1,066 | +60 | 1,126 | +44 | 1,170 |
| LARKIN, Alison (G.P.) | 298 | +10 | 308 | +37 | 345 | +18 | 363 | -363 | — | — | — | — | — | — | — | — | — |
| MACKIN, Denis (Lab.) | 522 | +112 | 634 | +14 | 648 | +19 | 667 | +70 | 737 | +18 | 755 | +126 | 881 | +159 | 1,040 | +49 | 1,089 |
| O'BRIEN, Michael J. (F.G.) | 224 | +4 | 228 | — | 228 | -228 | — | — | — | — | — | — | — | — | — | — | — |
| O'CONNOR, Geraldine (F.F.) | 577 | +7 | 584 | +2 | 586 | +21 | 607 | +19 | 626 | +141 | 767 | +52 | 819 | -819 | — | — | — |
| TAYLOR, Mervyn (Lab.) | 1,576 | -257 | 1,319 | — | 1,319 | — | 1,319 | — | 1,319 | — | 1,319 | — | 1,319 | — | 1,319 | — | 1,319 |
| TIPPING, Don (W.P.) | 912 | +54 | 966 | +29 | 995 | +25 | 1,020 | +87 | 1,107 | +31 | 1,138 | +168 | 1,306 | +51 | 1,357 | — | 1,357 |
| Non-transferable papers not effective | — | — | — | +16 | 16 | +6 | 22 | +44 | 66 | +35 | 101 | +155 | 256 | +80 | 336 | — | 336 |
| TOTAL: | 6,590 | — | 6,590 | — | 6,590 | — | 6,590 | — | 6,590 | — | 6,590 | — | 6,590 | — | 6,590 | — | 6,590 |

Elected: Taylor, Mervyn (Lab.); Farrell, Margaret (F.F.); Tipping, Don (W.P.); Keating, Michael (F.G.)

# LUCAN ELECTORAL AREA

TOTAL ELECTORATE 20,266. VALID POLL 9,895. NO. OF MEMBERS 4. QUOTA 1,980

| Names of Candidates | First Count Votes | Second Count Transfer of Kirwan's votes | Result | Third Count Transfer of Kavanagh's votes | Result | Fourth Count Transfer of O'Connor's votes | Result | Fifth Count Transfer of Brennan's votes | Result | Sixth Count Transfer of Ryan's votes | Result | Seventh Count Transfer of O'Connell's surplus | Result | Eighth Count Transfer of Finnegan's votes | Result | Ninth Count Transfer of McCann's votes | Result | Tenth Count Transfer of Lawlor's votes | Result | Eleventh Count Transfer of Hanrahan's surplus | Result |
|---|---|---|---|---|---|---|---|---|---|---|---|---|---|---|---|---|---|---|---|---|---|
| BRADY, Peter (F.G.) | 1,336 | +10 | 1,346 | +126 | 1,472 | +77 | 1,549 | +38 | 1,587 | +25 | 1,612 | +7 | 1,619 | +156 | 1,775 | +37 | 1,812 | +175 | 1,987 | — | 1,987 |
| BRENNAN, Michael (Lab.) | 497 | +37 | 534 | +29 | 563 | +35 | 598 | -598 | — | — | — | — | — | — | — | — | — | — | — | — | — |
| FINNEGAN, Anne (W.P.) | 665 | +6 | 671 | +6 | 677 | +71 | 748 | +29 | 777 | +22 | 799 | +4 | 803 | -803 | — | — | — | — | — | — | — |
| HANRAHAN, Finbarr (F.F.) | 1,119 | +7 | 1,126 | +19 | 1,145 | +37 | 1,182 | +33 | 1,215 | +225 | 1,440 | +19 | 1,459 | +55 | 1,514 | +93 | 1,607 | +755 | 2,362 | -382 | 1,980 |
| KAVANAGH, Tom (F.G.) | 311 | +5 | 316 | -316 | — | — | — | — | — | — | — | — | — | — | — | — | — | — | — | — | — |
| KIRWAN, Michael (Non-Party) | 200 | -200 | — | — | — | — | — | — | — | — | — | — | — | — | — | — | — | — | — | — | — |
| LAWLOR, Liam (F.F.) | 905 | +5 | 910 | +9 | 919 | +15 | 934 | +16 | 950 | +160 | 1,110 | +13 | 1,123 | +50 | 1,173 | +73 | 1,246 | -1,246 | — | — | — |
| McCANN, John (S.F.) | 783 | +6 | 789 | +8 | 797 | +11 | 808 | +7 | 815 | +13 | 828 | +2 | 830 | +89 | 919 | -919 | — | — | — | — | — |
| O'CONNELL, Guss (Non-Party) | 1,406 | +71 | 1,477 | +55 | 1,532 | +117 | 1,649 | +245 | 1,894 | +138 | 2,032 | -52 | 1,980 | — | 1,980 | — | 1,980 | — | 1,980 | — | 1,980 |
| O'CONNOR, Brídín (G.P.) | 492 | +20 | 512 | +19 | 531 | -531 | — | — | — | — | — | — | — | — | — | — | — | — | — | — | — |
| O'HALLORAN, John (Lab.) | 775 | +6 | 781 | +14 | 795 | +20 | 815 | +69 | 884 | +14 | 898 | +3 | 901 | +157 | 1,058 | +321 | 1,379 | +88 | 1,467 | +86 | 1,553 |
| RYAN, Deirdre (F.F.) | 580 | +11 | 591 | +18 | 609 | +21 | 630 | +45 | 675 | -675 | — | — | — | — | — | — | — | — | — | — | — |
| TUFFY, Eamon (Lab.) | 826 | +3 | 829 | +5 | 834 | +93 | 927 | +73 | 1,000 | +26 | 1,026 | +4 | 1,030 | +181 | 1,211 | +52 | 1,263 | +52 | 1,315 | +115 | 1,430 |
| Non-transferable papers not effective | — | +13 | 13 | +8 | 21 | +34 | 55 | +43 | 98 | +52 | 150 | — | 150 | +115 | 265 | +343 | 608 | +176 | 784 | +181 | 965 |
| TOTAL: | 9,895 | — | 9,895 | — | 9,895 | — | 9,895 | — | 9,895 | — | 9,895 | — | 9,895 | — | 9,895 | — | 9,895 | — | 9,895 | — | 9,895 |

Elected: O'Connell, Guss (Non-Party); Hanrahan, Finbarr (F.F.); Brady, Peter (F.G.); O'Halloran, John (Lab.)

# TALLAGHT - OLDBAWN ELECTORAL AREA

TOTAL ELECTORATE 18,163. VALID POLL 7,038. NO. OF MEMBERS 3. QUOTA 1,760

| Names of Candidates | First Count Votes | Second Count Transfer of Cunningham's votes | Result | Third Count Transfer of Ringland's votes | Result | Fourth Count Transfer of Dwane's votes | Result | Fifth Count Transfer of Murphy's votes | Result | Sixth Count Transfer of Barry's votes | Result | Seventh Count Transfer of Hannon's surplus | Result | Eighth Count Transfer of Crowe's votes | Result | Ninth Count Transfer of Maloney's votes | Result | Tenth Count Transfer of McMahon's votes | Result |
|---|---|---|---|---|---|---|---|---|---|---|---|---|---|---|---|---|---|---|---|
| BARRY, Jim (F.F.) | 389 | +5 | 394 | +1 | 395 | +35 | 430 | +4 | 434 | -434 | — | — | — | — | — | — | — | — | — |
| CASS, Breda (P.D.) | 892 | +8 | 900 | +16 | 916 | +4 | 920 | +49 | 969 | +29 | 998 | +23 | 1,021 | +41 | 1,062 | +69 | 1,131 | +370 | 1,501 |
| CROWE, Seán (S.F.) | 399 | +37 | 436 | +2 | 438 | +3 | 441 | +20 | 461 | +19 | 480 | +16 | 496 | -496 | — | — | — | — | — |
| CUNNINGHAM, Peter | 125 | -125 | — | — | — | — | — | — | — | — | — | — | — | — | — | — | — | — | — |
| DWANE, Pádraic (F.F.) | 178 | +1 | 179 | — | 179 | -179 | — | — | — | — | — | — | — | — | — | — | — | — | — |
| GIBBONS, Ned (Lab.) | 663 | +4 | 667 | +6 | 673 | +3 | 676 | +30 | 706 | +56 | 762 | +13 | 775 | +110 | 885 | +386 | 1,271 | +144 | 1,415 |
| HANNON, John (F.F.) | 1,572 | +7 | 1,579 | +11 | 1,590 | +73 | 1,663 | +21 | 1,684 | +231 | 1,915 | -155 | 1,760 | — | 1,760 | — | 1,760 | — | 1,760 |
| McMAHON, Larry (F.G.) | 789 | +10 | 799 | +90 | 889 | +23 | 912 | +30 | 942 | +22 | 964 | +24 | 988 | +21 | 1,009 | +74 | 1,083 | -1,083 | — |
| MALONEY, Eamonn (Lab.) | 667 | +10 | 677 | +12 | 689 | +14 | 703 | +38 | 741 | +7 | 748 | +8 | 756 | +45 | 801 | -801 | — | — | — |
| MURPHY, Malachy (G.P.) | 259 | +12 | 271 | +8 | 279 | +1 | 280 | -280 | — | — | — | — | — | — | — | — | — | — | — |
| RABBITTE, Pat (W.P.) | 947 | +20 | 967 | +13 | 980 | +14 | 994 | +72 | 1,066 | +36 | 1,102 | +23 | 1,125 | +130 | 1,255 | +217 | 1,472 | +264 | 1,736 |
| RINGLAND, Paul (F.G.) | 158 | +1 | 159 | -159 | — | — | — | — | — | — | — | — | — | — | — | — | — | — | — |
| Non-transferable papers not effective | — | +10 | 10 | — | 10 | +9 | 19 | +16 | 35 | +34 | 69 | +48 | 117 | +149 | 266 | +55 | 321 | +305 | 626 |
| TOTAL: | 7,038 | — | 7,038 | — | 7,038 | — | 7,038 | — | 7,038 | — | 7,038 | — | 7,038 | — | 7,038 | — | 7,038 | — | 7,038 |

Elected: Hannon, John (F.F.); Rabbitte, Pat (W.P.); Cass, Breda (P.D.).

# RATHFARNHAM ELECTORAL AREA

TOTAL ELECTORATE 20,175. VALID POLL 8,318. NO. OF MEMBERS 4. QUOTA 1,664.

| Names of Candidates | First Count Votes | Second Count Transfer of Corcoran's votes | Result | Third Count Transfer of Byrne's votes | Result | Fourth Count Transfer of Riney's votes | Result | Fifth Count Transfer of Ormonde's surplus | Result | Sixth Count Transfer of McBrien's votes | Result | Seventh Count Transfer of Kenny's votes | Result |
|---|---|---|---|---|---|---|---|---|---|---|---|---|---|
| BYRNE, Billy (Lab.) | 227 | +112 | 339 | -339 | — | — | — | — | — | — | — | — | — |
| CORCORAN, Graham (Lab.) | 154 | -154 | — | — | — | — | — | — | — | — | — | — | — |
| FEE, Damien (F.F.) | 882 | +2 | 884 | +13 | 897 | +92 | 989 | +153 | 1,142 | +81 | 1,223 | +102 | 1,325 |
| KENNY, Vincent (Non-Party) | 760 | +7 | 767 | +65 | 832 | +10 | 842 | +7 | 849 | +95 | 944 | -944 | — |
| McBRIEN, Ronnie (P.D.) | 719 | +2 | 721 | +39 | 760 | +18 | 778 | +10 | 788 | -788 | — | — | — |
| MULDOON, Mary (F.G.) | 1,161 | +5 | 1,166 | +28 | 1,194 | +12 | 1,206 | +7 | 1,213 | +142 | 1,355 | +267 | 1,622 |
| MULLARNEY, Maire (G.P.) | 1,163 | +13 | 1,176 | +113 | 1,289 | +24 | 1,313 | +14 | 1,327 | +184 | 1,511 | +366 | 1,877 |
| ORMONDE, Ann (F.F.) | 1,582 | +2 | 1,584 | +17 | 1,601 | +271 | 1,872 | -208 | 1,664 | — | 1,664 | — | 1,664 |
| RINEY, Stephen (F.F.) | 479 | — | 479 | +6 | 485 | -485 | — | — | — | — | — | — | — |
| SHATTER, Alan (F.G.) | 1,191 | +11 | 1,202 | +39 | 1,241 | +45 | 1,286 | +17 | 1,303 | +235 | 1,538 | +133 | 1,671 |
| Non-transferable papers not effective | — | — | — | +19 | 19 | +13 | 32 | — | 32 | +51 | 83 | +76 | 159 |
| TOTAL: | 8,318 | — | 8,318 | — | 8,318 | — | 8,318 | — | 8,318 | — | 8,318 | — | 8,318 |

Elected: Ormonde, Ann (F.F.); Mullarney, Marie (G.P.); Shatter, Alan (F.G.); Muldoon, Mary (F.G.).

# TALLAGHT - RATHCOOLE ELECTORAL AREA

TOTAL ELECTORATE 15,744. VALID POLL 6,003. NO. OF MEMBERS 3. QUOTA 1,501.

| Names of Candidates | First Count Votes | Second Count Transfer of Morton's votes | Result | Third Count Transfer of Lovett's votes | Result | Fourth Count Transfer of Smyth's votes | Result | Fifth Count Transfer of O'Mahony's votes | Result | Sixth Count Transfer of Flannery's votes | Result | Seventh Count Transfer of Corcoran's votes | Result | Eighth Count Transfer of Billane's surplus | Result | Ninth Count Transfer of Daly's votes | Result |
|---|---|---|---|---|---|---|---|---|---|---|---|---|---|---|---|---|---|
| BILLANE, Mick (W.P.) | 1,217 | +11 | 1,228 | +36 | 1,264 | +42 | 1,306 | +62 | 1,368 | +120 | 1,488 | +66 | 1,554 | -53 | 1,501 | — | 1,501 |
| CORCORAN, Pat (F.G.) | 384 | +4 | 388 | +63 | 451 | +12 | 463 | +21 | 484 | +35 | 519 | -519 | — | — | — | — | — |
| DALY, Jim (F.F.) | 741 | +16 | 757 | +2 | 759 | +5 | 764 | +19 | 783 | +49 | 832 | +72 | 904 | +10 | 914 | -914 | — |
| FLANNERY, Tony (S.F.) | 386 | +4 | 390 | +7 | 397 | +12 | 409 | +20 | 429 | -429 | — | — | — | — | — | — | — |
| INGLE, Maria (Lab.) | 694 | +6 | 700 | +12 | 712 | +29 | 741 | +74 | 815 | +71 | 886 | +50 | 936 | +18 | 954 | +74 | 1,028 |
| LOVETT, Jim (F.G.) | 177 | +1 | 178 | -178 | — | — | — | — | — | — | — | — | — | — | — | — | — |
| MORTON, Mary (F.F.) | 114 | -114 | — | — | — | — | — | — | — | — | — | — | — | — | — | — | — |
| O'CONNOR, Charles (F.F.) | 922 | +65 | 987 | +9 | 996 | +23 | 1,019 | +125 | 1,144 | +38 | 1,182 | +34 | 1,216 | +4 | 1,220 | +436 | 1,656 |
| O'MAHONY, John (Non-Party) | 359 | +4 | 363 | +11 | 374 | +15 | 389 | -389 | — | — | — | — | — | — | — | — | — |
| QUINN, Catherine (P.D.) | 785 | +1 | 786 | +10 | 796 | +93 | 889 | +45 | 934 | +48 | 982 | +217 | 1,199 | +9 | 1,208 | +213 | 1,421 |
| SMYTH, Martin (P.D.) | 224 | +2 | 226 | +22 | 248 | -248 | — | — | — | — | — | — | — | — | — | — | — |
| Non-transferable papers not effective | — | — | — | +6 | 6 | +17 | 23 | +23 | 46 | +68 | 114 | +80 | 194 | +12 | 206 | +191 | 397 |
| TOTAL: | 6,003 | — | 6,003 | — | 6,003 | — | 6,003 | — | 6,003 | — | 6,003 | — | 6,003 | — | 6,003 | — | 6,003 |

Elected: Billane, Mick (W.P.); O'Connor, Charles (F.F.); Quinn, Catherine (P.D.)

# TERENURE ELECTORAL AREA

TOTAL ELECTORATE 24,148. VALID POLL 10,333. NO. OF MEMBERS 5. QUOTA 1,723.

| Names of Candidates | First Count Votes | Second Count Transfer of O'Connell's votes | Result | Third Count Transfer of Mullally's votes | Result | Fourth Count Transfer of Ashe's votes | Result | Fifth Count Transfer of Tighe's votes | Result | Sixth Count Transfer of Stoke's votes | Result | Seventh Count Transfer of Ardagh's surplus | Result | Eighth Count Transfer of Murphy's votes | Result |
|---|---|---|---|---|---|---|---|---|---|---|---|---|---|---|---|
| ARDAGH, Sean (F.F.) | 1,070 | +5 | 1,075 | +193 | 1,268 | +43 | 1,311 | +229 | 1,540 | +542 | 2,082 | -359 | 1,723 | — | 1,723 |
| ASHE, Seamus | 532 | +29 | 561 | +5 | 566 | -566 | — | — | — | — | — | — | — | — | — |
| KEANE, Cáit (P.D.) | 1,128 | +31 | 1,159 | +14 | 1,173 | +45 | 1,218 | +49 | 1,267 | +50 | 1,317 | +59 | 1,376 | +166 | 1,542 |
| LAING, Stanley (F.G.) | 1,488 | +15 | 1,503 | +38 | 1,541 | +25 | 1,566 | +19 | 1,585 | +45 | 1,630 | +55 | 1,685 | +83 | 1,768 |
| LYNCH, Martin (F.G.) | 981 | +11 | 992 | +22 | 1,014 | +23 | 1,037 | +14 | 1,051 | +30 | 1,081 | +15 | 1,096 | +67 | 1,163 |
| MULLALLY, Gerry (F.F.) | 470 | +2 | 472 | -472 | — | — | — | — | — | — | — | — | — | — | — |
| MURPHY, Jim (G.P.) | 682 | +69 | 751 | +10 | 761 | +90 | 851 | +29 | 880 | +24 | 904 | +36 | 940 | -940 | — |
| O'CONNELL, Deirdre (W.P.) | 430 | -430 | — | — | — | — | — | — | — | — | — | — | — | — | — |
| STOKES, Michael J. (F.F.) | 555 | +9 | 564 | +77 | 641 | +34 | 675 | +173 | 848 | -848 | — | — | — | — | — |
| TIGHE, Molly (F.F.) | 550 | +9 | 559 | +56 | 615 | +56 | 671 | -671 | — | — | — | — | — | — | — |
| UPTON, Pat (Lab.) | 1,169 | +140 | 1,309 | +43 | 1,352 | +72 | 1,424 | +30 | 1,454 | +38 | 1,492 | +28 | 1,520 | +260 | 1,780 |
| WALSH, Eamonn (Lab.) | 1,278 | +104 | 1,382 | +2 | 1,384 | +143 | 1,527 | +98 | 1,625 | +31 | 1,656 | +22 | 1,678 | +167 | 1,845 |
| Non-transferable papers not effective | — | +6 | (6) | +12 | 18 | +35 | 53 | +30 | 83 | +88 | 171 | +144 | 315 | +197 | 512 |
| TOTAL: | 10,333 | — | 10,333 | — | 10,333 | — | 10,333 | — | 10,333 | — | 10,333 | — | 10,333 | — | 10,333 |

Elected: Ardagh, Sean (F.F.); Walsh, Eamonn (Lab.); Upton, Pat (Lab.); Laing, Stanley (F.G.); Keane, Cáit (P.D.)

# WHEN IT COMES TO EUROPE'S BEST, THE 'EYES' HAVE IT.

In a recent survey of Europe's 200* top circulating

newspapers only one Irish daily made the grade.

It will hardly be an eye-opener to you to learn that

'paper was the Irish Independent.

**Open your eyes
with the Irish Independent.**

*Source 'Newspaper Focus' Top 200. Vol 3 No. 9.

# GALWAY BOROUGH COUNCIL

## GALWAY BOROUGH COUNCIL RES.

| PARTY | 1991 % of votes | 1991 Seats obtained | 1985 % of votes | 1985 Seats obtained |
|---|---|---|---|---|
| Fianna Fail | 27.4 | 4 | 41.2 | 6 |
| Fine Gael | 20.2 | 4 | 29.0 | 5 |
| Labour | 13.2 | 2 | 9.6 | 1 |
| Progressive Dem. | 22.1 | 4 | — | — |
| Workers Party | 2.9 | — | 9.0 | 2 |
| Other | 14.2 | 1 | 10.0 | 1 |
| TOTAL SEATS | | 15 | | 15 |

## GALWAY

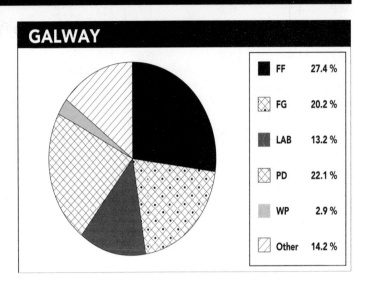

| | | |
|---|---|---|
| FF | 27.4 % |
| FG | 20.2 % |
| LAB | 13.2 % |
| PD | 22.1 % |
| WP | 2.9 % |
| Other | 14.2 % |

**Galway Corporation**
**City Hall, College Road**
**Galway**
**Telephone:(091) 68151**
**Fax:(091) 67493**
**Rateable valuation: £401,815.20**
**Municipal rate: £32.12**
**City Council meetings: First and third Monday of each month**

*Manager (Galway County and City):* S. Keating
*Assistant City Manager:* D. O'Donoghue
*Assistant Town Clerk:* D. J. Buggy
*City Engineer:* M. B. McCurtin
*Finance Officer:* S. Real
*Administrative Officer:* J. Tierney
*Senior Staff Officers:*
*Planning:* J. Cullen
*Capital:* M. T. Burke (Acting)
*Computer:* J. McGovern
*Senior Executive Engineers-Planners:*
*Roads and Sanitary Services:* M. P. Keaney
*Housing, Environment and General Urban:* M. Joyce
*Planning:* John A. Roche
*Executive Engineers:*
*Planning:* P. J. Kenny, B. Cahill
*Water and Sewerage:* P. Greaney
*Parks and Open Spaces:* M. Nugent (Acting)
*Housing:* G. O'Loughlin (Acting)
*Roads:* J. Waldron
*Traffic:* J. Tansey

Seamus Keating is a native of Tipperary where he was born in 1930. He has been Galway City and County Manager for over twenty years. He joined the public service at eighteen years of age as a Clerical Officer in Tipperary South Riding. At 23 he became a Staff Officer at Waterford County Council and then in 1963 returned to Tipperary South Riding as County Accountant.

In 1966 he became County Secretary in Donegal County Council and three years later was appointed Kerry County Manager. He moved from Kerry to Galway in 1973 and now has responsibility for over nine hundred staff and a budget of over forty million pounds.

Married to Mary Cleary with nine children. His hobbies include boating, reading and walking.

## NORTH EAST

|  | 1991 | 1985 | '85 to '91 Swing |
|---|---|---|---|
| FF | 27.3 | 45.7 | -18.4 |
| FG | 19.8 | 26.7 | -6.9 |
| LAB | 8.4 | 8.9 | -0.5 |
| WP | 4.5 | 6.2 | -1.7 |
| PD | 25.2 |  | 25.2 |
| SF | 2.9 |  | 2.9 |
| Ind | 11.9 | 12.5 | -0.6 |

COOGAN, Fintan,
Menlo Park,
Galway. (FG).
Lecturer. 091-64282

COSTELLO, Tom,
Kiloughter, Castlegar,
Galway. (Lab).
Bus Eireann Driver.

LEAHY, Michael (Ald),
15 Dublin Road, Renmore,
Galway. (FF)
Irish Rail Worker. 091-55395

McCORMACK, Pádraic,
3 Renmore Park,
Galway. (FG)
Dáil Deputy. 091-53992

McDONNELL, Declan (Ald),
Carnmore,
County Galway. (PD)
Accountant. 091-94300

O'CONNOR, Henry,
33 St. Bridget's Terrace, Prospect Hill,
Galway. (FF)
Company Director.

O'FLAHERTY, Bridie,
"San Jose",
15 Monivea Road, Mervue,
Galway. (PD)
Housewife. 091-55909

## SOUTH WARD

|  | 1991 | 1985 | '85 to '91 Swing |
|---|---|---|---|
| FF | 32.5 | 39.5 | -7.0 |
| FG | 21.6 | 41.0 | -19.4 |
| LAB | 13.2 | 6.6 | 6.6 |
| PD | 27.5 |  | 27.5 |
| Ind | 5.3 | 12.9 | -7.6 |

HIGGINS, Michael D. (Ald),
Letteragh, Rahoon,
Galway. (Lab)
Dail Deputy. 091-24513

LALLY, Paddy,
49 Davis Road, Shantalla,
Galway. (NP)
UCG Employee.

LUPTON, Angela,
Highfield Park,
Galway. (FG)
Public Representative. 091-23882

MADDEN, Liam,
Woodstock, Busy Park,
Galway. (PD)
Nurseryman. 091-24928

O'HIGGINS, Micheál,
Taylor's Hill,
Galway. (FF)
Company Director. 091-21080

## WEST WARD

|  | 1991 | 1985 | '85 to '91 Swing |
|---|---|---|---|
| FF | 24.5 | 36.3 | -11.8 |
| FG | 20.1 | 23.9 | -3.8 |
| LAB | 19.2 | 16.4 | 2.8 |
| WP | 2.4 | 19.0 | -16.6 |
| PD | 15.1 | — | 15.1 |
| SF | 1.3 | — | 1.3 |
| Ind | 17.3 | 4.4 | 12.9 |

CONNOLLY, Martin (Ald),
5 Frenchville, Grattan Road,
Galway. (PD)
Retired. 091-63704

MULHOLLAND, John,
1 Revagh Road, Salthill,
Galway. (FG)
Turf Accountant. 091-23739

COX, Tom,
7 Fr. Griffin Road,
Galway. (FF)
Company Director. 091-66892

**Bobby Molloy who is the Progressive Democrats' Director of Elections for the 1991 local elections pictured with one of his party's candidates.**

**Bridie O'Flaherty (PD)**
**Area No. 1**

**Angela Lupton (FG)**
**Area No. 2**

**Padraig McCormack (FG)**
**Area No. 1**

**Michael D. Higgins (Lab)**
**Area No. 2**

# The PD's are the big winners

The two big news stories from the Galway Corporation results were the performance of the Progressive Democrats and the almost total collapse of the Workers Party vote. Both issues require explanations.

The P.D.'s in their first Local Election contest had high hopes for Bobby Molloy's bailiwick and they were not to be disappointed. They were undoubtedly the big winners, securing four out of the fifteen seats, and taking 22.1% share of the vote.

Outgoing P.D. Councillor Bridie Flaherty who had joined them from Fianna Fail, came in second place in the North East Ward. The third seat in the Ward was taken up by P.D. colleague, accountant Declan McDonnell, to give the Party an unprecedented two out of seven seats. The Party's outgoing Councillor in the South Ward, Martin Connolly, topped the poll, while in the West Ward Liam Madden was elected for them on the last count.

Fianna Fail had hopes of regaining the six seats they had held on the Corporation before the P.D. split in 1986. Three of these six seats had gone to the P.D.'s. They, however, could only manage to return to the new Council with four seats.

Businessman Tom Cox after a close battle with running mate Dr. Tony O'Connor won back a seat for Fianna Fail in the South Ward to join outgoing Fianna Fail Councillor Michael Leahy and Micheal O'hUiginn as well as Henry O'Connor who regained the seat that he had lost in 1985. Leahy topped the poll in the North East Ward with 825 first preferences, while O'hUiginn came in second behind Micheal D. Higgins in the West Ward.

The Workers Party had won their first two seats in Galway in 1985. The 1991 results were a disaster for them however, due mainly to the collapse of the Party's Organisation in the City, following the resignation of former poll topper Jimmy Brick at the Workers Party 1990 Ard Fheis, after a highly publicised clash with the De Rossa leadership. Brick did not contest himself this time, and the Workers Party's candidate in the West Ward secured only 144 first preferences. The Party's outgoing Councillor in the North East Ward Liz Harkett polled over 340 votes on the first count and with only one third of a quota, lost her seat.

Overall in Galway Corporation, Fine Gael lost one of their seats, John Mulholland retained his seat in the South Ward. The Party's city T.D. Padraic McCormack struggled very hard to hold onto his seat in the North East Ward. Fintan Coogan who had been on the Party Ticket in the 1989 General Election with McCormack and had strongly challenged him for a Dail seat, outpolled him on the first count in these local elections.

The Labour Party also had much to celebrate, with a particularly fine performance by Deputy Michael D. Higgins who increased his first preference vote by 300 to top the poll in the West Ward, while Tom Costello took an extra seat for them, polling 360 first preferences in the North East Ward.

After the poll, the Fianna Fail and Fine Gael groups negotiated a pact to control the council. Their combined strength of eight gave them a majority on the 15 seat council and this denied the PD's of any of the fruits their fine performance might otherwise have

**Justin Flannery the youngest candidate in the Galway County Council and Borough Council Elections pictured with his brother and sister at the count in Loughrea.**

# NO. 1 ELECTORAL AREA

TOTAL ELECTORATE 15,295. VALID POLL 7,574. NO. OF MEMBERS 7. QUOTA 947

| Names of Candidates | First Count | Second Count Transfer of Manning's votes Result | Third Count Transfer of Joyce's votes Result | Fourth Count Transfer of McPhillip's votes Result | Fifth Count Transfer of Tierney's votes Result | Sixth Count Transfer of Fox's votes Result | Seventh Count Transfer of Leahy's surplus Result | Eighth Count Transfer of Hackett's votes Result | Ninth Count Transfer of McHugh's votes Result | Tenth Count Transfer of McDonnell's surplus Result | Eleventh Count Transfer of O'Flaherty's surplus Result | Twelfth Count Transfer of Nolan's votes Result | Thirteenth Count Transfer of McNamara's votes Result |
|---|---|---|---|---|---|---|---|---|---|---|---|---|---|
| COOGAN, Fintan (F.G.) | 604 | +7 611 | +11 622 | +11 633 | +66 699 | +33 732 | +3 735 | +60 795 | +48 843 | +15 858 | +7 865 | +31 896 | +109 1,005 |
| COSTELLO, Tom (Lab.) | 360 | +2 362 | +23 385 | +128 513 | +29 542 | +19 561 | +1 562 | +121 683 | +30 713 | +7 720 | +4 724 | +28 752 | +75 827 |
| FOX, Seán (F.F.) | 374 | — 374 | +6 380 | +6 386 | +9 395 | -395 — | — — | — — | — — | — — | — — | — — | — — |
| HACKETT, Liz (W.P.) | 340 | +2 342 | +25 367 | +39 406 | +9 415 | +19 434 | — 434 | -434 — | — — | — — | — — | — — | — — |
| JOYCE, Dave | 216 | +2 218 | -218 — | — — | — — | — — | — — | — — | — — | — — | — — | — — | — — |
| LEAHY, Michael (F.F.) | 825 | +3 828 | +14 842 | +11 853 | +23 876 | +150 1,026 | -79 947 | — 947 | — 947 | — 947 | — 947 | — 947 | — 947 |
| MANNING, Edward (Non-Party) | 58 | -58 — | — — | — — | — — | — — | — — | — — | — — | — — | — — | — — | — — |
| McCORMACK, Padraic (F.G.) | 556 | +6 562 | +7 569 | +10 579 | +67 646 | +8 654 | +1 655 | +19 674 | +42 716 | +6 722 | +4 726 | +36 762 | +54 816 |
| McDONNELL, Declan (P.D.) | 789 | +5 794 | +11 805 | +8 813 | +30 843 | +7 850 | +2 852 | +29 881 | +110 991 | -44 947 | — 947 | — 947 | — 947 |
| McHUGH, Martin (P.D.) | 418 | +1 419 | +5 424 | +10 434 | +27 461 | +6 467 | +1 468 | +22 490 | -490 — | — — | — — | — — | — — |
| McNAMARA, Pat (Non-Party) | 413 | +11 424 | +12 436 | +10 446 | +10 456 | +20 476 | +4 480 | +33 513 | +14 527 | +4 531 | +2 533 | +18 551 | -551 — |
| McPHILLIPS, Ivan Peter (Lab.) | 279 | +3 282 | +10 292 | -292 — | — — | — — | — — | — — | — — | — — | — — | — — | — — |
| NOLAN, Sean (F.F.) | 386 | +2 388 | +5 393 | +1 394 | +18 412 | +27 439 | +41 480 | +11 491 | +25 516 | +5 521 | +2 523 | -523 — | — — |
| O'CONNOR, Henry (F.F.) | 485 | +4 489 | +13 502 | +5 507 | +21 528 | +70 598 | +23 621 | +25 646 | +13 659 | +5 664 | +2 666 | +270 936 | +72 1,008 |
| O'FLAHERTY, Bridie (P.D.) | 698 | +6 704 | +19 723 | +19 742 | +32 774 | +13 787 | +2 789 | +33 822 | +149 971 | — 971 | -24 947 | — 947 | — 947 |
| SMITH, Brendan (Non-Party) | 433 | +2 435 | +32 467 | +16 483 | +15 498 | +9 507 | +1 508 | +43 551 | +35 586 | +2 588 | +3 591 | +20 611 | +72 683 |
| TIERNEY, Mary (F.G.) | 340 | +1 341 | +7 348 | +12 360 | -360 — | — — | — — | — — | — — | — — | — — | — — | — — |
| Non-transferable papers not effective | — | +1 1 | +18 19 | +6 25 | +4 29 | +14 43 | — 43 | +38 81 | +24 105 | — 105 | — 105 | +120 225 | +169 394 |
| TOTAL: | 7,574 | — 7,574 | — 7,574 | — 7,574 | — 7,574 | — 7,574 | — 7,574 | — 7,574 | — 7,574 | — 7,574 | — 7,574 | — 7,574 | — 7,574 |

Elected: Leahy, Michael (F.F.); McDonnell, Declan (P.D.); O'Flaherty, Bridie (P.D.); O'Connor, Henry (F.F.); Coogan, Fintan (F.G.); Costello, Tom (Lab.); McCormack, Padraic (F.G.)

# NO. 2 ELECTORAL AREA

TOTAL ELECTORATE 12,664. VALID POLL 5,992. NO. OF MEMBERS 5. QUOTA 999

| Names of Candidates | First Count Votes | Second Count Transfer of Egan's votes Result | Third Count Transfer of M. Lawless' votes Result | Fourth Count Transfer of Donnelly's votes Result | Fifth Count Transfer of Higgins' surplus Result | Sixth Count Transfer of Doolan's votes Result | Seventh Count Transfer of McCabe's votes Result | Eighth Count Transfer of Browne's votes Result | Ninth Count Transfer of O'Higgin's surplus Result | Tenth Count Transfer of Mullarkey's votes Result | Eleventh Count Transfer of Byrne's votes Result | Twelfth Count Transfer of Lyons' votes Result |
|---|---|---|---|---|---|---|---|---|---|---|---|---|
| BROWNE, Thomas A. (Non-Party) | 252 | +7 259 | +1 260 | +9 269 | +3 272 | +4 276 | +7 283 | -283 — | — — | — — | — — | — — |
| BYRNE, John Gerard (F.F.) | 324 | +2 326 | +19 345 | +1 346 | — 346 | +43 389 | +6 395 | +25 420 | +6 426 | +11 437 | -437 — | — — |
| DONNELLY, Michael J. (W.P.) | 144 | +12 156 | +1 157 | -157 — | — — | — — | — — | — — | — — | — — | — — | — — |
| DOOLAN, Jim (F.F.) | 202 | — 202 | +15 217 | +3 220 | — 220 | -220 — | — — | — — | — — | — — | — — | — — |
| EGAN, Mike (S.F.) | 80 | -80 — | — — | — — | — — | — — | — — | — — | — — | — — | — — | — — |
| HIGGINS, Michael D. (Lab.) | 940 | +19 959 | +9 968 | +65 1,033 | -34 999 | — 999 | — 999 | — 999 | — 999 | — 999 | — 999 | — 999 |
| LALLY, Paddy (Non-Party) | 554 | +10 564 | +3 567 | +17 584 | +3 587 | +7 594 | +44 638 | +84 722 | +7 729 | +82 811 | +98 909 | +63 972 |
| LAWLESS, Billy (F.G.) | 595 | +1 596 | +6 602 | +6 608 | +1 609 | +25 634 | +17 651 | +29 680 | +4 684 | +24 708 | +45 753 | +46 799 |
| LAWLESS, Mary (F.F.) | 111 | +3 114 | -114 — | — — | — — | — — | — — | — — | — — | — — | — — | — — |
| LUPTON, Angela (F.G.) | 608 | +3 611 | +10 621 | +10 631 | +1 632 | +11 643 | +23 666 | +27 693 | +6 699 | +24 723 | +49 772 | +73 845 |
| LYONS, Donal (P.D.) | 392 | +1 393 | +4 397 | +1 398 | +1 399 | +7 406 | +61 467 | +13 480 | +1 481 | +24 505 | +23 528 | -528 — |
| MADDEN, Liam (P.D.) | 513 | +1 514 | +4 518 | +1 519 | +1 520 | +21 541 | +27 568 | +16 584 | +2 586 | +29 615 | +42 657 | +249 906 |
| McCABE, Aidan (Non-Party) | 232 | — 232 | +4 236 | +1 237 | +1 238 | +5 243 | -243 — | — — | — — | — — | — — | — — |
| MULLARKEY, James (Lab.) | 213 | +10 223 | +3 226 | +27 253 | +22 275 | +5 280 | +13 293 | +20 313 | +1 314 | -314 — | — — | — — |
| O'HIGGINS, Mícheál (F.F.) | 832 | +5 837 | +31 868 | +11 879 | +1 880 | +81 961 | +28 989 | +37 1,026 | -27 999 | — 999 | — 999 | — 999 |
| Non-transferable papers not effective | — | +6 6 | +4 10 | +5 15 | — 15 | +11 26 | +17 43 | +32 75 | — 75 | +120 195 | +180 375 | +97 472 |
| TOTAL: | 5,992 | — 5,992 | — 5,992 | — 5,992 | — 5,992 | — 5,992 | — 5,992 | — 5,992 | — 5,992 | — 5,992 | — 5,992 | — 5,992 |

Elected: Higgins, Michael D. (Lab.); O'Higgins, Micheal (F.F.); Lally, Paddy (Non-Party); Madden, Liam (P.D.); Lupton, Angela (F.G.)

## NO. 3 ELECTORAL AREA

TOTAL ELECTORATE 7,004. VALID POLL 3,405. NO. OF MEMBERS 3. QUOTA 852

| Names of Candidates | First Count Votes | Second Count Transfer of Robinson's votes Result | Third Count Transfer of Manning's votes Result | Fourth Count Transfer of Garrett's votes Result | Fifth Count Transfer of Walsh's votes Result | Sixth Count Transfer of Cunningham's votes Result | Seventh Count Transfer of Burke's votes Result | Eighth Count Transfer of Connolly's surplus Result | Ninth Count Transfer of Mulholland's surplus Result |
|---|---|---|---|---|---|---|---|---|---|
| BURKE, Tom (P.D.) | 393 | +4 397 | +27 424 | +27 451 | +23 474 | +45 519 | -519 — | — — | — — |
| CONNOLLY, Martin (P.D.) | 543 | +9 552 | +10 562 | +13 575 | +16 591 | +102 693 | +311 1,004 | -152 852 | — 852 |
| COX, Tom (F.F.) | 455 | +6 461 | +24 485 | +49 534 | +17 551 | +86 637 | +17 654 | +81 735 | +27 762 |
| CUNNINGHAM, John Gerard (Lab.) | 324 | +76 400 | +26 426 | +6 432 | +14 446 | -446 — | — — | — — | — — |
| GARRETT, Carmel (F.F.) | 199 | +3 202 | +16 218 | -218 — | — — | — — | — — | — — | — — |
| MANNING, Eileen (Non-Party) | 179 | +9 188 | -188 — | — — | — — | — — | — — | — — | — — |
| MULHOLLAND, John (F.G.) | 527 | +10 537 | +32 569 | +30 599 | +130 729 | +78 807 | +102 909 | — 909 | -57 852 |
| O'CONNOR, Tony (F.F.) | 452 | +3 455 | +20 475 | +73 548 | +23 571 | +21 592 | +51 643 | +71 714 | +25 739 |
| ROBINSON, Noreen (Lab.) | 126 | -126 — | — — | — — | — — | — — | — — | — — | — — |
| WALSH, Michael (F.G.) | 207 | +3 210 | +17 227 | +8 235 | -235 — | — — | — — | — — | — — |
| Non-transferable papers not effective | — | +3 3 | +16 19 | +12 31 | +12 43 | +114 157 | +38 195 | — 195 | +5 200 |
| TOTAL: | 3,405 | — 3,405 | — 3,405 | — 3,405 | — 3,405 | — 3,405 | — 3,405 | — 3,405 | — 3,405 |

# GALWAY COUNTY COUNCIL

## GALWAY COUNTY COUNCIL RESULTS

| PARTY | 1991 % of votes | 1991 Seats obtained | 1985 % of votes | 1985 Seats obtained |
|---|---|---|---|---|
| Fianna Fail | 44.9 | 14 | 54.5 | 17 |
| Fine Gael | 28.0 | 10 | 28.0 | 9 |
| Labour | 0.5 | — | 0.2 | — |
| Progressive Dem. | 10.8 | 4 | — | — |
| Workers Party | 0.6 | — | 0.9 | — |
| Other | 15.2 | 2 | 16.4 | 4 |
| TOTAL SEATS | | 30 | | 30 |

## GALWAY

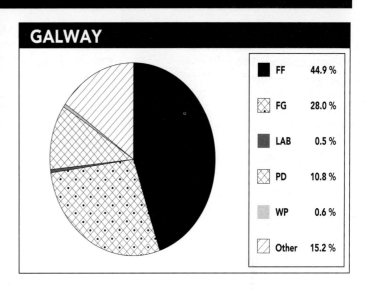

| | |
|---|---|
| ■ FF | 44.9 % |
| ⊠ FG | 28.0 % |
| ■ LAB | 0.5 % |
| ⊠ PD | 10.8 % |
| ▨ WP | 0.6 % |
| ▧ Other | 15.2 % |

**County Buildings, Prospect Hill, Galway**
**Telephone: (091) 63151**
**Fax: (091) 65817**
**Total population: 129,462**
**Rateable valuation: £755,084.15**
**County rate: £24.97**
**County Council meetings: Fourth Monday in each**
**month and the second Friday in each month**
*County and City Manager:* Seamus Keating
*Assistant County Managers:* Patrick J. Gavin, Donal
O'Donoghue
*County Secretary:* T. Kavanagh
*Finance Officer:* E. Lusby
*County Engineer:* P. Flood
*Administrative Officers:* T. Coughlan, G.Heneghan
*Senior Staff Officers:*
*General Purposes:* T. Murphy
*Accounts:* R. Curley
*Planning:* D. Barrett
*Engineering:* C. Wallace
*Rates:* B. Kennedy
County Development: F. Dawson
*County Librarian:* T. Sharkey
Island House, Galway
*Telephone:* (091) 65039
*Law Agent:* T. O'Donoghue
*County Coroners:*
Dr P. F. Joyce, Dr M. Costello, Dr C. McLoughlin
*Chief Fire Officer:* John A. O'Shaughnessey
*Senior Executive Engineers:*
*Roads:* P. Martyn, F. Cooke, R. Killeen
*Planning:* B. Callagy, L. Kavanagh
*Sanitary Services:* P. Ridge (Capital Schemes)
*Environment:* R. Faherty

Seamus Keating is a native of Tipperary where he was born in 1930. He has been Galway City and County Manager for over twenty years. He joined the public service at eighteen years of age as a Clerical Officer in Tipperary South Riding. At 23 he became a Staff Officer at Waterford County Council and then in 1963 returned to Tipperary South Riding as County Accountant.

In 1966 he became County Secretary in Donegal County Council and three years later was appointed Kerry County Manager. He moved from Kerry to Galway in 1973 and now has responsibility for over nine hundred staff and a budget of over forty million pounds.

Married to Mary Cleary with nine children. His hobbies include boating, reading and walking.

## BALLINASLOE

| | 1991 | 1985 | '85 to '91 Swing |
|---|---|---|---|
| FF | 60.8 | 57.7 | 3.1 |
| FG | 29.8 | 30.0 | -0.2 |
| Ind | 9.4 | 12.3 | -2.9 |

CALLANAN, Joe,
Calla, Kilconnell, Ballinasloe,
County Galway. (FF)
Farmer. 0905-86695

FINNERTY, Michael,
Tobergrellan, Ballinasloe,
County Galway. (FG)
Accounts Clerk. 0905-43010

KITT, Michael P.,
Castleblakeney, Ballinasloe,
County Galway. (FF)*

MULLINS, Michael,
Cleaghmore, Ballinasloe,
County Galway. (FG)
Personnel Manager. 0905-42728

O'SULLIVAN, Pat,
7 Kilgarve Park, Ballinasloe,
County Galway. (FF)
Teacher. 0905-43241

*Resigned when appointed Minister of
State, November 1991.
Replaced by
BRENNAN, Joseph,
Sarsfield Road,
Ballinasloe,
County Galway.

## CONNEMARA

| | 1991 | 1985 | '85 to '91 Swing |
|---|---|---|---|
| FF | 42.3 | 61.3 | -19.0 |
| FG | 21.2 | 24.6 | -3.4 |
| Ind | 22.8 | 14.1 | 8.7 |

MANNION, John M.,
Clifden,
County Galway. (FG)
Farmer. 095-21155

NÍ FHATHARTA, Connie,
Cladhnach,
An Cheathru Rua, (FF)
Co. na Gaillimhe.
Teacher. 091-72140

O' CUIV, Éamon,
Corr na Móna,
Co na Gaillimhe. (FF)
Senator. 092-48021

O'NEILL, Michael,
Tully, Renvyle,
County Galway. (PD)
Teacher. 0905-43241

O'TUATHAIL, Peadar,
Leitir Móir,
Co. na Gaillimhe. (NP)
Businessman. 091-81111

## GALWAY

| | 1991 | 1985 | '85 to '91 Swing |
|---|---|---|---|
| FF | 37.2 | 57.5 | -20.3 |
| FG | 31.6 | 27.9 | 3.7 |
| LAB | 2.7 | — | 2.7 |
| PD | 11.9 | — | 11.9 |
| SF | 0.0 | 11.8 | -11.8 |
| Ind | 16.6 | 2.8 | 13.8 |

GAVIN, Seamus,
Knockaunranny, Moycullen,
County Galway. (NP)
Teacher. 091-80366

MacDONAGH, Jarlath,
Turloughmore,
County Galway. (FG)
Teacher. 0905-97143

McCORMACK, Padraic,
3 Renmore Park,
Galway. (FG)
Dail Deputy. 0905-53992

McHUGH, Paddy T.,
Beaghmore, Caherlistrane, Belclare PO,
County Galway. (FF)
Planning Consultant. 093-55433

O'NEACHTAIN, Seán,
Spiddal,
County Galway. (FF)
Teacher. 091-83146

VARLEY, Evelyn,
The Square, Headford,
County Galway. (PD)
Publican. 093-35453

## LOUGHREA

| | 1991 | 1985 | '85 to '91 Swing |
|---|---|---|---|
| FF | 49.8 | 57.7 | -7.9 |
| FG | 27.0 | 32.8 | -5.8 |
| LAB | | 0.8 | -0.8 |
| WP | 2.3 | 1.5 | 0.8 |
| PD | 7.4 | | 7.4 |
| SF | 0.0 | 2.4 | -2.4 |
| Ind | 13.6 | 4.8 | 8.8 |

BURKE, Willie,
St. Josephs Road, Portumna,
County Galway. (PD)
Company Director. 0509-41163

BYRNE, Toddie,
Kinvara,
County Galway. (FG)
Teacher. 091-37121
CUNNINGHAM, Michael,
Galway Road, Gort,

**Evelyn Varley (PD)**
**Galway Rural**

**Jimmy McClearn (FG)**
**Loughrea**

**Pat Finnegan (FF)**
**Tuam**

**Paul Connaughton (FG)**
**Tuam**

County Galway. (FF)
Auctioneer. 091-31291

FAHY, Michael,
Caherduff, Ardrahan,
County Galway. (FF)
Insurance Representative. 091-35117

LOUGHNANE, Matt,
Dunsandle, Kiltulla,
County Galway. (FF)
Insurance Representative.
0905-48104

McCLEARN, Jimmy,
Killimor, Ballinasloe,
County Galway. (FG)
Electrician. 0905-76235

REGAN, Michael,
Ballinakill, Loughrea,
County Galway. (FF)
Company Representative. 0509-45071

| TUAM | | | |
|---|---|---|---|
| | 1991 | 1985 | '85 to '91 Swing |
| FF | 35.5 | 41.7 | -6.2 |
| FG | 30.3 | 23.3 | 7.0 |
| PD | 19.5 | — | 19.5 |
| SF | 6.2 | 8.2 | -2.0 |
| Ind | 8.5 | 26.9 | -18.4 |

BURKE, Joe,
Shop Street, Tuam,
County Galway. (PD)
Shopkeeper. 093-24146

CONNAUGHTON, Paul,
Mountbellew,
County Galway. (FG)
Dáil Deputy. 0905-79249

FINNEGAN, Patrick J.,
9 Curragh Park, Tuam,
County Galway. (FF)
Teacher. 093-24724

HUSSEY, Tom,
Patch, Glenamaddy,
County Galway. (FF)
Senator. 0907-59036

QUINN, Kathleen,
Ussey, Ballymoe,
County Galway. (FF)
Housewife. 0907-55058

RYAN, Michael,
Moate, Moylough, Ballinasloe,
County Galway. (FG)
Farmer. 0905-79285

WALSH, Tiarnan,
Ardeavin, Williamstown,
County Galway. (FG)
Farmer. 0907-55058

**Poll topping Councillor Joe Burke of the Progressive Democrats with some of his family and supporters after his election to Galway Councy Council.**

# Major surprises on Galway County Council

The lifetime of the 1986-91 Galway County Council was a dramatic time for Galway politics. The decision of Bobby Molloy to leave Fianna Fail to join Dessie O'Malley's new Progressive Democrats had totally transformed the political landscape in the Country's second largest County. Molloy had brought much of the Fianna Fail election team with him, and this was to be their first local contest in the P.D. colours. They performed remarkably well, contested four of the five electoral areas and secured four seats, giving Molloy a Local Government team to underpin his own strong General Election performances.

Overall the Galway results, counted at the Galway Tennis Club proved dramatic indeed, with the election of 13 new Councillors the ousting of seven sitting Councillors, the election of two Councillors who held office in previous terms and the election of three women Councillors. It had been twenty years since a women sat on Galway Council and the three, Kathleen Quinn. Evelyn Varley and Connie Ni Fhatharta represent the largest female delegation ever in Galway County Hall.

Some of the Councils longest serving personalities were among these who lost out, including outgoing Chairman Cllr. James Joyce of Fianna Fail whose seat was taken by fellow Party man Pat O'Sullivan of Ballinsloe U.D.C. Outgoing Fianna Fail County Councillors Tom Welby in Connemara, John Molloy in Galway Rural and Peter Raftery in Tuam also lost their seats. Fine Gael's Martin Lynch in Athenry, Republican Sinn Fein's Frank Glynn in Tuam and Ballinsloe Independent Cllr. Joe Brennan also lost out.

The Party make-up ended up as Fianna Fail with 14 seats, Fine Gael with 10 seats the P.D.'s with four and two Independents.

Joe Burke was the P.D. top performer in the County and indeed his first count

**Senator Eamon Ó Cuiv celebrates his election to Galway County Council.**

tally of 1,824 gave him the status of the P.D.'s biggest vote together in the Country. His success with the election of his name sake Willie Burke for the P.D.'s with 1,102 first preference in Loughrea, places the Party in a strong position in the Galway East three seater Dail Constituency.

The Party also pulled off a surprise in Galway Rural with the relatively unknown Evelyn Varley retaining Bobby Molloy's seat.

In Connemara the P.D.'s also took a seat, at the expense of Fianna Fail, with Michael O'Neil securing 607 first preference.

Connemara produced another surprise with the failure of outgoing Fine Gael Senator (now Independent) Pol O Foighil to secure a seat.

In Connemara, Senator Eamon O'Cuiv who had come so close to winning a Fianna Fail seat in the 1989 General Election, had failed to win a seat in the 1985 Local Elections. This time he made no mistake, topping the poll by nearly 300 votes while young Connie Ni Fharharta retained Nicholas O'Chonnchubair's seat for the Party. Comhacht, the Connemara Community

based Organisation held on to their seat with outgoing Councillor Peadar O' Tuatha.

Fianna Fail Deputy Michael Kitt topped the poll in Ballinasloe. In Galway Rural, Fianna Fail had won four out of six seats. One of them had since gone over to the P.D.'s in the form of Bobby Molloy, and to many peoples' surprise the P.D.'s held the seat with Headford Publican Evelyn Varley. Fianna Fail had not expected to lose another seat, however they did, due to the remarkable performance of Moycullen based Independent candidate, Seamus Gavin.

Gavin had campaigned on the roads and services issues, particularly on the West side of Lough Corrib and secured a massive 1,431 first preferences to take the second seat. Fianna Fail efforts were hampered by the absence of poll topper in 1985 Mark Killilea, now in Europe.

In Tuam, the big story was the phenomenal performance of controversial Fianna Fail candidate Michael "The Stroke" Fahey. Fahey had resigned the Fianna Fail whip after his failure to secure a Fianna Fail nomination in the 1987 General Election to run as an Independent. He rejoined Fianna Fail in late 1990. With 2,055, he had 500 votes to spare at the top of the poll, and was elected on the first count. It took 11 more counts before the next candidate was elected. Fianna Fail's Senator Tom Hussey was the other strong performer in Tuam, while newcomer Kathleen Quinn from Glinsk took the final seat for Fianna Fail although she had only .4 of a quota on the first count.

Fianna Fail fought the campaign in Loughrea, this time without its two big poll getters. Both Frank Fahey T.D. and Noel Treacy T.D. as Ministers of State could not contest, yet the Party still managed to hold on to four out of the seven seats.

Fine Gael's vote was down almost 6% and they lost a seat to the P.D.'s with outgoing Cllr. Martin Lynch losing out. A very tight vote management strategy had paid off.

Fine Gael Deputy Paul Connaghton got 1,650 first preferences and so was easily elected along with Party colleague Tiernan Walsh and Michael Ryan.

Fine Gael, the PD's and two independents negotiated a post election pack to control the chair of the new Council, their combined strength gave them sixteen of the council's thirty seats.

# BALLINASLOE ELECTORAL AREA

TOTAL ELECTORATE 15,564. VALID POLL 9,366. NO. OF MEMBERS 5. QUOTA 1,562.

| Names of Candidates | First Count Votes | Second Count Transfer of Kitt's surplus | Result | Third Count Transfer of Callanan's surplus | Result | Fourth Count Transfer of Brennan's votes | Result | Fifth Count Transfer of Mullins' surplus | Result | Sixth Count Transfer of Finnerty's surplus | Result |
|---|---|---|---|---|---|---|---|---|---|---|---|
| BRENNAN, Joe | 884 | +62 | 946 | +23 | 969 | -969 | — | — | — | — | — |
| CALLANAN, Joe (F.F.) | 1,751 | — | 1,751 | -189 | 1,562 | — | 1,562 | — | 1,562 | — | 1,562 |
| FINNERTY, Michael (F.G.) | 1,122 | +62 | 1,184 | +16 | 1,200 | +397 | 1,597 | — | 1,597 | -35 | 1,562 |
| JOYCE, James (F.F.) | 904 | +273 | 1,177 | +88 | 1,265 | +115 | 1,380 | +49 | 1,429 | +13 | 1,442 |
| KITT, Michael P. (F.F.) | 2,230 | -668 | 1,562 | — | 1,562 | — | 1,562 | — | 1,562 | — | 1,562 |
| MULLINS, Michael (F.G.) | 1,676 | — | 1,676 | — | 1,676 | — | 1,676 | -114 | 1,562 | — | 1,562 |
| O'SULLIVAN, Pat (F.F.) | 799 | +271 | 1,070 | +62 | 1,132 | +261 | 1,393 | +65 | 1,458 | +22 | 1,480 |
| Non-transferable papers not effective | — | — | — | — | — | +196 | 196 | — | 196 | — | 196 |
| TOTAL: | 9,366 | — | 9,366 | — | 9,366 | — | 9,366 | — | 9,366 | — | 9,366 |

Elected: Kitt, Michael P. (F.F.); Callanan, Joe (F.F.); Mullins, Michael (F.G.); Finnerty, Michael (F.G.); O'Sullivan, Pat (F.F.)

# CONNEMARA ELECTORAL AREA

TOTAL ELECTORATE 14,706. VALID POLL 8,840. NO. OF MEMBERS 5. QUOTA 1,474.

| Names of Candidates | First Count Votes | Second Count Transfer of Cuív's surplus | Result | Third Count Transfer of Molloy's votes | Result | Fourth Count Transfer of Gibbons' votes | Result | Fifth Count Transfer of Gorham's votes | Result | Sixth Count Transfer of King's votes | Result | Seventh Count Transfer of Geoghegan's votes | Result | Eighth Count Transfer of Mannion's surplus | Result | Ninth Count Transfer of Ó Foighil's votes | Result | Tenth Count Transfer of Cuaig's votes | Result |
|---|---|---|---|---|---|---|---|---|---|---|---|---|---|---|---|---|---|---|---|
| CUAIG, Seosamh Ó | 776 | +25 | 801 | +3 | 804 | +29 | 833 | +11 | 844 | +8 | 852 | +8 | 860 | — | 860 | +122 | 982 | -982 | — |
| CUÍV, Eamon Ó (F.F.) | 1,766 | -292 | 1,474 | — | 1,474 | — | 1,474 | — | 1,474 | — | 1,474 | — | 1,474 | — | 1,474 | — | 1,474 | — | 1,474 |
| GEOGHEGAN, Jimmy (P.D.) | 574 | +11 | 585 | +2 | 587 | +2 | 589 | +8 | 597 | +4 | 601 | -601 | — | — | — | — | — | — | — |
| GIBBONS, Erin | 228 | +7 | 235 | +5 | 240 | -240 | — | — | — | — | — | — | — | — | — | — | — | — | — |
| GORHAM, Michael | 266 | +4 | 270 | +1 | 271 | +38 | 309 | -309 | — | — | — | — | — | — | — | — | — | — | — |
| KING, Malachy (F.F.) | 384 | +33 | 417 | +2 | 419 | +20 | 439 | +30 | 469 | -469 | — | — | — | — | — | — | — | — | — |
| MANNION, John M. (F.G.) | 1,189 | +22 | 1,211 | +4 | 1,215 | +38 | 1,253 | +80 | 1,333 | +77 | 1,410 | +90 | 1,500 | -26 | 1,474 | — | 1,474 | — | 1,474 |
| MOLLOY, Joe | 35 | +6 | 41 | -41 | — | — | — | — | — | — | — | — | — | — | — | — | — | — | — |
| NÍ FHATHARTA, Connie (F.F.) | 890 | +58 | 948 | +4 | 952 | +3 | 955 | +3 | 958 | +84 | 1,042 | +15 | 1,057 | — | 1,057 | +79 | 1,136 | +148 | 1,284 |
| Ó FOIGHIL, Pól (F.G.) | 688 | +15 | 703 | +5 | 708 | +9 | 717 | +12 | 729 | +8 | 737 | +19 | 756 | +9 | 765 | -765 | — | — | — |
| O'NEILL, Michael (P.D.) | 647 | +9 | 656 | +2 | 658 | +38 | 696 | +69 | 765 | +71 | 836 | +343 | 1,179 | +12 | 1,191 | +67 | 1,258 | +49 | 1,307 |
| Ó TUATHAIL, Peadar | 708 | +10 | 718 | +4 | 722 | +30 | 752 | +17 | 769 | — | 769 | +13 | 782 | +2 | 784 | +227 | 1,011 | +480 | 1,491 |
| WELBY, Tom (F.F.) | 689 | +92 | 781 | +2 | 783 | +11 | 794 | +21 | 815 | +146 | 961 | +79 | 1,040 | +3 | 1,043 | +27 | 1,070 | +47 | 1,117 |
| Non-transferable papers not effective | — | — | — | +7 | 7 | +22 | 29 | +58 | 87 | +71 | 158 | +34 | 192 | — | 192 | +243 | 435 | +258 | 693 |
| TOTAL: | 8,840 | — | 8,840 | — | 8,840 | — | 8,840 | — | 8,840 | — | 8,840 | — | 8,840 | — | 8,840 | — | 8,840 | — | 8,840 |

Elected: Cuív, Eamon Ó (F.F.); Mannion, John M. (F.G.); Ó Tuathail, Peadar; O'Neill, Michael (P.D.); Ní Fhatharta, Connie (F.F.)

# LOUGHREA ELECTORAL AREA
## TOTAL ELECTORATE 22,731. VALID POLL 15,008. NO. OF MEMBERS 7. QUOTA 1,877

| Names of Candidates | First Count Votes | Second Count Transfer of Fahy's surplus | Result | Third Count Transfer of Murphy's votes | Result | Fourth Count Transfer of Baldwin's votes | Result | Fifth Count Transfer of Samuel's votes | Result | Sixth Count Transfer of Loughrey's votes | Result | Seventh Count Transfer of O'Meara's votes | Result |
|---|---|---|---|---|---|---|---|---|---|---|---|---|---|
| BALDWIN, P.J. | 146 | +4 | 150 | — | 150 | -150 | — | — | — | — | — | — | — |
| BURKE, Willie (P.D.) | 1,102 | +2 | 1,104 | +6 | 1,110 | +13 | 1,123 | +15 | 1,138 | +4 | 1,142 | +74 | 1,216 |
| BYRNE, Toddie (F.G.) | 867 | +16 | 883 | +7 | 890 | +13 | 903 | +13 | 916 | +11 | 927 | +3 | 930 |
| CUNNINGHAM, Michael (F.F.) | 890 | +48 | 938 | +6 | 944 | +26 | 970 | +6 | 976 | +49 | 1,025 | +3 | 1,028 |
| FAHY, Michael (F.F.) | 2,055 | -178 | 1,877 | — | 1,877 | — | 1,877 | — | 1,877 | — | 1,877 | — | 1,877 |
| FLANAGAN, Michael (F.F.) | 828 | +15 | 843 | +1 | 844 | +1 | 845 | +2 | 847 | +3 | 850 | +50 | 900 |
| FLANNERY, Justin (F.G.) | 792 | +15 | 807 | +6 | 813 | +10 | 823 | +9 | 832 | +23 | 855 | +8 | 863 |
| HYNES, Pat | 1,100 | +2 | 1,102 | +2 | 1,104 | +30 | 1,134 | +6 | 1,140 | +39 | 1,179 | +9 | 1,188 |
| LOUGHNANE, Matt (F.F.) | 1,484 | +27 | 1,511 | +7 | 1,518 | +5 | 1,523 | +7 | 1,530 | +21 | 1,551 | +29 | 1,580 |
| LOUGHREY, Michael (S.F.) | 232 | +5 | 237 | +1 | 238 | +14 | 252 | +8 | 260 | -260 | — | — | — |
| LYNCH, Martin (F.G.) | 1,018 | +3 | 1,021 | +6 | 1,027 | +4 | 1,031 | +11 | 1,042 | +14 | 1,056 | +13 | 1,069 |
| McCLEARN, Jimmy (F.G.) | 1,367 | — | 1,367 | — | 1,367 | +1 | 1,368 | +4 | 1,372 | +7 | 1,379 | +103 | 1,482 |
| MacEOIN, Stan (W.P.) | 338 | +6 | 344 | +6 | 350 | +10 | 360 | +43 | 403 | +28 | 431 | +2 | 433 |
| MURPHY, Margaret Mary | 72 | +2 | 74 | -74 | — | — | — | — | — | — | — | — | — |
| O'CONNOR, Bernie (F.F.) | 986 | +22 | 1,008 | +10 | 1,018 | +8 | 1,026 | +7 | 1,033 | +14 | 1,047 | +2 | 1,049 |
| O'MEARA, Donal | 342 | +1 | 343 | +1 | 344 | +2 | 346 | +7 | 353 | +1 | 354 | -354 | — |
| REGAN, Michael (F.F.) | 1,247 | +9 | 1,256 | +1 | 1,257 | +2 | 1,259 | +3 | 1,262 | +14 | 1,276 | +28 | 1,304 |
| SAMUEL, Malcolm Harry | 142 | +1 | 143 | +9 | 152 | +1 | 153 | -153 | — | — | — | — | — |
| Non-transferable papers not effective | — | — | — | +5 | 5 | +10 | 15 | +12 | 27 | +32 | 59 | +30 | 89 |
| TOTAL: | 15,008 | — | 15,008 | — | 15,008 | — | 15,008 | — | 15,008 | — | 15,008 | — | 15,008 |

| Eighth Count Transfer of MacEoin's votes | Result | Ninth Count Transfer of Flannery's votes | Result | Tenth Count Transfer of Flanagan's votes | Result | Eleventh Count Transfer of O'Connor's votes | Result | Twelfth Count Transfer of Loughnane's surplus | Result | Thirteenth Count Transfer of Lynch's votes | Result | Fourteenth Count Transfer of Byrne's surplus | Result |
|---|---|---|---|---|---|---|---|---|---|---|---|---|---|
| — | — | — | — | — | — | — | — | — | — | — | — | — | — |
| +36 | 1,252 | +45 | 1,297 | +53 | 1,350 | +69 | 1,419 | +7 | 1,426 | +136 | 1,562 | +18 | 1,580 |
| +143 | 1,073 | +252 | 1,325 | +27 | 1,352 | +127 | 1,479 | +7 | 1,486 | +501 | 1,987 | -110 | 1,877 |
| +27 | 1,055 | +72 | 1,127 | +67 | 1,194 | +278 | 1,472 | +74 | 1,546 | +59 | 1,605 | +4 | 1,609 |
| — | 1,877 | — | 1,877 | — | 1,877 | — | 1,877 | — | 1,877 | — | 1,877 | — | 1,877 |
| +8 | 908 | +52 | 960 | -960 | — | — | — | — | — | — | — | — | — |
| +26 | 889 | -889 | — | — | — | — | — | — | — | — | — | — | — |
| +28 | 1,216 | +55 | 1,271 | +86 | 1,357 | +16 | 1,373 | +1 | 1,374 | +53 | 1,427 | +5 | 1,432 |
| +6 | 1,586 | +37 | 1,623 | +238 | 1,861 | +258 | 2,119 | -242 | 1,877 | — | 1,877 | — | 1,877 |
| — | — | — | — | — | — | — | — | — | — | — | — | — | — |
| +11 | 1,080 | +130 | 1,210 | +11 | 1,221 | +77 | 1,298 | +16 | 1,314 | -1,314 | — | — | — |
| +3 | 1,485 | +133 | (1,618 | +67 | 1,685 | +5 | 1,690 | — | 1,690 | +158 | 1,848 | +83 | 1,931 |
| -433 | — | — | — | — | — | — | — | — | — | — | — | — | — |
| — | — | — | — | — | — | — | — | — | — | — | — | — | — |
| +32 | 1,081 | +23 | 1,104 | +29 | 1,133 | -1,133 | — | — | — | — | — | — | — |
| — | — | — | — | — | — | — | — | — | — | — | — | — | — |
| +5 | 1,309 | +20 | 1,329 | +281 | 1,610 | +123 | 1,733 | +68 | 1,801 | +88 | 1,889 | — | 1,889 |
| — | — | — | — | — | — | — | — | — | — | — | — | — | — |
| +108 | 197 | +70 | 267 | +101 | 368 | +180 | 548 | +69 | 617 | +319 | 936 | — | 936 |
| — | 15,008 | — | 15,008 | — | 15,008 | — | 15,008 | — | 15,008 | — | 15,008 | — | 15,008 |

Elected: Fahy, Michael (F.F.); Loughnane, Matt (F.F.); Byrne, Toddie (F.G.); Regan, Michael (F.F.); McClearn, Jimmy (F.G.); Cunningham, Michael (F.F.); Burke, Willie (P.D.)

# TUAM ELECTORAL AREA

TOTAL ELECTORATE 19,647. VALID POLL 13,066. NO. OF MEMBERS 7. QUOTA 1,634.

| Names of Candidates | First Count Votes | Second Count Transfer of Burke's surplus | Result | Third Count Transfer of Connaughton's surplus | Result | Fourth Count Transfer of Raftery's votes | Result | Fifth Count Transfer of Hehir's votes | Result | Sixth Count Transfer of Ward's votes | Result | Seventh Count Transfer of Hussey's surplus | Result | Eighth Count Transfer of Gormley's votes | Result | Ninth Count Transfer of Connolly's votes | Result | Tenth Count Transfer of Finnegan's surplus | Result |
|---|---|---|---|---|---|---|---|---|---|---|---|---|---|---|---|---|---|---|---|
| BURKE, Joe (P.D.) | 1,824 | -190 | 1,634 | — | 1,634 | — | 1,634 | — | 1,634 | — | 1,634 | — | 1,634 | — | 1,634 | — | 1,634 | — | 1,634 |
| CONNAUGHTON, Paul (F.G.) | 1,650 | — | 1,650 | -16 | 1,634 | — | 1,634 | — | 1,634 | — | 1,634 | — | 1,634 | — | 1,634 | — | 1,634 | — | 1,634 |
| CONNOLLY, Michael (F.F.) | 703 | +7 | 710 | +1 | 711 | +78 | 789 | +71 | 860 | +49 | 909 | +10 | 919 | +44 | 963 | -963 | — | — | — |
| FINNEGAN, Patrick J. (F.F.) | 1,274 | +36 | 1,310 | +1 | 1,311 | +31 | 1,342 | +71 | 1,413 | +49 | 1,462 | +12 | 1,474 | +126 | 1,600 | +286 | 1,886 | -252 | 1,634 |
| GLYNN, Frank | 810 | +19 | 829 | +1 | 830 | +12 | 842 | +31 | 873 | +72 | 945 | +1 | 946 | +201 | 1,147 | +47 | 1,194 | +23 | 1,217 |
| GORMLEY, T.J. (P.D.) | 719 | +86 | 805 | +1 | 806 | +4 | 810 | +45 | 855 | +44 | 899 | +1 | 900 | -900 | — | — | — | — | — |
| HEHIR, Sean (Non-Party) | 565 | +7 | 572 | — | 572 | +3 | 575 | -575 | — | — | — | — | — | — | — | — | — | — | — |
| HUSSEY, Tom (F.F.) | 1,440 | +15 | 1,455 | +1 | 1,456 | +154 | 1,610 | +58 | 1,668 | — | 1,668 | -34 | 1,634 | — | 1,634 | — | 1,634 | — | 1,634 |
| QUINN, Kathleen (F.F.) | 677 | +2 | 679 | +1 | 680 | +118 | 798 | +22 | 820 | +135 | 955 | +6 | 961 | +47 | 1,008 | +196 | 1,204 | +144 | 1,348 |
| RAFTERY, Peter (F.F.) | 547 | +1 | 548 | +1 | 549 | -549 | — | — | — | — | — | — | — | — | — | — | — | — | — |
| RYAN, Michael (F.G.) | 1,120 | +11 | 1,131 | +6 | 1,137 | +30 | 1,167 | +137 | 1,304 | +58 | 1,362 | +3 | 1,365 | +106 | 1,471 | +209 | 1,680 | — | 1,680 |
| WALSH, Tiarnan (F.G.) | 1,191 | +3 | 1,194 | +2 | 1,196 | +36 | 1,232 | +14 | 1,246 | +120 | 1,366 | +1 | 1,367 | +53 | 1,420 | +10 | 1,430 | +4 | 1,434 |
| WARD, Tom (Non-Party) | 546 | +3 | 549 | +1 | 550 | +46 | 596 | +58 | 654 | -654 | — | — | — | — | — | — | — | — | — |
| Non-transferable papers not effective | — | — | — | — | — | +37 | 37 | +68 | 105 | +127 | 232 | — | 232 | +323 | 555 | +215 | 770 | +81 | 851 |
| TOTAL: | 13,066 | — | 13,066 | — | 13,066 | — | 13,066 | — | 13,066 | — | 13,066 | — | 13,066 | — | 13,066 | — | 13,066 | — | 13,066 |

Elected: Burke, Joe (P.D.); Connaughton, Paul (F.G.); Hussey, Tom (F.F.); Finnegan, Patrick J. (F.F.); Ryan, Michael (F.G.); Walsh, Tiarnan (F.G.); Quinn Kathleen (F.F.)

# GALWAY ELECTORAL AREA

TOTAL ELECTORATE 18,636. VALID POLL 10,814. NO. OF MEMBERS 6. QUOTA 1,545.

| Names of Candidates | First Count Votes | Second Count Transfer of McDonagh's surplus | Result | Third Count Transfer of Cunningham's votes | Result | Fourth Count Transfer of Clancy's votes | Result | Fifth Count Transfer of Curran's votes | Result | Sixth Count Transfer of Molloy's votes | Result | Seventh Count Transfer of Halliday's votes | Result | Eighth Count Transfer of Hoade's votes | Result |
|---|---|---|---|---|---|---|---|---|---|---|---|---|---|---|---|
| CLANCY, Patsy (F.G.) | 298 | +31 | 329 | +20 | 349 | -349 | — | — | — | — | — | — | — | — | — |
| CUNNINGHAM, John G. (Lab.) | 300 | +5 | 305 | -305 | — | — | — | — | — | — | — | — | — | — | — |
| CURRAN, Tom | 390 | +6 | 396 | +31 | 427 | +50 | 477 | -477 | — | — | — | — | — | — | — |
| GAVIN, Seamus (Non-Party) | 1,431 | +5 | 1,436 | +61 | 1,497 | +54 | 1,551 | — | 1,551 | — | 1,551 | — | 1,551 | — | 1,551 |
| HALLIDAY, Marie (P.D.) | 453 | +5 | 458 | +30 | 488 | +44 | 532 | +56 | 588 | +13 | 601 | -601 | — | — | — |
| HOADE, Mary (F.F.) | 571 | +13 | 584 | +11 | 595 | +8 | 603 | +24 | 627 | +55 | 682 | +22 | 704 | -704 | — |
| McCORMACK, Padraic (F.G.) | 1,027 | +188 | 1,215 | +27 | 1,242 | +100 | 1,342 | +50 | 1,392 | +52 | 1,444 | +48 | 1,492 | +54 | 1,546 |
| McDONAGH, Jarlath (F.G.) | 1,971 | -426 | 1,545 | — | 1,545 | — | 1,545 | — | 1,545 | — | (1545) | — | 1,545 | — | 1,545 |
| McGRATH, Murty (F.F.) | 753 | +99 | 852 | +10 | 862 | +6 | 868 | +22 | 890 | +182 | 1,072 | +10 | 1,082 | +144 | 1,226 |
| McHUGH, Paddy T. (F.F.) | 1,095 | +29 | 1,124 | +20 | 1,144 | +2 | 1,146 | +16 | 1,162 | +54 | 1,216 | +3 | 1,219 | +335 | 1,554 |
| MOLLOY, John (F.F.) | 466 | +15 | 481 | +9 | 490 | +4 | 494 | +25 | 519 | -519 | — | — | — | — | — |
| Ó NEACHTAIN, Seán (F.F.) | 1,201 | +7 | 1,208 | +19 | 1,227 | +44 | 1,271 | +129 | 1,400 | +99 | 1,499 | +69 | 1,568 | — | 1,568 |
| VARLEY, Evelyn (P.D.) | 858 | +23 | 881 | +31 | 912 | +6 | 918 | +31 | 949 | +24 | 973 | +369 | 1,342 | +98 | 1,440 |
| Non-transferable papers not effective | — | — | — | +36 | 36 | +31 | 67 | +124 | 191 | +40 | 231 | +80 | 311 | +73 | 384 |
| TOTAL: | 10,814 | — | 10,814 | — | 10,814 | — | 10,814 | — | 10,814 | — | 10,814 | — | 10,814 | — | 10,814 |

Eelected: McDonagh, Jarlath (F.G.); Gavin, Seamus (Non-Party); Ó Neachtain, Seán (F.F.); McHugh, Paddy T. (F.F.); McCormack, Padraic (F.G.); Varley, Evelyn (P.D.)

# KERRY COUNTY COUNCIL

## KERRY COUNTY COUNCIL RESULTS

| PARTY | 1991 % of votes | 1991 Seats obtained | 1985 % of votes | 1985 Seats obtained |
|---|---|---|---|---|
| Fianna Fail | 44.1 | 13 | 46.7 | 13 |
| Fine Gael | 26.2 | 7 | 24.0 | 7 |
| Labour | 16.6 | 4 | 11.1 | 3 |
| Progressive Dem. | 0.7 | — | — | — |
| Workers Party | — | — | 2.4 | — |
| Other | 12.4 | 3 | 15.8 | 4 |
| | | | | |
| TOTAL SEATS | | 27 | | 27 |

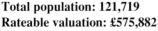

**Total population: 121,719**
**Rateable valuation: £575,882**
**County Council**
**2Aras an Chontae, Tralee**
**Telephone:(066) 21111**
**Fax:(066) 22466**
**Current county rate: £34.7535**
**County Council meetings: third Monday in each month**

## KERRY

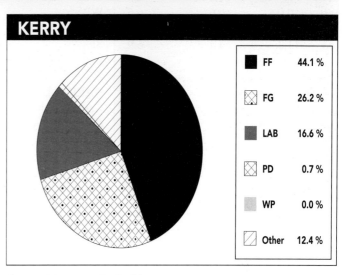

| | |
|---|---|
| FF | 44.1 % |
| FG | 26.2 % |
| LAB | 16.6 % |
| PD | 0.7 % |
| WP | 0.0 % |
| Other | 12.4 % |

*County Manager:* D. P. d'Arcy
*Assistant County Manager:* Vacant
*County Secretary:* John O'Connor (Acting)
*Finance Officer:* J. Ronayne
*County Engineer:* C. F. Kennelly
*County Solicitor:* John Daly
*County Development Officer:* Eamon O'Mahony
*Senior Staff Officers:*
*Accounts EDP:* P. Cronin
*County Development:* M. Collins, D. Cournane
*Environment and Sanitary Services:* B. O'Connor
*Personnel:* Yvonne Blennerhassett (Acting)
*Planning:* M. McMahon
*Revenue:* T. J. Riordan
*County Librarian:* Kathleen Browne,
*County Library,* Tralee. *Telephone:*(066) 21200
*County Coroner:* Dr D. F. O'Donovan
*Chief Fire Officer:* Kevin A. Caffrey
*Civil Defence Officer:* M. Forrest
*Veterinary Inspector:* J. D. PierseExecutive Chemist: Vacant
*Senior Executive Engineers:*
*Sanitary:* V. J. Dillon
*Environmental:* T. Carey
*Road Upkeep and General Purpose:* F. Dillon (Acting)
*Road Design:* A. P. B. Townsend
*Housing:* J. G. O'Sullivan
*Planning:* D. Daly

## KILLARNEY

| | 1991 | 1985 | '85 to '91 Swing |
|---|---|---|---|
| FF | 48.2 | 55.5 | -7.3 |
| FG | 28.3 | 22.0 | 6.3 |
| LAB | 8.7 | 11.5 | -2.8 |
| WP | 0.0 | 6.6 | -6.6 |
| GP | 3.6 | | 3.6 |
| Ind | 11.3 | 4.4 | 6.9 |

COGHLAN, Paul,
Ballydowney, Killarney,
County Kerry. (FG)
Auctioneer. 064-32106

CRONIN, P.J.,
Rathcommane, Ballyhar, Killarney,
County Kerry. (NP)
ESB Employee. 064-33534

FLEMING, Tom,
Scartaglen Village, Farranfore,
County Kerry. (FF)
Publican. 066-41384

HEALEY-RAE, Jackie,
Kilgarvan,
County Kerry. (FF)
Farmer. 064-85291

MOYNIHAN, Breeda,
10 Muckross Grove, Killarney,
County Kerry. (Lab)
Secretary. 064-31771

O'LEARY, John,
Beechcroft, Killarney,
County Kerry. (FF)
Dáil Deputy. 064-31565

## KILLORGLIN

| | 1991 | 1985 | '85 to '91 Swing |
|---|---|---|---|
| FF | 53.6 | 41.7 | 11.9 |
| FG | 34.9 | 31.2 | 3.7 |
| LAB | 8.2 | 5.5 | 2.7 |
| WP | — | 1.3 | -1.3 |
| PD | 3.4 | — | 3.4 |
| SF | — | 2.0 | -2.0 |
| Ind | — | 18.3 | -18.3 |

BARRY, Dan,
Carhan, Cahirciveen,
County Kerry. (FG)
Farmer. 066-72047

CAHILL, Michael,
Rossbeigh, Glenbeigh,
County Kerry. (FF)
Businessman. 066-68355

CONNOR-SCARTEEN, Michael,
5 Main Street, Kenmare,
County Kerry. (FG)
Insurance Broker. 064-41018

FINNEGAN, Pat,
Upper Bridge Street, Killorglin,
County Kerry. (FF)
Jeweller. 066-61330

KISSANE, Danny,
Carunahone, Beaufort,
County Kerry. (FG)
Farmer. 064-44264

O'DONOGHUE, John,
14 West Main Street, Cahirciveen,
County Kerry. (FF)*

*Resigned when appointed Minister for
State.
Replaced by
O'DONOGHUE, Paul,
Castlequin, Cahirciveen,
County Kerry. (FF)
066-618777

## LISTOWEL

| | 1991 | 1985 | '85 to '91 Swing |
|---|---|---|---|
| FF | 53.6 | 41.7 | 11.9 |
| FG | 34.9 | 31.2 | 3.7 |
| LAB | 15.4 | 14.0 | 1.4 |
| SF | — | 9.6 | -9.6 |
| Ind | 1.9 | — | 1.9 |

BRASSIL, Noel,
Dirtane, Ballyheigue,
County Kerry. (FF)
Businessman. 066-33112

BUCKLEY, Tim,
Knockane, Listowel,
County Kerry. (FG)
Farmer. 068-21159

DEENIHAN, Jimmy,
Finuge, Lixnaw,
County Kerry. (FG)
Dáil Deputy. 068-40235

KIELY, Dan,
Doonard, Tarbert,
County Kerry. (FF)
Senator. 068-36163

LEAHY, Pat,
Clounbrane, Moyvane,
County Kerry. (Lab)
Transport Driver.

O'SULLIVAN, Ned,
Cahirdown, Listowel,
County Kerry. (FF)
Teacher. 068-21831

**Tim Buckley (FG)**
**Listowel**

**Breeda Moynihan (Lab)**
**Killarney**

**Maeve Spring (Lab)**
**Mid Kerry**

**Michael Cahill (FF)**
**Killorglin**

## MID KERRY

|  | 1991 | 1985 | '85 to '91 Swing |
|---|---|---|---|
| FF | 41.6 | 39.5 | 2.1 |
| FG | 24.0 | 21.2 | 2.8 |
| LAB | 12.6 | 7.0 | 5.6 |
| SF | 0.0 | 4.9 | -4.9 |
| Ind | 21.9 | 27.4 | -5.5 |

COURTNEY, James,
Castlegregory,
County Kerry. (NP)
Farmer. 066-39120

MacGEARAILT, Breandán,
Marthain, Baile 'n Fhirteirigh,
Co. Ciarraí. (FF)
Teacher. 066-56174

McELLISTRIM, Tom,
Ahane, Ballymacelligott,
County Kerry. (FF)
Dail Deputy. 066-37127

O'CONNELL, Bobby,
15 Main Street, Castleisland,
County Kerry. (FG)
Publican. 066-41801

SPRING, Maeve,
37 Racecourse Lawn, Tralee,
County Kerry. (Lab)
Secretary

## TRALEE

|  | 1991 | 1985 | '85 to '91 Swing |
|---|---|---|---|
| FF | 28.4 | 51.1 | -22.7 |
| FG | 8.3 | 8.3 | 0.0 |
| LAB | 32.7 | 18.0 | 14.7 |
| WP | — | 4.3 | -4.3 |
| GP | 6.0 | — | 6.0 |
| SF | 7.9 | 9.3 | -1.4 |
| Ind | 16.8 | 9.0 | 7.8 |

FITZGERALD, Ted,
Clash Cross, Tralee,
County Kerry. (FF)
Builder. 066-22742

FOLEY, Tommy,
28 St. Johns Park, Tralee,
County Kerry. (FF)
Unemployed. 066-23587

FOLEY, Denis,
Staughton's Row, Tralee,
County Kerry. (FF)
Senator. 066-21174

SPRING, Dick,
Cloonanorig, Tralee,
County Kerry. (Lab)
Dail Deputy. 066-25337.

**Fine Gael Leader John Bruton emphasises his message during his first election campaign as party leader in June 1991.**

# General Election pointers in Kerry Local results

The Politics of Kerry have always attracted national attention. It incorporates the two three seater Dail Constituencies of Kerry North and Kerry South. The former is the base of Labour Leader Dick Spring, the latter holds the distinction of being one of only two Dail Constituencies in the country without a Fine Gael T.D.

In three seaters, surprises are usually unlikely, but as Dick Spring learned when,, as Tanaiste, he held onto his seat by just four votes in 1987. In Kerry politics, nothing can be taken for granted.

The results of the 1991 Local Elections therefore, in the 27 seat Kerry County Council are as significant for the next General Election as they are for the control of the County Council itself. All six T.D.'s, five of whom were outgoing Councillors contested.

Dick Spring, the only Party Leader actually contesting the Local Elections, raised many eyebrows by running with no team- mate in the Tralee Electoral Area. He topped the poll convincingly with almost 3,000 first preferences. Without a running mate, his 1,200 vote surplus was wasted and they came away with only one seat despite having almost 1.6 quotas. The Party did have a second candidate, who for combination of business and personal reasons, had withdrawn before the convention, and a last minute scramble to find a replacement second runner proved fruitless.

Spring's base was certainly solidified however, against a repeat of the 1987 near debacle with the victory of his sister and Constituency office worker Maeve, in getting a surprise seat for the Party in the Mid Kerry Electoral Area.

Across the border in Kerry South, implications for the sitting Labour Deputy Michael Moynihan were also mixed. Not being a member of the Out-going Council, the Killarney based Moynihan had decided to contest for the Labour Party in the Killorglin Electoral Area, while his daughter Breda contested for the Party in Killarney.

In Killorglin, Moynihan senior faced a direct head to head with Fianna Fail Deputy John O'Donoghue. On his home turf however, the Fianna Fail Cahirciveen Solicitor swept all before him. He got a massive 2,979 first preference in his second Local Government contest. With strong showings by Jack Carroll and Pat Finnegan, Fianna Fail took an extra seat leaving Moynihan in the wake with only 996 number ones, to face elimination on the fourth count.

> ## Dick Spring raised many eyebrows by running with no team-mate in the Tralee electoral area

Deputy Moynihan had some consolation however, in the performance of his daughter Breda back in Killarney. She took a surprise seat for the Party and stakes her claim as a future Dail contender now that her fathers retirement has been announced.

Back in Kerry North, the performance of Fianna Fail candidates may also have a bearing for any future Dail contest. Tralee based Senator and former T.D. Denis Foley, who had just lost out to Tom McEllistrim in 1989, put in a very strong showing with 1,845 first preferences and with Ted Fitzgerald held on to the Party's two seats in the area.

McEllistrim was running in the Mid Kerry Electoral Area, the only local area which stretches across both Dail constituencies. Despite this, he performed credibly although he came in behind running mate, Brendan McGearailt from Dingle. The absence of outgoing Councillor Michael Long on the Fianna Fail ticket and votes slippage meant that Fianna Fail were to lose a seat in Mid Kerry which was duly picked up by Maeve Spring.

The third man on the Fianna Fail 1989 General Election ticket had been Listowel Urban District Council member Ned O'Sullivan who was not a member of the outgoing Kerry County Council. The talking point of the 1991 Campaign in the Listowel Electoral area was the intense rivalry between O'Sullivan and Fianna Fail Senator Dan Kiely.

Fianna Fail had three out of the six seats in the Listowel area going in to the Election and it's four man ticket was made up of these three out-going Councillors and O'Sullivan. Despite a tight Fine Gael vote management strategy, Fianna Fail held on to it's three seats with Noel Brassil, the most comfortable, Ned O'Sullivan next and Kiely getting elected on the last count, with out-going Kieran Walsh losing out. Although failing to get three seats in Listowel, Fine Gael could take solace from the strong performance of Jimmy Dennihan T.D.

Overall in Kerry, Fine Gael held its seats. It had 7 on the old Council and it has 7 on the new. There were some changes in personnel however, including Listowel, where Paul Corcoran took a Fine Gael seat, held formerly by Christy McSweeney, who did not fight the election, having failed to win a nomination at convention. The other fact of note is that Fine Gael still have no Councillor in the Electoral area of the County's Capital town Tralee.

Neither did Fine Gael have much luck in attempting to blood a Dail Candidate in Kerry South. In controversial circumstances the Party top brass had imposed G.A.A. Board Chairman, Sean Kelly, on to the Party Ticket in the Killarney area. He performed worst of the Party's three candidates and was eliminated on the forth count.

The P.D.'s did not feature in Kerry. Their one out-going member Michael Ahern from Killorglin was elected as an independent candidate in 1985 but was not seeking re-election. Kenmare shop-keeper Maeve O'Sullivan was their only candidate and she was nowhere in the running.

Fianna Fail Killarney Deputy, John O'Leary, polled 2,222 votes in Killorglin and with Tom Fleming and the colourful Jackie Healy-Rae held on to FF's three seats.

# KILLARNEY ELECTORAL AREA

TOTAL ELECTORATE 20,677. VALID POLL 14,445. NO. OF MEMBERS 6. QUOTA 2,064

| Names of Candidates | First Count Votes | Second Count Transfer of Fleming's surplus | Result | Third Count Transfer of O'Leary's surplus | Result | Fourth Count Transfer of O'Shea's votes | Result | Fifth Count Transfer of O'Callaghan's votes | Result | Sixth Count Transfer of Kelly's votes | Result | Seventh Count Transfer of T. Gleeson's votes | Result |
|---|---|---|---|---|---|---|---|---|---|---|---|---|---|
| COGHLAN, Paul (F.G.) | 1,067 | +7 | 1,074 | +9 | 1,083 | +49 | 1,132 | +81 | 1,213 | +252 | 1,465 | +470 | 1,935 |
| CRONIN, P.J. | 1,629 | +42 | 1,671 | +16 | 1,687 | +103 | 1,790 | +104 | 1,894 | +117 | 2,011 | +140 | 2,151 |
| FLEMING, Tom (F.F.) | 2,291 | -227 | 2,064 | — | 2,064 | — | 2,064 | — | 2,064 | — | 2,064 | — | 2,064 |
| GLEESON, Michael (Lab.) | 1,254 | +9 | 1,263 | +7 | 1,270 | +75 | 1,345 | +70 | 1,415 | +86 | 1,501 | +183 | 1,684 |
| GLEESON, Tim (F.G.) | 944 | +18 | 962 | +4 | 966 | +22 | 988 | +44 | 1,032 | +264 | 1,296 | -1,296 | — |
| HEALY-RAE, Jackie (F.F.) | 1,906 | +86 | 1,992 | +73 | 2,065 | — | 2,065 | — | 2,065 | — | 2,065 | — | 2,065 |
| KELLY, Seán (F.G.) | 799 | +17 | 816 | +5 | 821 | +44 | 865 | +48 | 913 | -913 | — | — | — |
| MOYNIHAN, Breeda (Lab.) | 1,274 | +19 | 1,293 | +11 | 1,304 | +112 | 1,416 | +97 | 1,513 | +108 | 1,621 | +238 | 1,859 |
| O'CALLAGHAN, Dermot (F.F.) | 541 | +25 | 566 | +28 | 594 | +56 | 650 | -650 | — | — | — | — | — |
| O'LEARY, John (F.F.) | 2,222 | — | 2,222 | -158 | 2,064 | — | 2,064 | — | 2,064 | — | 2,064 | — | 2,064 |
| O'SHEA, Eugene (G.P.) | 518 | +4 | 522 | +5 | 527 | -527 | — | — | — | — | — | — | — |
| Non-transferable papers not effective | — | — | — | — | — | +66 | 66 | +206 | 272 | +86 | 358 | +265 | 623 |
| TOTAL: | 14,445 | — | 14,445 | — | 14,445 | — | 14,445 | — | 14,445 | — | 14,445 | — | 14,445 |

Elected: Fleming, Tom (F.F.); O'Leary, John (F.F.); Healy-Rae, Jackie (F.F.); Cronin, P.J.; Coghlan, Paul (F.G.); Moynihan, Breeda (Lab.)

# KILLORGLIN ELECTORAL AREA

TOTAL ELECTORATE 18,062. VALID POLL 12,018. NO. OF MEMBERS 6. QUOTA 1,717

| Names of Candidates | First Count Votes | Second Count Transfer of O'Donoghue's surplus | Result | Third Count Transfer of M. Cahill's surplus | Result | Fourth Count Transfer of O'Sullivan's votes | Result | Fifth Count Transfer of Connor-Scarteen's surplus | Result | Sixth Count Transfer of J. Cahill's votes | Result |
|---|---|---|---|---|---|---|---|---|---|---|---|
| BARRY, Dan (F.G.) | 1,238 | +420 | 1,658 | +13 | 1,671 | +35 | 1,706 | +18 | 1,724 | — | 1,724 |
| CAHILL, Jackie (F.F.) | 671 | +287 | 958 | +58 | 1,016 | +38 | 1,054 | +52 | 1,106 | -1,106 | — |
| CAHILL, Michael (F.F.) | 2,170 | — | 2,170 | -453 | 1,717 | — | 1,717 | — | 1,717 | — | 1,717 |
| CONNOR-SCARTEEN, Michael (F.G.) | 1,626 | +49 | 1,675 | +6 | 1,681 | +146 | 1,827 | -110 | 1,717 | — | 1,717 |
| FINNEGAN, Pat (F.F.) | 616 | +326 | 942 | +228 | 1,170 | +40 | 1,210 | +4 | 1,214 | +496 | 1,710 |
| KISSANE, Danny (F.G.) | 1,328 | +44 | 1,372 | +79 | 1,451 | +78 | 1,529 | +7 | 1,536 | +45 | 1,581 |
| MOYNIHAN, Michael (Lab.) | 986 | +101 | 1,087 | +54 | 1,141 | +74 | 1,215 | +29 | 1,244 | +132 | 1,376 |
| O'DONOGHUE, John (F.F.) | 2,979 | -1,262 | 1,717 | — | 1,717 | — | 1,717 | — | 1,717 | — | 1,717 |
| O'SULLIVAN, Marie (P.D.) | 404 | +35 | 439 | +15 | 454 | -454 | — | — | — | — | — |
| Non-transferable papers not effective | — | — | — | — | — | +43 | 43 | — | 43 | +433 | 476 |
| TOTAL: | 12,018 | — | 12,018 | — | 12,018 | — | 12,018 | — | 12,018 | — | 12,018 |

Elected: O'Donoghue, John (F.F.); Cahill, Michael (F.F.); Connor-Scarteen, Michael (F.G.); Barry, Dan (F.G.); Finnegan, Pat (F.F.); Kissane, Danny (F.G.)

# LISTOWEL ELECTORAL AREA

TOTAL ELECTORATE 21,584. VALID POLL 14,519. NO. OF MEMBERS 6. QUOTA 2,075.

| Names of Candidates | First Count Votes | Second Count Transfer of Deenihan's surplus | Result | Third Count Transfer of Halpin's votes | Result | Fourth Count Transfer of L. O'Sullivan's votes | Result | Fifth Count Transfer of Behan's votes | Result | Sixth Count Transfer of Buckley's surplus | Result | Seventh Count Transfer of Brassil's surplus | Result |
|---|---|---|---|---|---|---|---|---|---|---|---|---|---|
| BEHAN, Bernie (F.G.) | 1,170 | +78 | 1,248 | +12 | 1,260 | +121 | 1,381 | -1,381 | — | — | — | — | — |
| BRASSIL, Noel (F.F.) | 1,696 | +14 | 1,710 | +6 | 1,716 | +353 | 2,069 | +275 | 2,344 | — | 2,344 | -269 | 2,075 |
| BUCKLEY, Tim (F.G.) | 1,713 | +205 | 1,918 | +47 | 1,965 | +19 | 1,984 | +682 | 2,666 | -591 | 2,075 | — | 2,075 |
| DEENIHAN, Jimmy (F.G.) | 2,725 | -650 | 2,075 | — | 2,075 | — | 2,075 | — | 2,075 | — | 2,075 | — | 2,075 |
| HALPIN, James | 282 | +41 | 323 | -323 | — | — | — | — | — | — | — | — | — |
| KIELY, Dan (F.F.) | 1,593 | +54 | 1,647 | +30 | 1,677 | +55 | 1,732 | +56 | 1,788 | +44 | 1,832 | +51 | 1,883 |
| LEAHY, Pat (Lab.) | 1,090 | +64 | 1,154 | +64 | 1,218 | +477 | 1,695 | +85 | 1,780 | +138 | 1,918 | +14 | 1,932 |
| O'SULLIVAN, Liam (Lab.) | 1,150 | +31 | 1,181 | +14 | 1,195 | -1,195 | — | — | — | — | — | — | — |
| O'SULLIVAN, Ned (F.F.) | 1,743 | +105 | 1,848 | +80 | 1,928 | +54 | 1,982 | +35 | 2,017 | +24 | 2,041 | +16 | 2,057 |
| WALSH, Kieran (F.F.) | 1,357 | +58 | 1,415 | +36 | 1,451 | +31 | 1,482 | +38 | 1,520 | +47 | 1,567 | +16 | 1,583 |
| Non-transferable papers not effective | — | — | — | +34 | 34 | +85 | 119 | +210 | 329 | +338 | 667 | +172 | 839 |
| TOTAL: | 14,519 | — | 14,519 | — | 14,519 | — | 14,519 | — | 14,519 | — | 14,519 | — | 14,519 |

# MID-KERRY ELECTORAL AREA

TOTAL ELECTORATE 15,832. VALID POLL 10,604. NO. OF MEMBERS 5. QUOTA 1,768.

| Names of Candidates | First Count Votes | Second Count Transfer of MacGearailt's surplus | Result | Third Count Transfer of Courtney's surplus | Result | Fourth Count Transfer of McEllistrim's surplus | Result | Fifth Count Transfer of Lenihan's votes | Result | Sixth Count Transfer of Kenny's votes | Result |
|---|---|---|---|---|---|---|---|---|---|---|---|
| BEGLEY, Michael (F.G.) | 1,130 | +121 | 1,251 | +20 | 1,271 | +1 | 1,272 | +27 | 1,299 | +27 | 1,326 |
| COURTNEY, James | 1,746 | +89 | 1,835 | -67 | 1,768 | — | 1,768 | — | 1,768 | — | 1,768 |
| KENNY, Sile (F.F.) | 557 | +52 | 609 | +15 | 624 | +9 | 633 | +129 | 762 | -762 | — |
| LENIHAN, Arthur (Non-Party) | 574 | +8 | 582 | +6 | 588 | — | 588 | -588 | — | — | — |
| MacGEARAILT, Breandáin (F.F.) | 2,170 | -402 | 1,768 | — | 1,768 | — | 1,768 | — | 1,768 | — | 1,768 |
| McELLISTRIM, Tom (F.F.) | 1,683 | +95 | 1,778 | — | 1,778 | -10 | 1,768 | — | 1,768 | — | 1,768 |
| O'CONNELL, Bobby (F.G.) | 1,413 | +4 | 1,417 | — | 1,417 | — | 1,417 | +241 | 1,658 | +223 | 1,881 |
| SPRING, Maeve (Lab.) | 1,331 | +33 | 1,364 | +21 | 1,385 | — | 1,385 | +114 | 1,499 | +130 | 1,629 |
| Non-transferable papers not effective | — | — | — | +5 | (5) | — | (5) | +77 | 82 | +382 | 464 |
| TOTAL | 10,604 | — | 10,604 | — | 10,604 | — | 10,604 | — | 10,604 | — | 10,604 |

Elected: MacGearailt, Breandáin (F.F.); Courtney, James; McEllistrim, Tom (F.F.); O'Connell, Bobby, (F.G.); Spring, Maeve (Lab.)

# TRALEE ELECTORAL AREA

TOTAL ELECTORATE 16,826. VALID POLL 9,058. NO. OF MEMBERS 4. QUOTA 1,812.

| Names of Candidates | First Count Votes | Second Count Transfer of Spring's surplus | Result | Third Count Transfer of Donovan's votes | Result | Fourth Count Transfer of C. Fitzgerald's votes | Result | Fifth Count Transfer of Leen's votes | Result | Sixth Count Transfer of D. Foley's surplus | Result | Seventh Count Transfer of Blennerhassett's votes | Result |
|---|---|---|---|---|---|---|---|---|---|---|---|---|---|
| BLENNERHASSETT, John | 558 | +235 | 793 | +79 | 872 | +154 | 1,026 | +114 | 1,140 | +5 | 1,145 | -1,145 | — |
| DONOVAN, Michael (Non-Party) | 330 | +149 | 479 | -479 | — | — | — | — | — | — | — | — | — |
| FITZGERALD, Conor (G.P.) | 539 | +155 | 694 | +78 | 772 | -772 | — | — | — | — | — | — | — |
| FITZGERALD, Ted (F.F.) | 726 | +158 | 884 | +61 | 945 | +135 | 1,080 | +86 | 1,166 | +22 | 1,188 | +290 | 1,478 |
| FOLEY, Denis (F.F.) | 1,845 | — | 1,845 | — | 1,845 | — | 1,845 | — | 1,845 | -33 | 1,812 | — | 1,812 |
| FOLEY, Tommy (Non-Party) | 633 | +187 | 820 | +93 | 913 | +119 | 1,032 | +267 | 1,299 | +4 | 1,303 | +204 | 1,507 |
| KELLY, Jim (F.G.) | 752 | +177 | 929 | +47 | 976 | +131 | 1,107 | +62 | 1,169 | +2 | 1,171 | +294 | 1,465 |
| LEEN, Billy (S.F.) | 715 | +87 | 802 | +55 | 857 | +60 | 917 | -917 | — | — | — | — | — |
| SPRING, Dick (Lab.) | 2,960 | -1,148 | 1,812 | — | 1,812 | — | 1,812 | — | 1,812 | — | 1,812 | — | 1,812 |
| Non-transferable papers not effective | — | — | — | +66 | 66 | +173 | 239 | +388 | 627 | — | 627 | +357 | 984 |
| TOTAL: | 9,058 | — | 9,058 | — | 9,058 | — | 9,058 | — | 9,058 | — | 9,058 | — | 9,058 |

# EMPLOYERS

**If you employ someone who illegally claims Social Welfare**

**y<u>ou may be</u> <u>liable.</u>**

Have you full or part–time employees or sub–contractors? Under the law you must ensure they are not cheating other taxpayers by illegally claiming Social Welfare payments.

If you neglect to pay their PRSI or to keep proper documentation which enables them to cheat, it is all the more serious.
As their employer, you may be liable to pay back to the Department of Social Welfare any money they've defrauded.

**You could also be fined. You could even go to prison.**

Inspectors are checking on employers now, so be sure to get your records up-to-date.

If you allow your workers cheat the system - you're the one who'll pay!

Issued by
The Information Service,
Department of Social Welfare.

# KILDARE COUNTY COUNCIL

## KILDARE COUNTY COUNCIL RESULTS

| PARTY | 1991 % of votes | 1991 Seats obtained | 1985 % of votes | 1985 Seats obtained |
|---|---|---|---|---|
| Fianna Fail | 33.4 | 8 | 42.9 | 10 |
| Fine Gael | 20.8 | 7 | 23.2 | 7 |
| Labour | 17.7 | 3 | 21.3 | 5 |
| Progressive Dem. | 6.9 | 2 | — | — |
| Workers Party | 3.8 | 1 | 2.6 | 1 |
| Other | 17.4 | 4 | 10.0 | 2 |
| TOTAL SEATS | | 25 | | 25 |

## KILDARE

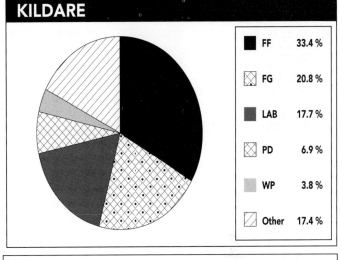

| | | |
|---|---|---|
| FF | 33.4 % |
| FG | 20.8 % |
| LAB | 17.7 % |
| PD | 6.9 % |
| WP | 3.8 % |
| Other | 17.4 % |

St Mary's, Naas, Co Kildare
Telephone:(045) 97071
Fax:(045) 76875/79772
Total population: 122,516
Rateable valuation: £780,820.60
Rate: £29.60
County Council meetings: Last Monday of each month

*County Manager:* J. G. Ward
*County Secretary:* H. Lyons
*County Finance Officer:* T. Keogh
*County Engineer:* J. A. Carrick
*County Development Officer:* B. N. Finn
*County Librarian:* Brigid A. Gleeson
*County Library*, Athgarvan Road, Newbridge.
*Telephone:*(045) 31486
*Chief Fire Officer:* M. P. Fitzsimons,
*Civil Defence Officer:* L. Coughlan,
*Senior Staff Officers:*
*County Secretary's Officer:* A. C. Talbot
*Accounts:* M. Bermingham
*Senior Executive Engineers:*
*Water Supply and Sewerage:* J. M. Murphy
*Development, Control and Housing:* B. White
*Road Maintenance:* L. Murphy
*Environmental Services:* M. Holligan
*Road Construction*: O. McCarthy
*Road Design:* R. Burke
*Senior Executive Architect:* D. Cogan
*Senior Executive Planner:* P. Jones

John Ward at 65 years of age is nearing retirement. He has been County Manager in Kildare since 1975. A prominent figure among County Managers he is both a past Chairman of the County and City Manager Association and is currently Chairman of the Board of the Institute of Public Administration.

His public service career can be traced through Clerical Officer 1948 - 1954 and Staff Officer with his native Donegal to five years with Limerick County Accountant 1962 - 67, followed by four years as Leitrim County Secretary 1967 - 1971 and then Manager of Mayo County Council from 1971 - 1975.

He was educated at the Presentation Brothers School Letter-kenny. He

**John Gerard Ward**

also holds a Diploma in Public Administration from IPA.

He is married to Kathleen Fallon and has three sons and two daughters. He has been known to list work as one of his hobbies but also enjoys reading and walking.

## ATHY

|     | 1991 | 1985 | '85 to '91 Swing |
|-----|------|------|------|
| FF  | 33.3 | 32.6 | 0.7 |
| FG  | 18.3 | 19.5 | -1.2 |
| LAB | 8.2  | 29.4 | -21.2 |
| WP  | 0.8  | —    | 0.8 |
| PD  | 5.4  | —    | 5.4 |
| GP  | 2.1  | —    | 2.1 |
| SF  | 12.6 | 12.8 | -0.2 |
| Ind | 19.3 | 5.7  | 13.6 |

BERMINGHAM, Joe,
Castlemitchell, Athy,
County Kildare. (NP)
Public Representative. 01-767571

HENDY, Rainsford,
Woodlawn, Timolin, Ballytore,
County Kildare. (FG)
Farmer. 0507-24155

MILEY, Martin,
Fontstown, Athy,
County Kildare. (FF)
Farmer. 0507-26132

WRIGHT, Paddy,
1 Clonmúllin, Athy,
County Kildare. (SF)
Labourer. 0507-38440

## CELBRIDGE

|     | 1991 | 1985 | '85 to '91 Swing |
|-----|------|------|------|
| FF  | 21.9 | 31.4 | -9.5 |
| FG  | 11.6 | 24.6 | -13.0 |
| LAB | 33.5 | 34.0 | -0.5 |
| WP  | 12.9 | 8.8  | 4.1 |
| PD  | 3.9  |      | 3.9 |
| GP  | 2.6  |      | 2.6 |
| Ind | 13.6 | 1.2  | 12.4 |

BRADY, Gerard,
Main Street, Maynooth,
County Kildare. (FF)
Auctioneer. 01-285257

DURKAN, Bernard,
Timard, Maynooth,
County Kildare. (FG)
Dáil Deputy. 01-6286063

MURPHY, Catherine,
46 Leixlip Park, Leixlip,
County Kildare. (Elected WP, now DL)
Clerical Worker.

PURCELL, Colm,
609 St. Mary's Park, Leixlip,
County Kildare. (Lab)
Sales Representative.

STAGG, Emmet,
Lodge Park, Straffan,
County Kildare. (Lab)
Dáil Deputy. 01-272169

## CLANE

|     | 1991 | 1985 | '85 to '91 Swing |
|-----|------|------|------|
| FF  | 40.1 | 52.3 | -12.2 |
| FG  | 34.1 | 27.6 | 6.5 |
| LAB | 18.6 | 20.1 | -1.5 |
| PD  | 4.0  | —    | 4.0 |
| GP  | 3.3  | —    | 3.3 |

DOYLE, Liam,
Ballybrack, Kilcock,
County Kildare. (FF)
Electrician. 01-6287629

REILLY, Sean,
Prosperous, Naas,
County Kildare. (FG)
Businessman. 045-68230

REILLY, Jim,
Ballinakill, Carbury,
County Kildare. (FG)
Clerk. 0405-53317

SHERIDAN, P.J.,
2 College Road, Clane,
County Kildare. (FF)
Milk Board Employee. 045-68580

## KILDARE

|     | 1991 | 1985 | '85 to '91 Swing |
|-----|------|------|------|
| FF  | 47.9 | 59.0 | -11.1 |
| FG  | 19.5 | 24.8 | -5.3 |
| LAB | 15.1 | 16.2 | -1.1 |
| PD  | 11.7 | —    | 11.7 |
| GP  | 2.7  | —    | 2.7 |
| Ind | 3.1  | —    | 3.1 |

DARDIS, John,
Belmont House, Athgarvan,
County Kildare. (PD)
Senator. 045-31665

KEANE, Jim,
Sheshoon, Curragh,
County Kildare. (Lab)
Unemployed. 045-41959

McWEY, Michael,
Round Tower House,
Kildare. (FG)
Auctioneer. 045-21398

O'FEARGHAIL, Sean,
Fenor,
Kildare. (FF)
Farmer. 045-21088

O'LOUGHLIN, Jimmy,
Cappanargid, Rathangan,
County Kildare. (FF)
Public Representative. 045-24318

**Bernard Durkan (FG)**
Celbridge

**John Dardis (PD)**
Kildare

**Emmet Stagg (Lab)**
Celbridge

## NAAS

|       | 1991 | 1985 | '85 to '91 Swing |
|-------|------|------|------|
| FF    | 32.8 | 41.7 | -8.9 |
| FG    | 20.3 | 20.6 | -0.3 |
| LAB   | 10.3 | 11.2 | -0.9 |
| WP    | 2.5  | 2.8  | -0.3 |
| PD    | 9.1  | —    | 9.1  |
| GP    | 6.7  | —    | 6.7  |
| Ind   | 18.2 | 23.7 | -5.5 |

CONWAY, Timmy,
Thomastown, Naas,
County Kildare. (PD)
Accountant. 045-79278

ENGLISH, Sean,
Station House, Naas,
County Kildare. (GP)
Publican. 045-79553

FRENCH, Mary,
6 Lakelands Drive,
Naas, County Kildare. (FG)
Teacher. 045-79379

LAWLOR, Patsy,
Johnstown, Naas,
County Kildare. (NP)
Public Representative.

NOLAN, Michael,
41 College Park, Newbridge,
County Kildare. (FG)
Council Employee.

O'NEILL, John,
Eyre Street, Newbridge,
County Kildare. (FF)
Stores Supervisor.

POWER, Paddy,
Caragh, Naas,
County Kildare. (FF)
Teacher. 045-97820

# Musical chairs in Kildare

Fianna Fail lost 2 seats in Kildare which was not surprising given, the emphasis placed by the other parties on the broken Fianna Fail promise over the imposition of local service charges. While the Labour Party played heavily on this issue, circulating 1985 Fianna Fail literature with 'Lies' printed over it, they did not benefit from the electorate's apathy. In fact Labour suffered a 2 seat loss in Kildare with the Progressive Democrats, Greens and Independents being the gainers from the Labour and Fianna Fail losses.

Kildare, however, was a case of musical chairs with 4 Councillors who were elected in 1985 being returned for different parties or groupings on this occasion. All 5 of the Councillors returned for Labour in 1985 were successful again this time out, although only 2 were re-elected under the Labour banner with one deflecting to the Progressive Democrats, one joining Fine Gael and another running as an Independent. In addition to the 2 outgoing Councillors returned for Labour, they won a third seat with the deflection of a former Worker's Party Councillor to the Labour ranks.

One of the former Labour Councillors, Joe Bermingham, topped the poll in the Athy Electoral Area. The former Kildare TD was returned on the third count. He was later joined by fellow outgoing Councillors Martin Miley of Fianna Fail and Sinn Fein's Paddy Wright. Fine Gael newcomer Rainsford Hendy took the final seat. Fianna Fail's hopes of taking a second seat in Athy were ruined by the decision to run 4 candidates, as their vote was too evenly spread among Miley's running mates who were too close to each other to stand a chance of taking a seat.

Emmet Stagg topped the poll in Celbridge, but unlike in 1985, when he had no running mate, a second Labour seat was taken in this area this time out. Colm Pursell was elected in 1985 for the Worker's Party, but subsequently joined Labour and was re-elected on the last count taking the last seat from the third Labour candidate John McGinley. The Worker's Party overcame the loss of Pursell with newcomer Catherine Murphy polling 1,242 first preferences as she comfortably took the third seat. Fine Gael's Bernard Durkan took the fourth seat although as a sitting Dail Deputy, he will have been disappointed with his performance, and that of his party, which lost a seat in Celbridge. Fianna Fail faired not much better with

their vote being down over 12%. Outgoing Councillor Gerry Brady was safely returned, but a second seat was never a reality in this area, where in 1985 only 5 votes deprived Fianna Fail of a second Council seat.

Fine Gael's Sean Reilly topped the poll in the Clane Area and was the only candidate in Kildare's 5 electoral areas to be returned on the first count. He was joined by party colleague Jim Reilly who had been elected for the Labour Party in 1985 but was a Fine Gael candidate on this occasion. Labour came close to holding their seat with their candidate only being beaten by Reilly by 63 votes. The other 2 seats in Clane were taken by Fianna Fail's outgoing Councillor Liam Doyle and his colleague PJ Sheridan who had been narrowly beaten in 1985.

Progressive Democrat Senator John Dardis took a seat in the Kildare Electoral Area at the expense of Fianna Fail's Paddy Aspell who had been a Councillor since 1974. Aspell's fellow outgoing Councillors were more fortunate with Sean O Fearghail topping the poll and Jimmy O'Loughlin taking the third seat. Michael McWey of Fine Gael was safely returned while Labour newcomer Jim Keane replaced party colleague Ciaran Coleman who was not a candidate on this occasion.

Labour were less successful in the Naas Area losing a seat with the deflection of former Senator Timmy Conway to the Progressive Democrats. Conway who had been elected for Labour in 1985 took the third seat this time out, to give the Progressive democrats their second seat in Kildare. Labour ruined whatever chances they had of regaining Conway's seat by spreading their vote over 3 candidates.

The poll was headed in Naas by former Fianna Fail Minister Paddy Power who was one vote ahead of Independent candidate Patsy Lawlor. A former member of Fine Gael, Lawlor comfortably retained his seat. Power was joined by party colleague John O'Neill, an outgoing Councillor. Fianna Fail's other Councillor elected in 1985, Paddy Behan lost out to Green Party candidate Sean English who climbed from ninth position on the first count with the help of cross party transfers to take the last seat in Naas on the fourteenth count. Fine Gael held their 2 seats although their was a change in lineup as Mary French defeated outgoing Councillor Billy Hillis.

**Catherine Murphy now a Democratic Left member, who was elected for the WP in the Celbridge area, Kildare.**

# ATHY ELECTORAL AREA

TOTAL ELECTORATE 12,209. VALID POLL 6,688. NO. OF MEMBERS 4. QUOTA 1,338

| Names of Candidates | First Count Votes | Second Count Transfer of Cullen's and Little's votes Result | | Third Count Transfer of Behan's votes Result | | Fourth Count Transfer of Cope's votes Result | | Fifth Count Transfer of Bermingham's surplus Result | | Sixth Count Transfer of Taaffe's votes Result | | Seventh Count Transfer of Keating's votes Result | | Eighth Count Transfer of Miley's surplus Result | | Ninth Count Transfer of Cunnane's votes Result | |
|---|---|---|---|---|---|---|---|---|---|---|---|---|---|---|---|---|---|
| BEHAN, Michael (F.F.) | 288 | +5 | 293 | -293 | — | — | — | — | — | — | — | — | — | — | — | — | — |
| BERMINGHAM, Joe (Non-Party) | 1,291 | +45 | 1,336 | +40 | 1,376 | — | 1,376 | -38 | 1,338 | — | 1,338 | — | 1,338 | — | 1,338 | — | 1,338 |
| COPE, David (P.D.) | 364 | +13 | 377 | +23 | 400 | -400 | — | — | — | — | — | — | — | — | — | — | — |
| CULLEN, Romie Dr. (G.P.) | 141 | -141 | — | — | — | — | — | — | — | — | — | — | — | — | — | — | — |
| CUNNANE, Sean (F.G.) | 520 | +13 | 533 | +23 | 556 | +34 | 590 | +4 | 594 | +85 | 679 | +77 | 756 | +3 | 759 | -759 | — |
| HENDY, Rainsford (F.G.) | 705 | +15 | 720 | +7 | 727 | +125 | 852 | +2 | 854 | +16 | 870 | +52 | 922 | +3 | 925 | +367 | 1,292 |
| KANE, Eamon (F.F.) | 503 | +2 | 505 | +56 | 561 | +80 | 641 | +7 | 648 | +68 | 716 | +55 | 771 | +5 | 776 | +60 | 836 |
| KEATING, John (Lab.) | 548 | +27 | 575 | +10 | 585 | +52 | 637 | +2 | 639 | +22 | 661 | -661 | — | — | — | — | — |
| LITTLE, Eugene (W.P.) | 51 | -51 | — | — | — | — | — | — | — | — | — | — | — | — | — | — | — |
| MILEY, Martin (F.F.) | 932 | +11 | 943 | +84 | 1,027 | +23 | 1,050 | +8 | 1,058 | +219 | 1,277 | +80 | 1,357 | -19 | 1,338 | — | 1,338 |
| TAAFFE, Frank (F.F.) | 502 | +13 | 515 | +34 | 549 | +14 | 563 | +2 | 565 | -565 | — | — | — | — | — | — | — |
| WRIGHT, Paddy (S.F.) | 843 | +36 | 879 | +11 | 890 | +20 | 910 | +6 | 916 | +91 | 1,007 | +161 | 1,168 | +8 | 1,176 | +136 | 1,312 |
| Non-transferable papers not effective | — | +12 | 12 | +5 | 17 | +52 | 69 | +7 | 76 | +64 | 140 | +236 | 376 | — | 376 | +196 | 572 |
| TOTAL: | 6,688 | — | 6,688 | — | 6,688 | — | 6,688 | — | 6,688 | — | 6,688 | — | 6,688 | — | 6,688 | — | 6,688 |

Elected: Bermingham, Joe (Non-Party); Miley, Martin (F.F.); Wright, Paddy (S.F.); Hendy, Rainsford (F.G.).

# CELBRIDGE ELECTORAL AREA

TOTAL ELECTORATE 20,088. VALID POLL 9,595. NO. OF MEMBERS 5. QUOTA 1,600

| Names of Candidates | First Count Votes | Second Count Transfer of Horan's votes Result | | Third Count Transfer of Gallery's votes Result | | Fourth Count Transfer of Leavy's votes Result | | Fifth Count Transfer of Power's votes Result | | Sixth Count Transfer of McGarry's votes Result | | Seventh Count Transfer of Hyland's votes Result | | Eighth Count Transfer of Stagg's surplus votes Result | | Ninth Count Transfer of Colgan's votes Result | | Tenth Count Transfer of Cotter's votes Result | | Eleventh Count Transfer of Byrne's votes Result | | Twelfth Count Transfer of Kelly's votes Result | |
|---|---|---|---|---|---|---|---|---|---|---|---|---|---|---|---|---|---|---|---|---|---|---|---|---|---|
| BRADY, Gerry (F.F.) | 817 | +7 | 824 | +3 | 827 | +27 | 854 | +7 | 861 | +8 | 869 | +25 | 894 | +5 | 899 | +33 | 932 | +230 | 1,162 | +445 | 1,607 | — | 1,607 |
| BYRNE, Mairead (F.F.) | 488 | — | 488 | +1 | 489 | +2 | 491 | +13 | 504 | +18 | 522 | +53 | 575 | +10 | 585 | +7 | 592 | +143 | 735 | -735 | — | — | — |
| COLGAN, John (Non-Party) | 447 | +3 | 450 | +12 | 462 | +13 | 475 | +30 | 505 | +7 | 512 | +27 | 539 | +2 | 541 | -541 | — | — | — | — | — | — | — |
| COTTER, Tim (F.F.) | 480 | +2 | 482 | +6 | 488 | — | 488 | +6 | 494 | +22 | 516 | +30 | 546 | +2 | 548 | +25 | 573 | -573 | — | — | — | — | — |
| DURKAN, Bernard (F.G.) | 923 | +5 | 928 | +96 | 1,024 | +34 | 1,058 | +16 | 1,074 | +184 | 1,258 | +73 | 1,331 | +21 | 1,352 | +77 | 1,429 | +70 | 1,499 | +88 | 1,587 | +158 | 1,745 |
| GALLERY, Gerard (F.G.) | 193 | +1 | 194 | -194 | — | — | — | — | — | — | — | — | — | — | — | — | — | — | — | — | — | — | — |
| HORAN, Sean 'Buggy' (Non-Party) | 107 | -107 | — | — | — | — | — | — | — | — | — | — | — | — | — | — | — | — | — | — | — | — | — |
| HYLAND, Mairin (P.D.) | 372 | +4 | 376 | +7 | 383 | +3 | 386 | +22 | 408 | +35 | 443 | -443 | — | — | — | — | — | — | — | — | — | — | — |
| KELLY, Finbarr (Non-Party) | 588 | +10 | 598 | +13 | 611 | +13 | 624 | +25 | 649 | +5 | 654 | +26 | 680 | +2 | 682 | +165 | 847 | +14 | 861 | +20 | 881 | -881 | — |
| LEAVY, Fred (Non-Party) | 163 | +34 | 197 | +1 | 198 | -198 | — | — | — | — | — | — | — | — | — | — | — | — | — | — | — | — | — |
| McGARRY, Catherine (F.G.) | 314 | — | 314 | +29 | 343 | — | 343 | +7 | 350 | -350 | — | — | — | — | — | — | — | — | — | — | — | — | — |
| McGINLEY, John (Lab.) | 799 | +14 | 813 | +1 | 814 | +39 | 853 | +20 | 873 | +2 | 875 | +13 | 888 | +9 | 897 | +34 | 931 | +5 | 936 | +12 | 948 | +33 | 981 |
| MURPHY, Catherine (W.P.) | 1,242 | +8 | 1,250 | +5 | 1,255 | +8 | 1,263 | +41 | 1,304 | +8 | 1,312 | +28 | 1,340 | +6 | 1,346 | +102 | 1,448 | +24 | 1,472 | +34 | 1,506 | +242 | 1,748 |
| POWER, Catherine (G.P.) | 248 | +3 | 251 | +3 | 254 | +9 | 263 | -263 | — | — | — | — | — | — | — | — | — | — | — | — | — | — | — |
| PURCELL, Colm (Lab.) | 965 | +4 | 969 | +10 | 979 | +7 | 986 | +24 | 1,010 | +2 | 1,012 | +19 | 1,031 | +20 | 1,051 | +50 | 1,101 | +30 | 1,131 | +15 | 1,146 | +247 | 1,393 |
| STAGG, Emmet (Lab.) | 1,449 | +11 | 1,460 | +4 | 1,464 | +24 | 1,488 | +39 | 1,527 | +47 | 1,574 | +103 | 1,677 | -77 | 1,600 | — | 1,600 | — | 1,600 | — | 1,600 | — | 1,600 |
| Non-transferable papers not effective | — | +1 | (1) | +3 | (4) | +19 | 23 | +13 | 36 | +12 | 48 | +46 | 94 | — | 94 | +48 | 142 | +57 | 199 | +121 | 320 | +201 | 521 |
| TOTAL: | 9,595 | — | 9,595 | — | 9,595 | — | 9,595 | — | 9,595 | — | 9,595 | — | 9,595 | — | 9,595 | — | 9,595 | — | 9,595 | — | 9,595 | — | 9,595 |

Elected: Stagg, Emmet (Lab.); Brady, Gerry (F.F.); Murphy, Catherine (W.P.); Durkan, Bernard (F.G.); Purcell, Colm (Lab.)

# CLANE LOCAL ELECTORAL AREA

TOTAL ELECTORATE 12,455. VALID POLL 6,614. NO. OF MEMBERS 4. QUOTA 1,323

| Names of Candidates | First Count Votes | Second Count Transfer of S. Reilly's surplus | Result | Third Count Transfer of Davenport's, Lyons' and O'Sullivan's votes | Result | Fourth Count Transfer of Murphy's votes | Result | Fifth Count Transfer of Fitzpatrick's votes | Result | Sixth Count Transfer of Doyle's surplus | Result |
|---|---|---|---|---|---|---|---|---|---|---|---|
| DAVENPORT, Daragh G.P.) | 112 | +1 | 113 | -113 | — | — | — | — | — | — | — |
| DOYLE, Liam F.F.) | 788 | +2 | 790 | +72 | 862 | +158 | 1,020 | +386 | 1,406 | -83 | 1,323 |
| FITZPATRICK, Michael F.F.) | 935 | +4 | 939 | +34 | 973 | +19 | 992 | -992 | — | — | — |
| LYONS, Noel P.D.) | 262 | +3 | 265 | -265 | — | — | — | — | — | — | — |
| McCORMACK, Michael J. Lab.) | 647 | +1 | 648 | +67 | 715 | +319 | 1,034 | +96 | 1,130 | +5 | 1,135 |
| MURPHY, Rose Lab.) | 584 | +4 | 588 | +85 | 673 | -673 | — | — | — | — | — |
| O'SULLIVAN, Deirdre G.P.) | 105 | +1 | 106 | -106 | — | — | — | — | — | — | — |
| REILLY, Jim F.G.) | 879 | +28 | 907 | +107 | 1,014 | +59 | 1,073 | +121 | 1,194 | +4 | 1,198 |
| REILLY, Sean F.G.) | 1,376 | -53 | 1,323 | — | 1,323 | — | 1,323 | — | 1,323 | — | 1,323 |
| SHERIDAN, P.J. F.F.) | 926 | +9 | 935 | +49 | 984 | +36 | 1,020 | +276 | 1,296 | +74 | 1,370 |
| Non-transferable papers not effective | — | — | — | +70 | 70 | +82 | 152 | +113 | 265 | — | 265 |
| TOTAL: | 6,614 | — | 6,614 | — | 6,614 | — | 6,614 | — | 6,614 | — | 6,614 |

Elected: Reilly, Sean (F.G.); Doyle, Liam (F.F.); Sheridan, P.J. (F.F.); Reilly, Jim (F.G.)

# KILDARE LOCAL ELECTORAL AREA

TOTAL ELECTORATE 14,895. VALID POLL 7,130. NO. OF MEMBERS 5. QUOTA 1,189.

| Names of Candidates | First Count Votes | Second Count Transfer of Brady's votes | Result | Third Count Transfer of Price's votes | Result | Fourth Count Transfer of Murphy's votes | Result | Fifth Count Transfer of Doyle's votes | Result | Sixth Count Transfer of Carr's votes | Result | Seventh Count Transfer of Kavanagh's votes | Result | Eighth Count Transfer of Mahon's votes | Result |
|---|---|---|---|---|---|---|---|---|---|---|---|---|---|---|---|
| ASPELL, Paddy (F.F.) | 643 | +15 | 658 | +23 | 681 | +1 | 682 | +119 | 801 | +8 | 809 | +14 | 823 | +95 | 918 |
| BRADY, Olive (G.P.) | 193 | -193 | — | — | — | — | — | — | — | — | — | — | — | — | — |
| CARR, Con (F.G.) | 408 | +11 | 419 | +1 | 420 | +35 | 455 | +8 | 463 | -463 | — | — | — | — | — |
| DARDIS, John (P.D.) | 835 | +38 | 873 | +40 | 913 | +41 | 954 | +45 | 999 | +38 | 1,037 | +34 | 1,071 | +66 | 1,137 |
| DOYLE, Angela (F.F.) | 406 | +21 | 427 | +7 | 434 | +1 | 435 | -435 | — | — | — | — | — | — | — |
| KAVANAGH, Mary (Lab.) | 414 | +26 | 440 | +13 | 453 | +7 | 460 | +18 | 478 | +25 | 503 | -503 | — | — | — |
| KEANE, Jim (Lab.) | 665 | +24 | 689 | +13 | 702 | +8 | 710 | +67 | 777 | +31 | 808 | +268 | 1,076 | +51 | 1,127 |
| MAHON, Denis (F.F.) | 566 | +8 | 574 | +6 | 580 | +1 | 581 | +27 | 608 | +141 | 749 | +8 | 757 | -757 | — |
| McWEY, Michael (F.G.) | 751 | +6 | 757 | +14 | 771 | +83 | 854 | +30 | 884 | +152 | 1,036 | +58 | 1,094 | +85 | 1,179 |
| MURPHY, John Joe (F.G.) | 230 | +5 | 235 | +23 | 258 | -258 | — | — | — | — | — | — | — | — | — |
| O FEARGHAIL, Sean (F.F.) | 1,012 | +9 | 1,021 | +13 | 1,034 | +16 | 1,050 | +72 | 1,122 | +27 | 1,149 | +62 | 1,211 | — | 1,211 |
| O'LOUGHLIN, Jimmy (F.F.) | 786 | +5 | 791 | +47 | 838 | +51 | 889 | +23 | 912 | +12 | 924 | +14 | 938 | +238 | 1,176 |

# NAAS ELECTORAL AREA

TOTAL ELECTORATE 24,361. VALID POLL 10,394. NO. OF MEMBERS 7. QUOTA 1,300.

| Names of Candidates | First Count Votes | Second Count Transfer of Kennedy's votes Result | Third Count Transfer of Sweetman's votes Result | Fourth Count Transfer of O'Sullivan's votes Result | Fifth Count Transfer of Kelly's votes Result | Sixth Count Transfer of Geoghegan's votes Result | Seventh Count Transfer of Larkin's votes Result |
|---|---|---|---|---|---|---|---|
| BEHAN, Paddy (F.F.) | 630 | +1 631 | +8 639 | — 639 | +45 684 | +12 696 | +8 704 |
| CONWAY, Timmy (P.D.) | 947 | +3 950 | +12 962 | +3 965 | +8 973 | +24 997 | +12 1,009 |
| CROKE, Norman (Lab.) | 465 | +3 468 | +3 471 | +7 478 | +7 485 | +60 545 | +36 581 |
| DONOHOE, Simon (Lab.) | 317 | +7 324 | +2 326 | +7 333 | — 333 | +62 395 | +44 439 |
| ENGLISH, Sean (G.P.) | 504 | +6 510 | +102 612 | +14 626 | +4 630 | +13 643 | +42 685 |
| FEENEY, Colm (Non-Party) | 472 | +14 486 | +10 496 | +45 541 | — 541 | +1 542 | +27 569 |
| FRENCH, Mary (F.G.) | 800 | +3 803 | +6 809 | +2 811 | +8 819 | +3 822 | +11 833 |
| GEOGHEGAN, Tom (Lab.) | 289 | +1 290 | +4 294 | +1 295 | +2 297 | -297 — | — — |
| HILLIS, Billy (F.G.) | 597 | +2 599 | +3 602 | + 603 | +2 605 | +64 669 | +5 674 |
| KELLY, Andy (F.F.) | 216 | +1 217 | — 217 | +2 219 | -219 — | — — | — — |
| KENNEDY, Peter (Non-Party) | 101 | -101 — | — — | — — | — — | — — | — — |
| LARKIN, Mary (W.P.) | 263 | +9 272 | +5 277 | +25 302 | +2 304 | +14 318 | -318 — |
| LAWLOR, Patsy | 1,145 | +5 1,150 | +14 1,164 | +7 1,171 | +46 1,217 | +12 1,229 | +36 1,265 |
| NOLAN, Michael (F.G.) | 717 | +8 725 | — 725 | +25 750 | +3 753 | +4 757 | +23 780 |
| O'NEILL, John (F.F.) | 977 | +9 986 | — 986 | +34 1,020 | +16 1,036 | +3 1,039 | +14 1,053 |
| O'SULLIVAN, Dan (Non-Party) | 175 | +21 196 | +7 203 | -203 — | — — | — — | — — |
| POWER, Paddy (F.F.) | 1,146 | +4 1,150 | +6 1,156 | +7 1,163 | +46 1,209 | +12 1,221 | +14 1,235 |
| ROBINSON, Mary (F.F.) | 444 | — 444 | +9 453 | +1 454 | +21 475 | +4 479 | +10 489 |
| SWEETMAN, Peter (G.P.) | 189 | +4 193 | -193 — | — — | — — | — — | — — |
| Non-transferable papers not effective | — | — — | +2 2 | +22 24 | +9 33 | +9 42 | +36 78 |
| TOTAL: | 10,394 | — 10,394 | — 10,394 | — 10,394 | — 10,394 | — 10,394 | — 10,394 |

| Names of Candidates | Eighth Count Transfer of Donohoe's votes Result | Ninth Count Transfer of Robinson's votes Result | Tenth Count Transfer of Power's surplus Result | Eleventh Count Transfer of Feeney's votes Result | Twelfth Count Transfer of Hillis' votes Result | Thirteenth Count Transfer of Lawlor's surplus Result | Fourteenth Count Transfer of Croke's votes Result |
|---|---|---|---|---|---|---|---|
| BEHAN, Paddy (F.F.) | +6 710 | +76 786 | +59 845 | +17 862 | +20 882 | +9 891 | +44 935 |
| CONWAY, Timmy (P.D.) | +22 1,031 | +43 1,074 | +9 1,083 | +69 1,152 | +75 1,227 | +12 1,239 | +102 1,341 |
| CROKE, Norman (Lab.) | +179 760 | +20 780 | +3 783 | +45 828 | +18 846 | +6 852 | -852 — |
| DONOHOE, Simon (Lab.) | -439 — | — — | — — | — — | — — | — — | — — |
| ENGLISH, Sean (G.P.) | +22 707 | +31 738 | +3 741 | +83 824 | +75 899 | +5 904 | +199 1,103 |
| FEENEY, Colm (Non-Party) | +41 610 | +2 612 | — 612 | -612 — | — — | — — | — — |
| FRENCH, Mary (F.G.) | +4 837 | +15 852 | +1 853 | +33 886 | +192 1,078 | +11 1,089 | +55 1,144 |
| GEOGHEGAN, Tom (Lab.) | — — | — — | — — | — — | — — | — — | — — |
| HILLIS, Billy (F.G.) | +9 683 | +6 689 | +1 690 | +13 703 | -703 — | — — | — — |
| KELLY, Andy (F.F.) | — — | — — | — — | — — | — — | — — | — — |
| KENNEDY, Peter (Non-Party) | — — | — — | — — | — — | — — | — — | — — |
| LARKIN, Mary (W.P.) | — — | — — | — — | — — | — — | — — | — — |
| LAWLOR, Patsy | +27 1,292 | +68 1,360 | — 1,360 | — 1,360 | — 1,360 | -60 1,300 | — 1,300 |
| NOLAN, Michael (F.G.) | +30 810 | +6 816 | — 816 | +126 942 | +139 1,081 | +2 1,083 | +47 1,130 |
| O'NEILL, John (F.F.) | +26 1,079 | +30 1,109 | +44 1,153 | +101 1,254 | +15 1,269 | +4 1,273 | +29 1,302 |
| O'SULLIVAN, Dan (Non-Party) | — — | — — | — — | — — | — — | — — | — — |
| POWER, Paddy (F.F.) | +18 1,253 | +167 1,420 | -120 1,300 | — 1,3000 | — 1,300 | — 1,300 | — 1,300 |
| ROBINSON, Mary (F.F.) | +7 496 | -496 — | — — | — — | — — | — — | — — |
| SWEETMAN, Peter (G.P.) | — — | — — | — — | — — | — — | — — | — — |
| Non-transferable papers not effective | +48 126 | +32 158 | — 158 | +125 283 | +169 452 | +11 463 | +376 839 |
| TOTAL: | — 10,394 | — 10,394 | — 10,394 | — 10,394 | — 10,394 | — 10,394 | — 10,394 |

# Making business
# a pleasure
# is our business!

At the Connemara Coast Hotel, you'll find an atmosphere that's as unique as our location.

Magnificently set overlooking Galway Bay just 6 miles from Galway, Europe's fastest growing city, the Connemara Coast provides a first class service for top business executives.

Our team of experts will co-ordinate your conference to the highest level of perfection, catering for a small business meeting or a forum of 500 people.

From the planning stages right through to the actual event, we are on hand to provide the professional advice required to ensure your conference is one hundred per cent successful.

Our state-of-the-art fully remote control conference facilities offers you the perfect setting to enhance your presentation. In addition we have the distinctive advantage of a variety of syndicate rooms available for additional meetings during the day.

Our fabulous new leisure centre is there to enjoy, following a day that has gone exactly as planned.

With quality, style and luxury at remarkably competitive prices, the Connemara Coast Hotel will provide the inspiration your team requires for a truly successful conference.

Call Ann Duggan or Conor Scott at (091) 92108 and see how we are making it our business to make your business a pleasure.

# Connemara Coast
### H O T E L
Furbo, Co. Galway. Tel: 091-92108. Fax: 091-92065.

*Making business a pleasure is our business!*

# KILKENNY COUNTY COUNCIL

## KILKENNY COUNTY COUNCIL RESULTS

| PARTY | 1991 % of votes | 1991 Seats obtained | 1985 % of votes | 1985 Seats obtained |
|---|---|---|---|---|
| Fianna Fail | 43.2 | 12 | 44.8 | 11 |
| Fine Gael | 33.3 | 10 | 35.4 | 10 |
| Labour | 16.0 | 4 | 10.7 | 3 |
| Progressive Dem. | 3.0 | — | — | — |
| Workers Party | 2.0 | — | 4.4 | 1 |
| Other | 2.5 | — | 4.7 | 1 |
| | | — | | — |
| TOTAL SEATS | | 26 | | 26 |

**Total population: 73,613**
**Rateable valuation:**
**County: £226,663.22**
**City: £63,593.90**
**County Council**
**John's Green, Kilkenny**
**Telephone: (056) 21196**
**Fax: (056) 63384**
**Rate: £20.91**
**County Council meetings: Third Monday of each month**
**except August**

*County Manager:* P. J. Donnelly
*County Secretary:* T. W. Boyle
*Finance Officer:* J. Magner
*County Engineer:* M. A. Barry
*County Development Officer:* A. Walsh
*Administrative Officers:*
*Engineering:* P. O'Neill
*Personnel and General Purposes:* P. Gibbs
*Senior Staff Officers:*
*Accounts:* M. Shortall
*Planning and Environment:* J. Gibbons
*Housing:* J. McCormack
*Internal Auditor:* M. Shortall
*County Librarian:* J. Fogarty
*County Library*, John Street, Kilkenny
*Telephone:*(056) 22021
*County Solicitor:* J. Harte,
Kilkenny. *Telephone:*(056) 21091
*County Coroner:* R. Hogan,
*Chief Fire Officer:* Captain H. Corrigan,
*Senior Executive Engineers:*
*Roads:* Vacant
*Sanitary Services:* F. Coughlan
*Planning and Environment:* O. Mannion
*Housing:* P. Foley
*Road Design:* F. O'Dwyer

## KILKENNY

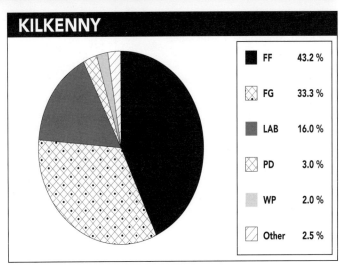

| | | |
|---|---|---|
| ■ FF | 43.2 % |
| ⊠ FG | 33.3 % |
| ■ LAB | 16.0 % |
| ⊠ PD | 3.0 % |
| ▨ WP | 2.0 % |
| ▧ Other | 2.5 % |

Patrick Donnelly, as well as being Kilkenny County Manager is also City Manager to Kilkenny Corporation. At 55, he is one of the Countries younger County Managers and also unusually began his career in the Department of Local Government. He actually entered the Public Services as a Clerical Officer in the Department of Finance at 18 years of age before moving to become an Executive Officer in the Customs House in 1959. He was Assistant Private Secretary between 1960 - 1964 and then acted as Private Secretary to the Minister for Local Government between 1964 - 1965. He was promoted to Higher Education Officer in the Department in 1965 and then to Assistant Principal Officer in 1969.

In 1973 he left the Department to become the County Secretary and temporary County Manager in Meath, 1975 - 1976 and then moved to his present post in Kilkenny County Council.

Donnelly is recognised for his work in relation to conservation and urban renewal in Kilkenny City and was a recipient of an award from the Quality Association of Ireland for such work in 1989. He is a member of a number of State Bodies and Boards and is Chairman of Kilkenny Civic Trust.

His education was in St. Josephs CBS in Drogheda, Trinity College and The Institute of Public Administration . He is married to Maura Collette Mc Elvenny and they have three children. His hobbies include swimming, walking and reading.

## BALLYRAGGET

| | 1991 | 1985 | '85 to '91 Swing |
|---|---|---|---|
| FF | 45.0 | 51.2 | -6.2 |
| FG | 35.4 | 36.5 | -1.1 |
| LAB | 15.1 | 12.3 | 2.8 |
| Ind | 4.5 | — | 4.5 |

BRENNAN, Dick,
New Road, Moneenroe, Castlecomer,
County Kilkenny. (Lab)
Retired. 056-42474

BRENNAN, John,
Crutt, Clogh, Castlecomer,
County Kilkenny. (FG)
Factory Worker. 056-42319

CAVANAGH, Mary Hilda,
Whiteswall, Crosspatrick,
County Kilkenny. (FG)
Housewife. 0505-46419

FITZPATRICK, Martin,
Borrismore, Johnstown,
County Kilkenny. (FF)
Farmer. 056-31386

MURPHY, John,
Oldtown, Ballyragget,
County Kilkenny. (FF)
Factory Worker. 056-42319

## KILKENNY

| | 1991 | 1985 | '85 to '91 Swing |
|---|---|---|---|
| FF | 37.7 | 31.4 | 6.3 |
| FG | 21.8 | 26.7 | -4.9 |
| LAB | 24.3 | 15.8 | 8.5 |
| WP | 5.8 | 3.9 | 1.9 |
| Ind | 10.4 | 22.2 | -11.8 |

CROTTY, Kieran,
"Ayrfield",
Kilkenny. (FG)
Baker. 056-21626
LANIGAN, Mick,
"St Judes", Chapel Avenue,
Kilkenny. (FF)
Senator. 056-22650

McGUINNESS, Michael J.,
11 O'Loughlin Road,
Kilkenny. (FF)
Business Manager. 056-21799

PATTISON, Seamus,
6 Upper New Street,
Kilkenny. (Lab)
Dail Deputy. 056-21295

## PILTOWN

| | 1991 | 1985 | '85 to '91 Swing |
|---|---|---|---|
| FF | 46.5 | 47.3 | -0.8 |
| FG | 39.3 | 34.1 | 5.2 |
| LAB | 9.3 | 5.3 | 4.0 |
| Ind | 0.0 | 13.3 | -13.3 |

AYLWARD, Liam,
Aghaviller, Hugginstown,
County Kilkenny. (FF)
Dail Deputy. 056-68703*

BLACKMORE, Anne,
Tybroughney, Pilltown,
County Kilkenny. (FF)
Part-time Worker.

COTTERELL, Andrew,
Kilmacshane,
Inistioge,
County Kilkenny. (FG)
Farmer. 056-58403

DOWLING, Richard,
"Glencara", Newrath via Waterford,
County Kilkenny. (FG)
Teacher. 051-73868

DUNPHY, Dick,
Luffany, Mooncoin,
County Kilkenny. (FF)
Farmer. 051-95141

MAHER, John,
Templeorum, Piltown,
County Kilkenny. (FG)
Farmer. 056-25234

WALSH, Joe,
Narabane, Kilmacow,
County Kilkenny. (Lab)
Supervisor.

*Resigned when appointed Minister of State,
Feb. 1992.
Replaced by
AYLWARD, Robert,
Knockmoylan, Mullinavat,
County Kilkenny. (FF)

## THOMASTOWN

| | 1991 | 1985 | '85 to '91 Swing |
|---|---|---|---|
| FF | 42.1 | 48.0 | -5.9 |
| FG | 28.3 | 34.2 | -5.9 |
| LAB | 22.6 | 13.9 | 8.7 |
| PD | 7.0 | — | 7.0 |
| SF | — | 3.9 | -3.9 |

BRETT, James J.,
Sheastown,
County Kilkenny. (FF)
Company Director. 056-27221

FENLON, Michael,
Miltown, Borris,
County Kilkenny. (FF)
Retired Farmer.

FENNELLY, Kevin,
Castleblanny, Mullinavat,
County Kilkenny. (FF)
Insurance Broker.056-68677

IRELAND, William,
Danesfort,
County Kilkenny. (FG)
Farmer.

MAHER, Tom,
Broadmore, Callan,
County Kilkenny. (FG)
Farmer. 056-25234

O'BRIEN, Michael T.,
Friars Hill, Thomastown,
County Kilkenny. (Lab)
Railway Employee. 056-24374

## TULLAROAN

| | 1991 | 1985 | '85 to '91 Swing |
|---|---|---|---|
| FF | 42.2 | 39.5 | 2.7 |
| FG | 38.8 | 47.7 | -8.9 |
| LAB | 10.6 | 7.3 | 3.3 |
| PD | 8.4 | — | 8.4 |
| Ind | — | 5.5 | -5.5 |

HOGAN, Philip,
25 The Sycamores,Freshford Road,
County Kilkenny. (FG)
Dail Deputy. 056-61572

McGUINNESS, John J.,
O'Loughlin Road,
Kilkenny. (FF)
Business Manager. 056-21331

MILLEA, Patrick,
Gaulstown, Tullaroan,
County Kilkenny. (FF)
Farmer. 056-69182

TYNAN, Margaret,
2 High Hayes Terrace,
Kilkenny. (FG)
Self-Employed. 056-22839

**Michael O'Brien (Lab)**
**Thomastown**

**Liam Aylward (FF)**
**Piltown**

**Philip Hogan (FG)**
**Tullaroan**

## Liquid effluent treatment

**Puraflo** liquid effluent treatment systems have been developed for a wide range of waste water treatment applications and have proven themselves in over one hundred and seventy applications over the past few years.

Comparative tests that we have carried out show that other systems such as bio-rotating disks and other aeration and chemical options fall far short of the performance of **Puraflo** systems.

**Puraflo** is the only system that does the job properly.

But why believe us, read the new SR6 document – the National Standards Authority recommends the type of system that **Puraflo** offers.

The **Puraflo** system is ideal for small developments of houses, pubs, hotels and holiday resorts.

ENVIRONMENTAL PRODUCTS

Newbridge, Co. Kildare, Ireland, Tel: 045-31201    Fax:045-31647

# BALLYRAGGET ELECTORAL AREA

TOTAL ELECTORATE 9,780. VALID POLL 6,918. NO. OF MEMBERS 5. QUOTA 1,154

| Names of Candidates | First Count Votes | Second Count Transfer of Bergin's votes Result | | Third Count Transfer of Wilson's votes Result | | Fourth Count Transfer of Phelan's votes Result | | Fifth Count Transfer of Connery's votes Result | | Sixth Count Transfer of Owens' votes Result | | Seventh Count Transfer of Murphy's surplus Result | | Eighth Count Transfer of J. Brennan's surplus Result | | Ninth Count Transfer of D. Brennan's surplus Result | |
|---|---|---|---|---|---|---|---|---|---|---|---|---|---|---|---|---|---|
| BERGIN, John Nicholas (Lab.) | 111 | -111 | — | — | — | — | — | — | — | — | — | — | — | — | — | — | — |
| BRENNAN, Dick (Lab.) | 931 | +50 | 981 | +7 | 988 | +23 | 1,011 | +38 | 1,049 | +142 | 1,191 | — | 1,191 | — | 1,191 | -37 | 1,154 |
| BRENNAN, John (F.G.) | 797 | +5 | 802 | +2 | 804 | +16 | 820 | +274 | 1,094 | +118 | 1,212 | — | 1,212 | -58 | 1,154 | — | 1,154 |
| CAVANAGH, Mary Hilda (F.G.) | 1,142 | +13 | 1,155 | — | 1,155 | — | 1,155 | — | 1,155 | — | 1,155 | — | 1,155 | — | 1,155 | — | 1,155 |
| CONNERY, Catherine (F.G.) | 509 | +4 | 513 | +6 | 519 | +36 | 555 | -555 | — | — | — | — | — | — | — | — | — |
| FITZPATRICK, Martin (F.F.) | 682 | +3 | 685 | +73 | 758 | +124 | 882 | +20 | 902 | +65 | 967 | +66 | 1,033 | +26 | 1,059 | +30 | 1,089 |
| MURPHY, Jack (F.F.) | 870 | +4 | 874 | +59 | 933 | +26 | 959 | +84 | 1,043 | +228 | 1,271 | -117 | 1,154 | — | 1,154 | — | 1,154 |
| O'DONNELL, Shem (F.F.) | 609 | +22 | 631 | +106 | 737 | +31 | 768 | +80 | 848 | +111 | 959 | +51 | 1,010 | +11 | 1,021 | +7 | 1,028 |
| OWENS, Patricia (F.F.) | 650 | +3 | 653 | +8 | 661 | +16 | 667 | +21 | 698 | -698 | — | — | — | — | — | — | — |
| PHELAN, Bríd (Non-Party) | 313 | +3 | 316 | +34 | 350 | -350 | — | — | — | — | — | — | — | — | — | — | — |
| WILSON, Michael (F.F.) | 304 | +2 | 306 | -306 | — | — | — | — | — | — | — | — | — | — | — | — | — |
| Non-transferable papers not effective | — | +2 | 2 | +11 | 13 | +78 | 91 | +38 | 129 | +34 | 163 | — | 163 | +21 | 184 | — | 184 |
| TOTAL: | 6,918 | — | 6,918 | — | 6,918 | — | 6,918 | — | 6,918 | — | 6,918 | — | 6,918 | — | 6,918 | — | 6,918 |

Elected: Cavanagh, Mary Hilda (F.G.); Murphy, Jack (F.F.); Brennan, John (F.G.); Brennan, Dick (Lab.); Fitzpatrick, Martin (F.F.)

# KILKENNY ELECTORAL AREA

TOTAL ELECTORATE 8,088. VALID POLL 4,648. NO. OF MEMBERS 4. QUOTA 930

| Names of Candidates | First Count Votes | Second Count Transfer of Pattison's surplus Result | | Third Count Transfer of McGrath's votes Result | | Fourth Count Transfer of Boyd's votes Result | | Fifth Count Transfer of Crotty's surplus Result | | Sixth Count Transfer of White's votes Result | | Seventh Count Transfer of Butler's votes Result | |
|---|---|---|---|---|---|---|---|---|---|---|---|---|---|
| BOLGER, John | 292 | +25 | 317 | +29 | 346 | +48 | 394 | +29 | 423 | +55 | 478 | +146 | 624 |
| BOYD, Carmel (F.G.) | 299 | +20 | 319 | +10 | 329 | -329 | — | — | — | — | — | — | — |
| BUTLER, Joe (W.P.) | 268 | +31 | 299 | +63 | 362 | +14 | 376 | +7 | 383 | +26 | 409 | -409 | — |
| CROTTY, Kieran (F.G.) | 715 | +47 | 762 | +29 | 791 | +192 | 983 | -53 | 930 | — | 930 | — | 930 |
| LANIGAN, Mick (F.F.) | 765 | +27 | 792 | +23 | 815 | +19 | 834 | +8 | 842 | +153 | 995 | — | 995 |
| McGRATH, Michael J. (Non-Party) | 193 | +13 | 206 | -206 | — | — | — | — | — | — | — | — | — |
| McGUINNESS, Michael J. (F.F.) | 680 | +21 | 701 | +12 | 713 | +24 | 737 | +4 | 741 | +92 | 833 | +84 | 917 |
| PATTISON, Seamus (Lab.) | 1,130 | -200 | 930 | — | 930 | — | 930 | — | 930 | — | 930 | — | 930 |
| WHITE, Evelyn M. (F.F.) | 306 | +16 | 322 | +20 | 342 | +19 | 361 | +5 | 366 | -366 | — | — | — |
| Non-transferable papers not effective | — | — | — | +20 | 20 | +13 | 33 | — | 33 | +40 | 73 | +179 | 252 |
| TOTAL: | 4,648 | — | 4,648 | — | 4,648 | — | 4,648 | — | 4,648 | — | 4,648 | — | 4,648 |

Elected: Pattison, Seamus (Lab.); Crotty, Kieran (F.G.); Lanigan, Mick (F.F.); McGuinness, Michael J. (F.F.)

# PILLTOWN ELECTORAL AREA

TOTAL ELECTORATE 12,979. VALID POLL 8,065. NO. OF MEMBERS 7. QUOTA 1,009

| Names of Candidates | First Count Votes | Second Count Transfer of Aylward's surplus | Result | Third Count Transfer of Dowling's surplus | Result | Fourth Count Transfer of Kennedy's votes | Result | Fifth Count Transfer of Byrne's votes | Result | Sixth Count Transfer of Kearns' votes | Result | Seventh Count Transfer of Maher's surplus | Result | Eighth Count Transfer of Cotterell's surplus | Result |
|---|---|---|---|---|---|---|---|---|---|---|---|---|---|---|---|
| AYLWARD, Liam (F.F.) | 1,906 | -897 | 1,009 | — | 1,009 | — | 1,009 | — | 1,009 | — | 1,009 | — | 1,009 | — | 1,009 |
| BLACKMORE, Ann (F.F.) | 456 | +222 | 678 | +4 | 682 | +20 | 702 | +121 | 823 | +35 | 858 | +26 | 884 | +6 | 890 |
| BYRNE, Albert Thomas (F.F.) | 335 | +110 | 445 | +10 | 455 | +36 | 491 | -491 | — | — | — | — | — | — | — |
| COTTERELL, Andrew (F.G.) | 763 | +49 | 812 | +84 | 896 | +18 | 914 | +17 | 931 | +138 | 1,069 | — | 1,069 | -60 | 1,009 |
| DOWLING, Richard (F.G.) | 1,229 | — | 1,229 | -220 | 1,009 | — | 1,009 | — | 1,009 | — | 1,009 | — | 1,009 | — | 1,009 |
| DREA, Margariet (F.F.) | 534 | +142 | 676 | +6 | 682 | +8 | 690 | +132 | 822 | +15 | 837 | +6 | 843 | +6 | 849 |
| DUNPHY, Dick (F.F.) | 517 | +222 | 739 | +9 | 748 | +6 | 754 | +101 | 855 | +67 | 922 | +40 | 962 | +19 | 981 |
| KEARNS, Catherine (F.G.) | 482 | +26 | 508 | +55 | 563 | +16 | 579 | +17 | 596 | -596 | — | — | — | — | — |
| KENNEDY, Martin (W.P.) | 396 | +25 | 421 | +13 | 434 | -434 | — | — | — | — | — | — | — | — | — |
| MAHER, John (F.G.) | 697 | +56 | 753 | +20 | 773 | +11 | 784 | +11 | 795 | +286 | 1,081 | -72 | 1,009 | — | 1,009 |
| WALSH, Joe (Lab.) | 750 | +45 | 795 | +19 | 814 | +231 | 1,045 | — | 1,045 | — | 1,045 | — | 1,045 | — | 1,045 |
| Non-transferable papers not effective | — | — | — | — | — | +88 | 88 | +92 | 180 | +55 | 235 | — | 235 | +29 | 264 |
| TOTAL: | 8,065 | — | 8,065 | — | 8,065 | — | 8,065 | — | 8,065 | — | 8,065 | — | 8,065 | — | 8,065 |

Elected: Alyward, Liam (F.F.); Dowling, Richard (F.G.); Walsh, Joe (Lab.); Maher, John (F.G.); Cotterell, Andrew (F.G.); Dunphy, Dick (F.F.); Blackmore, Ann (F.F.)

# THOMASTOWN ELECTORAL AREA

TOTAL ELECTORATE 11,771. VALID POLL 7,520. NO. OF MEMBERS 6. QUOTA 1,075.

| Names of Candidates | First Count Votes | Second Count Transfer of Brett's surplus | Result | Third Count Transfer of McDonald's votes | Result | Fourth Count Transfer of Crowley's votes | Result | Fifth Count Transfer of Somers' votes | Result | Sixth Count Transfer of Fennelly's surplus | Result | Seventh Count Transfer of Bolger's votes | Result |
|---|---|---|---|---|---|---|---|---|---|---|---|---|---|
| BOLGER, John (Lab.) | 647 | +1 | 648 | +9 | 657 | +32 | 689 | +14 | 703 | +5 | 708 | -708 | — |
| BRENNAN, Philip (F.G.) | 599 | +6 | 605 | +5 | 610 | +89 | 699 | +17 | 716 | +13 | 729 | +86 | 815 |
| BRETT, James J. (F.F.) | 1,179 | -104 | 1,075 | — | 1,075 | — | 1,075 | — | 1,075 | — | 1,075 | — | 1,075 |
| CROWLEY, Patrick (P.D.) | 350 | +10 | 360 | +74 | 434 | -434 | — | — | — | — | — | — | — |
| FENLON, Michael (F.F.) | 573 | +13 | 586 | +8 | 594 | +12 | 606 | +69 | 675 | +131 | 806 | +233 | 1,039 |
| FENNELLY, Kevin (F.F.) | 922 | +26 | 948 | +17 | 965 | +63 | 1,028 | +232 | 1,260 | -185 | 1,075 | — | 1,075 |
| IRELAND, Billy (F.G.) | 835 | +6 | 841 | +17 | 858 | +46 | 904 | +32 | 936 | +10 | 946 | +69 | 1,015 |
| McDONALD, Donal (P.D.) | 175 | +2 | 177 | -177 | — | — | — | — | — | — | — | — | — |
| MAHER, Tom (F.G.) | 692 | +9 | 701 | +16 | 717 | +63 | 780 | +160 | 940 | +20 | 960 | +31 | 991 |
| O'BRIEN, Michael Thomas (Lab.) | 1,055 | +6 | 1,061 | +14 | 1,075 | — | 1,075 | — | 1,075 | — | 1,075 | — | 1,075 |
| SOMERS, Breda (F.F.) | 493 | +25 | 518 | +10 | 528 | +70 | 598 | -598 | — | — | — | — | — |
| Non-transferable papers not effective | — | — | — | +7 | 7 | +59 | 66 | +74 | 140 | +6 | 146 | +289 | 435 |
| TOTAL: | 7,520 | — | 7,520 | — | 7,520 | — | 7,520 | — | 7,520 | — | 7,520 | — | 7,520 |

Elected: Brett, James J. (F.F.); O'Brien, Michael Thomas (Lab.); Fennelly, Kevin (F.F.); Fenlon, Michael (F.F.); Ireland, Billy (F.G.); Maher, Tom (F.G.)

# TULLAROAN ELECTORAL AREA

TOTAL ELECTORATE 8,832. VALID POLL 5,218. NO. OF MEMBERS 4. QUOTA 1,044.

| Names of Candidates | First Count Votes | Second Count Transfer of Hogan's surplus | Result | Third Count Transfer of Brennan's votes | Result | Fourth Count Transfer of Cuddihy's votes | Result | Fifth Count Transfer of Gibbons' votes | Result | Sixth Count Transfer of Rice's votes | Result | Seventh Count Transfer of Millea's surplus | Result |
|---|---|---|---|---|---|---|---|---|---|---|---|---|---|
| BRENNAN, Thomas (F.F.) | 337 | +1 | 338 | -338 | — | — | — | — | — | — | — | — | — |
| CUDDIHY, Paul (F.G.) | 376 | +9 | 385 | +12 | 397 | -397 | — | — | — | — | — | — | — |
| GIBBONS, Martin (P.D.) | 436 | +2 | 438 | +35 | 473 | +61 | 534 | -534 | — | — | — | — | — |
| HOGAN, Philip (F.G.) | 1,073 | -29 | 1,044 | — | 1,044 | — | 1,044 | — | 1,044 | — | 1,044 | — | 1,044 |
| McGUINNESS, John J. (F.F.) | 633 | +1 | 634 | +75 | 709 | +24 | 733 | +61 | 794 | +155 | 949 | +149 | 1,098 |
| MILLEA, Pat (F.F.) | 754 | +4 | 758 | +73 | 831 | +26 | 857 | +74 | 931 | +313 | 1,244 | -200 | 1,044 |
| PATTERSON, Tony (Lab.) | 555 | +2 | 557 | +23 | 580 | +67 | 647 | +92 | 739 | +50 | 789 | +27 | 816 |
| RICE, Joe (F.F.) | 476 | +1 | 477 | +84 | 561 | +25 | 586 | +79 | 665 | -665 | — | — | — |
| TYNAN, Margaret (F.G.) | 578 | +9 | 587 | +19 | 606 | +183 | 789 | +171 | 960 | +76 | 1,036 | +24 | 1,060 |
| Non-transferable papers not effective | — | — | — | +17 | 17 | +11 | 28 | +57 | 85 | +71 | 156 | — | 156 |
| TOTAL: | 5,218 | — | 5,218 | — | 5,218 | — | 5,218 | — | 5,218 | — | 5,218 | — | 5,218 |

Elected: Hogan, Philip (F.G.); Millea, Pat (F.F.); McGuinness, John J. (F.F.); Tynan, Margaret (F.G.)

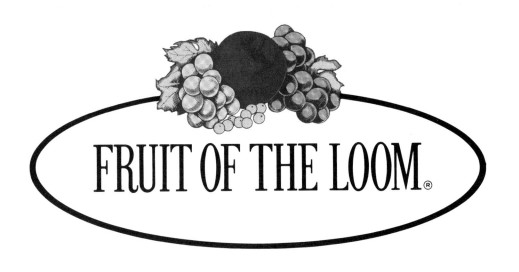

# Made in Ireland
# Styled in the U.S.A.

**Fruit of the Loom, America's finest quality leisurewear is now produced at our high-tech manufacturing plant in Buncrana, County Donegal, to supply the European market.**

For more information please contact:
Fruit of the Loom International, Ltd.,
Buncrana, Co. Donegal, Ireland.
Tel: 353 7762222. Fax: 353 7762333.

# LAOIGHIS COUNTY COUNCIL

## LAOIGHIS COUNTY COUNCIL RESULTS

| PARTY | 1991 % of votes | 1991 Seats obtained | 1985 % of votes | 1985 Seats obtained |
|---|---|---|---|---|
| Fianna Fail | 49.3 | 13 | 50.3 | 14 |
| Fine Gael | 34.1 | 9 | 35.7 | 9 |
| Labour | 7.2 | 1 | 6.1 | 1 |
| Progressive Dem. | 4.1 | 1 | — | — |
| Workers Party | — | — | — | — |
| Other | 5.3 | 1 | 7.9 | 1 |
| **TOTAL SEATS** | | **25** | | **25** |

## LAOIGHIS

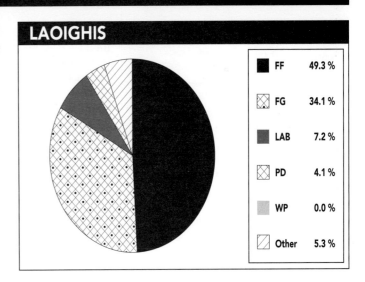

| | |
|---|---|
| FF | 49.3 % |
| FG | 34.1 % |
| LAB | 7.2 % |
| PD | 4.1 % |
| WP | 0.0 % |
| Other | 5.3 % |

**County Hall, Portlaoise**
**Telephone: (0502) 22044**
**Fax: (0502) 22313**
**Total population: 53,284**
**Rateable valuation: £375,454.05**
**Rate: £25.2007**
**County Council meetings: Last Monday of month**
**at 15.00**

*County Manager:* M. Deigan
*County Secretary:* J. Kennedy
*Finance Officer:* P. Scully
*County Engineer:* D. O'Riordan
*County Development Officer:* M. Frayne
*Administrative Officers:*
A. McQuillan, D. Byrne,
H. Fitzpatrick
*Senior Staff Officers:*
T. Costello, J. Daly
*County Librarian:* E. Phelan
*County Solicitor:* C. Murphy
*County Coroner:* P. Meagher
*Chief Fire Officer:* M. Collins
*Civil Defence Officer:* M. Cobbe
*Senior Executive Engineers:*
*Road Design:* C. Marshall, S. Mullins
*Roads:* M. White (Acting)
*Sanitary Services:* C. Tweney
*Housing:* D. O'Connor
*Senior Executive Planner:* G. Gibson
*Executive Planner:* P. Dolan

**Michal Deigan**

Michael Deigan was born in Kilkenny in 1931 and educated at the University of Edinburgh from where he received a masters degree in Civil Engineering. He is married to Peggy Gleeson and they have two sons.

Michael Deigan's career in local govern-ment spans four decades covering several county councils including Tipperary NR, where he worked as an engineer, and Roscom-monn where he was County Manager from 1978 to 1983.

He was appointed Laois County Manager in 1983 and today manages a staff of almost 400 with a budget in excess of £20 million.

Michael Deigan's hob-bies include garden-ing and golf.

## BORRIS-IN-OSSORY

|     | 1991 | 1985 | '85 to '91 Swing |
|-----|------|------|------|
| FF  | 47.2 | 50.2 | -3.0 |
| FG  | 27.8 | 31.6 | -3.8 |
| LAB | 8.8  | 5.5  | 3.3 |
| Ind | 16.2 | 12.7 | 3.5 |

HYLAND, Liam,
Fearagh, Ballacolla,
County Laois. (FF)*

KAVANAGH, Larry,
Rushin, Mountrath,
County Laois. (Lab)
Education Officer. 0502-32135

KELLY, James,
Main Street, Borris-in-Ossory,
County Laois. (NP)
Farmer. 0505-41138

MANSFIELD, William,
Cappalinnan, Rathdowney,
County Laois. (FG)
Auctioneer. 0505-46423

PHELAN, Kieran,
Raheen Upper, Donaghmore,
County Laois. (FF)
Farmer. 0505-46562

PHELAN, Martin,
Farren Eglish, Ballacolla,
County Laois. (FG)
Farmer. 0502-34032

RAFTER, Eamonn,
Knockanoran, Durrow,
County Laois. (FF)
Farmer. 0502-36145

*Resigned when appointed Minister of State,
Feb.1992. Replaced by
PHELAN, Fintan,
Knockbrack, Pike of Rushall,
County Laois. (FF)
0502-35223

## EMO

|     | 1991 | 1985 | '85 to '91 Swing |
|-----|------|------|------|
| FF  | 43.0 | 47.3 | -4.3 |
| FG  | 22.8 | 32.9 | -10.1 |
| LAB | 16.9 | 19.8 | -2.9 |
| PD  | 17.3 | —    | 17.3 |

BUGGIE, James,
Brockley Park, Stradbally,
County Laois. (FG)
Retired. 0502-25112

CRIBBIN, Raymond,
Main Street, Portarlington,
County Laois. (FF)
Estate Agent. 0502-23278

HONAN, Cathy,
"Austen House", Portarlington,
County Laois. (PD)
Accountant. 0502-23810

MULHARE, Teresa,
The Heath, Portlaoise,
County Laois. (FF)
Nurse. 0502-46777

## LUGGACURREN

|     | 1991 | 1985 | '85 to '91 Swing |
|-----|------|------|------|
| FF  | 54.0 | 55.7 | -1.7 |
| FG  | 37.7 | 21.0 | 16.7 |
| LAB | 7.9  | 5.2  | 2.7 |
| Ind | 0.4  | 18.1 | -17.7 |

COONEY, James,
Monamanry, Luggacurren,
County Laois. (FF)
Farmer. 0507-25510

DALY, James,
Garryglass, Timahoe.
County Laois. (FG)
Sales Representative. 0502-27101

MORAN, John,
Ballinagar, Ballylinan, Athy,
County Laois. (FG)
Farmer. 0503-45176

WHEATLEY, Mary,
Doonane, Crettyard,

Carlow. (FF)
Home Carer. 056-42144

## PORTLAOIGHISE

|     | 1991 | 1985 | '85 to '91 Swing |
|-----|------|------|------|
| FF  | 50.7 | 48.7 | 2.0 |
| FG  | 36.3 | 42.4 | -6.1 |
| LAB | 3.2  | 8.9  | -5.7 |
| PD  | 6.8  | —    | 6.8 |
| Ind | 3.0  | —    | 3.0 |

AIRD, William,
Nutgrove, Portlaoise,
County Laois. (FG)
Farmer. 0502-21131

DUNNE, Joseph,
"Knockbrack", New Road, Portlaoise,
County Laois. (FF)
Shopkeeper. 0502-22947

JACOB, Thomas,
"Ard na Greine", Glenside, Portlaoise,
County Laois. (FF)
Technician. 0502-21519

KEENAN, Thomas,
79 Marian Avenue, Portlaoise,
County Laois. (FG)
Public Representative. 0502-21573

LODGE, Jeremiah,
Ridge Road, Portlaoise,
County Laois. (FF)
Insurance Broker. 0502-21328

## TINNAHINCH

|     | 1991 | 1985 | '85 to '91 Swing |
|-----|------|------|------|
| FF  | 52.5 | 50.0 | 2.5 |
| FG  | 47.5 | 50.0 | -2.5 |

DIGAN, Joseph,
Coolagh, Clonaslee,
County Laois. (FF)
Farmer. 0502-28074

FLANAGAN, Charles,
6 Oaklawn Drive, Portlaoise,
County Laois. (FG)
Dáil Deputy. 0502-22100

LALOR, Michael,
Cardtown, Mountrath,
County Laois. (FG)
Coilte Teo Employee. 0502-35176

McDONALD, Seamus,
Drummond, Rosenallis,
County Laois. (FF)
Gravel Contractor. 0502-28547

MOLONEY, John Anthony,
27 Patrick Street, Mountmellick,
County Laois. (FF)
Publican. 0502-24391

**Charles Flanagan (FG)**
**Tinnahinch**

**Cahty Honan (PD)**
**Emo**

**Eamon Rafter (FF)**
**Borris-in-Ossory**

# Fianna Fail defy the national trend

Fianna Fail's performances in Laois went strongly against the National trend. They secured 49.3% of the first preference votes, their highest in the country and narrowly retained their overall majority on Laois County Council.

The eventual outcome left Fianna Fail with 13 of the 25 seats, making Laois one of only four Councils in which Fianna Fail held outright control after the June 1991 poll.

In the Emo Electoral area, Cathy Honan made a Local Government break through for the P.D.'s at the expense of Labour's Paddy Bray of Stradbally. Honan had been a very strong candidate for the Progressive Democrats in the previous two General Elections. She came very close to winning a Dail seat for the P.D.'s in Laois/Offaly in 1987 and also had a strong showing in the 1989 Election. The Portarlington based accountant got 652 first preferences to take the second seat in the Emo Electoral area, and now from the Councillors Chamber, is certain to contest the next election for the P.D.'s in Laois/Offaly.

The Election of Bridget Emerson in Offaly coupled with the strong performance by Assumpta Broomfield in the Portlaoise area, implies that, should the P.D.'s rise from their present opinion poll showing Honan could be one of their new T.D.'s.

Fine Gael too, held their own. They entered the race with nine Councillors and retained all nine seats. There were changes in personnel however, Martin J. Phelan replaced Patrick McMahon in Borris-in-Ossory. Michael Lalor who had lost out in 1989 by only 4 votes, replaced David Goodman in Tinnahinch.

In a major upset, former Fine Gael Senator and Leas Cathaoirleach of the Seanad, Charles McDonald lost his seat in the Luggacurran area and was replaced by party colleague James Daly, who at only 22, became the youngest Councillor on Laois County Council, and one of the youngest in the country. He reclaimed a seat once held by his father Johnny Daly as an Independent.

It was in the Luggacurran area also, that Fianna Fail had their only seat loss, from three seats to two, and in another major shock, it was outgoing Council Chairman Martin Rohan who lost out. He lost the last seat in Luggacurran to party colleague Mary Wheatley by just 11 votes. Outgoing James Cooney topped the poll for Fianna Fail with 600 votes.

In Emo Fianna Fail elected their second Women Councillor. Ray Cribbin topped the poll once again with 1,047 votes and was joined by newcomer Therese Mulhere. Mulhere, a Ward Sister, made it not only two Emo seats for Fianna Fail, but indeed with Cathy Honan, made it two Women Councillors out of the four in Emo.

The highest vote in the county was taken by outgoing Fianna Fail Portlaoise Councillor, Joe Dunne who with 1,316, had more than the combined vote of his Fine Gael rivals Tom Kennan and William Aird and was comfortably elected with almost 600 votes above the quota. Fianna Fail held onto their three seats here with newcomer Thomas Jacob replacing the outgoing John Fitzgibbons.

The other strong Fianna Fail preformance was that of John Moloney in Tinnahinch who topped the poll with 1,217 first preferences. The young Mountmellick publican and undertaker was over 600 votes in first preferences ahead of sitting Fine Gael T.D. Charles Flanagan.

In the seven seat Borris-in-Ossory electoral area, Carey Kavanagh salvaged Labour's pride in Laois, when he secured the Party's only Council seat in the election, following the defeat of outgoing Labour member Paddy Bray of Stradbally.

Laois Fianna Fail T.D., Liam Hyland topped the poll and Fianna Fail held on to their three seats, but Kieran Phelan of Rathdowney replaced fellow Party man and outgoing Mountrath Councillor Fintan Phelan. He was since co-opted to replace Liam Hyland on his appointment as Minister for State at the Department of Agricultural.

Laois's one outgoing Independent Councillor James Kelly retained his seat polling 828 votes to take the second seat on the second count in Borris-in-Ossory.

Fianna Fail Councillors topped the poll in all five electoral areas and they managed to keep their share of the vote despite an 8% decline in the party vote at national level.

**Former Taoiseach Charles Haughey congratulates Mary Wheatly who was successfully returned to Laois County Council for Fianna Fail**

# BORRIS-IN-OSSORY ELECTORAL AREA

TOTAL ELECTORATE 9,844. VALID POLL 6,776. NO. OF MEMBERS 7. QUOTA 848.

| Names of Candidates | First Count Votes | Second Count Transfer of Hyland's surplus | Result | Third Count Transfer of Kelly's surplus | Result | Fourth Count Transfer of Loughman's votes | Result | Fifth Count Transfer of K. Phelan's surplus | Result | Sixth Count Transfer of McMahon's votes | Result | Seventh Count Transfer of Mansfield's surplus | Result | Eighth Count Transfer of F. Phelan's votes | Result | Ninth Count Transfer of Murphy's votes | Result |
|---|---|---|---|---|---|---|---|---|---|---|---|---|---|---|---|---|---|
| FENNELLY, Thomas (F.F.) | 392 | +54 | 446 | +1 | 447 | +4 | 451 | — | 451 | +6 | 457 | — | 457 | +98 | 555 | +69 | 624 |
| HYLAND, Liam (F.F.) | 1,219 | -371 | 848 | — | 848 | — | 848 | — | 848 | — | 848 | — | 848 | — | 848 | — | 848 |
| KAVANAGH, Larry **Lab** | 594 | +23 | 617 | +1 | 618 | +12 | 630 | +1 | 631 | +98 | 729 | +6 | 735 | +109 | 844 | +73 | 917 |
| KELLY, James (Non-Party) | 828 | +28 | 856 | -8 | 848 | — | 848 | — | 848 | — | 848 | — | 848 | — | 848 | — | 848 |
| LOUGHMAN, Peter (Non-Party) | 267 | +8 | 275 | — | 275 | -275 | — | — | — | — | — | — | — | — | — | — | — |
| McMAHON, Patrick (F.G.) | 272 | +4 | 276 | — | 276 | +2 | 278 | — | 278 | -278 | — | — | — | — | — | — | — |
| MANSFIELD, William (F.G.) | 728 | +21 | 749 | +2 | 751 | +68 | 819 | +7 | 826 | +72 | 898 | -50 | 848 | — | 848 | — | 848 |
| MURPHY, Stephen (F.G.) | 411 | +14 | 425 | — | 425 | +8 | 433 | — | 433 | +22 | 455 | +32 | 487 | +9 | 496 | -496 | — |
| PHELAN, Fintan (F.F.) | 299 | +66 | 365 | +1 | 366 | +10 | 376 | +1 | 377 | +35 | 412 | +1 | 413 | -413 | — | — | — |
| PHELAN, Kieran (F.F.) | 751 | +65 | 816 | +2 | 818 | +43 | 861 | -13 | 848 | — | 848 | — | 848 | — | 848 | — | 848 |
| PHELAN, Martin J. (F.G.) | 476 | +37 | 513 | — | 513 | +63 | 576 | — | 576 | +25 | 601 | +11 | 612 | +32 | 644 | +258 | 902 |
| RAFTER, Eamon (F.F.) | 539 | +51 | 590 | +1 | 591 | +38 | 629 | +4 | 633 | +5 | 638 | — | 638 | +88 | 726 | +28 | 754 |
| Non-transferable papers not effective | — | — | — | — | — | +27 | 27 | — | 27 | +15 | 42 | — | 42 | +77 | 119 | +68 | 187 |
| TOTAL: | 6,776 | — | 6,776 | — | 6,776 | — | 6,776 | — | 6,776 | — | 6,776 | — | 6,776 | — | 6,776 | — | 6,776 |

Elected: Hyland, Liam (F.F.); Kelly, James (Non-Party); Phelan, Kieran (F.F.); Mansfield, William (F.G.); Kavanagh, Larry (Lab.); Phelan, Martin J. (F.G.); Rafter, Eamon (F.F.

# EMO ELECTORAL AREA

TOTAL ELECTORATE 6,431. VALID POLL 3,779. NO. OF MEMBERS 4. QUOTA 756

| Names of Candidates | First Count Votes | Second Count Transfer of Cribbin's surplus | Result | Third Count Transfer of Gee's and Martin's votes | Result |
|---|---|---|---|---|---|
| BRAY, Patrick (Lab.) | 512 | +3 | 515 | +75 | 590 |
| BUGGIE, JAMES (F.G.) | 616 | +8 | 624 | +126 | 750 |
| CRIBBIN, Raymond (F.F.) | 1,047 | -291 | 756 | — | 756 |
| GEE, Sam (F.G.) | 245 | +23 | 268 | -268 | — |
| HONAN, Cathy (P.D.) | 652 | +73 | 725 | +171 | 896 |
| MARTIN, Anthony (Lab.) | 128 | +21 | 149 | -149 | — |
| MULHARE, Teresa (F.F.) | 579 | +163 | 742 | +28 | 770 |
| Non-transferable papers not effective | — | — | — | +17 | 17 |
| TOTAL: | 3,779 | — | 3,779 | — | 3,779 |

Elected: Cribbin, Raymond (F.F.); Honan, Cathy (P.D.); Mulhare, Teresa (F.F.); Buggie, James (F.G.)

# LUGGACURREN ELECTORAL AREA

TOTAL ELECTORATE 5,972. VALID POLL 3,770. NO. OF MEMBERS 4. QUOTA 755.

| Names of Candidates | First Count Votes | Second Count Transfer of McCormack's and O'Brien's votes Result | | Third Count Transfer of Redmond's votes Result | | Fourth Count Transfer of McDonald's votes Result | | Fifth Count Transfer of Moran's surplus Result | | Sixth Count Transfer of Daly's surplus Result | |
|---|---|---|---|---|---|---|---|---|---|---|---|
| COONEY, James (F.F.) | 600 | +29 | 629 | +129 | 758 | — | 758 | — | 758 | — | 758 |
| DALY, James Francis (F.G.) | 478 | +74 | 552 | +23 | 575 | +167 | 742 | +80 | 822 | -67 | 755 |
| McCORMACK, Thomas (Non-Party) | 16 | -16 | — | — | — | — | — | — | — | — | — |
| McDONALD, Charles (F.G.) | 358 | +36 | 394 | +37 | 431 | -431 | — | — | — | — | — |
| MORAN, John Robert (F.G.) | 585 | +76 | 661 | +32 | 693 | +150 | 843 | -88 | 755 | — | 755 |
| O'BRIEN Tony (Lab.) | 299 | -299 | — | — | — | — | — | — | — | — | — |
| REDMOND, Mary (F.F.) | 368 | +14 | 382 | -382 | — | — | — | — | — | — | — |
| ROHAN, Martin (F.F.) | 575 | +6 | 581 | +45 | 626 | +37 | 663 | +4 | 667 | +12 | 679 |
| WHEATLEY, Mary (F.F.) | 491 | +47 | 538 | +93 | 631 | +43 | 674 | +4 | 678 | +12 | 690 |
| Non-transferable papers not effective | — | +33 | 33 | +23 | 56 | +34 | 90 | - | 90 | +43 | 133 |
| TOTAL: | | — | 3,770 | — | 3,770 | — | 3,770 | — | 3,770 | — | 3,770 |

Elected: Cooney, James (F.F.); Moran, John Robert (F.G.); Daly, James Francis (F.G.); Wheatley, Mary (F.F.)

# PORTLAOIGHISE LOCAL ELECTORAL AREA

TOTAL ELECTORATE 7,588. VALID POLL 4,312. NO. OF MEMBERS 5. QUOTA 719

| Names of Candidates | First Count Votes | Second Count Transfer of J. Dunne's surplus Result | | Third Count Transfer of Bannan's votes Result | | Fourth Count Transfer of McCormack's votes Result | | Fifth Count Transfer of A. Dunne's votes Result | | Sixth Count Transfer of Keenan's surplus Result | | Seventh Count Transfer of Aird's surplus Result | | Eighth Count Transfer of Phelan's votes Result | | Ninth Count Transfer of O'Donoghue's votes Result | | Tenth Count Transfer of Fitzgibbon's votes Result | |
|---|---|---|---|---|---|---|---|---|---|---|---|---|---|---|---|---|---|---|---|
| AIRD, Willie (F.G.) | 625 | +59 | 684 | +1 | 685 | +13 | 698 | +43 | 741 | — | 741 | -22 | 719 | — | 719 | — | 719 | — | 719 |
| BANNAN, Joseph Frederick (Non-Party) | 8 | +1 | 9 | -9 | — | — | — | — | — | — | — | — | — | — | — | — | — | — | — |
| BROOMFIELD, Assumpta Mary (P.D.) | 292 | +22 | 314 | — | 314 | +11 | 325 | +13 | 338 | +5 | 343 | +3 | 346 | +51 | 397 | +67 | 464 | +29 | 493 |
| DUNNE, Anthony (F.G.) | 129 | +21 | 150 | +2 | 152 | +13 | 165 | -165 | — | — | — | — | — | — | — | — | — | — | — |
| DUNNE, Joe (F.F.) | 1,316 | -597 | 719 | — | 719 | — | 719 | — | 719 | — | 719 | — | 719 | — | 719 | — | 719 | — | 719 |
| FITZGIBBON, John (F.F.) | 254 | +77 | 331 | — | 331 | +7 | 338 | +3 | 341 | +1 | 342 | — | 342 | +8 | 350 | +23 | 373 | -373 | — |
| JACOB, Thomas (F.F.) | 314 | +175 | 489 | — | 489 | +11 | 500 | +17 | 517 | +2 | 519 | +2 | 521 | +13 | 534 | +25 | 559 | +144 | 703 |
| KEENAN, Tom (F.G.) | 624 | +62 | 686 | +2 | 688 | +23 | 711 | +36 | 747 | -28 | 719 | — | 719 | — | 719 | — | 719 | — | 719 |
| LODGE, Jerry (F.F.) | 304 | +132 | 436 | — | 436 | +14 | 450 | +16 | 466 | +6 | 472 | +4 | 476 | +42 | 518 | +31 | 549 | +129 | 678 |
| McCORMACK, Joseph (Non-Party) | 120 | +25 | 145 | +4 | 149 | -149 | — | — | — | — | — | — | — | — | — | — | — | — | — |
| O'DONOGHUE, Ger (F.G.) | 187 | +11 | 198 | — | 198 | +7 | 205 | +16 | 221 | +12 | 233 | +13 | 246 | +21 | 267 | -267 | — | — | — |
| PHELAN, Tom (Lab.) | 139 | +12 | 151 | — | 151 | +27 | 178 | +6 | 184 | +2 | 186 | — | 186 | -186 | — | — | — | — | — |
| Non-transferable papers not effective | — | — | — | — | — | +23 | 23 | +15 | 38 | — | 38 | — | 38 | +51 | 89 | +121 | 210 | +71 | 281 |
| TOTAL: | 4,312 | — | 4,312 | — | 4,312 | — | 4,312 | — | 4,312 | — | 4,312 | — | 4,312 | — | 4,312 | — | 4,312 | — | 4,312 |

Elected: Dunne, Joe (F.F.); Keenan, Tom (F.G.); Aird, Willie (F.G.); Jacob, Thomas (F.F.); Lodge, Jerry (F.F.)

# TINNAHINCH ELECTORAL AREA

TOTAL ELECTORATE 6,381. VALID POLL 4,582. NO. OF MEMBERS 5. QUOTA 764.

| Names of Candidates | First Count<br>Votes | Second Count<br>Transfer of<br>Moloney's<br>surplus | Result | Third Count<br>Transfer of<br>McDonald's<br>surplus | Result | Fourth Count<br>Transfer of<br>Daly's<br>votes | Result |
|---|---|---|---|---|---|---|---|
| DALY, William (F.G.) | 340 | +5 | 345 | +1 | 346 | -346 | — |
| DIGAN, Joseph (F.F.) | 518 | +66 | 584 | +110 | 694 | +91 | 785 |
| FLANAGAN, Charles (F.G.) | 670 | +91 | 761 | +19 | 780 | — | 780 |
| GOODWIN, David (F.G.) | 462 | +36 | 498 | +11 | 509 | +85 | 594 |
| LALOR, Michael (F.G.) | 704 | +15 | 719 | +6 | 725 | +147 | 872 |
| McDONALD, Seamus (F.F.) | 671 | +240 | 911 | -147 | 764 | — | 764 |
| MOLONEY, John Anthony (F.F.) | 1,217 | -453 | 764 | — | 764 | — | 764 |
| Non-transferable papers not effective | — | — | — | — | — | +23 | 23 |
| TOTAL: | 4,582 | — | 4,582 | — | 4,582 | — | 4,582 |

Elected: Moloney, John Anthony (F.F.); McDonald, Seamus (F.F.); Flanagan, Charles (F.G.); Lalor, Michael (F.G.); Digan, Joseph (F.F.)

# LEITRIM COUNTY COUNCIL

## LEITRIM COUNTY COUNCIL RESULTS

| PARTY | 1991 % of votes | 1991 Seats obtained | 1985 % of votes | 1985 Seats obtained |
|---|---|---|---|---|
| Fianna Fail | 43.4 | 9 | 45.3 | 10 |
| Fine Gael | 35.4 | 9 | 34.6 | 8 |
| Labour | — | — | — | — |
| Progressive Dem. | — | — | — | — |
| Workers Party | — | — | — | — |
| Other | 21.2 | 4 | 20.1 | 4 |
| TOTAL SEATS | | 22 | | 22 |

**County Council**
**Courthouse, Carrick-on-Shannon**
**Telephone:(078) 20005**
**Fax:(078) 21023**
**Total population: 25,297**
**Rateable valuation: £183,500**
**Rate: £29.58**
**County Council meetings: Second Monday in**
**each month at 2.30 p.m.**

## LEITRIM

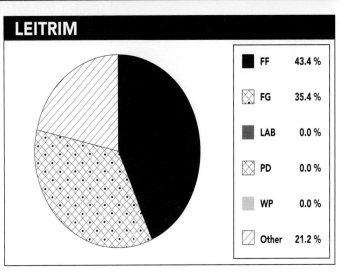

| | |
|---|---|
| FF | 43.4 % |
| FG | 35.4 % |
| LAB | 0.0 % |
| PD | 0.0 % |
| WP | 0.0 % |
| Other | 21.2 % |

*County Manager:* P. J. Doyle
*County Secretary:* Sean Kielty
*Finance Officer:* Patrick O'Meara
*County Engineer:* T. Murphy
*Administrative Officer:*
*(Environmental and Infrastructure):* Seamus Martin
*Senior Staff Officers:*
*Housing and Designated Training Officer:* Martin Dolan
*Engineering and Planning:* Michael Geelan
*County Development:* Dorothy Clarke
*County Librarian:* Se]an O'Suilleabháin, Ballinamore.
*Telephone:*(078) 44012
*Solicitor:* Gerard Gannon,
*County Coroner:* Michael P. Keane
*Chief Fire Officer:* Pat Forkan
*Civil Defence Officer:* Seamus Martin
*County Development Officer:* P. J. Martin
*Senior Executive Engineers:*
*Planning:* R. W. Walsh
*Sanitary Services and Water Pollution:*
JohnMcGuinness (Acting)
*Housing and Building:* Ken Moran (Acting)
*Roads:* Patrick Phelan
*Design and Construction:* Brian Kenny

## BALLINAMORE

|    | 1991 | 1985 | '85 to '91 Swing |
|----|------|------|------|
| FF | 42.1 | 40.9 | 1.2 |
| FG | 42.0 | 44.3 | -2.3 |
| SF | 16.0 | 14.8 | 1.2 |

BRENNAN, Damien,
Drumlegga, Cloone,
County Leitrim. (FG)
Teacher. 049-33492

ELLIS, John,
Fenagh,
County Leitrim. (FF)
Dail Deputy. 078-44252

McCARTIN, Thomas F.,
Mullyaster, Newtowngore,
County Leitrim. (FG)
Farmer. 049-33492

McGIRL, Liam,
Ballinamore,
County Leitrim. (SF)
Businessman. 078-44034

REYNOLDS, Gerard P.,
Main Street, Ballinamore,
County Leitrim, (FG)
Dail Deputy. 078-44016

SHORTT, James J.,
Lissagarvan, Ballinamore,
County Leitrim. (FF)
Farmer. 078-36050

## CARRICK-ON-SHANNON

|    | 1991 | 1985 | '85 to '91 Swing |
|----|------|------|------|
| FF | 44.0 | 46.5 | -2.5 |
| FG | 33.1 | 28.2 | 4.9 |
| SF | 6.7  | 7.3  | -0.6 |
| Ind | 16.1 | 18.0 | -1.9 |

FAUGHNAN, Thomas Patrick,
Corduff, Aughamore,
Carrick-on-Shannon,
County Leitrim. (FG)
Factory Worker. 078-31290

GUCKIAN, Michael,
Drumsna,
County Leitrim. (FF)
Retired. 078-20740

McELGUNN, Farrell,
Summerhill, Carrick-on-Shannon,
County Leitrim, (FF)
Teacher. 078-20215

McGOWAN, Sean,
Cloonturk, Dromod,
County Leitrim. (FF)
Plumber. 078-38357

McKEON, Pascal,
Drumdoo, Mohill,
County Leitrim. (NP)
078-31193*

MULLIGAN, Thomas,
Hyde Street, Mohill,
County Leitrim. (FG)
Farmer. 078-31142

*RIP. Replaced by McKEON, Pauline,
Drumdoo, Mohill, County Leitrim. (NP)

## DROMAHAIRE

|    | 1991 | 1985 | '85 to '91 Swing |
|----|------|------|------|
| FF | 43.4 | 49.1 | -5.7 |
| FG | 32.6 | 38.6 | -6.0 |
| SF | 5.4  | 12.3 | -6.9 |
| Ind | 18.7 | —   | 18.7 |

BOHAN, Mary,
Drumkeerin,
County Leitrim. (FF)
Postmistress. 078-48001

DOLAN, Gerry,
Carnashamsogue, Drumshanbo,
County Leitrim. (NP)
Farmer. 078-41278

McPADDEN, Jim,
Annagh Upper, Dowra,
County Leitrim. (FG)
Farmer. 078-43090

McTERNAN, John,
Market Street, Dromahaire,
County Leitrim. (FG)
Stone Mason. 071-64286

MOONEY, Pascal Canice,
Carrick Road, Drumshambo,
County Leitrim. (FF)
Senator. 078-41236

## MANORHAMILTON

|    | 1991 | 1985 | '85 to '91 Swing |
|----|------|------|------|
| FF | 44.5 | 45.6 | -1.1 |
| FG | 33.0 | 26.2 | 6.8 |
| SF | 11.0 | 8.8  | 2.2 |
| Ind | 11.5 | 19.4 | -7.9 |

CULLEN, Charlie,
Minkeragh, Glenfarne,
County Leitrim. (FG)
Farmer. 072-41806

FERGUSON, Tony,
Edenville, Kinlough,
County Leitrim. (FF)
Teacher. 072-41426

FLYNN, Aodh,
Deer Park, Manorhamilton,
County Leitrim. (FF)
Postmaster. 072-55001

McGLOIN, Siobhan Marie,
Ahanlish, Largydonnell,
County Leitrim. (FG)
Shop Assistant. 072-41806

McGOWAN, Larry,
Drummonds, Manorhamilton,
County Leitrim. (NP)
Farmer. 072-55197

**John Ellis (FF)**
**Leitrim**

**Gerry Reynolds (FG)**
**Ballinamore**

**Pascal Mooney (FF)**
**Dromahaire**

**Aodh Flynn (FF)**
**Manorhamilton**

# Leitrim once again has highest turnout

As in 1985, Leitrim County Council in the 1991 election, had the highest turnout in the country and, like many other areas, the proposed An Post viability plan was a central issue in the campaign. Surprisingly Fianna Fail only dropped 1.9% in their share of the vote. This was enough, however, for them to suffer a 1 seat loss in the Manorhamilton Area with a resulting Fine Gael gain. Sinn Fein had a disappointing campaign losing 1 of the 2 seats they won in 1985, while the election of Gerry Dolan in Dromahaire brought the number of Independents in Leitrim to 3 in the 22 member County Council.

There were only 7 candidates for the 6 seats in the Ballinmore Electoral Area with all 6 outgoing Councillors contesting the election. It was a relatively quiet affair as all 6 were returned - 4 on the first count and the remaining 2 by count 5. Dail Deputies Gerry Reynolds of Fine Gael and John Ellis of Fianna Fail, were both comfortably returned well above the quota. In terms of the next general election both will be happy with this outcome although the presence of Declan Bree on the Sligo-Leitrim ballot paper may be a possible source of concern, particularly for Ellis.

Reynolds, as in 1985, was the poll topper in Ballinmore. He was re-elected along with party colleagues Damien Brennan and Thomas McCartin. Fine Gael's vote management in Ballinamore was superior to Fianna Fail, who had 5 first preferences votes more than Fine Gael but ended up with a seat less. Thomas McCartin, a brother of Fine Gael MEP Joe McCartin held off the challenge of Fianna Fail's Paddy O'Rourke by 57 votes. Liam McGirl of Sinn Fein retained the seat won in 1985 by his late father John Joe McGirl. He was elected on the first count with 70 votes above the quota.

Party representation in Carrick-on-Shannon was the same as in 1985 with Fianna Fail holding their 3 seats, Fine Gael their 2, and Independent Councillor Pascal McKeon retaining his seat. 5 of the 6 outgoing Councillors were returned with the exception of Fianna Fail's Gerry McGee who was replaced on the Council by party colleague Sean McGowan. McGee was 95 votes behind McGowan.

The poll in Carrick-on Shannon was topped by Fine Gael's Thomas Mulligan but the first candidate elected was retired ESB worker Michael Guckian of Fianna Fail who was returned on the third count.

> ## Fine Gael's vote management in Ballinamore was superior to Fianna Fail

Former Fine Gael man Pascal McKeon, who had topped the poll as an Independent in 1985, did less impressively on this occasion being elected on the final count without reaching the quota.

Dromahaire proved to be the most interesting of the 4 electoral areas in Leitrim. Fianna Fail and Fine Gael took 2 seats each, as in 1985, while Independent candidate Gerry Dolan deprived Sinn Fein of the seat they won in this area at the last local elections.

Jim McPadden of Fine Gael topped the poll but he had to wait until the sixth count to become the first candidate elected. The distribution of his surplus narrowed the margin between 2 of the Fianna Fail candidates to a single vote. The distribution of Gerry Dolan's surplus of 4 votes, however, brought Francis Gilmartin level with party colleague Stasia Carre. In high drama Gilmartin was eliminated as he had less first preference votes than Carre. A recount was granted and introduced further excitement. On the second count of the re-count Gilmartin received 2 additional votes which placed him ahead of Carre on the vital sixth count and resultingly it was Carre who was eliminated on the re-count by a 2 vote margin.

It was all in vain for Fianna Fail's Gilmartin, however, as the elimination of Carre elected party colleagues Mary Bohan and Pascal Mooney along with Fine Gael's John McTernan. John McTernan benefited from Carre's elimination as he is a neighbour of Carre and, as such, transfers crossed party lines to the advantage of the Fine Gael man. It is possible that if Gilmartin had been eliminated Fianna Fail's remaining 3 candidates all would have been elected as his transfers would have had a stronger party allegiance.

Fine Gael gained a seat at the expense of Fianna Fail in Manorhamilton. In 1985 Fine Gael had narrowly missed out on the final seat by 30 votes. On this occasion they comfortably took the seat from Fianna Fail with the election of 25 year old Siobhan McGloin who was returned along with her running mate, outgoing Councillor, Charlie Cullen. Fianna Fail's Tony Ferguson again topped the poll in Manorhamilton. He was joined by party colleague Aodh Flynn who was re-elected despite a drop in his vote. Independent Larry McGowan held his

"Smiling for the camera" - Albert Reynolds on the campaign trail in Leitrim.

# BALLINAMORE ELECTORAL AREA

TOTAL ELECTORATE 5,674. VALID POLL 4,178. NO. OF MEMBERS 6. QUOTA 597.

| Names of Candidates | First Count Votes | Second Count Transfer of Reynolds' surplus Result | | Third Count Transfer of Ellis' surplus Result | | Fourth Count Transfer of Shortt's surplus Result | | Fifth Count Transfer of McGirl's surplus Result | |
|---|---|---|---|---|---|---|---|---|---|
| BRENNAN, Damian (F.G.) | 552 | +57 | 609 | — | 609 | — | 609 | — | 609 |
| ELLIS, John (F.F.) | 720 | — | 720 | -123 | 597 | — | 597 | — | 597 |
| McCARTIN, Thomas F. **F.G** | 435 | +100 | 535 | +28 | 563 | +16 | 579 | +40 | 619 |
| McGIRL, Liam (S.F.) | 667 | — | 667 | — | 667 | — | 667 | -70 | 597 |
| O'ROURKE, Paddy (F.F.) | 358 | +12 | 370 | +95 | 465 | +67 | 532 | +30 | 562 |
| REYNOLDS, Gerard Patrick (F.G.) | 766 | -169 | 597 | — | 597 | — | 597 | — | 597 |
| SHORTT, James Joseph (F.F.) | 680 | — | 680 | — | 680 | -83 | 597 | — | 597 |
| Non-transferable papers not effective | — | — | — | — | — | — | — | — | — |
| TOTAL: | 4,178 | — | 4,178 | — | 4,178 | — | 4,178 | — | 4,178 |

Elected: Reynolds, Gerard Patrick (F.G.); Ellis, John (F.F.); Shortt, James Joseph (F.F.); McGirl, Liam (S.F.); Brennan, Damian (F.G.); McCartin, Thomas F. (F.G.)

# CARRICK-ON-SHANNON ELECTORAL AREA

TOTAL ELECTORATE 5,574. VALID POLL 4,230. NO. OF MEMBERS 6. QUOTA 605.

| Names of Candidates | First Count Votes | Second Count Transfer of D. J. Guckian's votes Result | | Third Count Transfer of McTiernan's votes Result | | Fourth Count Transfer of M. Guckian's surplus Result | | Fifth Count Transfer of Harman's votes Result | | Sixth Count Transfer of Faughnan's surplus Result | |
|---|---|---|---|---|---|---|---|---|---|---|---|
| FAUGHNAN, Thomas Patrick (F.G.) | 497 | +38 | 535 | +29 | 564 | +7 | 571 | +130 | 701 | -96 | 605 |
| GUCKIAN, Desmond J. (Non-Party) | 187 | -187 | — | — | — | — | — | — | — | — | — |
| GUCKIAN, Michael (F.F.) | 563 | +33 | 596 | +43 | 639 | -34 | 605 | — | 605 | — | 605 |
| HARMAN, Ann (F.G.) | 339 | +21 | 360 | +55 | 415 | +5 | 420 | -420 | — | — | — |
| McELGUNN, Farrell (F.F.) | 400 | +8 | 408 | +75 | 483 | +16 | 499 | +186 | 685 | — | 685 |
| McGEE, Gerry (F.F.) | 420 | +1 | 421 | +10 | 431 | +1 | 432 | +5 | 437 | +13 | 450 |
| McGOWAN, Sean (F.F.) | 480 | +32 | 512 | +17 | 529 | +3 | 532 | +4 | 536 | +9 | 545 |
| McKEON, Pascal (Non-Party) | 494 | +18 | 512 | +20 | 532 | +2 | 534 | +13 | 547 | +26 | 573 |
| McTIERNAN, Martin (S.F.) | 285 | +17 | 302 | -302 | — | — | — | — | — | — | — |
| MULLIGAN, Thomas (F.G.) | 565 | +13 | 578 | +27 | 605 | — | 605 | — | 605 | — | 605 |
| Non-transferable papers not effective | — | +6 | 6 | +26 | 32 | — | 32 | +82 | 114 | +48 | 162 |
| TOTAL: | 4,230 | — | 4,230 | — | 4,230 | — | 4,230 | — | 4,230 | — | 4,230 |

Elected: Guckian, Michael (F.F.); Mulligan, Thomas (F.G.); Faughnan, Thomas Patrick (F.G.); McElgunn, Farrell (F.F.); McKeon, Pascal (Non-Party); McGowan, Sean (F.F.)

# DROMAHAIRE ELECTORAL AREA

TOTAL ELECTORATE 4,569. VALID POLL 3,594. NO. OF MEMBERS 5. QUOTA 600

| Names of Candidates | First Count Votes | Second Count Transfer of Gallagher's votes | Result | Third Count Transfer of Moran's votes | Result | Fourth Count Transfer of Guckian's votes | Result | Fifth Count Transfer of Wynne's votes | Result | Sixth Count Transfer of McPadden's surplus | Result | Seventh Count Transfer of Dolan's surplus | Result | Eighth Count Transfer of Carre's votes | Result |
|---|---|---|---|---|---|---|---|---|---|---|---|---|---|---|---|
| BOHAN, Mary (F.F.) | 437 | +41 | 478 | +5 | 483 | +7 | 490 | +20 | 510 | +4 | 514 | — | 514 | +149 | 663 |
| CARRE, Stasia (F.F.) | 385 | +16 | 401 | +1 | 402 | +3 | 405 | +6 | 411 | — | 411 | — | 411 | -411 | — |
| DOLAN, Gerry (Non-Party) | 344 | +28 | 372 | +46 | 418 | +111 | 529 | +75 | 604 | — | 604 | -4 | 600 | — | 600 |
| GALLAGHER, John (Non-Party) | 154 | -154 | — | — | — | — | — | — | — | — | — | — | — | — | — |
| GILMARTIN, Francis (F.F.) | 313 | +1 | 314 | +19 | 333 | +53 | 386 | +19 | 405 | +7 | 412 | +1 | 413 | +40 | 453 |
| GUCKIAN, Francis (S.F.) | 193 | +16 | 209 | +17 | 226 | -226 | — | — | — | — | — | — | — | — | — |
| McPADDEN, Jim (F.G.) | 479 | +22 | 501 | +26 | 527 | +12 | 539 | +99 | 638 | -38 | 600 | — | 600 | — | 600 |
| McTERNAN, John (F.G.) | 397 | +9 | 406 | +1 | 407 | +1 | 408 | +36 | 444 | +15 | 459 | +1 | 460 | +164 | 624 |
| MOONEY, Pascal Canice (F.F.) | 422 | +4 | 426 | +41 | 467 | +16 | 483 | +72 | 555 | +12 | 567 | +2 | 569 | +31 | 600 |
| MORAN, Michael | 175 | +7 | 182 | -182 | — | — | — | — | — | — | — | — | — | — | — |
| WYNNE, Sean (F.G.) | 295 | +7 | 302 | +24 | 326 | +14 | 340 | -340 | — | — | — | — | — | — | — |
| Non-transferable papers not effective | — | +3 | 3 | +2 | 5 | +9 | 14 | +13 | 27 | — | 27 | — | 27 | +27 | 54 |
| TOTAL: | 3,594 | — | 3,594 | — | 3,594 | — | 3,594 | — | 3,594 | — | 3,594 | — | 3,594 | — | 3,594 |

Elected: McPadden, Jim (F.G.); Dolan, Gerry (Non-Party); Bohan, Mary (F.F.); McTernan, John (F.G.); Mooney, Pascal Canice (F.F.)

# MANORHAMILTON ELECTORAL AREA

TOTAL ELECTORATE 4,791. VALID POLL 3,499. NO. OF MEMBERS 5. QUOTA 584.

| Names of Candidates | First Count Votes | Second Count Transfer of Ferguson's surplus | Result | Third Count Transfer of Curneen's votes | Result | Fourth Count Transfer of Colreavy's votes | Result | Fifth Count Transfer of Flynn's surplus | Result | Sixth Count Transfer of Dolan's votes | Result | Seventh Count Transfer of McGowan's surplus | Result |
|---|---|---|---|---|---|---|---|---|---|---|---|---|---|
| COLREAVY, Michael (S.F.) | 253 | +8 | 261 | +24 | 285 | -285 | — | — | — | — | — | — | — |
| CONNOLLY, Patsy (F.F.) | 304 | +45 | 349 | +16 | 365 | +22 | 387 | +4 | 391 | +18 | 409 | +33 | 442 |
| CULLEN, Charlie (F.G.) | 444 | +13 | 457 | +5 | 462 | +39 | 501 | +3 | 504 | +144 | 648 | — | 648 |
| CURNEEN, Declan | 131 | +7 | 138 | -138 | — | — | — | — | — | — | — | — | — |
| DOLAN, Frank (F.G.) | 361 | +5 | 366 | +3 | 369 | +17 | 386 | +2 | 388 | -388 | — | — | — |
| FERGUSON, Tony (F.F.) | 742 | -158 | 584 | — | 584 | — | 584 | — | 584 | — | 584 | — | 584 |
| FLYNN, Aodh (F.F.) | 511 | +31 | 542 | +6 | 548 | +54 | 602 | -18 | 584 | — | 584 | — | 584 |
| McGLOIN, Siobhán Marie (F.G.) | 351 | +30 | 381 | +39 | 420 | +36 | 456 | +2 | 458 | +68 | 526 | +26 | 552 |
| McGOWAN, Larry | 402 | +19 | 421 | +30 | 451 | +83 | 534 | +7 | 541 | +132 | 673 | -89 | 584 |
| Non-transferable papers not effective | — | — | — | +15 | 15 | +34 | (49 | — | 49 | +26 | 75 | +30 | 105 |
| TOTAL: | 3,499 | — | 3,499 | — | 3,499 | — | 3,499 | — | 3,499 | — | 3,499 | — | 3,499 |

Elected: Ferguson, Tony (F.F.); Flynn, Aodh (F.F.); McGowan, Larry; Cullen, Charlie (F.G.); McGloin, Siobhán Marie (F.G.)

# WHERE DO GREAT BEARS COME FROM?

# LIMERICK BOROUGH COUNCIL

## LIMERICK BOROUGH COUNCIL RES.

| PARTY | 1991 % of votes | 1991 Seats obtained | 1985 % of votes | 1985 Seats obtained |
|---|---|---|---|---|
| Fianna Fail | 20.3 | 2 | 28.0 | 5 |
| Fine Gael | 22.0 | 4 | 34.3 | 6 |
| Labour | 22.9 | 5 | 11.7 | 1 |
| Progressive Dem. | 13.1 | 3 | — | — |
| Workers Party | 3.6 | 1 | 1.8 | — |
| Other | 18.1 | 2 | 24.2 | 5 |
| TOTAL SEATS | | 17 | | 17 |

## LIMERICK

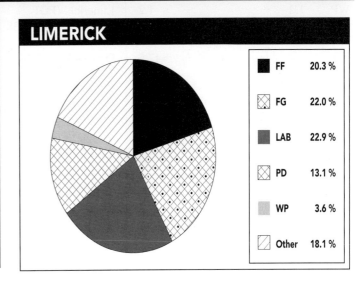

| | |
|---|---|
| FF | 20.3 % |
| FG | 22.0 % |
| LAB | 22.9 % |
| PD | 13.1 % |
| WP | 3.6 % |
| Other | 18.1 % |

**City Hall**
**Limerick**
**Telephone:(061) 415799**
**Fax: (061) 415266**
**Rateable valuation (city): £422,403.85**
**Municipal rate: £36.56**
**Borough Council meetings: Second Monday of each month**

*City Manager:* J. Higgins
*Finance Officer:* S. Real
*City Engineer:* M. B. McCurtin
*City Law Agent:* M. O'Floinn
*Administrative Officers:*
*Engineering and Allied Services:* W. G. O'Connell
*Estates:* E. Ryan
*Personnel:* R. 2O Domhnaill
*Planning:* B. Hayes
*Housing and Community:* S. Moran
*Senior Staff Officers:*
*Finance:* S. Real
*Senior Executive Engineers:*
*Housing/Building Control:* D. Toomey
*Planning:* L. Coyle
*Roads:* S. O'Sullivan
*Sanitary Services:* P. Eyres, F. Coppinger
*Environmental:* M. Donnellan
*Chief Veterinary Officer:* P. Flynn
*Senior Executive Planner:* R. Tobin
*Senior Executive Solicitor:* B. Rossiter
*Senior Architect:* J. Barrett
*Chief Fire Officer:* O. O'Loughlin
*City Coroner:* J. Lyons
*Civil Defence Officer:* P. McNamara
*City Librarian:* M. Flynn

## WARD 1

|     | 1991 | 1985 | '85 to '91 Swing |
|-----|------|------|------------------|
| FF  | 24.8 | 28.9 | -4.1 |
| FG  | 23.2 | 41.1 | -17.9 |
| LAB | 17.8 | 12.5 | 5.3 |
| WP  | 1.2  | —    | 1.2 |
| PD  | 28.4 | —    | 28.4 |
| SF  | 4.5  | —    | 4.5 |
| Ind | —    | 17.5 | -17.5 |

LEDDIN, Tim,
8 Eden Terrace, North Circular Road,
Limerick. (FG)
Retired. 061-52659

O'DEA, Willie,
2, Glenview Gardens, Farranshone,
Limerick. (FF)
Dail Deputy. 061-54488

Resigned when appointed Minister for
State, Feb. 1992.
Replaced by:
O'DONOGHUE, Judy,
6 Pineview Gardens, Moyross,
Limerick. (Lab)

PRENDERGAST, Frank,
121 Cratloe Road, Mayorstone Park,
Limerick. (Lab)
Trade Union Official. 061-52110

QUINN, John,
38 Ballynanty Road,
Limerick. (PD)
Law Clerk. 061-45301

## WARD 2

|     | 1991 | 1985 | '85 to '91 Swing |
|-----|------|------|------------------|
| FF  | 19.0 | 34.3 | -15.3 |
| FG  | 17.6 | 32.1 | -14.5 |
| LAB | 16.9 | 12.7 | 4.2 |
| WP  | 9.6  | —    | 9.6 |
| PD  | 12.5 | —    | 12.5 |
| GP  | 0.8  | —    | 0.8 |
| SF  | —    | 4.9  | -4.9 |
| Ind | 23.6 | 16.0 | 7.6 |

GILLIGAN, John (Ald),
36 Lee Estate, Island Road,
Limerick.
Unemployed.

O'DRISCOLL, Gus,
Corbally Bar, Corbally,
Limerick. (FG)
Publican. 061-44638

O'SULLIVAN, Jan,
7 Lanahrone Avenue, Corbally,
Limerick. (Lab)
Public Representative.

RYAN, John,
88 O'Dwyer Villas, Thomondgate,
Limerick. (Elected WP, now DL)
Lecturer. 061-53681

O'HANLON, Kieran,
Rhebogue, Dublin Road,
Limerick. (PD)
Supervisor. 061-40142

## WARD 3

|     | 1991 | 1985 | '85 to '91 Swing |
|-----|------|------|------------------|
| FF  | 21.1 | 20.1 | 1.0 |
| FG  | 11.8 | 21.1 | -9.3 |
| LAB | 41.6 | 9.3  | 32.3 |
| WP  | —    | 6.0  | -6.0 |
| SF  | —    | 3.6  | -3.6 |
| Ind | 25.6 | 39.9 | -14.3 |

BOURKE, Jack,
Roseville, Roxboro Road,
Limerick. (FF)
Public Representative. 061-418567

HARRINGTON, Joe,
109 Mountain View, O'Malley Park,
Limerick.
Health Board Worker. 061-310384

KEMMY, Jim (Ald),
c/o Mayors Office, City Hall,
Limerick. (Lab)
Dáil Deputy. 061-347270

LEDDIN, Frank,
Marie Ville, Roxboro Road,
Limerick. (Lab)
Telecom Eireann Employee

## WARD 4

|     | 1991 | 1985 | '85 to '91 Swing |
|-----|------|------|------------------|
| FF  | 19.6 | 26.8 | -7.2 |
| FG  | 35.1 | 43.6 | -8.5 |
| LAB | 19.4 | 12.1 | 7.3 |
| PD  | 11.2 | —    | 11.2 |
| SF  | 4.5  | —    | 4.5 |
| Ind | 14.7 | 17.5 | -2.8 |

BYRNE, Bobby,
3 O'Connell Avenue,
Limerick. (FG)
Publican. 061-316949

GRIFFIN, Sean (Ald),
98 Hyde Road, Prospect,
Limerick. (Lab)
Unemployed.

KENNEDY, Pat,
"Fortview", Greenpark,
South Circular Road,
Limerick. (FG)
Senator. 061-28731

SADLIER, Dick,
11 Plassy Grove, Castletroy,
Limerick. (PD)
Lecturer. 061-332637

**Jim Kemmy (Lab)**
**Ward 3**

**Jan O'Sullivan (Lab)**
**Ward 2**

**Jack Bourke (FF)**
**Ward 2**

**Willie O'Dea (FF)**
**Ward 1**

# The Lefts' Awake in Limerick City

It was always going to be difficult for Fianna Fail in Limerick, to improve on their showing of 1985, which itself was the lowest Fianna Fail vote in the country. The emergence of the Progressive Democrats and the rejuvenation of Labour, with the return to the fold of Jim Kemmy, were major obstacles to any Fianna Fail advance on the 5 seats won in 1985. Nobody, however, would have predicted an outcome which was to leave Fianna Fail with only 2 seats out of 17 on Limerick City Council following the June 1991 poll.

The election in Limerick was a triumph for the left and in particular Deputy Jim Kemmy who now heads the largest party on the Council with 5 Councillors returned. Forgotten in the drama of the Fianna Fail slump and the Left's triumph was the poor performance of Fine Gael, which in Limerick lost 2 seats and experienced a drop in their share of the first preference vote by more than 12%, even greater than the Fianna Fail fall of almost 8%. There can be no doubt that the controversial services charges issue resulted in huge difficulties for the 2 main parties particularly in the working class areas of Limerick.

The big issue in Ward 1 was the decision of Fianna Fail Deputy Willie O'Dea to contest the local elections. They had been left without a Councillor in the Ward following the defection of John Quinn, elected in 1985 for Fianna Fail, to the Progressive Democrats. The presence of O'Dea on the ticket guaranteed Fianna Fail at least one Councillor in Ward 1. O'Dea polled exceptionally well in heading the poll with over 150 votes above the quota. His running mate, however, was less successful, gaining a mere 87 votes. Councillor Quinn was returned for the Progressive Democrats but party colleague and outgoing Councillor Tim O'Driscoll was unsuccessful. O'Driscoll joined the PDs from Kemmy's old party, the DSP, for which he headed the poll in the 1985 local

elections. Fine Gael's Tim Leddin and Frank Prendergast of the Labour Party, both outgoing Councillors, were returned successfully in Ward 1.

The defeat of Mayor Paddy Madden in Ward 2, where Fianna Fail lost both of it's seats, and the successful showing by anti-service charge campaigners, John Ryan (WP) and John Gilligan (Ind.) were among the main talking points in Ward 2. Only 2 of the outgoing 5 Councillors were returned, Fine Gael's Gus O'Driscoll, and Jan O'Sullivan who was elected as a Labour Councillor having previously been

> There can be no doubt that the controversial services charges issue resulted in huge difficulties for the 2 main parties

a DSP Councillor.

The poll was headed to the surprise of many by John Gilligan who received an impressive 1,115 votes, thereby taking the Aldermanship in Ward 2. The anti-service charge message was also the basis for the election of Workers' Party candidate John Ryan. The Workers Party which admits to having less than 20 members in Limerick City, pulled off a remarkable achievement in getting Ryan elected. Kieran O'Hanlon of the Progressive Democrats pipped Fianna Fail Mayor, Paddy Madden by a mere eight votes for the last seat in Ward 2. Despite having a higher percentage vote

than any other party or group, Fianna Fail, with the failure of Madden and the other outgoing Councillor Larry Cross, now have no seat in Ward 2 in Limerick.

Fianna Fail lost a seat in Ward 3 with only former Mayor Jack Bourke being returned without reaching the quota. Undoubtedly Ward 3 was a success for Jim Kemmy who was elected with 1,418 votes which gave Labour 1.6 quotas. This was enough to safely see former Mayor Frank Leddin regain the seat he lost in 1985. Outgoing Fine Gael Councillor Ger Fahy, who ousted Leddin for the last seat in 1985, found the tables turned on this occasion, being beaten by Leddin by 145 votes for the final seat. Outgoing Independent Councillor Joe Harrington, who consistently opposed the introduction of services charges in Limerick, was re-elected along with Jim Kemmy on the first count.

Fianna Fail failed to win a seat in Ward 4 as their outgoing Councillor John O'Connor was beaten for the last seat by Dick Sadlier of the Progressive Democrats. Fine Gael's Bobby Burns held his seat while topping the poll. First elected, however, was Sean Griffin of the Labour Party who received sufficient transfers from eliminated candidate Noel Hannan to take the Aldermanship. Fine Gael Senator Patrick Kennedy was also returned in Ward 4 but must have been disappointed to have been replaced as poll topper by party colleague Bobby Burns, who received 179 more votes than Kennedy.

The poor performances from Fine Gael and Fianna Fail in particular, illustrates the resentment felt about the issue of Local Service Charges. The Left are the only ones to be happy with their performance in the 1991 elections. The Progressive Democrats returned three Councillors which was only a one seat gain in what is afterall Des O'Malley's backyard. O'Malley may yet regret this failure to make greater inroads in Limerick City, especially as the PD's second seat will be targeted by both Fianna Fail and the left in the next general election. While the results for Fianna Fail would appear to indicate that an extra seat is out of the question the strong performance of Deputy Willie O'Dea in the City, places them in a good position to gain, especially with the strong Fianna Fail base in the County Council area which is in the Limerick East constituency. This lack of County support may be enough to deprive Labour adding to Jim Kemmy's seat, even considering their excellent Local Election results.

# NO. 1 ELECTORAL AREA

TOTAL ELECTORATE 8,410. VALID POLL 4,793. NO. OF MEMBERS 4. QUOTA 959

| Names of Candidates | First Count Votes | Second Count Transfer of O'Dea's surplus | Result | Third Count Transfer of Lee's votes | Result | Fourth Count Transfer of Ryan's votes | Result | Fifth Count Transfer of O'Donoghue's votes | Result | Sixth Count Transfer of Clancy's votes | Result | Seventh Count Transfer of M. Prendergast's votes | Result | Eighth Count Transfer of O'Mahony's votes | Result |
|---|---|---|---|---|---|---|---|---|---|---|---|---|---|---|---|
| CLANCY, Thomas (S.F.) | 217 | +5 | 222 | +11 | 233 | +4 | 237 | +16 | 253 | -253 | — | — | — | — | — |
| LEDDIN, Tim (F.G.) | 827 | +16 | 843 | +3 | 846 | +17 | 863 | +4 | 867 | +9 | 876 | +88 | 964 | — | 964 |
| LEE, Dave (W.P.) | 58 | +2 | 60 | -60 | — | — | — | — | — | — | — | — | — | — | — |
| O'DEA, Willie (F.F.) | 1,104 | -145 | 959 | — | 959 | — | 959 | — | 959 | — | 959 | — | 959 | — | 959 |
| O'DONOGHUE, Judy (Lab.) | 134 | +4 | 138 | +15 | 153 | +2 | 155 | -155 | — | — | — | — | — | — | — |
| O'DRISCOLL, Tim (P.D.) | 489 | +13 | 502 | +9 | 511 | +21 | 532 | +25 | 557 | +71 | 628 | +28 | 656 | +100 | 756 |
| O'MAHONY, Frank (P.D.) | 349 | +8 | 357 | +4 | 361 | +11 | 372 | +3 | 375 | +2 | 377 | +36 | 413 | -413 | — |
| PRENDERGAST, Frank (Lab.) | 719 | +19 | 738 | +9 | 747 | +20 | 767 | +75 | 842 | +51 | 893 | +111 | 1,004 | — | 1,004 |
| PRENDERGAST, Mary (F.G.) | 286 | +7 | 293 | +5 | 298 | +13 | 311 | +13 | 324 | +10 | 334 | -334 | — | — | — |
| QUINN, John (P.D.) | 523 | +12 | 535 | +1 | 536 | +19 | 555 | +8 | 563 | +39 | 602 | +38 | 640 | +235 | 875 |
| RYAN, Garrett (F.F.) | 87 | +59 | 146 | +1 | 147 | -147 | — | — | — | — | — | — | — | — | — |
| Non-transferable papers not effective | — | — | — | +2 | 2 | +40 | 42 | +11 | 53 | +71 | 124 | +33 | 157 | +78 | 235 |
| TOTAL: | 4,793 | — | 4,793 | — | 4,793 | — | 4,793 | — | 4,793 | — | 4,793 | — | 4,793 | — | 4,793 |

Elected: O'Dea, Willie (F.F.); Prendergast, Frank (Lab.); Leddin, Tim (F.G.); Quinn, John (P.D.).

# NO. 2 ELECTORAL AREA

TOTAL ELECTORATE 12,063. VALID POLL 7,220. NO. OF MEMBERS 5. QUOTA 1,204

| Names of Candidates | First Count Votes | Second Count Transfer of O'Doherty's votes | Result | Third Count Transfer of Bennis' votes | Result | Fourth Count Transfer of R. Madden's votes | Result | Fifth Count Transfer of McInerney's votes | Result | Sixth Count Transfer of MacMahon's votes | Result | Seventh Count Transfer of Stockil's votes | Result | Eighth Count Transfer of P. Kiely's votes | Result | Ninth Count Transfer of K. Kiely's votes | Result | Tenth Count Transfer of Cross' votes | Result | Eleventh Count Transfer of Crowe's votes | Result | Twelfth Count Transfer of Gilligan's surplus | Result | Thirteenth Count Transfer of O'Sullivan's surplus | Result |
|---|---|---|---|---|---|---|---|---|---|---|---|---|---|---|---|---|---|---|---|---|---|---|---|---|---|
| BENNIS, Joseph (Lab.) | 139 | +1 | 140 | -140 | — | — | — | — | — | — | — | — | — | — | — | — | — | — | — | — | — | — | — | — | — |
| CROSS, Larry (F.F.) | 358 | +1 | 359 | +13 | 372 | +8 | 380 | +32 | 412 | +6 | 418 | +2 | 420 | +113 | 533 | +13 | 546 | -546 | — | — | — | — | — | — | — |
| CROWE, Mick | 588 | +4 | 592 | +12 | 604 | +15 | 619 | +24 | 643 | +11 | 654 | +17 | 671 | +24 | 695 | +104 | 799 | +32 | 831 | -831 | — | — | — | — | — |
| GILLIGAN, John | 1,115 | +11 | 1,126 | +12 | 1,138 | +9 | 1,147 | +13 | 1,160 | +14 | 1,174 | +14 | 1,188 | +24 | 1,212 | — | 1,212 | — | 1,212 | — | 1,212 | -8 | 1,204 | — | 1,204 |
| KIELY, Kevin (F.G.) | 443 | — | 443 | +8 | 451 | +23 | 474 | +12 | 486 | +2 | 488 | +6 | 494 | +13 | 507 | -507 | — | — | — | — | — | — | — | — | — |
| KIELY, Paddy (F.F.) | 362 | — | 362 | +2 | 364 | +11 | 375 | +28 | 403 | +5 | 408 | +7 | 415 | -415 | — | — | — | — | — | — | — | — | — | — | — |
| McINERNEY, Peggy (F.F.) | 212 | +2 | 214 | +4 | 218 | — | 218 | -218 | — | — | — | — | — | — | — | — | — | — | — | — | — | — | — | — | — |
| MacMAHON, Michael (Lab.) | 189 | +1 | 190 | +23 | 213 | +11 | 224 | +1 | 225 | -225 | — | — | — | — | — | — | — | — | — | — | — | — | — | — | — |
| MADDEN, Paddy (F.F.) | 435 | +3 | 438 | +2 | 440 | +7 | 447 | +41 | 488 | +19 | 507 | +9 | 516 | +120 | 636 | +39 | 675 | +243 | 918 | +107 | 1,025 | +3 | 1,028 | +1 | 1,029 |
| MADDEN, Ronnie (F.G.) | 160 | +4 | 164 | — | 164 | -164 | — | — | — | — | — | — | — | — | — | — | — | — | — | — | — | — | — | — | — |
| O'DOHERTY, Patrick (G.P.) | 61 | -61 | — | — | — | — | — | — | — | — | — | — | — | — | — | — | — | — | — | — | — | — | — | — | — |
| O'DRISCOLL, Gus (F.G.) | 668 | +6 | 674 | +5 | 679 | +34 | 713 | +6 | 719 | +10 | 729 | +76 | 805 | +23 | 828 | +158 | 986 | +50 | 1,036 | +93 | 1,129 | +2 | 1,131 | +4 | 1,135 |
| O'HANLON, Kieran (P.D.) | 539 | +2 | 541 | +4 | 545 | +15 | 560 | +7 | 567 | +49 | 616 | +184 | 800 | +32 | 832 | +19 | 851 | +67 | 918 | +117 | 1,035 | +1 | 1,036 | +1 | 1,037 |
| O'SULLIVAN, Jan (Lab.) | 895 | +12 | 907 | +35 | 942 | +11 | 953 | +17 | 970 | +92 | 1,062 | +56 | 1,118 | +26 | 1,144 | +39 | 1,183 | +30 | 1,213 | — | 1,213 | — | 1,213 | -9 | 1,204 |
| RYAN, John (W.P.) | 692 | +6 | 698 | +14 | 712 | +3 | 715 | +22 | 737 | +7 | 744 | +10 | 754 | +17 | 771 | +62 | 833 | +19 | 852 | +231 | 1,083 | +2 | 1,085 | +2 | 1,087 |
| STOCKIL, Joan (P.D.) | 364 | +5 | 369 | +2 | 371 | +10 | 381 | +8 | 389 | +4 | 393 | -393 | — | — | — | — | — | — | — | — | — | — | — | — | — |
| Non-transferable papers not effective | — | +3 | 3 | +4 | 7 | +7 | 14 | +7 | 21 | +6 | 27 | +12 | 39 | +23 | 62 | +73 | 135 | +105 | 240 | +283 | 523 | — | 523 | +1 | 524 |
| TOTAL: | 7,220 | — | 7,220 | — | 7,220 | — | 7,220 | — | 7,220 | — | 7,220 | — | 7,220 | — | 7,220 | — | 7,220 | — | 7,220 | — | 7,220 | — | 7,220 | — | 7,220 |

Elected: Gilligan, John; O'Sullivan, Jan (Lab.); O'Driscoll, Gus (F.G.); Ryan, John (W.P.); O'Hanlon, Kiernan (P.D.).

## NO. 3 ELECTORAL AREA

TOTAL ELECTORATE 8,405. VALID POLL 4,515. NO. OF MEMBERS 4. QUOTA 904

| Names of Candidates | First Count Votes | Second Count Transfer of Kemmy's surplus | Result | Third Count Transfer of O'Donovan's votes | Result | Fourth Count Transfer of O'Neill's votes | Result | Fifth Count Transfer of McMahon's votes | Result | Sixth Count Transfer of Morgan's votes | Result |
|---|---|---|---|---|---|---|---|---|---|---|---|
| BOURKE, Jack (F.F.) | 574 | +47 | 621 | +31 | 652 | +23 | 675 | +118 | 793 | +70 | 863 |
| FAHY, Ger (F.G.) | 533 | +56 | 589 | +5 | 594 | +43 | 637 | +15 | 652 | +66 | 718 |
| HARRINGTON, Joe | 905 | — | 905 | — | 905 | — | 905 | — | 905 | — | 905 |
| KEMMY, Jim (Lab.) | 1,418 | -514 | 904 | — | 904 | — | 904 | — | 904 | — | 904 |
| LEDDIN, Frank (Lab.) | 459 | +295 | 754 | +2 | 756 | +16 | 772 | +19 | 791 | +80 | 871 |
| McMAHON, Jim (F.F.) | 186 | +31 | 217 | +7 | 224 | +7 | 231 | -231 | — | — | — |
| MORGAN, Billy | 249 | +57 | 306 | +9 | 315 | +29 | 344 | +38 | 382 | -382 | — |
| O'DONOVAN, Paddy (F.F.) | 66 | +10 | 76 | -76 | — | — | — | — | — | — | — |
| O'NEILL, Anthony (F.G.) | 125 | +18 | 143 | +13 | 156 | -156 | — | — | — | — | — |
| Non-transferable papers not effective | — | — | — | +9 | 9 | +38 | 47 | +41 | 88 | +166 | 254 |
| TOTAL: | 4,515 | — | 4,515 | — | 4,515 | — | 4,515 | — | 4,515 | — | 4,515 |

Elected: Kemmy, Jim (Lab.); Harrington, Joe; Leddin, Frank (Lab.); Bourke, Jack (F.F.)

## NO. 4 ELECTORAL AREA

TOTAL ELECTORATE 8,003. VALID POLL 4,493. NO. OF MEMBERS 4. QUOTA 899

| Names of Candidates | First Count Votes | Second Count Transfer of Hannan's votes | Result | Third Count Transfer of Cremins' votes | Result | Fourth Count Transfer of McGrath's votes | Result | Fifth Count Transfer of Brazier's votes | Result | Sixth Count Transfer of Harrington's votes | Result | Seventh Count Transfer of Griffin's surplus | Result | Eighth Count Transfer of Byrne's surplus | Result | Ninth Count Transfer of Kennedy's surplus | Result |
|---|---|---|---|---|---|---|---|---|---|---|---|---|---|---|---|---|---|
| BRAZIER, Tom (F.F.) | 318 | +4 | 322 | +41 | 363 | +16 | 379 | -379 | — | — | — | — | — | — | — | — | — |
| BYRNE, Bobby (F.G.) | 879 | +4 | 883 | +6 | 889 | +18 | 907 | — | 907 | — | 907 | — | 907 | -8 | 899 | — | 899 |
| CREMINS, Michael (F.F.) | 101 | +3 | 104 | -104 | — | — | — | — | — | — | — | — | — | — | — | — | — |
| GRIFFIN, Seán (Lab.) | 870 | +43 | 913 | — | 913 | — | 913 | — | 913 | — | 913 | -14 | 899 | — | 899 | — | 899 |
| HANNAN, Noel | 98 | -98 | — | — | — | — | — | — | — | — | — | — | — | — | — | — | — |
| HARRINGTON, Win | 421 | +7 | 428 | +5 | 433 | +31 | 464 | +48 | 512 | -512 | — | — | — | — | — | — | — |
| KENNEDY, Patrick (F.G.) | 700 | +9 | 709 | +14 | 723 | +26 | 749 | +61 | 810 | +156 | 966 | — | 966 | — | 966 | -67 | 899 |
| McGRATH, John (Non-Party) | 142 | +14 | 156 | +7 | 163 | -163 | — | — | — | — | — | — | — | — | — | — | — |
| O'CONNOR, John (F.F.) | 463 | +8 | 471 | +22 | 493 | +9 | 502 | +160 | 662 | +73 | 735 | +2 | 737 | +2 | 739 | +24 | 763 |
| SADLIER, Dick (P.D.) | 501 | — | 501 | +2 | 503 | +29 | 532 | +45 | 577 | +162 | 739 | +5 | 744 | +6 | 750 | +43 | 793 |
| Non-transferable papers not effective | — | +6 | 6 | +7 | 13 | +34 | 47 | +65 | 112 | +121 | 233 | +7 | 240 | — | 240 | — | 240 |
| TOTAL: | 4,493 | — | 4,493 | — | 4,493 | — | 4,493 | — | 4,493 | — | 4,493 | — | 4,493 | — | 4,493 | — | 4,493 |

Eelected: Griffin, Sean (Lab.); Byrne, Bobby (F.G.); Kennedy, Patrick (F.G.); Sadlier, Dick (P.D.)

# LIMERICK COUNTY COUNCIL

## LIMERICK COUNTY COUNCIL RESULTS

| PARTY | 1991 % of votes | 1991 Seats obtained | 1985 % of votes | 1985 Seats obtained |
|---|---|---|---|---|
| Fianna Fail | 43.3 | 13 | 57.6 | 18 |
| Fine Gael | 32.1 | 10 | 37.4 | 10 |
| Labour | 4.1 | 1 | 1.7 | — |
| Progressive Dem. | 15.5 | 4 | — | — |
| Workers Party | — | — | — | — |
| Other | 5.0 | — | 3.3 | — |
| TOTAL SEATS | | 28 | | 28 |

Total population: 161,856
County (excl. Limerick city): 109,816
Limerick city: 52,040
Rateable valuation(county): £903,953.85
County Council, PO Box 53, County Buildings,
79-84 O'Connell Street, Limerick
Telephone:(061) 318477
Fax:(061) 318478
Rate: £27.2324
County Council meetings: Fourth Friday of month

## LIMERICK

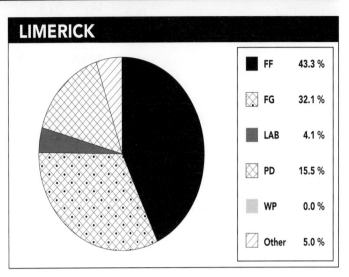

| | |
|---|---|
| ■ FF | 43.3 % |
| ⊠ FG | 32.1 % |
| ■ LAB | 4.1 % |
| ⊠ PD | 15.5 % |
| ▨ WP | 0.0 % |
| ▧ Other | 5.0 % |

*County Manager:* E. Gleeson
*Assistant County Manager:* P. O'Connor
*County Secretary:* J. Behan
*County Development Officer:* G. Behan
*County Finance Officer:* O. Killeen
*County Engineer:* A. O'Connell
*Administrative Officers:*
*Housing:* A. Hughes
*Roads:* M. O'Connor
*Senior Staff Officers:*
*Accounts:* M. Fitzgerald
*Personnel:* T. Barry
*General Administration:* K. Lehane
*Data Processing:* P. Fitzgerald
*County Librarian:* Damian Brady, 58 O'Connell Street, Limerick
*Telephone:* (061) 318692
*Senior Executive Planner:* G. Sheeran
*Senior Draughtsman:* S. Mulcahy
*Chief Fire Officer:* J. McGrath
*Civil Defence Officer:* P. O'Halloran
*County Solicitor:* W. Leahy
*County Veterinary Officer:* J. McCarthy
*County Coroners:* P. J. Meghen(West), Dr T. Casey (South East)
*Senior Executive Engineers:*
*Road Planning:* J. Tarpey
*Road Upkeep:* T. Curran
*Housing and Sanitary Services:* J. Condon
*Housing Development:* J. Lynch
*Environment:* J. O'Connell
*Road Design:* D. Brennan

## BRUFF

|     | 1991 | 1985 | '85 to '91 Swing |
| --- | --- | --- | --- |
| FF | 42.9 | 52.3 | -9.4 |
| FG | 31.3 | 43.3 | -12.0 |
| LAB | 6.9 | 2.5 | 4.4 |
| PD | 18.9 | — | 18.9 |
| Ind | — | 1.9 | -1.9 |

BRENNAN, Michael,
14 Park Avenue, Adare,
County Limerick. (FF)
Carpenter. 061-86408

CLIFFORD, John,
Crean, Bruff,
County Limerick. (FF)
Teacher. 061-399763

COLLINS, Michael J.,
"White Oaks",
Redhouse Hill, Patrickswell,
County Limerick. (FF)
Hotelier.

McCARTHY, Jim,
2 Willow Grove, Clonconare, Redgate,
Limerick. (FG)
Teacher.

NOONAN, Michael J.,
18 Gouldavoher Estate,
Father Russel Road,
Limerick. (FG)
Dail Deputy. 061-48686

O'MALLEY, Tim,
Regional Pharmacy, Dooradoyle,
County Limerick. (PD)
Pharmacist. 061-29401

## CASTLECONNELL

|     | 1991 | 1985 | '85 to '91 Swing |
| --- | --- | --- | --- |
| FF | 38.0 | 64.5 | -26.5 |
| FG | 21.8 | 33.9 | -12.1 |
| LAB | 4.8 | — | 4.8 |
| PD | 24.8 | — | 24.8 |
| Ind | 10.6 | 1.6 | 9.0 |

CLOHESSY, Peadar,
Fanningstown, Crecora,
County Limerick. (PD)
Dail Deputy. 061-351190

FINUCANE, John,
Sandylane, Caherconlish,
County Limerick. (PD)
Dairy Farmer. 061-351263

GLEESON, Noel,
Cullenagh, Cappamore,
County Limerick. (FF)
Farmer.

HOURIGAN, Paddy,
"The Orchards", Annagh, Lisnagry,
Limerick. (FG)
Farmer 061-378144

JACKMAN, Mary,
Newtown, Castletroy,
County Limerick. (FG)
Senator. 061-335511

WADE, Eddie,
Cahernorry, Drombanna,
County Limerick. (FF)
Salesman. 061-351467

## KILMALLOCK

|     | 1991 | 1985 | '85 to '91 Swing |
| --- | --- | --- | --- |
| FF | 36.3 | 52.8 | -16.5 |
| FG | 48.6 | 44.4 | 4.2 |
| LAB | — | 2.8 | -2.8 |
| PD | 15.2 | — | 15.2 |

BARRY, Michael,
Railway Road, Kilmallock,
County Limerick. (FF)
Self Employed. 063-98648

CALLAGHAN, Matt,
Glenroe, Kilmallock,
County Limerick. (FG)
Auctioneer.

CREIGHTON, Eddie,
9 St Josephs Terrace, Hospital,
County Limerick. (PD)
School Caretaker. 061-831779

HOULIHAN, James,
Stylepark, Bruree,
County Limerick. (FG)
Farmer. 061-89439

SAMPSON, William,
Spittle, Ballylanders,
County Limerick. (FF)
Farmer. 062-57024

## NEWCASTLE

|     | 1991 | 1985 | '85 to '91 Swing |
| --- | --- | --- | --- |
| FF | 49.2 | 57.5 | -8.3 |
| FG | 30.6 | 39.0 | -8.4 |
| LAB | 7.3 | 3.5 | 3.8 |
| PD | 8.5 | — | 8.5 |
| SF | 3.1 | — | 3.1 |
| Ind | 1.3 | — | 1.3 |

BRODERICK, Sean,
New Street, Abbeyfeale,
County Limerick. (FG)
Shopkeeper. (068) 31213

CREGAN, John,
Church Street, Dromcollogher,
County Limerick. (FF)
Telecom Technician.

**Maureen Barrett (FF)**
**Rathkeale**

**Michael Noonan (FG)**
**Limerick**

**Tim O'Malley (PD)**
**Bruff**

**Eddie Wade (FF)**
**Castleconnel**

FINUCANE, Michael,
Ardnacrohy, Newcastle West,
County Limerick. (FG)
Dáil Deputy. 069-62742

HEALY, Michael,
Ardnacrohy, Newcastle West,
County Limerick. (FF)
Teacher. 069-62140

KELLY, Mary,
Maiden Street, Newcastle,
County Limerick. (Lab)
Shopkeeper.

O'KELLY, Michael,
Tralee Road, Abbeyfeale,
County Limerick. (FF)
Teacher. 068-31221

## RATHKEALE

| | 1991 | 1985 | '85 to '91 Swing |
|---|---|---|---|
| FF | 50.4 | 59.4 | -9.0 |
| FG | 32.8 | 27.5 | 5.3 |
| LAB | — | 2.6 | -2.6 |
| PD | 7.7 | — | 7.7 |
| GP | 5.9 | — | 5.9 |
| SF | — | 10.5 | -10.5 |
| Ind | 3.1 | — | 3.1 |

BARRETT, Maureen,
Main Street, Glin,
County Limerick. (FF)
Housewife.

GRIFFIN, John,
Main Street, Rathkeale,
County Limerick. (FF)
Postmaster.

NAUGHTON, David,
Ballysteen, Askeaton,
County Limerick. (FG)
Farmer. 061-392206

NEVILLE, Dan,
Kiltannan, Croagh, Rathkeale,
County Limerick. (FG)
Senator. 061-86351

SHEAHAN, Kevin,
Cloonreash, Askeaton,
County Limerick. (FF)
Auctioneer. 061-392125

**Limerick Corporation Councillor John Gilligan gives the thumbs up to his election.**

# Heavy losses for FF in Limerick County

The Progressive Democrats were the main winners in Limerick County Council, taking 4 seats and over 15% of the first preference vote. Fianna Fail suffered heavy losses, dropping 5 seats on 1985, as their majority on the Council collapsed. Labour gained a seat in Newcastle by a mere 21 votes while Fine Gael's representation remained static holding 10 seats, as in 1985, on the 28 member Council.

Fine Gael lost a seat in the Bruff Electoral Area as Progressive Democrat candidate Tim O'Malley, a prominent member of the Mid-Western Health Board, was elected with the help of strong transfers from his 2 running mates. Fine Gael were at a disadvantage with the retirement of Councillor Michael Whelan and also former TD, Willie O'Brien

Former Justice Minister, Michael Noonan polled well and was elected along with outgoing Fine Gael Councillor Jim McCarthy. Fianna Fail ran only their 3 outgoing Councillors and all 3 were returned with strong first preference votes. A surprise was the poll topping performance of Fianna Fail's Michael Brennan, well ahead of party colleague, and outgoing Council Chairman, Councillor Michael Collins - a brother of the then Minister Gerry Collins, TD.

Castleconnell was the area where Fianna Fail suffered their heaviest losses with their vote being down over 25% as they lost 2 seats to the Progressive Democrats. The public outcry over a proposed halting site in Castletroy was one factor for this Fianna Fail decline. Although it must be noted that 1 of the seats dropped by Fianna Fail was lost prior to the election with the deflection of Deputy Peadar Clohessy to the PDs and Willie Keane only missed out being elected by a mere 11 votes. Fianna Fail's strategy of running 4 candidates can be questioned in the aftermath of the result. With a candidate less, Keane may not have been edged out by Clohessy's running mate John Finucane who actually polled 129 first preference votes less than Keane.

For probable Fianna Fail general election candidate in Limerick East, Eddie Wade, the outcome in Castleconnell was a success. Wade polled 2,039 votes on a quota of 1,632 votes, well over 400 votes ahead of Clohessy, the nearest candidate. The Fine Gael vote was down by some 12% but their strategy of running only 2

> ## Castleconnell was the area where Fianna Fail suffered their heaviest losses

candidates saw both outgoing Councillors - Mary Jackman and Paddy Hourigan - safely returned, leaving Fine Gael, the PDs and Fianna Fail all with 2 seats each in Castleconnell.

Eddie Creighton of the Progressive Democrats took a seat in Kilmallock at the expense of Fianna Fail whose vote dropped by over 16%. Outgoing Fianna Fail Councillor Alan Mee, who had been co-opted onto the Council to replace Michael Maguire, lost out, receiving the least number of votes of all 7 candidates in Kilmallock. Both Michael Barry and Willie Sampson of Fianna Fail were successfully returned.

Fine Gael polled 48.6% of the vote, one of the highest votes they received nationally. This strong vote was aided by the poll topping performance of outgoing Councillor Matt Callaghan who had almost 500 votes over the quota. Callaghan was elected on the first count with his running mate, outgoing Councillor, James Houlihan.

Labour, to the surprise of many, took a seat in Newcastle at the expense of Fianna Fail. The Labour candidate Mary Kelly was helped by transfers from both the Progressive Democrats and Fine Gael in

**Successful Progressive Democrat candidates in Limerick County celebrate.**

narrowly defeating outgoing Councillor Thomas Ahern by a 21 vote margin. Michael O'Kelly topped the poll for Fianna Fail and was returned along with Party colleagues Michael Healy and John Cregan.

Fine Gael Limerick West TD, Michael Finucane, was only 73 votes short of the quota on the first count and was elected with running mate Sean Broderick. A mere 43 votes short of being elected in 1985, Broderick was the third candidate returned on this occasion. The third Fine Gael candidate John Kelly, an outgoing Councillor, was less lucky with his first preference vote, dropping 445 votes. The Progressive Democrat challenge in Newcastle West failed to materialise. Sean Liston, who polled well in the 1989 general election, received only 525 votes while his running mate lost his deposit.

The Progressive Democrat's also performed poorly in the Rathkeale Electoral Area where their 2 candidates received a combined vote of 800 votes with a quota of 1,507 votes. Fianna Fail took 4 seats in Rathkeale in 1985. On this occasion they ran only 3 candidates and 2 of these, Maureen Barrett and John Griffin, were not far off being elected on the first count, along with Fianna Fail's first candidate home - Kevin Sheahan.

The Rathkeale poll was topped by Senator Dan Neville of Fine Gael who only scraped home by 17 votes in 1985. The seat gained by Fine Gael at Fianna Fail's expense was taken by David Naughton, whose father was chairman of Limerick County Council for three terms and was the man who welcomed President J. F. Kennedy to Shannon in 1963.

# BRUFF ELECTORAL AREA

TOTAL ELECTORATE 19,044. VALID POLL 10,767. NO. OF MEMBERS 6. QUOTA 1,539

| Names of Candidates | First Count Votes | Second Count Transfer of Brennan's surplus Result | | Third Count Transfer of Wright's votes Result | | Fourth Count Transfer of Penn's votes Result | | Fifth Count Transfer of O'Malley's surplus Result | | Sixth Count Transfer of Noonan's surplus Result | | Seventh Count Transfer of Dáson's votes Result | |
|---|---|---|---|---|---|---|---|---|---|---|---|---|---|
| BRENNAN, Michael (F.F.) | 1,976 | -437 | 1,539 | — | 1,539 | — | 1,539 | — | 1,539 | — | 1,539 | — | 1,539 |
| CLIFFORD, John (F.F.) | 1,316 | +149 | 1,465 | +14 | 1,479 | +29 | 1,508 | +14 | 1,522 | +3 | 1,525 | +121 | 1,646 |
| COLLINS, Michael J. (F.F.) | 1,328 | +169 | 1,497 | +8 | 1,505 | +40 | 1,545 | — | 1,545 | — | 1,545 | — | 1,545 |
| DÁSON, Noëlle (Lab.) | 740 | +8 | 748 | +32 | 780 | +42 | 822 | +39 | 861 | +8 | 869 | -869 | — |
| HANLEY, Charles (F.G.) | 855 | +56 | 911 | +7 | 918 | +51 | 969 | +27 | 996 | +9 | 1,005 | +94 | 1,099 |
| McCARTHY, Jim (F.G.) | 1,034 | +5 | 1,039 | +73 | 1,112 | +14 | 1,126 | +42 | 1,168 | +6 | 1,174 | +299 | 1,473 |
| NOONAN, Michael J. (F.G.) | 1,480 | +12 | 1,492 | +22 | 1,514 | +51 | 1,565 | — | 1,565 | -26 | 1,539 | — | 1,539 |
| O'MALLEY, Tim (P.D.) | 1,281 | +19 | 1,300 | +108 | 1,408 | +253 | 1,661 | -122 | 1,539 | — | 1,539 | — | 1,539 |
| PENN, Bobbie (P.D.) | 434 | +13 | 447 | +55 | 502 | -502 | — | — | — | — | — | — | — |
| WRIGHT, John (P.D.) | 323 | +6 | 329 | -329 | — | — | — | — | — | — | — | — | — |
| Non-transferable papers not effective | — | — | — | +10 | 10 | +22 | 32 | — | 32 | — | 32 | +355 | 387 |
| TOTAL: | 10,767 | — | 10,767 | — | 10,767 | — | 10,767 | — | 10,767 | — | 10,767 | — | 10,767 |

Elected: Brennan, Michael (F.F.); O'Malley, Tim (P.D.); Noonan, Michael J. (F.G.); Collins, Michael J. (F.F.); Clifford, John (F.F.); McCarthy, Jim (F.G.)

# CASTLECONNELL ELECTORAL AREA

TOTAL ELECTORATE 18,449. VALID POLL 11,421. NO. OF MEMBERS 6. QUOTA 1,632

| Names of Candidates | First Count Votes | Second Count Transfer of Wade's surplus Result | | Third Count Transfer of Clohessy's surplus Result | | Fourth Count Transfer of Duffy's votes Result | | Fifth Count Transfer of Jackman's surplus Result | | Sixth Count Transfer of Ryan's votes Result | | Seventh Count Transfer of Liston's votes Result | | Eighth Count Transfer of Long's votes Result | | Ninth Count Transfer of Meagher's votes Result | | Tenth Count Transfer of Gleeson's surplus Result | |
|---|---|---|---|---|---|---|---|---|---|---|---|---|---|---|---|---|---|---|---|---|---|
| CLOHESSY, Peadar (P.D.) | 1,623 | +99 | 1,722 | -90 | 1,632 | — | 1,632 | — | 1,632 | — | 1,632 | — | 1,632 | — | 1,632 | — | 1,632 | — | 1,632 |
| DUFFY, James (Non-Party) | 484 | +7 | 491 | +2 | 493 | -493 | — | — | — | — | — | — | — | — | — | — | — | — | — |
| FINUCANE, John (P.D.) | 631 | +29 | 660 | +20 | 680 | +62 | 742 | +17 | 759 | +201 | 960 | +84 | 1,044 | +55 | 1,099 | +112 | 1,211 | +18 | 1,229 |
| GLEESON, Noel (F.F.) | 934 | +64 | 998 | +8 | 1,006 | +11 | 1,017 | +2 | 1,019 | +148 | 1,167 | +26 | 1,193 | +274 | 1,467 | +230 | 1,697 | -65 | 1,632 |
| HOURIGAN, Patrick (F.G.) | 1,048 | +17 | 1,065 | +13 | 1,078 | +19 | 1,097 | +13 | 1,110 | +102 | 1,212 | +108 | 1,320 | +53 | 1,373 | +169 | 1,542 | +15 | 1,557 |
| JACKMAN, Mary (F.G.) | 1,443 | +22 | 1,465 | +12 | 1,477 | +225 | 1,702 | -70 | 1,632 | — | 1,632 | — | 1,632 | — | 1,632 | — | 1,632 | — | 1,632 |
| KEANE, Willie (F.F.) | 760 | +52 | 812 | +11 | 823 | +32 | 855 | +6 | 861 | +21 | 882 | +102 | 984 | +125 | 1,109 | +77 | 1,186 | +32 | 1,218 |
| LISTON, Jo (Lab.) | 552 | +10 | 562 | +6 | 568 | +36 | 604 | +19 | 623 | +16 | 639 | -639 | — | — | — | — | — | — | — |
| LONG, Tim (F.F.) | 612 | +80 | 692 | +12 | 704 | +11 | 715 | +3 | 718 | +30 | 748 | +31 | 779 | -779 | — | — | — | — | — |
| MEAGHER, William Joseph (Non-Party) | 721 | +12 | 733 | +3 | 736 | +30 | 766 | +4 | 770 | +34 | 804 | +109 | 913 | +126 | 1,039 | -1,039 | — | — | — |
| RYAN, Martin (P.D.) | 574 | +15 | 589 | +3 | 592 | +8 | 600 | +6 | 606 | -606 | — | — | — | — | — | — | — | — | — |
| WADE, Eddie (F.F.) | 2,039 | -407 | 1,632 | — | 1,632 | — | 1,632 | — | 1,632 | — | 1,632 | — | 1,632 | — | 1,632 | — | 1,632 | — | 1,632 |
| Non-transferable papers not effective | — | — | — | — | — | +59 | 59 | — | 59 | +54 | 113 | +179 | 292 | +146 | 438 | +451 | 889 | — | 889 |
| TOTAL: | 11,421 | — | 11,421 | — | 11,421 | — | 11,421 | — | 11,421 | — | 11,421 | — | 11,421 | — | 11,421 | — | 11,421 | — | 11,421 |

Elected: Wade, Eddie (F.F.); Clohessy, Peadar (P.D.); Jackman, Mary (F.G.); Gleeson, Noel (F.F.); Hourigan, Patrick (F.G.); Finucane, John (P.D.)

# KILMALLOCK ELECTORAL AREA

TOTAL ELECTORATE 12,482. VALID POLL 8,231. NO. OF MEMBERS 5. QUOTA 1,372

| Names of Candidates | First Count Votes | Second Count Transfer of Callaghan's surplus (Result | | Third Count Transfer of Houlihan's surplus (Result | | Fourth Count Transfer of Mee's votes (Result | |
|---|---|---|---|---|---|---|---|
| BARRY, Michael (F.F.) | 1,298 | +36 | (1,334 | +18 | (1,352 | +299 | (1,651 |
| CALLAGHAN, Matt (F.G.) | 1,865 | -493 | (1,372 | — | (1,372 | — | (1,372 |
| CREIGHTON, Eddie (P.D.) | 1,248 | +77 | (1,325 | +16 | (1,341 | +93 | (1,434 |
| HOULIHAN, James (F.G.) | 1,479 | — | (1,479 | -107 | (1,372 | — | (1,372 |
| MEE, Alan (F.F.) | 634 | +111 | (745 | +11 | (756 | -756 | (— |
| O'GRADY, John (F.G.) | 654 | +175 | (829 | +58 | (887 | +29 | (916 |
| SAMPSON, William (F.F.) | 1,053 | +94 | (1,147 | +4 | (1,151 | +238 | (1,389 |
| Non-transferable papers not effective | — | — | (— | — | (— | +97 | (97 |
| TOTAL: | 8,231 | — | (8,231 | — | (8,231 | — | (8,231 |

Elected: Callaghan, Matt (F.G.); Houlihan, James (F.G.); Barry, Michael (F.F.); Creighton, Eddie (P.D.); Sampson, William (F.F.).

# NEWCASTLE ELECTORAL AREA

TOTAL ELECTORATE 14,404. VALID POLL 9,609. NO. OF MEMBERS 6. QUOTA 1,373.

| Names of Candidates | First Count Votes | Second Count Transfer of O'Kelly's surplus Result | | Third Count Transfer of Flynn's votes Result | | Fourth Count Transfer of Hunt's votes Result | | Fifth Count Transfer of MacCurtáin's votes Result | | Sixth Count Transfer of Liston's votes Result | | Seventh Count Transfer of J. Kelly's votes Result | |
|---|---|---|---|---|---|---|---|---|---|---|---|---|---|
| AHERNE, Thomas T. (F.F.) | 976 | +133 | 1,109 | +10 | 1,119 | +10 | 1,129 | +18 | 1,147 | +24 | 1,171 | +37 | 1,208 |
| BRODERICK, Sean (F.G.) | 933 | +78 | 1,011 | +1 | 1,012 | +13 | 1,025 | +19 | 1,044 | +63 | 1,107 | +267 | 1,374 |
| CREGAN, John (F.F.) | 1,013 | +26 | 1,039 | +1 | 1,040 | +8 | 1,048 | +59 | 1,107 | +39 | 1,146 | +139 | 1,285 |
| FINUCANE, Michael (F.G.) | 1,300 | +9 | 1,309 | +22 | 1,331 | +51 | 1,382 | — | 1,382 | — | 1,382 | — | 1,382 |
| FLYNN, Michael (Non-Party) | 127 | — | 127 | -127 | — | — | — | — | — | — | — | — | — |
| HEALY, Michael (F.F.) | 1,075 | +31 | 1,106 | +19 | 1,125 | +45 | 1,170 | +26 | 1,196 | +85 | 1,281 | +73 | 1,354 |
| HUNT, Seamus (P.D.) | 288 | +4 | 292 | +9 | 301 | -301 | — | — | — | — | — | — | — |
| KELLY, John (F.G.) | 706 | +3 | 709 | +17 | 726 | +31 | 757 | +57 | 814 | +113 | 927 | -927 | — |
| KELLY, Mary (Lab.) | 698 | +6 | 704 | +32 | 736 | +47 | 783 | +62 | 845 | +164 | 1,009 | +220 | 1,229 |
| LISTON, Sean (P.D.) | 525 | +4 | 529 | +4 | 533 | +72 | 605 | +23 | 628 | +628 | — | — | — |
| MacCURTÁIN, Coireall (S.F.) | 300 | +1 | 301 | +3 | 304 | +7 | 311 | -311 | — | — | — | — | — |
| O'KELLY, Michael (F.F.) | 1,668 | -295 | 1,373 | — | 1,373 | — | 1,373 | — | 1,373 | — | 1,373 | — | 1,373 |
| Non-transferable papers not effective | — | — | — | +9 | 9 | +17 | 26 | +47 | 73 | +140 | 213 | +191 | 404 |
| TOTAL: | 9,609 | — | 9,609 | — | 9,609 | — | 9,609 | — | 9,609 | — | 9,609 | — | 9,609 |

Elected: O'Kelly, Michael (F.F.); Finucane, Michael (F.G.); Broderick, Sean (F.G.); Healy, Michael (F.F.); Cregan, John (F.F.); Kelly, Mary (Lab.)

# RATHKEALE ELECTORAL AREA

TOTAL ELECTORATE 12,705. VALID POLL 9,040. NO. OF MEMBERS 5. QUOTA 1,507.

| Names of Candidates | First Count Votes | Second Count Transfer of Neville's surplus Result | Third Count Transfer of Sheahan's surplus Result | Fourth Count Transfer of Griffin's surplus Result | Fifth Count Transfer of Sheehan's votes Result | Sixth Count Transfer of Fitzgibbon's votes Result | Seventh Count Transfer of O'Doherty's votes Result | Eighth Count Transfer of Reidy's votes Result |
|---|---|---|---|---|---|---|---|---|
| BARRETT, Maureen (F.F.) | 1,449 | +8 1,457 | +46 1,503 | +1 1,504 | +11 1,515 | — 1,515 | — 1,515 | — 1,515 |
| CARRIG, John (P.D.) | 564 | +21 585 | +19 604 | +3 607 | +44 651 | +70 721 | +175 896 | +175 1,071 |
| FITZGIBBON, Basil (Non-Party) | 284 | +7 291 | +17 308 | — 308 | +12 320 | -320 — | — — | — — |
| GRIFFIN, John (F.F.) | 1,493 | +29 1,522 | — 1,522 | -15 1,507 | — 1,507 | — 1,507 | — 1,507 | — 1,507 |
| NAUGHTON, David (F.G.) | 573 | +65 638 | +16 654 | +2 656 | +17 673 | +63 736 | +96 832 | +390 1,222 |
| NEVILLE, Dan (F.G.) | 1,699 | -192 1,507 | — 1,507 | — 1,507 | — 1,507 | — 1,507 | — 1,507 | — 1,507 |
| O'DOHERTY, Patrick (G.P.) | 532 | +19 551 | +4 555 | +3 558 | +23 581 | +54 635 | -635 — | — — |
| REIDY, Jimmie (F.G.) | 696 | +33 729 | +3 732 | — 732 | +5 737 | +38 775 | +46 821 | -821 — |
| SHEAHAN, Kevin (F.F.) | 1,614 | — 1,614 | -107 1,507 | — 1,507 | — 1,507 | — 1,507 | — 1,507 | — 1,507 |
| SHEEHAN, Patrick (P.D.) | 136 | +10 146 | +2 148 | +6 154 | -154 — | — — | — — | — — |
| Non-transferable papers not effective | — | — — | — — | — — | +42 42 | +95 137 | +318 455 | +256 711 |
| TOTAL: | 9,040 | — 9,040 | — 9,040 | — 9,040 | — 9,040 | — 9,040 | — 9,040 | — 9,040 |

Elected: Neville, Dan (F.G.); Sheahan, Kevin (F.F.); Griffin, John (F.F.); Barrett, Maureen (F.F.); Naughton, David (F.G.)

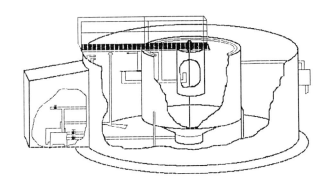

# LONGFORD COUNTY COUNCIL

## LONGFORD COUNTY COUNCIL RESULTS

| PARTY | 1991 % of votes | 1991 Seats obtained | 1985 % of votes | 1985 Seats obtained |
|---|---|---|---|---|
| Fianna Fail | 37.5 | 9 | 46.2 | 10 |
| Fine Gael | 40.7 | 8 | 38.2 | 9 |
| Labour | — | — | — | — |
| Progressive Dem. | 1.3 | — | — | — |
| Workers Party | — | — | — | — |
| Other | 20.5 | 4 | 15.6 | 2 |
| TOTAL SEATS | | 21 | | 21 |

**County Council**
**Longford**
**Telephone: (043) 46231**
**Fax: (043) 41233**
**Total population: 31,496**
**Rateable valuation: £204,167.75**
**Rate: £31.00**
**County Council meetings: Third Monday of each month**

*County Manager:* M. Killeen
*County Secretary:* P. A. Murphy
*Finance Officer:* T. McDonald
*County Engineer:* G. McGlinchey
*Senior Staff Officers:*
*Planning and Roads:* M. Clancy
*Sanitary and Housing:* J. Clarke (Acting)
*County Librarian:* M. Morrissey (Acting)
*County Library,* Longford
*Telephone:* (043) 41124
*County Solicitor:* E. C. Gearty
*County Coroner:* Dr G. McDonagh
*Chief Fire Officer:* Vincent Mulhern
*Civil Defence Officer:* M. Colreavy
*Senior Executive Engineers:*
*Sanitary Services:* J. Kilgallen
*Roads:* A. O'Sullivan
*Housing:* R. Timlin (Acting)
*Chief Assistant, Planning:* M. McCormack

## LONGFORD

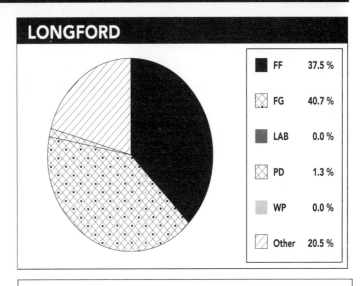

| | |
|---|---|
| ■ FF | 37.5 % |
| ▨ FG | 40.7 % |
| ■ LAB | 0.0 % |
| ▨ PD | 1.3 % |
| WP | 0.0 % |
| ▨ Other | 20.5 % |

**Michael Killeen**

Michael Killeen was born in Limerick in 1940 and is married to Eilish Slattery. They have three sons and one daughter. He was educated by the Christain Brothers in Limerick and by the Institute of Public Administration.

His career has been based in local government and the Health Boards. He was Town Clerk in Tullamore and an accountant with Laois County Council over the period 1968 to 1971. He spent the following seven years in the Midland and Western Health Boards before being appointed Longford County Manager in 1978. Today he has a staff of almost 350 and an annual budget of £12m million.

He enjoys jogging and is also interested in fishing and boating.

## BALLINALEE

|     | 1991 | 1985 | '85 to '91 Swing |
|-----|------|------|------------------|
| FF  | 60.5 | 54.5 | 6.0              |
| FG  | 39.5 | 36.0 | 3.5              |
| Ind | —    | 9.5  | -9.5             |

COYLE, Jimmy,
Cranley, Edgeworthstown,
County Longford. (FF)
Farmer. 043-71282

DOHERTY, Mickey,
Esker, Ballinalee,
County Longford. (FF)
Public Representative. 043-23188

KIERNAN, Victor,
Carrieglass,
Longford. (FG)
Farmer. 043-46857

## BALLYMAHON

|     | 1991 | 1985 | '85 to '91 Swing |
|-----|------|------|------------------|
| FF  | 28.9 | 40.3 | -11.4            |
| FG  | 55.6 | 45.0 | 10.6             |
| LAB | —    | 14.7 | -14.7            |
| Ind | 11.9 | —    | 11.9             |

BANNON, James,
Newtown, Legan,
County Longford. (FG)
Farmer. 044-57575

BELTON, Louis J.,
Kenagh,
County Longford. (FG)
Dáil Deputy. 042-22245

FARRELL, Adrian,
Lanesboro,
County Longford. (FG)
Publican.

FARRELL, Paddy,
Carrowbeg, Newtowncashel,
County Longford. (FF)
Farmer. 043-25126

NOLAN, John,
Castlerea, Moydow,
County Longford. (NP)
Bus Operator. 043-22228

STEELE, Barney,
Moigh, Ballymahon,
County Longford. (FF)
T.V. Engineer. 044-57575

## DRUMLISH

|     | 1991 | 1985 | '85 to '91 Swing |
|-----|------|------|------------------|
| FF  | 47.3 | 52.1 | -4.8             |
| FG  | 29.0 | 30.5 | -1.5             |
| SF  | 23.7 | 17.4 | 6.3              |
| Ind | 0.0  |      | 0.0              |

BRADY, Gerry,
Creenagh,
Longford. (FG)
Teacher. 043-45135

LYNCH, Sean,
Cleenrath,
Aughnacliffe,
County Longford. (NP)
Farmer. 043-84146

McENTIRE, Luie,
Annagh, Moyne,
County Longford. (FF)
Farmer. (049) 35147

## GRANARD

|     | 1991 | 1985 | '85 to '91 Swing |
|-----|------|------|------------------|
| FF  | —    | 59.5 | —                |
| FG  | —    | 36.5 | —                |
| SF  | —    | 4.0  | —                |

FLOOD, Fintan,
Granardkille, Granard,
County Longford. (FF)
Publican. 043-86025

KILBRIDE-HARKIN, Maura,
Cartron, Granard,
County Longford. (FG)
Housewife. 043-86015

LYNCH, Brian,
Carrickduff, Dring,
County Longford. (FF)
Farmer. 043-86182

*No election took place as there were only three candidates for the three seats. All three outgoing Councillors were returned.*

## LONGFORD

|     | 1991 | 1985 | '85 to '91 Swing |
|-----|------|------|------------------|
| FF  | 29.3 | 47.2 | -17.9            |
| FG  | 30.9 | 24.1 | 6.8              |
| SF  | 0.0  | 2.6  | -2.6             |
| Ind | 39.8 | 26.1 | 13.7             |

FINNAN, Seamus,
Kilnasavogue,
Longford. (FG)
Farmer. 043-41178

KELLY, Philo,
1 New Street,
Longford. (FG)
Clerk.

KELLY, Peter,
Main Street,
Longford. (FF)
Publican. 043-45181

MURPHY, Peter,
Moneylagan,
Longford. (NP)
Farmer. 043-46816

NEVIN, Michael,
Demense,
Longford. (FF)
Builder. 043-46749

SEXTON, Mae,
46 Demense,
Longford. (NP)
Secretary. 043-41142

**Louis J. Belton (FG)\
Ballymahon**

**Peter Kelly (FF)
Longford**

# Independents make gains in Longford

Longford County Council was the only Council in the country in which there was a revision of areas on those which existed for the local elections in 1985. 2 of the 5 electoral areas in Longford were changed with Ballinalee, being reduced from 4 to 3 seats and the Longford area gaining a seat to total 6 seats. The condition of roads in Longford and the 'junkets issue' were central to the dissatisfaction with the main two political parties as both Fine Gael and Fianna Fail lost one seat each, with Independents gaining at their expense.

Interestingly enough, 2 of the Independents elected to Longford Council have Fianna Fail connections. Mae Sexton, the popular poll topper in Longford is a daughter of Fianna Fail UDC member Tommy Breadon, while John Nolan, who was elected in Ballymahon, only opted to run as an Independent after failing to gain a Fianna Fail nomination.

Longford's electoral areas were easily the least competitive in the country. Both the Ballinalee and Drumlish areas had only 4 candidates each for their respective 3 seats while there was no election at all in the Granard area. As there were only 3 candidates proposed in Granard, when nominations closed, the 3, all outgoing Councillors - Brian Lynch and Fintan Flood of Fianna Fail and Fine Gael's Maura Harkin - were returned without having to face the Granard electorate.

In 1985 the 4 seats in Ballinalee were shared 2 apiece between Fianna Fail and Fine Gael. With only 3 seats in 1991, it was fairly predictable that Fianna Fail's 2 outgoing Councillors would be returned, especially as both had been elected on the first count in 1985, with Fine Gael only gaining their seats 4 counts later. The main issues this time around were which of Fianna Fail's outgoing Councillors, Jimmy Coyle or Mickey Doherty, would top the poll and which of the other 2 candidates would take the Fine Gael seat.

As in 1985, both Coyle and Doherty were elected on the first count, with Coyle again heading the poll narrowly ahead of his running mate. Victor Kiernan and Sean McEoin fought it out for the Fine Gael seat, with Kiernan having the edge after the first count and taking the seat with the help of stronger transfers from Doherty's surplus. The fact that Kiernan and Doherty are business partners in Kiernan-Doherty Auctioneers explains the 3:1 breakdown of Doherty's transfers in favour of his business partner but political foe.

Fianna Fail lost a seat in Drumlish as voter reaction to the condition of roads in the area reduced their vote and allowed Republican Sinn Fein's Sean Lynch to regain the Council seat he lost in 1985. Fianna Fail's Claire Brady-Casey, who had been co-opted onto the Council to replace Sean Mulleady, lost out to Lynch for the last seat by 64 votes. In a reversal of the 1985 outcome in Drumlish, Fine Gael's sole candidate Gerry Brady topped the poll, with Luie McEntire of Fianna Fail having to settle for the second seat this time out. The decline in McEntire's first preference vote by 265 votes, deprived his running mate of the transfers she required to edge ahead of Lynch.

Fine Gael and Fianna Fail both made

"Hands up" — Fine Gael's James Bannon who received 1,060 votes in the Ballymahon area.

mistakes in the Ballymahon Electoral Area which cost them each the chance of adding to their seats won in 1985. There was hope in Fine Gael circles that they would take 4 seats in Ballymahon. The party did increase their vote by over 10% and had the fourth seat within their grasp but in the end poor vote management cost them the last seat in Ballymahon by 96 votes. Outgoing Councillor James Bannon topped the poll for Fine Gael but the surplus from his high first preference vote did not transfer sufficiently well to give them their fourth seat. Bannon was returned along with party colleagues Adrian Farrell and Longford Deputy Louis Belton, both outgoing Councillors.

> "Mickey Doherty's transfers went in favour of his business partner but political foe."

Fianna Fail's Barney Steele and Paddy Farrell were also successfully returned in Ballymahon. They made the mistake of not running a candidate in the Lanesboro Area, thereby giving Aidan Farrell of Fine Gael a free run and with a more even spread of the Fine Gael vote they would have taken 4 seats. Fianna Fail could also be faulted for not putting coach operator John Nolan on their ticket. Having failed to gain a Fianna Fail nomination, Nolan ran as an Independent and he took the last seat in Ballymahon at the expense of Independent Councillor Michael Brennan, one of the more colourful members of the outgoing Council.

The big talking point in the Longford Electoral Area was the surprise poll topping performance of Independent candidate Mae Sexton. Mae Sexton, was well known for her letters to the local newspapers on issues such as 'political junkets'. Fine Gael held their 2 seats but outgoing Councillor Peter Clarke lost out to running mate Philo Kelly. A UDC member for 24 years, Kelly joins party colleague Seamus Finnan on the Council. An outgoing Councillor Finnan took the last seat without reaching the quota.

Fianna Fail's Peter Kelly was returned on the first count, as in 1985, although he was deprived of poll topping position on this occasion by Mae Sexton. There was a change in the Fianna Fail lineup with outgoing Councillor Noel McGeeney losing his seat to party colleague Michael Nevin who ran as an Independent in 1985 losing out, by 7 votes, to McGeeney.

# BALLINALEE ELECTORAL AREA

TOTAL ELECTORATE 3,294. VALID POLL 2,360. NO. OF MEMBERS 3. QUOTA 591.

| Names of Candidates | First Count Votes | Second Count Transfer of Coyle's surplus | Result | Third Count Transfer of Doherty's surplus | Result |
|---|---|---|---|---|---|
| COYLE, Jimmy (F.F.) | 719 | -128 | 591 | — | 591 |
| DOHERTY, Mickey (F.F.) | 709 | — | 709 | -118 | 591 |
| KIERNAN, Victor (F.G.) | 508 | +59 | 567 | +88 | 655 |
| MacEOIN, Sean (F.G.) | 424 | +69 | 493 | +30 | 523 |
| Non-transferable papers not effective | — | — | — | — | — |
| TOTAL: | 2,360 | — | 2,360 | — | 2,360 |

Elected: Coyle, Jimmy (F.F.); Doherty, Mickey (F.F.); Kiernan, Victor (F.G.)

# BALLYMAHON ELECTORAL AREA

TOTAL ELECTORATE 6,361. VALID POLL 4,746. NO. OF MEMBERS 6. QUOTA 679

| Names of Candidates | First Count Votes | Second Count Transfer of Bannon's surplus | Result | Third Count Transfer of Belton's surplus | Result | Fourth Count Transfer of Steele's surplus | Result | Fifth Count Transfer of Gilmore's votes | Result | Sixth Count Transfer of Brennan's votes | Result | Seventh Count Transfer of Carthy's votes | Result |
|---|---|---|---|---|---|---|---|---|---|---|---|---|---|
| BANNON, James (F.G.) | 1,060 | -381 | 679 | — | 679 | — | 679 | — | 679 | — | 679 | — | 679 |
| BELTON, Louis J. (F.G.) | 660 | +180 | 840 | -161 | 679 | — | 679 | — | 679 | — | 679 | — | 679 |
| BRENNAN, Michael (Non-Party) | 241 | +29 | 270 | +27 | 297 | +12 | 309 | +32 | 341 | -341 | — | — | — |
| CARTHY, Tony (F.F.) | 290 | +68 | 358 | +14 | 372 | +21 | 393 | +2 | 395 | +31 | 426 | -426 | — |
| FARRELL, Adrian (F.G.) | 612 | +11 | 623 | +45 | 668 | +1 | 669 | +24 | 693 | — | 693 | — | 693 |
| FARRELL, Paddy (F.F.) | 340 | +6 | 346 | +3 | 349 | +16 | 365 | +27 | 392 | +56 | 448 | +202 | 650 |
| FARRELL, Sean (F.G.) | 306 | +41 | 347 | +44 | 391 | +4 | 395 | +58 | 453 | +56 | 509 | +19 | 528 |
| GILMORE, Declan (P.D.) | 173 | +5 | 178 | +3 | 181 | — | 181 | -181 | — | — | — | — | — |
| NOLAN, John | 323 | +41 | 364 | +19 | 383 | +8 | 391 | +23 | 414 | +100 | 514 | +110 | 624 |
| STEELE, Barney (F.F.) | 741 | — | 741 | — | 741 | -62 | 679 | — | 679 | — | 679 | — | 679 |
| Non-transferable papers not effective | — | — | — | +6 | 6 | — | 6 | +15 | 21 | +98 | 119 | +95 | 214 |
| TOTAL: | 4,746 | — | 4,746 | — | 4,746 | — | 4,746 | — | 4,746 | — | 4,746 | — | 4,746 |

Elected: Bannon, James (F.G.); Steele, Barney (F.F.); Belton, Louis J. (F.G.); Farrell, Adrian (F.G.); Farrell, Paddy (F.F.); Nolan, John.

# DRUMLISH ELECTORAL AREA

TOTAL ELECTORATE 3,072. VALID POLL 2,260. NO. OF MEMBERS 3.

| Names of Candidates | First Count Votes | Second Count Transfer of G. Brady's surplus **Result** |
|---|---|---|
| BRADY, Gerry (F.G.) | 656 | -90  **566** |
| BRADY-CASEY, Claire (F.F.) | 480 | +41  **521** |
| LYNCH, Sean | 536 | +49  **585** |
| McENTIRE, Luie, (F.F.) | 588 | —  **588** |
| Non-transferable papers not effective | — | —  **—** |
| TOTAL: | **2,260** | —  **2,260** |

QUOTA 566

# GRANARD ELECTORAL AREA

TOTAL ELECTORATE  3,017
NO. OF MEMBERS  3

The number of candidates nominated for election was equal to the number of members to be elected for the Area. The candidates nominated were, accordingly, declared elected without taking a poll.

Names of candidates elected:

Flood, Fintan (F.F.);
Kilbride - Harkin, Maura (F.G.);
Lynch, Brian (F.F.).

# LONGFORD ELECTORAL AREA

TOTAL ELECTORATE 6,475. VALID POLL 4,263. NO. OF MEMBERS 6. QUOTA 610

| Names of Candidates | First Count Votes | Second Count Transfer of Sexton's surplus **Result** | Third Count Transfer of Peter Kelly's surplus **Result** | Fourth Count Transfer of Kane's votes **Result** | Fifth Count Transfer of Warnock's votes **Result** | Sixth Count Transfer of McGeeney's votes **Result** | Seventh Count Transfer of Clarke's votes **Result** |
|---|---|---|---|---|---|---|---|
| CLARKE, Peter (F.G.) | 278 | +12  **290** | +7  **297** | +28  **325** | +29  **354** | +50  **404** | -404  **—** |
| FINNAN, Seamus (F.G.) | 330 | +7  **337** | +4  **341** | +42  **383** | +15  **398** | +22  **420** | +168  **588** |
| KANE, James (F.G.) | 178 | +3  **181** | +2  **183** | -183  **—** | —  **—** | —  **—** | —  **—** |
| KELLY, Peter (F.F.) | 690 | —  **690** | -80  **610** | —  **610** | —  **610** | —  **610** | —  **610** |
| KELLY, Philo (F.G.) | 532 | +39  **571** | +9  **580** | +30  **610** | —  **610** | —  **610** | —  **610** |
| McDERMOTT, Brendan (NP) | 274 | +21  **295** | +6  **301** | +13  **314** | +55  **369** | +43  **412** | +61  **473** |
| McGEENEY, Noel (F.F.) | 261 | +7  **268** | +26  **294** | +9  **303** | +29  **332** | -332  **—** | —  **—** |
| MURPHY, Peter (Non-Party) | 426 | +18  **444** | +7  **451** | +12  **463** | +31  **494** | +36  **530** | +37  **567** |
| NEVIN, Michael (F.F.) | 299 | +11  **310** | +16  **326** | +24  **350** | +63  **413** | +125  **538** | +48  **586** |
| SEXTON, Mae (Non-Party) | 740 | -130  **610** | —  **610** | —  **610** | —  **610** | —  **610** | —  **610** |
| WARNOCK, Christy (Non-Party) | 255 | +12  **267** | +3  **270** | +10  **280** | -280  **—** | —  **—** | —  **—** |
| Non-transferable papers not effective | — | —  **—** | —  **—** | +15  **15** | +58  **73** | +56  **129** | +90  **219** |
| TOTAL: | **4,263** | —  **4,263** | —  **4,263** | —  **4,263** | —  **4,263** | —  **4,263** | —  **4,263** |

Elected: Sexton, Mae (Non-Party); Kelly, Peter (F.F.); Kelly, Philo (F.G.); Finnan, Seamus (F.G.); Nevin, Michael (F.F.); Murphy, Peter (Non-party)

# LOUTH COUNTY COUNCIL

## LOUTH COUNTY COUNCIL RESULTS

| Party | 1991 % of votes | 1991 Seats obtained | 1985 % of votes | 1985 Seats obtained |
|---|---|---|---|---|
| Fianna Fail | 37.0 | 12 | 43.4 | 12 |
| Fine Gael | 21.2 | 6 | 27.9 | 8 |
| Labour | 12.0 | 2 | 8.6 | 2 |
| Progressive Dem. | 4.6 | 2 | — | — |
| Workers Party | 0.7 | — | 1.0 | — |
| Other | 24.5 | 4 | 19.1 | 4 |
| TOTAL SEATS | | 26 | | 26 |

## LOUTH

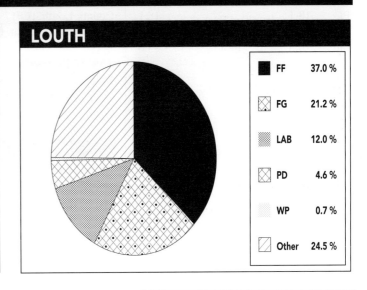

| | |
|---|---|
| ■ FF | 37.0 % |
| FG | 21.2 % |
| LAB | 12.0 % |
| PD | 4.6 % |
| WP | 0.7 % |
| Other | 24.5 % |

**County Offices, Dundalk**
**Telephone: (042) 35457**
**Fax: (042) 34549**
**Total population: 91,698**
**Area sq miles: 317.82**
**Rateable valuation: £297,999.00**
**Rate: £20.80**

*County Manager:* John Quinlivan
*County Secretary:* B. P. Gormley
*Finance Officer:* A. Davis
*County Engineer:* W. S. Bruen
*Administrative Officers:*
*Housing and Environment:* Vacant
*Planning and Development:* Vacant
*Senior Staff Officers:*
*Accounts:* B. Conlon
*Motor Tax:* J. Burns
*County Librarian:* Ann Ward
*County Coroner:* Dr S. Keenan
*Chief Fire Officer:* Eamon P. McGuire
*Civil Defence Officer:* P. Donnelly
*Veterinary Inspector:* Vacant
*Senior Executive Engineers:*
*Road Design:* P. Fallon
*Sanitary Services:* K. Spellman
*Senior Executive Planner:* P. N. Grimes
*Sanitary Services:* D. O'Neill
*Senior Executive Architect:* J. Gogarty
*Executive Planner:* M. Cummings
*Fire Prevention:* E. Curran
*Environmental Health Officers:* Aidan McDonnell,
Sean O'Connor

**John Quinlivan**

John Quinlivan was born in Limerick and educated at the C.B.S. in Limerick, as well as the Institute of Public Administration. He is married to Mary O'Loughlin and they have one son and one daughter.

John Quinlivan has held the position of Town Clerk in Cashel, Athy, Castlebar, Carlow and Dundalk. In 1979 he moved to Laois County Council where he was appointed County Secretary. In 1983 he was appointed Assistant County Manager in Wexford and five years later, in 1988, he became Louth County Manager. He is responsible for a staff of 750 and an annual budget in the region of £44 million.

John Quinlivan is a fan of most sports and enjoys long walks and music.

## ARDEE

|     | 1991 | 1985 | '85 to '91 Swing |
|-----|------|------|------------------|
| FF  | 40.3 | 42.1 | -1.8 |
| FG  | 22.5 | 28.4 | -5.9 |
| LAB | 8.3  | 7.7  | 0.6  |
| PD  | 18.1 | —    | 18.1 |
| SF  | —    | 7.4  | -7.4 |
| Ind | 10.8 | 14.4 | -3.6 |

CONLON, Hugh D.,
Main Street, Dunleer,
County Louth. (NP)
Decorator. 041-51537

MARKEY, Bernard,
Cappocksgreen, Ardee,
County Louth. (FG)
Accountant. 041-53510

McCABE, Nicholas,
Crinstown, Ardee,
County Louth. (FF)
Farmer. 041-53365

McCONVILLE, John,
Grangebellew, Drogheda,
County Louth. (FF)
Farmer. 041-51368

McCOY, Finnan,
Castle Street, Ardee,
County Louth. (PD)
Publican. 041-53151

## CARLINGFORD

|     | 1991 | 1985 | '85 to '91 Swing |
|-----|------|------|------------------|
| FF  | 42.7 | 33.3 | 9.4  |
| FG  | 33.6 | 31.1 | 2.5  |
| LAB | —    | 1.4  | -1.4 |
| PD  | 5.5  | —    | 5.5  |
| SF  | 12.4 | 17.9 | -5.5 |
| Ind | 5.9  | 16.3 | -10.4 |

BRENNAN, Terry,
Castlehill, Carlingford,
County Louth. (FG)
Engineering Officer. 042-73348

O'DONNELL, Miceal,
Mountpleasant, Dundalk,
County Louth. (FF)
Hardware Merchant. 042-71118

SAVAGE, Peter,
Millgrange, Greenore,
County Louth. (FF)
Company Director. 042-73260

## DROGHEDA (RURAL)

|     | 1991 | 1985 | '85 to '91 Swing |
|-----|------|------|------------------|
| FF  | 40.1 | 50.6 | -10.5 |
| FG  | 20.5 | 26.0 | -5.5  |
| LAB | 29.2 | 23.4 | 5.8   |
| Ind | 10.2 | —    | 10.2  |

BELL, Michael,
122 Newfield Park, Drogheda,
County Louth. (Lab)
Dail Deputy. 041-38573

GODFREY, Frank,
129 Ascal-a-hAon,
Yellowbatter, Drogheda,
County Louth. (FF)
Public Representative. 041-33892

MULROY, Jimmy,
1 Matson Lodge, Ballymakenny Road,
Drogheda,
County Louth. (FF)
Company Director. 041-36755

TULLY, Oliver,
Baltray, Drogheda,
County Louth. (FG)
Teacher. 041-22712

## DROGHEDA (URBAN)

|     | 1991 | 1985 | '85 to '91 Swing |
|-----|------|------|------------------|
| FF  | 32.4 | 49.5 | -17.1 |
| FG  | 13.9 | 20.5 | -6.6  |
| LAB | 28.6 | 16.5 | 12.1  |
| WP  | —    | 1.8  | -1.8  |
| PD  | 2.0  | —    | 2.0   |
| SF  | 6.7  | 7.0  | -0.3  |
| Ind | 16.3 | 4.7  | 11.6  |

BELL, Betty,
122 Newfield Park, Drogheda,
County Louth. (Lab)
Housewife. 041-38573

MURPHY, Tommy,
53 Pearse Park, Drogheda,
County Louth. (FF)
Social Worker. 041-36080

O'BRIEN, Con,
198 Marian Park, Drogheda,
County Louth. (FF)
Retired

O'DOWD, Fergus,
24 St. Mary's Villas, Drogheda,
County Louth. (FG)
Teacher. 041-33392

## DUNDALK (RURAL)

|     | 1991 | 1985 | '85 to '91 Swing |
|-----|------|------|------------------|
| FF  | 33.2 | 44.6 | -11.4 |
| FG  | 23.2 | 36.7 | -13.5 |
| LAB | 5.8  | 4.4  | 1.4   |
| WP  | —    | 2.0  | -2.0  |
| PD  | 9.0  | —    | 9.0   |
| SF  | 24.2 | 12.3 | 11.9  |
| Ind | 4.6  | —    | 4.6   |

AHERN, Dermot,
The Crescent, Blackrock,
County Louth. (FF)*

Con O'Brien (FF)
Drogheda Urban

Tommy Murphy (FF)
Drogheda Urban

Oliver Tully (FG)
Drogheda Rural

Dermot Ahern (FF)
Dundalk Rural

BREATHNACH, Declan,
Knockbridge, Dundalk,
County Louth. (FF)
Teacher.

COUSINS, Jim,
140 Ard Easmuinn, Dundalk,
County Louth. (PD)
Community Worker. 042-34724

LENNON, Jim,
Ballyroan, Louth, Dundalk,
County Dublin. (FG)
Farmer.

REILLY, Tommy,
Milltowngrange, Dromiskin,
Dundalk,
County Louth. (FF)
Farmer.

*Resigned when appointed Minister for
State, Nov. 1991.
Replaced by
LENNON, Noel,
Shore Road,
Dundalk,
County Louth. (FF)

### DUNDALK (URBAN)

|    | 1991 | 1985 | '85 to '91 Swing |
|----|------|------|------|
| FF | 23.3 | 40.5 | -17.2 |
| FG | 15.7 | 23.3 | -7.6 |
| LAB | 4.4 | 1.9 | 2.5 |
| WP | 3.5 | 1.8 | 1.7 |
| SF | 12.6 | 16.1 | -3.5 |
| Ind | 40.4 | 16.4 | 24.0 |

BELLEW, Tom,
Long Avenue, Dundalk,
County Louth. (NP)
Public Representative. 042-32568
BELLEW, Martin,
39 Meadow Grove, Dundalk,
County Louth. (NP)
Carpenter. 042-31549

KEELAN, Seamus,
Newry Road, Dundalk,
County Louth. (FF)
Accountant. 042-32093
KENNA, Sean,
200 Cedarwood Park, Dundalk,
County Louth. (SF)
Painter.

McGAHON, Conor,
4 Faughart Terrace, Dundalk,
County Louth. (FG)
Solicitor. 042-35920

"Ringing Bells" – Betty Bell celebrates with husband Michael. Both were returned for Labour to Louth County Council.

A celebration kiss for Jimmy Mulroy (FF) from his wife, Chris, at the count in Drogheda.

Crutches prove no handicap to the victorious Frank Godfrey in Louth.

# The Bells made news in Louth

While the Fianna Fail vote in Louth County Council may have dropped by over 6%, they successfully retained their 12 seats on the 26 member Council. One of the big talking points in the election in Louth was the poll-topping performances of Labour Deputy Michael Bell and his wife Betty Bell. The Bells made history as the first husband and wife team on Louth County Council. The Progressive Democrats can also be pleased with their performance in Louth, taking two seats at the expense of Fine Gael.

One of these PD gains was made in the Ardee Electoral area where Finnan McCoy edged out Fine Gael's outgoing Councillor Thomas McGrory, on the final count, by 42 votes. McGrory, himself, had taken the final seat in 1985 with only 8 votes to spare but on this occassion he was beaten by the stronger cross-party transfers received by the PD man. Interestingly enough, Fine Gael's vote in Ardee held up better than Fianna Fail's, but it was Fine Gael who lost a seat on 1985. The sole Fine Gael success, outgoing Councillor Bernard Markey, was safely returned despite a decline in his vote. Fianna Fail's Nicholas McCabe topped the poll even though his vote was also lower than in 1985. He was joined on the Council by fellow outgoing Councillor and party colleague, John McConville. Independent Hugh Conlon was also successfully returned in Ardee.

In 1985 Miceal O'Donnell was elected as an Independent in the Carlingford Electoral Area, with Fianna Fail and Fine Gael each taking one of the remaining two seats. O'Donnell subsequently joined Fianna Fail, and it was his presence on the FF ticket which boosted their vote in Carlingford by over 9%. O'Donnell consolidated his position on 1985, being returned on the first count and topping the poll. His running mate, outgoing Councillor Peter Savage took the third seat despite a drop in his own first preference vote.

Sinn Fein had been within 15 votes of the third seat in this area in 1985 but this time out ,Savage comfortably took the final seat from Arther Morgan of Sinn Fein. Fine Gael's outgoing Councillor Terence Brennan increased his share of the vote on 1985, but a second seat was never a real option for Fine Gael in Carlingford.

Labour TD Michael Bell was returned comfortably in the Drogheda Rural Area with a first preference vote of 1,309 on a quota of 1,014 votes. For the Louth deputy this was an increase on his 1985 total. Bell was followed by outgoing Fianna Fail Councillor, Jimmy Mulroy, who actually increased his own first preference vote despite the 10.5% decline in his party's vote in Drogheda Rural.

Outgoing Councillor Frank Godfrey had been elected to the Drogheda Urban Area in 1985 but was a candidate in the Rural electoral area on this occassion. Outgoing Drogheda Rural Councillor, Tommy Murphy, stood in the Urban area in place of his Fianna Fail colleague. Despite the rumours of a Fianna Fail rift over the move of Godfrey, they managed to hold the two seats won in 1985. Former Independent Councillor Godfrey polled poorly, but with strong transfers coming his way, he held off the challenge of fellow Fianna Fail candidate Michael Coyle by 67 votes. Fine Gael's vote declined by over 5.5% in Drogheda Rural but newcomer Oliver Tully took the seat previously held by retiring Councillor Tommy Donegan.

While Fianna Fail's Frank Godfrey was struggling in Drogheda Rural, his replace-ment in the Urban Drogheda Area, Tommy Murphy, was re-elected without undue difficulty. Murphy took the second seat and was returned along with fellow Fianna Fail candidate Con O'Brien who had been co-opted onto the council in the place of Aloysuis Farrell.

History was made with the election of Labour's Betty Bell to the Council. Along with her husband Deputy Micahel Bell not only are they the first husband and wife team on the Louth County Council, they are also interestingly the only two Labour Members sitting on the Council. Betty Bell, like her husband, was a poll topper, receiving 989 first preference votes in the Drogheda Urban Area. The final seat in this area was fought for until the thirteenth count with only 16 votes separating outgoing Fine Gael Councillor Fergus O'Brien from Independent candidate Tommy Boyle.

The second Progressive Democrat seat on Louth County Council was won in the Dundalk Rural Electoral Area. UDC member Jim Cousins, a former Fianna Fail member polled well and took the third seat in this area. Fianna Fail's Dermot Ahern TD received 1,550 votes in topping the poll, and was the first candidate returned in Dundalk Rural.

Ahern was joined by party colleagues Declan Breathnach and Tommy Reilly, both newcomers to Louth County Council. Reilly had to fight hard to gain a seat and only did so by edging out outgoing Councillor John MacGuinness of Fine Gael by 84 votes. Fine Gael's other candidate Jim Lennon who had been co-opted onto the Council, following the death of this brother Joe, was returned without reaching the quota.

The Fianna Fail vote declined by a huge 17% in the Dundalk Urban Area and the party lost one of the two seats that they had gained in 1985. Outgoing Councillor Seamus Keelan took the third seat, but with his three running mates polling poorly, one seat was all Fianna Fail could be content with.

Besides voter disquiet over unemployment and the future status of Dundalk Hospital, the Fianna Fail vote was heavily hit by the decision of former TD Tom Bellow, to run as an Independent candidate. Bellow, as in 1985, topped the poll on this occassion with 1,295 votes. So far was he ahead of the other candidates that it took an additional 10 counts to fill the next seat. The second seat was in fact taken for Fine Gael by Dundalk solicitor, Conor McGahon, a son of Louth Deputy Brendan McGahon. Although McGahon Junior received just half of the votes his father got in 1985. Sinn Fein held the seat won by Fran Browne in 1985. Their candidate Sean Kenna polled well, but suffered from lack of good transfers and was narrowly defeated by 21 votes by Independent Neil McCann, an outgoing Councillor. Kenna was himself five votes behind Independent Martin Bellew, no relation of the other Independent in Dundalk Urban namesake Tom Bellew. Martin Bellew was successful in regaining the seat he lost in 1985.

**John Little and Thomas Maguire celebrate the win of Oliver Tully (FG) in the local elections in Louth.**

# ARDEE ELECTORAL AREA

TOTAL ELECTORATE 11,626. VALID POLL 6,593. NO. OF MEMBERS 5. QUOTA 1,099

| Names of Candidates | First Count Votes | Second Count Transfer of Doherty's & Halpenny's votes | Results | Third Count Transfer of McGahon's votes | Results | Fourth Count Transfer of McShane's votes | Results | Fifth Count Transfer of Keenan's votes | Restults | Sixth Count Transfer of Butterly's votes | Results | Seventh Count Transfer of Taaffe's votes | Restults | Eighth Count Transfer of McCabe's surplus | Restults |
|---|---|---|---|---|---|---|---|---|---|---|---|---|---|---|---|
| BUTTERLY, Terry (Lab.) | 332 | +67 | 399 | +37 | 436 | +12 | 448 | +7 | 455 | -455 | — | — | — | — | — |
| CONLON, Hugh D. (Non-Party) | 692 | +15 | 707 | +64 | 771 | +81 | 852 | +8 | 860 | +98 | 958 | +137 | 1,095 | +2 | 1,097 |
| DOHERTY, Josephine (Non-Party) | 23 | -23 | — | — | — | — | — | — | — | — | — | — | — | — | — |
| HALPENNY, Gerry (Lab.) | 213 | -213 | — | — | — | — | — | — | — | — | — | — | — | — | — |
| KEENAN, Colm (F.F.) | 380 | +12 | 392 | +18 | 410 | +23 | 433 | -433 | — | — | — | — | — | — | — |
| MARKEY, Bernard (F.G.) | 812 | +28 | 840 | +13 | 853 | +9 | 862 | +39 | 901 | +27 | 928 | +162 | 1,090 | +5 | 1,095 |
| McCABE, Nicholas (F.F.) | 781 | +15 | 796 | +16 | 812 | +112 | 924 | +236 | 1,160 | — | 1,160 | — | 1,160 | -61 | 1,099 |
| McCONVILLE, John (F.F.) | 820 | +1 | 821 | +6 | 827 | +78 | 905 | +33 | 938 | +62 | 1,000 | +29 | 1,029 | +43 | 1,072 |
| McCOY, Finnan (P.D.) | 613 | +42 | 655 | +28 | 683 | +6 | 689 | +66 | 755 | +30 | 785 | +105 | 890 | +11 | 901 |
| McGAHON, Jackie (S.F.) | 333 | +13 | 346 | -346 | — | — | — | — | — | — | — | — | — | — | — |
| McGRORY, Thomas (F.G.) | 672 | +2 | 674 | +23 | 697 | +28 | 725 | +2 | 727 | +71 | 798 | +61 | 859 | — | 859 |
| McSHANE, Jimmy (F.F.) | 344 | +3 | 347 | +21 | 368 | -368 | — | — | — | — | — | — | — | — | — |
| TAAFFE, Dessie (Non-Party) | 578 | +31 | 609 | +46 | 655 | +5 | 660 | +16 | 676 | +32 | 708 | -708 | — | — | — |
| Non-transferable papers not effective | — | +7 | 7 | +74 | 81 | +14 | 95 | +26 | 121 | +135 | 256 | +214 | 470 | — | 470 |
| TOTAL: | 6,593 | — | 6,593 | — | 6,593 | — | 6,593 | — | 6,593 | — | 6,593 | — | 6,593 | — | 6,593 |

Elected: McCabe, Nicholas (F.F.); Conlon, Hugh D. (Non-Party); Markey, Bernard (F.G.); McConville, John (F.F.); McCoy, Finnan (P.D.)

# CARLINGFORD ELECTORAL AREA

TOTAL ELECTORATE 7,253. VALID POLL 4,712. NO. OF MEMBERS 3. QUOTA 1,179

| Names of Candidates | First Count Votes | Second Count Transfer of O'Donnell's surplus | Results | Third Count Transfer of Johnston's votes | Results | Fourth Count Transfer of Mulligan's votes | Results | Fifth Count Transfer of Elmore's votes | Results | Sixth Count Transfer of Brennan's surplus | Results |
|---|---|---|---|---|---|---|---|---|---|---|---|
| BRENNAN, Terry (F.G.) | 989 | +5 | 994 | +75 | 1,069 | +70 | 1,139 | +402 | 1,541 | -362 | 1,179 |
| ELMORE, Tommy (F.G.) | 592 | +3 | 595 | +43 | 638 | +42 | 680 | -680 | — | — | — |
| JOHNSTON, Don (P.D.) | 258 | +3 | 261 | -261 | — | — | — | — | — | — | — |
| MORGAN, Arthur (S.F.) | 582 | +5 | 587 | +29 | 616 | +91 | 707 | +96 | 803 | +76 | 879 |
| MULLIGAN, Peter (Non-Party) | 279 | +2 | 281 | +32 | 313 | -313 | — | — | — | — | — |
| O'DONNELL, Miceal (F.F.) | 1,226 | -47 | 1,179 | — | 1,179 | — | 1,179 | — | 1,179 | — | 1,179 |
| SAVAGE, Peter (F.F.) | 786 | +29 | 815 | +63 | 878 | +53 | 931 | +102 | 1,033 | +145 | 1,178 |
| Non-transferable papers not effective | — | — | — | +19 | 19 | +57 | 76 | +80 | 156 | +141 | 297 |
| TOTAL: | 4,712 | — | 4,712 | — | 4,712 | — | 4,712 | — | 4,712 | — | 4,712 |

Elected: O'Donnell, Miceal (F.F.); Brennan, Terry (F.G.); Savage, Peter (F.F.)

# DROGHEDA (RURAL) ELECTORAL AREA

TOTAL ELECTORATE 9,865. VALID POLL 5,065. NO. OF MEMBERS 4. QUOTA 1,014

| Names of Candidates | First Count Votes | Second Count Transfer of Bell's surplus Results | Third Count Transfer of O'hEochaidh's votes Results | Fourth Count Transfer of Mulroy's surplus Results | Fifth Count Transfer of Wood's votes Results | Sixth Count Transfer of Burke's votes Results | Seventh Count Transfer of Taaffe's votes Results | Eighth Count Transfer of Carroll-Holdcroft's votes Results | Ninth Count Transfer of Carr's votes Results |
|---|---|---|---|---|---|---|---|---|---|
| BELL, Michael (Lab.) | 1,309 | -295 1,014 | — 1,014 | — 1,014 | — 1,014 | — 1,014 | — 1,014 | — 1,014 | — 1,014 |
| BURKE, Pat (Lab.) | 169 | +132 301 | +17 318 | +3 321 | +7 328 | -328 — | — — | — — | — — |
| CARR, Patrick J (F.G.) | 306 | +24 330 | +11 341 | +3 344 | +99 443 | +57 500 | +15 515 | +62 577 | -577 — |
| CARROLL-HOLDCROFT, June (Non-Party) | 272 | +13 285 | +43 328 | +4 332 | +12 344 | +49 393 | +31 424 | -424 — | — — |
| COYLE, Michael (F.F.) | 397 | +14 411 | +31 442 | +13 455 | +11 466 | +31 497 | +118 615 | +39 654 | +61 715 |
| GODFREY, Frank (F.F.) | 358 | +29 387 | +24 411 | +12 423 | +14 437 | +67 504 | +117 621 | +93 714 | +68 782 |
| MULROY, Jimmy (F.F.) | 958 | +45 1,003 | +53 1,056 | -42 1,014 | — 1,014 | — 1,014 | — 1,014 | — 1,014 | — 1,014 |
| O'hEOCHAIDH, Tomas | 245 | +9 254 | -254 — | — — | — — | — — | — — | — — | — — |
| TAAFFE, Eamonn (F.F.) | 317 | +4 321 | +20 341 | +3 344 | +16 360 | +4 364 | -364 — | — — | — — |
| TULLY, Oliver (F.G.) | 443 | +16 459 | +21 (480 | +3 483 | +135 618 | +14 632 | +20 652 | +56 708 | +308 1,016 |
| WOODS, Dan (F.G.) | 291 | +9 300 | +11 311 | +1 312 | -312 — | — — | — — | — — | — — |
| Non-transferable papers not effective | — | — — | +23 23 | — 23 | +18 41 | +106 147 | +63 210 | +174 384 | +140 524 |
| TOTAL: | 5,065 | — 5,065 | — 5,065 | — 5,065 | — 5,065 | — 5,065 | — 5,065 | — 5,065 | — 5,065 |

Elected: Bell, Michael (Lab.); Mulroy, Jimmy (F.F.); Tully, Oliver (F.G.); Godfrey, Frank (F.F.)

# DROGHEDA (URBAN ) ELECTORAL AREA

TOTAL ELECTORATE 10,615. VALID POLL 5,578. NO. OF MEMBERS 4. QUOTA 1,116

| Names of Candidates | First Count Votes | Second Count Transfer of Reilly's votes Result | Third Count Transfer of Sheils' votes Result | Fourth Count Transfer of Coyle's votes Result | Fifth Count Transfer of MacRaghnaill's votes Result | Sixth Count Transfer of Nolan's votes Result | Seventh Count Transfer of Brannigan's votes Result | Eighth Count Transfer of E. Byrne's votes Result | Ninth Count Transfer of McShane's votes Result | Tenth Count Transfer of Collins' votes Result | Eleventh Count Transfer of Kirwan's votes Result | Twelfth Count Transfer of Murphy's surplus Result | Thirteenth Count Transfer of Bell's surplus Result |
|---|---|---|---|---|---|---|---|---|---|---|---|---|---|
| BELL, Betty (Lab.) | 989 | +5 994 | +31 1,025 | +15 1,040 | +31 1,071 | +9 1,080 | +32 1,112 | +38 1,150 | — 1,150 | — 1,150 | — 1,150 | — 1,150 | -34 1,116 |
| BRANNIGAN, Finian | 242 | +2 244 | +3 247 | +8 255 | +10 265 | +5 270 | -270 — | — — | — — | — — | — — | — — | — — |
| BYRNE, Eugene (F.G.) | 317 | +2 319 | +5 324 | +23 347 | +5 352 | +2 354 | +8 362 | -362 — | — — | — — | — — | — — | — — |
| BYRNE, Tommy (Non-Party) | 456 | +5 461 | +9 470 | +18 488 | +18 506 | +10 516 | +47 563 | +88 651 | +56 707 | +46 753 | +111 864 | +22 886 | +11 897 |
| COLLINS, Sean (F.F.) | 422 | +3 425 | +5 430 | +3 433 | +9 442 | +47 489 | +28 517 | +13 530 | +39 569 | -569 — | — — | — — | — — |
| COYLE, Rosemary (P.D.) | 113 | +1 114 | +5 119 | -119 — | — — | — — | — — | — — | — — | — — | — — | — — | — — |
| KIRWAN, Patsy (Lab.) | 510 | +6 516 | +26 542 | +11 553 | +8 561 | +9 570 | +18 588 | +17 605 | +37 642 | +50 692 | -692 — | — — | — — |
| MacRAGHNAILL, Donnchadha (Non-Party) | 149 | +7 156 | +2 158 | +6 164 | -164 — | — — | — — | — — | — — | — — | — — | — — | — — |
| McSHANE, Hugh (S.F.) | 372 | +10 382 | +2 384 | +3 387 | +28 415 | +3 418 | +16 434 | +8 442 | -442 — | — — | — — | — — | — — |
| MURPHY, Tommy (F.F.) | 689 | +9 698 | +4 702 | +4 706 | +15 721 | +48 769 | +26 795 | +24 819 | +60 879 | +201 1,080 | +108 1,188 | -72 1,116 | — 1,116 |
| NOLAN, Matt (F.F.) | 251 | +2 253 | +2 (255( | +1 256 | +1 257 | -257 — | — — | — — | — — | — — | — — | — — | — — |
| O'BRIEN, Con (F.F.) | 448 | — 448 | +2 450 | +3 453 | +4 457 | +104 561 | +30 591 | +13 604 | +41 645 | +128 773 | +120 893 | +40 933 | +3 936 |
| O'DOWD, Fergus (F.G.) | 461 | +6 467 | +2 469 | +15 484 | +21 505 | +15 520 | +43 563 | +139 702 | +49 751 | +66 817 | +77 894 | +9 903 | +10 913 |
| REILLY, John (Non-Party) | 62 | -62 — | — — | — — | — — | — — | — — | — — | — — | — — | — — | — — | — — |
| SHEILS, Joe (Lab.) | 97 | +2 99 | -99 — | — — | — — | — — | — — | — — | — — | — — | — — | — — | — — |
| Non-transferable papers not effective | — | +2 2 | +1 3 | +9 12 | +14 26 | +5 31 | +22 53 | +22 75 | +160 235 | +78 313 | +276 589 | +1 590 | +10 600 |
| TOTAL: | 5,578 | — 5,578 | — 5,578 | — 5,578 | — 5,578 | — (5,578 | — 5,578 | — 5,578 | — 5,578 | — 5,578 | — 5,578 | — 5,578 |

Elected: Bell, Betty (Lab.); Murphy, Tommy (F.F.); O'Brien, Con (F.F.); O'Dowd, Fergus (F.G.)

# DUNDALK (RURAL) ELECTORAL AREA

TOTAL ELECTORATE 13,563. VALID POLL 7,300. NO. OF MEMBERS 5. QUOTA 1,217

| Names of Candidates | First Count Votes | Second Count Transfer of Ahern's surplus (Result) | Third Count Transfer of Kenny's & Doherty's votes (Result) | Fourth Count Transfer of Taaffe's votes (Result) | Fifth Count Transfer of Burns' votes (Result) | Sixth Count Transfer of Carney's votes (Result) | Seventh Count Transfer of McEvoy's votes (Result) | Eighth Count Transfer of Breathnach's surplus (Result) | Ninth Count Transfer of Duffy's votes (Result) |
|---|---|---|---|---|---|---|---|---|---|
| AHERN, Dermot (F.F.) | 1,550 | -333 1,217 | — 1,217 | — 1,217 | — 1,217 | — 1,217 | — 1,217 | — 1,217 | — 1,217 |
| BREATHNACH, Declan (F.F.) | 875 | +107 982 | +41 1,023 | +40 1,063 | +32 1,095 | +57 1,152 | +203 1,355 | -138 1,217 | — 1,217 |
| BURNS, Stephen (F.G.) | 358 | +16 374 | +9 383 | +11 394 | -394 — | — — | — — | — — | — — |
| CARNEY, Frank (Lab.) | 422 | +10 432 | +14 446 | +27 473 | +30 503 | -503 — | — — | — — | — — |
| COUSINS, Jim (P.D.) | 659 | +25 684 | +13 697 | +21 718 | +87 805 | +146 951 | +97 1,048 | +20 1,068 | +116 1,184 |
| DOHERTY, Josephine (Non-Party) | 42 | +2 44 | -44 — | — — | — — | — — | — — | — — | — — |
| DUFFY, Frank (S.F.) | 602 | +16 618 | +21 639 | +6 645 | +23 668 | +41 709 | +20 729 | +5 734 | -734 — |
| KENNY, Paddy (F.F.) | 150 | +35 185 | -185 — | — — | — — | — — | — — | — — | — — |
| LENNON, Jim (F.G.) | 807 | +8 815 | +4 819 | +96 915 | +94 1,009 | +57 1,066 | +18 1,084 | +3 1,087 | +46 1,133 |
| MacGUINNESS, John (F.G.) | 530 | +59 589 | +12 601 | +19 620 | +90 710 | +74 784 | +44 828 | +4 832 | +55 887 |
| McEVOY, Jimmy (F.F.) | 448 | +33 481 | +55 536 | +9 545 | +15 560 | +22 582 | -582 — | — — | — — |
| REILLY, Tommy (F.F.) | 571 | +19 590 | +16 606 | +38 644 | +8 652 | +12 664 | | | |
| TAAFFE, Dessie (Non-Party) | 286 | +3 289 | +30 319 | -319 — | — — | — — | +125 789 | +106 895 | +76 971 |
| Non-transferable papers not effective | — | — — | +14 14 | +52 66 | +15 81 | +94 175 | +75 250 | — 250 | +441 691 |
| TOTAL: | 7,300 | — 7,300 | — 7,300 | — 7,300 | — 7,300 | — 7,300 | — 7,300 | — 7,300 | — 7,300 |

Elected: Ahern, Dermot (F.F.); Breathnach, Declan (F.F.); Cousins, Jim (P.D.); Lennon, Jim (F.G.); Reilly, Tommy (F.F.)

# DUNDALK (URBAN) ELECTORAL AREA

TOTAL ELECTORATE 12,373. VALID POLL 6,854. NO. OF MEMBERS 5. QUOTA 1,143

| Names of Candidates | First Count Votes | Second Count Transfer of T. Bellew's surplus (Result) | Third Count Transfer of Gallagher's votes (Result) | Fourth Count Transfer of Watters' votes (Result) | Fifth Count Transfer of Kerr's votes (Result) | Sixth Count Transfer of Short's votes (Result) | Seventh Count Transfer of Carroll's votes (Result) | Eighth Count Transfer of P. Bellew's votes (Result) | Ninth Count Transfer of O'Hanrahan's votes (Result) | Tenth Count Transfer of Callan's votes (Result) | Eleventh Count Transfer of Brennan's votes (Result) | Twelfth Count Transfer of Lennon's votes (Result) | Thirteenth Count Transfer of Keelan's surplus (Result) |
|---|---|---|---|---|---|---|---|---|---|---|---|---|---|
| BELLEW, Martin (Non-Party) | 419 | +21 440 | +7 447 | +7 454 | +24 478 | +26 504 | +33 537 | +103 640 | +18 658 | +91 749 | +89 838 | +61 899 | +46 945 |
| BELLEW, Paddy (Non-Party) | 266 | +17 283 | +2 285 | +4 289 | +10 299 | +19 318 | +32 350 | -350 — | — — | — — | — — | — — | — — |
| BELLEW, Tom (Non-Party) | 1,295 | -152 1,143 | — 1,143 | — 1,143 | — 1,143 | — 1,143 | — 1,143 | — 1,143 | — 1,143 | — 1,143 | — 1,143 | — 1,143 | — 1,143 |
| BRENNAN, Patrick (Lab.) | 305 | +10 315 | +4 319 | +1 320 | +6 326 | +56 382 | +24 406 | +28 434 | +12 446 | +25 471 | -471 — | — — | — — |
| CALLAN, Jimmy | 308 | +16 324 | +5 329 | +2 331 | +31 362 | +12 374 | +14 388 | +24 412 | +23 435 | -435 — | — — | — — | — — |
| CARROLL, John (F.G.) | 253 | +6 259 | +40 299 | +3 302 | +2 304 | +13 317 | -317 — | — — | — — | — — | — — | — — | — — |
| GALLAGHER, Joe (F.G.) | 144 | +6 150 | -150 — | — — | — — | — — | — — | — — | — — | — — | — — | — — | — — |
| KEELAN, Seamus (F.F.) | 753 | +13 766 | +9 775 | +68 843 | +4 847 | +4 851 | +22 873 | +29 902 | +113 1,015 | +54 1,069 | +44 1,113 | +310 1,423 | -280 1,143 |
| KENNA, Sean (S.F.) | 667 | +8 675 | +1 676 | +10 686 | +43 729 | +20 749 | +8 757 | +72 829 | +10 839 | +18 857 | +41 898 | +25 923 | +17 940 |
| KERR, Paddy | 199 | +4 203 | +1 204 | +3 207 | -207 — | — — | — — | — — | — — | — — | — — | — — | — — |
| LENNON, Noel (F.F.) | 344 | +5 349 | +4 353 | +30 383 | +8 391 | +14 405 | +9 414 | +4 418 | +126 544 | +48 592 | +31 623 | -623 — | — — |
| McCANN, Neil | 482 | +18 500 | +24 524 | +11 535 | +14 549 | +32 581 | +29 610 | +16 626 | +33 659 | +52 711 | +75 786 | +79 865 | +54 919 |
| McGAHON, Conor (F.G.) | 680 | +14 694 | +51 745 | +14 759 | +25 784 | +36 820 | +118 938 | +29 967 | +29 996 | +76 1,072 | +81 1,153 | — 1,153 | — 1,153 |
| O'HANRAHAN, Pearse (F.F.) | 304 | +6 310 | — 310 | +36 346 | +11 357 | +10 367 | +6 373 | +8 381 | -381 — | — — | — — | — — | — — |
| SHORT, Peter (W.P.) | 237 | +4 241 | +1 242 | +5 247 | +12 259 | -259 — | — — | — — | — — | — — | — — | — — | — — |
| WATTERS, Derek (F.F.) | 198 | +4 202 | — 202 | -202 — | — — | — — | — — | — — | — — | — — | — — | — — | — — |
| Non-transferable papers not effective | — | — — | +1 1 | +8 9 | +17 26 | +17 43 | +22 65 | +37 102 | +17 119 | +71 190 | +110 300 | +148 448 | +163 611 |
| TOTAL: | 6,854 | — 6,854 | — 6,854 | — 6,854 | — 6,854 | — 6,854 | — 6,854 | — 6,854 | — 6,854 | — 6,854 | — 6,854 | — 6,854 | — 6,854 |

Elected: Bellew, Tom (Non-Party); McGahon, Conor (F.G.); Keelan, Seamus (F.F.); Bellew, Martin (Non-Party); Kenna, Sean (S.F.).

# MAYO
# COUNTY COUNCIL

## MAYO COUNTY COUNCIL RESULTS

| PARTY | 1991 % of votes | 1991 Seats obtained | 1985 % of votes | 1985 Seat obtained |
|---|---|---|---|---|
| Fianna Fail | 47.3 | 15 | 52.6 | 15 |
| Fine Gael | 39.9 | 13 | 39.0 | 14 |
| Labour | 3.6 | 1 | 0.8 | — |
| Progressive Dem. | 2.8 | — | — | — |
| Workers Party | — | — | — | — |
| Other | 6.4 | 2 | 7.6 | 2 |
| TOTAL SEATS | | 31 | | 31 |

## MAYO

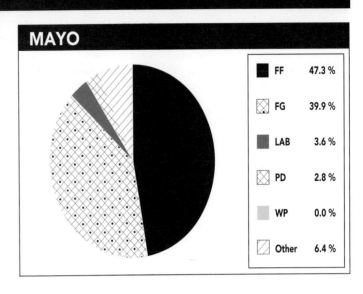

| | | |
|---|---|---|
| FF | 47.3 % | |
| FG | 39.9 % | |
| LAB | 3.6 % | |
| PD | 2.8 % | |
| WP | 0.0 % | |
| Other | 6.4 % | |

**Aras an Chontae**
**The Green**
**Castlebar**
**Telephone: (094) 24444**
**Fax: (094) 23937**
**Total population: 115,018**
**Rateable valuation: £547,899.60**
**Rate: £35.88**
**County Council meetings: Third Monday of each month,**
**except August**

*County Manager:* D. Mahon
*Assistant County Manager:* P. Fahey
*County Secretary:* P. Hughes
*Finance Officer:* T. Mullen
*County Engineer:* J. Beirne
*County Development Officer:* S. Smith
*Administrative Officers:* G. Groarke, B. Kelly,
S. Smyth, P. Commons
*Senior Staff Officers:* T. J. Loftus, P. McDermott, J. Loftus, P.
Carroll, M. Gormley
*County Librarian:* P. McMahon, County Library,
Castlebar. Telephone: (094) 21342
Fax: (094)24774
*County Solicitors:* Mary King, Michael Browne
*County Coroners:* M. Loftus, P. O'Connor, M. J. Egan, J. T.
O'Dwyer
*Chief Fire Officer:* S. Murphy
*Civil Defence Officer:* T. Duffy
*Senior Executive Architect:* P. Hynes
*Senior Executive Engineers:* B. O'Reilly (Acting),
N. Lonergan, F. X. Purcell, T. McNulty, R. Norton (Acting), M.
Mongan, P. Burke
*Senior Executive Planner:* S. Dunleavy

## BALLINA

| | 1991 | 1985 | '85 to '91 Swing |
|---|---|---|---|
| FF | 48.3 | 56.7 | -8.4 |
| FG | 43.3 | 43.3 | 0.0 |
| LAB | 2.2 | — | 2.2 |
| Ind | 6.2 | — | 6.2 |

BOURKE, Patrick,
Coolcran, Ballina,
County Mayo. (FF)
Furniture Maker. 096-70850

CAFFREY, Ernie,
Garden Street, Ballina,
County Mayo. (FG)
Publican. 096-22352

DEVANEY, Frank,
Lahardane, Ballina,
County Mayo. (FG)
Publican. 096-51001

MOLLOY, Stephen,
Scullibeen, Crossmolina,
County Mayo. (FF)
Electrician. 096-31300

REAPE, Annie May,
Pearse Street, Ballina,
County Mayo. (FF)
Personnel Assistant. 096-21154

STAUNTON, Eddie,
Ballynacloy, Crossmolina,
County Mayo. (FG)
Farmer. 096-21376

## CASTLEBAR

| | 1991 | 1985 | '85 to '91 Swing |
|---|---|---|---|
| FF | 49.0 | 43.6 | 5.4 |
| FG | 33.9 | 32.0 | 1.9 |
| LAB | 10.6 | 4.8 | 5.8 |
| PD | 6.5 | — | 6.5 |
| Ind | — | 19.6 | -19.6 |

BURKE, Patrick,
161 Knockaphunta, Castlebar,
County Mayo. (FG)
Businessman. 094-23009

KENNY, Enda,
Derrycoosh, Castlebar,
County Mayo. (FG)
Dáil Deputy. 094-22720

McDONNELL, AL,
Moorehall, Ballyglass, Claremorris,
County Mayo. (FF)
Company Director. 094-23799

MEE, Johnny,
20 St. Bridget's Crescent, Castlebar,
County Mayo. (Lab)
Typesetter. 094-21022

MORRIN, Richard,
Breaffy Road, Castlebar,
County Mayo. (FF)
Assurance Agent. 094-22726

## CLAREMORRIS

| | 1991 | 1985 | '85 to '91 Swing |
|---|---|---|---|
| FF | 38.9 | 48.1 | -9.2 |
| FG | 43.9 | 39.2 | 4.7 |
| LAB | 2.4 | — | 2.4 |
| PD | 5.5 | — | 5.5 |
| Ind | 9.4 | 12.7 | -3.3 |

FINN, Richard,
Birchfield, Claremorris,
County Mayo. (NP)
Teacher. 094-71593

HENEGHAN, J.
Bowgate Street, Ballinrobe,
County Mayo. (FF)
Insurance Agent. 092-41119.

HIGGINS, Jim Devlis,
Ballyhaunis,
County Mayo. (FG)
Dáil Deputy. 0907-30052

MANNION, Jim Frenchgrove,
Hollymount,
County Mayo. (FG)
Farmer. 093-47654

McHUGH, Pat,
Newtown, Ballindine,
County Mayo. (FF)
Company Director. 094-64149

MORLEY, P.J.
Bekan, Claremorris,
County Mayo. (FF)
Dail Deputy. 094-80217

RAFTERY, Michael,
Shrule,
County Mayo. (FG)
Retired. 093-31282

## KILLALA

| | 1991 | 1985 | '85 to '91 Swing |
|---|---|---|---|
| FF | 40.8 | 56.2 | -15.4 |
| FG | 33.2 | 43.8 | -10.6 |
| Ind | 25.9 | — | 25.9 |

CAREY, John N.
Attavalla, Bangor,
County Mayo. (FG)
ESB Employee. 097-83471

COSGRAVE, Paraic,
Cloontakilla, Bangor Erris, Ballina,
County Mayo. (NP)
Teacher. 097-83503

GOLDEN, Brian,
Ballina Road, Belmullet,
County Mayo. (FF)
Production Supervisor. 096-32009

QUINN, Tim,
Kilroe, Killala,
County Mayo. (FF)
Co-Op Manager. 097-81109

**Jim Higgins (FG)**
Claremorris

**Enda Kenny (FG)**
Castlebar

**Timothy Joseph Quinn (FF)**
Killala

**Annie May Reape (FF)**
Ballina

## SWINEFORD

|      | 1991 | 1985 | '85 to '91 Swing |
| ---- | ---- | ---- | ---- |
| FF   | 52.6 | 57.6 | -5.0 |
| FG   | 45.5 | 37.2 | 8.3 |
| SF   | 0.0  | 5.2  | -5.2 |
| Ind  | 1.9  |      | 1.9 |

FLANNERY, John,
Lavey, Charlestown,
County Mayo. (FG)
Farmer. 094-54193

MALONEY, Jimmy,
Ummoon, Foxford,
County Mayo. (FF)
Farmer. 094-56333

McEVOY, Sean,
Toomore, Foxford,
County Mayo. (FG)
Teacher. 094-56166

OLIVER, Paddy,
Tullinacurra, Swineford,
County Mayo. (FF)
ESB Employee. 094-51801

## WESTPORT

|      | 1991 | 1985 | '85 to '91 Swing |
| ---- | ---- | ---- | ---- |
| FF   | 55.8 | 57.5 | -1.7 |
| FG   | 37.4 | 39.0 | -1.6 |
| LAB  | 4.4  | —    | 4.4 |
| PD   | 2.3  | —    | 2.3 |
| SF   | —    | 3.5  | -3.5 |

CHAMBERS, Frank,
Georges Street, Newport,
County Mayo. (FF)
Auctioneer. 098-41327

HUGHES, Seamus,
Dún Maeve,
Newport Road, Westport,
County Mayo. (FF)
Solicitor. 098-26529

KILBANE, Pat,
New Road, Achill Sound,
County Mayo. (FG)
Teacher. 098-45206

O'TOOLE, Martin J.
Moneen, Louisburgh,
County Mayo. (FF)
Dail Deputy. 098-66154

RING, Michael,
The Paddock, Westport,
County Mayo. (FG)
Self-Employed. 098-25734

# Labour win their first seat ever in Mayo

The Mayo result provided two surprises. One was the Election of the Labour Party's first Councillor in Mayo since the 1930's, when Johnny Mee proved successful for the Party in Castlebar.

Many national commentators had put Mee's success down to a spin off from the Presidential Election victory for Labour in the home county of Mary Robinson. However Johnny Mee had contested the 1985 poll, and as a Castlebar U.D.C. member, had been gradually building his support. He got one short of a thousand first preferences and took the final seat in the Castlebar five seater.

The other news story was the performance of one outgoing Fianna Fail Councillor Paraic Cosgrove who topped the poll in Killala, this time as an Independent. He had failed to come through the Party's convention, ran as an Independent, and scored a massive 1,350 first preferences. He then went on to be elected Chairman of the new Council, ironically with Fianna Fail backing.

Overall, Fianna Fail managed to retain their 15 seats, one short of a majority in a performance which was very much against the national trend. Annie May Reape romped home for the Party in the Ballina electoral area, with 1,578 first preferences, helping the Party to hold on to its' three seats. Reape was the Constituency officer worker of Minister of State, Sean Calleary who could not contest.

Fianna Fail's two backbench T.D.'s, P.J. Morley and Martin J. O'Toole, were also both comfortably re-elected in Claremorris and Westport respectively.

Al McDonnell topped the poll for the Party in the Castlebar electoral area. He had been co-opted onto the Council to replace Minister Padraig Flynn, while Fianna Fail's other outgoing Councillor Dick Morrin was also comfortably returned.

Jimmy Moloney topped the poll for Fianna Fail in Swinford with 1,427 votes ,a very impressive performances for the first timer who had over 150 votes to spare above the quota.

> ## Cosgrove went on to take the Council chair, ironically with Fianna Fail backing

In this area outgoing Councillor Padraig Gavin had retired,, and the other outgoing candidate, Patsy Dunne, lost out to fellow Party man Paddy Oliver.

A second Independent member was elected in Claremorris. Fianna Fail had won the co-option in this area, on the death of the Independent Martin Finn. When the election came around however, his son Richard Finn contested as an Independent, got a massive vote of 1,141 and thus reclaimed the family seat, while Fianna Fail's Sean Fitzpatrick lost out.

Overall Fine Gael will be somewhat disappointed, as they lost one seat. This was in Killala where Cosgrove's performance upset the Party make-up and Fine Gael's Vinnie Munnelly lost his seat, despite being ahead of the two Fine Fail Councillors on the first count.

The Party's frontbench member, Jim Higgins T.D., topped the poll in Claremorris with almost 300 votes to spare and Fine Gael held its' three seats in this area, with Jim Mannion and Michael Raftery both also retaining their seats.

Fine Gael's other Mayo Deputy Enda Kenny came in second place in Castlebar with 1,327 votes and was easily elected.

The highest vote getter for the Party in the county was Michael Ring, one of Fine Gael candidates in the Westport areas. A Westport U.D.C. member for over 12 years, he had been selected to replace outgoing Fine Gael Councillor Patrick Durcan who retired. He polled a massive 2,063 to top the poll, some 431 votes above the quota.

**Padraig Flynn in conversation with his Fianna Fail colleagues, Charles Haughey and Bertie Ahern during the 1991 Local Elections.**

# BALLINA ELECTORAL AREA

TOTAL ELECTORATE 15,551. VALID POLL 10,107. NO. OF MEMBERS 6. QUOTA 1,444

| Names of Candidates | First Count Votes | Second Count Transfer of Melrose's votes Result | | Third Count Transfer of Reape's surplus Result | | Fourth Count Transfer of Durkan's votes Result | | Fifth Count Transfer of Naughton's votes Result | | Sixth Count Transfer of Bourke's surplus Result | | Seventh Count Transfer of Staunton's surplus Result | |
|---|---|---|---|---|---|---|---|---|---|---|---|---|---|
| BOURKE, Padraic (F.F.) | 1,244 | +23 | 1,267 | +47 | 1,314 | +57 | 1,371 | +200 | 1,571 | -127 | 1,444 | — | 1,444 |
| CAFFREY, Ernie (F.G.) | 1,284 | +62 | 1,346 | +30 | 1,376 | +128 | 1,504 | — | 1,504 | — | 1,504 | — | 1,504 |
| DEVANEY, Frank (F.G.) | 1,160 | +9 | 1,169 | +3 | 1,172 | +44 | 1,216 | +198 | 1,414 | +45 | 1,459 | — | 1,459 |
| DURKAN, Tony | 630 | +57 | 687 | +7 | 694 | -694 | — | — | — | — | — | — | — |
| GLACKEN, Jimmy (F.F.) | 857 | +22 | 879 | +24 | 903 | +222 | 1,125 | +37 | 1,162 | +27 | 1,189 | +11 | 1,200 |
| MELROSE, Dick (Lab.) | 221 | -221 | — | — | — | — | — | — | — | — | — | — | — |
| MOLLOY, Stephen (F.F.) | 1,200 | +6 | 1,206 | +12 | 1,218 | +20 | 1,238 | +15 | 1,253 | +22 | 1,275 | +15 | 1,290 |
| NAUGHTON, Patrick Joseph (F.G.) | 801 | +12 | 813 | +6 | 819 | +54 | 873 | -873 | — | — | — | — | — |
| REAPE, Annie May (F.F.) | 1,578 | — | 1,578 | -134 | 1,444 | — | 1,444 | — | 1,444 | — | 1,444 | — | 1,444 |
| STAUNTON, Eddie (F.G.) | 1,132 | +16 | 1,148 | +5 | 1,153 | +50 | 1,203 | +327 | 1,530 | — | 1,530 | -86 | 1,444 |
| Non-transferable papers not effective | — | +14 | 14 | — | 14 | +119 | 133 | +96 | 229 | +33 | 262 | +60 | 322 |
| TOTAL: | 10,107 | — | 10,107 | — | 10,107 | — | 10,107 | — | 10,107 | — | 10,107 | — | 10,107 |

Elected: Reape, Annie May (F.F.); Caffrey, Ernie (F.G.); Bourke, Padraic (F.F.); Staunton, Eddie (F.G.); Devaney, Frank (F.G.); Molloy, Stephen (F.F.)

# CASTLEBAR ELECTORAL AREA

TOTAL ELECTORATE 14,146. VALID POLL 9,394. NO. OF MEMBERS 5. QUOTA 1,566

| Names of Candidates | First Count Votes | Second Count Transfer of McDonnell's surplus Result | | Third Count Transfer of Bourke's votes Result | | Fourth Count Transfer of Mulrooney's votes Result | | Fifth Count Transfer of Coady's votes Result | | Sixth Count Transfer of Burke's surplus Result | |
|---|---|---|---|---|---|---|---|---|---|---|---|
| BOURKE, Kevin (P.D.) | 613 | +14 | 627 | -627 | — | — | — | — | — | — | — |
| BURKE, Paddy (F.G.) | 1,047 | +50 | 1,097 | +81 | 1,178 | +58 | 1,236 | +410 | 1,646 | -80 | 1,566 |
| COADY, Liam F. (F.G.) | 806 | +7 | 813 | +60 | 873 | +13 | 886 | -886 | — | — | — |
| KENNY, Enda (F.G.) | 1,327 | +16 | 1,343 | +154 | 1,497 | +131 | 1,628 | — | 1,628 | — | 1,628 |
| McDONNELL, AL. (F.F.) | 1,851 | -285 | 1,566 | — | 1,566 | — | 1,566 | — | 1,566 | — | 1,566 |
| MEE, Johnny (Lab.) | 999 | +7 | 1,006 | +155 | 1,161 | +49 | 1,210 | +231 | 1,441 | +67 | 1,508 |
| MORRIN, Dick (F.F.) | 1,204 | +80 | 1,284 | +78 | 1,362 | +203 | 1,565 | +76 | 1,641 | — | 1,641 |
| MULROONEY, Regina (F.F.) | 713 | +59 | 772 | +25 | 797 | -797 | — | — | — | — | — |
| O'MALLEY, George (F.F.) | 834 | +52 | 886 | +34 | 920 | +226 | 1,146 | +87 | 1,233 | +13 | 1,246 |
| Non-transferable papers not effective | — | — | — | +40 | 40 | +117 | 157 | +82 | 239 | — | 239 |
| TOTAL: | 9,394 | — | 9,394 | — | 9,394 | — | 9,394 | — | 9,394 | — | 9,394 |

Elected: McDonnell, AL (F.F.); Kenny, Enda (F.G.); Burke, Paddy (F.G.); Morrin, Dick (F.F.); Mee, Johnny (Lab.)

# CLAREMORRIS ELECTORAL AREA

TOTAL ELECTORATE 18,132. VALID POLL 12,586. NO. OF MEMBERS 7. QUOTA 1,574

| Names of Candidates | First Count Votes | Second Count Transfer of J. Higgins' surplus Result | | Third Count Transfer of Murphy's and Robinson's votes Result | | Fourth Count Transfer of Ryan's votes Result | | Fifth Count Transfer of Leonard's votes Result | | Sixth Count Transfer of Fitzpatrick's votes Result | | Seventh Count Transfer of McHugh's surplus Result | | Eighth Count Transfer of Finn's srplus Result | | Ninth Count Transfer of Heneghan's surplus Result | |
|---|---|---|---|---|---|---|---|---|---|---|---|---|---|---|---|---|---|
| FINN, Richard | 1,141 | +38 | 1,179 | +60 | 1,239 | +52 | 1,291 | +213 | 1,504 | +222 | 1,726 | — | 1,726 | -152 | 1,574 | — | 1,574 |
| FITZPATRICK, Sean (F.F.) | 913 | +3 | 916 | +33 | 949 | +26 | 975 | +110 | 1,085 | -1,085 | — | — | — | — | — | — | — |
| HENEGHAN, Jack (F.F.) | 1,209 | +2 | 1,211 | +25 | 1,236 | +141 | 1,377 | +11 | 1,388 | +153 | 1,541 | +168 | 1,709 | — | 1,709 | -135 | 1,574 |
| HIGGINS, Jim (F.G.) | 1,862 | -288 | 1,574 | — | 1,574 | — | 1,574 | — | 1,574 | — | 1,574 | — | 1,574 | — | 1,574 | — | 1,574 |
| HIGGINS, Tom (F.G.) | 860 | +86 | 946 | +16 | 962 | +13 | 975 | +127 | 1,102 | +36 | 1,138 | +11 | 1,149 | +25 | 1,174 | +14 | 1,188 |
| LEONARD, Ray (F.G.) | 761 | +51 | 812 | +50 | 862 | +29 | 891 | -891 | — | — | — | — | — | — | — | — | — |
| MANNION, Jim (F.G.) | 1,095 | +27 | 1,122 | +34 | 1,156 | +87 | 1,243 | +239 | 1,482 | +75 | 1,557 | +42 | 1,599 | — | 1,599 | — | 1,599 |
| McHUGH, Patrick (F.F.) | 1,254 | +6 | 1,260 | +11 | 1,271 | +21 | 1,292 | +78 | 1,370 | +431 | 1,801 | -227 | 1,574 | — | 1,574 | — | 1,574 |
| MORLEY, P.J. (F.F.) | 1,517 | +63 | 1,580 | — | 1,580 | — | 1,580 | — | 1,580 | — | 1,580 | — | 1,580 | — | 1,580 | — | 1,580 |
| MURPHY, John (Lab.) | 297 | +3 | 300 | -300 | — | — | — | — | — | — | — | — | — | — | — | — | — |
| RAFTERY, Michael (F.G.) | 942 | +4 | 946 | +24 | 970 | +235 | 1,205 | +32 | 1,237 | +7 | 1,244 | +4 | 1,248 | +4 | 1,252 | +5 | 1,257 |
| ROBINSON, Michael Kevin | 44 | +2 | 46 | -46 | — | — | — | — | — | — | — | — | — | — | — | — | — |
| RYAN, Michael (P.D.) | 691 | +3 | 694 | +45 | 739 | -739 | — | — | — | — | — | — | — | — | — | — | — |
| Non-transferable papers not effective | — | — | — | +48 | 48 | +135 | 183 | +81 | 264 | +161 | 425 | +2 | 427 | +123 | 550 | +116 | 666 |
| TOTAL: | 12,586 | — | 12,586 | — | 12,586 | — | 12,586 | — | 12,586 | — | 12,586 | — | 12,586 | — | 12,586 | — | 12,586 |

Elected: Higgins, Jim (F.G.); Morley, PJ (F.F.); McHugh, Patrick (F.F.); Finn, Richard; Heneghan, Jack (F.F.); Mannion, Jim (F.G.); Raftery, Michael (F.G.)

# KILLALA ELECTORAL AREA

TOTAL ELECTORATE 9,176. VALID POLL 5,971. NO. OF MEMBERS 4. QUOTA 1,195

| Names of Candidates | First Count Votes | Second Count Transfer of Tighe's and Mullarkey's votes Result | | Third Count Transfer of Goonan's votes Result | | Fourth Count Transfer of Cosgrove's surplus Result | | Fifth Count Transfer of Quinn's surplus Result | | Sixth Count Transfer of Carey's surplus Result | |
|---|---|---|---|---|---|---|---|---|---|---|---|
| CAREY, John Noel (F.G.) | 945 | +55 | 1,000 | +122 | 1,122 | +132 | 1,254 | — | 1,254 | -59 | 1,195 |
| COSGROVE, Paraic | 1,350 | — | 1,350 | — | 1,350 | -155 | 1,195 | — | 1,195 | — | 1,195 |
| GOLDEN, Brian (F.F.) | 949 | +14 | 963 | +42 | 1,005 | +14 | 1,019 | +108 | 1,127 | +12 | 1,139 |
| GOONAN, Michael (F.F.) | 496 | +15 | 511 | -511 | — | — | — | — | — | — | — |
| MULLARKEY, Tony (Non-Party) | 169 | -169 | — | — | — | — | — | — | — | — | — |
| MUNNELLY, Vinnie (F.G.) | 1,039 | +30 | 1,069 | +8 | 1,077 | +9 | 1,086 | +1 | 1,087 | +17 | 1,104 |
| QUINN, Tim (F.F.) | 994 | +47 | 1,041 | +268 | 1,309 | — | 1,309 | -114 | 1,195 | — | 1,195 |
| TIGHE, Martin | 29 | -29 | — | — | — | — | — | — | — | — | — |
| Non-transferable papers not effective | — | +37 | 37 | +71 | 108 | — | 108 | +5 | 113 | +30 | 143 |
| TOTAL: | 5,971 | — | 5,971 | — | 5,971 | — | 5,971 | — | 5,971 | — | 5,971 |

Elected: Cosgrove, Paraic; Quinn, Tim (F.F.); Carey, John Noel (F.G.); Golden, Brian (F.F.)

# SWINFORD ELECTORAL AREA

TOTAL ELECTORATE 9,877. VALID POLL 6,443. NO. OF MEMBERS 4. QUOTA 1,289

| Names of Candidates | First Count Votes | Second Count Transfer of McDonagh's votes | Result | Third Count Transfer of Maloney's surplus | Result | Fourth Count Transfer of Mellett's votes | Result |
|---|---|---|---|---|---|---|---|
| DUNNE, Patsy (F.F.) | 959 | +8 | 967 | +39 | 1,006 | +34 | 1,040 |
| FLANNERY, John (F.G.) | 1,200 | +11 | 1,211 | +4 | 1,215 | +168 | 1,383 |
| MALONEY, Jimmy (F.F.) | 1,423 | — | 1,423 | -134 | 1,289 | — | 1,289 |
| McDONAGH, Tony (Non-Party) | 121 | -121 | — | — | — | — | — |
| McEVOY, Sean (F.G.) | 901 | +23 | 924 | +32 | 956 | +386 | 1,342 |
| MELLETT, Joseph (F.G.) | 830 | +31 | 861 | +7 | 868 | -868 | — |
| OLIVER, Paddy, (F.F.) | 1,009 | +26 | 1,035 | +52 | 1,087 | +231 | 1,318 |
| Non-transferable papers not effective | — | +22 | 22 | — | 22 | +49 | 71 |
| TOTAL: | 6,443 | — | 6,443 | — | 6,443 | — | 6,443 |

Elected: Maloney, Jimmy (F.F.); Flannery, John (F.G.); McEvoy, Sean (F.G.); Oliver, Paddy (F.F.)

# WESTPORT ELECTORAL AREA

TOTAL ELECTORATE 13,691. VALID POLL 9,791. NO. OF MEMBERS 5. QUOTA 1,632

| Names of Candidates | First Count Votes | Second Count Transfer of Ring's surplus | Result | Third Count Transfer of Kilcoyne's votes | Result | Fourth Count Transfer of Rice's votes | Result |
|---|---|---|---|---|---|---|---|
| CHAMBERS, Frank (F.F.) | 1,538 | +26 | 1,564 | +20 | 1,584 | +78 | 1,662 |
| GALLAGHER, Denis (F.F.) | 989 | +18 | 1,007 | +28 | 1,035 | +95 | 1,130 |
| HUGHES, Seamus (F.F.) | 1,244 | +120 | 1,364 | +46 | 1,410 | +166 | 1,576 |
| KILBANE, Pat (F.G.) | 1,601 | +173 | 1,774 | — | 1,774 | — | 1,774 |
| KILCOYNE, John Joseph (P.D.) | 227 | +27 | 254 | -254 | — | — | — |
| O'TOOLE, Martin Joe (F.F.) | 1,697 | — | 1,697 | — | 1,697 | — | 1,697 |
| RICE, Maurice (Lab.) | 432 | +67 | 499 | +59 | 558 | -558 | — |
| RING, Michael (F.G.) | 2,063 | -431 | 1,632 | — | 1,632 | — | 1,632 |
| Non-transferable paper not effective | — | — | — | +101 | 101 | +219 | 320 |
| TOTAL: | 9,791 | — | 9,791 | — | 9,791 | — | 9,791 |

Elected: Ring, Michael (F.G.); O'Toole, Martin Joe (F.F.); Kilbane, Pat (F.G.); Chambers, Frank (F.F.); Hughes, Seamus (F.F.)

# MEATH COUNTY COUNCIL

## MEATH COUNTY COUNCIL RESULTS

| Party | 1991 | | 1985 | |
|---|---|---|---|---|
| | % of votes | Seats obtained | % of votes | Seat obtained |
| Fianna Fail | 44.8 | 12 | 50.6 | 17 |
| Fine Gael | 26.5 | 9 | 25.2 | 7 |
| Labour | 11.8 | 4 | 11.6 | 3 |
| Progressive Dem. | 3.1 | — | — | — |
| Workers Party | 2.9 | 1 | 1.5 | — |
| Other | 10.9 | 3 | 11.1 | 2 |
| TOTAL SEATS | | 31 | | 31 |

## MEATH

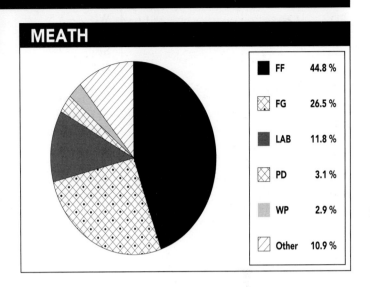

| | | |
|---|---|---|
| ■ | FF | 44.8 % |
| ▨ | FG | 26.5 % |
| ◼ | LAB | 11.8 % |
| ▨ | PD | 3.1 % |
| ▨ | WP | 2.9 % |
| ▨ | Other | 10.9 % |

County Hall, Navan
Telephone: (046) 21581
Fax: (046) 21463
Total population: 103,881
Rateable valuation: £840,453.60
Rate: £22.6152
County Council meetings: First Monday of each month at 14.00

*County Manager:* M.J. McFadden
*Assistant County Manager:* Vacant.
*County Secretary:* B. Keating
*Finance Officer:* J. Byrne
*County Engineer:* O. Perkins
*Administrative Officers:* J. O'Grady, H. Reilly, P.Minnock
*Senior Staff Officer:* H. Flanagan
*County Development Officer:* J. Donnellan
*County Librarian:* W. P. Smith
*County Coroner:* J. Lacy, Solicitor, Kells
*Chief Fire Officer:* M. Stack
*Civil Defence Officer:* J. O'Grady
*Senior Executive Engineers:*
*Road Design:* M. Jenkins
*Road Construction:* F. Burke, J. McLoughlin
*Sanitary Services:* P. Brady, C. McCarthy (Acting)
*Housing:* P. O'Rourke
*Planning:* R. Somers
*Urbans:* D. MacGowan

## CEANANNUS MÓR

| | 1991 | 1985 | '85 to '91 Swing |
|---|---|---|---|
| FF | 51.3 | 57.0 | -5.7 |
| FG | 29.9 | 26.8 | 3.1 |
| LAB | 6.2 | 7.2 | -1.0 |
| PD | 1.6 | | 1.6 |
| Ind | 8.5 | 9.0 | -0.5 |

BRADY, John,
Springville, Kilskyre, Kells,
County Meath. (FF)
Farmer. 046-40852

FARRELLY, John V.
Hurdlestown, Kells,
County Meath. (FG)
Dail Deputy. 046-41290

FITZSIMONS, Jack,
Kenlis Lodge, Kells,
County Meath. (NP)
Architect. 046-40117

GIBNEY, Gerry,
Moylagh, Oldcastle,
County Meath. (FG)
Officer Administrator. 049-41465

LYNCH, Michael,
Cogan Street, Oldcastle,
County Meath. (FF)
Publican. 049-41307

ROONEY, Sebastian (Sib),
Oristown, Kells,
County Meath. (FF)
Farmer. 046-40165

WELDON, Jimmy,
Rahood, Nobber,
County Meath. (FF)
Agricultural Contractor. 046-52312

## DUNSHAUGHLIN

| | 1991 | 1985 | '85 TO '91 Swing |
|---|---|---|---|
| FF | 45.2 | 51.5 | -6.3 |
| FG | 24.4 | 28.4 | -4.0 |
| LAB | 17.1 | 12.9 | 4.2 |
| WP | 5.5 | 3.2 | 2.3 |
| PD | 5.0 | | 5.0 |
| SF | 2.9 | 3.0 | -0.1 |
| Ind | 0.0 | 1.0 | -1.0 |

FANNING, John,
19 Castle Crescent, Ashbourne,
County Meath. (FG)
Airline Official.

FITZGERALD, Brian,
Warrenstown, Kilcock,
County Meath. (Lab)
Industrial Officer. 01-251847

SYLVER, Mary,
Piercetown, Dunboyne,
County Meath. (FG)
Housewife. 01-251652

TORMEY, Conor,
Milltown, Ashbourne,
County Meath. (FF)
Shopkeeper.

WALLACE, Mary,
Fairyhouse Road, Ratoath,
County Meath. (FF)
Dáil Deputy. 01-256259

## NAVAN

| | 1991 | 1985 | '85 TO '91 Swing |
|---|---|---|---|
| FF | 34.9 | 52.1 | -17.2 |
| FG | 22.8 | 23.4 | -0.6 |
| LAB | 11.6 | 10.7 | 0.9 |
| WP | 8.1 | 4.1 | 4.0 |
| PD | 7.3 | — | 7.3 |
| SF | 5.3 | 3.5 | 1.8 |
| Ind | 10.1 | 6.2 | 3.9 |

CLUSKER, Brendan,
16 Brews Hill, Navan,
County Meath. (Lab)
Retired.

FITZSIMONS, Patrick,
27 Trimgate Street, Navan,
County Meath. (FF)
Merchant. 046-21827

FOLEY, Noel,
32 Watergate Street, Navan,
County Meath. (FG)
Publican. 046-21827

GORMAN, Christy,
10 Clusker Park, Navan,
County Meath. (Elected WP, now DL)

HEANEY, Owen,
Castletown House, Castletown, Kilberry,
Navan,
County Meath. (FF)
Farmer. 046-21698

HEGARTY, Patricia,
35 St. Mary's Park, Navan,
County Meath. (NP)
Housewife.

O'NEILL, Patsy,
Wilkinstown, Navan,
County Meath. (FG)
Garage Owner. 046-21698

## SLANE

| | 1991 | 1985 | '85 TO '91 Swing |
|---|---|---|---|
| FF | 32.2 | 35.2 | -3.0 |
| FG | 32.1 | 25.0 | 7.1 |
| LAB | 15.1 | 6.2 | 8.9 |
| Ind | 20.5 | 33.6 | -13.1 |

CUDDEN, Jimmy,
23 St. Cianan's Villas, Dunleek,
County Meath. (Lab)
Bus Driver. 041-23353

Owen Heaney (FF)
Navan

Mary Wallace (FF)
Dunshaughlin

Christy Gorman (DL)
Navan

John Fanning (FG)
Dunshaughlin

GOUGH, Hugh,
Gilltown, Beauparc,
County Meath. (FF)
Maintenance Fitter. 041-25298

KELLY, Tom,
Laytown,
County Meath. (FG)
Pharmacist. 041-27163

LYNCH, Shaun,
Duleek,
County Meath. (FG)
Farmer.

MARRY, Gerry,
Duleek,
County Meath. (NP)
Auctioneer. 041-32856

| TRIM | | | |
|---|---|---|---|
| | | | '85 TO '91 |
| | 1991 | 1985 | Swing |
| FF | 60.8 | 54.2 | 6.6 |
| FG | 22.4 | 21.8 | 0.6 |
| LAB | 10.9 | 24.0 | -13.1 |
| GP | 3.9 | | 3.9 |
| SF | 1.6 | | 1.6 |
| Ind | 0.4 | | 0.4 |

CAREY, William,
Newcastle, Enfield,
County Meath. (FG)
Businessman. 0405-41064

CRIBBEN, Gabriel,
Boardsmill, Trim,
County Meath. (FF)
Farmer.

DEMPSEY, Noel,
Knightsbrook, Trim,
Co. Meath. (FF)
Dáil Deputy. 046-31146*

HILLIARD, Colm,
Ringlestown, Kilmessan,
County Meath. (FF)
Dáil Deputy. 046-25236

LOWE, Patrick,
Longwood,
County Meath. (Lab)
Retired. 0405-55066

*Resigned when appointed Minister of
State, Feb. 1992.
Replaced by:

MURRAY, Seamus,
Cullentra, Longwood,
County Meath. (FF)

# Left make gains in Meath

In 1985, for the first time in 20 years, Fianna Fáil won control of Meath County Counci,l taking 17 of the 29 seats available. This majority was, however, swept away in the 1991 election, with the party losing seats in all but 1 of the 5 electoral areas, resulting in an overall loss of 5 seats.

All other groupings gained at Fianna Fail's expense, with Fine Gael picking up 2 extra seats, bringing their total to 9. The success of the Independents and the left wing parties in Meath was not unexpected, especially with local services charges and travellers' halting sites being doorstep topics for canvassers.

The spotlight in the Kells Electoral Area was taken by Jack Fitzsimons, a Fianna Fail Senator from 1982 to 1989. Running as an Independent and campaigning on an anti-hare coursing ticket Fitzsimons, author of several best-selling books such as 'Bungalow Bliss', was strong enough to take a seat from his old party. Outgoing Councillor Fergus Muldoon, who was the unsuccessful Fianna Fail candidate, was eliminated on the seventh count.

Despite this loss, Fianna Fail's Michael Lynch again topped the poll, but with 446 votes less than in 1985. He was returned with party coleagues, and fellow outgoing Councillors, John Brady and Sebastian Rooney, along with newcomer James Weldon, who was elected on the last count without reaching the quota. Fine Gael held their 2 seats in Kells, although there was a change in the lineup, with outgoing Councillor Tom Bradley losing the seat he first won in 1974 to his running mate, 22 year old Gerry Gibney.

Although her first preference vote declined on 1985, Fianna Fail's Mary Wallace was returned in the Dunshaughlin Area, with a poll topping 1,469 votes. Fine Gael took a seat from Fianna Fail in Dunshaughlin, as outgoing Councillor Tadgh Delaney of Fianna Fail, lost out to Fine Gael newcomer John Fanning, an employee with Aer Lingus. Delaney joined his running mate Mary Sylver on the Council, with the strategy of running only 2 candidates bearing fruit for Fine Gael.

The seat formerly held by retiring Fianna Fail Councillor, and former Senator, Sean Conway was taken by his Ashbourne colleague, Conor Tormey. The closest candidate to Mary Wallace was Brian Fitzgerald of Labour, who went close to doubling the vote he received in 1985, and was only 68 votes short of the quota on the first count. This strong performance will give Labour hope of gaining a seat at the next General Election with Fitzgerald, unsuccessful in 1989, already the declared Labour candidate.

Christy Gorman of the Worker's Party and Independent candidate Patricia Hegarty both gained seats in the Navan Electoral Area, as Fianna Fail's vote fell by over 17% with the loss of 2 of their 4 seats won in 1985. The result was a victory for the anti-services charges campaign in which both Hegarty and Gorman were active. Gorman had been a regular picketer outside the County Hall, and had previously visited the Council Chamber to dump litter in protest at the privatisation of the refuse service in the County. With Gorman's election, the Worker's Party gained their first County Council seat in Meath. Hegarty had the backing of the Navan Combined Residents' Association, and successfully took the third seat well ahead of 5 outgoing Councillors, including Labour's Brendan Clusker, a Councillor since 1974, who was re-elected without reaching the quota.

In addition to the local charges issue, Fianna Fail's strategy in running 5 candidates in the Navan Area was to blame for their loss of 2 seats. They had 2.8 quotas between their 5 candidates and took 2 seats while in comparison, Fine Gael with just 1.8 quotas, also took 2 seats. Fine Gael's Patsy O'Neill increased his vote and was returned along with newcomer Noel Foley.

Paddy Fitzsimons of Fianna Fail again topped the poll in Navan, but on this occasion his vote was 594 lower than in 1985. He was joined on the Council by party colleague Owen Heaney who had been co-opted to replace Peter Finnegan. Heaney took the last seat in the Navan Area, having narrowly edged out fellow Fianna Fail candidate and outgoing Councillor, James Mangan.

The Heaney-Mangan tussle introduced much drama into the Navan count as on the 9th count just 1 vote separated Mangan from Heaney, with Heaney having the advantage. Mangan called for a recount, which continued into the small hours of the morning. When the results were announced, however, Mangan had in fact dropped by 2 votes with Heaney remaining the same. In the following count Heaney received 3 more votes than Mangan to take the final seat in the Navan Area by 6 votes, without reaching the quota.

In 1985 Fianna Fail and the Independents both took 2 seats apiece in the Slane Electoral area, with Fine Gael having 1 Councillor elected. One of these Independents, Jimmy Cudden, ran as a Labour Party candidate in 1991, and was returned with the help of transfers from running mate, Ken Lougheed. Gerry Marry, the other Independent, repeated his poll-topping performance of 1985. Marry, a former Fianna Fail member and chairperson of the National Anti-Rod License campaign, was 547 votes clear of outgoing Councillor Tom Kelly of Fine Gael, the nearest candidate. Kelly was joined on the Council by newcomer Shaun Lynch. Again Fine Gael's strategy proved successful. With essentially the same share of the first preference vote as Fianna Fail, but 1 candidate less, Fine Gael took 2 seats in Slane, while of Fianna Fail's 4 candidates, only 1 was elected. The sole Fianna Fail representative in Slane is marathon runner, Hugh Gough.

Trim was the only area in Meath where Fianna Fail did not lose any of their representatives elected in 1985. A large share of the credit for this result is attributable to the performance of Deputy Noel Dempsey, who received 2 quotas in topping the polling. He was 836 votes in front of the nearest candidate, party and Dail colleague, Colm Hillard. While Hillard's vote was down on his 1985 result, he was still elected on the first count.

The strength of the Fianna Fail vote, up over 6% on 1985 to nearly 61% of the total vote in Trim, was such to re-elect Gabriel Cribben from his base vote of only 278 first preferences giving him the third seat. Outgoing Councillor William Carey of Fine Gael received over 550 vote more then Cribben but was not returned until after Cribben. The final seat in Trim was filled by Patrick Lowe of the Labour Party. Despite the decrease in Labour's vote by 13% with the retirement of former TD Frank McLoughlin their seat was held by newcomer Lowe, with the help of strong transfers from his running mate Larry Murphy.

# CEANANNUS MÓR LOCAL ELECTORAL AREA

TOTAL ELECTORATE 16,291. VALID POLL 9,848. NO. OF MEMBERS 7. QUOTA 1,232

| Names of Candidates | First Count Votes | Second Count Transfer of Lynch's surplus Result | | Third Count Transfer of Farrelly's surplus Result | | Fourth Count Transfer of McCabe's votes Result | | Fifth Count Transfer of Maguire's votes Result | | Sixth Count Transfer of MhicDaeid's votes Result | | Seventh Count Transfer of O'Rourke's votes Result | | Eighth Count Transfer of Muldoon's votes Result | | Ninth Count Transfer of Brady's surplus Result | | Tenth Count Transfer of Grimes' votes Result | |
|---|---|---|---|---|---|---|---|---|---|---|---|---|---|---|---|---|---|---|---|
| BRADLEY, Tom (F.G.) | 672 | +11 | 683 | +26 | 709 | +2 | 711 | +5 | 716 | +71 | 787 | +5 | 792 | +34 | 826 | +3 | 829 | +87 | 916 |
| BRADY, John (F.F.) | 932 | +120 | 1,052 | +2 | 1,054 | +13 | 1,067 | +18 | 1,085 | +13 | 1,098 | +119 | 1,217 | +56 | 1,273 | -41 | 1,232 | — | 1,232 |
| FARRELLY, John V. (F.G.) | 1,293 | — | 1,293 | -61 | 1,232 | — | 1,232 | — | 1,232 | — | 1,232 | — | 1,232 | — | 1,232 | — | 1,232 | — | 1,232 |
| FITZSIMONS, Jack (Non-Party) | 648 | +16 | 664 | +4 | 668 | +32 | 700 | +31 | (731 | +63 | 794 | +26 | 820 | +59 | 879 | +2 | 881 | +246 | 1,127 |
| GIBNEY, Gerry (F.G.) | 980 | +89 | 1,069 | +9 | 1,078 | +19 | 1,097 | +4 | 1,101 | +18 | 1,119 | +3 | 1,122 | +8 | 1,130 | — | 1,130 | +50 | 1,180 |
| GRIMES, Tommy (Lab.) | 608 | +9 | 617 | +4 | 621 | +32 | 653 | +61 | 714 | +21 | 735 | +63 | 798 | +12 | 810 | — | 810 | -810 | — |
| LYNCH, Michael (F.F.) | 1,630 | -398 | 1,232 | — | 1,232 | — | 1,232 | — | 1,232 | — | 1,232 | — | 1,232 | — | 1,232 | — | 1,232 | — | 1,232 |
| MAGUIRE, John | 187 | +7 | 194 | +1 | 195 | +7 | 202 | -202 | — | — | — | — | — | — | — | — | — | — | — |
| McCABE, Patrick (S.F.) | 154 | +5 | 159 | — | 159 | -159 | — | — | — | — | — | — | — | — | — | — | — | — | — |
| MhicDAEID, Caroline (P.D.) | 254 | +4 | 258 | +1 | 259 | +3 | 262 | +3 | 265 | -265 | — | — | — | — | — | — | — | — | — |
| MULDOON, Fergus (F.F.) | 693 | +26 | 719 | +6 | 725 | +7 | 732 | +10 | 742 | +7 | 749 | +17 | 766 | -766 | — | — | — | — | — |
| O'ROURKE, James (F.F.) | 300 | +24 | 324 | +1 | 325 | +5 | 330 | +30 | 360 | +7 | 367 | -367 | — | — | — | — | — | — | — |
| ROONEY, Sebastian (Sib) (F.F.) | 780 | +54 | 834 | +2 | 836 | +10 | 846 | +18 | 864 | +31 | 895 | +95 | 990 | +137 | 1,127 | +22 | 1,149 | +136 | 1,285 |
| WELDON, James (F.F.) | 717 | +33 | 750 | +5 | 755 | +7 | 762 | +10 | 772 | +17 | 789 | +26 | 815 | +347 | 1,162 | +14 | 1,176 | +36 | 1,212 |
| Non-transferable papers not effective | — | — | — | — | — | +22 | 22 | +12 | 34 | +17 | 51 | +13 | 64 | +113 | 177 | — | 177 | +255 | 432 |
| TOTAL: | 9,848 | — | 9,848 | — | 9,848 | — | 9,848 | — | 9,848 | — | 9,848 | — | 9,848 | — | 9,848 | — | 9,848 | — | 9,848 |

Elected: Lynch, Michael (F.F.); Farrelly, John V. (F.G.); Brady, John (F.F.); Rooney, Sebastian (Sib) (F.F.); Weldon, James (F.F.); Gibney, Gerry (F.G.); Fitzsimons, Jack (Non-Party)

# NAVAN ELECTORAL AREA

TOTAL ELECTORATE 17,840. VALID POLL 8,227. NO. OF MEMBERS 7. QUOTA 1,029

| Names of Candidates | First Count Votes | Second Count Transfer of J. O'Brien's votes Result | | Third Count Transfer of McGoona's votes Result | | Fourth Count Transfer of McConnell's votes Result | | Fifth Count Transfer of S. O'Brien's votes Result | | Sixth Count Transfer of Reilly's votes Result | | Seventh Count Transfer of Carberry's votes Result | | Eighth Count Transfer of D'Arcy's votes Result | | Ninth Count Transfer of Andrews' votes Result | | Tenth Count Transfer of Fitzsimons' surplus Result | | Eleventh Count Transfer of Foley's surplus Result |
|---|---|---|---|---|---|---|---|---|---|---|---|---|---|---|---|---|---|---|---|---|
| ANDREWS, Patrick (P.D.) | 599 | +7 | 606 | +8 | 614 | +5 | 619 | +35 | 654 | +17 | 671 | +25 | 696 | +56 | 752 | -752 | — | — | — | — |
| CARBERRY, Frank (F.F.) | 424 | +2 | 426 | +52 | 478 | +6 | 484 | +10 | 494 | +16 | 510 | -510 | — | — | — | — | — | — | — | — |
| CLUSKER, Brendan (Lab.) | 533 | +33 | 566 | +20 | 586 | +11 | 597 | +124 | 721 | +45 | 766 | +65 | 831 | +38 | 869 | +120 | 989 | — | 989 | +17 | 1,006 |
| D'ARCY, Jim (F.G.) | 561 | +5 | 566 | — | 566 | +5 | 571 | +8 | 579 | +22 | 601 | +9 | 610 | -610 | — | — | — | — | — | — |
| FITZSIMONS, Patrick (F.F.) | 973 | +3 | 976 | +59 | 1,035 | — | 1,035 | — | 1,035 | — | 1,035 | — | 1,035 | — | 1,035 | -6 | 1,029 | — | 1,029 |
| FOLEY, Noel (F.G.) | 584 | +3 | 587 | +9 | 596 | +4 | 600 | +19 | 619 | +13 | 632 | +26 | 658 | +287 | 945 | +172 | 1,117 | — | 1,117 | -88 | 1,029 |
| GORMAN, Christy (W.P.) | 663 | +22 | 685 | +9 | 694 | +15 | 709 | +26 | 735 | +117 | 852 | +35 | 887 | +30 | 917 | +52 | 969 | — | 969 | +1 | 970 |
| HEANEY, Owen (F.F.) | 563 | — | 563 | +25 | 588 | +1 | 589 | +7 | 596 | +15 | 611 | +169 | 780 | +24 | 804 | +88 | 892 | +3 | 895 | +8 | 903 |
| HEGARTY, Patricia (Non-Party) | 556 | +16 | 572 | +4 | 576 | +220 | 796 | +29 | 825 | +41 | 866 | +38 | 904 | +30 | 934 | +90 | 1,024 | +1 | 1,025 | +8 | 1,033 |
| MANGAN, James (F.F.) | 689 | +3 | 692 | +21 | 713 | +2 | 715 | +15 | 730 | +13 | 743 | +38 | 904 | +30 | 934 | +90 | 1,024 | +1 | 1,025 | +8 | 1,033 |
| McCONNELL, Anthony (Non-Party) | 275 | +4 | 279 | +6 | 285 | -285 | — | — | — | — | — | +73 | 816 | +16 | 832 | +57 | 889 | +2 | 891 | +6 | 897 |
| McGOONA, Michael (F.F.) | 220 | +2 | 222 | -222 | — | — | — | — | — | — | — | — | — | — | — | — | — | — | — |
| O'BRIEN, Jim (Lab.) | 176 | -176 | — | — | — | — | — | — | — | — | — | — | — | — | — | — | — | — | — |
| O'BRIEN, Sean (Lab.) | 245 | +60 | 305 | +2 | 307 | +3 | 310 | -310 | — | — | — | — | — | — | — | — | — | — | — |
| O'NEILL, Patsy (F.G.) | 731 | +7 | 738 | +2 | 740 | +1 | 741 | +12 | 753 | +16 | 769 | +9 | 778 | +103 | 881 | +52 | 933 | — | 933 | +48 | 981 |
| REILLY, Joe (S.F.) | 435 | +5 | 440 | +3 | 443 | +6 | 449 | +10 | 459 | -459 | — | — | — | — | — | — | — | — | — |
| Non-transferable papers not effective | — | +4 | 4 | +2 | 6 | +6 | 12 | +15 | 27 | +144 | 171 | +61 | 232 | +26 | 258 | +121 | 379 | — | 379 | — | 379 |
| TOTAL: | 8,227 | — | 8,227 | — | 8,227 | — | 8,227 | — | 8,227 | — | 8,227 | — | 8,227 | — | 8,227 | — | 8,227 | — | 8,227 | — | 8,227 |

Elected: Fitzsimons, Patrick (F.F.); Foley, Noel (F.G.); Hegarty, Patricia (Non-Party); Clusker, Brendan (Lab.); O'Neill, Patsy (F.G.); Gorman, Christy (W.P.); Heaney, Owen (F.F.)

# DUNSHAUGHLIN LOCAL ELECTORAL AREA

TOTAL ELECTORATE 15,984. VALID POLL 7,582. NO. OF MEMBERS 5. QUOTA 1,264

| Names of Candidates | First Count Votes | Second Count Transfer of Wallace's surplus Result | | Third Count Transfer of Tuttle's votes Result | | Fourth Count Transfer of McDonnell's votes Result | | Fifth Count Transfer of Fitzgerald's surplus Result | | Sixth Count Transfer of Fernandez's votes Result | | Seventh Count Transfer of King's votes Result | | Eighth Count Transfer of Clynch's votes Result | |
|---|---|---|---|---|---|---|---|---|---|---|---|---|---|---|---|
| CLYNCH, Donal (F.F.) | 461 | +35 | 496 | +2 | 497 | +19 | 516 | +5 | 521 | +27 | 548 | +11 | 559 | -559 | — |
| DELANEY, Tadhg (F.F.) | 613 | +49 | 662 | +3 | 665 | +14 | 679 | +4 | 683 | +36 | 719 | +14 | 733 | +320 | 1,053 |
| FANNING, John (F.G.) | 855 | +7 | 862 | +14 | 876 | +6 | 882 | +1 | 883 | +101 | 984 | +167 | 1,151 | +33 | 1,184 |
| FERNANDEZ, Joe (P.D.) | 376 | +8 | 384 | +3 | 387 | +17 | 404 | +2 | 406 | -406 | — | — | — | — | — |
| FITZGERALD, Brian (Lab.) | 1,196 | +18 | 1,214 | +48 | 1,262 | +64 | 1,326 | -62 | 1,264 | — | 1,264 | — | 1,264 | — | 1,264 |
| KING, John (W.P.) | 417 | +2 | 419 | +11 | 430 | +22 | 452 | +7 | 459 | +37 | 496 | -496 | — | — | — |
| McDONNELL, Thomas (S.F.) | 219 | +4 | 223 | +1 | 224 | -224 | — | — | — | — | — | — | — | — | — |
| SYLVER, Mary (F.G.) | 994 | +15 | 1,009 | +5 | 1,014 | +16 | 1,030 | +9 | 1,039 | +118 | 1,157 | +41 | 1,198 | +32 | 1,230 |
| TORMEY, Conor (F.F.) | 885 | +64 | 949 | +4 | 953 | +16 | 969 | +2 | 971 | +23 | 994 | +115 | 1,109 | +83 | 1,192 |
| TUTTLE, Eamonn (Lab.) | 97 | +3 | 100 | -100 | — | — | — | — | — | — | — | — | — | — | — |
| WALLACE, Mary (F.F.) | 1,469 | -205 | 1,264 | — | 1,264 | — | 1,264 | — | 1,264 | — | 1,264 | — | 1,264 | — | 1,264 |
| Non-transferable papers not effective | — | — | — | +10 | (10) | +50 | (60) | +32 | (92) | +64 | 156 | +148 | 304 | +91 | 395 |
| TOTAL: | 7,582 | — | 7,582 | — | 7,582 | — | 7,582 | — | 7,582 | — | 7,582 | — | 7,582 | — | 7,582 |

Elected: Wallace, Mary (F.F.); Fitzgerald, Brian (Lab.); Sylver, Mary (F.G.); Tormey, Conor (F.F.); Fanning, John (F.G.)

# SLANE ELECTORAL AREA

TOTAL ELECTORATE 13,953. VALID POLL 6,878. NO. OF MEMBERS 5. QUOTA 1,147

| Names of Candidates | First Count Votes | Second Count Transfer of Marry's surplus Result | | Third Count Transfer of Halpin's votes Result | | Fourth Count Transfer of Lougheed's votes Result | | Fifth Count Transfer of Traynor's votes Result | | Sixth Count Transfer of Kelly's surplus Result | | Seventh Count Transfer of Meade's votes Result | | Eighth Count Transfer of Lynch's surplus Result | |
|---|---|---|---|---|---|---|---|---|---|---|---|---|---|---|---|
| CUDDEN, Jimmy (Lab.) | 659 | +60 | 719 | +11 | 730 | +191 | 921 | +25 | 946 | +14 | 960 | +54 | 1,014 | +57 | 1,071 |
| GOUGH, Hugh (F.F.) | 718 | +34 | 752 | +167 | 919 | +7 | 926 | +73 | 999 | +9 | 1,008 | +91 | 1,099 | +28 | 1,127 |
| HALPIN, Joe (F.F.) | 353 | +9 | 362 | -362 | — | — | — | — | — | — | — | — | — | — | — |
| KELLY, Tom (F.G.) | 865 | +22 | 887 | +4 | 891 | +113 | 1,004 | +199 | 1,203 | -56 | 1,147 | — | 1,147 | — | 1,147 |
| LOUGHEED, Kenneth (Lab.) | 382 | +15 | 397 | +5 | 402 | -402 | — | — | — | — | — | — | — | — | — |
| LYNCH, Shaun (F.G.) | 691 | +44 | 735 | +11 | 746 | +21 | 767 | +19 | 786 | +11 | 797 | +451 | 1,248 | -101 | 1,147 |
| MARRY, Gerry (Non-Party) | 1,412 | -265 | 1,147 | — | 1,147 | — | 1,147 | — | 1,147 | — | 1,147 | — | 1,147 | — | 1,147 |
| MEADE, Michael (F.G.) | 651 | +14 | 665 | +86 | 751 | +9 | 760 | +7 | 767 | +2 | 769 | -769 | — | — | — |
| MURRAY, Sean (F.F.) | 596 | +42 | 638 | +43 | 681 | +5 | 686 | +245 | 931 | +20 | 951 | +26 | 977 | +16 | 993 |
| TRAYNOR, Paddy (F.F.) | 551 | +25 | 576 | +19 | 595 | +32 | 627 | -627 | — | — | — | — | — | — | — |
| Non-transferable papers not effective | — | — | — | +16 | 16 | +24 | 40 | +59 | 99 | — | 99 | +147 | 246 | — | 246 |
| TOTAL: | 6,878 | — | 6,878 | — | 6,878 | — | 6,878 | — | 6,878 | — | 6,878 | — | 6,878 | — | 6,878 |

Elected:— Marry, Gerry (Non-Party); Kelly, Tom (F.G.); Lynch, Shaun (F.G.); Gough, Hugh (F.F.); Cudden, Jimmy (Lab.)

# TRIM ELECTORAL AREA

TOTAL ELECTORATE 12,858. VALID POLL 6,315. NO. OF MEMBERS 5. QUOTA 1,053

| Names of Candidates | First Count Votes | Second Count Transfer of Dempsey's surplus | Result | Third Count Transfer of Hilliard's surplus | Result | Fourth Count Transfer of Gormley's votes | Result | Fifth Count Transfer of Cumiskey's votes | Result | Sixth Count Transfer of Cummins' votes | Result | Seventh Count Transfer of Murphy's votes | Result | Eighth Count Transfer of Cribbin's surplus | Result | Ninth Count Transfer of Murray's votes | Result |
|---|---|---|---|---|---|---|---|---|---|---|---|---|---|---|---|---|---|
| CAREY, William (F.G.) | 858 | +55 | 913 | +17 | 930 | +3 | 933 | +2 | 935 | +42 | 977 | +60 | 1,037 | +29 | 1,066 | — | 1,066 |
| CRIBBIN, Gabriel (F.F.) | 278 | +490 | 768 | +87 | 855 | +5 | 860 | +13 | 873 | +31 | 904 | +214 | 1,118 | -65 | 1,053 | — | 1,053 |
| CUMISKEY, Lydia (S.F.) | 101 | +22 | 123 | +6 | 129 | +1 | 130 | -130 | — | — | — | — | — | — | — | — | — |
| CUMMINS, Patrick (G.P.) | 246 | +42 | 288 | +10 | 298 | +4 | 302 | +30 | 332 | -332 | — | — | — | — | — | — | — |
| DEMPSEY, Noel (F.F.) | 2,113 | -1,060 | 1,053 | — | 1,053 | — | 1,053 | — | 1,053 | — | 1,053 | — | 1,053 | — | 1,053 | — | 1,053 |
| EIVERS, Bernard (F.G.) | 555 | +81 | 636 | +22 | 658 | +3 | 661 | +7 | 668 | +44 | 712 | +7 | 719 | +10 | 729 | +62 | 791 |
| GORMLEY, John | 23 | +12 | 35 | +3 | 38 | -38 | — | — | — | — | — | — | — | — | — | — | — |
| HILLIARD, Colm (F.F.) | 1,277 | — | 1,277 | -224 | 1,053 | — | 1,053 | — | 1,053 | — | 1,053 | — | 1,053 | — | 1,053 | — | 1,053 |
| LOWE, Patrick (Lab.) | 409 | +82 | 491 | +23 | 514 | +7 | 521 | +18 | 539 | +68 | 607 | +24 | 631 | +9 | 640 | +251 | 891 |
| MURPHY, Syl (F.F.) | 173 | +187 | 360 | +43 | 403 | +3 | 406 | +7 | 413 | +20 | 433 | -433 | — | — | — | — | — |
| MURRAY, Larry (Lab.) | 282 | +89 | 371 | +13 | 384 | +4 | 388 | +12 | 400 | +42 | 442 | +15 | 457 | +10 | 467 | -467 | — |
| Non-transferable papers not effective | — | — | — | — | — | +8 | 8 | +41 | 49 | +85 | 134 | +113 | 247 | +7 | 254 | +154 | 408 |
| TOTAL: | 6,315 | — | 6,315 | — | 6,315 | — | 6,315 | — | 6,315 | — | 6,315 | — | 6,315 | — | 6,315 | — | 6,315 |

Elected: Dempsey, Noel (F.F.); Hilliard, Colm (F.F.); Cribbin, Gabriel (F.F.); Carey, William (F.G.); Lowe, Patrick (Lab.)

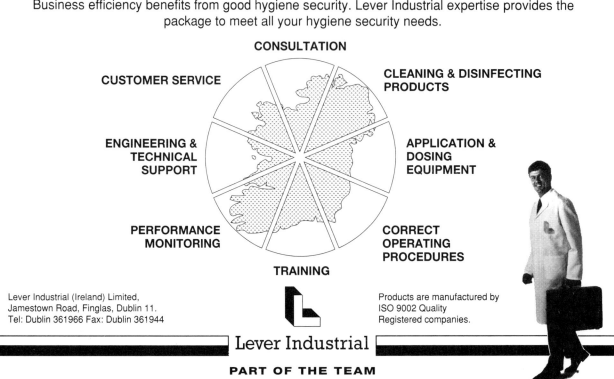

# MONAGHAN COUNTY COUNCIL

## MONAGHAN COUNTY COUNCIL RESULTS

| Party | 1991 % of votes | 1991 Seats obtained | 1985 % of votes | 1985 Seat obtained |
|---|---|---|---|---|
| Fianna Fail | 40.1 | 8 | 44.2 | 10 |
| Fine Gael | 32.8 | 7 | 33.5 | 7 |
| Labour | — | — | — | — |
| Progressive Dem. | — | — | — | — |
| Workers Party | 1.0 | — | 0.8 | — |
| Other | 26.1 | 5 | 21.5 | 3 |
| TOTAL SEATS | | 20 | | 20 |

## MONAGHAN

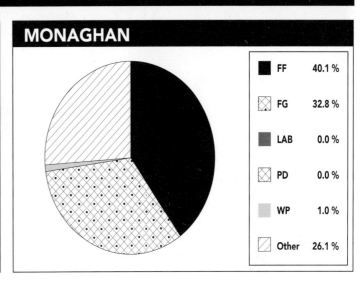

| | | |
|---|---|---|
| ■ | FF | 40.1 % |
| ▨ | FG | 32.8 % |
| ■ | LAB | 0.0 % |
| ▨ | PD | 0.0 % |
| ▨ | WP | 1.0 % |
| ▨ | Other | 26.1 % |

**County Offices, Monaghan**
**Telephone: (047) 82211**
**Total population: 51,361**
**Area sq miles: 499.83**
**Rateable valuation: £336,114.80**
**Rate: £26.19**
**County Council meetings: First Monday of each month**

*County Manager:* J. Gavin
*County Secretary:* A. J. Murphy
*Finance Officer:* E. Callaghan
*County Engineer:* J. Colleran
*Administrative Officer:* S. Finnan
*Senior Staff Officers:* G. O'Toole, K. McKenna
*County Librarian:* J. McElvaney (Acting), County
Library, Clones. Telephone: (047) 51143
*County Coroners:* P. J. O'Gara, Dr A. P. Roache
*Chief Fire Officer:* D. Treanor
*Civil Defence Officer:* S. Finnan
*Senior Executive Engineers:* F. Coyle,
P. Johnson, C. Boylan
*Senior Executive, Planning:* N. McCann

## CARRICKMACROSS

|      | 1991 | 1985 | '85 to '91 Swing |
|------|------|------|------|
| FF   | 46.8 | 46.7 | 0.1  |
| FG   | 35.0 | 34.5 | 0.5  |
| WP   | 3.9  | 2.8  | 1.1  |
| SF   | 4.7  | 8.0  | -3.3 |
| Ind  | 9.6  | 8.0  | 1.6  |

COTTER, Bill,
Cloughvalley, Carrickmacross,
County Monaghan. (FG)
Dail Deputy. 042-61422

JONES, Patrick,
Tonaneave,
Magheracloone, Carrickmacross,
Co. Monaghan. (FG)
Farmer. 042-69161

McNALLY, Padraig,
Nafferty, Carrickmacross,
County Monaghan. (FF)
Farmer. 042-61603

MURPHY, Peter,
Kednaminsha, Inniskeen,
County Monaghan.
Farmer. 042-78261

O'HANLON, Rosaleen,
28 Main Street, Carrickmacross,
County Monaghan. (FF)
Shop Owner. 042-61966

## CASTLEBLAYNEY

|      | 1991 | 1985 | '85 to '91 Swing |
|------|------|------|------|
| FF   | 44.5 | 50.1 | -5.6 |
| FG   | 44.3 | 48.1 | -3.8 |
| SF   | 6.4  | —    | 6.4  |
| Ind  | 4.8  | 1.8  | 3.0  |

CARVILLE, Arthur,
Annyalla, Castleblayney,
County Monaghan. (FG)
Farmer. 042-40183

CONLAN, John F.
Main Street, Ballybay,
County Monaghan. (FG)
Businessman. 042-41038

HUGHES, Brendan,
Kinnegan, Castleblayney,
County Monaghan. (FF)
Self Employed. 042-40463

KEENAN, Olivia,
Tonnyscallon House,
Doohamlet, Castleblayney,
County Monaghan. (FF)
Beauty Therapist. 047-83320

O'BRIEN, Francis,
Corwillan, Latton, Castleblayney,
County Monaghan. (FF)
Senator. 042-41152

## CLONES

|      | 1991 | 1985 | '85 to '91 Swing |
|------|------|------|------|
| FF   | 30.6 | 41.0 | -10.4 |
| FG   | 36.7 | 25.7 | 11.0  |
| SF   | 14.4 | 17.4 | -3.0  |
| Ind  | 18.2 | 15.8 | 2.4   |

CRAWFORD, Seymour,
Drumkeen, Aghabog,
County Monaghan. (FG)
Farmer. 047-54038

LEONARD, Jimmy,
Smithboro,
County Monaghan. (FF)
Dail Deputy. 047-57020

McELVANEY, Hugh,
Corcaghan,
Monaghan. (FG)
Company Director. 042-44844

PRINGLE, Walter,
Rawdeerpark, Clones,
County Monaghan. (NP)
Farmer. 047-51439

## MONAGHAN

|      | 1991 | 1985 | '85 to '91 Swing |
|------|------|------|------|
| FF   | 37.3 | 39.5 | -2.2 |
| FG   | 18.5 | 25.9 | -7.4 |
| SF   | 28.1 | 21.9 | 6.2  |
| Ind  | 16.1 | 12.7 | 3.4  |

MAXWELL, Noel,
Drumrutagh,
Monaghan. (NP)
Farmer. 047-81437

McAREE, Stephen,
Doogary, Tydavnet,
County Monaghan. (FG)
Retired. 047-87461

McKENNA, Willie,
Mullaghdun, Tydavnet Road,
Monaghan. (FF)
Building Society Manager. 047-82375

McKENNA, Brian,
Ivyhill, Emyvale,
County Monaghan. (SF)
Production Manager. 047-87849

O CAOLAIN, Caoimhghín,
60 Beechgrove Lawns,
Monaghan. (SF)
Public Representative. 047-83348

TREANOR, Patsy,
Latlurcan,
Monaghan. (FF)
Nurse. 047-82153

**Francis O'Brien (FF)**
**Castleblayney**

**Olivia Keenan, (FF)**
**Castleblayney**

**Peter Murphy**
**Carrickmacross**

**Jimmy Leonard (FF)**
**Clones**

# Sinn Fein and Protestant Association are the newsmakers

Fianna Fail won 10 of the 20 seats on Monaghan County Council in 1985 and in this election was to lose two of them. They lost one in Carrickmacross, and one in Clones with Fine Gael and the Monaghan Protestant Association gaining the seats.

Interesting from the Monaghan results was the performances of Sinn Fein. They have seven seats throughout the whole country and two of those are in Monaghan. They had won two seats in the county in 1985, one in the Monaghan electoral area and one in Clones. In Clane their outgoing Councillor, Pat Treanor, lost his seat, but in the Monaghan area, Caoimhghin O'Caolain topped the poll for Sinn Fein with 1,193 number ones while his running mate, Brian McKenna, polled 499 votes. O'Caolain's surplus transferred 80% to McKenna and in a major upset, the Party took two of the six seats.

The other surprise was the strength in the Monaghan Protestant Association. They had one seat in the outgoing County Council and had been regarded by some commentators as a spent force in Monaghan local politics. Noel Maxwell replaced James Wright to hold their seat in the Monaghan electoral area but in addition Walter Pringle, Secretary of Clones Co-operative Meats polled 913 votes in his first outgoing to take the second seat, behind Fianna Fail Deputy Jimmy Leonard and ahead of three sitting Councillors in Clones.

Monaghan County Council has 20 seats in four electoral areas. In Monaghan, Patsy Treanor and Willie McKenna were returned for Fianna Fail but Matt Caulfield, who had lost his seat by just 12 votes in 1985, failed to regain his seat. Fine Gael lost a seat with Tom O'Reilly not running, and Stephen McAree holding his seat.

In Clones, Fianna Fail Deputy Jimmy Leonard topped the poll with just 200 votes to spare above the quota. Hugh McElvaney retained his seat for Fine Gael and the party picked up an extra seat. They had wisely chosen former

IFA President, Seymour Crawford, to contest and he got 910 first preferences

> **Fine Gael wisely picked former IFA President Seymour Crawford to contest**

to take the forth and final seat.

In Castleblayney, local Fianna Fail Senator, Francie O'Brien, topped the poll and was elected on the first count, and the Party held its three seats, but only just. Brendan Hughes was also comfortably returned and newcomer, beautician Olivia Keenan just managed to win the final seat ahead of Fine Gael's Adam Armstrong initially by just one vote and then after a complete recount by just 4 votes. Fine Gael's two outgoing Castleblayney Councillors, Arthur Carville and John F. Conlon, both of them businessmen, won the Party two seats here.

In Carrickmacross, Fine Gael Deputy Bill Cotter topped the poll with 1,435 votes against a quota of 1,068 and in the absence of the Minister for Health Dr. Rory O'Hanlon, Fianna Fail lost a seat here to Independent Peter Murphy. Padraig McNally of Fianna Fail got 1,198 votes and was elected on the first count, while Rosaleen O'Hanlon (no relation) also held onto her seat, but Terence Freeman who had been co-opted to replace Rory O'Hanlon just lost out.

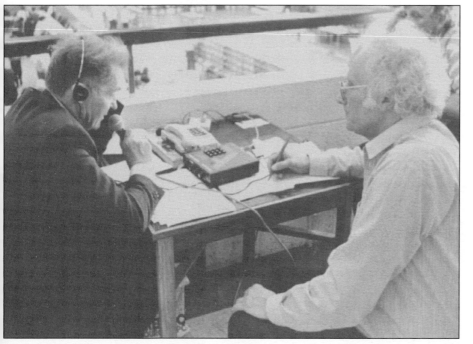

"And here is the vote of the Monaghan jury" — former Minister Rory O'Hanlon discussing the results for national radio.

# CRARRICKMACROSS ELECTORAL AREA

TOTAL ELECTORATE 9,384. VALID POLL 6,407. NO. OF MEMBERS 5. QUOTA 1,068

| Names of Candidates | First Count Votes | Second Count Transfer of Cotter's surplus | Result | Third Count Transfer of McNally's surplus | Result | Fourth Count Transfer of O'Donoghue's votes | Result | Fifth Count Transfer of Jones' surplus | Result | Sixth Count Transfer of O'Hanlon's surplus | Result | Seventh Count Transfer of B. Meegan's votes | Result | Eighth Count Transfer of J. Meegan's votes | Result |
|---|---|---|---|---|---|---|---|---|---|---|---|---|---|---|---|
| COTTER, Bill (F.G.) | 1,435 | -367 | 1,068 | — | 1,068 | — | 1,068 | — | 1,068 | — | 1,068 | — | 1,068 | — | 1,068 |
| FREEMAN, Thomas (F.F.) | 515 | +17 | 532 | +24 | 556 | +28 | 584 | +7 | 591 | +5 | 596 | +63 | 659 | +214 | 873 |
| JONES, Patrick (F.G.) | 808 | +223 | 1,031 | +10 | 1,041 | +51 | 1,092 | -24 | 1,068 | — | 1,068 | — | 1,068 | — | 1,068 |
| McNALLY, Padraig John (F.F.) | 1,198 | — | 1,198 | -130 | 1,068 | — | 1,068 | — | 1,068 | — | 1,068 | — | 1,068 | — | 1,068 |
| MEEGAN, Brian (S.F.) | 303 | +9 | 312 | +4 | 316 | +32 | 348 | +5 | 353 | +3 | 356 | -356 | — | — | — |
| MEEGAN, Joe (F.F.) | 367 | +15 | 382 | +21 | 403 | +32 | 435 | +5 | 440 | +5 | 445 | +64 | 509 | -509 | — |
| MURPHY, Peter | 615 | +32 | 647 | +6 | 653 | +38 | 691 | +7 | 698 | +6 | 704 | +98 | 802 | +124 | 926 |
| O'DONOGHUE, Francis (W.P.) | 249 | +23 | 272 | +6 | 278 | -278 | — | — | — | — | — | — | — | — | — |
| O'HANLON, Rosaleen (F.F.) | 917 | +48 | 965 | +59 | 1,024 | +63 | 1,087 | — | 1,087 | -19 | 1,068 | — | 1,068 | — | 1,068 |
| Non-transferable papers not effective | — | — | — | — | — | +34 | (34) | — | (34) | — | (34) | +131 | 165 | +171 | 336 |
| TOTAL: | 6,407 | — | 6,407 | — | 6,407 | — | 6,407 | — | 6,407 | — | 6,407 | — | 6,407 | — | 6,407 |

Elected: Cotter, Bill (F.G.); McNally, Padraig John (F.F.); Jones, Patrick (F.G.); O'Hanlon, Rosaleen (F.F.); Murphy, Peter

# CASTLEBLAYNEY ELECTORAL AREA

TOTAL ELECTORATE 8,895. VALID POLL 5,799. NO. OF MEMBERS 5. QUOTA 967.

| Names of Candidates | First Count Votes | Second Count Transfer of O'Brien's surplus | Result | Third Count Transfer of Carville's surplus | Result | Fourth Count Transfer of Duffy's votes | Result | Fifth Count Transfer of Woods' votes | Result | Sixth Count Transfer of Hughes' surplus | Result | Seventh Count Transfer of Conlan's surplus | Result |
|---|---|---|---|---|---|---|---|---|---|---|---|---|---|
| ARMSTRONG, Adam (F.G.) | 710 | +6 | 716 | +41 | 757 | +24 | 781 | +30 | 811 | +17 | 828 | +19 | 847 |
| CARVILLE, Arthur (F.G.) | 1,080 | — | 1,080 | -113 | 967 | — | 967 | — | 967 | — | 967 | — | 967 |
| CONLAN, John F. (F.G.) | 777 | +28 | 805 | +36 | 841 | +98 | 939 | +63 | 1,002 | — | 1,002 | -35 | 967 |
| DUFFY, Talbot (Non-Party) | 280 | +12 | 292 | +2 | 294 | -294 | — | — | — | — | — | — | — |
| HUGHES, Brendan (F.F.) | 879 | +32 | 911 | +18 | 929 | +15 | 944 | +105 | 1,049 | -82 | 967 | — | 967 |
| KEENAN, Olivia (F.F.) | 598 | +52 | 650 | +11 | 661 | +53 | 714 | +83 | 797 | +39 | 836 | +16 | 852 |
| O'BRIEN, Francis (F.F.) | 1,105 | -138 | 967 | — | 967 | — | 967 | — | 967 | — | 967 | — | 967 |
| WOODS, Malachy (S.F.) | 370 | +8 | 378 | +5 | 383 | +73 | 456 | -456 | — | — | — | — | — |
| Non-transferable papers not effective | — | — | — | — | — | +31 | 31 | +175 | 206 | +26 | 232 | — | 232 |
| TOTAL: | 5,799 | — | 5,799 | — | 5,799 | — | 5,799 | — | 5,799 | — | 5,799 | — | 5,799 |

Elected: O'Brien, Francis (F.F.); Carville, Arthur (F.G.); Hughes, Brendan (F.F.); Conlan, John F. (F.G.); Keenan, Olivia (F.F.)

# CLONES ELECTORAL AREA

TOTAL ELECTORATE 7,736. VALID POLL 5,072. NO. OF MEMBERS 4. QUOTA 1,015.

| Names of Candidates | First Count Votes | Second Count Transfer of Leonard's surplus Result | | Third Count Transfer of Duffy's and McKenna's votes Result | |
|---|---|---|---|---|---|
| CRAWFORD, Seymour (F.G.) | 910 | +26 | 936 | +37 | 973 |
| DUFFY, Joe | 12 | +1 | 13 | -13 | — |
| LEONARD, Jimmy (F.F.) | 1,314 | -299 | 1,015 | — | 1,015 |
| McELVANEY, Hugh (F.G.) | 952 | +34 | 986 | +49 | 1,035 |
| McKENNA, Pat (F.F.) | 239 | +190 | 429 | -429 | — |
| PRINGLE, Walter (Non-Party) | 913 | +25 | 938 | +99 | 1,037 |
| TREANOR, Pat (S.F.) | 732 | +23 | 755 | +77 | 832 |
| Non-transferable papers not effective | — | — | — | +180 | 180 |
| TOTAL: | 5,072 | — | 5,072 | — | 5,072 |

Elected: Leonard, Jimmy (F.F.); Pringle, Walter (Non-Party); McElvaney, Hugh (F.G.); Crawford, Seymour (F.G.)

# MONAGHAN ELECTORAL AREA

TOTAL ELECTORATE 11,796. VALID POLL 7,089. NO. OF MEMBERS 6. QUOTA 1,013.

| Names of Candidates | First Count Votes | Second Count Transfer of Ó Caoláin's surplus Result | | Third Count Transfer of Treanor's surplus Result | | Fourth Count Transfer of P. McKenna's votes Result | | Fifth Count Transfer of O'Hanrahan's votes Result | |
|---|---|---|---|---|---|---|---|---|---|
| CAULFIELD, Matt (F.F.) | 499 | +8 | 507 | +67 | 574 | +43 | 617 | +27 | 644 |
| MAXWELL, Noel (Non-Party) | 877 | +5 | 882 | +5 | 887 | +38 | 925 | +44 | 969 |
| McAREE, Stephen (F.G.) | 899 | +6 | 905 | +16 | 921 | +57 | 978 | +291 | 1,269 |
| McKENNA, Brian (S.F.) | 798 | +144 | 942 | +11 | 953 | +50 | 1,003 | +14 | 1,017 |
| McKENNA, Plunkett (Non-Party) | 267 | +10 | 277 | +7 | 284 | -284 | — | — | — |
| McKENNA, Willie (F.F.) | 1,019 | — | 1,019 | — | 1,019 | — | 1,019 | — | 1,019 |
| O CAOLAIN, Caoimhghin (S.F.) | 1,193 | -180 | 1,013 | — | 1,013 | — | 1,013 | — | 1,013 |
| O'HANRAHAN, Timothy Colman (F.G.) | 410 | +7 | 417 | +8 | 425 | +18 | 443 | -443 | — |
| TREANOR, Patsy (F.F.) | 1,127 | — | 1,127 | -114 | 1,013 | — | 1,013 | — | 1,013 |
| Non-transferable papers not effective | — | — | — | — | — | +78 | (78) | +67 | 145 |
| TOTAL: | 7,089 | — | 7,089 | — | 7,089 | — | 7,089 | — | 7,089 |

Elected: Ó Caolain, Caoimhghin (S.F.); Treanor, Patsy (F.F.); McKenna, Willie (F.F.); McAree, Stephen (F.G.); McKenna, Brian (S.F.); Maxwell, Noel (Non-Party)

# OFFALY COUNTY COUNCIL

## OFFALY COUNTY COUNCIL RESULTS

| Party | 1991 % of votes | 1991 Seats obtained | 1985 % of votes | 1985 Seat obtained |
|---|---|---|---|---|
| Fianna Fail | 41.4 | 10 | 49.7 | 12 |
| Fine Gael | 31.1 | 6 | 32.7 | 6 |
| Labour | 6.8 | 1 | 4.1 | — |
| Progressive Dem. | 4.1 | 1 | — | — |
| Workers Party | — | — | — | — |
| Other | 16.6 | 3 | 13.5 | 3 |
| TOTAL SEATS | | 21 | | 21 |

## OFFALY

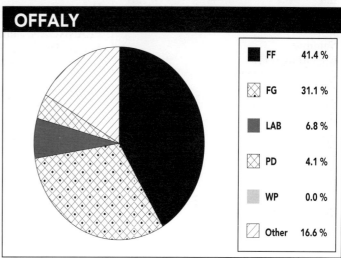

| | |
|---|---|
| ■ FF | 41.4 % |
| ⊠ FG | 31.1 % |
| ■ LAB | 6.8 % |
| ⊠ PD | 4.1 % |
| ▨ WP | 0.0 % |
| ▨ Other | 16.6 % |

**Courthouse, Tullamore**

**Telephone: (0506) 21419**

**Fax: (0506) 41160**

**Total population: 59,835**

**Rateable valuation: £348,040.95**

**Courthouse, Tullamore**

**Telephone: (0506) 21419**

**Fax: (0506) 41160**

**Rate: £24.4719**

**County Council meetings: Third Monday of each month except August**

*County Manager:* S. P. MacCarthy

*County Secretary:* Declan Nelson

*Finance Officer:* Brian Colgan

*County Engineer:* William Wall

*County Development Officer:* Seán Ryan

*Administrative Officers:* R. Carroll, A. O'Gorman

*Senior Staff Officers:* S. Ryan, H. O'Donoghue

*Training Officer:* Ambrose O'Gorman

*County Checker:* J. Price (Acting)

*County Librarian:* A. Coughlan

*County Solicitor:* B. J. Mahon (Acting)

*County Coroner:* Dr P. J. Grealy

*Chief Fire Officer:* D. Ó Céilleachair

*Civil Defence Officer:* E. A. Colville (Acting)

*Senior Executive Engineers:*

*Roads:* T. Fitzpatrick

*Planning:* V. Hussey

*Housing and Sanitary:* J. Keyes

*Urbans:* P. Rouse

**Sean P. McCarthy**

A Civil Engineer by education and profession, Sean Mc Carthy worked originally in the private sector with MIS Barrett & Sons in Cork before joining Local Government.

He worked as a Civil Engineer with Waterford, Tipperary North Riding, Laois, Cork County Council and Corporation respectively before becoming Offaly County Engineer in 1975. In 1982 he was promoted to rank of County Manager, firstly briefly with Donegal and then returning to Offaly.

Born in Cork in 1933 he was educated at the Presentation Brothers College and then UCD, BE(Civil). He is married to Marie Cashman and has five children. His hobbies include reading, walking and listening to music.

He is noted for job creation initiatives in the Council. His chairman of Offaly's Task Force and is a founder member of the Offaly Enterprise Board.

## BIRR

|     | 1991 | 1985 | '85 to '91 Swing |
| --- | --- | --- | --- |
| FF  | 55.9 | 50.2 | 5.7 |
| FG  | 39.0 | 42.1 | -3.1 |
| SF  | —    | 4.5  | -4.5 |
| Ind | 5.1  | —    | 5.1 |

CLEAR, Joe,
Shinrone,
Co. Offaly (FG)
Retired 0505-47239*

DOOLEY, Joseph,
Lisheen, Birr,
County Offaly. (FF)
Retired. 0509-20590

ENRIGHT, Tom,
3 John's Mall, Birr,
County Offaly. (FG)
Dail Deputy. 0509-20293

LOUGHNANE, Seamus,
5 Woodlands Drive, Birr,
County Offaly. (FF)
Civil Engineer. 0509-20094

MOYLAN, Patrick J.
Harbour Road, Banagher,
County Offaly. (FF)
Sales Representative. 0509-51113

*RIP. Replaced by
CLENDENNEN, Percy,
Kinnity, Birr,
County Offaly. (FG)

## EDENDERRY

|     | 1991 | 1985 | '85 to '91 Swing |
| --- | --- | --- | --- |
| FF  | 35.4 | 51.6 | -16.2 |
| FG  | 21.8 | 30.5 | -8.7 |
| LAB | 4.9  | —    | 4.9 |
| PD  | 17.3 | —    | 17.3 |
| GP  | 5.1  | —    | 5.1 |
| Ind | 15.5 | 17.9 | -2.4 |

BOURKE, Noel,
Killane, Edenderry,
County Offaly. (FF)
Bord-na-Mona Official.

EMERSON, Brigid,
Bishopswood Road, Portarlington,
County Offaly. (PD)
Housewife.

FLANAGAN, James,
Francis Street, Edenderry,
County Offaly. (NP)
Engineer.

FOX, Michael,
Kilmurry, Ballinagar, Tullamore,
County Offaly. (FG)
Farmer. 0506-21530

WEIR, Francis,
Cushina,
Portarlington,
County Offaly. (FF)
Farmer. 0502-23294

## FERBANE

|     | 1991 | 1985 | '85 to '91 Swing |
| --- | --- | --- | --- |
| FF  | 41.4 | 50.2 | -8.8 |
| FG  | 43.0 | 42.0 | 1.0 |
| Ind | 15.7 | 7.8  | 7.9 |

BUTTERFIELD, John,
Ballincanty, Blueball, Tullamore,
County Offaly. (NP)
Farmer. 0506-54027

CORCORAN, Bernard,
Ballyclare, Ferbane,
County Offaly. (FG)
Victualler. 0902-54304

DOOLEY, Edward J.
21 St. Cynoc's Terrace, Ferbane,
County Offaly. (FF)
Retired. 0902-54198

FEIGHERY, Tom,
Freagh, Kilcormac,
County Offaly. (FF)
Bord-na-Mona Official. 0509-35091

HANNIFFY, Connie,
Doon, Ballinahoun, Athlone,
County Offaly. (FG)
Businesswoman. 0902-30106

## TULLAMORE

|     | 1991 | 1985 | '85 to '91 Swing |
| --- | --- | --- | --- |
| FF  | 42.1 | 47.5 | -5.4 |
| FG  | 24.0 | 20.1 | 3.9 |
| LAB | 18.4 | 10.9 | 7.5 |
| Ind | 15.5 | 21.5 | -6.0 |

COWEN Brian,
28, Hophill Grove,
Tullamore,
Co. Offaly (FF)*

DOLAN, Thomas C.
Market Square, Clara,
County Offaly. (NP)
Publican. 0506-31408

FLANAGAN, John,
Batchlor's Walk, Tullamore,
County Offaly. (FF)
Builder. 0506-21570

GALLAGHER, Pat,
4 Henry Street, Tullamore,
County Offaly. (Lab)
Commercial Manager.

McKEIGUE, Tommy,
Spollanstown, Tullamore,
County Offaly. (FG)
ESB Employee. 0506-41519

O'CALLAGHAN, Miriam,
Collin's Lane, Tullamore,
County Offaly. (FF)
Health Board Official. 0506-41757

*Resigned when appointed to Cabinet
Feb. 1992. Replaced by:
COWEN, Barry,
River Street, Clara,
County Offaly. (FF)

**Tommy McKeigue, FG**
**Tullamore**

**Tom Enright, FG**
**Birr**

**Brian Cowen, FF**
**Tullamore**

# Labour and PDs win their first seats in Offaly

Offaly accounts for three of the T.D.'s in the five seat Constituency of Laois/Offaly. One of them, Ger Connolly, could not contest since he was then Minister of State at the Department of Environment. The other Fianna Fail T.D. Brian Cowen, since appointed Minister for Labour was the biggest Offaly vote-getter in these local elections. He polled 1,141 first preferences, 700 less than in 1987 but again topped the poll in the Tullamore area and was elected on the first count.

The Fine Gael Deputy Tom Enright topped the poll in Birr, 70 votes short of the quota, but was comfortably elected on the third count.

Offaly, like many counties has four electoral areas and, forty-three candidates in total contested the 21 seats.

In Tullamore, Fianna Fail held their three seats, John Flanagan was elected after Brian Cowen and Miriam O'Callaghan. Fine Gael took just one seat despite having almost one and three quarters quota in first preferences and newcomer Tommy McKeigue replaced outgoing Frank Feery.

Labour made yet another breakthrough to pick up a seat on Offaly County Council. They ran four candidates in Tullamore. Pat Gallagher was the strongest on first preferences and with over 48% transfer rates from his three running mates, he took the third seat.

In Birr, all was as is, no change in Party seats here or indeed in personnel. However, Fine Gael newcomer Percy Clendennen came unbelievably close to unseating outgoing Party colleague Joe

Clear, it was undoubtedly the closest finish in the county, he was deemed elected without reaching the quota on the 8th count ahead of Percy Clendennen by just one single vote. All four Fianna Fail candidates came in close together with the outgoing Seamus Loughnane, Patrick J. Moylan and Joseph Dooley retaining their seats.

In Edenderry, the Progressive Democratic made a historic breakthrough. Bridget Emerson took their first seat ever on the Council. Her Party colleague, Tom O'Connell had been more fancied and indeed got 143 more first preferences then her, but she faired better in transfers and took the fourth and final seat.

In this area Michael Fox topped the poll for Fine Gael and took their only seat in the area. Fianna Fail lost a seat. Newcomers Noel Burke and Fred Weir were elected for the main Government Party, but outgoing Councillor Patrick Scully lost out. Outgoing Independent John Flanagan maintained his good 1985 showing to take the second seat in the area.

In Ferbane, Fianna Fail were also to lose a seat, this time to Independent John Butterfield, who despite having switched electoral area from Tullamore, still got 829 first preferences and took the third seat.

Outgoing Fianna Fail Councillor Patrick Mahon was the one who lost out in this case, with Eddie Dooley and Tom Feighery taking the Parties two seats. For Fine Gael, Connie Hannify topped the poll, while Bernard Corcoran held his vote, both of them outgoing, retained there seats.

Fianna Fail's overall loss of two seats meant that they lost control of the County Council.

# BIRR ELECTORAL AREA

TOTAL ELECTORATE 9,171. VALID POLL 5,960. NO. OF MEMBERS 5. QUOTA 994

| Names of Candidates | First Count Votes | Second Count Transfer of Kavanagh Neavyn's votes | Result | Third Count Transfer of Carroll's votes | Result | Fourth Count Transfer of Enright's surplus | Result | Fifth Count Transfer of McLoughney's votes | Result | Sixth Count Transfer of Loughnane's surplus | Result | Seventh Count Transfer of Moylan's surplus | Result | Eighth Count Transfer of Dooley's surplus | Result |
|---|---|---|---|---|---|---|---|---|---|---|---|---|---|---|---|
| CARROLL, John (S.F.) | 570 | +31 | 601 | -601 | — | — | — | — | — | — | — | — | — | — | — |
| CLEAR, Joe (F.G.) | 657 | +21 | 678 | +71 | 749 | +10 | 759 | +114 | 873 | +23 | 896 | +8 | 904 | +3 | 907 |
| CLENDENNEN, Percy (F.G.) | 742 | +18 | 760 | +41 | 801 | +19 | 820 | +56 | 876 | +20 | 896 | +8 | 904 | +2 | 906 |
| DOOLEY, Joseph (F.F.) | 635 | +53 | 688 | +108 | 796 | +16 | 812 | +187 | 999 | — | 999 | — | 999 | -5 | 994 |
| ENRIGHT, Tom (F.G.) | 924 | +42 | 966 | +110 | 1,076 | -82 | 994 | — | 994 | — | 994 | — | 994 | — | 994 |
| KAVANAGH NEAVYN, Philomena S. (Non-Party) | 304 | -304 | — | — | — | — | — | — | — | — | — | — | — | — | — |
| LOUGHNANE, Seamus (F.F.) | 681 | +44 | 725 | +69 | 794 | +19 | 813 | +224 | 1,037 | -43 | 994 | — | 994 | — | 994 |
| McLOUGHNEY, Pat (F.F.) | 658 | +31 | 689 | +43 | 732 | +8 | 740 | -740 | — | — | — | — | — | — | — |
| MOYLAN, Patrick J. (F.F.) | 789 | +34 | 823 | +75 | 898 | +10 | 908 | +102 | 1,010 | — | 1,010 | -16 | 994 | — | 994 |
| Non-transferable papers not effective | — | +30 | 30 | +84 | 114 | — | 114 | +57 | 171 | — | 171 | — | 171 | — | 171 |
| TOTAL: | 5,960 | — | 5,960 | — | 5,960 | — | 5,960 | — | 5,960 | — | 5,960 | — | 5,960 | — | 5,960 |

Elected: Enright, Tom (F.G.); Loughnane, Seamus (F.F.); Moylan, Patrick J. (F.F.); Dooley, Joseph (F.F.); Clear, Joe (F.G.)

# EDENDERRY ELECTORAL AREA

TOTAL ELECTORATE 10,007. VALID POLL 5,861. NO. OF MEMBERS 5. QUOTA 977

| Names of Candidates | First Count Votes | Second Count Transfer of Brereton's votes | Result | Third Count Transfer of Coughlan's votes | Result | Fourth Count Transfer of Dolan's votes | Result | Fifth Count Transfer of Dunne's votes | Result | Sixth Count Transfer of Fox's surplus | Result | Seventh Count Transfer of O'Connell's votes | Result | Eighth Count Transfer of Flanagan's surplus | Result |
|---|---|---|---|---|---|---|---|---|---|---|---|---|---|---|---|
| BOURKE, Noel (F.F.) | 681 | +20 | 701 | +12 | 713 | +20 | 733 | +13 | 746 | +6 | 752 | +152 | 904 | +78 | 982 |
| BRERETON, Willie (Non-Party) | 111 | -111 | — | — | — | — | — | — | — | — | — | — | — | — | — |
| COUGHLAN, Sean (Lab.) | 289 | +3 | 292 | -292 | — | — | — | — | — | — | — | — | — | — | — |
| DOLAN, Anthony (G.P.) | 299 | +6 | 305 | +28 | 333 | -333 | — | — | — | — | — | — | — | — | — |
| DUNNE, Jack (F.G.) | 361 | +2 | 363 | +25 | 388 | +37 | 425 | -425 | — | — | — | — | — | — | — |
| EMERSON, Brigid (P.D.) | 436 | +2 | 438 | +68 | 506 | +35 | 541 | +134 | 675 | +10 | 685 | +147 | 832 | +35 | 867 |
| FLANAGAN, James (Non-Party) | 795 | +49 | 844 | +26 | 870 | +40 | 910 | +32 | 942 | +9 | 951 | +243 | 1,194 | -217 | 977 |
| FOX, Michael (F.G.) | 915 | +2 | 917 | +20 | 937 | +101 | 1,038 | — | 1,038 | -61 | 977 | — | 977 | — | 977 |
| O'CONNELL, Tom (P.D.) | 579 | +18 | 597 | +11 | 608 | +34 | 642 | +18 | 660 | +13 | 673 | -673 | — | — | — |
| SCULLY, Patrick (F.F.) | 677 | +1 | 678 | +6 | 684 | +25 | 709 | +19 | 728 | +19 | 747 | +26 | 773 | +8 | 781 |
| WEIR, Francis (F.F.) | 718 | — | 718 | +73 | 791 | +15 | 806 | +88 | 894 | +4 | 898 | +22 | 920 | +6 | 926 |
| Non-transferable papers not effective | — | +8 | (8) | +23 | 31 | +26 | 57 | +121 | 178 | — | 178 | +83 | 261 | +90 | 351 |
| TOTAL: | 5,861 | — | 5,861 | — | 5,861 | — | 5,861 | — | 5,861 | — | 5,861 | — | 5,861 | — | 5,861 |

Elected: Fox, Michael (F.G.); Flanagan, James (Non-Party); Bourke, Noel (F.F.); Weir, Francis (F.F.); Emerson, Brigid (P.D.)

# FERBANE ELECTORAL AREA

TOTAL ELECTORATE 8,914. VALID POLL 5,292. NO. OF MEMBERS 5. QUOTA 883

| Names of Candidates | First Count Votes | Second Count Transfer of Hanniffy's surplus | Result | Third Count Transfer of Troy's votes | Result | Fourth Count Transfer of Corcoran's surplus | Result |
|---|---|---|---|---|---|---|---|
| BUTTERFIELD, John (Non-Party) | 829 | +57 | 886 | — | 886 | — | 886 |
| CORCORAN, Bernard (F.G.) | 673 | +167 | 840 | +221 | 1,061 | -178 | 883 |
| DOOLEY, Edward J. (F.F.) | 966 | — | 966 | — | 966 | — | 966 |
| FEIGHERY, Tom (F.F.) | 680 | +15 | 695 | +109 | 804 | +41 | 845 |
| HANNIFFY, Connie (F.G.) | 1,183 | -300 | 883 | — | 883 | — | 883 |
| MAHON, Patrick (F.F.) | 544 | +18 | 562 | +40 | 602 | +6 | 608 |
| TROY, Pat (F.G.) | 417 | +43 | 460 | -460 | — | — | — |
| Non-transferable papers not effective | — | — | — | +90 | 90 | +131 | 221 |
| TOTAL: | 5,292 | — | 5,292 | — | 5,292 | — | 5,292 |

Elected: Hanniffy, Connie (F.G.); Dooley, Edward J. (F.F.); Butterfield, John (Non-Party); Corcoran, Bernard (F.G.); Feighery, Tom (F.F.)

# TULLAMORE ELECTORAL AREA

TOTAL ELECTORATE 12,610. VALID POLL 7,609. NO. OF MEMBERS 6. QUOTA 1,088

| Names of Candidates | First Count Votes | Second Count Transfer of Gaffey's, M. Keeley's & P. Keeley's votes | Result | Third Count Transfer of Cowen's surplus | Result | Fourth Count Transfer of O'Brien's votes | Result | Fifth Count Transfer of O'Toole's votes | Result | Sixth Count Transfer of Byrne's votes | Result | Seventh Count Transfer of Wrafter's votes | Result | Eighth Count Transfer of McGuire's votes | Result | Ninth Count Transfer of Lynam's votes | Result |
|---|---|---|---|---|---|---|---|---|---|---|---|---|---|---|---|---|---|
| BYRNE, Laurence (Lab.) | 250 | +8 | 258 | +1 | 259 | +11 | 270 | +10 | 280 | -280 | — | — | — | — | — | — | — |
| COWEN, Brian (F.F.) | 1,141 | — | 1,141 | -53 | 1,088 | — | 1,088 | — | 1,088 | — | 1,088 | — | 1,088 | — | 1,088 | — | 1,088 |
| DOLAN, Thomas C. (Non-Party) | 844 | +16 | 860 | +15 | 875 | +4 | 879 | +23 | 902 | +24 | 926 | +24 | 950 | +16 | 966 | +47 | 1,013 |
| FEERY, Frank (F.G.) | 708 | +4 | 712 | +7 | 719 | +3 | 722 | +2 | 724 | +13 | 737 | +61 | 798 | +12 | 810 | +38 | 848 |
| FLANAGAN, John (F.F.) | 953 | +12 | 965 | +16 | 981 | +13 | 994 | +24 | 1,018 | +54 | 1,072 | +41 | 1,113 | — | 1,113 | — | 1,113 |
| GAFFEY, Nellie | 26 | -26 | — | — | — | — | — | — | — | — | — | — | — | — | — | — | — |
| GALLAGHER, Pat (Lab.) | 722 | +20 | 742 | +1 | 743 | +65 | 808 | +34 | 842 | +52 | 894 | +27 | 921 | +178 | 1,099 | — | 1,099 |
| KEELEY, May (Non-Party) | 41 | -41 | — | — | — | — | — | — | — | — | — | — | — | — | — | — | — |
| KEELEY, Peadar (Non-Party) | 78 | -78 | — | — | — | — | — | — | — | — | — | — | — | — | — | — | — |
| LYNAM, Michael (F.F.) | 403 | +2 | 405 | +3 | 408 | +4 | 412 | +10 | 422 | +8 | 430 | +11 | 441 | +7 | 448 | -448 | — |
| McGUIRE, Ernest (Lab.) | 223 | +9 | 232 | +1 | 233 | +32 | 265 | +27 | 292 | +68 | 360 | +8 | 368 | -368 | — | — | — |
| McKEIGUE, Tommy (F.G.) | 830 | +24 | 854 | +1 | 855 | +27 | 882 | +31 | 913 | +33 | 946 | +111 | 1,057 | +61 | 1,118 | — | 1,118 |
| O'BRIEN, Sean (Lab.) | 202 | +2 | 204 | — | 204 | -204 | — | — | — | — | — | — | — | — | — | — | — |
| O'CALLAGHAN, Miriam (F.F.) | 706 | +16 | 722 | +7 | 729 | +18 | 747 | +34 | 781 | +16 | 797 | +19 | 816 | +35 | 851 | +225 | 1,076 |
| O'TOOLE, Anne (Non-Party) | 193 | +14 | 207 | — | 207 | +12 | 219 | -219 | — | — | — | — | — | — | — | — | — |
| WRAFTER, Kevin Gerard (F.G.) | 289 | +9 | 298 | +1 | 299 | +5 | 304 | +5 | 309 | +1 | 310 | -310 | — | — | — | — | — |
| Non-transferable papers not effective | — | +9 | 9 | — | 9 | +10 | 19 | +19 | 38 | +11 | 49 | +8 | 57 | +59 | 116 | +138 | 254 |
| TOTAL: | 7,609 | — | 7,609 | — | 7,609 | — | 7,609 | — | 7,609 | — | 7,609 | — | 7,609 | — | 7,609 | — | 7,609 |

Elected: Cowen, Brian (F.F.); Flanagan, John (F.F.); McKeigue, Tommy (F.G.); Gallagher, Pat (Lab.); O'Callaghan, Miriam (F.F.); Dolan, Thomas C. (Non-Party)

# Always check before you go.

Now you can call "Weatherdial" to get the latest Met Service weather forecast anywhere in Ireland - 24 hours a day - 7 days a week. For the weather in your area just call the appropriate number opposite:

| | |
|---|---|
| **Munster** | 1550 123 626 |
| **Leinster** | 1550 123 627 |
| **Connaught** | 1550 123 628 |
| **Ulster** | 1550 123 629 |
| **Dublin** | 1550 123 630 |
| **Sea Area** | 1550 123 631 |

**WEATHERDIAL**

FROM THE MET SERVICE

# ROSCOMMON COUNTY COUNCIL

## ROSCOMMON COUNTY COUNCIL RESULTS

| PARTY | 1991 % of votes | 1991 Seats obtained | 1985 % of votes | 1985 Seat obtained |
|---|---|---|---|---|
| Fianna Fail | 40.2 | 10 | 43.6 | 13 |
| Fine Gael | 40.3 | 11 | 37.4 | 8 |
| Labour | — | — | — | — |
| Progressive Dem. | — | — | — | — |
| Workers Party | — | — | — | — |
| Other | 19.5 | 5 | 19.0 | 5 |
| **TOTAL SEATS** | | **26** | | **26** |

## ROSCOMMON

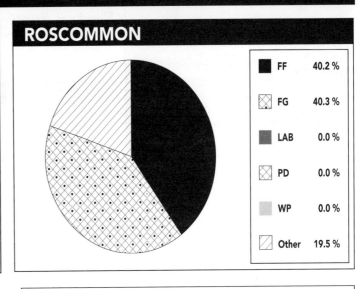

| | |
|---|---|
| ■ FF | 40.2 % |
| ⊠ FG | 40.3 % |
| ■ LAB | 0.0 % |
| ⊠ PD | 0.0 % |
| WP | 0.0 % |
| ⁄ Other | 19.5 % |

Courthouse, Roscommon
Telephone: (0903) 26100
Total population: 54,592
Rateable valuation: £432,824
Rate: £31.33
County Council meetings: Fourth Monday,
January to November (excl. August); Third Monday in
December

*County Manager:* Donal Connolly
*County Secretary:* Derry O'Donnell
*Finance Officer:* M. Doyle
*County Engineer:* Vincent Brennan
*Administrative Officers:*
*General and Personnel:* F. C. Friel
*Planning and Sanitary Services:* W. Halligan
*Planning and Environment:* B. McGrath
*Senior Staff Officers:*
*Accounts:* Tony Robinson
*Roads and Engineering:* Michael Nolan
*County Development Team:* Gerry Finn
*Motor Taxation:* Thomas Flanagan
*County Librarian:* Helen Kilcline,
Abbey Street, Roscommon
*County Solicitor:* Dermot M. MacDermot,
*County Coroner:* P. Desmond O'Connor, Solicitor,
Ballaghaderreen
*Civil Defence Officer:* Michael J. Cunnane (Acting)
*Chief Fire Officer:* Cathal McConn
*County Development Officer:* Thomas Lynch
*Senior Executive Engineers:*
*Road Design:* John Cunningham
*Roads:* Frank Gleeson
*Sanitary Services:* John Vincent Kyne
*Environment:* Joe Walsh
*Housing:* Albert Looby (Acting)
*Senior Executive (Planning):* Michael O'Donnell

Donal Connolly, a native of Waterford, was born in 1932 and worked as a Clerical Officer with CIE before joining Local Government, with Cork County Council in 1962 as a Clerical Officer. In 1969 he became Staff Officer with Tipperary North Riding County Council and held the same post with Waterford County Council from 1970 - 1972.

In 1972 he became County Accountant with Tipperary South Riding until he was appointed County Secretary with Westmeath County Council in 1977. He later served as Assistant County Manager in Tippperary South Riding until 1985 when he was appointed Roscommon County Manager.

He has educational qualifications from both

**Donal Connolly**

the ACIS and the IPA from which he holds a Diploma in Public Administration.

He is married to Cathy Curran, they have four daughters and four sons. His hobbies include golf and the G.A.A.

## ATHLONE

|    | 1991 | 1985 | '85 to '91 Swing |
|----|------|------|------|
| FF | 53.4 | 37.8 | 15.6 |
| FG | 46.6 | 37.8 | 8.8 |
| LAB | — | 24.4 | -24.4 |

FINNERAN, Michael,
Feevagh, Taughmaconnell, Ballinasloe,
County Roscommon (FF)
Senator. 0903-42117

MOORE, Patrick,
7 Riverside Place, Galway Road,
Athlone,
County Roscommon. (FG)
Storeman. 0902-92580

MORRIS, Jim,
Purts, Kiltoom,
County Roscommon. (FF)
Retired. 0902-39116

NAUGHTEN, Liam,
Drum, Athlone,
County Roscommon. (FG)
Senator. 0902-37100

## BALLAGHADERREEN

|    | 1991 | 1985 | '85 to '91 Swing |
|----|------|------|------|
| FF | 34.4 | 44.1 | -9.7 |
| FG | 48.0 | 42.8 | 5.2 |
| IND | 17.6 | 13.1 | 4.5 |

CONNOR, John,
Cloonshanville, Frenchpark,
County Roscommon. (FG)
Dáil Deputy. 0907-71043

DOONEY, Patrick,
Green Road, Cairns Hill,
Sligo. (FF)
Teacher. 0907-60173

LYNCH, Paul,
Loughglynn,
Castlerea,
County Roscommon. (FF)
Building Contractor. 0907-80011

SCALLY, Michael,
Sligo Road, Ballaghaderreen,
County Roscommon. (FG)
Teacher. 0907-60284

## BOYLE

|    | 1991 | 1985 | '85 to '91 Swing |
|----|------|------|------|
| FF | 36.4 | 52.1 | -15.7 |
| FG | 48.0 | 42.8 | 5.2 |
| SF | — | 5.4 | -5.4 |
| Ind | 15.6 | — | 15.6 |

BEIRNE, Paul,
St. Patrick's Street, Boyle,
County Roscommon. (NP)
Butcher.

DUIGNAN, Kitty,
Rathallen, Boyle,
County Roscommon. (FG)
Housewife. 079-68035

HOPKINS, Charlie,
Derriniskey, Arigna,
County Roscommon. (FG)
Small Farmer. 078-46044

McQUAID, Sean,
Deerpark, Sligo Road, Boyle,
County Roscommon. (FF)
Retired. 079-62273

O'DONNELL, Colm,
Keadue, Boyle,
County Roscommon. (FF)
Electrical Contractor. 078-47216

## CASTLEREA

|    | 1991 | 1985 | '85 to '91 Swing |
|----|------|------|------|
| FF | 23.6 | 27.9 | -4.3 |
| FG | 35.7 | 27.1 | 8.6 |
| IND | 40.7 | 45.0 | -4.3 |

BURKE, Danny,
Barrack Street, Castlerea,
County Roscommon. (NP)
Postman

CALLAGHAN, Thomas,
Rathmoyle, Lisalway, Castlerea,
County Roscommon. (FG)
Farmer. 0907-51040

McGREAL, Michael,
Carrick, Ballinlough,
County Roscommon. (FG)
Draughtsman. 0907-40079

MOYLAN, Patrick,
Ballinlough,
County Roscommon. (NP)
Farmer. 0907-40026

## ROSCOMMON

|    | 1991 | 1985 | '85 to '91 Swing |
|----|------|------|------|
| FF | 35.8 | 48.6 | -12.8 |
| FG | 26.5 | 32.9 | -6.4 |
| IND | 37.6 | 18.6 | 19.0 |

BRUEN, Des,
Ballinagard,
Roscommon. (FF)
Insurance Broker. 0903-26138

CONNOLLY, Domnick,
Fuerty,
Roscommon. (FG)
Creamery Manager.

**Michael McGreal (FG)**
Castlerea

**Tommy Crosby (FF)**
Strokestown

**Michael Finneran (FF)**
Athlone

**Liam Naughton (FG)**
Athlone

DONNELLY, Gerard,
Rahara, Athleague,
County Roscommon. (FG)
Farmer. 0902-88224

FOXE, Tom,
Athlone Road,
Roscommon. (NP)
Dail Deputy. 0903-26507

QUINN, Eithne,
Crubyhill,
Roscommon. (NP)
Public Representative.

Jim Moris (FF), Athlone

John Connor (FG)
Roscommon

## STROKESTOWN

|     | 1991 | 1985 | '85 to '91 Swing |
| --- | --- | --- | --- |
| FF  | 52.2 | 47.4 | 4.8 |
| FG  | 37.3 | 39.9 | -2.6 |
| SF  | 10.5 | 12.7 | -2.2 |

BEIRNE, Sean,
Derryphatten, Strokestown,
County Roscommon. (FG)
Farmer.

CROSBY, Tommy,
Tarmonbarry,
County Roscommon. (FF)
Publican. 043-26021

MULLOOLY, Brian,
Church Street, Strokestown,
County Roscommon. (FF)
Senator. 078-35112

MURPHY, Eugene,
Scramogue,
County Roscommon. (FF)
Horticultural Advisor.

# The 'Foxe Factor' in Roscommon

Throughout the country, Independents running on specific issues, such as local service charges, polled extremely well and were elected in many cases. In Roscommon, since the election of publican Tom Foxe to Dail Eireann in 1989, the success of such candidates is loosely called the 'Foxe Factor'. Five Independents who had campaigned specifically on local services, which are under threat, were elected to Roscommon County Council. This number was the same as in 1985 only there were several changes in faces. Fine Gael were the real gainers in Roscommon, winning 3 new seats, all at the expense of Fianna Fail, and thereby becoming the largest party in the County Council, with 11 of the 26 seats.

With outgoing Independent Councillor, Paddy Lenihan, a brother of Fianna Fail's Brian Lenihan and Mary O'Rourke, not in the field on this occasion the way was clear for Fine Gael to regain the seat they lost to Lenihan in 1985. The Fine Gael newcomer, Patrick Moore, polled well and took the third seat with a margin of 73 votes from Michael O'Faolain of Fianna Fail. Moore was helped by good transfers from his party colleague Senator Liam Naughten, who increased his 1985 outcome by 207 votes. The poll was topped by Fianna Fail's Michael Finneran. The Ballinasloe based Senator had 1.6 quotas and was returned along with running mate and fellow outgoing Councillor James Morris. Despite the 15% increase in Fianna Fail's vote, as 1985 Lenihan supporters came back to FF, the chances of a third seat were always remote.

In Ballaghaderreen, Fine Gael again gained an extra seat at the expense of an Independent. This time it was outgoing Councillor Tom McGarry who lost out. In 1985, the Independent, McGarry, had defeated Fine Gael's Michael Scally by a mere 2 votes. Scally had his revenge, however, on this occasion topping the poll and being elected on the first count. The Fine Gael teacher was joined by party colleague John Connor who was also successfully returned on the first count. The other two seats in

Ballaghaderreen were filled by Fianna Fail's two outgoing Councillors, Patrick Dooney and Paul Lynch.

The absence of Senator Sean Doherty from the ballot paper in the Boyle Electoral Area was bound to affect the Fianna Fail vote, especially as he had topped the poll with 1,263 votes in 1985. Fianna Fail's share of the vote declined by a sizeable 15.7% and one of the three FF seats was conceded. Outgoing Councillors, Colm O'Donnell and Sean McQuaid, were returned on the final count neither of them reaching the quota. Interestingly, O'Donnell and McQuaid were the only Councillors elected in 1985 who sought re-election on this occassion in Boyle.

The poll in Boyle was headed by Fine Gael's Kitty Duignan, widow of the late Councillor Charlie Duignan. She was returned along with running mate Charlie Hopkins who made amends for his 1985 defeat. Duignan was closely followed by 22 year old Paul Beirne who received an impressive 775 votes. Beirne fought the election on the proposed downgrading of postal services.

Fianna Fail lost its only seat in Castlerea to Fine Gael, and the area is now one of only four areas throughout the country without Fianna Fail representation. The retirement of outgoing Councillor Johnny Costello was a contributing factor, although the decision to run 3 candidates was a poor strategic one, and was a big factor in the Fianna Fail loss. Fine Gael increased their vote by over 8% and Thomas Callaghan made amends for the disappointment of 1985 by taking the last seat. His party colleague, Michael McGreal added 169 votes to his 1985 total and was only 7 votes short of a first count victory.

Castlerea returned two Independent Councillors. Despite a drop in his vote, outgoing Independent Councillor, Patrick Moylan, successfully took the second seat in this four seat area. Independent Danny Burke was the second successful candidate to win a seat in Roscommon County Council by fighting against postal service cut-backs. However, Burke's

achievement was offset as outgoing Independent Councillor, Paddy Concannon, lost out, thus ending 46 years of uninterrupted service on Roscommon Council.

In running two candidates in the Roscommon Electoral Area, the Roscommon Hospital Action Committee were seen as taking a big risk. Nevertheless it was a risk that paid off, with Dail Deputy, Tom Foxe and outgoing Councillor, Eithne Quinn taking the first two seats. Foxe received 1,232 votes and obviously strengthened his base for the next general election in the new Roscommon-Westmeath constituency. Quinn's first preference vote was down on 1985 but with the help of Foxe's transfers was safely returned.

The losers in the Roscommon Area were Fianna Fail dropping 2 of the 3 seats they won in 1985. Without the presence of Deputy Terry Leydon, the FF vote was down by a sizable 12.7%, but again the mistake of spreading their vote over too many candidates was costly. With 2.1 quotas and 4 candidates, Fianna Fail took a single seat while Fine Gael returned 2 of their 3 candidates with only 1.59 quotas. Outgoing Councillor Desmond Bruen was the only Fianna Fail success in the Roscommon Area.

Fine Gael picked up an extra seat at Fianna Fail's expense despite the 6.8% drop in their vote. Outgoing Councillor Patrick Walshe was defeated as his 2 running mates, newcomers Gerard Donnelly and Domnick Connolly were elected on the last count without reaching the quota.

The Stokestown Electoral Area brought some good news for Fianna Fail as a seat was gained at the expense of Fine Gael. Internal Fine Gael transfers were weak and the seat they won by a 46 vote margin in 1985, was taken on this occasion by Fianna Fail's Tommy Crosby, who received an unusually high number of transfers from Fine Gael to edge out Noel Collins of Fine Gael for the last seat. With such a slender victory in 1985 Fine Gael would have been better off with only 2 candidates in Stokestown to ensure stronger transfers between their candidates.

The poll in Stokestown was headed by Fianna Fail Senator, Brian Mullooly, who was returned along with colleagues Eugene Murphy and Tommy Crosby. The newly elected Fianna Fail Councillors, along with Fine Gael's Sean Beirne, were all returned on the third count.

# ATHLONE ELECTORAL AREA

TOTAL ELECTORATE 7,031. VALID POLL 5,204. NO. OF MEMBERS 4. QUOTA 1,041

| Names of Candidates | First Count Votes | Second Count Transfer of Finneran's surplus | Result | Third Count Transfer of Naughten's surplus | Result | Fourth Count Transfer of Moore's surplus | Result |
|---|---|---|---|---|---|---|---|
| FINNERAN, Michael Joseph (F.F.) | 1,635 | -594 | **1,041** | — | **1,041** | — | **1,041** |
| MOORE, Patrick (F.G.) | 841 | +155 | **996** | +409 | **1,405** | -364 | **1,041** |
| MORRIS, James (F.F.) | 592 | +265 | **857** | +47 | **904** | +76 | **980** |
| NAUGHTEN, Liam (F.G.) | 1,586 | — | **1,586** | -545 | **1,041** | — | **1,041** |
| O'FAOLAIN, Mich´eal (F.F.) | 550 | +174 | **724** | +89 | **813** | +94 | **907** |
| Non-transferable papers not effective | — | — | — | — | — | +194 | **194** |
| TOTAL: | **5,204** | — | **5,204** | — | **5,204** | — | **5,204** |

Elected: Finneran, Michael Joseph (F.F.); Naughten, Liam (F.G.); Moore, Patrick (F.G.); Morris, James (F.F.)

# BALLAGHADERREEN ELECTORAL AREA

TOTAL ELECTORATE 5,583. VALID POLL 4,068. NO. OF MEMBERS 4. QUOTA 814

| Names of Candidates | First Count Votes | Second Count Transfer of Scally's surplus | Result | Third Count Transfer of Creighton's votes | Result | Fourth Count Transfer of McGarry's votes | Result |
|---|---|---|---|---|---|---|---|
| ALLMAN, Dermot | 430 | +54 | **484** | +68 | **552** | +100 | **652** |
| CONNOR, John (F.G.) | 839 | — | **839** | — | **839** | — | **839** |
| CREIGHTON, Ml. Joe (F.F.) | 252 | +25 | **277** | -277 | — | — | — |
| DOONEY, Patrick F. (F.F.) | 550 | +80 | **630** | +60 | **690** | +113 | **803** |
| LYNCH, Paul (F.F.) | 599 | +73 | **672** | +71 | **743** | +52 | **795** |
| McGARRY, Tom | 286 | +65 | **351** | +38 | **389** | -389 | — |
| SCALLY, Michael (F.G.) | 1,112 | -298 | **814** | — | **814** | — | **814** |
| Non-transferable papers not effective | — | +1 | **1** | +40 | **41** | +124 | **165** |
| TOTAL: | **4,068** | — | **4,068** | — | **4,068** | — | **4,068** |

Elected: Scally, Michael (F.G.); Connor, John (F.G.); Dooney, Patrick F. (F.F.); Lynch, Paul (F.F.)

# BOYLE ELECTORAL AREA

TOTAL ELECTORATE 6,955. VALID POLL 4,963. NO. OF MEMBERS 5. QUOTA 828

| Names of Candidates | First Count Votes | Second Count Transfer of Carty's votes Result | | Third Count Transfer of Duignan's surplus Result | | Fourth Count Transfer of Clifford's votes Result | | Fifth Count Transfer of Kelly's votes Result | |
|---|---|---|---|---|---|---|---|---|---|
| BEIRNE, Paul Vincent | 775 | +65 | 840 | — | 840 | — | 840 | — | 840 |
| CARTY, Michael (F.G.) | 368 | -368 | — | — | — | — | — | — | — |
| CLIFFORD, Mary (F.F.) | 369 | +21 | 390 | +6 | 396 | -396 | — | — | — |
| DUIGNAN, Kitty (F.G.) | 813 | +172 | 985 | -157 | 828 | — | 828 | — | 828 |
| HOPKINS, Charlie (F.G.) | 671 | +62 | 733 | +69 | 802 | +42 | 844 | — | 844 |
| KELLY, Tommy (F.F.) | 452 | — | 452 | +2 | 454 | +65 | 519 | -519 | — |
| McQUAID, Sean J. (F.F.) | 457 | +22 | 479 | +19 | 498 | +129 | 627 | +165 | 792 |
| O'BEIRNE, Joseph (F.G.) | 529 | +14 | 543 | +44 | 587 | +12 | 599 | +127 | 726 |
| O'DONNELL, Colm (F.F.) | 529 | +8 | 537 | +8 | 545 | +104 | 649 | +165 | 814 |
| Non-transferable paper not effective | — | +4 | 4 | +9 | 13 | +44 | 57 | +62 | 119 |
| TOTAL: | 4,963 | — | 4,963 | — | 4,963 | — | 4,963 | — | 4,963 |

Elected: Duignan, Kitty (F.G.); Beirne, Paul Vincent; Hopkins, Charlie (F.G.); O'Donnell, Colm (F.F.); McQuaid, Sean J. (F.F.)

# CASTLEREAGH ELECTORAL AREA

TOTAL ELECTORATE 5,175. VALID POLL 3,771. NO. OF MEMBERS 4. QUOTA 755

| Names of Candidates | First Count Votes | Second Count Transfer of Sloyan's vote Result | | Third Count Transfer of Satchwell's votes Result | | Fourth Count Transfer of Concannon's votes Result | |
|---|---|---|---|---|---|---|---|
| BURKE, Danny (Non-Party) | 579 | +19 | 598 | +46 | 644 | +112 | 756 |
| CALLAGHAN, Thomas (F.G.) | 600 | +8 | 608 | +40 | 648 | +104 | 752 |
| CONCANNON, Patrick (Non-Party) | 372 | +9 | 381 | +29 | 410 | -410 | — |
| McGREAL, Michael (F.G.) | 748 | +45 | 793 | — | 793 | — | 793 |
| MOYLAN, Patrick (Non-Party) | 583 | +66 | 649 | +35 | (684 | +103 | 787 |
| SATCHWELL, Liam (F.F.) | 257 | +43 | 300 | -300 | — | — | — |
| SLOYAN, Seamus (F.F.) | 250 | -250 | — | — | — | — | — |
| WALDRON, Tony (F.F.) | 382 | +50 | 432 | +138 | 570 | +53 | 623 |
| Non-transferable papers not effective | — | +10 | 10 | +12 | 22 | +38 | 60 |
| TOTAL: | 3,771 | — | 3,771 | — | 3,771 | — | 3,771 |

Elected: McGreal, Michael (F.G.); Moylan, Patrick (Non-Party); Burke, Danny (Non-Party); Callaghan, Thomas (F.G.)

# ROSCOMMON ELECTORAL AREA

TOTAL ELECTORATE 7,411. VALID POLL 5,072. NO. OF MEMBERS 5. QUOTA 846

| Names of Candidates | First Count Votes | Second Count Transfer of Foxe's surplus | Result | Third Count Transfer of Murray's votes | Result | Fourth Count Transfer of Walshe's surplus | Result | Fifth Count Transfer of Kilduff's votes | Result | Sixth Count Transfer of Bruen's surplus | Result |
|---|---|---|---|---|---|---|---|---|---|---|---|
| BRUEN, Desmond (F.F.) | 608 | +48 | 656 | +90 | 746 | +53 | 799 | +124 | 923 | -77 | 846 |
| CONNOLLY, Domnick (F.G.) | 578 | +29 | 607 | +47 | 654 | +91 | 745 | +20 | 765 | +2 | 767 |
| DONNELLY, Gerard (F.G.) | 436 | +14 | 450 | +43 | 493 | +111 | 604 | +180 | 784 | +18 | 802 |
| FOXE, Tom | 1,232 | -386 | 846 | — | 846 | — | 846 | — | 846 | — | 846 |
| KILDUFF, Paddy (F.F.) | 439 | +11 | 450 | +48 | 498 | +25 | 523 | -523 | — | — | — |
| McDERMOTT, Seamus (F.F.) | 476 | +30 | 506 | +32 | 538 | +37 | 575 | +89 | 664 | +55 | 719 |
| MURRAY, Anthony (F.F.) | 295 | +9 | 304 | -304 | — | — | — | — | — | — | — |
| QUINN, Eithne | 677 | +213 | 890 | — | 890 | — | 890 | — | 890 | — | 890 |
| WALSHE, Patrick (F.G.) | 331 | +32 | 363 | +14 | 377 | -377 | — | — | — | — | — |
| non-transferable papers not effective | — | — | — | +30 | 30 | +60 | 90 | +110 | 200 | +2 | 202 |
| TOTAL: | 5,072 | — | 5,072 | — | 5,072 | — | 5,072 | — | 5,072 | — | 5,072 |

Elected:— Foxe, Tom; Quinn, Eithne; Bruen, Desmond (F.F.); Donnelly, Gerard (F.G.); Connolly, Domnick (F.G.)

# STROKESTOWN ELECTORAL AREA

TOTAL ELECTORATE 6,219. VALID POLL 4,762. NO. OF MEMBERS 4. QUOTA 953

| Names of Candidates | First Count Votes | Second Count Transfer of Curley's votes | Result | Third Count Transfer of D. Mullooly's votes | Result |
|---|---|---|---|---|---|
| BEIRNE, Sean (F.G.) | 773 | +108 | 881 | +89 | 970 |
| COLLINS, Noel A. (F.G.) | 614 | +43 | 657 | +65 | 722 |
| CROSBY, Tommy (F.F.) | 759 | +59 | 818 | +91 | 909 |
| CURLEY, Frank (F.G.) | 390 | -390 | — | — | — |
| MULLOOLY, Brian (F.F.) | 899 | +38 | 937 | +122 | 1,059 |
| MULLOOLY, Dermot | 500 | +25 | 525 | -525 | — |
| MURPHY, Eugene M. (F.F.) | 827 | +101 | 928 | +86 | 1,014 |
| Non-transferable papers not effective | — | +16 | 16 | +72 | 88 |
| TOTAL: | 4,762 | — | 4,762 | — | 4,762 |

Elected: Mullooly, Brian (F.F.); Murphy, Eugene M. (F.F.); Beirne, Sean (F.G.); Crosby, Tommy (F.F.)

# SLIGO COUNTY COUNCIL

## SLIGO COUNTY COUNCIL RESULTS

| Party | 1991 % of votes | 1991 Seats obtained | 1985 % of votes | 1985 Seat obtained |
|---|---|---|---|---|
| Fianna Fail | 44.4 | 11 | 45.6 | 11 |
| Fine Gael | 34.3 | 11 | 37.9 | 9 |
| Labour | 3.3 | — | 2.9 | 1 |
| Progressive Dem. | 1.0 | — | — | — |
| Workers Party | — | — | — | — |
| Other | 17.0 | 3 | 13.6 | 4 |
| TOTAL SEATS | | 25 | | 25 |

## SLIGO

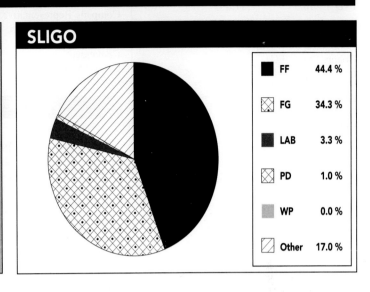

| | | |
|---|---|---|
| ■ | FF | 44.4 % |
| ⊠ | FG | 34.3 % |
| ■ | LAB | 3.3 % |
| ⊠ | PD | 1.0 % |
| ▨ | WP | 0.0 % |
| ⧄ | Other | 17.0 % |

**Riverside, Sligo**
**Telephone: (071) 43221**
**Total population: 55,979**
**Area sq miles: 709**
**Rateable valuation: £274,014**
**Rate: £25.78**

*County Manager:* P. Byrne
*County Secretary:* B. Byrne
*Finance Officer:* A. P. McConnell
*County Engineer:* S. Stewart
*County Development Officer:* T. Byrne
*Assistant County Development Officer:* C. Leonard
*Administrative Officers:*
*Housing:* Monica P. Foran
*Miscellaneous Services, Sanitary Services:*
Denis O'Donovan
*Senior Staff Officers:*
*Finance:* D. Breen
*Planning and Development:* W. McGonagle
*County Librarian:* J. McTernan
*County Solicitor:* Bryan Armstrong
*County Coroner:* Dr D. Moran
*Chief Fire Officer:* P. Forkan
*Civil Defence Officer:* S. McManus
*Senior Executive Engineers:*
*Sanitary Services:* D. O'Rourke
*Roads:* N. Farrell
*Planning:* J. McHugh (Acting)
*Road Design:* P. Canning (Acting)
*Housing:* J. Harney

A Longford man, Paul Byrne was born in 1932 and is married to Nora Mc Gee, they have four children. He was educated at Maiest Brothers in Sligo, Summer Hill College, Sligo and then UCG where he took a Diploma in Social Science.

He entered local government at 17 years of age as a Clerical Officer with Sligo County Council and was Ceannais Mor Town Clerk in Meath from 1960 - 1962. He was Donegal County Council Staff Officer from 1962 - 1968, Donegal County Accountant from 1968 - 1970 and County Secretary with the same Council from 1970 - 1972. He then became Programme Manager with the North West

**Paul Byrne**

Health Board from 1972 - 1975 , before becoming Roscommon County Manager in 1975. Two years later he took up the Sligo County Managers position.

He is a keen photographer, who also enjoys reading and listenting to music.

## BALLYMOTE

|  | 1991 | 1985 | '85 to '91 Swing |
|---|---|---|---|
| FF | 47.3 | 44.5 | 2.8 |
| FG | 40.4 | 43.9 | -3.5 |
| LAB | 2.0 | — | 2.0 |
| IND | 10.3 | 11.6 | -1.3 |

CONLON, Leo,
Coolmurla, Geevagh,
County Sligo. (FG)
Farmer. 078-47112

CONLON, Michael "Boxer",
Rinnatruffane, Geevagh,
County Sligo. (FF)
Farmer.

LAVIN, Tommy,
Lord Edward Street, Ballymote,
County Sligo. (FG)
Businessman. 071-83354

McLOUGHLIN, Tony,
Beechlawn, Barnsraghy,
Sligo. (FG)
Sales Representative. 071-60768

MURRAY, Gerry,
Calterane, Gurteen,
County Sligo. (FG)
Farmer. 071-82016

SCANLON, Eamon,
Keenaghan, Ballymote,
County Sligo. (FF)
Farmer. 071-83113

SHERLOCK, John,
Knox Park, Ballisodare,
County Sligo. (FF)
Contractor. 071-67506

## DROMORE

|  | 1991 | 1985 | '85 to '91 Swing |
|---|---|---|---|
| FF | 58.6 | 51.1 | 7.5 |
| FG | 41.4 | 48.9 | -7.5 |

BARRETT, Mary,
Ardabrone, Dromard,
County Sligo. (FG)
Nurse.

CONMY, Paul,
Meenaun, Culleens,
County Sligo. (FG)
Farmer. 096-36499

CONWAY, Patrick,
Bartra, Enniscrone,
County Sligo. (FF)
Company Representative. 096-36196

MULLIGAN, Syl,
Coolaney,
County Sligo. (FF)
Fitter. 071-67794

## DRUMCLIFF

|  | 1991 | 1985 | '85 to '91 Swing |
|---|---|---|---|
| FF | 38.1 | 43.2 | -5.1 |
| FG | 30.2 | 36.8 | -6.6 |
| LAB | 7.9 | 6.9 | 1.0 |
| PD | 4.6 |  | 4.6 |
| IND | 19.2 | 13.1 | 6.1 |

CARROLL, Michael,
Carney,
County Sligo. (NP)
Shopkeeper. 071-63036

DEVINS, Jimmy,
"Lia-Fail", Calry Road,
Sligo. (FF)
Doctor. 071-42317

FARRELL, Willie,
Silverhill, Ballinfull,
County Sligo. (FF)
Senator. 071-63119

FOX, Ita,
Colgagh, Calry,
County Sligo. (FG)
Housewife. 071-5013

LEONARD, Joe,
Cloonaghbawn, Ballinfull,
County Sligo. (FG)
Teacher. 071-63443

## SLIGO

|  | 1991 | 1985 | '85 to '91 Swing |
|---|---|---|---|
| FF | 38.9 | 41.9 | -3.0 |
| FG | 28.2 | 22.5 | 5.7 |
| LAB | 5.8 | 8.5 | -2.8 |
| SF | 8.3 | 6.8 | 1.5 |
| IND | 18.8 | 20.3 | -1.5 |

BREE, Declan,
1 High Street,
Sligo. (Elected NP< now Lab.)
Public Representative.

HEALY, Gerry,
"Beezies", O'Connell Street,
Sligo. (FF)
Businessman. 071-60284

HENRY, Peter,
"Blue Lagoon", Riverside,
Sligo. (FG)
Vintner. 071-2530

McGARRY, Jim,
44 St. Bridget's Place,
Sligo. (FG)
Sales Clerk.

McMANUS, Sean,
15 Highfield Road,
Sligo. (FF)
Health Board Official. 071-62985

## TOBBERCURRY

|  | 1991 | 1985 | '85 to '91 Swing |
|---|---|---|---|
| FF | 40.7 | 48.7 | -8.0 |
| FG | 29.6 | 34.1 | -4.5 |
| IND | 29.8 | 17.2 | 12.6 |

BRENNAN, Matthew,
Ragoora, Cloonacool, Tobbercurry,
County Sligo. (FF)
Dáil Deputy. 071-85136

CAWLEY, P.J.
Emmet Street, Tubbercurry,
County Sligo. (FG)
Publican. 071-85025

COLLEARY, Aidan A.
Cully, Curry, Charlestown P.O.
County Sligo. (FF)
Farmer. 094-54222

GORMLEY, Margaret,
Carrowloughlin, Bunninadden,
County Sligo (NP)
Farmer.

**Mattie Brennan (FF)**
**Tobercurry**

**Willie Farrell (FF)**
**Drumcliff**

**Gerry Healy (FF)**
**Sligo**

**Eamon Scanlon (FF)**
**Ballymote**

# FF - FG share spoils in Sligo

Despite a drop in their vote of over 3%, Fine Gael gained 2 seats, bringing their number of Councillors on Sligo County Council to 11, the same number as Fianna Fail. The Labour Party lost their sole seat while the performance of Declan Bree's Socialist Party was unexceptional, placing a doubt over Bree's own chances of building on his 1989 election, result for the next general election, although his recent membership of the Labour Party might aid his cause.

Pat Carty won a seat in Ballymote in 1985 as an Independent candidate, having failed to get a Fianna Fail nomination. He was, however, on the Fianna Fail ticket in 1991, and they went into the 1991 election with 4 sitting Councillors. John Sherlock was the only one of these Councillors returned in June 1991 with Tom Deignan, Joe Shannon and Pat Carty all losing their seats. Sherlock was joined on the Council by party colleagues Eamon Scanlon and Michael Conlon. In taking the second seat in Ballymote, Conlon made up for the disappointment of 1985 when he lost his seat. Possibly, running 6 candidates was partly to blame for the Fianna Fail seat loss, as Fine Gael with a lower percentage of the vote returned their 4 candidates as Councillors.

Fine Gael's performance in Ballymote was impressive. They took 4 seats out of 7 on only 3.2 quotas. Outgoing Councillor, Tony McLaughlin, topped the poll, 8 votes short of the quota. Both Tommy Lavin and Leo Conlon were also successfully returned, while newcomer Gerry Murray took the final seat by 74 votes from Fianna Fail's Tommy Deignan.

Fianna Fail were within shooting distance of taking 3 seats out of 4 in Dromore, but as in Ballymote, too many candidates hindered such aspirations. If Fianna Fail had done what Fine Gael did in Ballymote, in running the same number of candidates as the seat they sought, it is possible that they could have returned 3 Councillors. Both sitting Fianna Fail Councillors Syl Mulligan and Patrick Conway were returned. Mulligan, who had been co-opted onto the Council prior to the election, failed to get a nomination but was added to the FF ticket by the party hierarchy.

> Fianna Fail newcomer, Gerald Healy, headed the poll in the Sligo Area with an impressive 1,043 votes

The poll was topped, as in 1985, by Fine Gael's Paul Conmy. Strategically Fine Gael did well in deciding to run only 2 candidates in Dromore, as Conmy's running mate, Mary Barrett, took the third seat. Barrett was elected with the help of transfers from Fianna Fail's Michael Clarke, more of whose transfers went to Barrett than to his party colleagues.

There was no change in the distribution of seats in the Drumcliff Area, with both Fine Gael and Fianna Fail taking 2 seats each and Independent Councillor Michael Carroll retaining his seat. Senator Willie Farrell had topped the poll for Fianna Fail in 1985, but on this ocassion, his vote was down by 322 votes and he was returned on the last count without reaching the quota. Outgoing Councillor John Mulrooney's vote decreased substantially and he lost both his seat and deposit. Mulrooney was replaced by party colleague, Jimmy Devins who took the second seat, impressively for a newcomer, with 749 first preference votes.

The poll was headed in Drumcliff by Fine Gael's Joe Leonard who was elected on the first count, receiving 205 more first preferences than in 1985. He was joined by fellow party member and outgoing Councillor, Ita Foxe who was returned on the last count without reaching the quota.

Fianna Fail newcomer, Gerald Healy, headed the poll in the Sligo Area with an impressive 1,043 votes, almost 200 above the quota. His Fianna Fail running mate Sean McManus, an outgoing Councillor, took the fourth seat while the man Healy replaced for Fianna Fail, John Monaghan, lost his deposit along with his seat.

In 1985 Tommy Higgins was the only Labour Councillor elected to Sligo County Council. His vote dropped to 266 first preferences in 1991 and his seat was always under threat. Fine Gael's Jim McGarry was the candidate to benefit at the expense of the Labour man. McGarry, a newcomer for Fine Gael, was elected before party colleague Peter Henry, who took the last seat on this occasion. For Declan Bree the outcome was mixed. While regaining his seat, the vote he received was 285 less than in 1985 and Fianna Fail's Gerard Healy replaced him as poll topper on this occassion.

Independent Councillor Margaret Gormley headed the poll in Tubbercurry. Gormley had been elected in 1985 on the last count by a 38 vote margin, so her performance in June 1991 was particularly good. She was narrowly ahead of local Fianna Fail TD Mattie Brennan whom she dislodged as poll topper. Brennan was returned along with his running mate Aidan Colleary who held off the challenge of Fine Gael's Michael Fleming by 59 votes in taking the last seat. Patrick Cawley of Fine Gael increased his vote on his 1985 showing and comfortably took the third seat in Tubbercurry.

# BALLYMOTE ELECTORAL AREA

TOTAL ELECTORATE 10,555. VALID POLL 7,343. NO. OF MEMBERS 7. QUOTA 918

| Names of Candidates | First Count Votes | Second Count Transfer of Masiacz's votes | Result | Third Count Transfer of McCarrick's votes | Result | Fourth Count Transfer of Shannon's votes | Result | Fifth Count Transfer of Parke's votes | Result | Sixth Count Transfer of Carty's votes | Result |
|---|---|---|---|---|---|---|---|---|---|---|---|
| CARTY, Patrick (Mixer) (F.F.) | 554 | +5 | 559 | +31 | 590 | +26 | 616 | +33 | 649 | -649 | — |
| CONLON, Leo (F.G.) | 691 | +10 | 701 | +24 | 725 | +5 | 730 | +98 | 828 | +55 | 883 |
| CONLON, Michael (Boxer) (F.F.) | 699 | +7 | 706 | +27 | 733 | +26 | 759 | +79 | 838 | +111 | 949 |
| DEIGNAN, Tommy (F.F.) | 595 | +7 | 602 | +13 | 615 | +27 | 642 | +74 | 716 | +60 | 776 |
| LAVIN, Tommy (F.G.) | 703 | +14 | 717 | +26 | 743 | +25 | 768 | +83 | 851 | +28 | 879 |
| McCARRICK, John (I.S.P.) | 271 | +36 | 307 | -307 | — | — | — | — | — | — | — |
| McLOUGHLIN, Tony (F.G.) | 910 | +25 | 935 | — | 935 | — | 935 | — | 935 | — | 935 |
| MASIACZ, Catherine Elizabeth (Lab.) | 150 | -150 | — | — | — | — | — | — | — | — | — |
| MURRAY, Gerry (F.G.) | 663 | +6 | 669 | +14 | 683 | +107 | 790 | +41 | 831 | +19 | 850 |
| PARKE, Alfie | 484 | +18 | 502 | +62 | 564 | +20 | 584 | -584 | — | — | — |
| SCANLON, Eamon (F.F.) | 680 | +14 | 694 | +31 | 725 | +62 | 787 | +53 | 840 | +45 | 885 |
| SHANNON, Joseph (F.F.) | 372 | +1 | 373 | +12 | 385 | -385 | — | — | — | — | — |
| SHERLOCK, John (F.F.) | 571 | +4 | 575 | +32 | 607 | +75 | 682 | +57 | 739 | +181 | 920 |
| Non-transferable papers not effective | — | +3 | 3 | +35 | 38 | +12 | 50 | +66 | 116 | +150 | 266 |
| TOTAL: | 7,343 | — | 7,343 | — | 7,343 | — | 7,343 | — | 7,343 | — | 7,343 |

Elected: McLoughlin, Tony (F.G.); Conlon, Michael (Boxer) (F.F.); Sherlock, John (F.F.); Scanlon, Eamon (F.F.); Conlon, Leo (F.G.); Lavin, Tommy (F.G.); Murray, Gerry (F.G.)

# DROMORE ELECTORAL AREA

TOTAL ELECTORATE 5,920. VALID POLL 4,206. NO. OF MEMBERS 4. QUOTA 842

| Names of Candidates | First Count Votes | Second Count Transfer of Conmy's surplus | Result | Third Count Transfer of Clarke's votes | Result | Fourth Count Transfer of Conway's surplus | Result | Fifth Count Transfer of Barrett's surplus | Result |
|---|---|---|---|---|---|---|---|---|---|
| BARRETT, Mary (F.G.) | 643 | +130 | 773 | +158 | 931 | — | 931 | -89 | 842 |
| CLARKE, Michael (F.F.) | 541 | +22 | 563 | -563 | — | — | — | — | — |
| CONMY, Paul (F.G.) | 1,102 | -260 | 842 | — | 842 | — | 842 | — | 842 |
| CONWAY, Patrick A. (F.F.) | 781 | +56 | 837 | +157 | 994 | -152 | 842 | — | 842 |
| HEALY, Gabriel (F.F.) | 531 | +40 | 571 | +96 | 667 | +68 | 735 | +34 | 769 |
| MULLIGAN, Syl (F.F.) | 608 | +12 | 620 | +126 | 746 | +42 | 788 | +52 | 840 |
| Non-transferable papers not effective | — | — | — | +26 | 26 | +42 | 68 | +3 | 71 |
| TOTAL: | 4,206 | — | 4,206 | — | 4,206 | — | 4,206 | — | 4,206 |

Elected: Conmy, Paul (F.G.); Conway, Patrick A. (F.F.); Barrett, Mary (F.G.); Mulligan, Syl (F.F.)

# DRUMCLIFF LOCAL ELECTORAL AREA

TOTAL ELECTORATE 9,182. VALID POLL 5,628. NO. OF MEMBERS 5. QUOTA 939

| Names of Candidates | First Count Votes | Second Count Transfer of Dobbs' votesvotes Result | | Third Count Transfer of Regan's votes Result | | Fourth Count Transfer of Hanly's votes Result | | Fifth Count Transfer of Mulrooney's votes Result | | Sixth Count Transfer of Leonard's surplus Result | | Seventh Count Transfer of Slevin's votes Result | | Eighth Count Transfer of Harrison's votes Result | | Ninth Count Transfer of McDonagh's Result | |
|---|---|---|---|---|---|---|---|---|---|---|---|---|---|---|---|---|---|
| CARROLL, Michael Noel (Non-Party) | 475 | +9 | 484 | +34 | 518 | +25 | 543 | +37 | 580 | +2 | 582 | +84 | 666 | +55 | 721 | +235 | 956 |
| DEVINS, Jimmy (F.F.) | 749 | +9 | 758 | +3 | 761 | +33 | 794 | +58 | 852 | +1 | 853 | +47 | 900 | +32 | 932 | +88 | 1,020 |
| DOBBS, Frank **I.S.P.** | 117 | -117 | — | — | — | — | — | — | — | — | — | — | — | — | — | — | — |
| FARRELL, Willie (F.F.) | 605 | +4 | 609 | +11 | 620 | +9 | 629 | +76 | 705 | +2 | 707 | +21 | 728 | +82 | 810 | +26 | 836 |
| FOX, Ita (F.G.) | 570 | +11 | 581 | +75 | 656 | +30 | 686 | +7 | 693 | +5 | 698 | +62 | 760 | +45 | 805 | +90 | 895 |
| HANLY, Sheelagh (Non-Party) | 206 | +3 | 209 | +3 | 212 | -212 | — | — | — | — | — | — | — | — | — | — | — |
| HARRISON, John (I.S.P.) | 282 | +34 | 316 | +18 | 334 | +5 | 339 | +3 | 342 | +2 | 344 | +17 | 361 | -361 | — | — | — |
| LEONARD, Joe (F.G.) | 952 | — | 952 | — | 952 | — | 952 | — | 952 | -13 | 939 | — | 939 | — | 939 | — | 939 |
| McDONAGH, Stephen Patrick (Lab.) | 445 | +16 | 461 | +5 | 466 | +44 | 510 | +12 | 522 | — | 522 | +25 | 547 | +33 | 580 | -580 | — |
| MULROONEY, John (F.F.) | 244 | +3 | 247 | +6 | 253 | +2 | 255 | -255 | — | — | — | — | — | — | — | — | — |
| O'ROURKE, Felim (F.F.) | 549 | +8 | 557 | +5 | 562 | +26 | 588 | +40 | 628 | — | 628 | +32 | 660 | +14 | 674 | +54 | 728 |
| REGAN, Maureen (F.G.) | 177 | +4 | 181 | -181 | — | — | — | — | — | — | — | — | — | — | — | — | — |
| SLEVIN, Hugh James (P.D.) | 257 | +11 | 268 | +16 | 284 | +17 | 301 | +11 | 312 | +1 | 313 | -313 | — | — | — | — | — |
| Non-transferable paper not effective | — | +5 | 5 | +5 | 10 | +21 | 31 | +11 | 42 | — | 42 | +25 | 67 | +100 | 167 | +87 | 254 |
| TOTAL: | 5,628 | — | 5,628 | — | 5,628 | — | 5,628 | — | 5,628 | — | 5,628 | — | 5,628 | — | 5,628 | — | 5,628 |

Eelected: Leonard, Joe (F.G.); Devins, Jimmy (F.F.); Carroll, Michael Noel (Non-Party); Fox, Ita (F.G.); Farrell, Willie (F.F.)

# SLIGO ELECTORAL AREA

TOTAL ELECTORATE 8,247. VALID POLL 5,200. NO. OF MEMBERS 5. QUOTA 867.

| Names of Candidates | First Count Votes | Second Count Transfer of Healy's surplus Result | | Third Count Transfer of Fallon's votes Result | | Fourth Count Transfer of Monaghan's votes Result | | Fifth Count Transfer of Gillen's votes Result | | Sixth Count Transfer of Lyons' votes Result | | Seventh Count Transfer of Higgins' votes Result | | Eighth Count Transfer of McGuinn's votes Result | |
|---|---|---|---|---|---|---|---|---|---|---|---|---|---|---|---|
| BREE, Declan (I.S.P.) | 675 | +22 | 697 | +90 | 787 | +24 | 811 | +64 | 875 | — | 875 | — | 875 | — | 875 |
| FALLON, Pat (I.S.P.) | 111 | +2 | 113 | -113 | — | — | — | — | — | — | — | — | — | — | — |
| GILLEN, Michael J. (Non-Party) | 194 | +5 | 199 | +3 | 202 | +6 | 208 | -208 | — | — | — | — | — | — | — |
| HEALY, Gerald (Gerry) (F.F.) | 1,043 | -176 | 867 | — | 867 | — | 867 | — | 867 | — | 867 | — | 867 | — | 867 |
| HENRY, Peter (F.G.) | 430 | +14 | 444 | +2 | 446 | +8 | 454 | +14 | 468 | +150 | 618 | +59 | 677 | +75 | 752 |
| HIGGINS, Tommy (Lab.) | 299 | +6 | 305 | +5 | 310 | +5 | 315 | +19 | 334 | +39 | 373 | -373 | — | — | — |
| LYONS, Matt (F.G.) | 267 | +7 | 274 | — | 274 | +4 | 278 | +8 | 286 | -286 | — | — | — | — | — |
| McGARRY, Jim (F.G.) | 769 | +26 | 795 | +6 | 801 | +33 | 834 | +39 | 873 | — | 873 | — | 873 | — | 873 |
| McGUINN, Roddy (F.F.) | 307 | +38 | 345 | — | 345 | +43 | 388 | +22 | 410 | +27 | 437 | +56 | 493 | -493 | — |
| MacMANUS, Sean (S.F.) | 431 | +10 | 441 | +1 | 442 | +15 | 457 | +21 | 478 | +12 | 490 | +90 | 580 | +57 | 637 |
| McMANUIS, Sean (F.F.) | 506 | +25 | 531 | +3 | 534 | +44 | 578 | +8 | 586 | +29 | 615 | +55 | 670 | +209 | 879 |
| MONAGHAN, John (F.F.) | 168 | +21 | 189 | +1 | 190 | -190 | — | — | — | — | — | — | — | — | — |
| Non-transferable papers not effective | — | — | — | +2 | 2 | +8 | 10 | +13 | 23 | +29 | 52 | +113 | 165 | +152 | 317 |
| TOTAL: | 5,200 | — | 5,200 | — | 5,200 | — | 5,200 | — | 5,200 | — | 5,200 | — | 5,200 | — | 5,200 |

Elected: Healy, Gerald (Gerry) (F.F.); Bree, Declan (I.S.P.); McGarry, Jim (F.G.); McManus, Sean (F.F.); Henry, Peter (F.G.)

# TOBERCURRY ELECTORAL AREA

TOTAL ELECTORATE 5,618. VALID POLL 4,312. NO. OF MEMBERS 4. QUOTA 863

| Names of Candidates | First Count Votes | Second Count Transfer of Gormley's surplus | Result | Third Count Transfer of Brennan's surplus | Result | Fourth Count Transfer of O'Hara's votes | Result | Fifth Count Transfer of McKeon's votes | Result |
|---|---|---|---|---|---|---|---|---|---|
| BRENNAN, Matt (F.F.) | 1,009 | — | 1,009 | -146 | 863 | — | 863 | — | 863 |
| CAWLEY , Patrick Joseph (F.G.) | 747 | +77 | 824 | +48 | 872 | — | 872 | — | 872 |
| COLLEARY, Aidan (F.F.) | 547 | +29 | 576 | +61 | 637 | +71 | 708 | +118 | 826 |
| FLEMING, Michael (F.G.) | 527 | +68 | 595 | +19 | 614 | +81 | 695 | +72 | 767 |
| GORMLEY, Margaret (Non-Party) | 1,107 | -244 | 863 | — | 863 | — | 863 | — | 863 |
| McKEON, Peter (F.F.) | 199 | +62 | 261 | +14 | 275 | +8 | 283 | -283 | — |
| O'HARA, Denis | 176 | +8 | 184 | +4 | 188 | -188 | — | — | — |
| Non-transferable papers not effective | — | — | — | — | — | +28 | 28 | +93 | 121 |
| TOTAL: | 4,312 | — | 4,312 | — | 4,312 | — | 4,312 | — | 4,312 |

Elected: Gormley, Margaret (Non-Party); Brennan, Matt (F.F.); Cawley, Patrick Joseph (F.G.); Colleary, Aidan (F.F.)

# TIPPERARY NORTH RIDING

## TIPPERARY N.R. CO. COUNCIL RESULTS

| Party | 1991 % of votes | 1991 Seats obtained | 1985 % of votes | 1985 Seat obtained |
|---|---|---|---|---|
| Fianna Fail | 45.4 | 11 | 52.8 | 12 |
| Fine Gael | 35.9 | 7 | 29.1 | 6 |
| Labour | 10.1 | 2 | 12.6 | 1 |
| Progressive Dem. | 3.8 | — | — | — |
| Workers Party | — | — | — | — |
| Other | 4.8 | 1 | 5.5 | 2 |
| **TOTAL SEATS** | | **21** | | **21** |

## TIPPERARY NORTH

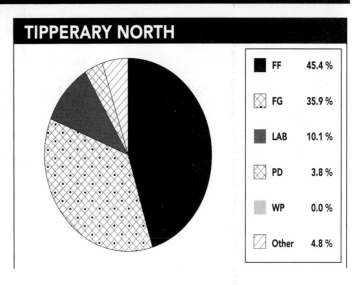

| | |
|---|---|
| ■ FF | 45.4 % |
| ▨ FG | 35.9 % |
| ▨ LAB | 10.1 % |
| ▨ PD | 3.8 % |
| ▨ WP | 0.0 % |
| ▧ Other | 4.8 % |

Courthouse, Nenagh
Telephone: (067) 31771
Fax: (067) 33134
Tipperary (NR)
Total population: 57,829
Rateable valuation: £458,992
Rate: £28.0347
County Council meetings: Fourth Tuesday in each month

*County Manager:* John McGinley
*County Secretary:* Michael Malone
*Finance Officer:* T. Kirwan
*County Engineer:* J. S. Malone
*Administrative Officers:*
Roads, Personnel, General Purposes,
*Development:* T. Kirby
Finance Section: P. Hogan
*Senior Staff Officers:*
*Planning and Development:* P. Heffernan
*Housing:* P. Roche
*Accounts:* N. Cleary
*County Librarian:* Martin Maher
*County Coroners:* Dr L. B. D. Courtney,
James Kelly (Solicitor)
*Chief Fire Officer:* Karl Cashen
*Civil Defence Officer:* L. Daly (Acting)
*Senior Executive Engineers:*
*Roads:* T. Haugh
*Housing/Planning:* J. Gaffney
*Sanitary Services:* P. Crowe

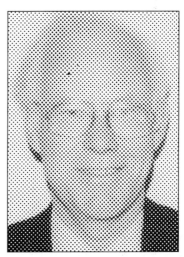

**John McGinley**

John Mc Ginley has been County Manger for Tipperary NR since 1978.

Born in Leetown in County Meath and was educated at Drogheda CBS, and at Rathmines College of Commerce (ACIS) along with the Institute of Public Administration (Diploma in Social Studies in Local Government).

He worked initially as a Clerk with Bord Uisce Mhara and then as a Court Clerk with The Department of Justice, before joining local government service as Cavan County Clerk, 1960 - 1962. He became Sligo Burough Accountant in 1962, Town Clerk in Ballina in 1965, Drogheda Town Clerk in 1970 and Clare County Secretary in 1975 - 1978.

He is married to Mairead Ruttleage, they have four daughters and in his spare time he enjoys boating and tennis.

## BORRISOKANE

|     | 1991 | 1985 | '85 to '91 Swing |
| --- | --- | --- | --- |
| FF | 51.9 | 60.8 | -8.9 |
| FG | 34.1 | 29.5 | 4.6 |
| LAB | 10.0 | 9.7 | 0.3 |
| PD | 4.0 | — | 4.0 |

CASEY, Jim,
Knocknacree, Cloughjordan,
County Tipperary. (FF)
Farmer. 0505-42276

DARCY, Gerard,
Clashateeaun, Ardcroney,
County Tipperary. (FG)
Farmer. 067-38149

HOUGH, Michael,
Coorevan, Borrisokane,
County Tipperary. (FF)
Farmer. 067-27269

McKENNA, Tony,
Ballyhaden, Borrisokane,
County Tipperary. (FF)
Senator. 067-27221

## NENAGH

|     | 1991 | 1985 | '85 to '91 Swing |
| --- | --- | --- | --- |
| FF | 37.7 | 47.0 | -9.3 |
| FG | 33.1 | 26.3 | 6.8 |
| LAB | 15.5 | 17.5 | -2.0 |
| PD | 2.2 | — | 2.2 |
| SF | 3.7 | — | 3.7 |
| IND | 7.7 | 9.2 | -1.5 |

HARRINGTON, Tom,
Upper Knockalton, Nenagh,
County Tipperary. (FF)
Creamery Manager. 067-32661

KENNEDY, Willie,
Glastrigen, Borrisoleigh, Thurles,
County Tipperary. (FG)
Farmer. 0504-52122

O'CONNOR, Joseph,
Tyone, Nenagh,
County Tipperary. (NP)
Company Director. 067-31318

RYAN, John,
26 Patrick's Terrace, Nenagh,
County Tipperary. (Lab)
Senator. 067-31905

RYAN, Tom,
Rathnaleen, Nenagh,
County Tipperary. (FG)
Telecom Official. 067-32010

RYAN, Mattie (Coole),
Coolecarra, Kilcommon, Thurles,
County Tipperary. (FF)
Farmer. 062-78134

SHEEHY, John,
Garryneel, Ballina, Killaloe,
County Tipperary. (FF)
Farmer. 061-376547

## TEMPLEMORE

|     | 1991 | 1985 | '85 to '91 Swing |
| --- | --- | --- | --- |
| FF | 44.7 | 57.9 | -13.2 |
| FG | 47.1 | 31.6 | 15.5 |
| LAB | 5.3 | 10.5 | -5.2 |
| PD | 2.9 | — | 2.9 |

COONAN, Noel,
Gortnagoona, Roscrea,
County Tipperary. (FG)
Farmer. 0505-43382

EGAN, John,
Inch House, Bouladuff, Thurles,
County Tipperary. (FF)
Farmer. 0504-51348

MULROONEY, Sean,
Millpark, Roscrea,
County Tipperary. (FF)
Company Manager. 0505-21997

RYAN, Denis,
Parkmore, Roscrea,
County Tipperary. (FG)
Butcher. 0505-21207

SMITH, Dan,
Timeighter, Roscrea,
County Tipperary. (FF)
Teacher. 0505-21051

## THURLES

|     | 1991 | 1985 | '85 to '91 Swing |
| --- | --- | --- | --- |
| FF | 42.6 | 49.3 | -6.7 |
| FG | 40.1 | 30.5 | 9.6 |
| LAB | 6.7 | 10.0 | -3.3 |
| PD | 6.9 | — | 6.9 |
| IND | 3.6 | 10.2 | -6.6 |

HANAFIN, Jane (Binkie),
Parnell Street, Thurles,
County Tipperary. (FF)
Secretary. 0504-21060

KENNEDY, Martin,
Castlemeadows, Gortataggart, Thurles,
County Tipperary. (Lab)
Ambulance Driver. 0504-22487

LOWRY, Michael,
The Green, Holycross, Thurles,
County Tippeary. (FG)
Dáil Deputy. 0504-43182

QUINN, Mae,
Rossestown, Thurles,
County Tipperary. (FG)
Teacher. 0504-22191

RYAN, Harry,
Galboola, Littleton, Thurles,
County Tipperary. (FF)
Inseminator. 0504-21273

**John Ryan (Lab)**
**Nenagh**

**Michael Lowry (FG)**
**Thurles**

**Tony McKenna (FF)**
**Borisokane**

**Sean Mulrooney (FF)**
**Roscrea**

# FF hold Tipperary NR

Tipperary (N.R.) County Council is 1 of only 4 local authorities in the country over which Fianna Fail maintained control, following the 1991 local elections. It was a surprising outcome, especially given that the result achieved in 1985 was the first time in 18 years that they were in a majority in Tipperary North.

It was in the Thurles electoral area that Fianna Fail lost the seat which saw it's numbers on the Council drop from 12 to 11, out of a total of 21. Also losing out in Thurles was Progressive Democrat, Frank Dwan, who was elected as an Independent in 1985.

Fianna Fail's slippage may have been as a result of the lingering bad feeling about the closure of the town's sugar plant and the Government's failure to reassure voters about the future status of Thurles Hospital. Nevertheless, these issues did not stop Fine Gael deputy, Michael Lowry from being elected on the first count along with Jane 'Binkie' Hanafin, a sister of prominent Fianna Fail Senator Des Hanafin.

Poll topper Lowry had enough transfers to bring in Thurles Urban Councillor , May Quinn, whose husband is an Uncle of Irish striker Niall Quinn. The other newcomer was Labour's Martin Kennedy, a member of the national executive of SIPTU. Kennedy did well to fight off the challenge of former Labour

Constituency Council, Sec. Din Ryan, who ran as an Independent.

The Borrisokane Area returned 3 out of 4 of it's outgoing Councillors. Losing out was Fine Gael's Liam Whyte, a Councillor of thirty years, who was replaced on the Council by party colleague Gerard Darcy.

> All in all there are now three  Ryans representing  the Nenagh electoral area with five Ryans in total sitting on Tipp. NR Council

There was also a change in the Fine Gael personnel in the Templemore Electoral Area, with Noel Coonan taking the seat of retiring Councillor, Denis Meagher. Dan Smith who was co-opted onto the Council in the place of Tipperary North Deputy, Michael Smith, was also

successful.  Fine Gael could only count themselves unlucky not to have gained an additional seat in Templemore, as their candidate Johnny Butler was denied election by a mere 18 votes, with Fianna Fail's Sean Mulrooney holding on by the narrowest of margins.

While the future of the local  hospital was an issue in the Nenagh electoral area, the breakdown of seats was as in 1985 with 3 FF, 2 FG, 1 Lab. and 1 other. Mairead Ryan, grand-daughter of former Fianna Fail TD's Martin Ryan and Mary Bridget Ryan, who topped the poll in 1985 did not contest the 1991 elections and was replaced by party colleague and namesake, Matt Ryan. There was also a change in the Fine Gael lineout  as outgoing Councillor Tom Berkery lost out to Part colleague Tom Ryan. All in all there are now 3 Ryans representing the Nenagh electoral area with 5 Ryans in total sitting on the Tipperary NR County Council.

The best known of these Ryans is probably Labour Senator John Ryan, who did his chances of a return to Dail Eireann no harm, with a solid result in Nenagh. Nevertheless the chances of a change in the present 2-FF, 1-FG lineup would appear unlikely given the    strong performance of Michael Lowry, which would seem to auger well for the Fine Gael deputy, while the replacement of Michael O'Kennedy by Michael Smith in the Reynolds shake-up still leaves the constituency with a cabinet presence.

Nevertheless in a constituency which only needs a 0.1% swing against Fianna Fail to see that party lose a seat  much can happen and Fianna Fail will again have to fight off the challenge of Senator John Ryan who represented the constituency as deputy from 1973 until the 1987 election.

**Charles Haughey and Michael Smith discuss strategy for Tipperary North**

# NENAGH LOCAL ELECTORAL AREA

TOTAL ELECTORATE 14,173. VALID POLL 9,898. NO. OF MEMBERS 7. QUOTA 1,238

| Names of Candidates | First Count Votes | Second Count Transfer of English's votes Result | Third Count Transfer of Coleman's votes Result | Fourth Count Transfer of Flannery's votes Result | Fifth Count Transfer of Matt. Ryan's votes Result | Sixth Count Transfer of J. Ryan's surplus Result | Seventh Count Transfer of Nolan's votes Result | Eighth Count Transfer of O'Sullivan's votes Result | Ninth Count Transfer of G. Ryan's votes Result | Tenth Count Transfer of Boland's votes Result |
|---|---|---|---|---|---|---|---|---|---|---|
| BERKERY, Tom (F.G.) | 673 | +4 677 | +3 680 | +44 724 | +22 746 | +22 768 | +14 782 | +146 928 | +16 944 | +70 1,014 |
| BOLAND, Sean (F.F.) | 564 | +2 566 | +22 588 | +6 594 | +8 602 | +2 604 | +11 615 | +149 764 | +32 796 | -796 — |
| COLEMAN, Patrick (Lab.) | 148 | +1 149 | -149 — | — — | — — | — — | — — | — — | — — | — — |
| ENGLISH, John (P.D.) | 68 | -68 — | — — | — — | — — | — — | — — | — — | — — | — — |
| FLANNERY, Michael (P.D.) | 154 | +25 179 | +1 180 | -180 — | — — | — — | — — | — — | — — | — — |
| HARRINGTON, Tom (F.F.) | 998 | +1 999 | +2 1,001 | +17 1,018 | +18 1,036 | +4 1,040 | +29 1,069 | +24 1,093 | +174 1,267 | — 1,267 |
| KENNEDY, Willie (F.G.) | 1,182 | — 1,182 | +2 1,184 | +12 1,196 | +38 1,234 | +15 1,249 | — 1,249 | — 1,249 | — 1,249 | — 1,249 |
| NOLAN, Jimmy (S.F.) | 364 | — 364 | — 364 | +12 376 | +8 384 | +2 386 | -386 — | — — | — — | — — |
| O'CONNOR, Joseph Peter (Non-Party) | 767 | +7 774 | +5 779 | +11 790 | +7 797 | +14 811 | +116 927 | +28 955 | +88 1,043 | +98 1,141 |
| O'SULLIVAN, Martin (F.G.) | 467 | +16 483 | +38 521 | +6 527 | +1 528 | +2 530 | +9 539 | -539 — | — — | — — |
| RYAN, Ger (F.F.) | 570 | — 570 | +1 571 | +5 576 | +11 587 | +9 596 | +45 641 | +9 650 | -650 — | — — |
| RYAN, John (Lab.) | 1,107 | +7 1,114 | +42 1,156 | +23 1,179 | +146 1,325 | -87 1,238 | — 1,238 | — 1,238 | — 1,238 | — 1,238 |
| RYAN, Matt (Lab.) | 283 | +2 285 | +14 299 | +2 301 | -301 — | — — | — — | — — | — — | — — |
| RYAN (Coole), Mattie (F.F.) | 795 | +1 796 | +1 797 | +5 802 | +21 823 | +3 826 | +25 851 | +19 870 | +104 974 | +180 1,154 |
| RYAN, Tom (F.G.) | 950 | +1 951 | +1 952 | +20 972 | +9 981 | +14 995 | +47 1,042 | +32 1,074 | +74 1,148 | +16 1,164 |
| SHEEHY, John (F.F.) | 808 | — 808 | +12 820 | +13 833 | +7 840 | — 840 | +23 863 | +60 923 | +96 1,019 | +216 1,235 |
| Non-transferable papers not effective | — | +1 1 | +5 6 | +4 10 | +5 15 | — 15 | +67 82 | +72 154 | +66 220 | +216 436 |
| TOTAL: | 9,898 | — 9,898 | — 9,898 | — 9,898 | — 9,898 | — 9,898 | — 9,898 | — 9,898 | — 9,898 | — 9,898 |

Names of candidates elected:— Ryan, John (Lab.); Kennedy, Willie (F.G.); Harrington, Tom (F.F.); Sheehy, John (F.F.); Ryan, Tom (F.G.); Ryan (Coole), Mattie (F.F.); O'Connor, Joseph Peter (Non-Party)

# BORRISOKANE ELECTORAL AREA

TOTAL ELECTORATE 7,902. VALID POLL 5,642. NO. OF MEMBERS 4. QUOTA 1,129.

| Names of Candidates | First Count Votes | Second Count Transfer of Esmonde's votes Result | Third Count Transfer of Casey's surplus Result | Fourth Count Transfer of Dunne's votes Result | Fifth Count Transfer of Carroll's votes Result |
|---|---|---|---|---|---|
| CASEY, Jim (F.F.) | 1,212 | — 1,212 | -83 1,129 | — 1,129 | — 1,129 |
| CARROLL, John Martin (F.F.) | 630 | +12 642 | +14 656 | +82 738 | -738 — |
| DARCY, Gerard (F.G.) | 681 | +37 718 | +9 727 | +157 884 | +115 999 |
| DUNNE, Larry (Lab.) | 567 | +53 620 | +5 625 | -625 — | — — |
| ESMONDE, Tony (P.D.) | 224 | -224 — | — — | — — | — — |
| HOUGH, Michael (F.F.) | 745 | +18 763 | +28 791 | +93 884 | +345 1,229 |
| McKENNA, Tony (F.F.) | 970 | +37 1,007 | +21 1,028 | +111 1,139 | — 1,139 |
| WHYTE, Liam (F.G.) | 613 | +59 672 | +6 678 | +127 805 | +53 858 |
| Non-transferable papers not effective | — | +8 8 | — 8 | +55 63 | +225 288 |
| TOTAL: | 5,642 | — 5,642 | — 5,642 | — 5,642 | — 5,642 |

Elected: Casey, Jim (F.F.); McKenna, Tony (F.F.); Hough, Michael (F.F.); Darcy, Gerard (F.F.)

# TEMPLEMORE ELECTORAL AREA

TOTAL ELECTORATE 9,941. VALID POLL 6,684. NO. OF MEMBERS 5. QUOTA 1,115.

| Names of Candidates | First Count Votes | Second Count Transfer of Ryan's surplus | Result | Third Count Transfer of Treacy's votes | Result | Fourth Count Transfer of Leahy's votes | Result | Fifth Count Transfer of Smith's surplus | Result |
|---|---|---|---|---|---|---|---|---|---|
| BUTLER, Johnny (F.G.) | 821 | +70 | 891 | +27 | 918 | +107 | 1,025 | +3 | 1,028 |
| COONAN, Noel (F.G.) | 879 | +100 | 979 | +33 | 1,012 | +102 | 1,114 | +2 | 1,116 |
| EGAN, John (F.F.) | 1,086 | +9 | 1,095 | +35 | 1,130 | — | 1,130 | — | 1,130 |
| LEAHY, Liam (Lab.) | 356 | +20 | 376 | +36 | 412 | -412 | — | — | — |
| MULROONEY, Sean (F.F.) | 916 | +73 | 989 | +23 | 1,012 | +31 | 1,043 | +3 | 1,046 |
| RYAN, Denis (F.G.) | 1,446 | -331 | 1,115 | — | 1,115 | — | 1,115 | — | 1,115 |
| SMITH, Daniel A. (F.F.) | 988 | +45 | 1,033 | +27 | 1,060 | +79 | 1,139 | +24 | 1,115 |
| TREACY, Michael (P.D.) | 192 | +14 | 206 | -206 | — | — | — | — | — |
| Non-transferable papers not effective | — | — | — | +25 | 25 | +93 | 118 | +16 | 134 |
| TOTAL: | 6,684 | — | 6,684 | — | 6,684 | — | 6,684 | — | 6,684 |

Elected  Ryan, Denis (F.G.); Egan, John (F.F.); Smith, Daniel A. (F.F.); Coonan, Noel (F.G.); Mulrooney, Sean (F.F.)

# THURLES ELECTORAL AREA

TOTAL ELECTORATE 10,367. VALID POLL 6,364. NO. OF MEMBERS 5. QUOTA 1,061

| Names of Candidates | First Count Votes | Second Count Transfer of Lowry's surplus | Result | Third Count Transfer of Hanafin's surplus | Result | Fourth Count Transfer of Quinn's surplus | Result | Fifth Count Transfer of D. Ryan's votes | Result | Sixth Count Transfer of Dwan's votes | Result |
|---|---|---|---|---|---|---|---|---|---|---|---|
| DWAN, Frank (P.D.) | 442 | +63 | 505 | +24 | 529 | +28 | 557 | +57 | 614 | (-614) | — |
| HANAFIN, Jane (Binkie) (F.F.) | 1,204 | — | 1,204 | -143 | 1,061 | — | 1,061 | — | 1,061 | — | 1,061 |
| KENNEDY, Martin (Lab.) | 427 | +85 | 512 | +14 | 526 | +25 | 551 | +117 | 668 | +250 | 918 |
| LOOBY, Larry (F.F.) | 584 | +64 | 648 | +61 | 709 | +8 | 717 | +36 | 753 | +120 | 873 |
| LOWRY, Michael (F.G.) | 1,958 | -897 | 1,061 | — | 1,061 | — | 1,061 | — | 1,061 | — | 1,061 |
| QUINN, Mae (F.G.) | 596 | +553 | 1,149 | — | 1,149 | -88 | 1,061 | — | 1,061 | — | 1,061 |
| RYAN, Denis (Din) (Non-Party) | 227 | +49 | 276 | +7 | 283 | +12 | 295 | -295 | — | — | — |
| RYAN, Harry (F.F.) | 926 | +83 | 1,009 | +37 | 1,046 | +15 | 1,061 | — | 1,061 | — | 1,061 |
| Non-transferable papers not effective | — | — | — | — | — | — | — | +85 | 85 | +244 | 329 |
| TOTAL: | 6,364 | — | 6,364 | — | 6,364 | — | 6,364 | — | 6,364 | — | 6,364 |

Elected: Lowry, Michael (F.G.); Hanafin, Jane (Binkie) (F.F.); Quinn, Mae (F.G.); Ryan, Harry (F.F.); Kennedy, Martin (Lab.)

# TIPPERARY SOUTH RIDING

## TIPPERARY S.R. CO. COUNCIL RESULTS

| Party | 1991 % of votes | 1991 Seats obtained | 1985 % of votes | 1985 Seat obtained |
|---|---|---|---|---|
| Fianna Fail | 37.9 | 10 | 43.8 | 14 |
| Fine Gael | 27.2 | 9 | 28.9 | 8 |
| Labour | 18.8 | 4 | 12.0 | 3 |
| Progressive Dem. | 4.4 | — | — | — |
| Workers Party | — | — | 2.9 | — |
| Other | 10.5 | 3 | 12.4 | 1 |
| **TOTAL SEATS** | | 26 | | 26 |

## TIPPERARY SOUTH

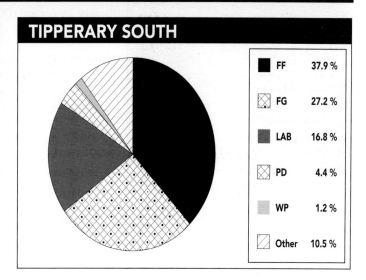

| | |
|---|---|
| ■ FF | 37.9 % |
| ▨ FG | 27.2 % |
| ■ LAB | 16.8 % |
| ▨ PD | 4.4 % |
| WP | 1.2 % |
| ▨ Other | 10.5 % |

Emmet Street, Clonmel
Telephone: (052) 21399
Fax: (052) 24355
Total population: 77,051
Rateable valuation: £476,646
Rate: £26.1409
County Council meetings: First Monday in each month

*County Manager:* S. Hayes
*Assistant County Manager:* N. O'Connor
*County Secretary:* A. Fleming
*Finance Officer:* R. Grant
*County Engineer:* J. Ó'Callaghan
*Administrative Officers:*
Environment, Planning, Sanitary and Fire:
B. Doyle
*Finance:* K. Conway
*Roads:* T. Byrne
*Senior Staff Officers:*
*Housing:* J. Harney
*Personnel and General Purposes:* D. Commins
*Internal Audit:* T. Hayes
*County Solicitor:* D. Binchy
*County Coroner:* P. Morris
*Chief Fire Officer:* C. Murphy
*Civil Defence Officer:* E. Cooney
*County Development Officer:* C. O'Brien
*Senior Executive Engineers:*
*Housing:* W. McEvoy
*Sanitary:* M. Nolan
*Planning:* M. McCarthy (Acting)
*Roads Design/Roads Maintenance:* M. O'Malley
*Environment:* W. Moore

**Seamus Hayes**

Seamus Hayes formally held posts of County Accountant and County Secretary and assistant County Manager with various local authorities including Longford County Council, Kerry Council and Wicklow County Council before being appointed Tipperary South County Manager.

Born in Cappawhite, Tipperary in 1930, he is married to Una Powell and they have six children. His hobbies include golf and following GAA.

## CAHIR

| | 1991 | 1985 | '85 to '91 Swing |
|---|---|---|---|
| FF | 52.5 | 57.9 | -5.4 |
| FG | 30.5 | 29.2 | 1.3 |
| LAB | 10.4 | 7.6 | 2.8 |
| PD | 6.6 | — | 6.6 |
| SF | — | 2.1 | -2.1 |
| IND | — | 3.2 | -3.2 |

AHERN, Theresa,
Ballindoney, Grange, Clonmel,
County Tipperary. (FG)
Dail Deputy. 052-38142

ANGLIM, Michael,
Ballylaffin, Ardfinnan,
County Tipperary. (FF)
Farmer. 052-66170

BYRNE, Sean,
Tubrid, Ballylooby, Cahir,
County Tipperary. (FF)
Senator. 052-65132

DONOVAN, Con,
Main Street, Ballyporeen, Cahir,
County Tipperary. (FF)
Farmer. 052-67106

SAMPSON, Sean,
The Mall, Cahir,
County Tipperary. (FG)
Shopkeeper. 052-41823

## CASHEL

| | 1991 | 1985 | '85 to '91 Swing |
|---|---|---|---|
| FF | 42.8 | 48.9 | -6.1 |
| FG | 49.6 | 38.2 | 11.4 |
| WP | — | 4.1 | -4.1 |
| PD | 4.8 | — | 4.8 |
| SF | 2.9 | — | 2.9 |
| IND | — | 8.8 | -8.8 |

CROWE, Jack,
Convent Cross, Dundrum,
County Tipperary. (FG)
Farmer. 062-71162

HAYES, Tom,
Cahervillahow, Golden,
County Tipperary. (FG)
Farmer. 062-72194

HAMMERSLEY, Tim,
Clonoulty, Cashel,
County Tipperary. (FF)
Farmer. 0504-42111

McCARTHY, Sean,
John Street, Cashel,
County Tipperary. (FF)
Senator. 062-61754

WOOD, Tom,
12 Old Road, Cashel,
County Tipperary. (FG)
Supervisor

## CLONMEL

| | 1991 | 1985 | '85 to '91 Swing |
|---|---|---|---|
| FF | 29.4 | 36.1 | -6.7 |
| FG | 12.8 | 17.8 | -5.0 |
| LAB | 15.1 | 10.7 | 4.4 |
| PD | 6.3 | — | 6.3 |
| IND | 36.5 | 35.4 | 1.1 |

AMBROSE, Tom,
"Dun Mhuire", 7 Melview, Clonmel,
County Tipperary. (FF)
Teacher. 052-22581

BOYLE, Ted,
140 Elm Park, Clonmel,
County Tipperary. (NP)
Insurance Agent

HEALY, Seamus,
Scrouthea, Old Bridge, Clonmel,
County Tipperary. (NP)
Health Board Worker.

LYONS, Sean,
20 Powerstown Road, Clonmel,
County Tipperary. (Lab)
Trade Union Official. 052-22747

DAVERN, Noel,
TANNERSRATH,
Fethard Road,
Clonmel. (FF)*
Dail Deputy. 0502-22991

*Resigned when appointed to Cabinet,
Nov. 1991.
Replaced by:

NORRIS, Patrick,
Rathronan, Clonmel,
County Tipperary. (FF)
052-22878

## FETHARD

| | 1991 | 1985 | '85 to '91 Swing |
|---|---|---|---|
| FF | 40.3 | 41.3 | -1.0 |
| FG | 24.4 | 32.8 | -8.4 |
| LAB | 26.6 | 16.5 | 10.1 |
| WP | — | 2.0 | -2.0 |
| PD | 4.4 | — | 4.4 |
| SF | — | 5.0 | -5.0 |
| IND | 4.2 | 2.4 | 1.8 |

BOURKE, Denis,
1 Castle Street, Carrick-on-Suir,
County Tipperary. (FF)
Insurance Broker.

BRENNAN, Edmond,
Pike Street, Killenaule,
County Tipperary. (Lab)
Public Representative.

HOGAN, Jimmy,
7 Dunbane, Carrick-on-Suir,
County Tipperary. (FG)
Semi-Retired. 051-40398

Tom Hayes (FG) Cashel

Sean Byrne (FF) Cahir

Theresa Ahearn (FG) Cahir

Sean McCarthy (FF) Cashel

HOLOHAN, John,
Ballinard, Fethard,
County Tipperary. (FG)
Farmer. 052-31249

LANDY, Denis,
Greystone Street, Carrick-on-Suir,
County Tipperary. (Lab)
Clerical Officer. 051-40888

MEAGHER, Edward Francis,
Shangarry, Ballingarry,
County Tipperary. (FF)
Farmer. 052-54163

### TIPPERARY

| | 1991 | 1985 | '85 to '91 Swing |
|---|---|---|---|
| FF | 26.1 | 37.0 | -10.9 |
| FG | 29.4 | 26.2 | 3.2 |
| LAB | 32.4 | 23.7 | 8.7 |
| WP | 1.2 | 8.9 | -7.7 |
| SF | — | 4.2 | -4.2 |
| IND | 10.9 | | 10.9 |

FERRIS, Michael,
Rosanna,
Tipperary. (Lab)
Dáil Deputy. 062-52265

Noel Davern (FF) was elected for the Clonmel area but subsequently resigned his seat when appointed to cabinet in November 1991.

FITZGERALD, Michael,
Rathclogheen, Golden,
County Tipperary. (FG)
Farmer. 062-72136

GRIFFIN, Brendan,
"Cnoc Pio", St. Michael Street,
Tipperary. (FG)
Public Representative. 062-51595

Labour Deputy Michael Ferris who received 1,820 first preference votes in being elected to Tipperary SR County Council.

KINAHAN, Christy,
19 Cashel Road,
Tipperary. (NP)
Creamery Worker.

MAGUIRE, Michael,
Lattin,
Tipperary. (FF)
A.I. Technician. 062-55129

Tipperary South Senator and Councillor for Cahir, Sean Byrne in conversation with fellow Fianna Fail Senators, Willie Farrell, Batt O'Keeffe and Sean Haughey all of whom also hold local authority seats.

# Independents gain in South Tipperary

Fianna Fail suffered major losses on South Tipperary County Council, losing 5 of their seats and thereby relinquishing the control they had gained, for the first time in 25 years, in the poll of 1985. Independent candidates were the biggest gainers taking 3 seats while both Fine Gael and Labour each gained 1 additional seat.

Of South Tipperary's 5 electoral areas, Cahir was the only one in which Fianna Fail held it's own, with the breakdown of seats remaining, 3 - FF, 2 - FG, as it was in 1985. On this occasion Fianna Fail Senator Sean Byrne was replaced as poll topper by Fine Gael's Theresa Ahern, whose good performance should help her consolidate the Dail seat which she won in 1989. Fianna Fail newcomer Michael Anglim polled extremely well to hold the third Fianna Fail seat.

> Indeed, in total, Labour received over 26% of the vote in Fethard - almost 2.5% higher than Fine Gael obtained

Fine Gael won an additional seat in the Cashel electoral area, at the expense of Fianna Fail, even though Fianna Fail actually received a larger share of the first preference vote. The Fianna Fail campaign was made all the more difficult by the decision to run 5 candidates in Cashel. With 1 less name on the ticket, or even only the 3 outgoing Councillors, William McInerney of Fianna Fail may have not have lost the seat he gained by co-option prior to 1991.

One of the interesting features of the results in Cashel, was the failure of the 3 women candidates to be elected, continuing the historical fact that no woman from the area has ever been elected to Tipperary SR County Council from the Cashel area. Fianna Fail's Josephine Quinlan, who was elected to the Council in1985 for the Tipperary Electoral area was unsuccessful in 1991, when she moved areas to contest the Cashel area which can be blamed on poor strategy by her party.

Clonmel was the most exciting of the 5 electoral areas in South Tipperary. In 1985, former Labour Deputy Sean Tracy was elected as an Independent Councillor but upon his election as Ceann Comhairle in 1987, his seat on Tipperary SR Council was taken by Fianna Fail's Michael Kennedy. In the 1991 election Kennedy not only lost his seat but also his deposit. Both Tom Ambrose and Noel Davern were re-elected for Fianna Fail although Dail Deputy Davern was replaced as poll topper by Independent candidate Seamus Healy who placed the unemployment problem as the major plank of his campaign .

Fine Gael representation was reduce with outgoing Councillor Johnny Kehoe failing to be re-elected. The party did, however, suffer by the presence on the ballot paper of former Fine Gael member Ted Boyle, an Independent candidate, who polled almost two hundred more votes than Kehoe.

3 of the 6 seats in the Fethard electoral area were filled on the first count as 3 outgoing Councillors - Edward Francis Meagher (FF), Edmond Brennan (Lab) and John Holohan (FG) - all passed the quota. Fianna Fail's Edward F. Meagher topped the poll and was later joined by fellow party colleague and outgoing Councillor Denis Bourke. Fine Gael's two outgoing Councillors were also both successfully returned.

Fethard was successful hunting ground for the Labour Party, returning once again Edmond Brennan while his running mate Denis Landy took a second seat for Labour at the expense of Fianna Fail. Indeed, in total Labour received over 26% of the vote in Fethard - almost 2.5% higher than Fine Gael obtained.

Fianna Fail performed badly in the Tipperary Electoral Area, dropping from 3 seats in 1985 to a mere 1 in 1991. The party was not helped by the decision of former Senator and Councillor of forty years, Willie Ryan of Golden, to bow out of local politics. Also sitting Councillor Josephine Quinlan moved, unsuccessfully, to the Cashel area. Neither of the two new candidates made good these departures, leaving Michael Maguire as the sole Fianna Fail Councillor in the area.

Fine Gael's Michael Fitzgerald was re-elected, as the Fine Gael representation in the Tipperary Electoral Area was increased with the election of former TD Brendan Griffen. Running as an Independent this time out, Christy Kinahan, a Workers' Party candidate in 1986, was also successfully elected.

Deputy Michael Ferris of Labour headed the poll with 600 votes above the quota. The weakness of Ferris's transfers, however, ruled out any possibility of a second seat for Labour in this area.

With Sean Treacy automatically returned because he is Ceann Comhairle Tipperary South is effectively a three seat constituency returning in 1989 Noel Davern (FF), Theresa Ahearn (FG) and Michael Ferris (Lab). It is unlikely on the basis of the local election results that any significant change will occur in the next general election although Ahearn, an Alan Dukes prodigy, may face a renewed challenge from party colleague, Brendan Griffin, whom she ousted in 1989.

**Senator Tony McKenna and former Taoiseach Charles Haughey.**

# CAHER ELECTORAL AREA

TOTAL ELECTORATE 9,103. VALID POLL 9,343. NO. OF MEMBERS 5. QUOTA 1,058

| Names of Candidates | First Count Votes | Second Count Transfer of Ahearn's surplus Result | | Third Count Transfer of Lonergan's votes Result | | Fourth Count Transfer of Byrne's surplus Result | | Fifth Count Transfer of Alton's votes Result | |
|---|---|---|---|---|---|---|---|---|---|
| AHEARN, Theresa (F.G.) | 1,334 | -276 | **1,058** | — | **1,058** | — | **1,058** | — | **1,058** |
| ALTON, Ernest V. (Lab.) | 662 | +24 | **686** | +59 | **745** | +3 | **748** | -748 | — |
| ANGLIM, Michael (F.F.) | 807 | +33 | **840** | +104 | **944** | +21 | **965** | +117 | **1,082** |
| BYRNE, Sean (F.F.) | 994 | +35 | **1,029** | +77 | **1,106** | -48 | **1,058** | — | **1,058** |
| DONOVAN, Con (F.F.) | 837 | +26 | **863** | +29 | **892** | +9 | **901** | +78 | **979** |
| LONERGAN, Tom (P.D.) | 419 | +45 | **464** | -464 | — | — | — | — | — |
| McGRATH, Mattie (F.F.) | 691 | +23 | **714** | +73 | **787** | +12 | **799** | +52 | **851** |
| SAMPSON, Sean (F.G.) | 599 | +90 | **689** | +77 | **766** | +3 | **769** | +371 | **1,140** |
| Non-transferable papers not effective | — | — | — | +45 | **45** | — | **45** | +130 | **175** |
| TOTAL: | 6,343 | — | **6,343** | — | **6,343** | — | **6,343** | — | **6,343** |

Elected:— Ahearn, Theresa (F.G.); Byrne, Sean (F.F.); Anglim, Michael (F.F.); Sampson, Sean (F.G.); Donovan, Con (F.F.)

# CASHEL ELECTORAL AREA

TOTAL ELECTORATE 9,963. VALID POLL 6,685. NO. OF MEMBERS 5. QUOTA 1,115

| Names of Candidates | First Count Votes | Second Count Transfer of Crowe's surplus Result | | Third Count Transfer of Browne's votes Result | | Fourth Count Transfer of McCarthy's surplus Result | | Fifth Count Transfer of Bergin's votes Result | | Sixth Count Transfer of Kennedy's votes Result | | Seventh Count Transfer of McLoughlin's votes Result | | Eighth Count Transfer of McInerney's votes Result | | Ninth Count Transfer of Quinlan's votes Result | |
|---|---|---|---|---|---|---|---|---|---|---|---|---|---|---|---|---|---|
| BERGIN, John (P.D.) | 321 | +5 | **326** | +3 | **329** | +3 | **332** | -332 | — | — | — | — | — | — | — | — | — |
| BROWNE, Michael Joseph (S.F.) | 193 | +6 | **199** | -199 | — | — | — | — | — | — | — | — | — | — | — | — | — |
| CROWE, Jack (F.G.) | 1,298 | -183 | **1,115** | — | **1,115** | — | **1,115** | — | **1,115** | — | **1,115** | — | **1,115** | — | **1,115** | — | **1,115** |
| HAMMERSLEY, Tim (F.F.) | 520 | +23 | **543** | +26 | **569** | +16 | **585** | +33 | **618** | +111 | **729** | +32 | **761** | +197 | **958** | +300 | **1,258** |
| HAYES, Tom (F.G.) | 525 | +61 | **586** | +12 | **598** | +5 | **603** | +52 | **655** | +33 | **688** | +140 | **828** | +52 | **880** | +79 | **959** |
| KENNEDY, Roger (F.F.) | 311 | +12 | **323** | +24 | **347** | +17 | **364** | +34 | **398** | -398 | — | — | — | — | — | — | — |
| McCARTHY, Sean (F.F.) | 1,226 | — | **1,226** | — | **1,226** | -111 | **1,115** | — | **1,115** | — | **1,115** | — | **1,115** | — | **1,115** | — | **1,115** |
| McINERNEY, William (F.F.) | 320 | +6 | **326** | +42 | **368** | +37 | **405** | +39 | **444** | +112 | **556** | +24 | **580** | -580 | — | — | — |
| McLOUGHLIN, Catherine (F.G.) | 352 | +15 | **367** | +4 | **371** | +4 | **375** | +76 | **451** | +15 | **466** | -466 | — | — | — | — | — |
| O'DONOGHUE, Maureen (Lab.) | 501 | +8 | **509** | +51 | **560** | +8 | **568** | +20 | **588** | +29 | **617** | +25 | **642** | +78 | **720** | +74 | **794** |
| QUINLAN, Josephine (F.F.) | 481 | +21 | **502** | +16 | **518** | +11 | **529** | +13 | **542** | +46 | **588** | +25 | **613** | +75 | **688** | -688 | — |
| WOOD, Tom (F.G.) | 637 | +26 | **663** | +13 | **676** | +10 | **686** | +45 | **731** | +28 | **759** | +191 | **950** | +80 | **1,030** | +58 | **1,088** |
| Non-transferable papers not effective | — | — | — | +8 | **8** | — | **8** | +20 | **28** | +24 | **52** | +29 | **81** | +98 | **179** | +177 | **356** |
| TOTAL: | 6,685 | — | **6,685** | — | **6,685** | — | **6,685** | — | **6,685** | — | **6,685** | — | **6,685** | — | **6,685** | — | **6,685** |

Elected: Crowe, Jack (F.G.); McCarthy, Sean (F.F.); Hammersley, Tim (F.F.); Wood, Tom (F.G.); Hayes, Tom (F.G.)

# CLONMEL ELECTORAL AREA

TOTAL ELECTORATE 12,368. VALID POLL 7,545. NO. OF MEMBERS 5. QUOTA 1,258

| Names of Candidates | First Count Votes | Second Count Transfer of Healy's surplus | Result | Third Count Transfer of Burke's votes | Result | Fourth Count Transfer of Keating's votes | Result | Fifth Count Transfer of Kennedy's votes | Result | Sixth Count Transfer of O'Hara's votes | Result | Seventh Count Transfer of Dennehy's votes | Result | Eighth Count Transfer of Kehoe's votes | Result |
|---|---|---|---|---|---|---|---|---|---|---|---|---|---|---|---|
| AMBROSE, Tom (F.F.) | 796 | +11 | 807 | +23 | 830 | +17 | 847 | +125 | 972 | +45 | 1,017 | +113 | 1,130 | +141 | 1,271 |
| BOYLE, Ted (Non-Party) | 718 | +33 | 751 | +34 | 785 | +79 | 864 | +35 | 899 | +70 | 969 | +163 | 1,132 | +276 | 1,408 |
| BURKE, Mary Ann (Lab.) | 296 | +13 | 309 | -309 | — | — | — | — | — | — | — | — | — | — | — |
| DAVERN, Noel (F.F.) | 1,066 | +19 | 1,085 | +42 | 1,127 | +29 | 1,156 | +120 | 1,276 | — | 1,276 | — | 1,276 | — | 1,276 |
| DENNEHY, Niall (P.D.) | 472 | +17 | 489 | +21 | 510 | +25 | 535 | +21 | 556 | +65 | 621 | -621 | — | — | — |
| HEALY, Seamus (Non-Party) | 1,582 | -324 | 1,258 | — | 1,258 | — | 1,258 | — | 1,258 | — | 1,258 | — | 1,258 | — | 1,258 |
| KEATING, James (Lab.) | 303 | +20 | 323 | +45 | 368 | -368 | — | — | — | — | — | — | — | — | — |
| KEHOE, Johnny (F.G.) | 527 | +3 | 530 | +19 | 549 | +11 | 560 | +8 | 568 | +172 | 740 | +71 | 811 | -811 | — |
| KENNEDY, Michael (Ken) (F.F.) | 354 | +9 | 363 | +9 | 372 | +20 | 392 | -392 | — | — | — | — | — | — | — |
| LYONS, Sean (Lab.) | 537 | +25 | 562 | +68 | 630 | +104 | 734 | +32 | 766 | +55 | 821 | +104 | 925 | +191 | 1,116 |
| O'DONNELL, Brian (Non-Party) | 452 | +169 | 621 | +23 | 644 | +56 | 700 | +24 | 724 | +37 | 761 | +74 | 835 | +39 | 871 |
| O'HARA, Dominic (F.G.) | 442 | +5 | 447 | +19 | 466 | +13 | 479 | +7 | 486 | -486 | — | — | — | — | — |
| Non-transferable papers not effective | — | — | — | +6 | 6 | +14 | 20 | +20 | 40 | +42 | 82 | +96 | 178 | +164 | 342 |
| TOTAL: | 7,545 | — | 7,545 | — | 7,545 | — | 7,545 | — | 7,545 | — | 7,545 | — | 7,545 | — | 7,545 |

Elected: Healy, Seamus (Non-Party); Davern, Noel (F.F.); Boyle, Ted (Non-Party); Ambrose, Tom (F.F.); Lyons, Sean (Lab.)

# FETHARD ELECTORAL AREA

TOTAL ELECTORATE 12,561. VALID POLL 8,186. NO. OF MEMBERS 6. QUOTA 1,170.

| Names of Candidates | First Count Votes | Second Count Transfer of Meagher's surplus | Result | Third Count Transfer of Brennan's surplus | Result | Fourth Count Transfer of Holohan's surplus | Result | Fifth Count Transfer of Lalor's votes | Result | Sixth Count Transfer of J. Murphy's votes | Result | Seventh Count Transfer of P. Murphy's votes | Result | Eighth Count Transfer of Landy's surplus | Result |
|---|---|---|---|---|---|---|---|---|---|---|---|---|---|---|---|
| BOURKE, Denis (F.F.) | 675 | +44 | 719 | +9 | 728 | +3 | 731 | +62 | 793 | +44 | 837 | +237 | 1,074 | +29 | 1,103 |
| BRENNAN, Edmond (Lab.) | 1,360 | — | 1,360 | -190 | 1,170 | — | 1,170 | — | 1,170 | — | 1,170 | — | 1,170 | — | 1,170 |
| HOGAN, Jimmy (F.G.) | 649 | +8 | 657 | +16 | 673 | +71 | 744 | +77 | 821 | +98 | 919 | +118 | 1,037 | +28 | 1,065 |
| HOLOHAN, John (F.G.) | 1,314 | — | 1,314 | — | 1,314 | -144 | 1,170 | — | 1,170 | — | 1,170 | — | 1,170 | — | 1,170 |
| LALOR, Jack (Non-Party) | 368 | +3 | 371 | +5 | 376 | +4 | 380 | -380 | — | — | — | — | — | — | — |
| LANDY, Denis (Lab.) | 788 | +5 | 793 | +89 | 882 | +5 | 887 | +101 | 988 | +60 | 1,048 | +186 | 1,234 | -64 | 1,170 |
| MEAGHER, Edward Francis (F.F.) | 1,449 | -279 | 1,170 | — | 1,170 | — | 1,170 | — | 1,170 | — | 1,170 | — | 1,170 | — | 1,170 |
| MURPHY, Jack (P.D.) | 375 | +80 | 455 | +49 | 504 | +33 | 537 | +21 | 558 | -558 | — | — | — | — | — |
| MURPHY, Patsy (F.F.) | 580 | +37 | 617 | +6 | 623 | +5 | 628 | +84 | 712 | +38 | 750 | -750 | — | — | — |
| TOBIN, Dick (F.F.) | 628 | +102 | 730 | +16 | 746 | +23 | 769 | +12 | 781 | +96 | 877 | +125 | 1,002 | +7 | 1,009 |
| Non-transferable papers not effective | — | — | — | — | — | — | — | +23 | 23 | +222 | 245 | +84 | 329 | — | 329 |
| TOTAL: | 8,186 | — | 8,186 | — | 8,186 | — | 8,186 | — | 8,186 | — | 8,186 | — | 8,186 | — | 8,186 |

# TIPPERARY ELECTORAL AREA

TOTAL ELECTORATE 10,571. VALID POLL 7,064. NO. OF MEMBERS 5. QUOTA 1,178

| Names of Candidates | First Count Votes | Second Count Transfer of Ferris's surplus | Result | Third Count Transfer of O'Donnell's votes | Result | Fourth Count Transfer of O'Keeffe's votes | Result | Fifth Count Transfer of Maher's votes | Result | Sixth Count Transfer of Byrne's votes | Result | Seventh Count Transfer of Griffin's surplus | Result |
|---|---|---|---|---|---|---|---|---|---|---|---|---|---|
| BYRNES, Thady (Lab.) | 469 | +183 | 652 | +22 | 674 | +8 | 682 | +50 | 732 | -732 | — | — | — |
| FERRIS, Michael (Lab.) | 1,820 | -642 | 1,178 | — | 1,178 | — | 1,178 | — | 1,178 | — | 1,178 | — | 1,178 |
| FITZGERALD, Michael (F.G.) | 812 | +68 | 880 | +5 | 885 | +89 | 974 | +96 | 1,070 | +80 | 1,150 | +31 | 1,181 |
| GRIFFIN, Brendan (F.G.) | 838 | +116 | 954 | +12 | 966 | +9 | 975 | +153 | 1,128 | +124 | (1,252 | -74 | 1,178 |
| KINAHAN, Christy (Non-Party) | 766 | +106 | 872 | +32 | 904 | +14 | 918 | +18 | 936 | +144 | 1,080 | +26 | 1,106 |
| MAGUIRE, Michael (F.F.) | 811 | +56 | 867 | +2 | 869 | +131 | 1,000 | +73 | 1,073 | +147 | 1,220 | — | 1,220 |
| MAHER, P.J. (F.G.) | 427 | +24 | 451 | +1 | 452 | +4 | 456 | -456 | — | — | — | — | — |
| O'DONNELL, Peadar (W.P.) | 83 | +14 | 97 | -97 | — | — | — | — | — | — | — | — | — |
| O'KEEFFE, Dan (F.F.) | 348 | +15 | 363 | +2 | 365 | -365 | — | — | — | — | — | — | — |
| WALLACE, John Joseph (F.F.) | 690 | +60 | 750 | +14 | 764 | +98 | 862 | +53 | 915 | +108 | (1,023 | +17 | 1,040 |
| Nontransferable papers not effective | — | — | — | +7 | 7 | +12 | 19 | +13 | 32 | +129 | 161 | — | 161 |
| TOTAL: | 7,064 | — | 7,064 | — | 7,064 | — | 7,064 | — | 7,064 | — | 7,064 | — | 7,064 |

Elected: Ferris, Michael (Lab.); Griffin, Brendan (F.G.); Maguire, Michael (F.F.); Fitzgerald, Michael (F.G.); Kinahan, Christy (Non-Party)

# Fortwilton Ltd

CHAMCO HOUSE,
SHANKILL BUSINESS CENTRE,
SHANKILL, CO. DUBLIN.

Tel:**2823688** Fax:**2826311** Telex:**90228**

LITTER

# WATERFORD BOROUGH COUNCIL

## WATERFORD BOROUGH COUNCIL RES.

| Party | 1991 | | 1985 | |
| --- | --- | --- | --- | --- |
| | % of votes | Seats obtained | % of votes | Seat obtained |
| Fianna Fail | 19.0 | 3 | 30.2 | 5 |
| Fine Gael | 13.3 | 2 | 23.0 | 4 |
| Labour | 20.6 | 3 | 9.3 | 2 |
| Progressive Dem. | 8.2 | 2 | — | — |
| Workers Party | 22.0 | 3 | 10.3 | 2 |
| Other | 16.9 | 2 | 27.2 | 2 |
| TOTAL SEATS | | 15 | | 15 |

## WATERFORD

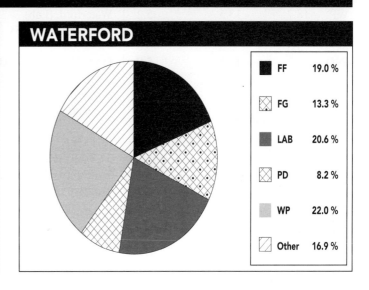

| | | |
| --- | --- | --- |
| ■ | FF | 19.0 % |
| ▨ | FG | 13.3 % |
| ■ | LAB | 20.6 % |
| ▨ | PD | 8.2 % |
| ▨ | WP | 22.0 % |
| ▨ | Other | 16.9 % |

**City Hall, Waterford**
**Telephone: (051) 73501**
**Fax: (051) 79124**
**Rateable valuation: £319,384**
**Municipal rate: £32.1586**
**City Council meetings: Second Monday in each month**

*City Manager and Town Clerk:* Michael Doody
*Assistant Town Clerk:* Terry O'Sullivan
*Finance Officer:* M. Moran
*City Engineer:* Gerard O'Byrne
*Administrative Officers:*
*Estate:* Richard Brennan
*Housing:* Patrick Power
*Senior Staff Officers:*
*Personnel:* Thomas F. Ryan
*General Purposes:* Anthony F. McElroy
*Finance:* Mary Quigley
*Senior Executive Engineer (Sanitary Services):*
Liam O'Donnell
*Senior Executive Engineer (Roads):* Tom Mackey
*Senior Executive Architect:* Barry Hennessy
*Senior Executive (Planning):* Vacant
*Chief Fire Officer:* Anthony Gleeson
*City Law Adviser:* I. Farrell (Acting)
*Veterinary Inspector:* T. Cronin
*Coroner:* John P. Goff
*City Librarian:* Vacant
*Civil Defence Officer:* M. A. Gleeson

## WARD 1

|     | 1991 | 1985 | '85 to '91 Swing |
|-----|------|------|------------------|
| FF  | 19.2 | 33.3 | -14.1 |
| FG  | 22.6 | 30.7 | -8.1 |
| LAB | 19.9 | 5.5  | 14.4 |
| WP  | 18.7 | 13.5 | 5.2 |
| PD  | 8.4  |      | 8.4 |
| SF  | 5.5  | 5.5  | -0.0 |
| IND | 5.7  | 11.5 | -5.8 |

CULLEN, Martin,
Abbey House, Ferrybank,
Waterford. (PD)
Senator. 051-5112

HAYES, Pat (Ald),
7 Keane's Road,
Waterford. (Lab)
Post Office Worker. 051-75315

POWER, Pat,
67 Doyle Street,
Waterford. (FF)
Civil Servant. 051-74866

QUINLAN, Hillary,
24 Daisy Terrace,
Waterford. (FG)
Self-employed

WALSH, Davy (Ald),
30 Ard Mhuire, Ferrybank,
Waterford. (WP)
Company Director

## WARD 2

|     | 1991 | 1985 | '85 to '91 Swing |
|-----|------|------|------------------|
| FF  | 18.4 | 26.5 | -8.1 |
| FG  | 9.1  | 23.4 | -14.3 |
| LAB | 15.8 | 12.6 | 3.2 |
| WP  | 8.9  | 2.3  | 6.6 |
| PD  | 10.6 |      | 10.6 |
| IND | 37.2 | 35.3 | 1.9 |

CUNNINGHAM, Thomas,
197 Viewmount Park,
Waterford. (PD)
General Manager. 051-73717

CURHAM, Liam (Ald),
19 The Folly,
Waterford. (Lab)
Teacher. 051-73051

DANIELS, David (Ald),
"St Anthony's", 32 Viewmount Park,
Waterford. (NP)
Company Representative. 051-76003

ROGERS, Stephen,
31 Viewmount Park,
Waterford. (NP)
Transport Engineer

SWIFT, Brian,
12 Comeragh Green, Lismore Heights,
Waterford. (FF)
*Replaced Brendan Kenneally who
resigned when appointed Minister for
State in February 1992.

## WARD 3

|     | 1991 | 1985 | '85 to '91 Swing |
|-----|------|------|------------------|
| FF  | 19.4 | 31.0 | -11.6 |
| FG  | 9.6  | 13.7 | -4.1 |
| LAB | 25.1 | 9.9  | 15.2 |
| WP  | 36.3 | 16.0 | 20.3 |
| PD  | 5.8  | —    | 5.8 |
| SF  | 3.0  | —    | 3.0 |
| IND | 0.7  | 29.4 | -28.7 |

BROWNE, Thomas,
Ballyknock, Tramore,
County Waterford. (FF)
Teacher. 051-81283

CUMMINS, Maurice,
34 Ursuline Court,
Waterford. (FG)
Claims Manager

GALLAGHER, Paddy (Ald),
4 Thomond Green, Lismore Lawn,
Waterford. (DL)
Journalist

O'REGAN, Martin,
210 Clonard Park, Ballybeg,
Waterford. (WP)
Unemployed

O'SHEA, Brian (Ald),
61 Sweetbriar Lawn, Tramore,
County Waterford. (Lab)
Dail Deputy. 51-81913

**Brendan Kenneally (FF)**
**Ward 2**

**Paddy Gallagher (DL)**
**Ward 3**

**Tom Browne (FF)**
**Ward 2**

**Paddy Hayes (Lab)**
**Ward 1**

# Service Charges hit FF

Waterford Corporation was a disaster for Fianna Fail and Fine Gael, both of which lost 2 seats each on their 1985 performance. In the case of both parties, their share of the first preference vote was less than 20%. The big gainers were the parties of the left, which played heavily on the local services charge issue throughout the campaign.

Following the results of the 1991 local elections, both Labour and the Worker's Party have 3 Councillors each on the Corporation the same number as Fianna Fail. The Progressive Democrats and Fine Gael each have 2 councillors while 2 Independents were also returned.

The poll was topped in Ward 1 by Labour's Pat Hayes who polled some 328 votes more than the nearest candidate, outgoing Councillor, Davy Walsh of the Worker's Party. Fine Gael's Hilary Quinlan was re-elected but her running mate, James Brett, was less successful losing his Council seat to Martin Cullen of the Progressive Democrats. The PD Senator was unsuccessful in the County Council elections, where he was also a candidate, losing out by 42 votes. He held off Brett in the City to take the final seat with 63 votes to spare, although this performance does not

auger well for a possible challenge for a Dail seat at the next general election.

Fianna Fail's vote was down by 14.2% in Ward 1 and with 1.15 quotas, it was inevitable that one of their seats was lost. Outgoing Councillor Larry Dower was eliminated on the fifth count and his

transfers helped running mate Pat Power retain his seat.

Fine Gael won 2 seats in Ward 2 in 1985, but on this occasion, one of these Councillors Katherine Bulbulia did not contest the election, while the other Stephen Rodgers ran as an Independent. The two newcomers for Fine Gael polled poorly and failed to gain election leaving Fine Gael without a representative on the Corporation from Ward 2. As an Independent Stephen Rodgers increased his vote and was returned on the sixth count. The poll was headed in Ward 2 by another

Independent, outgoing Councillor Davy Daniels who was 312 votes ahead of the nearest candidate.

Daniels was followed by Labour's Liam Curham, who was only 47 votes short of the quota on the first count. The Progressive Democrats' second seat on Waterford Corporation was taken in Ward 2 by newcomer Bryan Cunningham, who was elected on the last count without reaching the quota. The Fianna Fail vote was down by 8% but they retained the seat won in 1985. Deputy Brendan Kenneally was returned on the fifth count with an increase of 173 votes on his 1985 performance.

The Worker's Party were the big winners in Ward 3, where they received over 36% of the first preference vote. Former TD Paddy Gallagher was re-elected to the Council and was joined by party colleague Martin O'Reagan, who had been returned as an Independent in 1985. Labour's Brian O'Shea headed the poll with 1,556 first preference votes. The Labour Dail Deputy was also successfully elected to Waterford County Council.

Fine Gael won no seat in Ward 3 in 1985, but they made no mistake this time, running only one candidate, Maurice Cummins who made up for the disappointment of 1985 when he was beaten for the last seat by 15 votes. Fianna Fail's vote was down by over 11% in Ward 3, and they lost a seat with former TD Brian Swift failing to be re-elected to the Council.

# NO. 1 ELECTORAL AREA

TOTAL ELECTORATE 7,945. VALID POLL 5,000. NO. OF MEMBERS 5. QUOTA 834

| Names of Candidates | First Count Votes | Second Count Transfer of Hayes' surplus | Result | Third Count Transfer of Guilfoyle's votes | Result | Fourth Count Transfer of Ryan's votes | Result | Fifth Count Transfer of White's votes | Result | Sixth Count Transfer of Dower's votes | Result | Seventh Count Transfer of McCarthy's votes | Result |
|---|---|---|---|---|---|---|---|---|---|---|---|---|---|
| BRETT, James (F.G.) | 463 | +9 | 472 | +7 | 479 | +7 | 486 | +7 | 493 | +22 | 515 | +22 | 537 |
| CULLEN, Martin (P.D.) | 419 | +18 | 437 | +12 | 449 | +18 | 467 | +48 | 515 | +30 | 545 | +55 | 600 |
| DOWER, Larry (F.F.) | 299 | +6 | 305 | +62 | 367 | +13 | 380 | +21 | 401 | -401 | — | — | — |
| GUILFOYLE, Joe (F.F.) | 201 | +6 | 207 | -207 | — | — | — | — | — | — | — | — | — |
| HAYES, Pat (Lab.) | 997 | -163 | 834 | — | 834 | — | 834 | — | 834 | — | 834 | — | 834 |
| McCARTHY, Billy (W.P.) | 309 | +28 | 337 | +4 | 341 | +42 | 383 | +50 | 433 | +9 | 442 | -442 | — |
| POWER, Patrick (F.F.) | 459 | +13 | 472 | +53 | 525 | +24 | 549 | +16 | 565 | +244 | 809 | +40 | 849 |
| QUINLAN, Hilary (F.G.) | 669 | +25 | 694 | +21 | 715 | +24 | 739 | +58 | 797 | +37 | 834 | — | 834 |
| RYAN, Noel (S.F.) | 273 | +8 | 281 | +7 | 288 | -288 | — | — | — | — | — | — | — |
| WALSH, Davy (W.P.) | 625 | +33 | 658 | +12 | 670 | +72 | 742 | +86 | 828 | +15 | 843 | — | 843 |
| WHITE, Val (Non-Party) | 286 | +17 | 303 | +20 | 323 | +37 | 360 | -360 | — | — | — | — | — |
| Non-transferable paper not effective | — | — | — | +9 | 9 | +51 | 60 | +74 | 134 | +44 | 178 | +325 | 503 |
| TOTAL: | 5,000 | — | 5,000 | — | 5,000 | — | 5,000 | — | 5,000 | — | 5,000 | — | 5,000 |

Elected: Hayes, Pat (Lab.); Walsh, Davy (W.P.); Quinlan, Hilary (F.G.); Power, Patrick (F.F.); Cullen, Martin (P.D.)

# NO. 2 ELECTORAL AREA

TOTAL ELECTORATE 9,189. VALID POLL 5,450. NO. OF MEMBERS 5. QUOTA 909

| Names of Candidates | First Count Votes | Second Count Transfer of Daniels' surplus | Result | Third Count Transfer of Power's votes | Result | Fourth Count Transfer of Jones' votes | Result | Fifth Count Transfer of King's votes | Result | Sixth Count Transfer of Lane's votes | Result | Seventh Count Transfer of Rogers' surplus | Result |
|---|---|---|---|---|---|---|---|---|---|---|---|---|---|
| CUNNINGHAM, Bryan (P.D.) | 579 | +28 | 607 | +21 | 628 | +40 | 668 | +19 | 687 | +142 | 829 | +67 | 896 |
| CURHAM, Liam (Lab.) | 862 | +54 | 916 | — | 916 | — | 916 | — | 916 | — | 916 | — | 916 |
| DANIELS, David (Non-Party) | 1,174 | -265 | 909 | — | 909 | — | 909 | — | 909 | — | 909 | — | 909 |
| JONES, Bryan (Non-Party) | 257 | +21 | 278 | +7 | 285 | -285 | — | — | — | — | — | — | — |
| KENNEALLY, Brendan (F.F.) | 720 | +41 | 761 | +8 | 769 | +34 | 803 | +171 | 974 | — | 974 | — | 974 |
| KING, Frank (F.F.) | 283 | +15 | 298 | +10 | 308 | +14 | 322 | -322 | — | — | — | — | — |
| LANE, Michael J. (F.G.) | 319 | +16 | 335 | +72 | 407 | +39 | 446 | +20 | 466 | -466 | — | — | — |
| POWER, George (F.G.) | 175 | +8 | 183 | -183 | — | — | — | — | — | — | — | — | — |
| REDMOND, Dr. Olga (W.P.) | 484 | +17 | 501 | +26 | 527 | +53 | 580 | +17 | 597 | +79 | 676 | +15 | 691 |
| ROGERS, Stephen (Non-Party) | 597 | +65 | 662 | +32 | 694 | +75 | 769 | +60 | 829 | +162 | 991 | -82 | 909 |
| Non-transferable papers not effective | — | — | — | +7 | 7 | +30 | 37 | +35 | 72 | +83 | 155 | — | 155 |
| TOTAL: | 5,450 | — | 5,450 | — | 5,450 | — | 5,450 | — | 5,450 | — | 5,450 | — | 5,450 |

Elected: Daniels, David (Non-Party); Curham, Liam (Lab.); Kenneally, Brendan (F.F.); Rogers, Stephen (Non-Party); Cunningham, Bryan (P.D.)

# NO. 3 ELECTORAL AREA

TOTAL ELECTORATE 10,360. VALID POLL 6,195. NO. OF MEMBERS 5. QUOTA 1,033

| Names of Candidates | First Count Votes | Second Count Transfer of O'Shea's surplus | Result | Third Count Transfer of Sweeney's & O'Brien's votes | Result | Fourth Count Transfer of Gallagher's surplus | Result | Fifth Count Transfer of Swift's votes | Result | Sixth Count Transfer of Murphy's votes | Result | Seventh Count Transfer of O'Regan's surplus | Result | Eighth Count Transfer of Halligan's votes | Result |
|---|---|---|---|---|---|---|---|---|---|---|---|---|---|---|---|
| BROWNE, Thomas (F.F.) | 482 | +50 | 532 | +28 | 560 | +2 | 562 | +158 | 720 | +238 | 958 | +14 | 972 | +56 | 1,028 |
| CUMMINS, Maurice (F.G.) | 594 | +105 | 699 | +21 | 720 | +4 | 724 | +36 | 760 | +38 | 798 | +3 | 801 | +84 | 885 |
| GALLAGHER, Patrick (W.P.) | 1,082 | — | 1,082 | — | 1,082 | -49 | 1,033 | — | 1,033 | — | 1,033 | — | 1,033 | — | 1,033 |
| HALLIGAN, John (W.P.) | 384 | +77 | 461 | +37 | 498 | +17 | 515 | +21 | 536 | +16 | 552 | +9 | 561 | -561 | — |
| MURPHY, Tom (F.F.) | 386 | +24 | 410 | +10 | 420 | +1 | 421 | +62 | 483 | -483 | — | — | — | — | — |
| O'BRIEN, Denis (S.F.) | 187 | +17 | 204 | -204 | — | — | — | — | — | — | — | — | — | — | — |
| O'NEILL, Michelle (P.D.) | 359 | +73 | 432 | +36 | 468 | +5 | 473 | +38 | 511 | +50 | 561 | +20 | 581 | +117 | 698 |
| O'REGAN, Martin (W.P.) | 784 | +114 | 898 | +55 | 953 | +18 | 971 | +38 | 1,009 | +89 | 1,098 | -65 | 1,033 | — | 1,033 |
| O'SHEA, Brian (Lab.) | 1,556 | -523 | 1,033 | — | 1,033 | — | 1,033 | — | 1,033 | — | 1,033 | — | 1,033 | — | 1,033 |
| SWEENEY, Paidi (Non-Party) | 46 | +16 | 62 | -62 | — | — | — | — | — | — | — | — | — | — | — |
| SWIFT, Brian (F.F.) | 335 | +47 | 382 | +20 | 402 | +2 | 404 | -404 | — | — | — | — | — | — | — |
| Non-transferable papers not effective | — | — | — | +59 | 59 | — | 59 | +51 | 110 | +52 | 162 | +19 | 181 | +304 | 485 |
| TOTAL: | 6,195 | — | 6,195 | — | 6,195 | — | 6,195 | — | 6,195 | — | 6,195 | — | 6,195 | — | 6,195 |

Elected: O'Shea, Brian (Lab.); Gallagher, Patrick (W.P.); O'Regan, Martin (W.P.); Browne, Thomas (F.F.); Cummins, Maurice (F.G.)

# WATERFORD COUNTY COUNCIL

## WATERFORD COUNTY COUNCIL RESULTS

| Party | 1991 % of votes | 1991 Seats obtained | 1985 % of votes | 1985 Seat obtained |
|---|---|---|---|---|
| Fianna Fail | 43.3 | 10 | 48.7 | 11 |
| Fine Gael | 32.3 | 9 | 38.1 | 10 |
| Labour | 14.0 | 3 | 7.7 | 2 |
| Progressive Dem. | 3.1 | — | — | — |
| Workers Party | 2.7 | 1 | 1.1 | — |
| Other | 4.6 | — | 4.4 | — |
| **TOTAL SEATS** | | 23 | | 23 |

## WATERFORD

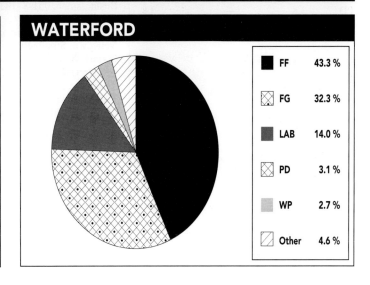

| | | |
|---|---|---|
| ■ | FF | 43.3 % |
| ▨ | FG | 32.3 % |
| ■ | LAB | 14.0 % |
| ▨ | PD | 3.1 % |
| ▨ | WP | 2.7 % |
| ▨ | Other | 4.6 % |

**Waterford**
**County: 51,622**
**Rateable valuation (county):**
**£369,408.50**
**County Council**
**Davitt's Quay, Dungarvan**
**Telephone: (058) 42822**
**Fax: (058) 42911**
**County rate: £29.0113**
**County Council meetings: Second Monday in each month**

*County Manager:* D. Hurley
*County Secretary:* B. J. McNally
*Finance Officer:* Paul Clerkin
*County Engineer:* John O'Flynn
*County Development Officer:* M. McHugh
*Administrative Officer:* T. Cunningham
*Senior Staff Officers:*
*Housing:* John Ahearn
*Roads:* G. Enright
*Environment:* G. Enright
*County Librarian:* D. Brady
County Library Headquarters, Lismore.
*Telephone:* (058) 54128
*County Solicitor:* M. M. Halley
*County Coroners:* Dr E. Maughan, Dr D. F. Cantillon
*Chief Fire Officer:* T. A. McCarthy
*Civil Defence Officer:* Colm Bannon
*Senior Executive Engineers:*
*Roads:* T. Lineen
*Design:* D. O'Sullivan
*Water Supplies:* E. Mansfield
*Planning:* J. M. Shine
*Environment:* D. McCarthy

Daniel Hurley was born in 1932 and is married to Betty Walsh, they have two sons. He was educated at the Cork School of Commerce and University College, Cork.

Prior to his appointment as Manager of Waterford County Council He has held positions in both the public and private sectors. He was Industrial Relations Officer of the Irish Dunlop Company and Programme Manager of the Mid-Western Health Board. A former Assistant Manager of Cork City he has also been Manager of Westmeath County Council.

As well as presently being Manager of the Waterford County Council, Daniel Hurley is a director of Waterford Regional Airport and several other local companies with interests in the tourism area.

## DUNGARVAN

| | 1991 | 1985 | '85 to '91 Swing |
|---|---|---|---|
| FF | 31.5 | 39.8 | -8.3 |
| FG | 26.6 | 38.5 | -11.9 |
| LAB | 21.9 | 14.1 | 7.8 |
| WP | 7.0 | 2.5 | 4.5 |
| PD | 3.8 | — | 3.8 |
| SF | — | 2.9 | -2.9 |
| IND | 9.2 | 2.2 | 7.0 |

FLYNN, Austin,
Ballinamuck West, Dungarvan,
County Waterford. (FF)
Teacher. 058-43449

HARTE, Lar,
66 Congress Villas, Dungarvan,
County Waterford. (Lab)
Unemployed.

KENNEALLY, Patrick,
Curradarra, Aglish, Cappoquin,
County Waterford. (FF)
Farmer. 024-96215

KYNE, Billy,
5 Parklane Drive, Abbeyside, Dungarvan,
County Waterford. (Lab)
Fitter.

O'HALLORAN, Garry,
Laurentum House, Clashmore,
County Waterford. (FG)
Farmer. 024-96205

WALSH, Ritchie,
Abbeyside, Dungarvan,
County Waterford. (FG)
Retired. 058-41345

WRIGHT, Tony,
13 Mitchell Terrace, Dungarvan,
County Waterford. (Elected WP, now DL)
Co-op Employee.

## KILMACTHOMAS

| | 1991 | 1985 | '85 to '91 Swing |
|---|---|---|---|
| FF | 56.9 | 65.2 | -8.3 |
| FG | 26.6 | 30.4 | -3.8 |
| LAB | 13.7 | — | 13.7 |
| SF | — | 4.4 | -4.4 |
| IND | 2.7 | — | 2.7 |

COFFEY, Oliver,
Shanbally, Leamybrien,
County Waterford. (FG)
Farmer. 051-91102

COFFEY, Patrick,
Coolfin, Portlaw,
County Waterford. (FG)
Businessman. 051-87183

CUNNINGHAM, Thomas,
Newtown, Stradbally,
County Waterford. (FF)
Farmer. 051-93210

FAHY, Jackie,
95 Springfield, Dungarvan,
County Waterford. (FF)
Dail Deputy. 058-42514

O'RYAN, Kieran,
Knockalisheen, Ballymacarbry,
Clonmel,
County Tipperary. (FF)
Farmer. 052-36137

## LISMORE

| | 1991 | 1985 | '85 to '91 Swing |
|---|---|---|---|
| FF | 52.3 | 53.1 | -0.8 |
| FG | 47.7 | 42.4 | 5.3 |
| LAB | — | 4.4 | -4.4 |

FLYNN, Nora,
Main Street, Cappaquinn,
County Waterford. (FG)
Publican.

McDONNELL, William,
Convent View, Tallow,
County Waterford. (FG)
Farmer. 058-56253

QUIRKE, James,
Inchinleamy, Ballyduff Upper,
County Waterford. (FF)
Farmer. 058-60245

WILKINSON, Ollie,
Killahala, Cappoquin,
County Waterford. (FF)
Farmer. 058-54413

## TRAMORE

| | 1991 | 1985 | '85 to '91 Swing |
|---|---|---|---|
| FF | 39.8 | 43.8 | -4.0 |
| FG | 33.0 | 40.4 | -7.4 |
| LAB | 14.8 | 8.2 | 6.6 |
| WP | 2.1 | — | 2.1 |
| PD | 6.3 | 1.2 | 5.1 |
| IND | 4.0 | 6.4 | -2.4 |

CAREY, John,
Passage East,
County Waterford. (FG)
Shopkeeper. 051-82352

CASEY, Con,
Newtown, Tramore,
County Waterford. (FG)
Engineer. 051-75376

COWMAN, Dan,
42 Mounloun, Tramore,
County Waterford. (FF)
051-86792

LEAHY, Patrick,
Blackknock, Kilmeaden,
County Waterford. (FF)
Co-Op Manager.

O'SHEA, Brian,
61 Sweetbriar Lawn, Tramore,
County Waterford. (Lab)
Dail Deputy. 051-81913

POWER, Geoffrey,
2 Woodview, Dunmore East,
County Waterford. (FF)
Factory Worker.

QUEALLY, Michael,
Grenan Upper, Kilmacthomas,
County Waterford. (FG)
Farmer. 051-94149

**John Carey (FG)**
**Tramore**

**Jackie Fahey (FF)**
**Kilmacthomas**

**Ritchie Walsh (FG)**
**Dungarvan**

**Lar Hart (Lab)**
**Dungarvan**

# Fine Gael do well to hold on in Waterford

The Labour Party and the Worker's Party made gains in Waterford County Council, as both Fianna Fail and Fine Gael each lost a seat on their 1985 outcome. Despite this loss Fianna Fail remain the largest party on the Council with 10 seats, while the result for Fine Gael could easily have been much worse, as they only narrowly retained their 2 and 3 seats in Kilmacthomas and Tramore respectively.

The parties of the left made big gains in the Dungarvan Electoral Area. Labour picked up a second seat through Lar Hart who was helped by the poll topping performance of his running mate, outgoing Councillor, Billy Kyne. The Worker's Party took their first ever seat on Waterford County council with the election of Tony Wright. It was a narrow win for Wright who held off outgoing Councillor Sean Whelan by a mere 3 votes. Whelan had been elected for Fianna Fail in 1985, but ran unsuccessfully as an Independent this time out.

In 1985 Fianna Fail took 3 seats in Dungarvan but with the deflection of Whelan and the decision of Deputy Jackie Fahey to move to the Kilmacthomas Area they were left with only one of these outgoing Councillors on their Dungarvan ticket. Patrick Kenneally increased his vote from 1985 and took the second seat on this occasion. He was returned along with his Fianna Fail colleague Austin Flynn who benefitted from the transfers of the other 2 Fianna Fail candidates on the ballot paper.

The Fine Gael vote was down almost 12% in Dungarvan, and they lost one of the seats taken in 1985. Michael O'Riordan, an outgoing Councillor, was eliminated on the tenth count by 3 votes. Fine Gael's other Councillor who sought re-election, Garry O'Halloran, was returned on the eight count. He was joined by UDC member of 40 years, Richie Walsh, who was successfully returned at 75 years of age after several previously unsuccessful attempts.

.. SHO WHERE BETTER TO SHTART THE LOCAL ELECTION CAMPAIGN THAN THE LOCAL..

In 1985, the 5 seats in Kilmacthomas were split 3-Fianna Fail and 2-Fine Gael. There was no change on this situation in 1991, with the only personnel change being the election of Jackie Fahey, TD for Fianna Fail, in the place of Sean Fahey. The Dail Deputy, who topped the poll in 1985 in Dungarvan, repeated this performance in the Kilmacthomas Area receiving 1,066 votes on a quota of 849 votes. The next 2 seats were filled by Fahey's Fianna Fail colleagues, Tony Cunningham and Kieran O'Ryan, both outgoing Councillors. Fine Gael's Patrick Coffey and namesake Oliver Coffey took the final 2 seats in Kilmacthomas.

Fine Gael's vote increased by over 5% in Lismore, as they held their 2 seats. While Willie McDonnell was replaced as poll topper on this occasion by Fianna Fail's Ollie Wilkinson, he was safely returned along with Fine Gael newcomer Nora Flynn, who defeated party colleague Matthew Power by 35 votes. Power had in fact been 3 votes ahead of Flynn on the first count. Jimmy Quirke of Fianna Fail was also returned in Lismore, despite a drop of 293 votes on his 1985 performance.

Labour Deputy Brian O'Shea strengthened his Dail base in topping the poll in the Tramore Area, as he also did in Area 3 of Waterford Corporation. He was, however, only ahead in Tramore by a single vote from Fianna Fail newcomer Paddy Leahy, who received 1,093 first preference votes. Only 1 of the 3 Councillors elected in this area in 1985 for Fianna Fail was a candidate on this occasion. Outgoing Councillor Seamus Dunphy was, however, well beaten, as Dan Cowman and Geoff Power joined Paddy Leahy on the Council. All 3 outgoing Fine Gael Councillors were success-fully returned, with Con Casey taking the last seat from Progressive Democrat, Senator Martin Cullen, by 42 votes.

# DUNGARVAN ELECTORAL AREA

TOTAL ELECTORATE 10,669. VALID POLL 6,860. NO. OF MEMBERS 7. QUOTA 858

| Names of Candidates | First Count Votes | Second Count Transfer of Kyne's surplus Result | Third Count Transfer of P. Kenneally's surplus Result | Fourth Count Transfer of Queally's votes Result | Fifth Count Transfer of W. J. Kenneally's votes Result | Sixth Count Transfer of Dineen's votes Result | Seventh Count Transfer of Flavin's votes Result | Eighth Count Transfer of Coll's votes Result | Ninth Count Transfer of Ryan's votes Result | Tenth Count Transfer of O'Keeffe's votes Result | Eleventh Count Transfer of O'Riordan's votes Result | Twelfth Count Transfer of Walsh's surplus Result |
|---|---|---|---|---|---|---|---|---|---|---|---|---|
| COLL, James (P.D.) | 263 | +2 265 | +5 270 | +1 271 | +5 276 | +11 287 | +12 299 | -299 — | — — | — — | — — | — — |
| DINEEN, Dan | 181 | +6 187 | +1 188 | +6 194 | +6 200 | -200 — | — — | — — | — — | — — | — — | — — |
| FLAVIN, Mario (F.G.) | 221 | +4 225 | +3 228 | +1 229 | +2 231 | +16 247 | -247 — | — — | — — | — — | — — | — — |
| FLYNN, Austin (F.F.) | 382 | +8 390 | +9 399 | +3 402 | +39 441 | +13 454 | +19 473 | +18 491 | +120 611 | +144 755 | +45 800 | +5 805 |
| HART, Lar (Lab.) | 491 | +52 543 | +1 544 | — 544 | +16 560 | +23 583 | +11 594 | +16 610 | +21 631 | +11 642 | +74 716 | +8 724 |
| KENNEALLY, Patrick (F.F.) | 969 | — 969 | -111 858 | — 858 | — 858 | — 858 | — 858 | — 858 | — 858 | — 858 | — 858 | — 858 |
| KENNEALLY, Willie John (F.F.) | 154 | +8 162 | +22 184 | — 184 | -184 — | — — | — — | — — | — — | — — | — — | — — |
| KYNE, Billy (Lab.) | 1,009 | -151 858 | — 858 | — 858 | — 858 | — 858 | — 858 | — 858 | — 858 | — 858 | — 858 | — 858 |
| O'HALLORAN, Garrett (F.G.) | 686 | +4 690 | +19 709 | — 709 | +9 718 | +6 724 | +59 783 | +75 858 | — 858 | — 858 | — 858 | — 858 |
| O'KEEFFE, Paud (F.F.) | 349 | +2 351 | +26 377 | — 377 | +25 402 | +3 405 | +4 409 | +31 440 | +59 499 | -499 — | — — | — — |
| O'RIORDAN, Michael (F.G.) | 446 | +17 463 | +1 464 | +1 465 | +7 472 | +20 492 | +50 542 | +15 557 | +35 592 | +14 606 | -606 — | — — |
| QUEALLY, Benny | 30 | +1 31 | — 31 | -31 — | — — | — — | — — | — — | — — | — — | — — | — — |
| RYAN, Nuala (F.F.) | 306 | +9 315 | +11 326 | +5 331 | +43 374 | +10 384 | +4 388 | +18 406 | -406 — | — — | — — | — — |
| WALSH, Richie (F.G.) | 469 | +10 479 | +3 482 | +4 486 | +4 490 | +26 516 | +58 574 | +36 610 | +33 643 | +19 662 | +225 887 | -29 858 |
| WHELAN, Sean | 422 | +5 427 | +8 435 | +4 439 | +11 450 | +22 472 | +10 482 | +30 512 | +70 582 | +58 640 | +50 690 | +9 699 |
| WRIGHT, Tony (W.P.) | 482 | +23 505 | +2 507 | +3 510 | +6 516 | +29 545 | +11 556 | +11 567 | +29 596 | +13 609 | +86 695 | +7 702 |
| Non-transferable papers not effective | — | — — | — — | +3 3 | +11 14 | +21 35 | +9 44 | +49 93 | +39 132 | +240 372 | +126 498 | — 498 |
| TOTAL: | 6,860 | — 6,860 | — 6,860 | — 6,860 | — 6,860 | — 6,860 | — 6,860 | — 6,860 | — 6,860 | — 6,860 | — 6,860 | — 6,860 |

Elected: Kyne, Billy (Lab.); Kenneally, Patrick (F.F.); O'Halloran, Garrett (F.G.); Walsh, Richie (F.G.); Flynn, Austin (F.F.); Hart, Lar (Lab.); Wright, Tony (W.P.)

# KILMACTHOMAS ELECTORAL AREA

TOTAL ELECTORATE 8,239. VALID POLL 5,092. NO. OF MEMBERS 5. QUOTA 849

| Names of Candidates | First Count Votes | Second Count Transfer of Fahey's surplus Result | Third Count Transfer of O'Ryan's surplus Result | Fourth Count Transfer of P. Kelly's votes Result | Fifth Count Transfer of Dineen's votes Result | Sixth Count Transfer of R. Kelly's votes Result | Seventh Count Transfer of Whelan's votes Result | Eighth Count Transfer of Cunningham's surplus Result |
|---|---|---|---|---|---|---|---|---|
| BOWERS, Victor (Lab.) | 493 | +9 502 | +1 503 | +26 529 | +17 546 | +72 618 | +24 642 | +19 661 |
| COFFEY, Oliver (F.G.) | 703 | +13 716 | — 716 | +4 720 | +54 774 | +27 801 | +54 855 | — 855 |
| COFFEY, Patrick (F.G.) | 654 | +12 666 | +2 668 | +39 707 | +8 715 | +15 730 | +32 762 | +27 789 |
| CUNNINGHAM, Tom (F.F.) | 582 | +47 629 | +10 639 | +19 658 | +39 697 | +42 739 | +237 976 | -127 849 |
| DINEEN, Dan | 140 | +8 148 | — 148 | — 148 | — 148 | — — | — — | — — |
| FAHEY, Jackie (F.F.) | 1,066 | -217 849 | — 849 | — 849 | — 849 | — 849 | — 849 | — 849 |
| KELLY, Paul (F.F.) | 125 | +20 145 | +3 148 | -148 — | — — | — — | — — | — — |
| KELLY, Raymond (Lab.) | 204 | +8 212 | — 212 | +1 213 | +4 217 | -217 — | — — | — — |
| O'RYAN, Kieran (F.F.) | 807 | +69 876 | -27 849 | — 849 | — 849 | — 849 | — 849 | — 849 |
| WHELAN, Kathleen (F.F.) | 318 | +31 349 | +11 360 | +44 404 | +12 416 | +46 462 | -462 — | — — |
| Non-transferable papers not effective | — | — — | — — | +15 15 | +14 29 | +15 44 | +115 159 | +81 240 |
| TOTAL: | 5,092 | — 5,092 | — 5,092 | — 5,092 | — 5,092 | — 5,092 | — 5,092 | — 5,092 |

Elected: Fahey, Jackie (F.F.); O'Ryan, Kieran (F.F.); Cunningham, Tom (F.F.); Coffey, Oliver (F.G.); Coffey, Patrick (F.G.)

# LISMORE ELECTORAL AREA

TOTAL ELECTORATE 6,263. VALID POLL 4,115. NO. OF MEMBERS 4. QUOTA 824

| Names of Candidates | First Count Votes | Second Count Transfer of Wilkinson's surplus | Result | Third Count Transfer of McDonnell's surplus | Result | Fourth Count Transfer of Ryan's votes | Result |
|---|---|---|---|---|---|---|---|
| FLYNN, Nora (F.G.) | 421 | +82 | 503 | +134 | 637 | +79 | 716 |
| McDONNELL, Willie (F.G.) | 1,116 | — | 1,116 | -292 | 824 | — | 824 |
| POWER, Mathew (F.G.) | 424 | +73 | 497 | +104 | 601 | +80 | 681 |
| QUIRKE, Jimmy (F.F.) | 660 | +182 | 842 | — | 842 | — | 842 |
| RYAN, Mary (F.F.) | 207 | +126 | 333 | +54 | 387 | -387 | — |
| WILKINSON, Ollie (F.F.) | 1,287 | -463 | 824 | — | 824 | — | 824 |
| Non-transferable papers not effective | — | — | — | — | — | +228 | 228 |
| TOTAL: | 4,115 | — | 4,115 | — | 4,115 | — | 4,115 |

Elected: Wilkinson, Ollie (F.F.); McDonnell, Willie (F.G.); Quirke, Jimmy (F.F.); Flynn, Nora (F.G.)

# TRAMORE ELECTORAL AREA

TOTAL ELECTORATE 12,642. VALID POLL 7,408. NO. OF MEMBERS 7. QUOTA 927

| Names of Candidates | First Count Votes | Second Count Transfer of O'Shea's surplus Result | Third Count Transfer of Leahy's surplus Result | Fourth Count Transfer of Gahan's votes Result | Fifth Count Transfer of Dunphy's votes Result | Sixth Count Transfer of Griffin's votes Result | Seventh Count Transfer of O'Carroll's votes Result | Eighth Count Transfer of Queally's surplus Result | Ninth Count Transfer of Hutchinson's votes Result | Tenth Count Transfer of McDonagh's votes Result | Eleventh Count Transfer of Cowman's surplus Result | Twelfth Count Transfer of Carey's surplus Result |
|---|---|---|---|---|---|---|---|---|---|---|---|---|
| CAREY, John (F.G.) | 755 | +9 764 | +2 766 | +7 773 | +7 780 | +11 791 | +13 804 | +2 806 | +21 827 | +184 1,011 | — 1,011 | -84 927 |
| CASEY, Con (F.G.) | 422 | +27 449 | +3 452 | +9 461 | +19 480 | +16 496 | +94 590 | +3 593 | +67 660 | +60 720 | +22 742 | +53 795 |
| COWMAN, Dan (F.F.) | 560 | +33 593 | +22 615 | +12 627 | +68 695 | +53 748 | +53 801 | +3 804 | +191 995 | — 995 | -68 927 | — 927 |
| CULLEN, Martin (P.D.) | 469 | +19 488 | +7 495 | +16 511 | +9 520 | +40 560 | +79 639 | +3 642 | +45 687 | +50 737 | +9 746 | +7 753 |
| DUNPHY, Seamus (F.F.) | 215 | +9 224 | +27 251 | +6 257 | -257 — | — — | — — | — — | — — | — — | — — | — — |
| GAHAN, Edward (W.P.) | 154 | +15 169 | +18 187 | -187 — | — — | — — | — — | — — | — — | — — | — — | — — |
| GRIFFIN, Peter, (F.F.) | 213 | +5 218 | +22 240 | +30 270 | +21 291 | -291 — | — — | — — | — — | — — | — — | — — |
| HUTCHINSON, Billy (F.F.) | 336 | +14 350 | +9 359 | +10 369 | +28 397 | +35 432 | +49 481 | — 481 | -481 — | — — | — — | — — |
| LEAHY, Pat (F.F.) | 1,093 | — 1,093 | -166 927 | — 927 | — 927 | — 927 | — 927 | — 927 | — 927 | — 927 | — 927 | — 927 |
| McDONAGH, Noel (F.G.) | 454 | +5 459 | +3 462 | +8 470 | +4 474 | +4 478 | +14 492 | — 492 | +7 499 | -499 — | — — | — — |
| O'CARROLL, Maureen (Non-Party) | 294 | +21 315 | +2 317 | +26 343 | +17 360 | +22 382 | -382 — | — — | — — | — — | — — | — — |
| O'SHEA, Brian (Lab.) | 1,094 | -167 927 | — 927 | — 927 | — 927 | — 927 | — 927 | — 927 | — 927 | — 927 | — 927 | — 927 |
| POWER, Geoff (F.F.) | 533 | +4 537 | +15 552 | +5 557 | +23 580 | +20 600 | +14 614 | +2 616 | +59 675 | +146 821 | +37 858 | +24 882 |
| QUEALLY, Michael (F.G.) | 816 | +6 822 | +36 858 | +14 872 | +38 910 | +30 940 | — 940 | -13 927 | — 927 | — 927 | — 927 | — 927 |
| Non-transferable papers not effective | — | — — | — — | +44 44 | +23 67 | +60 127 | +66 193 | — 193 | +91 284 | +59 343 | — 343 | — 343 |
| TOTAL: | 7,408 | — 7,408 | — 7,408 | — 7,408 | — 7,408 | — 7,408 | — 7,408 | — 7,408 | — 7,408 | — 7,408 | — 7,408 | — 7,408 |

Elected: O'Shea, Brian (Lab.); Leahy, Pat (F.F.); Queally, Michael (F.G.); Cowman, Dan (F.F.); Carey, John (F.G.); Power, Geoff (F.F.); Casey, Con (F.G.)

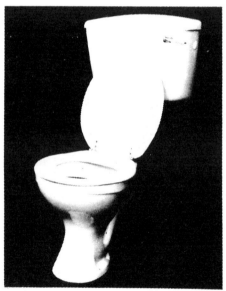

# WESTMEATH COUNTY COUNCIL

## WESTMEATH COUNTY COUNCIL RESULTS

| Party | 1991 % of votes | 1991 Seats obtained | 1985 % of votes | 1985 Seat obtained |
|---|---|---|---|---|
| Fianna Fail | 43.8 | 12 | 48.1 | 13 |
| Fine Gael | 27.3 | 6 | 27.9 | 5 |
| Labour | 18.3 | 4 | 12.8 | 3 |
| Progressive Dem. | 1.8 | — | — | — |
| Workers Party | 0.1 | — | — | — |
| Other | 8.7 | 1 | 11.2 | 2 |
| TOTAL SEATS | | 23 | | 23 |

## WESTMEATH

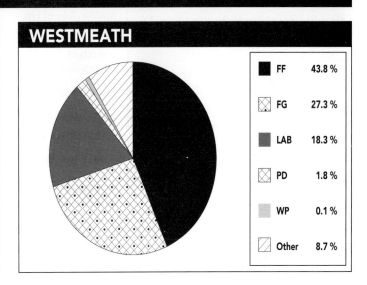

| | |
|---|---|
| FF | 43.8 % |
| FG | 27.3 % |
| LAB | 18.3 % |
| PD | 1.8 % |
| WP | 0.1 % |
| Other | 8.7 % |

**Mullingar**
**Telephone: (044) 40861/5**
**Fax: (044) 42330**
**Total population: 63,306**
**Rateable valuation: £509,824.80**
**County Council**
**Rate: £23.96**
**County Council meetings: Last Monday of each month**

*County Manager:* J. Taaffe
*County Secretary:* C. McGrath
*County Engineer:* J. Hearn
*Finance Officer:* M. Timoney
*Senior Executive Engineers:*
*Roads:* Noel Fay
*Housing/Sanitary Services:* Gary Walshe
*Road Design:* Ray Kenny
*Planning:* Vacant
*Road Projects:* John Ahearn (Acting)
*County Development Officer:* C. Kiernan
*Administrative Officers:*
*Housing and Sanitary:* G. Lambden
*Administration and General Purposes:* E. Hynes
*Senior Staff Officers:*
*Accounts:* Liam Kelly
*Planning:* Gerry Murphy
*Roads:* Nicholas Smyth (Acting)
*County Solicitor:* N. J. Downes
*County Coroner:* Dr P. Mangan
*Civil Defence Officer:* Brian Gillen
*Chief Fire Officer:* Murty Hanly
*Assistant Chief Fire Officers:*
D. Stuart (Prevention), E. Fayne (Operations)
*County Librarian:* Marian Keaney
Telephone: (044) 40781/2/3

**John Taaffe**

John Taaffe was born in Mayo in 1933 and is married with six children. he was educated in Athy C.B.S. and the School of Commerce, Rathmines. He is the holder of a Diploma in Administration from the I.P.A..

John Taaffe has worked for several County Councils including those in Carlow, Kildare and Roscommon where he served as Finance Secretary between 1971 and 1973. He is a former County Secretary in Laois County Council. In 1978 he was apppointed Assistant County Manager in Laois. He has been Westmeath County Manager since 1981.

He is interested in most sports and is an avid follower of gaelic games.

## ATHLONE

|  | 1991 | 1985 | '85 to '91 Swing |
|---|---|---|---|
| FF | 45.9 | 49.0` | -3.1 |
| FG | 24.5 | 25.1 | -0.6 |
| LAB | 7.7 | 8.2 | -0.5 |
| PD | 4.1 | — | 4.1 |
| SF | 0.0 | 3.4 | -3.4 |
| IND | 17.7 | 14.3 | 3.4 |

ALLEN, George,
Fardrum, Athlone,
County Westmeath. (FG)
Farmer. 0902-72840

COGHILL, P.J.
Waterstown, Glasson, Athlone,
County Westmeath. (FF)
Self-employed. 0902-85137

FALLON, Sean,
Clonown Road, Athlone,
County Westmeath. (FF)
Senator. 0902-74158

McFADDEN, Brendan,
5 Dunard, The Batteries, Athlone,
County Westmeath. (FG)
ESB Employee. 0902-72611

MOLLOY, Kieran,
Connolly Street, Athlone,
County Westmeath. (FF)
ESB Employee. 0902-72611

PRICE, Stephen,
18 Station Road, Moate,
County Westmeath. (NP)
Retired. 0902-81314

TEMPLE, Ciaran,
Ballymahon Road, Athlone,
County Westmeath. (FF)
Company Director. 0902-72390

## COOLE

|  | 1991 | 1985 | '85 to '91 Swing |
|---|---|---|---|
| FF | 53.4 | 65.5 | -12.1 |
| FG | 31.1 | 30.1 | 1.0 |
| LAB | 10.3 | 4.4 | 5.9 |
| IND | 5.2 | — | 5.2 |

BOURKE, Thomas,
"The Covert", Ballinafid, Mullingar,
County Westmeath. (FF)
Farmer. 044-71127

CASSIDY, Donie,
The Square,
Castlepollard,
County Westmeath. (FF)
Senator. 044-61176

McDERMOTT, Frank,
Ankerland, Fore,
Castlepollard,
County Westmeath. (FG)
Farmer. 044-66338

O'SHAUGHNESSY, Patrick,
Delvin,
County Westmeath. (FF)
Shopkeeper. 044-64121

## KILBEGGAN

|  | 1991 | 1985 | '85 to '91 Swing |
|---|---|---|---|
| FF | 41.8 | 44.1 | -2.3 |
| FG | 36.8 | 40.9 | -4.1 |
| LAB | 16.9 | | 16.9 |
| IND | 4.5 | 15.0 | -10.5 |

COWLEY, Tom,
Kilbeggan, Mullingar,
County Westmeath. (FF)
Self-employed. 0506-32146

FLANAGAN, Joseph,
Moyvoughley, Moate,
County Westmeath. (FG)
Company Representative. 0902-81235

NUGENT, Mark,
Carrick, Dalystown,
Mullingar,
County Westmeath. (Lab)
Board na Mona Worker. 044-23341

RYAN, Michael,
Newtown, Ballymore, Mullingar,
County Westmeath. (FF)
Farmer. 044-56231

## MULLINGAR (LOUGH OWEL)

|  | 1991 | 1985 | '85 to '91 Swing |
|---|---|---|---|
| FF | 43.8 | 45.3 | -1.5 |
| FG | 28.8 | 26.5 | 2.3 |
| LAB | 24.1 | 28.2 | -4.1 |
| IND | 3.3 | — | 3.3 |

ABBOTT, Henry,
Monilea, Mullingar,
County Westmeath. (FF)
Barrister. 044-72110

KEEGAN, John H,
Edmondstown, Killucan,
County Westmeath. (FG)
Farmer. 044-74102

PENROSE, Willie,
Ballintue, Ballynacargy, Mullingar,
County Westmeath. (Lab)
Barrister. 044-41577

WRIGHT, Thomas,
Gaybrook, Mullingar,
County Westmeath. (FF)
Self-employed. 044-22157

## MULLINGAR (URBAN)

|  | 1991 | 1985 | '85 to '91 Swing |
|---|---|---|---|
| FF | 32.3 | 32.5 | -0.2 |
| FG | 15.5 | 16.5 | -1.0 |
| LAB | 44.1 | 32.2 | 11.9 |
| WP | 0.4 | | 0.4 |
| PD | 3.3 | | 3.3 |
| SF | 0.0 | 2.7 | -2.7 |
| IND | 4.3 | 16.1 | -11.8 |

DOLLARD, Michael,
15 Beechgrove, Mullingar,
County Westmeath. (Lab)
Health Board Worker. 044-42105

GLYNN, Camillus,
8 Newbrook Road, Clonmore, Mullingar,
County Westmeath. (FF)
Nurse. 044-40116

COLEMAN, Des,
40 Great Oaks, Mullinar,
County Westmeath. (Lab)
Communications Officer. 044-40132

McGRATH, Paul,
"Carna", Irishtown, Mullingar,
County Westmeath. (FG)
Dail Deputy. 044-40746

**Paul McGrath (FG)**
**Mullingar Urban**

**Tom Bourke (FF)**
**Coole**

**John M. Keegan (FG)**
**Mullingar Rural**

**Sean Fallon (FF)**
**Athlone**

# Despite seat loss, Fianna Fáil hold majority

Despite losing one seat, Fianna Fáil regained control of Westmeath County Council, winning 12 of the 23 seats which make up the Council. Fine Gael gained a seat on 1985, to bring their number to 6 but came nowhere near regaining the 9 seats they held in 1979. The Labour Party increased their share of the vote by over 5% and their number of Council seats to 4.

The Athlone Electoral Area not only had the largest number of candidates (21) but also needed the greatest number of counts (14) to elect it's 7 seats. There was no change in party representation in Athlone, with only George Ledwith failing to hold the seat he was co-opted into with the retirement from the Council, due to Ministerial obligations, of Mary O'Rourke, the 1985 poll topper in this area. Ledwith lost out to party colleague Kieran Molloy who was Chairman of Athlone UDC. Fianna Fáil's other co-opted outgoing Councillor Cieran Temple, who replaced Padraic Dunne, held his seat by a margin of 44 votes from running mate Egbert Moran.

The star performer in Athlone was that from Fianna Fáil Senator Seán Fallon, who was first elected, topping the poll by a huge margin over the next placed candidate Brendan McFadden of Fine Gael, who was only returned on the eleventh count. McFadden was joined by party colleague outgoing Councillor George Allen. Independent candidate Stephen Price saw his first preference vote drop on 1985, but good transfers from all parties was enough to ensure his re-election.

All 4 outgoing candidates in the Coole Electoral Area were returned. Fianna Fáil Senator Donnie Cassidy topped the poll as in 1985. He did so, however, with a drop of 387 in his first preference vote and had to wait until the fourth count to be deemed re-elected. Cassidy was returned along with fellow Fianna Fáil Councillors, Patrick O'Shaughnessy and Thomas Bourke.

Fine Gael's Frank McDermott was safely re-elected, although it has to be said that with 3 candidates in this area Fine Gael themselves ruined their chances of taking a seat from Fianna Fáil. With only 2 candidates, it is possible that Fine Gael could have added to McDermott's seat in Coole.

The Labour Party gained a seat in the Kilbeggan Electoral Area at the expense of Fine Gael. Mark Nugent had been co-opted onto Westmeath County Council in place of Helena McAuliffe-Ennis, who won a seat for Labour in Mullingar (Lough Owel) in 1985, but later defected to join the Progressive Democrats. Nugent was a candidate in the Kilbeggan Area and captured almost 17% of the vote for Labour which giving the second seat on the fifth count.

The poll was topped by Fine Gael's Joseph Flanagan, but with a 4% decline in their vote, holding the second seat won in 1985 was never really on. Seán Keegan

> ## The big talking point in Mullingar Urban was the outstanding performance of Labour's Michael Dollard

who topped the poll for Fianna Fáil in 1985 was not a candidate on this occasion. His place as that party's chief vote getter was taken by newcomer Tom Cowley, who was elected along with, outgoing Councillor and party colleague, Michael Ryan.

Service charges were one of the central issues in Mullingar and it was not surprising that it was in Mullingar Urban that Fianna Fáil suffered their only seat loss in the 5 electoral areas. In 1985 Fianna Fáil took 2 seats with 1 Independent and 1 Labour. Fine Gael were without representation in 1985 in this area, missing out on the last seat by 3 votes to Fianna Fáil's Martin Hynes. This situation was reversed this time out, with the election to the Council of Deputy Paul McGrath, in the place of Hynes. The Fine Gael TD's performance was, however, a poor one taking the last seat without reaching the quota, and it may spell trouble ahead for the former National School Teacher in the new 3 seater Westmeath constituency.

The big talking point in Mullingar Urban was the outstanding performance of Labour's Michael Dollard, who topped the poll with 1,688 votes, some 835 votes above the quota and 1085 votes ahead of the nearest candidate. This vote getting achievement was matched by the 58% transfer of Dollard's surplus to his running mate, Des Coleman. With this transfer, Coleman went from a first preference vote of 190, to taking the third seat on the final count. The Labour vote, of 44% in Mullingar Urban, was the highest they achieved in the entire country.

A Labour candidate also topped the poll in Mullingar Lough Owel. Outgoing Councillor Willie Penrose went from taking the last seat by a mere 5 votes in 1985, to poll topper this time out. Labour took 2 seats in this area in 1985 and a repeat of this result was never a serious option, especially with the defection of Helena Mac Auliffe-Ennis to the Progressive Democrats. Her replacement on the Council, Mark Nugent, was, however, elected in the Kilbeggan Area. Fine Gael, having failed to take a seat in 1985, made no mistake this time out. John Keegan who was beaten for the last seat by 5 votes was safely returned, taking the third seat. Fianna Fáil safely held their 2 seats. Outgoing Councillor Shay Callaghan was replaced on the Council by running mate Thomas Wright, while former TD Henry Abbott, increased his vote on 1985 to be elected on the first count.

Abbott, will be seeking to build on this result to regain the Dail seat he lost in 1989 to Fine Gael's Paul McGrath, who could be in real trouble if his Mullingar Urban result is any thing to go by. Westmeath will be a 3 seater next time out, and Fianna Fáil's Mary O'Rourke is safely assured of re-election. The other two seats will be between Fianna Fáil, Fine Gael and possibly Labour as a long shot. Interestingly there was no Labour candidate in the old Longford-Westmeath in 1989, so if nothing else, the strong performance of Labour in Westmeath in the 1991 locals will add spice to this constituency at the next general election.

# ATHLONE ELECTORAL AREA

TOTAL ELECTORATE 15,815. VALID POLL 8,791. NO. OF MEMBERS 7. QUOTA 1,099

| Names of Candidates | First Count Votes | Second Count Transfer of Fallon's surplus Result | Third Count Transfer of Cooney's & Dolan's votes Result | Fourth Count Transfer of Kearney's votes Result | Fifth Count Transfer of Gavin's votes Result | Sixth Count Transfer of O'Brien's votes Result | Seventh Count Transfer of Keenehan's votes Result | Eighth Count Transfer of Berry's votes Result |
|---|---|---|---|---|---|---|---|---|
| ALLEN, George (F.G.) | 415 | +1 416 | +7 423 | +1 424 | +11 435 | +42 477 | +3 480 | +4 484 |
| BEAUMONT, Patsy (Non-Party) | 255 | +2 257 | +6 263 | +19 282 | +45 327 | +3 330 | +33 363 | +87 450 |
| BERRY, Austin (Non-Party) | 234 | +1 235 | +10 245 | +40 285 | +36 321 | +3 324 | +13 337 | -337 — |
| COGHILL, P.J. (F.F.) | 737 | +3 740 | +2 742 | +4 746 | +7 753 | +5 758 | +4 762 | +2 764 |
| COGHLAN, Pauline (F.G.) | 381 | +1 382 | +10 392 | +1 393 | +1 394 | +23 417 | — 417 | +5 422 |
| COONEY, Benedict Oliver (Non-Party) | 43 | — 43 | -43 — | — — | — — | — — | — — | — — |
| DOLAN, David Thomas (Lab.) | 82 | — 82 | -82 — | — — | — — | — — | — — | — — |
| DOOLEY, Vincent (F.G.) | 332 | +1 333 | +3 336 | +1 337 | +15 352 | +15 367 | +4 371 | +8 379 |
| FALLON, Sean (F.F.) | 1,140 | -41 1,099 | — 1,099 | — 1,099 | — 1,099 | — 1,099 | — 1,099 | — 1,099 |
| GAVIN, Oliver John (Non-Party) | 209 | +1 210 | +7 217 | +9 226 | -226 — | — — | — — | — — |
| HENSON, John (Lab.) | 377 | +2 379 | +21 400 | +10 410 | +17 427 | +14 441 | +66 507 | +26 533 |
| KEARNEY, Joan (Non-Party) | 144 | +1 145 | +2 147 | -147 — | — — | — — | — — | — — |
| KEENEHAN, John (Lab.) | 230 | +1 231 | +6 237 | +7 244 | +6 250 | — 250 | -250 — | — — |
| LEDWITH, George (F.F.) | 399 | +2 401 | +6 407 | +1 408 | +6 414 | +2 416 | +3 419 | +6 425 |
| LYNCH, Des (P.D.) | 364 | +1 365 | +2 367 | +5 372 | +5 377 | +25 402 | +10 412 | +13 425 |
| McFADDEN, Brendan (F.G.) | 817 | +4 821 | +10 831 | +8 839 | +21 860 | +46 906 | +56 962 | +26 988 |
| MOLLOY, Kieran (F.F.) | 660 | +8 668 | +3 671 | +13 684 | +17 701 | +6 707 | +27 734 | +32 766 |
| MORAN, Egbert (F.F.) | 463 | +4 467 | +2 469 | +8 477 | +3 480 | +30 510 | +7 517 | +5 522 |
| O'BRIEN, Dick (F.G.) | 241 | — 241 | +2 243 | +1 244 | +2 246 | -246 — | — — | — — |
| PRICE, Stephen (Non-Party) | 693 | +1 694 | +19 713 | +6 719 | +10 729 | +7 736 | +6 742 | +36 778 |
| TEMPLE, Cieran (F.F.) | 575 | +7 582 | +1 583 | +7 590 | +10 600 | +21 621 | +8 629 | +12 641 |
| Non-transferable papers not effective | — | — — | +6 6 | +6 12 | +14 26 | +4 30 | +10 40 | +75 115 |
| TOTAL: | 8,791 | — 8,791 | — 8,791 | — 8,791 | — 8,791 | — 8,791 | — 8,791 | — 8,791 |

| Ninth Count Transfer of Dooley's votes Result | Tenth Count Transfer of Ledwith's votes Result | Eleventh Count Transfer of Lynch's votes Result | Twelfth Count Transfer of McFadden's surplus Result | Thirteenth Count Transfer of Beaumont's votes Result | Fourteenth Count Transfer of Coghlan's votes Result | Fifteenth Count Transfer of Price's surplus Result | Sixteenth Count Transfer of Henson's votes Result |
|---|---|---|---|---|---|---|---|
| +53 537 | +44 581 | +55 636 | +16 652 | +12 664 | +173 837 | +58 895 | +103 998 |
| +10 460 | +2 462 | +22 484 | +7 491 | -491 — | — — | — — | — — |
| — — | — — | — — | — — | — — | — — | — — | — — |
| +70 834 | +48 882 | +14 896 | +1 897 | +15 912 | +20 932 | +8 940 | +41 981 |
| +64 486 | +39 525 | +20 545 | +13 558 | +9 567 | -567 — | — — | — — |
| — — | — — | — — | — — | — — | — — | — — | — — |
| — — | — — | — — | — — | — — | — — | — — | — — |
| -379 — | — — | — — | — — | — — | — — | — — | — — |
| — 1,099 | — 1,099 | — 1,099 | — 1,099 | — 1,099 | — 1,099 | — 1,099 | — 1,099 |
| — — | — — | — — | — — | — — | — — | — — | — — |
| +22 555 | +8 563 | +24 587 | +7 594 | +52 646 | +24 670 | +3 673 | -673 — |
| — — | — — | — — | — — | — — | — — | — — | — — |
| — — | — — | — — | — — | — — | — — | — — | — — |
| +7 432 | -432 — | — — | — — | — — | — — | — — | — — |
| +12 437 | +8 445 | -445 — | — — | — — | — — | — — | — — |
| +76 1,064 | +6 1,070 | +110 1,180 | -81 1,099 | — 1,099 | — 1,099 | — 1,099 | — 1,099 |
| +8 774 | +38 812 | +34 846 | +11 857 | +86 943 | +16 959 | +7 966 | +67 1,033 |
| +9 531 | +60 591 | +52 643 | +5 648 | +14 662 | +13 675 | +5 680 | +102 782 |
| — — | — — | — — | — — | — — | — — | — — | — — |
| +14 792 | +139 931 | +21 952 | +4 956 | +53 1,009 | +219 1,228 | -129 1,099 | — 1,099 |
| +6 647 | +25 672 | +40 712 | +17 729 | +35 764 | +10 774 | +8 782 | +44 826 |
| +28 143 | +15 158 | +53 211 | — 211 | +215 426 | +92 518 | +40 558 | +316 874 |
| — 8,791 | — 8,791 | — 8,791 | — 8,791 | — 8,791 | — 8,791 | — 8,791 | — 8,791 |

Elected: Fallon, Seán (F.F.); McFadden, Brendan (F.G.); Price, Stephen (Non-Party); Molloy, Kieran (F.F.); Allen, George (F.G.); Coghill, P.J. (F.F.); Temple, Cieran (F.F.)

# COOLE ELECTORAL AREA

TOTAL ELECTORATE 7,178. VALID POLL 4,905. NO. OF MEMBERS 4. QUOTA 982

| Names of Candidates | First Count Votes | Second Count Transfer of McCormack's votes Result | | Third Count Transfer of Boyhan's votes Result | | Fourth Count Transfer of Cahill's votes Result | | Fifth Count Transfer of Cassidy's surplus Result | | Sixth Count Transfer of Penrose's votes Result | | Seventh Count Transfer of Drum's votes Result | |
|---|---|---|---|---|---|---|---|---|---|---|---|---|---|
| BOURKE, Thomas (F.F.) | 628 | +2 | 630 | +84 | 714 | +39 | 753 | +15 | 768 | +102 | 870 | +8 | 878 |
| BOYHAN, Kevin | 255 | +3 | 258 | -258 | — | — | — | — | — | — | — | — | — |
| BRENNAN, Phil (F.G.) | 504 | +3 | 507 | +54 | 561 | +17 | 578 | +2 | 580 | +92 | 672 | +76 | 748 |
| CAHILL, Molly (F.F.) | 372 | +13 | 385 | +6 | 391 | -391 | — | — | — | — | — | — | — |
| CASSIDY, Donie (F.F.) | 897 | +24 | 921 | +12 | 933 | +138 | 1,071 | -89 | 982 | — | 982 | — | 982 |
| DRUM, Maura (F.G.) | 429 | +6 | 435 | +8 | 443 | +23 | 466 | +4 | 470 | +23 | 493 | -493 | — |
| McCORMACK, John (Lab.) | 125 | -125 | — | — | — | — | — | — | — | — | — | — | — |
| McDERMOTT, Frank (F.G.) | 594 | +23 | 617 | +27 | 644 | +58 | 702 | +26 | 728 | +36 | 764 | +243 | 1,007 |
| O'SHAUGHNESSY, Patrick (F.F.) | 720 | +5 | 725 | +6 | 731 | +85 | 816 | +41 | 857 | +23 | 880 | +120 | 1,000 |
| PENROSE, John (Lab.) | 381 | +40 | 421 | +42 | 463 | +6 | 469 | +1 | 470 | -470 | — | — | — |
| Non-transferable papers not effective | — | +6 | 6 | +19 | 25 | +25 | 50 | — | 50 | +194 | 244 | +46 | 290 |
| TOTAL: | 4,905 | — | 4,905 | — | 4,905 | — | 4,905 | — | 4,905 | — | 4,905 | — | 4,905 |

Elected: Cassidy, Donie (F.F.); McDermott, Frank (F.G.); O'Shaughnessy, Patrick (F.F.); Bourke, Thomas (F.F.)

# KILBEGGAN ELECTORAL AREA

TOTAL ELECTORATE 7,331. VALID POLL 4,848. NO. OF MEMBERS 4. QUOTA 970

| Names of Candidates | First Count Votes | Second Count Transfer of Flanagan's surplus Result | | Third Count Transfer of Cooney's votes Result | | Fourth Count Transfer of Henry's votes Result | | Fifth Count Transfer of Bradley's votes Result | | Sixth Count Transfer of Nugent's surplus Result | | Seventh Count Transfer of Cowley's surplus Result | |
|---|---|---|---|---|---|---|---|---|---|---|---|---|---|
| BRADLEY, Christo (F.F.) | 529 | +7 | 536 | +11 | 547 | +46 | 593 | -593 | — | — | — | — | — |
| COONEY, Gerard Christopher (Non-Party) | 218 | +4 | 222 | -222 | — | — | — | — | — | — | — | — | — |
| COWLEY, Tom (F.F.) | 837 | +4 | 841 | +84 | 925 | +17 | 942 | +221 | 1,163 | — | 1,163 | -193 | 970 |
| FALLON, Mary (F.G.) | 340 | +57 | 397 | +43 | 440 | +190 | 630 | +14 | 644 | +34 | 678 | +4 | 682 |
| FLANAGAN, Joseph (F.G.) | 1,124 | -154 | 970 | — | 970 | — | 970 | — | 970 | — | 970 | — | 970 |
| HENRY, Mary (F.G.) | 321 | +24 | 345 | +15 | 360 | -360 | — | — | — | — | — | — | — |
| NUGENT, Mark (Lab.) | 820 | +12 | 832 | +42 | 874 | +80 | 954 | +234 | 1,188 | -218 | 970 | — | 970 |
| RYAN, Michael (F.F.) | 659 | +46 | 705 | +13 | 718 | +6 | 724 | +91 | 815 | +51 | 866 | +177 | 1,043 |
| Non-transferable papers not effective | — | — | — | +14 | 14 | +21 | 35 | +33 | 68 | +133 | (201 | +12 | 213 |
| TOTAL: | 4,848 | — | 4,848 | — | 4,848 | — | 4,848 | — | 4,848 | — | 4,848 | — | 4,848 |

Elected: Flanagan, Joseph (F.G.); Nugent, Mark (Lab.); Cowley, Tom (F.F.); Ryan, Michael (F.F.)

# MULLINGAR (LOUGH OWEL) ELECTORAL AREA

TOTAL ELECTORATE 8,054. VALID POLL 4,864. NO. OF MEMBERS 4. QUOTA 973

| Names of Candidates | First Count Votes | Second Count Transfer of Penrose's surplus | Result | Third Count Transfer of Abbott's surplus | Result | Fourth Count Transfer of Bagnall's votes | Result | Fifth Count Transfer of Moughty's votes | Result | Sixth Count Transfer of Keegan's surplus | Result | Seventh Count Transfer of Callaghan's votes | Result |
|---|---|---|---|---|---|---|---|---|---|---|---|---|---|
| ABBOTT, Henry (F.F.) | 1,101 | — | 1101 | -128 | 973 | — | 973 | — | 973 | — | 973 | — | 973 |
| BAGNALL, Robert Joseph | 160 | +24 | 184 | +6 | 190 | -190 | — | — | — | — | — | — | — |
| CALLAGHAN, Shay (F.F.) | 444 | +26 | 470 | +57 | 527 | +41 | 568 | +6 | 574 | — | 574 | -574 | — |
| KEEGAN, John H. (F.G.) | 821 | +33 | 854 | +10 | 864 | +45 | 909 | +69 | 978 | -5 | 973 | — | 973 |
| MOUGHTY, Thomas Patrick (F.G.) | 210 | +29 | 239 | +4 | 243 | +4 | 247 | -247 | — | — | — | — | — |
| PENROSE, Willie (Lab.) | 1,170 | -197 | 973 | — | 973 | — | 973 | — | 973 | — | 973 | — | 973 |
| WALLACE, Frank J. (F.G.) | 371 | +53 | 424 | +16 | 440 | +15 | 455 | +119 | 574 | +5 | 579 | +45 | 624 |
| HT, Thomas Joseph (F.F.) | 587 | +32 | 619 | +35 | 654 | +35 | 689 | +11 | 700 | — | 700 | +343 | 1,043 |
| Non-transferable papers not effective | — | — | — | — | — | +50 | 50 | +42 | 92 | — | 92 | +186 | 278 |
| TOTAL: | 4,864 | — | 4,864 | — | 4,864 | — | 4,864 | — | 4,864 | — | 4,864 | — | 4,864 |

Elected: Penrose, Willie (Lab.); Abbott, Henry (F.F.); Keegan, John H. (F.G.); Wright, Thomas Joseph (F.F.)

# MULLINGAR (URBAN) ELECTORAL AREA

TOTAL ELECTORATE 7,870. VALID POLL 4,263. NO. OF MEMBERS 4. QUOTA 853

| Names of Candidates | First Count Votes | Second Count Transfer of Dollard's surplus | Result | Third Count Transfer of Cooney's votes | Result | Fourth Count Transfer of Boyce's votes | Result | Fifth Count Transfer of Whelan's votes | Result | Sixth Count Transfer of Guinan's votes | Result | Seventh Count Transfer of McIntyre's votes | Result | Eighth Count Transfer of Bourke's votes | Result |
|---|---|---|---|---|---|---|---|---|---|---|---|---|---|---|---|
| BOURKE, Jim (F.F.) | 275 | +29 | 304 | — | 304 | — | 304 | +24 | 328 | +21 | 349 | +23 | 372 | -372 | — |
| BOYCE, Patrick (W.P.) | 19 | +11 | 30 | +1 | 31 | -31 | — | — | — | — | — | — | — | — | — |
| COLEMAN, Des (Lab.) | 190 | +488 | 678 | +1 | 679 | +10 | 689 | +21 | 710 | +22 | 732 | +78 | 810 | +35 | 845 |
| COONEY, Benedict Oliver (Non-Party) | 2 | +5 | 7 | -7 | — | — | — | — | — | — | — | — | — | — | — |
| DOLLARD, Michael (Lab.) | 1,688 | -835 | 853 | — | 853 | — | 853 | — | 853 | — | 853 | — | 853 | — | 853 |
| GLYNN, Camillus (F.F.) | 603 | +71 | 674 | — | 674 | +5 | 679 | +21 | 700 | +14 | 714 | +50 | 764 | +110 | 874 |
| GUINAN, Jim (F.G.) | 144 | +16 | 160 | +1 | 161 | +3 | 164 | +13 | 177 | -177 | — | — | — | — | — |
| HYNES, Martin (F.F.) | 501 | +52 | 553 | +1 | 554 | +1 | 555 | +10 | 565 | +11 | 576 | +47 | 623 | +96 | 719 |
| McGRATH, Paul (F.G.) | 517 | +61 | 578 | — | 578 | +1 | 579 | +36 | 615 | +80 | 695 | +52 | 747 | +89 | 836 |
| McINTYRE, Frank | 183 | +83 | 266 | +2 | 268 | +4 | 272 | +18 | 290 | +17 | 307 | -307 | — | — | — |
| WHELAN, Patrick (P.D.) | 141 | +19 | 160 | — | 160 | +3 | 163 | -163 | — | — | — | — | — | — | — |
| Non-transferable papers not effective | — | — | — | +1 | 1 | +4 | 5 | +20 | 25 | +12 | 37 | +57 | 94 | +42 | 136 |
| TOTAL: | 4,263 | — | 4,263 | — | 4,263 | — | 4,263 | — | 4,263 | — | 4,263 | — | 4,263 | — | 4,263 |

Elected: Dollard, Michael (Lab.); Glynn, Camillus (F.F.); Coleman, Des (Lab.); McGrath, Paul (F.G.)

# WEXFORD COUNTY COUNCIL

## WEXFORD COUNTY COUNCIL RESULTS

| Party | 1991 % of votes | 1991 Seats obtained | 1985 % of votes | 1985 Seats obtained |
|---|---|---|---|---|
| Fianna Fail | 40.2 | 8 | 46.3 | 11 |
| Fine Gael | 30.2 | 8 | 28.3 | 6 |
| Labour | 12.6 | 1 | 8.3 | 1 |
| Progressive Dem. | 2.5 | — | — | — |
| Workers Party | 2.1 | — | 1.8 | — |
| Other | 12.4 | 4 | 15.3 | 3 |
| TOTAL SEATS | | 21 | | 21 |

## WEXFORD

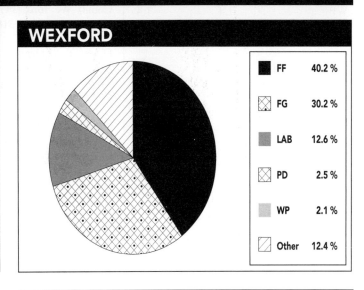

| | |
|---|---|
| ■ FF | 40.2 % |
| ▨ FG | 30.2 % |
| ■ LAB | 12.6 % |
| ▨ PD | 2.5 % |
| ▨ WP | 2.1 % |
| ▨ Other | 12.4 % |

County Hall,
Spawell Road, Wexford
Telephone: (053) 22211
Fax: (053) 23406
Total population: 102,456
Rateable valuation: £525,816.70
Rate: £29.00
County Council meetings: Second Monday of each month

*County Manager:* Michael N. Dillon
*Assistant County Manager:* Vacant.
*County Secretary:* W. P. Creedon
*Fi nance Officer:* A. Doyle
*County Engineer:* P. Callery
*Development Officer:* W. Ringwood
*Administrative Officers:* James O'Leary, John Pierce, Gerard Leahy
*Senior Staff Officers:* Niall McDonnell, Thomas Skehan, Anthony Larkin, Vacancy
*County Librarian:* C. O'Ruairc, Abbey Street, Wexford.
*Telephone:* (053) 22211
*County Solicitor:* Messrs J. A. Sinnott and Co.
*County Coroners:* Dr J. P. Nixon  J. Murphy, Solicitor
*Civil Defence Officer:* Gabrielle Willis
*Senior Executive Engineers:*
*Roads:* J. N. Casey
*Sanitary Services:* Don O'Sullivan
*Environmental:* P. Wilson (Acting)
*Planning:* Ms R. Nixon
*Borough of Wexford:* T. Fahey
*Senior Executive Architect*: W. A. Rahilly
*Chief Fire Officer:* S. McDermott

Michael Dillion as he is generally known has been County Manager since 1976. He is a native of Cork where he was born in 1936. He was educated at the Presentation College and then University College Cork, where he took a Diploma in Commerce and Diploma in Public Administration (Gold Medal Winner). He is a Fellow of the Chartered Institute of Secretaries and Administrators.

**Michael Noel Dillon**

He has been Staff Officer and Finance Officer with Limerick County Council 1967 - 1971. County Secretary with Limerick County Council in 1971 - 1975 and Assistant County Manager from 1975.

He is married to Delia Barrett and they have five children. He enjoys all sports but especially golf and angling. He was captain of Highfield, Cork and Corinthians, Galway Rugby Club in his day.

He is a member of many National Bodies and is Director of the National Building Agency and Deputy Chairman of the Fire Service Council. His greatest achievement probably would be seen to be the opening of a National Heritage Park at Ferrycarrig on the outskirts of Wexford Town.

## ENNISCORTHY

|     | 1991 | 1985 | '85 to '91 Swing |
|-----|------|------|------|
| FF  | 44.6 | 47.6 | -3.0 |
| FG  | 35.9 | 34.2 | 1.7 |
| LAB | 4.5  | 4.9  | -0.4 |
| WP  | —    | 1.4  | -1.4 |
| IND | 15.0 | 11.9 | 3.1 |

BOLGER, Jack,
Marshaltown, Enniscorthy,
County Wexford. (FG)
Farmer. 054-88583

BROWNE, John,
Kilcannon, Enniscorthy,
Co. Wexford (FF)*
Dail Deputy. 054-35046
*Resigned when appointed
Minister of State. Replaced by:

BYRNE, Peter,
Boormount, Enniscorthy,
County Wexford. (FF)

DOYLE, Sean,
2 Esmonde Road, Enniscorthy,
County Wexford. (NP)
Nurse.

SINNOTT, Michael,
Garrywilliam House, Crossabeg,
County Wexford. (FF)
Famer. 053-28136

YATES, Ivan,
Blackstoops, Enniscorthy,
County Wexford. (FG)
Dail Deputy. 054-33793

## GOREY

|     | 1991 | 1985 | '85 to '91 Swing |
|-----|------|------|------|
| FF  | 38.9 | 50.1 | -11.2 |
| FG  | 45.4 | 39.0 | 6.4 |
| LAB | 15.7 | 8.4  | 7.3 |
| IND | 0.0  | 2.5  | -2.5 |

ALLEN, Lorcan,
Raheenagurren, Gorey,
County Wexford. (FF)
Farmer. 055-21114

BOLGER, Deirdre,
Millmount, Gorey,
County Wexford. (FG)
Housewife. 055-21318

D'ARCY, Michael,
Annagh Lower, Inch, Gorey,
County Wexford. (FG)
Dail Deputy. 055-28177

GAHAN, James,
Ballycarrigeen, Ferns,
County Wexford. (FG)
Farmer. 054-66214

MURPHY, Rory,
Ballinavocran, Bunclody,
County Wexford. (FF)
Farmer. 054-77158

## NEW ROSS

|     | 1991 | 1985 | '85 to '91 Swing |
|-----|------|------|------|
| FF  | 56.5 | 63.4 | -6.9 |
| FG  | 21.5 | 23.8 | -2.3 |
| LAB | 13.6 | 6.5  | 7.1 |
| WP  | —    | 1.5  | -1.5 |
| PD  | 8.4  | —    | 8.4 |
| SF  | —    | 4.6  | -4.6 |
| IND | —    | 0.2  | -0.2 |

BROWNE, John T.
Foulkesmills, New Ross,
County Wexford. (FG)
Public Representative. 051-28326

BYRNE, Hugh,
Air-Hill, Fethard-on-Sea, New Ross,
County Wexford. (FF)
Senator. 051-97125

CURTIS, Jimmy,
Loughnageer, Foulksmills,
County Wexford. (FF)
Farmer. 051-62130

WALSH, Jim,
Parkfield, New Ross,
County Wexford. (FF)
Manager.

O'BRIEN, Laurence,
Ballinamona, Campile, New Ross,
County Wexford. (FG)
Car Sales Manager. 051-88331

## WEXFORD DISTRICT

|     | 1991 | 1985 | '85 to '91 Swing |
|-----|------|------|------|
| FF  | 24.2 | 28.5 | -4.3 |
| FG  | 20.1 | 18.2 | 1.9 |
| LAB | 15.8 | 12.6 | 3.2 |
| WP  | 7.3  | 3.9  | 3.4 |
| SF  | —    | 2.6  | -2.6 |
| IND | 30.7 | 34.2 | -3.5 |

BYRNE, Gus,
19 Thomas Clarke Place,
Wexford. (FF)
Ambulance Driver. 053-22408

CARTHY, Leo,
Lake View, Airdowns, Broadway,
County Wexford. (NP)
Salesman. 053-31235

CORISH, Helen,
"Woodhelven", 7 Parkview,
Wexford. (NP)
Teacher. 053-41571

DOYLE, Avril,
Kitestown House, Crossabeg,
County Wexford. (FG)
Senator. 053-42873

HOWLIN, Brendan,
7 Upper William Street,
Wexford. (Lab)
Dail Deputy. 053-22848

RECK, Padge,
Mulgannon,
Wexford. (NP)
Unemployed. 053-44666

**Ivan Yates (FG)**
**Enniscorthy**

**Gus Byrne (FF)**
**Wexford**

**Hugh Byrne (FF)**
**New Ross**

**Michael D'Arcy**
**Gorey**

# Fine Gael make big gains in Wexford

Neither Fianna Fail nor the Labour Party, will have been pleased with their respective performances in the elections for Wexford County Council. Fianna Fail lost 3 seats and their control of the Council, while the Labour Party failed to make any inroads, and Deputy Brendan Howlin remains their only Councillor in Wexford. The big winners were Fine Gael, who ran only 10 candidates, with 8 of them being successfully returned. Fine Gael now have the same number of seats as Fianna Fail, with 4 Independents and a single Labour representative.

The Enniscorthy Electoral Area returned the same five Councillors who were elected in 1985, with TD's John Browne and Ivan Yates both being elected on the first count. Fianna Fail's John Browne polled almost 500 votes above the quota and he was returned along with party colleague, Michael Sinnott. Fine Gael's vote was up slightly on 1985, and outgoing Councillors Ivan Yates TD and Jack Bolger were never in any danger. The final seat in Enniscorthy was comfortably filled by Independent Sean Doyle, who was returned without reaching the quota.

The results from the Gorey Electoral Area were a success for Fine Gael Deputy Michael D'Arcy, who topped the poll with 2,469 first preference votes. With the help of strong transfers from his surplus, and the eliminated Labour candidate, D'Arcy's two running mates, outgoing Councillor Deirdre Bolger and newcomer James Gannon were successfully returned. This Fine Gael gain was made at the expense of Fianna Fail, whose vote dropped by over 11%. Their 1985 poll topper in this area, Lorcan Allen, saw his vote decline by a 1,148 votes. Allen, a former Oireachtas member, was returned on the fourth count with party colleague Rory Murphy joining him two counts later. Rory Murphy, who filled the last seat in Enniscorthy, replaced namesake Joe Murphy, an outgoing Councillor, by a mere 29 votes.

Fianna Fail took 4 out of a possible 5 seats in the New Ross Electoral Area in 1985, and their chances of repeating this performance were always going to be remote. Senator Hugh Byrne polled remarkably well, receiving 2,200 first preference votes, but with the Fianna Fail vote down over 6% in Ross, the fourth seat was never likely, and outgoing Councillor Seamus Whelan

> ## The big winners were Fine Gael who ran only 10 candidates with 8 of them being successfully returned

was the losing FF candidate. Byrne's performance made him the largest Fianna Fail vote getter in Wexford and re-establishes the former TD in terms of a Dail return. His other two party colleagues, Jimmy Curtis and Jim Walsh, both outgoing Councillors, were re-elected to the Council.

The Fine Gael candidate to gain at the expense of Fianna Fail in Ross, was haulier Larry O'Brien, who was a well known local figure having come to prominence following his heroic deeds at the 1987 Zebrugge Ferry disaster. O'Brien polled 1,134 votes and was elected on the last count along with his running mate, outgoing Fine Gael Councillor, John T. Browne. The Labour Party, which had targetted Ross as an area where they would make gains, increased their vote by over 7%. However, with weak transfers and possibly one candidate too many, they suffered and neither of their 2 candidates were in the running.

The Wexford Electoral Area was possibly the most interesting of all the four areas in this constituency, with big mistakes being made by both Fianna Fail and the Labour Party. The decision of sitting TD, Seamus Cullimore not to contest the local elections was a costly one for his party, as Fianna Fail lost a seat leaving Gus Byrne as their sole Councillor in the Wexford area. Strategically Fianna Fail lost the seat themselves, through a combination of not having Cullimore on the ticket and also spreading their vote over four candidates. Fianna Fail had 1.7 quotas and took a single seat while the Independents won 3 seats with 1.9 quotas. Even without Cullimore, a candidate less may have resulted in less slippage in internal transfers, and possibly an extra seat.

Fianna Fail were not the only ones shooting themselves in the foot in the Wexford Area. The Labour Party threw away a second seat in the area by not selecting Helen Corish as a candidate alongside outgoing Councillor Brendan Howlin TD. Believing she was the candidate to take a second 'left' seat, Corish ran as an Independent and received 1,301 first preference votes, almost 1,000 votes more than the candidate Labour selected instead of her. Labour made the second mistake of choosing two urban based candidates with Vincent Browne being completely overshadowed by Howlin. A rural based candidate might have somewhat counteracted the Corish threat. Labour's failure in Wexford, as in the three other areas in the constituency, may be regretted at the next general election, where Corish as an Independent, or even a Green Party candidate, may cause Deputy Howlin trouble.

Fine Gael's Avril Doyle was re-elected for the Wexford area, and having lost her Dail seat in 1989 the result can be counted as a comeback but Doyle's vote was well down on her poll topping 1985 performance. Doyle's running mate Pat Codd put up a good performance, but was beaten for the final seat in Wexford by outgoing Independent Councillor Leo Carty.

# ENNISCORTHY ELECTORAL AREA

TOTAL ELECTORATE 17,954. VALID POLL 10,044. NO. OF MEMBERS 5. QUOTA 1,675

| Names of Candidates | First Count Votes | Second Count Transfer of Browne's surplus | Result | Third Count Transfer of Yates' surplus | Result | Fourth Count Transfer of Murphy's votes | Result | Fifth Count Transfer of Sinnott's surplus | Result | Sixth Count Transfer of O'Connor's votes | Result | Seventh Count Transfer of Walsh's votes | Result |
|---|---|---|---|---|---|---|---|---|---|---|---|---|---|
| BOLGER, John (F.G.) | 1,000 | +20 | 1,020 | +24 | 1,044 | +58 | 1,102 | +2 | 1,104 | +62 | 1,166 | +650 | 1,816 |
| BROWNE, John A. (F.F.) | 2,167 | -492 | 1,675 | — | 1,675 | — | 1,675 | — | 1,675 | — | 1,675 | — | 1,675 |
| DOYLE, Sean | 1,075 | +126 | 1,201 | +12 | 1,213 | +85 | 1,298 | +4 | 1,302 | +215 | 1,517 | +42 | 1,559 |
| HIPWELL, Henry G. (F.F.) | 845 | +151 | 996 | +2 | 998 | +37 | 1,035 | +16 | 1,051 | +29 | 1,080 | +60 | 1,140 |
| MURPHY, Pat | 432 | +27 | 459 | +3 | 462 | -462 | — | — | — | — | — | — | — |
| O'CONNOR, Francis (Lab.) | 454 | +31 | 485 | +5 | 490 | +47 | 537 | — | 537 | -537 | — | — | — |
| SINNOTT, Michael Joseph (F.F.) | 1,470 | +132 | 1,602 | +4 | 1,606 | +98 | 1,704 | -29 | 1,675 | — | 1,675 | — | 1,675 |
| WALSH, John (F.G.) | 861 | +5 | 866 | +15 | 881 | +53 | 934 | +7 | 941 | +69 | 1,010 | -1,010 | — |
| YATES, Ivan (F.G.) | 1,740 | — | 1,740 | -65 | 1,675 | — | 1,675 | — | 1,675 | — | 1,675 | — | 1,675 |
| Non-transferable paper not effective | — | — | — | — | — | +84 | 84 | — | 84 | +162 | 246 | +258 | 504 |
| TOTAL: | 10,044 | — | 10,044 | — | 10,044 | — | 10,044 | — | 10,044 | — | 10,044 | — | 10,044 |

Elected: Browne, John A. (F.F.); Yates, Ivan (F.G.); Sinnott, Michael Joseph (F.F.); Bolger, John (F.G.); Doyle, Sean

# GOREY ELECTORAL AREA

TOTAL ELECTORATE 16,825. VALID POLL 10,107. NO. OF MEMBERS 5. QUOTA 1,685

| Names of Candidates | First Count Votes | Second Count Transfer of D'Arcy's surplus | Result | Third Count Transfer of Ireton's votes | Result | Fourth Count Transfer of Murray's votes | Result | Fifth Count Transfer of Bolger's surplus | Result | Sixth Count Transfer of Allen's surplus | Result |
|---|---|---|---|---|---|---|---|---|---|---|---|
| ALLEN, Lorcan (F.F.) | 1,406 | +97 | 1,503 | +117 | 1,620 | +113 | 1,733 | — | 1,733 | -48 | 1,685 |
| BOLGER, Deirdre (F.G.) | 1,029 | +354 | 1,383 | +121 | 1,504 | +243 | 1,747 | -62 | 1,685 | — | 1,685 |
| D'ARCY, Michael J. (F.G.) | 2,469 | -784 | 1,685 | — | 1,685 | — | 1,685 | — | 1,685 | — | 1,685 |
| GAHAN, James (F.G.) | 1,092 | +184 | 1,276 | +40 | 1,316 | +302 | 1,618 | +50 | 1,668 | +20 | 1,688 |
| IRETON, Rober (Bob) (Lab.) | 714 | +64 | 778 | -778 | — | — | — | — | — | — | — |
| MURPHY, Joe (F.F.) | 1,230 | +30 | 1,260 | +50 | 1,310 | +106 | 1,416 | +8 | 1,424 | +18 | 1,442 |
| MURPHY, Rory (F.F.) | 1,297 | +22 | 1,319 | +26 | 1,345 | +112 | 1,457 | +4 | 1,461 | +10 | 1,471 |
| MURRAY, Paddy (Lab.) | 870 | +33 | 903 | +376 | 1,279 | -1,279 | — | — | — | — | — |
| Non-transferable papers not effective | — | — | — | +48 | 48 | +403 | 451 | — | 451 | — | 451 |
| TOTAL: | 10,107 | — | 10,107 | — | 10,107 | — | 10,107 | — | 10,107 | — | 10,107 |

Elected: D'Arcy, Michael J. (F.G.); Bolger, Deirdre (F.G.); Allen, Lorcan (F.F.); Gahan, James (F.G.); Murphy, Rory (F.F.)

# WEXFORD ELECTORAL AREA

### TOTAL ELECTORATE 22,875. VALID POLL 12,177. NO. OF MEMBERS 6. QUOTA 1,740

| Names of Candidates | First Count Votes | Second Count Transfer of Roche's votes | Result | Third Count Transfer of V. Byrne's votes | Result | Fourth Count Transfer of Howlin's surplus | Result | Fifth Count Transfer of Murphy's votes | Result | Sixth Count Transfer of Molloy's votes | Result | Seventh Count Transfer of Nolan's votes | Result | Eighth Count Transfer of J. Doyle's votes | Result | Ninth Count Transfer of G. Byrne's surplus | Result | Tenth Count Transfer of Enright's votes | Result |
|---|---|---|---|---|---|---|---|---|---|---|---|---|---|---|---|---|---|---|---|
| BYRNE, Gus (F.F.) | 992 | +20 | 1,012 | +16 | 1,028 | +3 | 1,031 | +66 | 1,097 | +149 | 1,246 | +288 | 1,534 | +607 | 2,141 | -401 | 1,740 | — | 1,740 |
| BYRNE, Vincent (Lab.) | 323 | +8 | 331 | -331 | — | — | — | — | — | — | — | — | — | — | — | — | — | — | — |
| CARTHY, Leo (Non-Party) | 1,032 | +13 | 1,045 | +15 | 1,060 | +8 | 1,068 | +65 | 1,133 | +20 | 1,153 | +7 | 1,160 | +180 | 1,340 | +115 | 1,455 | +72 | 1,527 |
| CODD, Pat (F.G.) | 1,013 | +6 | 1,019 | +9 | 1,028 | +3 | 1,031 | +39 | 1,070 | +112 | 1,182 | +4 | 1,186 | +37 | 1,223 | +13 | 1,236 | +14 | 1,250 |
| CORISH, Helen | 1,301 | +43 | 1,344 | +19 | 1,363 | +12 | 1,375 | +69 | 1,444 | +27 | 1,471 | +62 | 1,533 | +50 | 1,583 | +37 | 1,620 | +298 | 1,918 |
| DOYLE, Avril (F.G.) | 1,431 | +36 | 1,467 | +16 | 1,483 | +5 | 1,488 | +67 | 1,555 | +21 | 1,576 | +43 | 1,619 | +53 | 1,672 | +17 | 1,689 | +127 | 1,816 |
| DOYLE, Jo (Josephine) (F.F.) | 811 | +2 | 813 | +5 | 818 | — | 818 | +28 | 846 | +133 | 979 | +68 | 1,047 | -1,047 | — | — | — | — | — |
| ENRIGHT, Michael (W.P.) | 893 | +14 | 907 | +25 | 932 | +19 | 951 | +8 | 959 | +10 | 969 | +79 | 1,048 | +8 | 1,056 | +4 | 1,060 | -1,060 | — |
| HOWLIN, Brendan (Lab.) | 1,597 | +27 | 1,624 | +179 | 1,803 | -63 | 1,740 | — | 1,740 | — | 1,740 | — | 1,740 | — | 1,740 | — | 1,740 | — | 1,740 |
| MOLLOY, Brigid (F.F.) | 537 | +3 | 540 | +2 | 542 | — | 542 | +25 | 567 | -567 | — | — | — | — | — | — | — | — | — |
| MURPHY, Pat | 472 | +4 | 476 | +5 | 481 | — | 481 | -481 | — | — | — | — | — | — | — | — | — | — | — |
| NOLAN, Patrick (F.F.) | 610 | +5 | 615 | +4 | 619 | +2 | 621 | +11 | 632 | +54 | 686 | -686 | — | — | — | — | — | — | — |
| RECK, Padge (Non-Party) | 931 | +44 | 975 | +29 | 1,004 | +11 | 1,015 | +76 | 1,091 | +12 | 1,103 | +84 | 1,187 | +25 | 1,212 | +10 | 1,222 | +303 | 1,525 |
| ROCHE, John (P.D.) | 234 | -234 | — | — | — | — | — | — | — | — | — | — | — | — | — | — | — | — | — |
| Non-transferable papers not effective | — | +9 | 9 | +7 | 16 | — | 16 | +27 | 43 | +29 | 72 | +51 | 123 | +87 | 210 | +205 | 415 | +246 | 661 |
| TOTAL: | 12,177 | — | 12,177 | — | 12,177 | — | 12,177 | — | 12,177 | — | 12,177 | — | 12,177 | — | 12,177 | — | 12,177 | — | 12,177 |

Elected: Howlin, Brendan (Lab.); Byrne, Gus (F.F.); Corish, Helen; Doyle Avril (F.G.); Carthy, Leo (Non-Party); Reck, Padge (Non-Party)

# NEW ROSS ELECTORAL AREA

### TOTAL ELECTORATE 16,815. VALID POLL 10,108. NO. OF MEMBERS 5. QUOTA 1,685

| Names of Candidates | First Count Votes | Second Count Transfer of Byrne's surplus | Result | Third Count Transfer of P. Doyle's votes | Result | Fourth Count Transfer of Walsh's surplus | Result | Fifth Count Transfer of Whelan's votes | Result | Sixth Count Transfer of Curtis' surplus | Result | Seventh Count Transfer of Minihan's votes | Result |
|---|---|---|---|---|---|---|---|---|---|---|---|---|---|
| BROWNE, John T. (F.G.) | 1,037 | +22 | 1,059 | +31 | 1,090 | +6 | 1,096 | +71 | 1,167 | +50 | 1,217 | +300 | 1,517 |
| BYRNE, Hugh (F.F.) | 2,200 | -515 | 1,685 | — | 1,685 | — | 1,685 | — | 1,685 | — | 1,685 | — | 1,685 |
| CURTIS, Jimmie (F.F.) | 1,192 | +160 | 1,352 | +9 | 1,361 | +1 | 1,362 | +565 | 1,927 | -242 | 1,685 | — | 1,685 |
| DOYLE, John Jude (Lab.) | 827 | +20 | 847 | +212 | 1,059 | +10 | 1,069 | +31 | 1,100 | +13 | 1,113 | +163 | 1,276 |
| DOYLE, Patrick (Lab.) | 546 | +12 | 558 | -558 | — | — | — | — | — | — | — | — | — |
| MINIHAN, Eoin (P.D.) | 849 | +34 | 883 | +105 | 988 | +26 | 1,014 | +57 | 1,071 | +31 | (1,102) | -1,102 | — |
| O'BRIEN, Laurence (F.G.) | 1,134 | +50 | 1,184 | +44 | 1,228 | +6 | 1,234 | +128 | 1,362 | +53 | 1,415 | +333 | 1,748 |
| WALSH, Jim (F.F.) | 1,525 | +77 | 1,602 | +134 | 1,736 | -51 | 1,685 | — | 1,685 | — | 1,685 | — | 1,685 |
| WHELAN, Seamus (F.F.) | 798 | +140 | 938 | +7 | 945 | +2 | 947 | -947 | — | — | — | — | — |
| Non-transferable papers not effective | — | — | — | +16 | 16 | — | 16 | +95 | 111 | +95 | 206 | +306 | 512 |
| TOTAL: | 10,108 | — | 10,108 | — | 10,108 | — | 10,108 | — | 10,108 | — | 10,108 | — | 10,108 |

Elected: Byrne, Hugh (F.F.); Walsh, Jim (F.F.); Curtis, Jimmie (F.F.); O'Brien, Laurence (F.G.); Browne, John T. (F.G.)

# WICKLOW COUNTY COUNCIL

## WICKLOW COUNTY COUNCIL RESULTS

| Party | 1991 % of votes | 1991 Seats obtained | 1985 % of votes | 1985 Seat obtained |
|---|---|---|---|---|
| Fianna Fail | 32.2 | 9 | 40.6 | 13 |
| Fine Gael | 14.6 | 4 | 26.7 | 5 |
| Labour | 19.2 | 5 | 18.2 | 4 |
| Progressive Dem. | 3.4 | — | — | — |
| Workers Party | 5.3 | 1 | 6.3 | 1 |
| Other | 25.3 | 5 | 8.2 | 1 |
| **TOTAL SEATS** | | **24** | | **24** |

**County Buildings, Wicklow**
**Telephone: (0404) 67324**
**Fax: (0404) 67792**
**Total population: 94,542**
**Rateable valuation: £704,298.55**
**Rate: £29.50**
**County Council meetings: First and second Mondays in each month.**

*County Manager:* Blaise Treacy
*Assistant County Manager:* Edward Breen
*County Secretary:* R.T. Ó Niadh
*Finance Officer:* Anselm Fidgeon
*County Engineer:* J. Maloney
*County Development Officer:* Tom Broderick
*Law Agent:* Maurice Cassidy
*Administrative Officers:* Ultan McCabe,Louis Brennan
*Senior Staff Officers:* K. Roberts, F. O'Toole
*County Librarian:* J.Hayes, County Library,
Greystones. Telephone: (01) 2874387
*Civil Defence Officer:* B. Downes
*Road Safety Officer:* K. Roberts (Acting)
*Senior Executive Engineers:*
*Roads:* J. Molony, T. Gorman, J. Solon
*Environment/Sanitary Services:* M. O'Keeffe
*Housing:* S. O'Neill (Acting)
*Chief Fire Officer:* J. F. Moran
*Senior Executive Planner:* F. Ó Gallachor

## WICKLOW

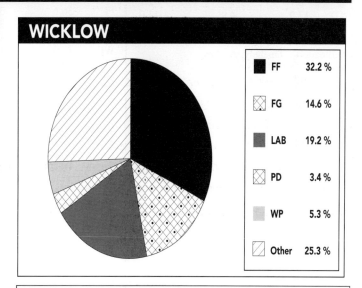

| | |
|---|---|
| ■ FF | 32.2 % |
| ▨ FG | 14.6 % |
| ▨ LAB | 19.2 % |
| ▨ PD | 3.4 % |
| ▨ WP | 5.3 % |
| ▨ Other | 25.3 % |

**Blaise Treacy**

Blaise Treacy was born in 1935 and is married with four sons and one daughter. He is the holder of a Diploma in Local Government Administration from the I.P.A..

He has been Town Clerk in Dundalk, Carlow and Carrickmacross. He served in Kerry County Council as County Secretary over the period 1976 to 1978. He joined Clare County Council in 1978 where he was Assistant County Manager. He later became County Manager in Clare before his appointment as Wicklow County Manager in 1984.

He is involved in several local initatives being on the boards of both Horizon Radio and Cospoir.

Blaise Treacy has an interest in both horse racing and golf.

## ARKLOW

| | 1991 | 1985 | '85 to '91 Swing |
|---|---|---|---|
| FF | 40.0 | 48.7 | -8.7 |
| FG | 18.8 | 26.4 | -7.6 |
| LAB | 18.2 | 20.0 | -1.8 |
| WP | 2.5 | — | 2.5 |
| PD | 2.7 | — | 2.7 |
| IND | 17.9 | 4.9 | 13.0 |

BLAKE, Vincent,
Mullinacuffe, Tinahely, Arklow,
County Wicklow. (FG)
Retired. 0402-38254

HONAN, Thomas,
Ferrybank, Arklow,
County Wicklow. (FG)
Solicitor. 0402-32649

KEENAN, Tom,
1 Lourdes Crescent, Aughrim,
County Wicklow. (FF)
Builder. 0402-36131

McELHERON, Vincent,
2 South Quay, Arklow,
County Wicklow. (NP)
Journalist. 0402-32173

O'CONNELL, James W.
Vale Road, Arklow,
County Wicklow. (FF)
Doctor. 0402-32264

RYAN, Kevin,
Hilltop Nurseries, Carnew,
County Wicklow. (Lab)
Nurseryman. 055-26387

## BALTINGLASS

| | 1991 | 1985 | '85 to '91 Swing |
|---|---|---|---|
| FF | 46.5 | 37.9 | 8.6 |
| FG | 26.9 | 39.9 | -13.0 |
| LAB | 17.5 | 14.5 | 3.0 |
| SF | 4.9 | 5.8 | -0.9 |
| IND | 4.2 | 1.9 | 2.3 |

CULLEN, Thomas,
Deerpark, Baltinglass,
County Wickow. (Lab)
Fisheries Consultant. 0508-81513

RUTTLE, James,
Lisheen, Manor Kilbride, Blessington,
County Wicklow. (NP)
Agriculture Inspector. 01-582234

TIMMINS, Godfrey,
Weavers Square, Baltinglass,
County Wicklow. (FG)
Dail Deputy. 0508-81016

## BRAY

| | 1991 | 1985 | '85 to '91 Swing |
|---|---|---|---|
| FF | 36.6 | 39.1 | -2.5 |
| FG | 11.3 | 22.6 | -11.3 |
| LAB | 13.8 | 19.5 | -5.7 |
| WP | 19.0 | 18.8 | 0.2 |
| PD | 4.3 | — | 4.3 |
| GP | 3.6 | — | 3.6 |
| SF | 4.5 | — | 4.5 |
| Ind | 7.0 | — | 7.0 |

BEHAN, Joe,
59 Richmond Park, Bray,
County Wicklow. (FF)
Teacher. 01-2867388

BYRNE, John,
1 Roselawn Park, Bray,
County Wicklow. (Lab)
Fire Control Operator. 01-2829861

LAWLOR, Michael D.
26 Rectory Slopes, Herbert Road, Bray,
County Wicklow. (FF)
Computer Analyst. 01-2829861

McMANUS, Liz,
1 Martello Terrace, Bray,
County Wicklow. (Elected WP now DL)
Journalist. 01-2868407

ROSS, Shane,
Askefield, Dublin Road, Bray,
County Wicklow. (FG)
Senator. 01-2821896

VANCE, Pat,
Beachmount, Putland Road, Bray,
County Wicklow. (FF)
Shoe-Repairer. 01-2868169

## GREYSTONES

| | 1991 | 1985 | '85 to '91 Swing |
|---|---|---|---|
| FF | 31.6 | 40.5 | -8.9 |
| FG | 6.2 | 32.2 | -26.0 |
| LAB | 9.3 | 10.5 | -1.2 |
| WP | 4.1 | — | 4.1 |
| PD | 2.7 | — | 2.7 |
| GP | 9.5 | — | 9.5 |
| SF | 0.0 | 8.1 | -8.1 |
| IND | 36.5 | 8.7 | 27.8 |

AHERN, Nuala,
80 Heathervue, Greystones,
County Wicklow. (GP)
Psychologist.

FOX, John,
Calary Lower, Kilmacanogue, Bray,
County Wicklow. (FF)
Farmer. 01-2876386

JONES, George,
103 Applewood Heights, Greystones,
County Wicklow. (NP)
Insurance Manager. 01-2875678

ROCHE, Dick,
2 Herbert Terrace, Herbert Road, Bray,
County Wicklow. (FF)
Dail Deputy. 01-2861206

## WICKLOW

| | 1991 | 1985 | '85 to '91 Swing |
|---|---|---|---|
| FF | 32.0 | 34.9 | -2.9 |
| FG | 11.6 | 17.9 | -6.3 |
| LAB | 34.7 | 24.6 | 10.1 |
| PD | 6.2 | — | 6.2 |
| SF | 0.0 | 2.8 | -2.8 |
| IND | 15.4 | 19.8 | -4.4 |

VANCE, Pat,
Killadreenan,
Newtownmountkennedy,
County Wicklow. (FF)

HYNES, Frank,
Milltown North, Ashford,
County Wicklow. (Lab)
Retired. 0404-40339

JACOB, Joseph,
Main Street, Rathdrum,
County Wicklow. (FF)
Dail Deputy. 0404-46282

KAVANAGH, Liam,
Mount Carmel,
Wicklow. (Lab)
Dail Deputy. 0404-67582

PHILIPS, Susan,
Ballinacoola, Glenealy,
County Wicklow. (NP)
Public Representative. 0404-40339

**Godfrey Timmins (FG)**
**Baltinglass**

**Joe Jacob (FF)**
**Wicklow**

**Nuala Ahern (Greens)**
**Greystones**

**Liz McManus (DL)**
**Bray**

# Main parties suffer in Wicklow

Following the revision of Dail constituencies in 1991, Wicklow will be one of the few areas in the Country which will have an extra Dail seat in the next General Election. The new 5 seat constituency will encompass all of the Wicklow's four Council areas and a section of East Kildare.

Fine Gael had hoped that the local's would provide them with an opportunity to "blood" their new Dail candidate for Wicklow, former independent Senator Shane Ross, who had joined the Party a few months previously. His imposition onto the Party's Local Election Ticket in Bray provoked a storm from the Fine Gael organisation in North Wicklow. Three of their sitting Councillors Jane Murphy, George Jones and John Leeson resigned from the Party in protest and ran as Independents in the June Poll with disasterous consequences for the Party in Bray and Greystones.

In the Greystones area Fine Gael had held two of the four seats but when Jones and Leeson resigned, the Party scrambled to find a replacement candidate. Breda Allen was selected, she polled just 436 preferences and the Party lost both of it's seats. The two new Independents had mixed performances, George Jones comfortably held on to his seat as an Independent but the other John Leeson lost out.

The Fine Gael battle in Bray provided one of the most interesting counts in the country. It took 15 hours to complete. Former Fine Gael Councillor, Jane Murphy, had polled 574 first preferences Senator Ross was ahead of her by just 68 votes and in a battle where transfers were crucial, Ross was declared elected on the 13th and final count without reaching the quota.

Fine Gael's problems were compounded by the victory of Vincent McElheron in Arklow. He had failed to get a Fine Gael nomination at Convention, but went on to contest an Independent, getting an impressive 1,205 first preferences, just 79 votes short of the quota.

Overall Fine Gael vote dropped over 12% in the County, they ended up loosing one seat to return with only four

**Erin Lawlor congratulates her dad Michael who was successful in Bray.**

members on the new Council, having no Councillor in Wicklow or Greystones. New comer Thomas Honan and outgoing Vincent Blake, held the Party's 2 seats in Arklow, despite battling against McElheron, while local Fine Gael Deputy Godfrey Timmons came in second in Baltinglass, to become the longest serving member on the new Council.

Fianna Fail too had its problems in Wicklow. Baltinglass, in particular proved a disaster for them. Here former Senator and outgoing Fianna Fail Councillor Jim Ruttle had failed to get a nomination, and ran as an Independent and topped the poll with a massive 1,905 first preferences, a total of 711 votes above Deputy Timmons. Fianna Fail's troubles worsened when the Party's other outgoing Councillor Hugh O'Keeffe polled just 684 votes and lost his seat. Baltinglass then became one of only four electoral areas in the county where Fianna Fail had no seat.

Fianna Fail went into the election with four out of the six seats in the Arklow Electoral area. Popular Arklow Doctor, Bill O'Connell, again topped the poll, his voting holding up well with 1,267 first preferences. Party colleague Tom Keenan also held his seat but with the Party vote in the area down by almost 9% both Pat Power and Pat Sweeney lost out.

In West Wicklow Fianna Fail Deputy Joe Jacob, got 1,422 first preferences and was comfortably elected but

Newmountkennedy man, Pat Doyle, replaced James Giff as the Party's second local representative in the area.

In Greystones, Fianna Fail also held their own, with both outgoing Councillors returned.

There was consolation for Fianna Fail in their very strong showing in Bray. They had won three seats here in 1985, but since then, Councillor Ciaran Murphy had joined the P.D.'s. Murphy's vote collapsed almost completely in the election however. He got only 250 first preferences - and lost the seat at an early stage. Fianna Fail however had their three candidates closely bunched together and sitting Councillor Michael Lawlor and his two Bray colleagues, Pat Lance and Joe Behan, took the seats.

For the Labour Party, Wicklow had another success, with a strong personal triumph for local Labour T.D. Liam Kavanagh. He topped the poll in West Wicklow with 1,927 first preferences, almost 500 votes to spare above the quota, and ahead of Fianna Fail T.D., Joe Jacob. Frank Hynes took the final seat, so the Party returned two out of five in this area. John Byrne was returned in Bray, while Kevin Ryan regained the seat he had lost to Labour Party colleague, Sean Wallace, in 1985. The Party increased its representation on the new Council from four to five, with a historic victory by Tommy Cullen in Baltinglass, to take the Party's first seat in the area for 42 years.

The Greens too, had a spectaculator victory when, despite only getting 663 first preferences, Nuala Ahern took the Party's first seat ever on Wicklow County Council in the Greystones area. Her husband had run for the Greens in Bray, but never featured in the final shake-up.

The Workers Party's Liz McManus topped the poll in Bray with a 1,047 first preferences. She has since transferred to the Democratic Left and although she is the parties' only Councillor in the county, her high profile, the overall strength of the Left/ Green vote in Wicklow, coupled with the internal problems thrown up for Fine Gael and Fianna Fail in these elections, means that she will certainly be in with a good chance of picking up that extra seat in Wicklow/East Kildare whenever the next election comes.

# BALTINGLASS ELECTORAL AREA

TOTAL ELECTORATE 8,692. VALID POLL 6,143. NO. OF MEMBERS 3. QUOTA 1,536

| Names of Candidates | First Count Votes | Second Count Transfer of Ruttle's surplus | Result | Third Count Transfer of Scanlon's and Williams' votes | Result | Fourth Count Transfer of McGrath's votes | Result | Fifth Count Transfer of O'Neill's votes | Result | Sixth Count Transfer of Deering's votes | Result | Seventh Count Transfer of Timmins' surplus | Result |
|---|---|---|---|---|---|---|---|---|---|---|---|---|---|
| CULLEN, Tommy (Lab.) | 1,077 | +36 | 1,113 | +56 | 1,169 | +13 | 1,182 | +59 | 1,241 | +92 | 1,333 | +98 | 1,431 |
| DEERING, Paschal (F.G.) | 460 | +54 | 514 | +94 | 608 | +45 | 653 | +35 | 688 | -688 | — | — | — |
| McGRATH, Anne (F.F.) | 266 | +41 | 307 | +16 | 323 | -323 | — | — | — | — | — | — | — |
| O'KEFFFE, Hugh (F.F.) | 687 | +31 | 718 | +12 | 730 | +192 | 922 | +55 | 977 | +64 | 1,041 | +99 | 1,140 |
| O'NEILL, Gerry (S.F.) | 302 | +40 | 342 | +23 | 365 | +12 | 377 | -377 | — | — | — | — | — |
| RUTTLE, James | 1,905 | -369 | 1,536 | — | 1,536 | — | 1,536 | — | 1,536 | — | 1,536 | — | 1,536 |
| SCANLON, Michael (Non-Party) | 27 | +12 | 39 | -39 | — | — | — | — | — | — | — | — | — |
| TIMMINS, Godfrey (F.G.) | 1,190 | +120 | 1,310 | +36 | 1,346 | +34 | 1,380 | +73 | 1,453 | +401 | 1,854 | -318 | 1,536 |
| WILLIAMS, Adrian Vincent | 229 | +35 | 264 | -264 | — | — | — | — | — | — | — | — | — |
| Non-transferable papers not effective | — | — | — | +66 | 66 | +27 | 93 | +155 | 248 | +131 | 379 | +121 | 500 |
| TOTAL: | 6,143 | — | 6,143 | — | 6,143 | — | 6,143 | — | 6,143 | — | 6,143 | — | 6,143 |

Eelected: Ruttle, James; Timmins, Godfrey (F.G.); Cullen, Tommy (Lab.)

# ARKLOW ELECTORAL AREA

TOTAL ELECTORATE 13,867. VALID POLL 8,998. NO. OF MEMBERS 6. QUOTA 1,286

| Names of Candidates | First Count Votes | Second Count Transfer of Kinsella's votes | Result | Third Count Transfer of O'Connell's surplus | Result | Fourth Count Transfer of Byrne's votes | Result | Fifth Count Transfer of Keogh's votes | Result | Sixth Count Transfer of Horsman's votes | Result | Seventh Count Transfer of Sweeney's votes | Result | Eighth Count Transfer of Wolohan's votes | Result | Ninth Count Transfer of Ryan's surplus | Result |
|---|---|---|---|---|---|---|---|---|---|---|---|---|---|---|---|---|---|
| BLAKE, Vincent (F.G.) | 1,020 | +2 | 1,022 | — | 1,022 | +34 | 1,056 | +20 | 1,076 | +25 | 1,101 | +6 | 1,107 | +20 | 1,127 | +13 | 1,140 |
| BYRNE, Catherine (Non-Party) | 212 | +6 | 218 | +1 | 219 | -219 | — | — | — | — | — | — | — | — | — | — | — |
| DORAN, Pat (F.F.) | 977 | +1 | 978 | — | 978 | +27 | 1,005 | +6 | 1,011 | +5 | 1,016 | +58 | 1,074 | +13 | 1,087 | +3 | 1,090 |
| HONAN, Thomas (F.G.) | 671 | +11 | 682 | +6 | 688 | +17 | 705 | +35 | 740 | +107 | 847 | +72 | 919 | +224 | 1,143 | +33 | 1,176 |
| HORSMAN, Michael (P.D.) | 241 | +7 | 248 | — | 248 | +17 | 265 | +10 | 275 | -275 | — | — | — | — | — | — | — |
| KEENAN, Tom (F.F.) | 914 | +7 | 921 | +2 | 923 | +22 | 945 | +27 | 972 | +14 | 986 | +146 | 1,132 | +63 | 1,195 | +17 | 1,212 |
| KEOGH, Michael (W.P.) | 225 | +2 | 227 | — | 227 | +4 | 231 | -231 | — | — | — | — | — | — | — | — | — |
| KINSELLA, Denis | 190 | -190 | — | — | — | — | — | — | — | — | — | — | — | — | — | — | — |
| McELHERON, Vincent (Non-Party) | 1,205 | +57 | 1,262 | +6 | 1,268 | +22 | 1,290 | — | 1,290 | — | 1,290 | — | 1,290 | — | 1,290 | — | 1,290 |
| O'CONNELL, Dr. Bill (F.F.) | 1,267 | +44 | 1,311 | -25 | 1,286 | — | 1,286 | — | 1,286 | — | 1,286 | — | 1,286 | — | 1,286 | — | 1,286 |
| RYAN, Kevin (Lab.) | 1,079 | +5 | 1,084 | — | 1,084 | +12 | 1,096 | +42 | 1,138 | +14 | 1,152 | +6 | 1,158 | +194 | 1,352 | -66 | 1,286 |
| SWEENEY, Patrick (F.F.) | 440 | +9 | 449 | +8 | 457 | +20 | 477 | +11 | 488 | +25 | 513 | -513 | — | — | — | — | — |
| WOLOHAN, Sean (Lab.) | 557 | +30 | 587 | +2 | 589 | +17 | 606 | +59 | 665 | +47 | 712 | +135 | 847 | -847 | — | — | — |
| Non-transferable papers not effective | — | +9 | 9 | — | 9 | +27 | 36 | +21 | 57 | +38 | 95 | +90 | 185 | +333 | 518 | — | 518 |
| TOTAL: | 8,998 | — | 8,998 | — | 8,998 | — | 8,998 | — | 8,998 | — | 8,998 | — | 8,998 | — | 8,998 | — | 8,998 |

Elected: O'Connell, Bill Dr. (F.F.); McElheron, Vincent (Non-Party); Ryan, Kevin, (Lab.); Keenan, Tom (F.F.); Honan, Thomas (F.G.); Blake, Vincent (F.G.)

# BRAY ELECTORAL AREA

TOTAL ELECTORATE 18,099. VALID POLL 8,225. NO. OF MEMBERS 6. QUOTA 1,176

| Names of Candidates | First Count Votes | Second Count Transfer of Noble's votes Result) | Third Count Transfer of McKenna's votes Result | Fourth Count Transfer of Egan's votes Result | Fifth Count Transfer of McManus's surplus Result | Sixth Count Transfer of C. Murphy's votes Result | Seventh Count Transfer of Tobin's votes Result | Eighth Count Transfer of Byrne's surplus Result | Ninth Count Transfer of Kennedy's votes Result | Tenth Count Transfer of Ahern's votes Result | Eleventh Count Transfer of Ledwidge's votes Result | Twelfth Count Transfer of McDonnell's votes Result | Thirteenth Count Transfer of Keyes' votes Result |
|---|---|---|---|---|---|---|---|---|---|---|---|---|---|
| AHERN, Barry (G.P.) | 297 | +3 300 | +10 310 | +5 315 | +1 316 | +13 329 | +29 358 | +14 372 | +24 396 | -396 — | — — | — — | — — |
| BEHAN, Joe (F.F.) | 687 | +4 691 | +4 695 | +5 700 | — 700 | +22 722 | +17 739 | +2 741 | +11 752 | +33 785 | +59 844 | +27 871 | +110 981 |
| BYRNE, John (Lab.) | 978 | +1 979 | +74 1,053 | +17 1,070 | — 1,070 | +24 1,094 | +115 1,209 | -33 1,176 | — 1,176 | — 1,176 | — 1,176 | — 1,176 | — 1,176 |
| EGAN, Anne (W.P.) | 256 | — 256 | +8 264 | -264 — | — — | — — | — — | — — | — — | — — | — — | — — | — — |
| KENNEDY, Michael (F.G.) | 286 | +4 290 | +3 293 | +6 299 | — 299 | +31 330 | +7 337 | +1 338 | -338 — | — — | — — | — — | — — |
| KEYES, Noel Patrick (F.F.) | 602 | +4 606 | +2 608 | +21 629 | +2 631 | +10 641 | +12 653 | +4 657 | +16 673 | +17 690 | +60 750 | +41 791 | -791 — |
| LAWLOR, Michael D. (F.F.) | 767 | +2 769 | +1 770 | +10 780 | +1 781 | +22 803 | +10 813 | +3 816 | +8 824 | +15 839 | +94 933 | +39 972 | +195 1,167 |
| LEDWIDGE, Michael (F.F.) | 379 | +1 380 | +1 381 | +5 386 | — 386 | +18 404 | +3 407 | +1 408 | +12 420 | +16 436 | -436 — | — — | — — |
| McDONNELL, Gerry (S.F.) | 371 | +2 373 | +3 376 | +17 393 | +1 394 | +4 398 | +12 410 | +2 412 | +3 415 | +27 442 | +4 446 | -446 — | — — |
| McKENNA, Carmel (Lab.) | 153 | +3 156 | -156 — | — — | — — | — — | — — | — — | — — | — — | — — | — — | — — |
| McMANUS, Liz (W.P.) | 1,047 | +16 1,063 | +20 1,083 | +111 1,194 | -18 1,176 | — 1,176 | — 1,176 | — 1,176 | — 1,176 | — 1,176 | — 1,176 | — 1,176 | — 1,176 |
| MURPHY, Ciaran (P.D.) | 250 | +41 291 | +3 294 | +2 296 | +1 297 | -297 — | — — | — — | — — | — — | — — | — — | — — |
| MURPHY, Jane | 574 | +2 576 | +6 582 | +10 592 | +1 593 | +50 643 | +23 666 | +2 668 | +33 701 | +75 776 | +40 816 | +47 863 | +66 929 |
| NOBLE, Michael (P.D.) | 101 | -101 — | — — | — — | — — | — — | — — | — — | — — | — — | — — | — — | — — |
| ROSS, Shane (F.G.) | 642 | +8 650 | +10 660 | +5 665 | — 665 | +38 703 | +12 715 | +2 717 | +181 898 | +67 965 | +24 989 | +22 1,011 | +47 1,058 |
| TOBIN, Dermot (W.P.) | 259 | +5 264 | +2 266 | +36 302 | +11 313 | +15 328 | -328 — | — — | — — | — — | — — | — — | — — |
| VANCE, Pat (F.F.) | 576 | +4 580 | +5 585 | +8 593 | — 593 | +25 618 | +17 635 | +2 637 | +19 656 | +28 684 | +118 802 | +39 841 | +214 1,055 |
| Non-transferable papers not effective | — | +1 1 | +4 5 | +6 11 | — 11 | +25 36 | +71 107 | — 107 | +31 138 | +118 256 | +37 293 | +231 524 | +159 683 |
| TOTAL: | 8,225 | — 8,225 | — 8,225 | — 8,225 | — 8,225 | — 8,225 | — 8,225 | — 8,225 | — 8,225 | — 8,225 | — 8,225 | — 8,225 | — 8,225 |

Elected: McManus, Liz (W.P.); Byrne, John (Lab.); Lawlor, Michael D. (F.F.); Ross, Shane (F.G.); Vance, Pat (F.F.); Behan, Joe (F.F.)

# GREYSTONES ELECTORAL AREA

TOTAL ELECTORATE 13,645. VALID POLL 6,997. NO. OF MEMBERS 4. QUOTA 1,400

| Names of Candidates | First Count Votes | Second Count Transfer of Hogan's votes Result | Third Count Transfer of Lalor's votes Result | Fourth Count Transfer of Devlin's votes Result | Fifth Count Transfer of Sweeney's votes Result | Sixth Count Transfer of Allen's votes Result | Seventh Count Transfer of Keddy's votes Result | Eighth Count Transfer of Murnane's votes Result | Ninth Count Transfer of Jones' surplus Result |
|---|---|---|---|---|---|---|---|---|---|
| AHERN, Nuala (G.P.)(663) | 663 | +8 671 | +33 704 | +31 735 | +16 751 | +114 865 | +124 989 | +248 1,237 | +46 1,283 |
| ALLEN, Breda (F.G.) | 436 | +4 440 | +24 464 | +5 469 | +5 474 | -474 — | — — | — — | — — |
| DEVLIN, Christy (W.P.) | 181 | +32 213 | +1 214 | -214 — | — — | — — | — — | — — | — — |
| FOX, Johnny (F.F.) | 1,205 | +10 1,215 | +10 1,225 | +52 1,277 | +29 1,306 | +29 1,335 | +90 1,425 | — 1,425 | — 1,425 |
| HOGAN, James Francis (W.P.) | 109 | -109 — | — — | — — | — — | — — | — — | — — | — — |
| JONES, George | 955 | +13 968 | +43 1,011 | +6 1,017 | +33 1,050 | +111 1,161 | +87 1,248 | +279 1,527 | -127 1,400 |
| KEDDY, Charlie (Lab.) | 411 | +2 413 | +7 420 | +31 451 | +110 561 | +45 606 | -606 — | — — | — — |
| LALOR, Joseph (P.D.) | 188 | +2 190 | -190 — | — — | — — | — — | — — | — — | — — |
| LEESON, John | 921 | +4 925 | +21 946 | +45 991 | +4 995 | +43 1,038 | +15 1,053 | +39 1,092 | +39 1,131 |
| MURNANE, John (Jack) (Non-Party) | 679 | +17 696 | +17 713 | +11 724 | +46 770 | +48 818 | +75 893 | -893 — | — — |
| ROCHE, Dick (F.F.) | 1,008 | +6 1,014 | +19 1,033 | +9 1,042 | +13 1,055 | +44 1,099 | +70 1,169 | +157 1,326 | +42 1,368 |
| SWEENEY, Joe (Lab.) | 241 | +10 251 | +7 258 | +13 271 | -271 — | — — | — — | — — | — — |
| Non-transferable papers not effective | — | +1 1 | +8 9 | +11 20 | +15 35 | +40 75 | +145 220 | +170 390 | — 390 |
| TOTAL: | 6,997 | — 6,997 | — 6,997 | — 6,997 | — 6,997 | — 6,997 | — 6,997 | — 6,997 | — 6,997 |

Eelected: Fox, Johnny (F.F.); Jones, George; Roche, Dick (F.F.); Ahern, Nuala (G.P.)

# WICKLOW ELECTORAL AREA

TOTAL ELECTORATE 14,989. VALID POLL 8,571. NO. OF MEMBERS 5. QUOTA 1,429

| Names of Candidates | First Count Votes | Second Count Transfer of Kavanagh's surplus | Result | Third Count Transfer of Jacob's surplus | Result | Fourth Count Transfer of Lalor's votes | Result | Fifth Count Transfer of O'Shaughnessy's votes | Result | Sixth Count Transfer of Kearns' votes | Result | Seventh Count Transfer of Larkin's votes | Result | Eighth Count Transfer of Giff's votes | Result |
|---|---|---|---|---|---|---|---|---|---|---|---|---|---|---|---|
| DOYLE, Pat (F.F.) | 835 | +10 | 845 | +2 | 847 | +5 | 852 | +3 | 855 | +7 | 862 | +163 | 1,025 | +286 | 1,311 |
| GIFF, James (F.F.) | 489 | +49 | 538 | +7 | 545 | +41 | 586 | +13 | 599 | +116 | 715 | +57 | 772 | -772 | — |
| HYNES, Frank (Lab.) | 726 | +153 | 879 | +6 | 885 | +17 | 902 | +156 | 1,058 | +71 | 1,129 | +70 | 1,199 | +78 | 1,277 |
| JACOB, Joe (F.F.) | 1,422 | +31 | 1,453 | -24 | 1,429 | — | 1,429 | — | 1,429 | — | 1,429 | — | 1,429 | — | 1,429 |
| KAVANAGH, Liam (Lab.) | 1,927 | -498 | 1,429 | — | 1,429 | — | 1,429 | — | 1,429 | — | 1,429 | — | 1,429 | — | 1,429 |
| KEARNS, Robert (Non-Party) | 358 | +51 | 409 | +1 | 410 | +48 | 458 | +17 | 475 | -475 | — | — | — | — | — |
| LALOR, Oliver Joseph (F.G.) | 339 | +43 | 382 | — | 382 | -382 | — | — | — | — | — | — | — | — | — |
| LARKIN, John (P.D.) | 532 | +27 | 559 | — | 559 | +23 | 582 | +11 | 593 | +19 | 612 | -612 | — | — | — |
| MILEY, Mary (F.G.) | 652 | +15 | 667 | +4 | 671 | +158 | 829 | +96 | 925 | +29 | 954 | +81 | 1,035 | +43 | 1,078 |
| O'SHAUGHNESSY, James (Lab.) | 325 | +69 | 394 | +3 | 397 | +14 | 411 | -411 | — | — | — | — | — | — | — |
| PHILIPS, Susan (Non-Party) | 966 | +50 | 1,016 | +1 | 1,017 | +51 | 1,068 | +53 | 1,121 | +105 | 1,226 | +170 | 1,396 | +134 | 1,530 |
| Non-transferable papers not effective | — | — | — | — | — | +25 | 25 | +62 | 87 | +128 | 215 | +71 | 286 | +231 | 517 |
| TOTAL: | 8,571 | — | 8,571 | — | 8,571 | — | 8,571 | — | 8,571 | — | 8,571 | — | 8,571 | — | 8,571 |

Elected: Kavanagh, Liam (Lab.); Jacob, Joe (F.F.); Philips, Susan (Non-Party); Doyle, Pat (F.F.); Hynes, Frank (Lab.)

## Arklow

CLANDILLON, Tom, 3A South Quay, Arklow, Co. Wicklow. (FF)
FORTUNE, Paul, 59 Connolly Street, Arklow, County Wicklow. (NP)
KAVANAGH, Patrick, 42 St. Peter's Place, Arklow, Co. Wicklow (Lab)
KINSELLA, Denis, 20 Mellow's Avenue, Arklow, County Wicklow.
McELHERON, Vincent, 2 South Quay, Arklow, County Wicklow.
MILLS, Peter, 1 Seaview Heights, Arklow, Co. Wicklow. (FF)
O'CONNELL, Dr. James W. Vale Road, Arklow, County Wicklow. (FF)
SWEENEY, Patrick, 31 Ferrybank, Arklow, County Wicklow. (FF)
WOLOHAN, Sean, 14 St. Patrick's Terrace, Arklow Co. Wicklow. (Lab)

## Athlone

BEAUMONT, Patsy, 89 Battery Heights, Athlone, County Westmeath. (NP)
BUTLER, John, 30 St. Kieran's Terrace, Athlone, County Westmeath. (FF)
FALLON, Sean, Clonown Road, Athlone, County Westmeath. (FF)
GAVIN, O. 105 Sarsfield Square, Athlone, County Westmeath. (NP)
LYNCH, Des, "Tisment", Bonavalley, Athlone, County Westmeath. (PD)
McFADDEN, Brendan, Dunard, The Batteries, Athlone, County Westmeath. (FG)
MOLLOY, Kieran, Connolly Street, Athlone, County Westmeath. (FF)
ROWAN, Breffni, 13 West Lodge, Athlone, County Westmeath. (NP)
TEMPLE, Ciaran, Ballymahon Road, Athlone, County Westmeath. (FF)

## Athy

CHANDERS, Patrick, 1 Carbery Park, Athy, County Kildare. (FG)
DOOLEY, Kieran, 18 Avondale Drive, Athy, County Kildare. (FF)
ENGLISH, Frank, Church Road, Athy, County Kildare. (FF)
LALOR, Reggie, 34 Leinster Street, Athy, County Kildare. (FG)
LAWLER, John, c/o 3 Woodstock Street, Athy, County Kildare. (FF)
O'ROURKE-GLYNN, Lenore, 8 Beasley House, Punchestown Gate, Dublin Road, Naas, County Kildare. (FF)
PENDER, Brian, 27A Forest Park, Athy, County Kildare. (Lab)
TAAFFE, Frank, Ardreigh, Athy, County Kildare. (FF)
WRIGHT, Paddy, 1 Clonmullin, Athy, County Kildare. (SF)

## Ballina

CAFFREY, Ernest, Garden Street, Ballina, County Mayo. (FG)
McLOUGHLIN, Sean, 34 Tyrawley Terrace, Ballina, County Mayo. (FF).
DIAMOND, Pat, Tone Street, Ballina, County Mayo. (NP)
DOHERTY, Neil, c/o Dunnes Shopping Mall, Pearse Street, Ballina, County Mayo. (FF)
DOWNEY, Patrick, Barrett St. Ballina, Co Mayo. (FF)
KILCULLEN, Anne, Kilmore, Ballina, County Mayo. (WP)
LYNCH, Henry, The Brook, Ardnaree, Ballina, County Mayo. (FF)
MOORE, Gerry, 37 Corcoran Terrace, Ballina, County Mayo. (FF)
TROY, Vincent, Shanaghy, Ballina, County Mayo. (FG)

## Ballinasloe

BRODERICK, Lily, Brackernagh, Ballinasloe, County Galway. (FG)
CONNELL, Stephen, 39 St. Grellan's Terrace, Ballinasloe, County Galway. (Lab)
FINNERTY, Michael, Tobergrellan, Ballinasloe, County Galway. (FG)
GERAGHTY, Patsy, St. Michael's Square, Ballinasloe, County Galway. (FF)
GUIDER, Seamus, 12 Brackernagh, Ballinasloe, County Galway. (FF)
HURLEY, Sean Óg, "Beechwood", Garbally, Ballinasloe, County Galway. (FG)
O'BAOILL, Tomás, Deerrpark, Ballinasloe, County Galway. (FF)
O'SULLIVAN, Pat, 7 Kilgarve Park, Ballinasloe, County Galway. (FF)
PARKER, Brian, Creagh, Ballinasloe, County Galway. (NP)

## Birr

CAMPBELL, Sadie, Moorpark, Birr, County Offaly. (FG)
CARROLL, John, "The Ring", Birr, County Offaly. (SF)
ENRIGHT, Edward J. Emmet Square, Birr, County Offaly. (FG)
FANNERAN, Seamus, Whiteford, Birr, County Offaly. (Lab)
GARAHY, Patrick, Seffin, Birr, County Offaly. (NP)
HARTE, John, Emmet Square, Birr, County Offaly. (FG)
LOUGHNANE, Seamus, Woodland Drive, Birr, County Offaly. (NP)
MOLLOY, John, Hillside, Birr, County Offaly. (FF)
RYAN, Sean, Newbridge Street, Birr, County Offaly. (FG)

## Bray

### NO. 1 ELECTORAL AREA
HANNON, Brigid, 62 Beech Road, Bray, County Wicklow. (NP)
KEYES, Noel P. 3 Kilery Terrace, Upper Dargle Road, Bray, County Wicklow. (FF)
McMANUS, John, 1 Martello Terrace, Strand Road, Bray, County Wicklow. (DL)

### NO. 2 ELECTORAL AREA
LEDWIDGE, Michael, "Ashbury", Killarney Road, Bray, County Wicklow. (FF)
McMANUS, Liz, 1 Martello Terrace, Strand Road, Bray, County Wicklow. (DL)
MURPHY, Jane, "De-Porres", Meath Road, Bray, County Wicklow. (NP)
VANCE, Patrick, Beachmount, Putland Road, Bray, County Wicklow. (FF)

### NO. 3 ELECTORAL AREA
BEHAN, Joe, 59 Richmond Park, Herbert Road, Bray, County Wicklow. (FF)
BYRNE, John, 1 Roselawn Park, Bray, County Wicklow. (Lab)
GILSENAN, Aedin, 27 Rectory Slopes, Bray, County Wicklow. (FG)
MURPHY, Ciaran P. "Goilin", Dargle Vale, Bray, County Wicklow. (PD)
TOBIN, Dermot, 77 O'Byrne Road, Bray, County Wicklow. (DL)

## Buncrana

BONNER, Brid, Swilly Road, Buncrana, County Donegal. (FF)
DIGGIN, Philip, Church Street, Buncrana, County Donegal. (NP)
DOHERTY, Joseph, Rockfield Terrace, Buncrana, County Donegal. (FF)
FERRY, Jim, 21 Upper Main Street, Buncrana, County Donegal. (SF)
GILL, Anne, Castle Avenue, Buncrana, County Donegal. (NP)
GILL, Seamus, Lower Main Street, Buncrana, County Donegal. (FG)
McLAUGHLIN, Peter, Upper Main Street, Buncrana, County Donegal. (FG)
Nic LOCHLAINN, Sinéad, Maginn Avenue, Buncrana, County Donegal. (FF)
McLAUGHLIN, Dermot, Upper Main Street, Buncrana, Co. Donegal. (FF)

## Bundoran

McELHINNEY, Michael J. West End, Bundoran, County Donegal. (FG)
McENIFF, Sean, "Derlua", Church Road, Bundoran, County Donegal. (FF)
McGLOIN, Patrick, East End, Bundoran, County Donegal. (FF)
McGLYNN, Mary, 10 Brighton Terrace, Bundoran, County Donegal. (FF)
McGOWAN, Hugh J. Northern Counties, West End, Bundoran, Co. Donegal. (FF)
MULHERN, Michael D. 9 St Bridget's Terrace, Bundoran, County Donegal. (NP)
O'GORMAN, Frankie, East End, Bundoran, County Donegal. (NP)
O'KELLY, Francis J. Bundrowes House, Bundoran, County Donegal. (FG)
O'NEILL, Joseph, 76 Main Street, Bundoran, County Donegal. (SF)

## Carlow

ALCOCK, Declan, 96 Pearse Road, Graiguecullen, Carlow. (FG)
BRADY, James, 52 New Oak Estate, Carlow. (FF)
CARPENTER, Patrick, Barrack Street, Carlow. (FF)
FOLEY, Kieran, 2 John Street, Carlow. (FF)
GOVERNEY, Patrick, "Erindale", Kilkenny Road, Carlow. (FG)
LACEY, Walter, 68 Green Road, Carlow. (PD)
McDONALD, Joe, 2 Pinewood Avenue, Rathnapish, Carlow. (FF)
MURNANE, James, 80 Maher Road, Graiguecullen, Carlow. (FF)
WHELAN, Sean, 4 Montgomery Street, Carlow. (FG)

## Carrickmacross

HANRATTY, Thomas, Cloughvalley House, Carrickmacross, Co.Monaghan. (NP)
MAGGS, Gerard, Mullinarry, Carrickmacross, County Monaghan. (FF)
MATTHEWS, Hugh, 30 St. Macartan's Villas, Carrickmacross, County Monaghan. (FG)
McCARTNEY, Thomas, Farney Street, Carrickmacross, County Monaghan. (FF)
McENEANEY, Patrick, 11 Highfield Estate, Carrickmacross, County Monaghan. (FF)
McKEEVER, Brendan, 26 St Macartan's Villas, Carrickmacross, Co. Monaghan. (NP)
McMAHON, James, 16 O'Neill Street, Carrickmacross, County Monaghan. (FF)
NELSON, James, Nafferty, Carrickmacross, County Monaghan. (FG)
O'DONOGHUE, Francie, Magheross, Carrickmacross, Co Monaghan. (WP)
O'FARRELL, Kevin, Creery, Carrickmacross, Co. Monaghan (FF)

## Carrick-on-Suir

BOURKE, Denis, 1 New Street, Carrick-on-Suir, County Tipperary. (FF)
DWYER, Liam, 70 St Molerans, Carrick-Beg, Carrick-on-Suir, Co Tipperary. (NP)
FOGARTY, Seamus, Poulmaleen, Carrick-on-Suir, County Tipperary. (NP)
HOGAN, James, 7 Dunbane, Carrick-on-Suir, County Tipperary. (FG)
LALOR, John, Waterford Road, Carrick-on-Suir, County Tipperary. (NP)
MURPHY, Patrick, 30 Woodland Heights, Carrick-on-Suir, County Tipperary. (FF)
LANDY, Denis, Greystone Street, Carrick-on-Suir, County Tipperary. (Lab)
RYAN, Patrick, 24 O'Mahony Avenue, Carrick-on-Suir, County Tipperary. (FF)
TORPEY, Noel, 25 Woodland Heights, Carrick-on-Suir, County Tipperary. (FF)

## Cashel

BROWNE, Martin, Dualla Road, Cashel, County Tipperary. (NP)
BROWNE, Michael, 41 Oliver Plunkett Park, Cashel, County Tipperary. (SF)
FINNERTY, Mattie, The Green, Cashel, County Tipperary. (FF)
HILL, Sean, Palmers Hill, Cashel, County Tipperary. (WP)
MALONEY, Joe, 30 Cathal Brugha St. Cashel, County Tipperary. (FF)
McINERNEY, William, Camas Road, Cashel, County Tipperary. (FF)
O'DONOGHUE, Maureen, 1 Upper Friar Street, Cashel, Co. Tipperary. (Lab)
WOOD, Richard, 10 Ard Mhuire, Cashel, County Tipperary. (FG)
WOOD, Thomas, 12 Old Road, Cashel, County Tipperary. (FG)

## Castlebar

AINSWORTH, Jude, 14 Rathbawn Drive, Castlebar, County Mayo. (FF)
BOURKE, Sean, Snugboro, Castlebar, County Mayo. (FF)
COADY, Liam, Knockthomas, Castlebar, County Mayo. (FG)
DURCAN, Frank, Westport Road, Castlebar, County Mayo. (NP)
JOYCE, Eamonn, Knockthomas, Castlebar, County Mayo. (FF)
McGUINNESS, Paddy, Main Street, Castlebar, County Mayo. (NP)
MEE, Johnny, 20 St. Bridget's Crescent, Castlebar, County Mayo. (Lab)
O'MALLEY, George, Mountain View, Castlebar, County Mayo. (FF)
EGAN, Eanya, Mountains View, Castlebar, County Mayo. (NP)

## Castleblayney

ATKINSON, Kevin, Main Street, Castleblayney, County Monaghan. (NP)
DUFFY, James, Lake View, Castleblayney, County Monaghan. (FF)
HUGHES, Brendan, Main Street, Castleblayney, County Monaghan. (FF)
LYNCH, Peter, 5 Ashling Grove, Castleblayney, County Monaghan. (FF)
McCOOEY, Sean, Main Street, Castleblayney, County Monaghan. (FF)
McGINN, Sean, Lake View, Castleblayney, County Monaghan. (SF)
McHUGH, Michael, Muckno Street, Castleblayney, County Monaghan. (FG)
McNALLY, Pat, Bree, Castleblayney, County Monaghan. (FF)
NUGENT, Edward P. Muckno Street, Castleblayney, County Monaghan. (NP)

## Cavan

ARGUE, Terry, Keadue, Cavan. (FG)
CONATY, Patrick, Killynebber, Cavan. (FF)
CROWE, George, Drumalee, Cavan. (FF)
DOLAN, Paul, 2 Owen Roe Terrace, Cavan. (NP)
GAFFNEY, Angela, Kilnavara, Cavan. (FF)
MALONE, Oliver, Coras Point, Cavan. (FG)
McDWYER, Dr. Eamonn, Farnham Street, Cavan. (FF)
O'REILLY, Patrick, 79 Church Street, Cavan. (FG)
WILSON, Thomas, "American Bar" Main Street, Cavan. (FG)

## Ceanuas Mór

CAFFREY, John, 22 Father McCullen Park, Ceanannus Mor, Co. Meath. (FF)
COLE, Cyril, Moynalty Road, Ceanannus Mór, County Meath. (FF)
GRIMES, Tommy, 14 Father McCullen Park, Ceanannus Mór, Co. Meath. (Lab)
GRIMES, Seamus, Church Lane, Ceanannus Mór, County Meath. (FG)
MAGUIRE, John, 9 Blackwater Heights, Ceanannus Mór, County Meath. (NP)
MOLONEY, Anne, 8 Upper Gardenrath Rd, Ceanannus Mór, Co. Meath. (FF)
O'ROURKE, James, "St Cecilia's", Moynalty Road, County Meath. (FF)
REILLY, Bryan, Rockfield Road, Ceanannus Mór, County Meath. (FF)
DARDIS, Noel, 29 Fr. McCullen Park, Ceanannus Mór, Co. Meath (FG)

## Clonakilty

CULLINANE, Charles R. Tawnies Cottage, Clonakilty, County Cork. (FF)
CULLINANE, Donal, 12 Pearse Street, Clonakilty, County Cork. (FF)
HARTE, Gerald, Clarke Street, Clonakilty, County Cork. (FG)
O'DONOVAN, Michael, Lower Tubbereen Road, Clonakilty, Co. Cork. (NP)
O'DONOVAN, Gretta, The Miles, Clonakilty, County Cork. (FF)
O'NEILL, Raymond, Glenbrook, Kilgarriffe, Clonakilty, County Cork. (PD)
O'REGAN, James P. Tawnies Upper, Clonakilty, County Cork. (NP)
O'REGAN, Michael, 22 Assumption Place, Clonakilty, County Cork. (NP)
WALSH, Nora, Rossa Street, Clonakilty, County Cork. (FG)

## Clones

DONOHOE, Patricia, 16 Beechgrove, Clones, County Monaghan. (FG)
FLANAGAN, John, 15 O'Neill Park, Clones, County Monaghan. (FF)
GUNN, Michael, Fermanagh Street, Clones, County Monaghan. (FF)
MacALEER, Peter, 11 Cherry Park, Clones, County Monaghan. (SF)
MEALIFF, Jim, Analore Street, Clones, County Monaghan. (Ind)
MULLIGAN, Peter, 6 Carn Heights, Clones, County Monaghan. (FG)
QUIGLEY, Patrick, The Diamond, Clones, County Monaghan. (FG)
MacPHILLIPS, Fintan, 59 O'Neill Park, Clones, Co. Monaghan. (SF)
McKENNA, Pat, Cara Street, Clones, County Monaghan (FF)

## Cobh

ANDERSON, Terence C. 24 Bishop Street, Cobh, County Cork. (FG)
FOSTER, Kevin, 7 Harbour Terrace, Cobh, County Cork. (FF)
LYNCH, Con, "Ringlee" Rushbrooke, Cobh, County Cork. (NP)
MEADE, Stella, Fort Villas, High Road, Cobh, County Cork. (FG)
O'CONNOR, Sean, 3 "Oakdene" Carricknajoy, Cobh, County Cork. (FF)
O'DEE, Eamonn, 16 Assumption Place, Cobh, County Cork. (NP)
O'MAHONY, Patrick, Bunkerhill, Rushbrooke, Cobh, Co. Cork. (FF)
OWENS, Leo, 7 Springfield Park, Cobh, County Cork. (WP)
POWER, Kevin, 18 Midleton Street, Cobh, County Cork. (FF)

## Dundalk

BELLEW, Tomás, Long Avenue, Dundalk, County Louth. (NP).
BELLEW, Patrick, 144 Cedarwood Park, Dundalk, County Louth. (NP)
BROWNE, Fra, 63 Oakland Park, Dundalk, County Louth. (SF)
BURNS, Stephen, "The Nook", Mount Avenue, Dundalk, County Louth. (FG)
CALLAN, J. Cherry Brook, 83 Seafield Lawns, Dundalk, County Louth. (NP)
COUSINS, Jim, "Monabri", 140 Ard Easmuinn, Dundalk, County Louth. (PD)
DUFFY, Frank, 46 Slieve Foy Park, Muirhevnamor, Dundalk, County Louth. (SF)
GALLAGHER, J. Marsh Road, Bellurgan, Dundalk, County Louth. (FG)
McCANN, Neil, 6 Batchelor's Walk, Dundalk, County Louth. (NP)
McGAHON, Brendan, 4 Faughart Terrace, St Mary's Rd, Dundalk, Co Louth. (FG)
MURRAY, Lucia, 411 Beechmount Drive, Dundalk, County Louth. (NP)
KEELAN, Seamus, Oaklands, Newry Road, Dundalk, County Lough. (FF)

## Dungarvan

DIXON, Mary, 9 T.J. Murphy Place, Abbeyside, Dungarvan, Co. Waterford. (NP)
GOODE, Declan, 17 Church Street, Dungarvan, County Waterford. (FF)
HALLAHAN, Austin, Youghal Road, Dungarvan, County Waterford. (NP)
KYNE, Billy, 5 Parklane Drive, Abbeyside, Dungarvan, County Waterford. (Lab)
O'RIORDAN, Michael, 32 Pinewood Lawn, Abbeyside, Dungarvan, Co Waterford. (FG)
POWER, Patrick, 4 Lower King Street, Abbeyside, Dungarvan, Co Waterford. (Lab)
RYAN, Nuala, 9 Kyne Park, Abbeyside, Dungarvan, County Waterford. (FF)
WALSH, Richie A, New Line, Abbeyside, Dungarvan, County Waterford. (FG)
WRIGHT, Tony, 13 Mitchel Terrace, Dungarvan, County Waterford. (DL)

## Ennis

ARTHUR-O'BRIEN, Anne, Gort Road, Ennis, County Clare. (FF)
BRENNAN, Thomas, "Prairie House", Clonroadmore, Ennis, Co. Clare. (NP)
CONSIDINE, Peter, 26 Abbey Street, Ennis, County Clare. (FF)
GREENE, Raymond, Cloughleigh, Ennis, County Clare. (FF)
GUILFOYLE, Michael, 50 McNamara Park, Ennis, County Clare. (FF)
HONAN, Tras, "Heather Lea", Cusack Road, Ennis, County Clare. (FF)
MULQUEEN, Anna, 2 Parnell Street, Ennis, County Clare. (FG)
RYAN, Mary, 1 Kincora Park, Ennis, County Clare. (FG)
SHERIDAN, Aoner, Kilrush Road, Ennis, County Clare. (PD)

## Enniscorthy

BROWNE, John, Kilcannon, Enniscorthy, County Wexford. (FF)
BYRNE, Peter, Brownswood, Enniscorthy, County Wexford. (FF)
DOYLE, Andy, Scarawalsh, Enniscorthy, County Wexford. (Lab)
DOYLE, Sean, 2 Esmonde Road, Enniscorthy, County Wexford. (NP)
KAVANAGH, Charlie, 11/13 Templeshannon, Enniscorthy, Co. Wexford. (FG)
McCAULEY, Sam, Rectory Road, Enniscorthy, County Wexford. (NP)
SHEAHAN, Sean, Millpark Road, Enniscorthy, County Wexford. (FF)
WILDES, Paddy, 15 Armstrong's Range, Enniscorthy, County Wexford. (NP)

YATES, Ivan, Blackstoops, Enniscorthy, County Wexford. (FG)
MURPHY, John, "Hillcrest", Summerhill, Enniscorthy, Co. Wexford. (FF)

## Fermoy

BARTLEY, Jim, Pike Road, Rathealy, Fermoy, County Cork. (GP)
EGAN, Thomas, 46 St Bernard's Place, Fermoy, County Cork. (WP)
GUINEVAN, John, Ballinarmma, Glanworth, County Cork. (PD)
HANLEY, Michael J, Duntaheen Road, Fermoy, County Cork. (FG)
LONERGAN, Roger, 6 McCurtain Street, Fermoy, County Cork. (FG)
MURPHY, John, 7 Quarry Lane, Chapel Hill, Fermoy, County Cork. (FF)
O'DONOVAN, Tadhg, 8 St Mary's Crescent, Fermoy, County Cork. (WP)
PHELAN, Tom, Richmond Hill, Fermoy, County Cork. (FG)
PYNE, Aileen, Kerrymist, Duntahane Road, Fermoy, County Cork. (FG)

## Killarney

COGHLAN, Paul, Ballydowney, Killarney, County Kerry. (FG)
LUCEY, Michael, Gortagullane, Muckross, Killarney, County Kerry. (GP)
COURTNEY, Michael B. Ardshanavooly Estate, Killarney, Co Kerry. (NP)
HORGAN, Christy, 39 New Street, Killarney, County Kerry. (Lab)
MOYNIHAN, M. Ballydowney, Killarney, County Kerry. (Lab)
O'CALLAGHAN, Dermot, Failte Family Inn, College Street, Killarney. (FF)
O'DONOGHUE, Maurice, Mill Road, Killarney, County Kerry. (NP)
O'GRADY, Sean, Ardshanavooly, Killarney, County Kerry. (DL)
O'SHEA, Mort, 18 Marian Terrace, Killarney, County Kerry. (FF)

## Kilrush

DUNLEAVY, Sean, Moore St., Kilrush, County Clare. (FG)
FENNELL, John, Henry Street, Kilrush, County Clare. (NP)
FLYNN, Michael, Moore Street, Kilrush, County Clare. (FF)
HANRAHAN, Patrick J. Pella Road, Kilrush, County Clare. (NP)
O'MALLEY, Gerard, 59 Shannon Heights, Kilrush, County Clare. (FF)
PRENDEVILLE, Tom, Cappa, Kilrush, County Clare. (FF)
SWEENEY, Gerry, Moore Street, Kilrush, County Clare. (FG)

## Kinsale

ACTON, Robert, Ardkilly, Sandycove, Kinsale, County Cork. (FG)
COLLINS, Dermot, Harbour Heights, Kinsale, County Cork. (FG)
COTTER, Joe, Pie Road, Kinsale, County Cork. (FF)
FRAWLEY, Michael, Pears Street, Kinsale, County Cork. (FF)
HOGAN, Eddie, Cork Street, Kinsale, County Cork. (FG)
O'BRIEN, Tim, 8 Friars Street, Kinsale, County Cork. (NP)
O'CONNELL, John, 10 Ardbrack, Kinsale, County Cork. (FG)
RYAN, Dermot, Winters Hill, Kinsale, County Cork. (NP)
SHEEHAN, Jeremiah, Ardbrack, Kinsale, County Cork. (FF)

## Letterkenny

BLAKE, Laurence, Covehill, Port Road, Letterkenny, County Donegal. (FG)
BLAKE, Patrick J. 3 Gartan Avenue, Letterkenny, County Donegal. (NP)
CULBERT, Tadhg, 5 Sprackburn Drive, Letterkenny, County Donegal. (NP)
DORRIAN, Hugh, College Road, Glencar, Letterkenny, County Donegal. (NP)
FISHER, Victor, 5 McNeely Villas, Letterkenny, County Donegal. (FF)
LARKIN, James, 112 Lower Main Street, Letterkenny, County Donegal. (NP)
LYNCH, James A. Dromore, Letterkenny, County Donegal. (NP)
McCLOSKEY, Liam, Kiltoy, Letterkenny, County Donegal. (FG)
McGLINCHEY, Bernard, Bluebanks, Kilmacrenan, County Donegal. (FF)

## Listowel

BEASLEY, James, "Loughcrew", Curaghatoosane, Listowel, Co. Kerry. (FG)
GUERIN, Michael, Clieveragh, Listowel, County Kerry. (Lab)
KELLIHER, Donal, 90 Ballygalogue Park, Listowel, County Kerry. (SF)
KENNEDY, Albert, Convent Street, Listowel, County Kerry. (NP)
O'CALLAGHAN, Tony, Cahirdown, Listowel, County Kerry. (FF)
O'SULLIVAN, Ned, "Fernhill," Cahirdown, Listowel, County Kerry. (FF)
PIERSE, Robert, Cahirdown, Listowel, County Kerry. (FG)
STACK, Denis, Cahirdown, Listowel, County Kerry. (FG)
WALSH, Thomas, 47 Church Street, Listowel, County Kerry. (FF)

## Longford

BARRY, John, Aughadegnan, Longford. (FF)
BREADEN, Thomas, Glack, Park Road, Longford. (FF)
CARBERRY, Tony, 13 St. Mel's Road, Longford.
CLARKE, Peter, Dublin Street, Longford. (FG)
KANE, James, Ballymahon Street, Longford. (FG)
KELLY, Philo, 1 New Street, Longford. (FG)
McDERMOTT, Brendan, Farnagh Hill, Longford.
SHEDWELL, Joseph, 8 Demense, Longford. (FF)
WARNOCK, Christy, 26 Annaly Park, Longford. (NP)

## Macroom

BROWNE, John, Codrum, Macroom, County Cork. (FF)
CULLINANE, Murphy, 32 Barrett Place, Macroom, County Cork. (NP)
KELLEHER, Cornelius, Mountmassey, Macroom, County Cork. (FG)
KELLEHER, Timothy, 5 Masseytown, Macroom, County Cork. (FF)
KELLEHER, Denis, Masseytown, Macroom, County Cork. (NP)
LEAHY, William, Gurteenroe, Macroom, County Cork. (FF)
MURPHY, Con, 30 St. Colman's Park, Macroom, County Cork. (FF)
MURRAY, Nora, Main Street, Macroom, County Cork. (FG)
O'CONNOR, Stephen, Coolcower, Macroom, County Cork. (FF)

## Mallow

CONROY, Thomas, Ivermore, Lacknalooha, Mallow, County Cork. (NP)
CURTIS, Tadhg, 51 Rockbrook Lawn, Mallow, County Cork. (Lab)
HEALY, Gerard, Ballydahin, Mallow, County Cork. (NP)
KAVANAGH, Con, 36 Sean Moylan Park, Mallow, County Cork. (FF)
O'MAHONY, Dan, Bellevue, Mallow, County Cork. (FF)
O'RIORDAN, Ted, 22 Lisheen, Mallow, County Cork. (FF)
SHERLOCK, Joe, 20 Blackwater Drive, Mallow, County Cork. (DL)
WILLIS, David, Lower Bearforest, Mallow, County Cork. (FF)
WRIGHT, Sean, 46 Dromore Drive, Mallow, County Cork. (FG)

## Midleton

COLLINS, Noel, "St. Judes", Midleton, County Cork. (NP)
HURLEY, John, "Maryville", The Rock, Midleton, County Cork. (FF)
JOY, Michael, Westbrook Court, Midleton, County Cork. (PD)
MURPHY, Ted, Upper Road, Ballinacurra, Midleton, County Cork. (FF)
RONAYNE, Charlie, 21 Ahern Terrace, Midleton, County Cork. (SF)
WALL, Donal, 71 Rosary Place, Midleton, County Cork. (NP)
WALLIS, Jerry, 74 Main Street, Midleton, County Cork. (FF)
WOODS, Mary, "Whiterock", Riverside Estate, Midleton, County Cork. (FG)
WOULFE, Kathleen, Railway House, Midleton, County Cork. (FG)

## Monaghan

CLERKIN, John, 20 Highfield Close, Killygoan, Monaghan. (FF)
GRAHAM, Heather, Dernagrew, Monaghan.
MACKLIN, Francis, 18 Cortlvin View, Monaghan. (FG)
McCARRON, Bridie, 32 Mullaghmatt, Monaghan. (FG)
McCARRON, Francis T. Old Cross Square, Monaghan. (NP)
MYLES, Thomas, 8 Glaslough Street, Monaghan. (FG)
SMYTH, Owen, Church Square, Monaghan. (SF)
TREANOR, Patsy, Latlurcan, Monaghan. (FF)
Uí MHURCHADHA, Pádraigín, 21 Park Street, Monaghan. (SF)

## Naas

BEHAN, Patrick, 34 Ashgrove Avenue, Naas, County Kildare. (FF)
BRACKEN, Evelyn, Harbour View, Naas, County Kildare. (NP)
LAWLOR, Patsy, Johnstown House, Naas, County Kildare. (NP)
CALLAGHAN, William, 26 Esmondale Estate, Naas, County Kildare. (FF)
CORCORAN, Donal, 18 Lakeside Park, Naas, County Kildare. (NP)
CONWAY, Timmy, Thomastown, Naas, County Kildare. (PD)
BRYNE, Charles, 31 Lakeside Park, Naas, County Kildare. (FF)
O'REILLY, Patrick, 8 Lakeside Park, Naas, County Kildare. (FG)
FRENCH, Mary, 37 Ashgrove Crescent, Naas, County Kildare. (FG)

## Navan

CARBERRY, Frank, 4 Abbeyland Crescent, Navan, County Meath. (FF)
CLUSKER, Brendan, Brews Hill, Navan, County Meath. (Lab)
D'ARCY, Jim, Allenstown, Kells, County Meath. (FG)
FITZPATRICK, Danny J. Abbeylands, Navan, County Meath. (FF)
FITZSIMONS, Paddy, 27 Trimgate Street, Navan, County Meath. (FF)
FOLEY, Noel, Watergate Street, Navan, County Meath. (FG)
McGOONA, Michael, Sheetrim House, Trim Road, Navan, Co. Meath. (FF)
MURTAGH, John, 24 St. Brigid's Villas, Navan, County Meath. (FF)
O'BRIEN, James, 66 Parnell Park, Navan, County Meath. (Lab)

## Nenagh

GARDINER, Sally, 11 St. Patrick's Terrace, Nenagh, County Tipperary. (Lab)
MORAN, James, Sun View, Ciamaltha Road, Nenagh, County Tipperary. (FF)
NOLAN, Jimmy, Cunnahurt, Nenagh, County Tipperary. (NP)
O'CONNOR, Joseph, Tyone, Nenagh, County Tipperary. (NP)
RICHARDSON, Paddy, 1 Orchard Heights, Nenagh, County Tipperary. (NP)
RYAN, Ger, 3 Mitchel Street, Nenagh, County Tipperary. (FF)
RYAN, John, 26 St. Patrick's Terrace, Nenagh, County Tipperary. (Lab)
RYAN, Tom, Rathnaleen, Nenagh, County Tipperary. (FG)
WHITE, Jack, "Santa Maria", Yewston, Nenagh, County Tipperary. (FG)

## New Ross

CLARKIN, Tom F. Henry Street, New Ross, County Wexford. (FF)
DOYLE, Paddy, 8 Chapel Street, New Ross, County Wexford. (Lab)
DWYER, Jim, 15 Mount Carmel, New Ross, County Wexford. (FF)
FURNESS, V. 52 Pondfields, New Ross, County Wexford. (FG)
HENNESSY, L. 15 Southknock, New Ross, County Wexford. (FG)
KEHOE, Jim, c/o Court Arms, Cross Street, New Ross, County Wexford. (NP)
O'BRIEN, Nick, Corner House, Rosbercon, New Ross, Co Wexford. (FF)
RYAN, Francis M. "The Maudlins", New Ross, County Wexford. (FF)
WALSH, Jim, 5 Parkfield, New Ross, County Wexford. (FF)

## Skibbereen

BAKER, Laetitia, 64 North Street, Skibbereen, County Cork. (FF)
BURKE, Mary, 31 Bridge Street, Skibbereen, County Cork. (FG)
CARTHY, Richard, Coronea, Skibbereen, County Cork. (Lab)
DWYER, Michael, 6 North Street, Skibbereen, County Cork. (FG)
McCARTHY, Donal, 24 Riverdale, Skibbereen, County Cork. (FF)
O'BRIEN, Seamus, Coronea, Skibbereen, County Cork. (FF)
O'KEEFFE, Catherine, Baltimore, Skibbereen, County Cork. (FG)
O'SULLIVAN, D.F. Schull Road, Skibbereen, County Cork. (FF)
SWANTON, Jerry, 18 High Street, Skibbereen, County Cork. (NP)

## Templemore

COSTELLO, John, 58 Lacey Avenue, Templemore, County Tipperary. (FF)
CURLEY, Michael, 31 Park Road, Templemore, County Tipperary. (FG)
GLEESON, Thomas, 4 Lacey Avenue, Templemore, County Tipperary. (NP)
HANLEY, Jack, Main Street, Templemore, County Tipperary. (FG)
HOGAN, Patrick, Church Avenue, Templemore, County Tipperary. (FF)
MEAGHER, Edward, "Ros", Richmond Gve, Templemore, Co. Tipperary. (NP)
MEAGHER, Mary, Patrick Street, Templemore, County Tipperary. (FF)
SHELLY, Tony, 13 Park Avenue West, Templemore, County Tipperary. (FF)
YOUNG, Henry, Patrick Street, Templemore, County Tipperary. (FG)

## Thurles

CALLANAN, Andrew, 19 Iona Avenue, Thurles, County Tipperary. (Lab)
FOGARTY, Mary, 4 Beechwood Grove, Kickham Street, Thurles, Co. Tipperary. (FG)
DURACK, Patrick, 7 Hillview Drive, Thurles, County Tipperary. (FF)
O'BRIAIN, Antoin, "Caragh", Brittas Road, Thurles, County Tipperary. (FF)
O'DWYER, Kevin, Kickham Street, Thurles, County Tipperary. (FF)
QUINN, Mae, Rossestown, Thurles, County Tipperary. (FG)
RYAN, Martin, 6 Fontenoy Terrace, Stradavoher, Thurles, Co. Tipperary. (FG)
SCULLY, Maura, Cathedral Street, Thurles, County Tipperary. (FF)

## Tipperary

ALLEN, Anne, 7 Abbey Street, Tipperary. (FF)
FERRIS, Michael, Rosanna Road, Tipperary. (Lab)
GRIFFIN, Brendan, "Cnoc Pio", St. Michael's Street, Tipperary. (FG)
KINAHAN, Christy, 19 Cashel Road, Tipperary. (NP)
CRONIN, Thomas, 33 Canon Hayes Park, County Tipperary. (FG)
LEAHY, Denis, 4 Davis Street, Tipperary.
McGRATH, Jimmy, 17 Canon Hayes Park, Tipperary. (FF)
O'SHEA, Jimmy, Davis Street, Tipperary. (FF)
PRICE, Richie, 14 O'Connell Road, Tipperary. (Lab)

## Tralee

BLENNERHASSETT, John, Ballinorig, Tralee, County Kerry. (NP)
DONOVAN, Michael, Foley's Glen, Ballyard, Tralee, County Kerry. (NP)
FINUCANE, Jim, 3 Cloondara, Clounalour, Tralee, County Kerry. (FG)
FITZGERALD, Ted, Clash Cross, Tralee, County Kerry. (FF)
FOLEY, Denis, 3 St. Joseph's Estate, Spa Road, Tralee, County Kerry. (NP)
FOLEY, Tommy, 28 St John's Park, Tralee, County Kerry. (NP)
HALLORAN, Mary, Upper Oakpark, Tralee, County Kerry. (FF)
HOARE, Joe C. 41 Connolly Park, Tralee, County Kerry. (FF)
LEEN, Billy, c/o Mason's Bar, Upper Castle Street, Tralee, Co. Kerry. (SF)
O'CONNOR, Maurice, 19 Racecourse Lawn, Tralee, County Kerry. (NP)
O'REGAN, Michael, 36 Moyderwell, Tralee, County Kerry. (Lab)
WALL, Johnny, 8 Ballinorig Estate, Tralee, County Kerry. (FF)

## Trim

ANDERSON, Frankie, Crowpark, Trim, County Meath. (Lab)
ALLEN, Babs, 28 St. Patrick's Park, Trim, County Meath. (FF)
DEMPSEY, Tom, Navangate, Trim, County Meath. (FF)
GRIFFITH, Robbie, Griffin Park, Trim, County Meath. (Lab)
KELLY, Brian, 123 Boyne View, Avondale, Trim, County Meath. (FG)
MURRAY, Larry, 45 Griffin Park, Trim, County Meath. (Lab)
POWER, Maurice, Robinstown, Navan, County Meath. (FF)
McHUGH, Vincent, 3 St. Johns, Trim, County Meath. (FF)

## Tullamore

BYRNE, Laurence, O'Brien Street, Tullamore, County Offaly. (Lab)
DUNNE, Laurence, "Roselawn", High Street, Tullamore, County Offaly. (FG)
FLANAGAN, John, New Road, Tullamore, County Offaly. (FF)
KEELEY, May, Clara Road, Tullamore, County Offaly. (NP)
MANSOOR, Ann, Church Road, Tullamore, County Offaly. (FF)
McGUIRE, Ernest J. 39 Clontarf Road, Tullamore, County Offaly. (Lab)
McKEIGUE, Tommy, Spollanstown, Tullamore, County Offaly. (FG)
O'TOOLE, Anne, 12 Pearse Park, Tullamore, Co Offaly. (NP)
Ui CHEALLACHAIN, M, Collins Lane, Tullamore, County Offaly. (FF)

## Westport

ADAMS, Margaret, Kings Hill, Westport, County Mayo. (FF)
CAMPBELL, J.P. Bridge Street, Westport, County Mayo. (FG)
DURCAN, Patrick, James Street, Westport, County Mayo. (FG)
HUGHES, Seamus, The Fairgreen, Westport, County Mayo. (FF)
HUGHES, Cormac, Altamount Street, Westport, County Mayo. (FF)
O'MALLEY, John J. Horkan's Hill, Westport, County Mayo. (FF)
RICE, Maurice, Belclare, Westport, County Mayo. (Lab)
RING, Michael, The Paddock, Westport, County Mayo. (FG)
STAUNTON, Sean, Streamstown, Westport, County Mayo. (FF)

## Wicklow

BYRNE, Tom, 3 Kilmantin Road, Wicklow. (Lab)
CONWAY, Roy, Woodlands, Blainroe Upper, Wicklow. (NP)
DUNNE, Teddy, 131 Mount Carmel, Wicklow. (NP)
FITZPATRICK, Nora, The Mall, Wicklow. (FG)
GIFF, Jim, 11 St. Laurences Road, Wicklow. (FF)
KEARNS, Robert, 4 Castlepark, Wicklow. (NP)
LALOR, Oliver, Dunbur Park, Wicklow. (FG)
O'BRIEN, John, 123 Mount Carmel Avenue, Wicklow. (Lab)
TEEVAN, Denis, 1 Wentworth Villas, Wicklow. (FF)

## Youghal

BICKERDIKE, Bob, 32 Raheen Park, Youghal, County Cork. (NP)
BROSNAN, John, c/o John Brosnan & Co., Solicitors, Friar Street, Youghal, County Cork. (FF)
KENEFICK, William, 17 Raheen Park, Youghal, County Cork. (NP)
LINEHAN, Paddy, Market Square, Youghal, County Cork. (FF)
LOUGHMAN, David, 24 Friar Street, Youghal, County Cork. (FF)
MURPHY, Denis, 9 Knockaverry, Youghal, County Cork. (FF)
RING, Paddy, 68 Sarsfield Terrace, Youghal, County Cork. (FF)
RUSSELL, Jerry, Whitebarn, Youghal, County Cork. (FG)
WALSH, Alice, South Abbey, O'Brien's Place, Youghal, County Cork. (FG)

## Ardee

BRADLEY, James, 5 Lambes Terrace, Ardee, Co. Louth. (PD)
BURKE, Tony, 26 Sliabh Breagh, Ardee, County Louth. (FG)
KERR, Val, Irish Street, Ardee, County Louth.
KERR, Val, 37 Sliabh Breagh, Ardee, County Louth. (FF)
MAGUIRE, John, Moorehall, Ardee, County Louth. (FF)
MALONE, Fintan, 84 Cherrybrook, Ardee, County Louth. (FF)
McCOY, Finnan, Riverstown, Ardee, County Louth. (FF)
ROONEY, Seamus, 22 Market Street, Ardee, Co. Louth. (SF)
McKENNY, Padraig, Dundalk Road, Ardee, Co. Louth (FF)

## Balbriggan

DAVIS, Joseph, 191, Lambeecher Estate, Balbriggan, Co. Dublin. (Lab)
GALLEN, Patricia, Mill House, Balbriggan, County Dublin. (FG)
HARFORD, Monica, 186 Lambeecher Estate, Balbriggan, Dublin. (Lab)
LAWLESS, Stephen, 6 Derham Park, Balbriggan, County Dublin. (FF)
MURRAY, David, 109 Hampton Cove, Balbriggan, Co. Dublin. (PD)
PURCELL, Brian L, St Judes, Seapoint, Balbriggan, Co. Dublin. (FF)
TUITE, Breige, 94 Lambeecher Estate, Balbriggan, Co. Dublin. (SF)

## Ballybay

CONLON, John F, Main Street, Ballybay, Co. Monaghan. (FG)
DUFFY, Talbot, 4 Lake View Terrace, Ballybay, County Monaghan. (NP)
LEONARD, James, 5 Pearse Place, Ballybay, County Monaghan. (FG)
McAVINEY, Martin, Hall Street, Ballybay, Co. Monaghan. (FF)
McSKEANE, Annie, 33 O'Duffy Terrace, Ballybay, Co. Monaghan. (FF)
SMYTH, Philip, Main Street, Ballybay, Co. Monaghan. (FG)
TRAYNOR, Gerard, 28 O'Duffy Terrace, Ballybay, Co. Monaghan. (FF)
TRAYNOR, Joseph, The Square, Ballybay, Co. Monaghan. (FF)

## Ballyshannon

KEANE, Jim, 9 East Rock, Ballyshannon, County Donegal. (FF)
LEE, John, 33 Cluain Barron, Ballyshannon, County Donegal.
McGLOIN, Ann, The Mall, Ballyshannon, County Donegal. (FG)
McINTYRE, John, 59 Assaroe Heights, Ballyshannon, Co. Donegal. (FF)
O'MALLEY, Pat, 23 Assaroe Heights, Ballyshannon, Co. Donegal. (FF)
SWEENEY, John, Westport, Ballyshannon, County Donegal. (FG)
TRAVERS, Phonsie, 56 Cluain Barron, Ballyshannon, Co. Donegal. (FG)
WYNNE, Val, 2 Erne Street, Ballyshannon, County Donegal.

## Bandon

COLEMAN, Andrew, Hill Terrace, Bandon, County COrk. (FG)
CANTY, Kathleen, North Main Street, Bandon, County Cork. (FF)
CONNOLLY, Paddy, Clancoolmore, Bandon, Co. Cork. (FF)
LOONEY, Cornelius, 17 Connolly Street, Bandon, County Cork. (Lab)
O'SULLIVAN, Kathleen, Allan Square, Bandon, County Cork. (FG)
MURPHY, Con, Cork Road, Bandon, County Cork. (FF)
O'BRIEN, Dominic, St Patricks Hill, Bandon, County Cork. (NP)
O'DONOVAN, Tim, Kilbrogan Hill, Bandon, County Cork. (FG)
TRAYNOR, Patrick F, 5 Knockbrogan Park, Bandon, County Cork. (FF)

## Bantry

BARRY, Patrick J, Marino Street, Bantry, County Cork. (FF)
CONNOLLY, John J, Cahernacrin, Bantry, County Cork. (FG)
CONNOLLY, John M, Reenrour Road, Bantry, County Cork. (Lab)
HOLLAND, Thomas, 59 Bishop Lucey Place, Bantry, County Cork. (FF)
MILNER, Michael, Newtown, Bantry, County Cork. (PD)
O'LEARY, Con, Seafield, Bantry, County Cork. (FG)
O'SHEA, John P, 33 Bishop Lucey Place, Bantry, County Cork. (FG)
O'SULLIVAN, Tom, Milleencoola, Bantry, County Cork. (FF)
KINGSTON, Matt, Newtown, Bantry, County Cork. (NP)

## Belturbet

BRADY, James C, Kilconny, Belturbet, County Cavan. (FF)
FITZPATRICK, Seamus, Creeny, Belturbet, County Cavan. (FG)
GORBY, Desmond, Railway Road, Belturbet, County Cavan. (FF)
HARRIS, Richard, Naughen, Belturbet, County Cavan. (NP)
McDWYER, Thomas, Main Street, Belturbet, County Cavan. (FF)
McGINLEY, Lily, "Mill Hill House" Belturbet, County Cavan. (FG)
REHILL, Patrick, Grilly, Belturbet, County Cavan. (FF)
VESEY, Anthony P, Kilconny., Belturbet, County Cavan. (FF)
WALSH, Bridget, Sugarloaf, Belturbet, County Cavan. (FF)

## Boyle

BEIRNE, Paul, St Patrick Street, Boyle, County Roscommon. (NP)
BEIRNE, Malachy, St Patrick Street, Boyle, County Roscommon. (FF)
DODD, Dennis, The Crescent, Boyle, County Roscommon. (FG)
FLAHERTY, Seamus, Station Road, Boyle, County Roscommon. (FF)
GEELAN, Francis, 9 Hanly Avenue, Boyle, County Roscommon. (NP)
McTIERNAN, James, Church View, Boyle, County Roscommon. (FG)
MURPHY, John J, 11 Termon Road, Boyle, County Roscommon. (FF)
SHANNON, Kitty, Station Road, Boyle, County Roscommon. (FF)
SHERIDAN, Eithne, Lowparks Street, Boyle, County Roscommon. (FF)

## Cootehill

BOYLE, Aiden, Main Street, Cootehill, County Cavan. (FG)
BRENNAN, Nuala M, Corbeagh, Cootehill, County Cavan. (FF)
CONNOLLY, Brendan, 9 Cavan Road, Cootehill, County Cavan. (FG)
McNALLY, Bridie, 19 Drumnaveil, Cootehill, County Cavan. (FG)
OWENS, Margot, Alpha House, Cootehill, County Cavan. (FF)
PILKINGTON, John, 67 Church Street, Cootehill, County Cavan. (FF)
SHERLOCK, Hugh, Errigal, Cootehill, County Cavan. (FF)
SMITH, Michael, Main Street, Cootehill, County Cavan. (FF)

## Droichead Nua

FEENEY, Colm, 63 Moorefield Drive, Droichead Nua, Co. Kildare. (NP)
KEARNS, Joe, Main Street, Droichead Nua, County Kildare. (FG)
MULLANE, Maria, 2687 Dara Park, Newbridge, County Kildare. (Lab)
NOLAN, Michael, 41 College Park, DroicheaD Nua, Co.Kildare. (FG)
O'BRIEN, Ray, 19 Ballymany Park, Newbridge, County Kildare. (PD)
O'NEILL, John, Middle Eyre Street, Droichead Nua, County Kildare. (FF)
PLANT, P. Hawkfield, Droichead Nua, Co. Kildare. (FF)
RYAN, Michael, 1773 Pairc Mhuire, Newbridge, County Kildare. (FF)
WHYTE, John, 1827 Pairc Mhuire, Droichead Nua, Co. Kildare, (NP)

## Edenderry

BRERETON, William, St Annes, Tunnell, Edenderry, Co. Offaly. (NP)
BYRNE, Frank, Windsor Lodge, Edenderry, County Offaly. (FG)
FLANAGAN, James, Francis Street, Edenderry, County Offaly. (NP)
McDONNELL, Fergus, 12 Castleview Park, Edenderry, Co. Offaly. (FF)
McGUINNESS, Barney, St Olivers, Edenderry, County Offaly. (FF)
MORRISSEY, Thomas, 40 Castle View, Edenderry, County Offaly. (NP)
O'CONNOR, Eileen, Cahareens, Killane, Edenderry, County Offaly. (NP)
O'DONOGHUE, Damien, 1 Fr Kearns Street, Edenderry, Co. Offaly. (FF)
O'NEILL, Eamon, 181 Derries, Edenderry, County Offaly. (FF)

## Gorey

ALLEN, Lorcan, Raheenagurren, Gorey, County Wexford. (FF)
BOLGER, Deirdre, Millmount, Gorey, County Wexford. (FG)
FUNGE, Joseph, Hollyfort Road, Gorey, Co. Wexford. (FF)
HOBBS, Michael, 2 Ramsfort Avenue, Gorey, County Wexford. (FG)
LEACY, Kevin, Courtown Road, Gorey, County Wexford. (NP)
MULHALL, James, 37A, Garden City, Gorey, County Wexford. (FF)
O'GORMAN, Anthony, Mount Alexander, Gorey, County Wexford. (NP)
SHEEHAN, John, St Michaels Road, Gorey, Co Wexford. (SF)
SWORDS, Kevin, Gorey Hill, Gorey, County Wexford. (FF)

## Granard

CAMPBELL, Francis, Market Street, Granard, County Longford. (NP)
DONOGHUE, James, Main Street, Granard, County Longford. (NP)
HIGGINS, Patrick M, Moxham Street, Granard, County Longford. (NP)
KIERNAN, Thomas S Springlawn, Granard, County Longford. (NP)
KILBRIDE-HARKIN, Maura, Cartron, Granard, County Longford. (FG)
LEE, Connie, Church View, Granard, County Longford. (NP)
SMITH, TP, Barrack Street, Granard, County Longford. (NP)
SMYTH, Philip, Main Street, Granard, County Longford. (NP)
WALSH, Benny, Main Street, Granard, County Longford. (NP)
BRENNAN, Edward, 18 Mill Grove, Greystones, County Wicklow. (NP)

## Greystones

BRENNAN, James, 'Glenties', Church Lane, Greystones, Wicklow. (NP)
DAVIDSON, Alex, 76 Hillside, Greystones, County Wicklow. (NP)
JONES, George, 103 Applewood Heights, Greystones, Wicklow. (NP)
MOLONEY, Geraldine, 166 Applewood Hhts, Greystones, Wicklow. (FF)
MURNANE, Jack, 24 Heathervue, Greystones, County Wicklow. (NP)
ROCHE, Dick, 2 Herbert Terrace, Herbert Road, Bray, Co. Wicklow. (FF)
SWEENEY, Joseph, 'The Paddock', Beech Road, Wicklow. (Lab)
KILLALEA, Pat, 29 Bellevue Park, Greystones, Wicklow. (FF)

## Kilkee

BURKE, Annette, 'Carnashee', Kilrush Road, Kilkee, County Clare. (FG)
CLOHESSY, Eamonn, Geraldine Place, Kilkee, County Clare. (FF)
DI LUCIA, Manuel, Corbally, Kilkee, County Clare.
FURLONG, Jimmy, Railway Road, Kilkee, County Clare. (FF)
HAUGH, Claire, 21 Marian Estate, Kilkee, County Clare. (FF)
KELLY, Michael, 22 St Patrick's Terrace, Kilkee, County Clare. (FF)
MARRINAN, Sean, Miltown Road, Kilkee, County Clare. (FG)
O'SHEA, Tony, Grattan Street, Kilkee, County Clare.
RYAN, Michael Sraide Line, Kilkee, Co. Clare. (FF)

## Leixlip

BARDON, Jim, Mountainview, Leixlip Gate, Leixlip. (NP)
COLGAN, John, 6 Highfield Park, Leixlip. (NP)
KEARNEY, David, 634 River Forest, Leixlip. (FG)
KELLY, Finbar, 41 River Forest, Leixlip. (NP)
KELLY, Paul, Rye Cottage, 99 Main Street, Leixlip. (FF)
MURPHY, Catherine, 46 Leixlip Park, Leixlip. (DL)
O'NEILL, Frank, 460 Green Lane, Leixlip. (Lab)
PURCELL, Colm, 609 St Mary's Park, Leixlip. (Lab)
PURCELL, Sean, 69 Newtown Park, Leixlip. (DL)

## Lismore

BOLGER, Joan, Deerpark Road, Lismore, Co. Waterford (FG)
DOWD, Peter, East Main Street, Lismore, County Waterford. (FF)
MORRISSEY, Mary, Bank Field, Lismore, County Waterford. (NP)
GEOGHEGAN, Frank, Fairfield, Lismore, County Waterford. (Lab)
HICKEY, Noel, Curaheen, Lismore, County Waterford.(FG)
MADDEN, Owen, South Mall, Lismore, Co.Waterford.(FG)
O'CONNELL, Mona, Chapel Street, Lismore, County Waterford. (NP)
ROCHE, Joseph, Monatarrive, Lismore, County Waterford. (FG)
RYAN, Mary, Townsparks, Lismore, County Waterford. (FF)

## Loughrea

BARRETT, Oliver, Caheronaun, Loughrea, County Galway. (FG)
BURKE, Gabriel, Main Street, Loughrea, County Galway. (FF)
DONNELLAN, Brendan, Westbridge, Loughrea, County Galway. (FF)
HYNES, Pat, 78 St Laurances Field's, Loughrea, County Galway. (NP)
KELLY, Thomas R, Cross Street, Loughrea, County Galway. (FG)
LOUGHNANE, Matthew, Dunsandle, Loughrea, County Galway. (FF)
McNALLY-FULLARD, Perlie, Athenry Road, Co. Galway. (NP)
MORGAN, Norman, Bride Street, Loughrea, County Galway. (NP)
REILLY, John, 16 Mount Carmel Crescent, Loughrea, Co. Galway. (FG)

## Mountmellick

BOWE, Patrick, Manor Road, Mountmellick, County Laois. (FG)
BRACKEN, Patrick J, Garoon Road, Mountmellick, County Laois. (FF)
CONROY, Oliver, Brittas, Mountmellick, County Laois. (PD)
CONROY, John, 11 Emmet Terrace, Mountmellick, County Laois. (FG)
CULLITON, Thomas, Acragar House, Mountmellick, County Laois. (FF)
FLANAGAN, Charles, Oaklawn, Portlaoise, County Laois. (FG)
GORMAN, Carmel, 12 Connolly Street, Mountmellick, Co. Laois. (FF)
GORMLEY, Michael, Parnell Street, Mountmellick, County Laois. (FF)
MOLONEY, John, Patrick Street, Mountmellick, County Laois. (FF)

## Muineheag

BAMBRICK, Patrick, Royal Oak Road, Muinebheag, Co. Carlow. (FG)
CLARKE, John, 22 Pairc Mhuire, Muinebheag, County Carlow. (Lab)
CUSHEN, Margaret, 14 Pairc Mhuire, Muinebheag, County Carlow. (FF)
FOLEY, Denis, Long Range Muinebheag, County Carlow. (FG)

# TOWN COMMISSIONERS

HICKEY, Thomas, 12 St Brigid's Crescent, Muinebheag, Carlow. (NP)
MANNING, Joseph, Market Square, Muinebheag, County Carlow. (FG)
McDONALD, Arthur, Kilcarrig Street, Muinebheag, County Carlow. (FF)
McNALLY, John, 9 Barrett Street, Muinebheag, County Carlow (Lab)
NOLAN, Enda, Park, Tinryland, Muinebheag, County Carlow. (FF)

## Mullingar

BROPHY, Vincent, 14 Ginnell Terrace, Mullingar, Co. Westmeath. (FG)
BURKE, Denis J, Cullen Beg, Mullingar, County Westmeath. (NP)
COLEMAN, Des, 40 Great Oaks, Mullinar, County Westmeath. (Lab)
DOLLARD, Michael, 15 Beechgrove, Mullingar, Co. Westmeath. (Lab)
DOWD, Christopher, 14 Grand Parade, Mullingar, Co. Westmeath. (FF)
FEELY, Joseph J, 16 Oliver Plunkett Street, Co. Westmeath. (FF)
GLYNN, Camillus, Newbrook Road, Mullingar, County Westmeath. (FF)
HYNES, Martin, 3 Lynnderry Court, Mullingar, Co Westmeath. (FF)
McINTYRE, Frank, 18 Mount Street, Mullingar, Co. Westmeath. (NP)

## Passage West

BROWN, Phyl, Rock Farm, Ringaskiddy, County Cork. (FG)
GREENE, William, 18 Maple Dr., Pembroke Wood, Passage West. (FF)
HENNESSY, Charles, Castlehouse, Monkstown, County Cork.
HILL, David, Thornhill Cottage, Ballinlough Road, County Cork. (NP)
MEE, Jim, 11 Desmond Villas, Passage West, County Cork. (SF)
MURPHY, Jim, 8 Pembroke Wood, Passage West, County Cork. (Lab)
O'BRIEN, David, Beech Road, Passage West, County Cork. (FF)
QUIGLEY, Pat, Beachcout, Passage West, County Cork. (FG)
MURPHY, Michael, Pembroke, Passage West, Cork. (FF)
AIRD, William, Nutgrove, Portlaoise, County Laois. (FG)

## Portlaoighise

BREEN, Liam, 49 Beladd, Portlaoise, County Laois. (FF)
COLGAN, Thomas, Beladd, Portlaoise, County Laois. (FF)
DUNNE, Anthony J, 8 St Brigid's Place, Portlaoise, County Laois. (FG)
DUNNE, Joseph, New Road, Portlaoise, County Laois. (FF)
JACOB, Thomas, Glenside Portlaoise, County Laois. (FF)
LODGE, Jerry, Ridge Road, Portlaoise, County Laois. (FF)
McCORMACK, Joseph, 87 Marian Place, Portlaoise, County Laois.
O'BRIEN, Cathleen, Mill View, Portlaoise, Co. Laois. (FG)
DRISCOLL, Sean, Limerick Road, Newmarket-on-Fergus, Clare. (FF)

## Shannon

HAMMOND, Dermot, 23 Gleann na Smol, Shannon, County Clare. (FG)
LAMBERT, Geraldine, 6 Allen Park, Shannon, County Clare. (FF)
MAKOWSKI, Brigid, 16 Tradaree Court, Shannon, County Clare. (NP)
McCARTHY, Patricia, 13 Caragh Park, Shannon, County Clare. (NP)
McKEE, Michael, 12 Inis Fail, Shannon, County Clare. (SF)
O'BRIEN, Pat, 50 Cill Chais, Shannon, County Clare. (FF)
O'SHAUGHNESSY, Tom, 43 Finian Park, Shannon, County Clare. (Lab)
RYAN, Kathleen, 4 Fergus Road, Drumgeely, Shannon, Co. Clare. (FF)

## Tramore

BRENNAN, Sean, Upper Branch Road, Tramore, County Waterford. (FF)
CASEY, Con, Seafield, Newtown Hill, Tramore, County Waterford. (FG)
CLARKE-RELLIS, Maura, Talbot Place, Tramore, Co. Waterford. (FG)
COWMAN, Dan, 42 Moonloun, Tramore, County Waterford. (FF)
HEALY, Tom, Cliff Road, Tramore, County Waterford. (FF)
HUTCHINSON, BIlly, 140 Sweetbriar Lawn, Tramore, Waterford. (FF)
O'CARROLL, Maureen, Mary Mount, Tramore, County Waterford. (NP)
O'DONOGHUE, Frank, Ballinattin, Tramore, County Waterford. (PD)
O'SHEA, Brian, 61 Sweetbriar Lawn, Tramore, County Waterford. (Lab)

## Tuam

BIGGINS, Frank, Fair Green, Tuam, County Galway. (Lab)
BROWNE-LANE, Gilleesa, Fairgreen Heights, Tuam, County Galway.
BURKE, Joe, Shop Street, Tuam, County Galway. (PD)
FLAHERTY, John, Ryehill Tuam, County Galway. (NP)
HALION, Nora, High Street, Tuam, County Galway. (FG)
KELLY, Michael, Church View, Tuam, County Galway. (NP)
O'GRADY, Midie, Millstream Park, Tuam, County Galway. (FG)
O'MARA, James, Tullinadaly Road, Tuam, County Galway. (FF)
STAPLETON, PM, Vicar Street, Tuam, County Galway. (FF)

## CLONMEL

AMBROSE, Tom (Ald),
"Dún Mhuire", Melview, Clonmel,
County Tipperary. (FF)

BOYLE, Edward,
140 Elm Park, Clonmel,
County Tipperary. (NP)

BYRNE, William,
31 Geoffrey Baron Park, Clonmel,
County Tipperary. (Lab)

DARMODY, Terry,
11 Cherrymount, Clonmel,
County Tipperary. (FG)

HEALY, Seamus,
Scrouthea, Old Bridge, Clonmel,
County Tipperary. (NP)

HEWITT, Vera,
Glenconnor, Clonmel,
County Tipperary. (FF)

KENNEDY, John,
72 Ard-na-Gréine, Clonmel,
County Tipperary. (FF)

LYONS, Sean (Ald),
20 Powerstown Road, Clonmel,
County Tipperary. (Lab)

NORRIS, Thomas,
Coleville Road, Clonmel,
County Tipperary. (FF)

NYHAM, Sean,
5 Davis Avenue, Clonmel,
County Tipperary. (FG)

O'BRIEN, Michael,
42 Oliver Plunkett Terrace, Clonmel,
County Tipperary. (FF)

O'HARA, Dominick,
52 Highfield Grove, Clonmel,
County Tipperary. (FG)

## DROGHEDA

### NO. 1 ELECTORAL AREA

DEMPSEY, Raymond,
91 College Rise, Drogheda,
County Louth. (FG)

GODFREY, Frank,
129 Avenue One, Yellowbatter,
Drogheda,
County Louth. (FF)

MOORE, Thomas,
31 Glenmore Drive, Drogheda,
County Louth. (NP)

MURPHY, Tommy (Ald),
53 Pearse Park, Drogheda,
County Louth. (FF)

### NO. 2 ELECTORAL AREA

BELL, Michael,
110 Brookville Park, Drogheda,
County Louth. (Lab)

CARR, Patrick,
Crosslanes, Drogheda,
County Louth. (FG)

MULROY, Jimmy (Ald),
1 Matson Lodge, Ballymakenny Road,
Drogheda,
County Louth. (FF)

MURRAY, M.J.
Edenville, Lower Mall, Drogheda,
County Louth. (FF)

### NO. 3 ELECTORAL AREA

BELL, Betty,
110 Brookville Park, Drogheda,
County Louth. (Lab)

NOLAN, Matthew P,
Barrick Street, Drogheda,
County Louth. (FF)

O'BRIEN, Con (Ald),
198 Marian Park, Drogheda,
County Louth. (FF)

O'DOWD, Fergus (Ald),
24 St Mary's Villas, Drogheda,
County Louth. (FG)

## DUN LAOGHAIRE

BHREATHNACH, Niamh,
12 Anglesea Avenue, Blackrock,
County Dublin. (Lab)

BREATHNACH, Colm,
41 Montpelier Parade, Monkstown,
County Dublin. (DL)

COFFEY, Betty,
Rear of 40 Northumberland Avenue,
Dun Laoghaire,
County Dublin. (FF)

CONROY, Richard,
Silveracre House, Grange Road,
Dublin 16. (FF)

COSGRAVE, Liam,
33 Hillside, Dalkey,
County Dublin. (FG)

DILLON-BYRNE, Jane,
Silchester House, Silchester Road,
Glenageary,
County Dublin. (Lab)

DOCKRELL, John,
13 Knocksinna Crescent, Foxrock,
Dublin 18. (FG)

GILMORE, Eamon,
24 Corbawn Close, Shankill,
County Dublin. (DL)

KEOGH, Helen,
12 Beech Court, Killiney,
County Dublin. (PD)

LOHAN, Larry,
3 Woodlands Avenue, Dun Laoghaire,
County Dublin. (PD)

MADIGAN, Paddy,
"Algoa", Westminster Road, Foxrock,
Dublin 18. (FF)

MARREN, Donal,
17 Rock Lodge, Killiney,
County Dublin. (FG)

REEVES, Betty,
16 Rosehill, Careysfort Avenue,
Blackrock,
County Dublin. (GP)

SMYTH, Frank,
Brookeville, Commons Road,
Loughlinstown,
County Dublin. (Lab)

## KILKENNY

BOLGER, John,
"Clologue", Blackmill Street,
Kilkenny. (NP)

BOYD, Carmel,
7 Patrick Street,
Kilkenny. (FG)

BYRNE, Grace,
9 John Street,
Kilkenny (NP)

CROTTY, Thoma,
"The Bower", Coolgrange,
Kilkenny. (FG)

CROTTY, Kieran (Ald),
Ayrfield, Granges Road,
Kilkenny. (FG)

DELANEY, Tomas,
19 Circular Road,
Kilkenny. (FF)

LANIGAN, Mick (Ald),
"St Judes", Chapel Avenue,
Kilkenny. (FF)

McGUINNESS, Michael J,
11 O'Loughlin Road,
Kilkenny. (FF)

McGUINNESS, John J,
11 O'Loughlin Road,
Kilkenny. (FF)

PATTISON, Seamus (Ald),
6 Upper New Street,
Kilkenny. (Lab)

QUIGLEY, Liam,
40 Dean Cavanagh Place,
Kilkenny. (NP)

TYNAN, Margaret,
2 High Hayes Terrace,
Kilkenny. (FG)

## SLIGO

### NO. 1 ELECORAL AREA

CARROLL, Michael,
Carney,
Sligo.

HANLEY, Sheelagh (Ald),
13 Cartron Heights,
Sligo.

McDONAGH, Stephen,
1 St. John's Terrace,
Sligo. (Lab)

McGOLDRICK, Kathleen,
"Avondale", Strandhill Road,
Sligo. (FG)

### NO. 2 ELECTORAL AREA

BREE, Declan (Ald),
1 High Street, Sligo. (Lab)

McGUINN, Roddy,
19 Langan Drive, Cranmore,
Sligo. (FF)

McLOUGHLIN, Tony,
"Beechlawn", Barnasraghy,
Sligo. (FG)

McMANUS, Sean,
15 Highfield Road,
Sligo (FF)

### NO. 3 ELECTORAL AREA

HARRISON, John (Ald),
55 Greenfort Estate,
Sligo. (FF)

HIGGINS, Tommy (Ald),
82 Treacy Avenue,
Sligo. (Lab)

LYONS, Matt,
5 Rosehill,
Sligo. (FG)

McGARRY, Jim,
44 St. Brigid's Place,
Sligo. (FG)

## WEXFORD

BYRNE, Vincent,
"Erin Cottage", St Peter's Square,
Wexford. (Lab)

BYRNE, Gus (Ald),
19 Thomas Clarke Place,
Wexford. (FF)

CORISH, Helen,
"Woodhelven", 7 Parkview,
Wexford.

ENRIGHT, Michael,
Ballyduskar Lane, Killinick,
County Wexford. (DL)

HOWLIN, Brendan (Ald),
7 Upper William Street,
Wexford. (Lab)

KAVANAGH, Nicholas,
Mulgannon,
Wexford. (FG)

KIERNAN, Dominic M (Ald),
Avondale Drive,
Wexford. (FF)

MAHONEY, J,
84 Bishopswater,
Wexford.

NOLAN, Paddy,
9 Hantoon Road, Maudlintown,
Wexford. (FF)

O'FLAHERTY, John,
37 McDermott Terrace, Hill Street,
Wexford. (FF)

RECK, Padge (Ald),
"Sunrise", Mulgannon,
Wexford.

ROCHE, Peter,
53 William Street,
Wexford. (Lab)